ALSO BY GARY FISHGALL

Gregory Peck: A Biography
Pieces of Time: The Life of James Stewart
Against Type: The Biography of Burt Lancaster

Gonna Do Great Things

THE LIFE OF SAMMY DAVIS, JR.

Gary Fishgall

A LISA DREW BOOK

SCRIBNER

NEW YORK   LONDON   TORONTO   SYDNEY   SINGAPORE

A LISA DREW BOOK/SCRIBNER
1230 Avenue of the Americas
New York, NY 10020

For information about special discounts for bulk purchases,
please contact Simon & Schuster Special Sales:
1-800-456-6798 or business@simonandschuster.com

Designed by Colin Joh
Text set in Fairfield

Manufactured in the United States of America

1 3 5 7 9 10 8 6 4 2

Library of Congress Cataloging-in-Publication Data is available.

ISBN 0-7432-2741-7

For this is my moment
My destiny calls me,
And, tho' it may be just once in my life time
I'm gonna do great things.

—"Once in a Lifetime" by Leslie Bricusse/Anthony Newley;
recorded by Sammy Davis, Jr., 1962
(*What Kind of Fool Am I?—And Other Show Stoppers*)

Contents

Contents

Acknowledgments

Exploring Sammy Davis, Jr.'s life and career has been a thoroughly engaging experience. Even though I'd written three previously published biographies—of Burt Lancaster, James Stewart, and Gregory Peck—nothing had quite prepared me for the twists and turns in Davis' story. Part of the difference lay in the fact that Sammy was a more emotional, more vulnerable person than any of my previous subjects. Another factor was his involvement in so many aspects of show business: not just TV, films, and theater, which had engaged Lancaster, Stewart, and Peck as well, but also vaudeville, burlesque, nightclubs, and recordings. And then there was the additional issue of race, with Davis' life playing out against an evolving tapestry of black-white relations in America.

Any biography is a daunting undertaking and this one was no different, requiring the assistance of hundreds of people, many of whom are remembered with gratitude below. But I would be remiss if I didn't start by offering my profound thanks to Burt Boyar, Davis' friend and the coauthor (with Sammy and Burt's wife, Jane) of the entertainer's two autobiographies, *Yes I Can* and *Why Me?*, published by Farrar, Straus and Giroux in 1965 and 1989, respectively. Without a moment's concern about another writer's interest in the subject to which he'd devoted so much of his own career, Burt cheerfully lent me every possible assistance, from hours of interview time to moral encouragement to connecting me with a number of other people who played important roles in Davis' life. Paramount among the latter were Sammy's second wife, May Britt Ringquist, who doubtless wouldn't have agreed to talk with me had Burt not encouraged her to do so; Davis' oldest son, Mark; and the two closest surviving members of Sammy's inner circle, his longtime agent and business partner, Sy Marsh, and his office manager and then manager, Shirley Rhodes. Mark, Shirley, and Sy, in turn, cheered me with their encouragement and their kindness.

But Burt remained a case apart. Not only do I consider him a friend, but I also have enormous respect for the books he, his wife, and Davis created, particularly *Yes I Can*, a landmark among celebrity autobiographies and an important record of the black experience in the United States between the end of the 1920s and the outset of the 1960s. I was

especially grateful for the book's detailed coverage of Sammy's forma-
tive years, for, by the time I started my project, information along these
lines from other sources was difficult to locate.

Useful as it was, *Yes I Can* could take me only so far. It is a memory
piece, with virtually no dates. In quite a few instances, the chronology of
the narrative doesn't conform to events that I have been able to validate.
I doubt very much that Burt or Jane consulted outside printed sources to
support what they were being told in the interviews they conducted.
Thus, I have used the book for what I—and Burt—consider its principal
strength, its ability to record the emotional truths of Sammy Davis, Jr.'s
life, from his youth to his mid-thirties, but not as a reliable indicator of
what Davis did and when. In some instances, where the narrative
doesn't conform to the facts as I found them, I simply ignored what I
read and moved on. Where warranted, in my opinion, I have pointed
out, in my narrative or in notes, places of divergence. This is not to
diminish or denigrate *Yes I Can*, but simply to clarify the record in case
the reader is familiar with the relevant passage in the book or reads it in
conjunction with this one.

In addition to the volumes attributed to Sammy himself, I consulted
dozens of other books and hundreds, perhaps even thousands, of periodicals (see the bibliography for specifics). For helping me access these
materials, I am grateful to several specialized libraries in New York and
Los Angeles and the kind experts employed by those institutions. These
include the Billy Rose Collection, the New York Public Library for the
Performing Arts; the Schomburg Center for Research in Black Culture,
the New York Public Library; the Cinema-TV Library of the Doheney
Library, University of Southern California, directed by the always supportive Ned Comstock; the Warner Bros. Collection at USC, under the
supervision of Noelle Carter and Randi Hockett; and the Academy of
Motion Picture Arts and Sciences' Center for Motion Picture Study,
housed in the beautiful Margaret Herrick Library, with particular thanks
to Barbara Hall, Howard Prouty, and Sandra Archer. I also want to
acknowledge my hometown institutions, the St. Louis Public Library
and the St. Louis County Public Library, for their extensive general collections, which, in the case of the former, includes a microfilm set of
Variety back issues, and for arranging the occasional interlibrary loan.

In addition to the voluminous reading matter, I watched virtually all
of Davis' features, made-for-TV films, and dramatic work on television,
as well as numerous sitcom and variety show appearances, including
about half of the episodes of the short-lived *Sammy Davis Jr. Show*. For
helping me to locate and view these materials, I must thank Donovan
Brandt, manager, Eddie Brandt's Saturday Matinee Video, North Holly-

wood, California; the Film and Television Archive, Archive Research and Study Center, Powell Library, University of California, Los Angeles; Paul Hrisko, Paramount Television; the Museum of Television & Radio, New York, Ron Simon, curator, Ned Kulakowski, press officer, and Jane Klain, manager, research services; and Madeline Matz, research librarian, the Motion Picture Broadcasting and Recorded Sound Division of the Library of Congress, Washington, D.C.

Davis recorded more than fifty LPs during his lifetime. Given this body of work, I felt it important to assess his contributions as a recording artist, even though he considered himself first and foremost a live entertainer, one whose busy touring schedule didn't allow much time in the studio. For assistance in obtaining CDs and other information pertaining to Sammy's recording career, I am grateful to Judy Kerr, Capitol Records publicity; David McKees, Rhino Entertainment; Gregg Geller, the producer of Rhino's outstanding four-CD box set *Yes I Can! The Sammy Davis, Jr. Story*; Kyle Cazazza and Marissa Kurtz, Universal Music Enterprises' publicity department, Barry Korkin, Universal's resident historian, and Henry Weinger, Universal's resident Motown expert; Mark Goldstein, Warner Bros. Records; and Bryan E. Cornell, reference librarian, Recorded Sound Reference Center, Motion Picture Broadcasting and Recorded Sound Division, Library of Congress.

For helping me in my attempt to understand Davis' complicated military experience, I owe a debt of gratitude to Eric Voelz, Records Reconstruction Branch, Military Personnel Records, National Personnel Records Center, St. Louis, Missouri; Mary Haynes, a historian with the U.S. Army History Center in Washington, D.C., specializing in the African American experience during World War II; Jeffrey B. Bohn, M/Sgt., United States Air Force, Ft. Warren AFB, Wyoming; Richard W. Peuser, National Archives, Washington, D.C.; Kenneth Schlesinger, Modern Military Records, Textual Archives Services Division, National Archives, College Park, Maryland; and David Neimeyer, an independent researcher who perused the relevant material at the National Archives' College Park facility on my behalf.

I also interviewed dozens of people who knew and worked with Davis. Particular thanks are due to Arthur Silber, Jr., the entertainer's earliest friend, who spent hours with me, patiently answering questions and sharing recollections, even though he was putting the finishing touches on his own memoir about Sammy. In addition to Arthur, I am enormously grateful to the following individuals for their kindness and insights: Earl Bellamy, Jay Bernstein, Jerry Bock, Leslie Bricusse, Peter Brown, Robert Brown, Doug Buschauser, James Caan, Diahann Carroll, Nick Castle, Jr., Gary Catona, John Climaco, Bill Coker, Robert Conrad,

Acknowledgments

Norm Crosby, Robert Culp, Mike Curb, Dom DeLouise, Barbara Eden, Hillard Elkins, Gloria Franks, Rabbi Allen Freehling, Ben Gazzara, William Gibson, Carl Gottlieb, Buddy Greco, Shecky Greene, Harry Harris, Naura Hayden, Holmes Hendricksen, Ethel Kennedy, Buz Kohan, Arnold Laven, Marc Lawrence, Ruta Lee, Janet Leigh, Jerry Lewis, Eric Lieber, Lorna Luft, Shirley MacLaine, Ed McMahon, Meg Myles, Marian Mercer, Mrs. Corbell (Barbara) Monica, Nichelle Nichols, Arthur Penn, Stephanie Powers, Jess Rand, Deke Richards, Chita Rivera, Isabel Sanford, George Schlatter, Arthur Allen Seidelman, Mel Shapiro, Mrs. George (Corrine) Sidney, Gary Smith, Aaron Spelling, David Steinberg, Sally Struthers, Joseph Stein, Rip Taylor, Leslie Uggams, Mort Viner, Luddy Waters, and several people who wished to remain anonymous. I am also grateful to the agency departments of the Allied Federation of Television and Radio Artists and the Screen Actors Guild for providing me with contact information and the assistants, managers, and agents who helped me reach these individuals. I am additionally indebted to Gregory Peck for giving me a wonderful letter of recommendation.

For a variety of other types of research assistance, I want to thank the following: authors Sam Kashner, Edward Mapp, Armand Fields, and Herbert Goldman; Howard Rosenberg; John M. Kelso, Jr., section chief, Freedom of Information Privacy Acts Section, Office of Public and Congressional Affairs, Federal Bureau of Investigation; Jennifer Cavins, administrative assistant, Tax and License Division, and Joanie Jacka, administrative coordinator, Administration Division of the State of Nevada Gaming Control Board, Carson City, Nevada; David Schwartz and Su Kim Chung, University of Nevada, Las Vegas; Frank Cullen, the American Vaudeville Museum, an Internet Web site; Susan Nolte, curator, Richard Nixon Library and Birthplace, Yorba Linda, California; Daurie Hole, reference consultant, U.S. and Canada, Reference Family History Library; Chris Hunter, archivist, Schenectady Museum, Schenectady, New York; and Gerald C. Weinberg, senior vice president and director of field organization, Muscular Dystrophy Association.

Finally, for research assistance in New York, London, and Las Vegas, I am indebted to Arlene Graston, Sandra Archer, and Diane E. Greene and Heather Nobles. And, on a personal note, I want to thank my mother, Sylvia Fishgall, and my friend Daniel DiPlacido for their early reviews of portions of the manuscript; my friends Arlene Graston and Charles Mathes for moral support; and, as always, my agent, Alexander Hoyt, my editor, Lisa Drew, and Lisa's assistant, Erin Curler, for innumerable instances of help and support.

Introduction

"Whata ya say we go camping?" a pal once asked Sammy Davis, Jr. "We'll rough it."

"Rough it?" the entertainer replied. "My idea of roughing it is when room service is slow."

The fact is, Sammy loved the good life. He relished palatial homes, good food, premium booze, fast cars, pretty women, fancy guns, and the latest in electronic gadgetry. If it was expensive, he wanted it. At home, he steeped himself in a treasure trove of quality merchandise. Not just for his own enjoyment, but also for that of his guests, for he was, indeed, a generous host who constantly surrounded himself with people. A journalist once likened his home to "Penn Station at rush hour."

When he traveled, he took his life with him. His fleet of suitcases and trunks—naturally, by Gucci or the equivalent—typically included a stereo record player and dozens of record albums, a motion picture projector and films (later replaced by a VCR and videotapes), photography equipment (later replaced by cooking paraphernalia), and, of course, clothes: outfits for every occasion imaginable, with hats ranging from Stetsons to derbies. As to the places he stayed, he was fond of saying, "They haven't built a hotel glamorous enough to suit me."

Keeping himself in the style to which he'd become accustomed was a costly proposition, but Sammy Davis was up to the challenge. "I'm not going to hang onto my money until I retire," he once said, "then sit back like an old man, burping, and say: 'I got $42 million in the bank, burp, burp.'" He raised spending money to the level of high art. He didn't just buy one suit at a time, or two or five. He bought twenty. He had enough watches to open his own store. His many pairs of shoes were housed in their own closet. And his jewelry collection—rings, medallions, gold chains, and the like—was legendary.

Davis was a collector of people as well. Hating to be alone, he made friends easily. As singer/actress Meg Myles put it, "Sammy treated everybody like a pal." He got a particular kick out of all the celebrities who were his buddies. His friendship with Frank Sinatra was a thing apart. But, at various times, he also hobnobbed with Elvis Presley, James Dean, Marilyn Monroe, Clint Eastwood, Laurence Olivier, Richard Burton and Elizabeth Taylor, the Kennedy clan, Richard Nixon, and

Michael Jackson, to name just a few. He didn't take such relationships for granted; he'd think to himself with unabashed glee, "Hey, dig this: I'm having dinner with Elizabeth fucking Taylor. Cool, baby."

Of course, *he* was as big a celebrity as any of them. And, God, how he loved it. Being Sammy Davis, Jr., was the most important thing in the world to him. Not only did fame bring in the money that gave him the life he craved; it was a major kick. When he walked down the street in New York or anywhere else in the world and people called out, "Hey, Sammy," he knew that he was esteemed. He could never get enough adoration. As his friend Shirley MacLaine once put it, "Sammy was a man who would do anything to be loved, and we all knew it." Why else would he regularly perform on stage for two hours, two and a half hours, three hours or more—when sixty to ninety minutes was expected? He didn't want to leave the stage because he didn't want the applause, the cheers, and the approval to end. He was so addicted to the spotlight, comedians liked to say, that when he opened his refrigerator, the light would come on, and he'd do twenty minutes.

Late in his life, Sammy told reporter Lerone Bennett, Jr., "I didn't like me." To which his friend actress Nichelle Nichols added, "There was a private Sammy that ached and resented the way the world worked."

His need for the limelight and the fans, the large coterie of friends, and the nonstop spending all seem symptomatic of a fragile ego, the origin of which can be traced directly to his childhood, which was anything but normal. From an impoverished, broken home, he lacked even a single day of formal education. Nor did he experience any of the traditional joys of youth—sports, dances, hanging out with friends, dating. He also had to confront his tiny stature and unconventional facial features. Not to mention the color of his skin. Being black in a country where many people considered African Americans second-class citizens at best was his ultimate reality. The result: a man afraid to be alone, driven to succeed, wanting desperately to be chic, a nonstop fireball of energy with an overwhelming desire to please, to be where it was happening, to define who he was by what he owned—and what he could accomplish.

Fortunately, Davis could do almost anything on a stage that people would pay to see. From the sixties on, he was best known as a song stylist. But he started his career as a hoofer, then added impressions of famous actors and singers, filled in with turns on the drums, the trumpet, and other musical instruments, and even threw in the occasional display of gunmanship, demonstrating his ability to draw, twirl, flip, toss, and catch a pair of six-shooters. The depth and breadth of his talent was overwhelming, all rendered with such force and energy that he left audiences breathless. Such was his skill that *Los Angeles Times* entertainment reporter Charles Champlin once described him as "all the floats in the big parade, a cast of hundreds (it sometimes seemed) contained in one slight frame."

Davis also had the gift of gab, entertaining audiences with anecdotes about his life and his take on current events. Talking, in fact, may have been his single greatest skill. His ability to get on a stage and to present himself in a way that people found funny and endearing became the glue with which he appended all of his other talents. To be sure, he had a delightful sense of humor. His jokes, aimed first and foremost at himself, often had a racial cast, particularly from the sixties on.

But he did more than joke about race. When Martin Luther King, Jr., and his colleagues forced a nation to examine its conscience and change, Sammy became a familiar presence at rallies, marches, and demonstrations. He also gave generously to the cause. But his greatest contribution lay in who he was. Arguably the first African American superstar, he opened doors for the many other entertainers who followed. By refusing to acknowledge that there were places he couldn't go, things he couldn't do, people he couldn't befriend, date, or marry, his *very existence* became a political statement. Any time the world said, "You can't do this or that," Sammy said, "Yes, I can" and moved ahead undaunted, with his head held high. So much so that "Yes I Can" became the title of a tune written for him by Charles Strouse and Lee Adams and the title of his first autobiography. It was the credo by which he lived his life.

During the heyday of the civil rights era, from the late fifties to the mid-sixties, the man was everywhere. Not just at sociopolitical events, but also in nightclubs, on records, at charity gigs, on television, at book signings, treading the Broadway stage. Everything he touched, it seemed, turned to the gold he craved so badly. He was a powerhouse entertainer, a charter member of the Rat Pack, and the epitome of cool. By the mid-seventies, however, the Sammy Davis persona was somewhat different: he was the cat who donned Nehru jackets, sported rings on every finger, and peppered his language with words like "groovy" and "far out" long after they were passé. He hugged Nixon and laughed too hard at unfunny jokes. He'd become so cool he was cold. Worse, he'd grown overly fond of cocaine, was addicted to booze, enjoyed kinky sex, and even dabbled in Satanism.

Sammy still had legions of devoted fans; his concert engagements still sold out. But his performances suffered. In time, he was able to kick the excesses—except smoking and spending money. But the impression of a sycophantic Uncle Tom, epitomized by Billy Crystal's skits on *Saturday Night Live*—rendered in black face, yet—lingered. The worldwide idol was now an object of ridicule.

Who knows what further turns his life would have taken had Sammy Davis, Jr., pressed on into the nineties. But cancer cut short his life at the age of sixty-four.

Ironically, shortly before he died, he'd celebrated his sixth decade in show business at a gala carried on network television. It featured virtually a Who's Who of American entertainment. During those tumultuous years, Davis had known more triumphs—and hurts and disappointments—than most people could even imagine. Up or down, he remained a figure of great controversy. As Sammy himself observed, there "is something in my makeup that causes strong reactions, something makes people care about me." Although he was hailed for his talent, he was almost always vilified by somebody or other for something he said or didn't say, something he did or didn't do, or something someone *thought* he should have said or done. Why couldn't he stay in his place? they wanted to know. Did he want to be white? How dare he date a white movie star? Why didn't he stick to black women? Why did he spend so much money? How could he hang with Richard Nixon? Was he joking with that Jewish business? And on and on and on. An avid TV buff, Sammy knew what was being said about him. Many of the attacks hurt him badly, but he was who he was. The son of show folk, a child of show business himself, he was completely at home on a stage, in a concert hall, behind the mike in a recording studio, or in front of a television or movie camera. These realms are all about glamour and make-believe, fantasy and illusion. Daily life was another matter. There, it often helped to have a cool head, sound judgment, and the ability to postpone immediate gratification. Sammy was somewhat deficient in these areas. He was perhaps first getting a handle on the real world as he neared his sixth decade—and shortly thereafter, he was gone.

But right or wrong, good or bad, he was Sammy Davis, Jr. He was a husband, a father, and a very good friend. He was a complex human being: driven, loving, insecure, generous, needy, kind, thrilled with his life and yet never fully satisfied. He was a civil rights pioneer and a humanitarian. But, above all, he was, as it says on his tombstone, an entertainer, one whom comic Alan King called "the greatest entertainer of all."

Perhaps his friend, television producer George Schlatter, put it best: "Sammy was a phenomenon. There was never anything like him before and there hasn't been anything like him since. There were people who approached it in different areas before. There was Bill Robinson. There was certainly Nat Cole. There were singers, there were dancers, there were comedians. No one performer encompassed it all the way Sammy did. Sammy created the need for new superlatives. Just talented, just genius, just legend doesn't quite cover it, because the totality of what made up Sammy Davis, the story—his beginnings, his early life, his experiences in the army, the environment, the climate, the evolution of show business, and the evolution of the black race—all came together to create this phenomenon. The phenomenon that became known as Sammy Davis, Jr."

This is that story.

PART ONE

Growing Up in the Country of Show Business

CHAPTER 1

Harlem and the Road

For most of its history, Harlem was white. Established in 1658 by Dutch settlers under Peter Stuyvesant, the enclave in upper Manhattan was originally known as Nieuw Haarlem. For about two hundred years, it was farmland. After its annexation to New York City in 1873, it became a genteel suburb, whose tidy, well-designed row houses, stately apartment buildings, and occasional mansion were occupied by solid middle-class families, mostly of Irish, German, and Jewish descent.

The black influx began around 1900. After the city announced the construction of a new subway along Lenox Avenue, one of Harlem's principal north-south thoroughfares, speculators purchased property in the surrounding area and began constructing apartment houses to meet the anticipated population boom. But the flood of newcomers never materialized. Faced with one empty building after another, the landlords responded to the appeal of Philip A. Payton, Jr., a college-educated black man who offered to fill the vacancies with African American families living in uneasy proximity to hostile whites in tenements on the West Side of Manhattan.

Soon, Harlem became a magnet for African Americans from all over the United States, notably the South. Negroes came as well from the Caribbean, South America, and Africa. In 1914, the National Urban League estimated the community's black population at nearly 50,000, rising to a whopping 200,000 by 1930.

By then, Harlem was home to all of the city's African American institutions: churches, newspapers, clubs, fraternal orders, even the National Association for the Advancement of Colored People (NAACP), the National Urban League, and a variety of black nationalist organizations. Not surprisingly, professionals of all kinds followed these institutions—writers, musicians, actors, lawyers, doctors, preachers, and businessmen. By the 1920s, the presence of so much talent in the relatively confined space between 110th and 155th Streets gave rise to what became known as the Harlem Renaissance. Thanks to poet Langston Hughes and novelist Zora Neale Hurston, painter Aaron Douglas and sculptor Augusta Savage, actors-singers Paul Robeson and Ethel Waters, jazz pioneers Duke Ellington, Fats Waller, and Fletcher Henderson, and their contemporaries, the arts were flourishing uptown.

So, too, were lesser pursuits. By 1915, nearly one hundred saloons and liquor stores had taken root in Harlem; playing the numbers had become a local mania. Indeed, the community had become a haven not only to black artists and the intelligentsia, but also to gamblers, prostitutes, street rowdies, and gang members. The twenties were roaring and one could find just about anything one wanted in Harlem. Such was its reputation that affluent downtown whites began trekking north to savor the community's exotic nightlife. Several of the local high-toned cabarets, including Connie's Inn and the Cotton Club, wouldn't even serve people of color. More democratic was the always jumping Savoy Ballroom, which opened on Lenox between 140th and 141st Streets in 1926.

Whichever side of the law one was on, most of the community's residents were happy to be where they were. As Harlem journalist Floyd Nelson noted, "Many Harlemites lived more spaciously, confidently, and comfortably than did others of their race in the black precincts of most large cities. Such people felt that there was not a better place than Harlem anywhere—no place they would rather have been."

Given its panache, talent, flash, bravado, and humanity, Harlem was the ideal place to give rise to the showman who would one day embody so many of those qualities. Sammy Davis, Jr., entered the world smack in the middle of the decade, December 8, 1925, at Harlem Hospital, located on fashionable Lenox Avenue and 135th Street.

Not everyone in Harlem was flashy or stylish. Thousands of Harlemites were ordinary people, who, social historian Jervis Anderson noted, "thought of little besides their struggle to make ends meet." Such was the case with Sammy's paternal grandmother, Rosa B. Davis. Born in 1880, Rosa B. was a strong, practical, loving woman who worked as a maid in the same household for about twenty years. Her income enabled her to maintain a modest apartment at 2632 Eighth Avenue (at 140th Street). It was not in a stylish part of Harlem, but it was only one flight up and in the front. Rosa would joke that she could open her living room window and catch a breeze coming off the Hudson River—by way of the gutter.

Seeking a better life up north from the woes of the segregated South (in her case, Wilmington, North Carolina), Rosa Davis was, like many women of her generation, the family anchor who lent support—moral, spiritual, and often financial—to her children and grandchildren. Her son, Sammy's father, Sam Davis, Sr., was a sweet, even-tempered man of no particular distinction. About 5 feet 10 inches with a broad frame, he was moderately attractive with a wonderful smile. In all likelihood, he had no formal education. Fashionable clothes, lively women, booze, and the horses were his passions. He supported these pastimes variously as a cook, a shoeshine man, a stoker on the Erie Railroad, a taxicab driver, and an elevator operator at the Roseland Dance Hall in Manhattan. Around 1920, when he was nineteen years old, he won a Charleston contest. This honorarium brought him to the attention of an African American impresario by the name of Will Mastin.* From then on, Sam's career was show business.

Like Sam Davis, Will Mastin hailed from the South, in his case, Huntsville, Alabama. Born around 1879, twenty-two years before Davis and only a few years after the end of Reconstruction, Mastin is reputed to have entered show business as a child, touring in a variety of black musical shows as part of what was called a "pick" (for "pickaninny") chorus. Striking out on his own, he became a dancer and, by 1916, was half of an act known as Mastin and Richards. A rather large, bulky man, Will's style of dancing was athletic rather than elegant. But he was a good showman. Sporting a straw hat and cane, he made up in bravado what he lacked in talent.

Mastin served in the army during World War I. Shortly after his discharge, he met Sam Davis, and for a brief period the two men did a double act. But where Sam was easygoing, a spendthrift, and lacking in drive, Will, described by one journalist as "steely-eyed" and "lantern jawed," was reserved, eager to succeed, and thrifty. Such was his ambition that, in around 1920, he produced as well as danced in his own show, an all-black musical revue called *Holiday in Dixieland*.

Holiday in Dixieland was in the tradition of *A Trip to Coontown,* the sensation of 1898, and other New York hits during the twentieth century's first two decades, shows that were written, produced, managed, and staged by African Americans, featuring all-black casts. Such musicals were credited with popularizing the Lindy Hop, Charleston, and other dance crazes and introducing such hit songs as "I'm Just Wild about Harry," "Dinah," and "Ain't Misbehavin.'" To be successful, an all-black show had to attract both white and African American audiences. This meant, according to Henry T. Sampson, author of *Blacks in Black-*

*In time, Sammy Davis, Jr., would refer to Will Mastin as his uncle, but, in fact, the two men were not related by blood or marriage.

face: A Source Book on Early Black Musical Shows, that "the black show producer had to retain enough of the 'plantation' element in his shows to appeal to whites and to convince managers of white houses to book the show while at the same time not make the show so demeaning that it would not appeal to blacks."

During the 1910s and twenties, quite a few black revues patterned on the Broadway model flourished in the hinterlands. Of course, they were written by lesser composers than the giants of the day—Will Marion Cook, Eubie Blake, and Fats Waller—and starred performers who were not on par with such great stars as Florence Mills, Bert Williams and George Walker, and Ethel Waters. But they were entertaining enough to appeal to less sophisticated audiences in the South and Midwest. Booking engagements in these regions became easier around the time Will Mastin launched *Holiday in Dixieland,* for, in 1920, a host of theaters catering exclusively to black audiences joined an outfit called the Theatre Owners and Booking Association (TOBA). Organized in Chattanooga, Tennessee in 1920, the TOBA, which was quickly dubbed the "chitlin' circuit," came to include show houses in more than eighty southern and midwestern cities, from Birmingham to St. Louis and Jacksonville, Florida to Detroit.

Holiday in Dixieland was probably no better or worse than most of its contemporaries. With a cast of fifteen—among them, Sam Davis—the revue featured the expected stereotypical characters and situations and included songs, sketches, and comedy, plus a dance novelty that was sweeping the nation, the "Texas Tommy." Such was its success that Will revived it the following year. The next season, he replaced it with a similar show called *Shake Your Feet*. Once again, Sam Davis was a featured member of the dance ensemble. Also in the cast was an attractive, light-skinned chorus girl who stood about 5 feet 7 inches named Elvera Sanchez. She and Sam Davis were soon a couple.

It is commonly thought that Elvera hailed from Puerto Rico, but the obituary of her mother in the *New Amsterdam News* in 1996 indicates that both of her parents were Cuban. Elvera's mother, Louisa, was born in Havana, the daughter of a Cuban cigar maker and a half Native American–half African woman who died giving birth to her. Moving to New York with her dad, Louisa married Elvera's father, a Cuban émigré named Marco Sanchez, when she was only fourteen. Louisa and Marco had four children, two of whom died in infancy. When Louisa was twenty-one, Marco also died, leaving her with the two surviving kids, Elvera and her sister, Julia. To support herself, Louisa took a variety of jobs, including, according to her obituary, that of personal maid to the celebrated actress Laurette Taylor.

Elvera, better known as "Baby," had a more direct connection to show business than her mother; she joined the chorus line at Harlem's Lafayette Theater when she was sixteen. Like Sam Davis and Will Mastin, she probably spent little, if any, time in school. When she caught Mastin's eye, she was between gigs, checking hats in a nightclub. Will immediately asked her to join his company. "He hadn't even seen me dance," Elvera recalled. "He hadn't even seen my *feet*. I had never taken any lessons. But I didn't waste any time saying yes."

According to Elvera, she and Sam Davis married in 1924, the year after she joined the Mastin company. But Arthur Silber, Jr., one of Sammy's closest friends in the 1940s and 1950s, maintained that the two were never wed. Burt Boyar, Sammy's pal and coauthor of his autobiographies *Yes I Can* and *Why Me?*, conceded the possibility, saying, "It could well be that they weren't married."

Officially Mrs. Davis or not, Elvera became pregnant early in 1925. She stayed with *Shake Your Feet* until two weeks before she was due and then retired to Harlem, staying in all likelihood with Sam's mother, Rosa. Elvera named her baby after his dad. His official name was not Sam or Samuel. It was Sammy, with no middle name or initial.

Elvera promptly returned to *Shake Your Feet*, leaving the infant with friends in Brooklyn. One day, Rosa B. came to visit the baby. "I never saw a dirtier child in my life," she wrote her son. "They leave Sammy alone all day so I've taken him with me. I'm going to make a home for that child." As his father called Rosa "Mama," Sammy dubbed her that, too. She served as both mother and father to the boy during his first two and a half years. His real mother and father would spend time with him whenever they played Manhattan or its environs. Such an occasion came when Sammy was one year old. "My first birthday," he told *Ebony* magazine in 1960, "was celebrated in a specially-contoured crib made up of suitcases in a dressing room at the old Hippodrome Theater in New York City."

Meanwhile, in 1927, Will Mastin launched a new musical entitled *Struttin' Hannah from Savannah*. Both Sam Sr. and Elvera were in the cast, which totaled twenty-four, Will's largest troupe yet. The plot, typical for its time, focused on a group of African Americans in New Orleans, all playing the numbers and trying to win on the same combination.

While *Struttin' Hannah* was on the boards, Elvera became pregnant once again. This time she gave birth to a girl, whom she and Sam called Ramona. Placing her daughter in the care of her mother, Elvera once more rejoined the Mastin troupe. A few months later, she left the company to join a rival show, *Connor's Hot Chocolate*. Her departure marked the end of her relationship with Sam Davis as well.

Initially, Sam feared that Elvera might lay claim to their son, so he went to Harlem to remove him from her potential grasp. Rosa argued that Sammy was too young to go on the road, but his dad insisted. It wasn't just fear that motivated him; he genuinely wanted his boy with him. "From the beginning, he was his daddy's baby," Elvera said many years later, perhaps with some bitterness.

Elvera Sanchez would continue as a chorus girl, serving for six years at Harlem's Apollo Theater. When the famed showplace abandoned its line of beauties in the early forties, she retired as a performer, becoming a barmaid and eventually settling in Atlantic City.

Sammy's first stop on the road was Pittsburgh. *Struttin' Hannah from Savannah* was booked in the town's Pitheon Theater, and the toddler spent every afternoon and evening backstage with his father. But after the final performance of the night, Sam would typically leave the boy alone at their rooming house while he went out drinking or gambling. On those occasions, sober, responsible Will Mastin took over, bathing Sammy in the sink and serving him breakfast: Horlick's malted milk mixed with hot tap water. The impresario genuinely liked the boy. "We were great friends," said Sammy. "He spent hours making funny faces at me and I loved making the same faces right back at him."

One thing Sammy and Will had in common was their love of show business. At each performance of *Struttin' Hannah*, the tiny toddler, roughly three years old, would position himself in the wings to savor the lively dances as well as the show's corny comic bits and renderings of current pop songs. A natural mimic, Sammy quickly absorbed everything he saw—as he proved one Sunday when the company was enjoying a day off in Asheville, North Carolina. That afternoon, he was in the parlor of the troupe's rooming house, amusing himself while pianist Obie Smith rehearsed on an upright piano. Suddenly, the kid started acting out parts of the show. One of the dancers, Rastus "Airship" Murray, quietly left the room, returning with Sam Sr. and Mastin. Pretty soon, other boarders began drifting in. As they watched in amazement, Sammy proceeded to render the whole hour-and-twenty-minute revue, including all of the dances, songs, and gags. When he finished, Mastin, laughing and applauding, told him that he'd find him a spot onstage for real. Then his father picked him up and carried him around the room, introducing him to all of the players he'd been traveling with but had never met.

What Sammy ended up doing in *Struttin' Hannah from Savannah* varies somewhat from account to account. According to one version, he would poke his head through a backdrop with a fence painted on it, prompting the actress playing Hannah to ask, "Are you a little kid or a midget?" In his autobiography, *Yes I Can,* Sammy recalled that Will had him sitting on the lead actress' lap while she sang one of Al Jolson's biggest hits, "Sonny Boy." "Keep singing no matter what happens," Will told her the first time he included Sammy in the number. As the actress started the song, Mastin positioned himself in the wings where the boy could see him. He began rolling his eyes and shaking his head, knowing that Sammy would imitate him, which he did. When the singer hit a high note, Will held his nose. Sammy did likewise. That got a big laugh. His unexpected antics were so unnerving that the poor singer's lips began to tremble, her jaw started to quiver, and her chest began to heave. Sammy imitated those actions as well, which pleased the audience even more. He left the stage to the sound of applause. He was hooked. In the wings, Mastin knelt beside him and told him how well he'd done. His ecstatic father exclaimed, "You're a born mugger, son, a born mugger."

Of course, both versions of Sammy's entry into show business could be true. He might have started by poking his head through the backdrop and then graduated to sitting on the leading lady's lap. In any event, he was now a full-fledged member of the company. Proof of his status came when they arrived at the next town on the tour. At each venue, a restaurant would customarily issue meal tickets so the performers could eat regularly during their engagement and settle up with the management on payday. Will gave Sam Sr. his meal ticket and then handed one to Sammy, bestowing on him a nickname, "Mose Gastin." Sammy never found out who Mose Gastin was or why Will chose to call him that, but he knew the name was a sign of affection from a man who didn't bestow tenderness on just anyone. Unwittingly, Sammy gave the boss a nickname in return. Unable to say Mastin, he said, "Thanks, Massey," as he took the meal ticket. From then on, that's who they were to one another: Mose Gastin and Massey.

Little Sammy was only a bit player in *Struttin' Hannah from Savannah,* but he took center stage when the Mastin troupe played the Standard Theater in Philadelphia. The management was sponsoring an amateur dance contest for children the day after the company's final performance. The three-year-old trouper decided to try his luck, even though there were more than a dozen older contestants. He was undaunted by the competition, and he knew his confidence hadn't been misplaced when he saw the other children doing stately fox-trots. By contrast, he came on with athletic bravado, his little legs flying. Not surprisingly, he was awarded the winner's cup—and ten dollars. "My father," Sammy recalled, "took me straight over to A. S. Beck's shoe store and bought me a pair of black pumps with taps."

* * *

Will Mastin was a tough businessman who kept steady pressure on the bookers in New York, Chattanooga, and elsewhere to keep his troupe employed. But, every so often, he would hit a dry patch. Such was the case after the Philadelphia engagement. With no money coming in, Sam was forced to phone his mother for a loan. She told him that if he had to ask for her help, it was time to come in off the road. Reluctantly, Sam agreed, bid a tearful farewell to Will, and returned with Sammy to Harlem.

"Mama was waiting for us when we got home," said Sammy. "I put on my shoes and ran into the front room to show them to her. My father proudly explained how I'd won them." Rosa then turned on her player piano and Sammy demonstrated his routine. "My, oh my!" she exclaimed, smiling. "You're a real dancer now."

Every day, Sam went out to look for work, but each evening he'd come home empty-handed. Having no desire to do anything outside of show business, his heart simply wasn't in his job search. Most days he'd find himself drawn to a downtown theater where some friends were performing. Back at the apartment, he would promise Rosa that the following day would be different, but it never was. Finally, in a desperate act of self-preservation, he sent a telegram to Mastin, hoping his old boss would be able to use him again. Rosa wasn't happy with her son's defiance, but, for once, Sam stood up to her. "It's better to go hungry when you're happy," he asserted, "than to eat regular when you're dead. And I'm good as dead out of show business."

A few days later, a special delivery letter arrived from Will—with an offer of employment. Initially, Davis had been planning on leaving his son with his mother. But, as he pulled his suitcase from beneath his bed, the boy ran to his closet to fetch his precious black pumps, which he then placed in Sam's suitcase, next to his dad's tap shoes. Davis looked at his son, whom he called "Poppa," probably a humorous tribute to the boy's adult-like proficiency onstage, smiled that delightful smile, slapped him on the back, and said, "Okay, you're coming too."

Father and son were back in show business!

In 1929, Will retired *Struttin' Hannah from Savannah* and launched a new show called *Miss Creola*. The cast included Sam Davis and Little Sammy and numerous other Mastin regulars. In October of that year, the stock market crashed, giving rise to the Great Depression. With the economy in dire straits, one might expect black musicals to suffer dramatically at the box office, but Mastin was able to keep *Miss Creola* running for a year or so.

But the nation's economic woes eventually forced him to shut down the show, his last full-scale revue. Instead, the impresario put together a vaudeville troupe of dancers known as Will Mastin's Gang. Depending on bookings, the size of the company would vary from as few as five members to as many as fifteen. But there would always be a place for Sam. And Sammy.

Will Mastin's Gang played a wide variety of venues: vaudeville theaters of all sizes and descriptions—black only, white only, big time, small time, popular, and downtrodden—as well as burlesque houses, carnivals, road houses, and anywhere else they could get a booking. Their travels took them from New England and the mid-Atlantic states to the Midwest and the South. Each engagement generally lasted no more than a week or two, which meant that the troupe spent a considerable amount of time on trains. Sammy later estimated that he'd visited ten states and played more than fifty cities by the age of four. He learned early that personal possessions could make a strange place feel like home. At the time, about all he owned was a makeup kit and mirror, a few items of clothing, and his tap shoes. As an adult, he'd transport a dozen or more trunks with him wherever he performed.

Sharing cheap hotel rooms in town after town forged a tight bond between Sammy and his dad. The elder Davis, something of a big kid himself, loved to tease and play games with his son, and his funny faces always made Sammy laugh. The boy lacked the same ease with his mother. At one town, Elvera showed up for a rare visit, and Sammy didn't even know who she was until Sam Sr. told him. Sammy found her captivating, much prettier than the girls in the Mastin troupe. Wanting her to admire him as well, he proudly demonstrated his proficiency as a dancer. With tears in her eyes, she told him he was every bit as good as his father.

Given the night off so he could spend time with his mother, Sammy took Elvera's hand and they strolled down the street. She offered to buy him an ice cream soda, but he declined. Then, spying a toy store, she went inside and got him a ball. Back outside, she tossed the ball to him. But Sammy, having never played catch before, didn't know what to do with his hands. Consequently, it hit him in the cheek and, although it didn't hurt, it frightened him. The ball rolled away, but he refused to go after it, even when his mother ordered him to do so. They continued to walk. Finally, Elvera said, "Is there anything you'd like to do?" When Sammy didn't answer, she gave up.

Returning to the theater, Sammy discovered that the act had yet to go on, so he quickly donned his costume and makeup. He asked Elvera to stay and watch him work. "As I danced, I saw her watching me from the wings and smiling," he recalled. But by the time he came offstage, she was gone. His father carried him to the dressing room, saying, "Your mother had to leave. She said to tell you she loves you." At that point, Sammy started to cry.

Elvera's departure that night virtually marked the end of her relationship with her oldest child. She noted years later, "I didn't spend a lot of time with my son, but I felt we had a close relationship." In actuality, she and the boy had almost no contact—until she reentered Sammy's life after he became famous. Testament to her relative lack of importance during his developmental years is the fact that there isn't a single photo of her in his autobiography, *Yes I Can,* until the mid-1950s, by which time he was a star.

Although Davis said little about Elvera's absence during his youth and was extremely tolerant of her presence as an adult, the lack of a loving, full-time mother was perhaps the single most painful element of his extremely unusual childhood. Even though he had a supportive father and a doting grandmother, Elvera's disappearance created a void that no other human being could fill.

Moreover, Elvera's visit to the theater that evening reveals several other key elements in the formation of Sammy Davis, Jr.'s personality. First, his awkwardness with the ball demonstrates just how deficient he was in the ordinary experiences of childhood. He had virtually no contact with youngsters his own age and, therefore, no opportunity to develop the social skills that come with such encounters. Second, Sammy's insistence on demonstrating his dancing prowess for his mother twice, once in private and once onstage during the act, suggests that he had already discovered at this early age that the best way to get approval—from family members as well as from strangers—was to perform. When it came to his talent, he was secure. Offstage was another matter.

CHAPTER 2

The Forty-four-year-old Midget

Enthusiastic audiences were teaching the four-year-old the value of being talented. Even at this early age, Sammy Davis, Jr., was a crowd pleaser. Part of his popularity derived from his appearance. "I was the most pint-sized, wide-eyed kid you ever saw," he explained, noting that "in those days my size added to the act because people thought it was cute." He also danced like his life depended on each performance.

A quick learner, he picked up a variety of steps from his father and Will. He also expanded his repertoire by watching the other acts that shared the bill with the Mastin troupe. "I was developing a feeling for 'timing,'" he recalled. "I could watch other acts perform and anticipate when a gesture, a fall, or an attitude would or would not work. I remembered everything I saw."

Recognizing Sammy's audience appeal, Will gave the lad a solo spot, during which the youngster's burgeoning showmanship often prompted people to toss coins on the stage. One night, Sammy stuffed so much money in his pockets he could barely participate in the act's finale. In his dressing room, he proudly showed his father his take: $28.50. Swinging the boy in the air, Sam Sr. declared, "You're the breadwinner, Poppa." They decided to treat themselves to a fancy restaurant dinner. Then, in the middle of the meal, Sam got drunk and turned on his son, accusing him of holding back some of the money. "Before I could deny it," Sammy said, "he slapped me and I fell off the chair." When he opened his eyes, he saw his father standing over him, his hands at his sides and tears streaming down his cheeks. Sam bent down, picked the boy up, and carried him out of the restaurant, apologizing profusely.

As this incident suggests, Sammy's relationship with his father was far from idyllic. To begin with, the elder Davis spent money freely when he was flush. Nothing was going to interfere with his pleasure, not even parenting. And he was not above using Sammy to further the act. Although undoubtedly proud of his son, Sam may have also been jealous of the youngster's greater audience appeal; certainly, his talent never equaled that of his offspring, and he knew it. Finally, although Sam wasn't an alcoholic, he drank to excess. He would often leave his son alone while he threw back some "skull-busters," as he called them. Once, Sammy asked Will why his father drank. "Your daddy's lonely," Mastin explained, meaning Sam lacked a wife or steady girlfriend. "There's no one he cares about and it makes him feel bad. The whisky makes him feel better." For years after he reached maturity, Sammy avoided alcohol, preferring Coca-Cola instead—at least until difficulties in his own life made an alcoholic buzz more attractive than frightening.

The night after the incident in the restaurant, the kid's solo spot lacked its usual sparkle. Afterward, Will took him aside. "Now I know you're troubling," he said, "and you're worried about Big Sam, but you can't take any thoughts onstage with you except the show you're doing. That's the first rule of show business." Sammy apologized. Then Will put his arms around the boy and said, "We all have troubles sometimes, Mose Gastin, but those people out front don't want to know 'em. No matter how bad you're hurting, leave your troubles here in the wings and come on smiling." It was a lesson Davis took to heart.

As time went on, Sammy's audience appeal became a significant factor in distinguishing the Mastin troupe from other dance acts, so much so that the act became known as Will Mastin's Gang Featuring Little Sammy. But there was a problem. In 1931, the boy reached school age. He thus became a target for an organization known as the Society for the Prevention of Cruelty to Children, informally dubbed the "Gerry Society," after its founder, Judge Elbridge T. Gerry. Children, the jurist fervently maintained, should be at home getting decent meals and plenty of sleep and in school learning, not performing in dirty, drafty, disease-ridden theaters. He didn't blame the youngsters for enjoying the spotlight. He blamed their parents for electing to profit by their children's talents rather than looking out for their best interests. Sam Davis and Will Mastin made every effort to keep Sammy out of the hands of these "do-gooders," even going so far as to blacken the lad's face so his features were harder to see. Then they dressed him as an adult, stuck a cigar in his mouth, and billed him as a silent forty-four-year-old midget.

Their schemes were mostly successful. Once, in Lansing, Michigan, however, a Gerry Society member raised such a fuss over Sam and Will's "mistreatment" of little Sammy that the manager of the theater where they were performing discharged the act. For some time, they were unable to get another booking anywhere in the state.

In February 1931, while the Mastin troupe was playing the Republic Theatre in Manhattan, Sam again ran afoul of the Gerry Society; New York, the show business capital of the country, was a focal point for the organization's activities. This time Sam was arrested. Although he was given a suspended sentence, the embarrassing incident was reported in *Variety* a few months later.

Away from the theater, there were similar perils—from the police. Once, when Sammy and his dad were staying with his grandmother, a truant officer came to the apartment to find out why the boy wasn't in school. Rosa B. promised to enroll Sammy the following day, but she had no intention of doing so. She made sure that Sammy knew how to elude the police thereafter, telling him that if he heard a knock on the door he was to remain absolutely still until the unwanted visitor went away.

Although educating Sammy wasn't a high priority for the Davises, Sam and Will tried to locate people in the venues where they played who could help the boy. From these "tutors," Sammy did master the rudiments of reading and writing, but not much else. Even in his late teens, he was only barely literate, and throughout his life, he avoided personalizing autographs for fear of misspelling a fan's name.

Far more interesting to Sammy than his makeshift tutoring was what he learned from the silver screen. When he was about five, he discovered what was to be a lifelong passion: the cinema. The first picture he ever saw was *Dracula,* starring Bela Lugosi. The horror film terrified but fascinated him. Thereafter, he saw every picture he could. Movies provided escape and adventure and were also a surrogate education. As Sammy put it, "To me Robin Hood and Abe Lincoln were equally important to the development of mankind, for I believed everything I saw on film. I learned all my vocabulary from Clark Gable and Errol Flynn."

A couple of years after Sam Davis' arrest in Manhattan, he was again targeted by the Gerry Society. As on the previous occasion, the Mastin troupe was playing New York, this time in Minsky's Burlesque. Once again, Davis was hauled off to jail.

His tearful son ran home to Rosa B. Sammy was so upset he couldn't even explain why he was crying. When Sam arrived, having been bailed out by Minsky's stage manager, Bert Jonas, he told his mother that he was going to be arraigned the following day. He decided to get out of town; naturally, he planned on taking Sammy with him. But Rosa B. refused to let the boy go. "You got no booking," she pointed out, "you got no money, you got no nothing. You think I'm gonna let you take this child running from the bulls, wandering to beg food with no place to sleep? Not while I'm willing and able to work."

Accepting defeat, Sam took off alone for parts unknown. The following day, Rosa showed up at her son's hearing, having arranged for her employer to phone the court and give her a good character reference. Between this ex-officio testimony and the absence of either parent, the judge awarded custody of Sammy to his grandmother. From then on, she informed Mastin and later her son that they would need to get her permission before taking her ward anywhere. As it happened, Will had managed to book the act in Boston the following week. "I wanted desperately to go with them," said Sammy, and his grandmother knew it. Reluctantly, she agreed, but she laid down the law to Will and Sam, insisting that they feed the boy well and give him three daily doses of Scott's Emulsion to keep him from catching cold.

Over the ensuing years, Sammy saw his surrogate mother with increasing regularity, because as the Depression deepened, Mastin had a harder time keeping his troupe on the road. When ensconced at the apartment on Eighth Avenue and 141st Street, Sammy tended to stay close to home. In the evenings, he would often play pinochle with his father, even though the old man cheated, as Sammy well knew. Once, when he caught Sam dealing from the bottom of the deck, the elder Davis insisted that he was doing so to teach his son a valuable lesson. "That way," he asserted, "when you grow up and I'm not around to protect you, you won't get taken."

Sammy preferred playing cards with a loving cheat to hanging out with boys his own age. His encounters with children usually ended badly. Once, when he had $10 in his pocket, he went down to the candy store below his grandmother's apartment to buy some comic books. Some neighborhood boys were sitting around, trading cards with pictures on them. Sammy was totally unfamiliar with these objects until one of the kids disdainfully informed him that they were penny baseball cards. In a great display of bravado, Sammy went over to Mr. Peterson, the owner of the store, and purchased a hundred cards. That made him the richest guy in the room. Suddenly, the aloof youngsters were his pals. One of them even offered to trade three of his cards for a like number of Sammy's. Davis agreed to the trade and, after it was completed, the kid and his buddies roared with laughter. "Boy, you are really dumb," one of them told Sammy. "Anybody who'd give up a Babe Ruth or a Lou Gehrig for less'n five cards—boy, that's the dumbest thing I ever saw."

Ashamed, Sammy ran out of the store, leaving his cards behind. "I closed the door to my room," he said, "and played a record, loud, so Mama couldn't hear me crying." Then he remembered he hadn't gotten the comic books. Even though he hated the idea of facing those boys again, he marched back down to the store and picked out a host of his favorite comics. The astonished kids wanted to know how he had so much money. Sammy proudly told them he was in show business, offering a few tap steps to quiet the doubters. They were less impressed by his talent, however, than by his hoard. "Can we see them after you're through?" one of his new pals asked. "You can have these," Sammy replied, demonstrating the combination of generosity and disregard for money that would be a hallmark throughout his life. He then went back to Mr. Peterson and bought a new stack of comics for himself.

Over the next few days, he'd see the boys outside the store. At first, they were nice to him, but pretty soon he was again an object of scorn. Then a new batch of comic books arrived and they were his bosom chums again. By then, Sammy was no longer interested in winning their approval. He knew "how I could make them like me again if ever I wanted to."

Unfortunately, Davis was no more successful with young girls. Once, in Peterson's store, he was browsing through the racks of comic books while some girls were sitting at a table drinking Cokes. Certain they had been staring at him, he sauntered over. Quickly, they reached for a yellow piece of paper in the center of the table, ripped it up, and dropped the pieces on the floor. After they dashed out of the store, Sammy gathered up the pieces and took them home with him. When he put them together, he saw that one of the girls had drawn a picture of him, emphasizing his large head and flat nose, and had written the word "Ugly." Hurt and humiliated, he tore up the pieces of paper and flushed them down the toilet. But when he studied himself in the mirror, he had to agree. He hated what he saw.

After that, he didn't go back to the candy store. Instead, he started accompanying Will on his rounds of booking agents. Teaching Sammy about business was a good idea, but, when it came to finances, the lad was more like his father than his boss. A businessman he would never be.

But he was getting better and better at the "show" part of show business. Such was his proficiency that when he was seven, he even landed a role in a short feature produced by Warner Bros.' Vitaphone division and shot at the studio's sound stages in Brooklyn.*

Rufus Jones for President was one of many featurettes that showcased African American artists during the late 1920s and early 1930s. Such talents as Chick Webb, the Mills Brothers, Billie Holiday, Jimmie Lunce-

---

*During the 1930s, picture palaces offered a variety of short subjects—dramas, comedies, animations, newsreels—before showing a feature film. By the mid-1940s, the practice was largely abandoned in favor of the double feature, that is, two full-length films.

ford, and Bessie Smith were among those who graced these largely forgettable outings. The principal star of *Rufus Jones* was the gifted Broadway star Ethel Waters. She played the title character's tough but loving mother while Sammy, as Rufus, dreams he is elected president of the United States.

Viewed today, *Rufus Jones* is about as politically incorrect as a film could be. It plays to all of the worst black stereotypes of the era. There are references to watermelon and chicken; members of the U.S. Senate, most of whom are African American, appear to be lazy and/or corrupt; and Waters, sporting a shapeless house dress and a bandana on her head, resembles Aunt Jemima. The only reason to watch the short today is to glimpse Sammy Davis, Jr., as a youngster, for he is absolutely adorable: agile, adept, and brimming with confidence. He sings the Louis Armstrong hit "I'll Be Glad When You're Dead, You Rascal You" and tap dances with all the bravado of an old pro. Unfortunately, no one in Hollywood at the time was remotely interested in making a movie star out of a young black kid.

Instead, he was cast in one more Vitaphone short. His role in *Seasoned Greetings*—released, like *Rufus Jones,* in 1933—was far more modest than that of the boy president. Lita Grey Chaplin, the ex-wife of Charlie Chaplin, played the owner of a failing greeting card store who gets a hot idea: talking greeting cards in the form of records. Little Sammy is one of her customers.

Although *Seasoned Greetings* was a musical, Davis didn't get to sing or dance in this one. Nevertheless, his undeniable self-confidence and captivating charm made him stand out. Apparently he was quite a hit with Lita Grey Chaplin as well. On the last day of filming, she offered to adopt the boy, take him to Hollywood, and get him a contract with a studio. But neither Sam nor Rosa B. was interested in giving him up.

Outside of the Vitaphone shorts, probably the most exciting experience of Sammy's childhood came about two years later, when he was nine. The Mastin troupe was performing in Boston, as was Bill "Bojangles" Robinson, the celebrated African American tap dancer who headlined at the Palace and commanded a salary of $3,500 a week. Mastin took his protégé to meet the great vaudevillian.* For Sammy, watching Bojangles work was a revelation, for his performance style was vastly different from the Mastin approach. "We'd exhaust ourselves trying," he explained, "arms and legs flying six ways to the moon and come off limp and wet. But Mr. Robinson had his hands in his pockets and he was

---

*Shortly after his encounter with Davis, Bill Robinson would embark on the series of feature films with Shirley Temple for which he is best remembered today.

going up and down a flight of stairs and around the stage like he was taking a stroll set to music. He wasn't even trying to get the audience, yet
I'd never seen anyone go over so big."

Offstage, Robinson was just as cool. When Will and Sammy came to his
dressing room, he was eating ice cream and sporting a beautiful robe
bearing his initials, his valet nearby. Moreover, his clothes closet revealed
a dozen or more pairs of shoes, which astounded Sammy. One day, Bojangles' shoe collection would represent a tiny fraction of his own.

Will asked Sammy to show the great man what he could do, and
Sammy happily complied. Robinson complimented him, then showed him
a few steps of his own, which the youngster immediately mimicked—to
Bojangles' slight dismay. Later, Sammy realized that he shouldn't have
shown off, but when it came to his talent, he was loaded with confidence. More than the tap steps, Sammy learned something about style from
the fabled vaudevillian. As he put it, "What Bill Robinson really taught me
was that when you're a tap dancer . . . you talk to the audience with your
feet."

By the time Sammy met Bojangles, stage shows featuring a wide variety
of performers—singers, dancers, acrobats, jugglers, children's acts, animal acts—were in dire trouble. A combination of factors was reponsible:
the Great Depression, the advent of talking pictures, and the formation
of national radio networks which brought live entertainment into people's homes for the first time. The demise of the great vaudeville tradition wasn't lost on Sammy. "Wherever we went," he said years later, "for
meals or between shows in the Green room, backstage, there was none
of the usual atmosphere of clowning around that had always been so
much fun. Everybody seemed afraid and they spoke only of acts that had
been forced to quit the business."

By the mid-thirties, many variety houses had become motion picture
theaters. The best of these kept some vaudevillians working, as they
treated patrons to modified live shows before or after the feature. But these
stage offerings in no way compensated for the disappearance of the variety houses. And, of course, the smaller and less prestigious movie theaters
couldn't afford to book live entertainment at all.

Will Mastin and his gang of dancers were badly hurt by the demise of
vaudeville. Mastin was able to get the occasional movie house gig, and
he continued to play burlesque houses and whatever other venues he
could book. But, by 1936, with vaudeville totally dead, economics forced
him to pare the act down to a threesome—himself, Sam Davis, and
young Sammy—which he dubbed the Will Mastin Trio.

The Will Mastin Trio was a "flash" act. In contrast to the elegance of a

Bill Robinson or Fred Astaire, Will, Sam, and Sammy would hit the stage in a burst of energy, accompanied by lively, uptempo music. Seeking to quickly captivate an audience, they would proceed with a display of stamina and athleticism, featuring moves drawn from traditional tap dancing as well as ballet, folk dancing, and even gymnastics. During the routine, each member of the act would get an opportunity to display his specialty moves, after which the trio would close with a final rousing group display.

Mastin and the two Davises were fine flash dancers, but so, too, were numerous other such entertainers, including the two Nicholas Brothers, the three Berry Brothers, and the four Step Brothers. No doubt, Mastin's doggedness, reputation for reliability, and insistence that he and his partners look sharp and neat no matter how dire their economic situation did as much to secure bookings for the Trio as did their onstage appeal.

Struggling at the lower end of the show business food chain, the Trio took what they could get. They often played in rundown theaters—or worse—before mean-spirited audiences. As Sammy later put it, "We had to fight for our lives every time the lights went up. We knew that we were booked on the strength of our reputation as a clean act that could be depended on for fast and furious flash dancing. Probably fifty percent of our flash came from our dread of the word 'Cancelled.'"

Knowing and caring only about show business and limited by their talent, their skin color, and their economic circumstances, Will, Sam, and Sammy carried on as best they could for the next nine or ten years. "By the time I was fifteen," Sammy said, "we'd crossed the country twenty-three times and played so much time in Canada that we were considered residents of Montreal." On more than one occasion, they lacked the requisite money for a boarding room and had to camp out in a bus or train station. Sometimes, they couldn't even afford a decent meal; dinner was a candy bar for each. Whenever possible, however, Will and Sam made sure their charge ate properly, even if they starved.

During these years, Sammy went from a precocious eleven-year-old to a physically mature eighteen. He continued to be almost childlike in his stature, and thin, but he was strong. Even within the rough-and-tumble world of flash dancing, he exhibited a grace and fluidity of movement that his older, chunkier partners lacked. In time, he became a superlative dancer. "He did steps nobody ever did before," asserted producer George Schlatter. "Because he was little and he was light. So he could get such elevation and such speed. . . . Sammy's taps were like nano-seconds." Mel Torme agreed, calling Sammy "the best tap dancer I have ever seen."

Sammy knew he was becoming an accomplished performer, but he wanted to become even better. Offstage, he remained what he had been as a boy: a sweet, kind, generous soul who liked people and craved their approval. But he was also terribly insecure about his height and his looks. He had a good brain, and traveling around the country gave him a worldliness that his contemporaries in Harlem lacked. But, restricted to the insularity of show business and comic books and with no teachers or other adults to stimulate his thinking, he remained emotionally and intellectually stunted.

One thing he learned during these lean years was the nature of prejudice. His first recorded exposure came after a particularly satisfying performance in Joplin, Missouri. Will and Sam decided to treat themselves to a good meal at a restaurant near the theater. They invited the members of a duo on the same bill, Vern and Kissel, to join them. The counterman cordially greeted Vern and Kissel, who were white, but told Sam, Will, and Sammy that "niggers" had to sit at the rear portion of the counter. The quintet protested, saying they had come in together and wanted to dine together, but the counterman would entertain no deviation from the restaurant's standard policy. Vern wanted to leave, but Mastin, always the pragmatist, pointed out that they might not find another open restaurant. So they reluctantly sat down, Vern and Kissel moving as close to the black end of the counter as possible, Will, Sam, and Sammy doing likewise on the white end. In point of fact, they weren't very far apart, but no one felt like talking.

Back at the theater, Vern and Kissel told the stage manager what had transpired. He profusely apologized to the Trio. In the dressing room, Sammy asked Will what a "nigger" was. "That's just a nasty word some people use about us," Mastin replied softly. "About show people?" Sammy asked. "No," the older man said. "It's a word some white people use about colored people. People like us whose skin is brown." Then Sam sought to deflect the uncomfortable conversation by making a funny face, which, as usual, broke his son up.

Sammy couldn't forget the counterman's attitude. Almost all of the white folks he'd encountered to that point had been in show business, and they mostly judged people by their talent. He had no experience with those who valued others only by their skin color, and the realization came as a shock.

Around the same time, Sammy experienced a different, more personal kind of prejudice. A friend of his grandmother had a daughter, and Mama convinced Sammy to take the young lady out on one of his layovers in Harlem. Since the encounter with the kids in the candy store, Sammy had avoided girls, figuring that he was too ugly to be of interest to anyone. This date, however, had been set up in advance—by his grandmother, yet—and he was eager to go.

He decided to take the girl downtown to one of Manhattan's premiere picture palaces, the Capitol. After the stage show, the pair repaired to the lobby, where the girl excused herself to go to the ladies' room. When she didn't return after twenty minutes, Sammy asked an usher to check on her. The usher reported that the girl wasn't there. Sammy couldn't imagine where she was, but, feeling responsible for her, he waited in the lobby for another two hours. Then, finally, he saw Sam approach the foyer. Running up to his dad, Sammy explained what had happened, but Sam already knew; the girl's mother had come to Rosa B.'s apartment a little while earlier to say that her daughter had bumped into some friends in the ladies' room and decided to leave with them. Sam broke the news to his son as gently as he could, but Sammy knew the truth: the girl ditched him because he wasn't good-looking enough for her. His only consolation was to close his eyes, picture himself, like Bill Robinson, headlining the Palace, and this dumb girl sitting out in the audience, in awe of his talent. It was a pleasant fantasy, but it didn't take away the sting of being abandoned on his very first date, a hurt he would never forget.

As the thirties waned, the Trio hit rock bottom. One stretch of unemployment lasted a full five months, which Sammy and his dad naturally waited out at Mama's. During the same time, the family Rosa worked for moved away, and she, too, was out of work. Money became so tight in the Davis household that Rosa was forced to serve inexpensive chicken neckbones and collard greens every night for a week. "For the first time in our lives," said Sammy, "we were on relief, waiting helplessly for the checks to arrive, hoping every day that Will would come running up the stairs, and say, 'We're booked.'" Finally, Sam turned for help to a close friend named Nathan Crawford, who worked as a foreman in a factory in the garment industry. "Once a week he arrived at Mama's," Sammy recalled, "and turned over half of his thirty-five-dollar-a-week salary as if she were his own mother. He wanted nothing in return."

Even with Crawford's help, the Davises had to pawn virtually everything they owned in order to get by. The sole item they refused to sell was their radio, which Sammy later called "the last link between us and show business." Every evening, he and his father would sit in the kitchen, listening to the era's popular dramatic serials, comedies, and musical programs. Sammy particularly relished the celebrity interview show hosted by Jack Eigen that originated from a posh midtown Manhattan nightclub called the Copacabana. "I never tired of listening to the celebrities," he said, "when they talked show business. They weren't dreaming as we always were. These people were making movies, hit records, doing radio, and starring on Broadway. Eigen's slogan or catch phrase was 'I'm at the Copa, where are you?' That killed me."

Sammy occasionally talked his dad into walking downtown to the Copa at E. 60th Street just off Fifth Avenue to gawk as the rich folks disembarked from their limos and cabs. "They had everything," he recalled, "importance, clothes and jewelry like I'd never seen anywhere but in movies. God, they were beautiful." He promised himself that someday he would be a star at the Copa, with Mama watching him at ringside.

Finally, the dry spell broke. Among the Trio's bookings was a gig at the Michigan Theater in Detroit, where the headliner was trombonist Tommy Dorsey and his Orchestra. Will, Sam, and Sammy were filling in for Dorsey's regular opening act, a dance team known as Tip, Tap, & Toe. When they arrived, they were greeted by a skinny young man in his twenties, who stuck out his hand and said, "Hi'ya. My name's Frank. I sing with Dorsey." "That might sound like nothing much," Sammy later told writer Alex Haley, "but the average top vocalist in those days wouldn't give the time of day to a Negro supporting act."

Sammy already knew who Frank was: the vocalist who appeared on most of his Tommy Dorsey records, Frank Sinatra. During each performance, Sammy stood in the wings at the Michigan Theater, watching the unique young singer work. Frank wasn't a belter. He rendered melodies in a simple, easy manner and, at the same time, effectively communicated the meanings of the lyrics. Sammy was in awe. For his part, Sinatra took a liking to the dancer, ten years his junior. Between shows, the two passed the time chatting on the dressing room stairs or grabbing a bite to eat at a nearby restaurant. After three days, Tip, Tap, & Toe returned, and Sammy left town with his uncle and dad, unaware of the significant role Frank Sinatra would play in his future.

Shortly after the Trio's 1941 Detroit engagement, the Japanese bombed Pearl Harbor and America was thrust into World War II.

At sixty-one and forty, respectively, Will and Sam were well past the target age for military service, and Sammy turned a mere sixteen the day after the attack. So they simply carried on with the act.

Two years later, however, Sammy reached eighteen and the situation changed. At 5 feet 4 inches and under 120 pounds, he wasn't exactly the ideal warrior. Moreover, his eyesight was less than perfect, and he was barely literate. At the outset of the war, he might not have been taken even if he had been of age. But, after two and a half years of combat with no end in sight, America needed every man to fuel the war machine. Accordingly, near the end of August 1944, while the Trio was performing at the Fortune Club in Reno, Sammy received orders to report to the Presidio of Monterey, the army's induction center for the San Francisco area. He had been drafted.

In *Yes I Can*, Sammy indicated that he was somewhat exhilarated at the thought of being on his own, away from his dad and Will for a change. But, about five years before the publication of his autobiography, he told Pete Martin of the *Saturday Evening Post* that he "wanted to go in the army like I'd love to jump out of this building. First of all, I was mad because I felt, what am I fighting for? I'm a Negro. Ain't nobody ever giving me no kind of chance, and I was as bitter as it's possible to be." Moreover, he believed that the depletion of entertainers due to the draft might have given the Trio a boost had he been able to stay in civilian life.

Sammy's attitude toward his induction might be a matter of debate, but there is little doubt that Will and his father were stunned. They were certain that his departure would spell the end of the act. Nevertheless, they rallied, pooling their money to buy Sammy a state-of-the-art watch, a $150 chronograph that he'd been drooling over for a year. "We always had the name of the best-dressed colored act in show business," Will said when they made the presentation. "Can't let 'em think different about us in the Army."

The two old pros accompanied Sammy to the induction center early one Saturday morning, bidding their awkward goodbyes out front. Will told him to treat his new gig just like show business, to give it his best, to which his father added, "You'll meet all kinds of people, but just do your job like you're supposed to and nobody can bother you."

The leave-taking was painful. Sammy wasn't just saying goodbye to his loved ones, he was bidding farewell to his youth as well. It certainly hadn't been a typical childhood—no contemporary pals, not a single day of formal education, no exposure whatsoever to sports, games, and other recreational activities, virtually no dating, a complete absence of maternal affection. On the other hand, he'd had the equivalent of two fathers and a loving grandmother; he'd also enjoyed the company of a host of performers. Beyond these pleasant associations, he relished the ambience of show business: watching other acts perform and learning from them, getting into costume and makeup, feeling the rush inside as curtain time drew near, and, of course, hearing the applause roll over the footlights.

Looking back from the remove of adulthood, Sammy himself was always quick to point out the fun of being a child in show business, but he also admitted that he'd never had an opportunity to even consider other career alternatives. He also mourned his lack of education and the simpler elements of childhood that he missed. He wistfully recalled a time when he looked out of a theater window at a playground down below. "There were little kids like me playing," he said. "That was something I had never done, because I lived in an adult world. I never had toys or any friends my age."

Because of such deprivations, the adult Davis harbored conflicted feelings toward his parents. According to his friend Diahann Carroll, he felt an obligation toward his mother and helped support her financially, but he could barely stand to be in a room with her. By contrast, he adored his father, the man who had been his constant companion, indeed his bedmate, from the time he was two and a half until he was eighteen. But he knew that his dad had used him to further his own career. Occasionally, his rage over this abuse overcame his love. Indeed, according to Sy Marsh, Davis' longtime agent and business partner, Sammy once grabbed a gun and set out to kill Sam Sr. Fortunately, he calmed down—or was subdued—before he could carry out his plan.

And what about Harlem, the backdrop to Sammy's youth? To what extent did the Black Mecca influence the entertainer's development? "I don't think Harlem had any impact on Sammy at all," said Burt Boyar, "because it was just a place where he stopped and changed his clothes, really. Yes, he did live there with Mama for a number of years, but she kept him so sheltered that he didn't live the Harlem street kid life at all. . . . So he didn't know he was in Harlem."

"Home" to young Davis was show business. And "his people" weren't blacks, they were fellow troupers. Given this perspective, it is perhaps not surprising that the young Sammy Davis had no real racial consciousness at all. "He never felt black," Boyar maintained, "until people made him feel that way. His only black identity was the color of his skin. It was forced on him, to be an African American." Because Sammy traveled so extensively around the United States and Canada from the age of two and a half on, he developed a universal outlook: he considered himself an American, pure and simple.

Harlem may not have fostered Davis' sense of self, other people, or the world, but it nevertheless granted him membership in its homogeneous community. When he was on the road, he entered another closed society, the world of entertainers. If Harlemites accepted him for his skin color, show people welcomed him for his talent. Of the two groups, clearly it was the world of show business that influenced his style and manner—the way he dressed, the way he learned to speak, and the kind of music to which he responded. He may have come into conflict with individual members of one community or the other, but never, as he was growing up, was he made to feel outside the mainstream as he knew it.

That would change entirely when he entered yet a third insular community, the U.S. Army. His self-image, his identity as an African American, indeed his life would be threatened, shaken, and altered in ways he could not possibly have imagined on that Saturday in December 1944 in Monterey. When he reentered the world he had known, he would be a different man.

PART TWO

Breaking All the Rules

CHAPTER 3

Fort Warren

From the induction center in Monterey, Sammy was shipped to Fort Francis E. Warren, an army training facility outside of Cheyenne, Wyoming.

Today, Warren Air Force Base is one of three strategic missile sites in the United States, but its roots go back to 1867, when Wyoming was still a territory. The outpost, then known as Fort D. A. Russell, for a hero of the Civil War, was charged with protecting workers of the Union Pacific Railroad from hostile Indians. The fort's name was changed in 1930 at the instigation of President Herbert Hoover, to honor Wyoming's first state governor (later U.S. senator), Medal of Honor winner Francis E. Warren. By then, the small frontier outpost had become one of the largest military installations in the country, encompassing sufficient brick barracks, office buildings, mess halls, recreational facilities, and support structures to house a brigade. During World War II, Fort Warren served in excess of 240,000 infantrymen, as well as thousands of prisoners of war.

During the fort's wild frontier days, it had played host to three of the army's four African American regiments (two cavalry, two infantry), popularly known as the "Buffalo Soldiers." Despite that exposure, Fort Warren and, for that matter, Cheyenne, with its tiny black population, retained an uneasy relationship with the Negroes assigned to them during World War II. Indeed, the fort's first contingent of blacks, a group of five hundred trainees inducted during an early civilian call-up in June 1941, was transferred to another base as a result of local tensions. But by the end of 1942, with nearly half a million blacks in uniform (compared with 3,640 in August 1939), a base the size of Fort Warren simply had to be used to house and train new African American inductees.

The post commander, Brig. Gen. John A. Warden, was hardly a friend of the black enlisted men assigned to him. Judge William H. Hastie, a civilian aide to the secretary of war, reported after visiting the fort in

May 1942, "I found the Negro soldiers very bitter with reference to alleged manifestations of racial prejudice" by the general. Not only did Warden refuse to fill vacancies in the ranks of noncommissioned officers within his African American training cadres, but he frequently referred to the trainees as "niggers." At the time of Hastie's visit, the contingent of African Americans on the post numbered around two thousand, a sizable group, though small in comparison to the fort's white population.

Although Gen. Warden was transferred to the Pacific theater of operations in March 1943, the uneasy climate between whites and blacks, on the post and in the town, remained unchanged at the time of Sammy Davis, Jr.'s arrival. Indeed, according to *Yes I Can*, he endured a number of racial attacks during his tenure in Wyoming. Some of these came as a direct result of his living with white soldiers. He recalled, for example, being yanked out of line while waiting for a washroom sink by a trainee from Texas, who told him, "Where I come from, niggers stand in the back of the line, behind the white people." Davis slugged the man with his toilet kit. Lying on the ground, bleeding, the fellow looked up, grinned, and said, "But you're still a nigger." In another instance, a barracks mate named Jennings viciously destroyed the precious watch given Sammy by his dad and Will, stomping it with the heel of his boot when it accidentally fell to the floor.

Beyond these specifics, Davis conveyed in his book the feeling of being completely cut off, almost suffocated, at Fort Warren and was certainly enraged by his circumstances. He felt isolated and friendless, surrounded by people who, at best, had no use for him and, at worst, were out to do him harm.

There is no question that the general climate in the army and in the United States at large in 1944 would have supported the kind of experiences Davis recounted. For a biographer, however, there is a problem with some of the incidents he described, dramatic and heartbreaking as they are. The fact is that during World War II, the army was rigidly segregated along racial lines. There were separate barracks, mess halls, and, in most cases, recreational facilities at each installation for each race. The goal was to avoid precisely the kinds of situations described by Davis in his book. Even in combat, where the exigencies of battle might have mitigated against such care, every effort was made to keep blacks and whites from intermingling.

There is no reason to think that Sammy's experience was different from that of hundreds of thousands of his peers. Indeed, he told Jim Cook, who wrote an extensive series of articles about him in the *New York Post* in 1956, that he had been assigned to an all-black training regiment. Burt Boyar, his *Yes I Can* collaborator, told this author that he seemed to recall Sammy mentioning something similar. But Boyar also insisted that Sammy was one of two Negroes assigned to an otherwise white training regiment, the first integrated unit in the entire U.S. Army. Davis told the same thing to the *Saturday Evening Post*'s Pete Martin about five years prior to his autobiography's publication.

Despite Sammy's assertions, a thorough examination of the relevant documents at the National Archives in College Park, Maryland, turned up nothing to indicate the presence of an integrated unit at Fort Warren—or anywhere else, for that matter. Unfortunately, this can't be determined with absolute certainty, because all of the World War II records of the domestic military installations were destroyed in the 1950s, and, unlike combat outfits, training regiments maintain no group histories or alumni associations.

But even if, by some strange chance, Sammy did find himself one of two blacks in an otherwise white outfit, this still wouldn't account for the overwhelming feeling of being trapped that permeates the relevant passages of *Yes I Can*. There would have been thousands of other African Americans on the base with him, men he could have befriended during his off-hours, GIs who might have watched his back when protection seemed advisable. Moreover, a single incident, like that with the Texan in the latrine or the one with Jennings and the watch, would have resulted in Sammy's transfer into a regular segregated unit. Put simply, the general environment on the base as well as the specifics described by Davis in his book seem more in keeping with the experiences of African American enlisted men after the army was integrated by President Truman in the postwar period, not the army of 1944–45.

This having been said, if one sets aside the racial incidents that supposedly occurred in Davis' sleeping, bathing, and dining quarters, there remain examples of brutal physical abuse and humiliation in settings that would not necessarily have been precluded by segregation. From these alone, one can easily conclude that Davis' military service provided the crucible for the extreme consciousness-raising he described in his book.

To begin with, Sammy had a difficult time adjusting to army life, even without the racial tensions. A soldier's day starts at dawn, and he was—and always would be—a night person. Furthermore, he had no experience being part of a group or the regimentation that accompanies such social interactions. He found the experience so intimidating that he cried in his bed his first night in camp. His sobs caught the attention of the company master sergeant, a white fellow named Gene Williams. "He took me to his room and we talked for a couple of hours," Sammy recalled. In the manner of Will Mastin, Williams tried to bolster the trainee's resolve, telling him, "A man can do anything he wants if he tries. Give the Army a try. If you have any serious problems come to see me."

Sgt. Williams would play a pivotal role in Sammy's life over the next few months. Not only did he offer the young trainee a sympathetic ear, but he also fostered Sammy's intellectual development. Davis discovered that the master sergeant was an avid reader and was intrigued by his large collection of books. When he asked to borrow one, Williams suggested he try *The Picture of Dorian Gray* by Oscar Wilde. Intrigued but puzzled by the many words he didn't understand, Sammy read the book from cover to cover, using a pocket dictionary he bought at the PX to guide him. "When I finished it," he recalled, "I gave it back to Sergeant Williams and we discussed it. He handed me three more and told me in what order to read them and we had long discussions after each one as I finished it."

Under Williams' tutelage, Davis opened his mind to a vast, exciting, and hitherto unsuspected world of adventures, events, people, and ideas. He eventually worked his way through *The Complete Works of William Shakespeare,* Carl Sandburg's multivolume biography of Abraham Lincoln, a history of the United States, tales by Poe, Dumas, Dickens, and Twain, and Edmond Rostand's play about an ugly man with a beautiful soul, *Cyrano de Bergerac,* with which Sammy felt a keen sense of identification. "The more education Sergeant Williams gave me," the entertainer recalled, "through his books and our discussions, the greater hunger I developed for it. When I ran out of his books, I found others at the Post Library and then reread the ones he had." Particularly memorable was his first book about the African American experience, Richard Wright's recently published *Black Boy*. It gave him a new perspective on his own life and the unfortunate plight of Negroes in the United States at the time.

Williams helped in yet another way. Despite the influence of Clark Gable and Errol Flynn, Sammy spoke with a thick black dialect. The sergeant suggested that they read aloud to one another as a way of helping Sammy improve his speech. "Before long," Davis told reporter Jim Cook, "I lost the accent and had a pretty good vocabulary."

Improving his manner of speaking was particularly important to Sammy because, with Williams' encouragement, he began to perform in the camp variety shows held at the white service club on Friday night. As a professional entertainer, Davis quickly became an obvious standout. More important in terms of his future, these shows, far removed from critics and paying audiences, enabled him to move beyond his career as a hoofer. He could try a little humor, sing the occasional song, and render some rudimentary impressions of popular actors and singers. The guys didn't care if he was black and the stars he imitated were white; what he was doing onstage was amusing. Exposed to nonpaying audiences for the first time in his career, Sammy quickly realized that performing could be a way of reaching out to people.

He felt particularly gratified after a show when a group of white trainees invited him to join them for a drink, even though African Americans, performers included, had their own recreational facilities on the base. After about an hour, Sammy said goodnight and headed for the door. En route, another group of soldiers invited him to join them. Among this bunch was Jennings, the white trainee who, according to Sammy, destroyed his watch in the barracks they shared. In light of his history with this particular crowd, Davis was reluctant to accept the invitation, but he was finally persuaded to sit down. Effusive over Sammy's talent, Jennings offered him a beer. In those days, the entertainer drank only Cokes, but he didn't want to be rude. Raising his own bottle in a toast, Jennings encouraged Sammy to take a big swig. The entertainer had the bottle halfway to his mouth when he realized it was warm. Then he got a whiff of the contents and discovered it was urine.

Trying to rein in his fury, Sammy placed the bottle on the table and got up to leave. But Jennings turned the bottle upside down so that the urine ran all over Sammy's uniform. Then he stood up and shouted to the others in the club, "Silly niggers can't even control themselves. This little fella got so excited sittin' with white men—look what he did to himself." At that point, Sammy attacked. "I had my hands on his throat," he said, "with every intention of killing him. I loved seeing the sneer fall from his face and be replaced by dumb shock as I squeezed tighter and tighter, my thumbs against his windpipe." Finally, the bully, a foot taller and at least sixty pounds heavier, extricated himself from Sammy's grasp, and the fight was on. It wasn't much of a contest. "His fist smashed into my face," the entertainer recalled. "Then I just stood there watching his other fist come at me, helpless to make myself move out of the way. I felt my nose crumble as if he'd hit an apple with a sledge hammer. The blood spurted out and I smelled a dry horrible dusty smell." Back at the barracks, Sgt. Williams wanted to send Davis to the infirmary, but Sammy refused to go. Later, he learned with grim satisfaction that Jennings had been hospitalized, but he realized that no amount of fighting would make certain whites see him as anything more than subhuman. It was a rude awakening.

According to Sammy, the battle royal led to other fights with other guys—about one every other day, in his estimation. (Once again, the reader is reminded that if Davis were, indeed, in a segregated unit, the preponderance of these encounters must be called into question. He couldn't have had that many fights after club shows, which were the only places he would have regularly encountered white enlisted men; the shows, after all, were offered only once a week.) Sammy's propensity for sticking up for himself led to repeated injuries, notably to his nose, which, as he put it, was "getting flatter all the time." Finally, Sgt. Williams told him what he already knew, that he wasn't going to be able to pound people into liking him. "You can't hope to change a man's ideas," the sergeant pointed out, "except with another, better idea. You've got to fight with your brains, Sammy, not your fists."

Like all GIs, Davis had been drafted to fight America's enemies abroad, not the haters at home. To that end, his first eight weeks at Fort Warren consisted of an unrelenting regimen of physical exercise plus instructions about how to march, shoot, and handle a weapon. As a dancer, he was in better condition than most of his peers and thus adjusted to the rigors of basic training with relative ease.

After completing the eight-week course, Davis and his peers were given physical exams to determine their fitness for combat. In *Yes I Can,* Sammy indicated that he was not posted to a fighting unit because it was discovered that he had an "athletic heart," meaning that his heart occasionally beat a couple times more per minute than the norm. However, there is nothing in his service record, which is on file at the National Personnel Record Center in St. Louis, to support this contention. Rather, it was persistent headaches that kept him from being shipped to Europe or the Pacific.

GIs exempt from combat duty were typically trained for service roles, of which there were many, ranging from clerk-typist to hospital orderly to cook to motor pool mechanic. Instead of drawing such an assignment, however, Davis was ordered to repeat basic training. Having done so, eight weeks later he went through basic training yet again. And even a fourth time. None of the military historians consulted by this author could offer a reasonable explanation for why he would have drawn such repetitive, fruitless duty, one that benefited neither him nor the army. Typically, such assignments would have derived from a physical problem—a broken leg during training, for example—or a mental deficiency or psychological breakdown. But Davis suffered from none of these. In fact, he was being considered for the Good Conduct Medal at the time of his discharge (he simply hadn't served long enough to receive the award).

The singular benefit of Davis' prolonged stay at Fort Warren was his continued involvement in the weekly camp shows. One evening, he came offstage to find a corporal waiting for him. After congratulating him on his performance, the fellow introduced himself as George M. Cohan, Jr., son of the great songwriter-actor-director. Over a drink, Cohan said that each army base was creating a show for an intercamp competition. He wanted Sammy to help him mount Fort Warren's entry. Davis was delighted. All they needed, Cohan added, was permission from the base commander.

A few days later, Cohan told Sammy that the general had agreed to give them an audition at the officers' club. They cobbled together a mini-version of the show they had in mind, using guys who performed at the officers' club on Friday nights plus a few others. Sammy's contributions included an impression of Frank Sinatra. Pleased with what he saw but aware of several others angling for the plumb assignment, the general wanted to hear the rest of Davis and Cohan's ideas for the show. At a meeting arranged for that purpose, it became clear that the commander's adjutant, a WAC captain, would have a key vote in deciding which team would get to represent the fort. Consequently, Sammy and George began courting her, paying her compliments and showering her with flowers and candy. Their plan seemed to be working—to the extent that the captain asked the energetic duo to submit a budget for sets, costumes, and props.

But the plan also resulted in a horrible incident, which happened after Sammy dropped off the budget at the captain's office. As he headed back to his barracks, a PFC and another fellow, both headquarters clerks, told him that the captain was waiting for him in an unused barracks about half a mile away. Sammy was puzzled by the information but thought perhaps the barracks was being used to store scenery. So he followed the clerks. When they entered the barracks, they shoved him into the latrine, saying, "Sorry, nigger, but your lady love won't be here." There had been nothing romantic in his relationship with the captain, but neither the two clerks nor the four other guys waiting in the latrine were in the mood for explanations.

Pinning Sammy's arms behind him, they ripped open his shirt, dragged him before a mirror so he could watch what was happening to him, and brought forth a can of white paint. The PFC then dipped a small brush into the paint can and wrote, "I'm a nigger!" across Sammy's chest. With a larger brush, he began to cover the helpless entertainer's arms and hands, adding "Coon" across his forehead. Then, while the paint dried, Davis was ordered to dance. At first he refused, but the PFC punched him in the stomach. Finally, he complied. "That's better, Sambo," the hateful clerk oozed. "Keep it going. And a little faster."

Sammy picked up the tempo, but he couldn't seem to go fast enough to satisfy his tormentors, which earned him another punch in the stomach. Finally, with the paint dry, the PFC drove home the point of the exercise: that Sammy might think he was white, but he wasn't. To prove it, he poured turpentine on a rag and began wiping the white paint off one of the entertainer's arms. "When my skin showed through the paint," Davis said, "he grinned. 'There. Y'see. Just as black 'n' ugly as ever!'" Then the PFC rubbed turpentine on his own arm, illustrating the fact that no matter how hard he pressed, his skin remained white. Finally, after threatening to repeat the lesson in even more dramatic fashion if the incident were reported, the soldiers left, taking the turpentine with them.

"I looked at myself in one of the mirrors," Sammy recalled. "I wanted to crawl into the walls and die. I sat down on the floor and cried." Finally, after an hour or so, he left the latrine, humiliated and confused, his skin itching terribly. He had no choice but to return to his own barracks with the paint intact. As night had fallen by then, he was at least able to cross the post grounds unseen. Finally, when he arrived at his destination, Sgt. Williams sent to the motor pool for some turpentine and helped him clean up. When Sammy finally crawled into bed that night, he vowed that no one would ever do anything like that to him again.

Davis and Cohan did win the coveted camp show assignment. After rehearsing their offering for a month, they performed it for a week at the fort. But the incident with the paint had ruined the experience for Sammy. On opening night, he didn't even want to go on. Looking out at the audience before the start of the show, he thought to himself, "How can you run out and smile at people who despise you?" But, in the time-honored tradition of show business, he persevered. Later, as he was taking his curtain call, he observed a certain measure of respect on the white faces looking back at him. He had already learned that performing could endear him to people, strangers as well as those he knew well. But now he began to realize that he had an even more powerful gift. As he saw it, his "talent was the weapon, the power, the way for me to fight. It was the only way I might hope to affect a man's thinking."

Throughout the week of performances, Sammy repeatedly felt the same sensation he experienced on opening night, that his only outlet for change lay in his skill as an entertainer. "While I was performing," he noted, "they forgot what I was and there were times when even I could forget it. Sometimes off-stage I passed a guy I didn't know and he said, 'Good show last night.' It was as though my talent was giving me a pass which excluded me from their prejudice. I didn't hope for camaraderie.

All I wanted was to walk into a room without hearing the conversation slow down, and it was happening. I was developing an identity around camp and it was buying me a little chunk of peace."

Thereafter, he was driven to achieve. As he put it, "I dug down deeper every day, looking for new material, inventing it, stealing it, switching it—any way that I could find new things to make my shows better—and I lived twenty-four hours a day for that hour or two at night when I could stand on that stage, facing the audience, knowing I was dancing down the barriers between us."

In *Yes I Can*, Sammy indicated that after the camp show he was transferred to Special Services, the army's entertainment branch, and that he spent the final eight months of his military service performing on posts around the country. But this assertion is not borne out by his army personnel record. According to this document, he was eventually classified as an entertainment specialist, but he never progressed beyond a training regiment and never left Fort Warren. Moreover, his entire period of service lasted a mere ten months. On May 29, 1945, he was hospitalized for his persistent headaches. Three days later, while he was still in the infirmary, he received his discharge. By then, the war in Europe had been over for some three weeks.

The duration of Sammy's military service is of relatively little consequence, as is the question of whether or not he was ever in Special Services. Of far greater importance are the things he learned at Fort Warren and how those discoveries impacted his future. As was his youth, his military career was a mixed blessing.

On the plus side, Sgt. Gene Williams imbued Sammy with an interest in reading and a thirst for knowledge that remained with him for the rest of his life. Moreover, he significantly improved his way of speaking, which would serve him well when he reentered the world of show business after his discharge.

In addition, performing in camp shows significantly enlarged Sammy's sense of himself as an entertainer. Once he started plumbing hitherto unexplored pockets of talent, he wanted to push the boundaries of what he could do onstage as far as they would go. Arguably, had it not been for Fort Warren, the world might never have heard of Sammy Davis, Jr., for it is inconceivable that he would have become a star as one-third of a Negro flash dance act.

Of course, he paid a heavy price for these broadening experiences. The hurt and humiliation he felt at the hands of the racists he encountered in Wyoming, whether in an integrated training unit or not, left scars on his psyche that were profound. For the first time, he realized that there were people who would define him solely by his race and that being a Negro in and of itself could produce undisguised, sustained, and virulent antipathy. As he later explained, "Until the Army, nobody white had ever just *looked* at me and *hated* me—and didn't even *know* me." The discovery was, in his words, "horrible and very, very frightening."

Ultimately, he concluded that the single best weapon at his command was his talent. Combined with the concurrent broadening of his performance skills, this realization became the defining moment of Sammy Davis, Jr.'s entire life. Everything that he would do and be thereafter can be traced to this single concept that, once conceived, lodged in the very depth of his heart, soul, and mind. Long after he put the walls of Fort Warren behind him, he would seek to quell the haters by wowing them with his gifts. No matter how long he had to remain onstage to do so, he wanted everyone to love him.

CHAPTER 4

"Hungry and Mad"

Despite their fears, Will and Sam Sr. were able to keep the act going while Sammy was in uniform. Initially, they tried performing as a duo, but they hadn't carried an engagement by themselves in nearly twenty years, and they no longer had the stamina for it. All of their 1940s material was geared toward a threesome, so they hired a girl to fill in for Sammy. Later, they replaced her with a roller skater named Joe Smythe. Either way, as Sam told his son when they spoke on the phone, they were just "killing time" until he could rejoin them.

They were in Los Angeles when Sammy's discharge came through. "Get my clothes cleaned and pressed," he jubilantly told his father. "I'm coming back into the act." He was so energized that he didn't sleep at all on the train from Wyoming. All he could think about was getting the Trio back on its feet and becoming a star.

Following a joyful reunion at Union Station, Will and Sam accompanied the kid back to their downtown hotel, the Chetwood, where he immediately changed out of his uniform. Neither man questioned him too closely about his military experiences; indeed, Sammy would grimace any time he thought about the army.

Initially, the Davises and Mastin returned to the type of flash dance act they had offered prior to Sammy's induction. But now, in addition to movie palaces, burlesque houses, road houses, and carnivals, they focused on bookings in a different type of venue: nightclubs.

Nightclubs were not new. They had been a part of the American scene since the early years of the twentieth century. But they had faltered during the Depression, and only a few elite spots, such as New York's Copa, remained unscathed by the dismal U.S. economy. During the war years, however, cabarets enjoyed a major resurgence. People eagerly flocked to places where, for a few moments, they could dress up and forget the realities of the world around them. In major metropolises, like New York, Chicago, and San Francisco, the town's swankiest cabarets became magnets for celebrities, mavens of society and their debutante daughters, wealthy businesspeople, and other movers and shakers. Columnists like New York's Cholly Knickerbocker made it their business to follow the doings of what they called café society.

In the immediate postwar years, nightclubs continued to flourish as the domestic economy boomed and Americans sought to put the carnage behind them. Of course, not every club could count on the patronage of Clark Gable or Brenda Frazier or Aly Khan. Many operated on a more mundane level, with customers who were boringly middle class or, worse, downright seedy. There were also clubs that catered exclusively to African Americans, establishments with exotic names like the Rum Boogie and the Club De Lisa. The Will Mastin Trio wasn't hip enough for the black clubs or prominent enough for the elite clubs. They played what was left over.

Such a place was L.A.'s Cricket Club, the Trio's first booking on Sammy's return. It was a job, but such gigs were never going to take Sammy where he wanted to go. "Who the hell's gonna see us at the Cricket Club?" he asked Will. "My God, we played better places than that before I went into the army." Mastin didn't share Sammy's impatience. Remembering the dark days during the Depression, he reasoned that their $250 a week was a lot better than nothing.

Following their stint in Los Angeles, Will put together a series of bookings in the Northwest for the same sum, $250 a week. To Sammy, these engagements were just more dead ends. Mastin continued to argue in favor of such bookings. Not only did the aging hoofer not share Davis' quest for stardom, but he didn't even understand it. Complaints about their engagements left him puzzled and hurt, and Sammy invariably found himself apologizing to his mentor for his lack of gratitude.

If Mastin was mystified by Sammy's insistence on playing better venues, he was equally perplexed by his protégé's persistence about adding some of his impressions to the act. Will was perfectly content doing a traditional flash dance routine. Nevertheless, he reluctantly agreed to let Sammy try his hand at the likes of Step'n'Fetchit, Billy Eckstine, and Louis Armstrong. But when the kid said he wanted to impersonate Edward G. Robinson, James Cagney, and Jimmy Durante, Mastin exploded. "No colored performer ever did white people in front of white people," he insisted. Davis pointed out how popular those impressions had been at Fort Warren, but Will was unmoved. He knew that the bored GIs who were getting entertainment for free were no measure of what paying nightclub audiences would accept.

As if young Davis weren't unhappy enough with Mastin's bookings and the confinements Will placed on the act, he had also begun to resent the fact that, in most of the venues the Trio played, he had to stay in hotels and rooming houses that catered exclusively to African Americans. That had been the case since he was a child, but before the war, he hadn't noticed. Since his return to civilian life, such restrictions rankled. Being older and having grown up in the South, Will and, for that matter, Sam Sr. quietly accepted what Sammy could not. Their passivity angered him even more. Most days, he was, in his words, "hungry and mad, baby."

His fury reached its zenith when the Trio played Spokane, Washington. Discovering that all of the colored hotels and rooming houses were booked up, Sam and Will resigned themselves to sleeping in their dressing room. But Sammy vowed to find them rooms in, as he put it, "the whitest goddamned hotel in town." He was unsuccessful. In fact, he even got into a fight with a bellboy at a posh establishment, who told him, "Go back where you belong." Sheepishly, Sammy returned to the theater, his face bloody, and joined his dad and Mastin on the dressing room floor.

Following the Northwest tour, Davis and his partners returned to Los Angeles, which had become their permanent base of operations. Having saved a bit of money on the road, they decided to move from the Chetwood to a better black hotel, the Morris, on Fifth Avenue downtown. Sammy was even given a room of his own for the first time in his life.

Unfortunately, he had more time than he wished to hang out at the Morris, because Mastin hit a booking slump. To fill the time, Sammy bought a pair of bongos, which he taught himself to play, figuring that if he got proficient enough, he might eventually work them into the act. One day, he strolled into a penny arcade that featured a booth in which one could record one's voice for a quarter. He ended up making several records. Back at the Morris, he played the disks for his father. "That's not bad singin', Poppa," Sam told him, "not bad at all." Then he added, dryly, "Course it'd help if you could do it where you won't pick up the sound of cars goin' by." As far as Davis Sr. was concerned, he, Will, and Sammy were hoofers. Period.

One evening, boredom drove Sammy to the studio of KFWB, the radio station from which Frank Sinatra's CBS radio program originated. He didn't expect Sinatra to remember him; he just wanted to watch the singer work.

After the show, he hurried over to the stage door, where about five hundred others were waiting. When Frank emerged, he was engulfed by the crowd, mostly swooning girls. But he calmly signed autographs. Catching a glimpse of Sammy, he asked, "Don't I know you?" Surprised, Davis reminded him of the 1941 Detroit gig. Nodding his head, Frank invited him to come back and see the show the following week, even leaving a ticket for him at the box office. Sammy showed up, and afterward found himself being escorted to the singer's immense dressing room. Watching Frank with the other well-wishers was as magical to Sammy as that long-ago occasion when he had met Bill Robinson. Even more than the vaudevillian, Sinatra was smooth and confident; he had, in Sammy's words, "the aura of a king about him." Not knowing what to say, the younger entertainer remained in the background, observing, not even sure Frank remembered him from the previous week. Then Sinatra turned to him, put his arm around him, and said, "So long, Sam. Keep in touch."

One day, around the early part of 1946, Will and Sam Sr. decided to look up a friend from vaudeville named Arthur Silber. Once part of a double act called Silber and North, he had retired as a performer in the mid-thirties. Becoming a booking agent for the prestigious Pantages Circuit, he eventually went out on his own and, by the mid-forties, had emerged as one of the biggest talent bookers on the West Coast. Happy to see his old colleagues, Silber signed the Mastin Trio, an omen of good things to come.

Indeed, a few months later, in April 1946, Silber managed to take Sammy, Sam, and Will to a new level by getting them into Slapsie Maxie's, a Los Angeles nightspot popular with members of the movie community.* By now, the act showcased Sammy's growing skill on the drums. Moreover, he had finally won Will's permission to do his impressions of white movie stars.

The impressions, in particular, were a rousing success. With his natural skill for mimicry, Davis had an uncanny ability to not only sound like Cagney and Robinson and the others he introduced a bit later on (such as Jimmy Stewart and Cary Grant), but also to move like them and even look like them. When he came offstage after the first time, with the audience laughing and clapping, his dad hugged him and Will cheerfully admitted he had been wrong.

Thus, Sammy was well positioned to make an impression at Slapsie Maxie's, even though the headliner was the sad-faced clown Ben Blue, a part owner of the club.† Indeed, his impressions of movie stars went over extremely well with the home crowd. Beyond Cagney and Robinson and a few other actors, he was also offering musical impressions. Typically, he'd pick a song and render a verse in the style of one pop singer, Billy Eck-

---

*The club was named for one of its owners, Max Rosenbloom, the former boxing champ who occasionally played punchdrunk pugs in films.

†Primarily a stage performer, Blue appeared in more than twenty films during the 1930s and 1940s, but he is perhaps best remembered today for his late-career roles in *It's a Mad, Mad, Mad, Mad World*, *The Russians Are Coming*, and *A Guide for the Married Man*.

stine, for example, then do the next verse as someone else—Sinatra, perhaps, or Nat King Cole—and the next verse as yet a third performer. Sometimes he would even end the tune with a few bars in his own voice. The musical renderings were slightly exaggerated to emphasize each singer's idiosyncrasies, making them not only accurate but also amusing. When, for example, Davis added Tony Bennett a few years later, he emphasized, to a comically excruciating degree, Bennett's barely perceptible lisp.

It was during this L.A. stint that Davis started referring to Will Mastin as his uncle. One night, he stepped forward at the end of the act to thank the audience, something he'd never done before, and found himself saying, "Ladies and gentlemen, you can't imagine what this means to me, my father and . . ." He didn't want to say "Mr. Mastin" or "our friend Will," so he said "my uncle." Mastin retained the honorific for the rest of his life. Indeed, as Sammy's celebrity grew, Will's new status became such a given that, even in Hollywood, only those very close to the Davises realized the old hoofer was not, in fact, a relative.

Mastin had agreed to the gig at Slapsie Maxie's even though it paid only $200 a week in the hope that influential people would catch the act. The gamble paid off because Arthur Silber next booked the Trio into San Francisco's Golden Gate Theater with the celebrated drummer Buddy Rich and his Orchestra, followed in June by a tour of U.S. military bases in Hawaii. The junket, which featured a number of other acts, yielded Sammy, his dad, and Will $400 a week, the most money they'd ever earned. Even their fear of flying couldn't dampen their excitement.

Accompanying them was Silber's teenage son, Arthur Jr. Although Arthur was about five years younger than Sammy and was still in high school, he and the entertainer quickly became friends. Silber, in fact, was the first peer that Sammy could truly call a pal. Figuring out things to do in the daytime is always tough for an entertainer. To amuse themselves on the tour, Sammy and Arthur started teaching themselves how to "fake fight," that is, orchestrating battles like those staged by stuntmen for the movies. "Neither one of us knew what the heck we were doing," Silber admitted, but they enjoyed themselves, inventing everything as they went along. On occasion, their enthusiasm got the better of them. "We broke up a restaurant in Honolulu," Silber recalled. "Tables and chairs went flying. We caught holy hell from our fathers—and from Will."

After the tour, the Trio hit a booking slump. Sammy spent some of the time visiting Arthur Jr. at the Silber home in the San Fernando Valley, sleeping overnight on the floor in his friend's bedroom. Growing bored with just fake fighting, they bought a couple of foils and added swordplay to the mix.

Finally, Mastin decided they should try their luck in New York; the Trio hit the road, taking whatever small-time gigs they could along the way. Back in Harlem, Rosa B. was still on relief and still getting help from Sam Sr.'s old friend, Nathan Crawford, even though the garment factory where Crawford worked was experiencing a severe economic downturn, requiring him to take a cut in pay.

New York proved a bust, so Will, Sam, and Sammy moved on to Chicago. After two months of stagnating at the old Ritz, a hotel on the South Side, the act remained without a booking, while a friend of Sammy's dad, Ossie Wilson, fronted their rent. Because Wilson ran poker games for a living, Sammy and his partners were dependent on his good fortune. During the day, they'd hang around the hotel lobby, reading the trade papers. One of the acts they read about was Dick and Gene Wesson, old pals who had just opened at a club downtown. Desperate to get out of Chicago, Will, Sammy, and Sam went over to the club to ask the Wessons for a loan, enough money to take them somewhere else. The Wessons gave them the money, but their manager, Sam Stefel, did something even better. He booked the Trio as the opening act for another of his clients, Mickey Rooney, who was fresh out of the army and about to embark on a tour of the RKO movie theater circuit.

Born Joe Yule, Jr., in 1920, five years before Sammy, Mickey Rooney had been a major movie star since he was a teenager, thanks to a series of MGM films about an all-American boy named Andy Hardy as well as several backyard let's-put-on-a-show musicals with Judy Garland. In 1939, Rooney was the most popular motion picture actor in America. But, by 1946, he was no longer a juvenile and, after his release from the service, he needed to jump-start his career. Hence the tour.

Two short, cocky guys, both children of vaudeville, Rooney and Davis hit it off instantly, so much so that Mickey encouraged Sammy to do impressions even though they were also featured in Mickey's act. Sam Stefel wasn't keen to have an unknown draw attention away from the star. Nevertheless, when the show opened in Boston in October 1946, Rooney told Sammy to sneak in a few bits, and Davis happily complied.

When he wasn't performing, Sammy stood in the wings watching Mickey sing, dance, tell jokes, do impressions, and play musical instruments. No doubt, Rooney's versatility fueled Sammy's own resolve to be a multiple-threat performer.

The tour was grueling, with seven shows a day, starting at 9:30 in the morning, but Sammy was having a ball. Between performances, he and Mickey hung out backstage, playing gin rummy and listening to records. As the tour progressed and the two troupers became closer, Mickey told

Sam Stefel to use more shots of Sammy, Sam, and Will in advertising posters. He also generously extended the Trio's stage time, so that Sammy could include more impressions. "He was taking time away from himself to make room for me," Davis recalled. Every time he tried to thank the star, Rooney would cut him off, saying, "Let's not get sickening about this."

The tour was interrupted in December because Mickey's wife, Betty Jane, was pregnant, and he wanted to be home in time for the child's birth. Before leaving, Rooney told Davis that he was slated to do a feature for Metro called *Killer McCoy,* a remake of the boxing film *The Crowd Roars.* In it was the part of a fighter for which he thought Sammy would be perfect. "I'll talk to them as soon as I get out there," he promised.

Envisioning himself in front of a motion picture camera for the first time since the 1933 Vitaphone shorts, Sammy spent weeks practicing shadow boxing. But, when Rooney rejoined the tour in early 1947, he sadly confessed that he couldn't persuade Metro to use a black man for the role. Sammy was devastated. That MGM wasn't even willing to test him stung. When the two young troupers parted in New York, Mickey again told Sammy how disappointed he was about the film, but he admitted that he no longer wielded much clout at MGM. He shook Sammy's hand, saying, "So long, buddy. What the hell. Maybe one day we'll get our innings."

Sammy had hoped the tour with Mickey Rooney would be the Trio's big break, but that wasn't the case. He, his dad, and Will had to settle for several gigs at second-rate clubs in New England, taking home less than a quarter of what they'd earned with Mickey. And when those engagements ran out, they found themselves back at Mama's in Harlem.

While he was in New York, Sammy reconnected with Buddy Rich. Like a pair of kids, the duo formed a secret society with Marty Mills, a friend of Rich whose father owned a music publishing company. Adopting code names and brandishing gold badges, the three men liked going into hotels and pretending they were house detectives, often fooling even the real gumshoes. They also enjoyed taunting another friend, singer Mel Torme, who was eager to join their select club. Torme merited only a probationary silver badge.

But Mel had something Davis didn't: a Colt .45 revolver and a beautiful Western holster in which to keep it. One evening, he strapped on the rig and demonstrated his ability to quickly draw the weapon and twirl it around his finger. Davis was captivated. Mel let him try on the holster, but Sammy discovered that drawing and spinning the gun wasn't as easy as it looked. He spent the entire evening practicing, prompting Torme to declare, "You're hooked!"

Indeed, he was. Soon he would have a Western rig of his own and would practice endlessly at the foot of his bed (so that, when he dropped the gun, it fell without harm on the mattress). Eventually, Sammy became so proficient at drawing, twirling, and flipping a six-shooter that, in addition to singing, dancing, doing impressions, and playing a musical instrument, he could dazzle nightclub audiences with this unusual and somewhat dubious talent.

One evening, Sammy decided to take in a movie at the Strand Theater downtown. Lucky Millander's band was headlining the live show, but a black comedy act was also on the bill. The fellows in the act were funny, but they were doing the same sort of shtick that African Americans had been offering white audiences since the days of minstrelsy (and that two white guys had recently turned to gold on the *Amos and Andy* radio program): slurring their words, moving at a snail's pace, acting shiftless yet crafty. Suddenly, like a blinding flash, it hit Sammy: he was guilty of playing to the same stereotypes. "They were an automatic part of our personalities onstage," he later explained. "It was the way people expected Negro acts to be so that's the way we were." But, in that Manhattan movie theater, he saw the behavior anew, and it made him sick. Why, he asked himself, couldn't those black comedians speak English properly? Why did they have to downgrade themselves to get laughs?

He began checking out other Negro acts. As Davis put it, "They were all shuffling around, 'Yassuhing' all over the stage. Does the public really want this? It doesn't seem possible. If the joke is funny won't they still laugh if we call them 'Gentlemen' [instead of slurring the word]? They don't expect every Jew to have a long nose and a heavy accent; not every Irish performer has to do 'Pat and Mike' jokes so why must every Negro be an Uncle Tom?"

Then he realized something even more insidious. Black performers failed to make any personal contact whatsoever with their audiences. They substituted interaction with *each other* for direct involvement with those who were paying to see them. It was, he thought, "as if they didn't have the right to communicate with the people out front. It was the total reverse of the way Mickey played, directly to the people, talking to them, kidding them, communicating with them." He ruefully acknowledged that he, his father, and Will were also guilty of this. "It didn't matter," he said, "how many instruments I learned to play, how many impressions I learned to do, or how much I perfected them—we were still doing *Holiday in Dixieland*—still a flash act. That was how we set ourselves up so that was how the audiences would see us." Which, in his opinion, explained why the tour with Rooney had failed to take him to a higher level of success. If he wanted to be a star, he suddenly knew with absolute certainty that he would have to engage audiences directly, the way Rooney did, the way Sinatra did, the way every successful white performer did.

This epiphany was probably the most important realization of his career.

Certain he was onto something important, he excitedly explained his thinking to his father and Will. Surprisingly, Will was willing to let Sammy try his new approach, telling him, "Take a straight eight minutes in the middle of the act and use it however you want." But he conceded that he and Sam Sr. were too old to change.

As 1946 gave way to a new year, bookings at more desirable venues began to open up.

First, in February, the Trio made its Las Vegas debut, at the El Rancho Vegas. For $500 a week, Sammy and his partners were second-billed behind the team of Baker and Carroll, Harry Carroll being the composer of such hit tunes as "I'm Always Chasing Rainbows." Negroes represented a tiny fraction of the Nevada population at the time; in fact, Las Vegas was known as the Mississippi of the West. But Sammy offered no objections to the booking. In 1947, the desert outpost was on the move.*

The Nevada city's history dates back to 1829, when a party of travelers heading for Los Angeles on the Old Spanish Trail discovered an artesian spring in a desert area west of the established route. This find enabled travelers to journey *through* the desert rather than go around it, thereby shortening the trip to the coast. Thereafter, a sleepy village rose up around the spring. For about two years in the 1850s, the population took a dramatic upturn, as Mormons from Salt Lake City, seeking to expand their Utah empire, established a fort in the Las Vegas Valley. This outpost still stands; in fact, it's the oldest structure in town. But the Mormon experiment that gave rise to it lasted a mere two years. For the rest of the nineteenth century, Las Vegas remained a quiet backwater.

Things picked up in 1905, thanks to the San Pedro, Los Angeles, and Salt Lake Railroad, which made Vegas a watering stop on its run to and from the coast. Then, in 1928, the federal government earmarked $165

---

*Many press releases, CD liner notes, and the like place Sammy Davis' first appearance in Las Vegas in 1945. Although no date is given in *Yes I Can*, the story's place in the narrative would suggest that it fell in 1945 as well. However, a week-by-week review of the acts appearing at the El Rancho Vegas as listed in the Vegas newspapers for the period between June 1945 and early 1947 showed no appearance by the Will Mastin Trio until that cited above. No one consulted by this author, in Las Vegas or elsewhere, could refute this conclusion.

million to construct a dam in Boulder Canyon, and thousands of job seekers flocked to the valley. In 1935, the completion of the facility, called Hoover Dam, with its virtually endless supply of electric power, contributed significantly to local growth, as did the subsequent establishment of the Las Vegas Arial Gunnery School. By then, downtown Vegas boasted several luxury hotels and numerous successful gaming clubs, gambling having been legalized in Nevada in 1931.

A major development occurred in April 1941 when a California motel operator named Thomas Hull opened a Western-style resort on fifty-two acres of land on rural Highway 91, about three miles outside of downtown. Designed by architect Wayne McAllister and beckoning visitors with a tall, neon windmill signpost, the El Rancho Vegas, as Hull's hotel-casino was called, featured rustic air-conditioned cabins and inviting green lawns, an outdoor swimming pool, a showroom, a chuck wagon buffet, and a twenty-four-hour coffee shop—the first place in town to offer all of these amenities. Less than two years later, an even more lavish place called the Last Frontier joined the El Rancho Vegas on Highway 91, soon to be known as the Strip, and the building boom was on.

In its determination to become known as the Entertainment Capital of the World, Vegas began actively courting nightclub performers in the mid-1940s. Mastin and the Davises had heard that the new establishments provided entertainers with free lodging and meals, and, of course, Sam Sr. was eager to check out the gaming tables. But when they arrived at the El Rancho Vegas, they quickly learned that whatever the perks were for white performers, blacks faced an entirely different set of working conditions. Not only were they not given *free* room and board, but they weren't allowed to stay at the hotels where they performed *under any circumstances*. Nor were they permitted to enjoy any of the amenities on the grounds, including the casinos, dining facilities, and swimming pools. They couldn't even attend other performers' shows, white or black, as the showrooms catered only to whites. Indeed, black entertainers were expected to enter their places of business like hired help—through the kitchen—and disappear as soon as they finished performing.

Moreover, they were required to make their own living arrangements. In the mid-forties, Vegas had a small Negro section called Westside, which Davis likened to Erskine Caldwell's Tobacco Road. In the cab that initially took the Trio through the area, Sammy was sickened by the sight of shacks made of wood and cardboard and young children walking around naked. Westside boasted a few nicer boarding houses, and the owner of one of them, a woman named Cartwright, was happy to provide the Trio with rooms—at about triple the going rate whites paid at the El Rancho Vegas.

Not only were such accommodations less than desirable and the working conditions demeaning, but Sammy found little to do in his spare time. His father and Will were content with a Negro barbecue place and a bar with a few games of chance, but Sammy chafed at being told where he could and couldn't go. So he spent most of his free time in his room, listening to records and teaching himself to play the trumpet.

The Mississippi of the West may have fueled Sammy's anger, but appearing at the bustling El Rancho Vegas was a major step forward. The Trio weren't the headliners, but they were seen by important people, and Sammy took full advantage of that fact. Indeed, he lived for the moments when he could get onstage, trying to perform his way out of his entrapment.

In May, three months after the Vegas gig, came another important engagement: the Trio was invited to appear at the Capitol Theater in Manhattan, site of Sammy's horrible first date. But this time he would be opening for Frank Sinatra. If this news weren't exciting enough, Sammy, his dad, and Will would earn an unprecedented $1,250 a week during the three-week gig. Later, Davis learned that Sinatra himself had been responsible for the booking. For $1,250 a week, the Capitol could have hired a far more celebrated act, but the singer had insisted on the Will Mastin Trio. When Sammy and Frank met at rehearsal, Sinatra simply said, "Hi'ya, Sam. Glad we're working together." He never even hinted at his part in bringing Davis to New York.

Sammy was determined to maximize the opportunity, but the movie palace's general manager, Alan Zede, restricted the Trio to flash dancing. There simply wasn't time for Sammy's impressions or banter with the audience.

Naturally, Davis was disappointed. Still, the Capitol was a big deal, and Sinatra was supportive, even ensuring that the Trio's name appeared on the theater's marquee along with his own. During the run, the two entertainers renewed their burgeoning friendship, chatting in Frank's dressing room between shows and occasionally sharing dinner. As in Detroit six years earlier, Davis caught every Sinatra performance from the wings, admiring the star's commanding stage presence as well as his musical gifts.

The day before the end of the run, Frank threw a party for the company in the theater's rehearsal hall. During the meal, someone asked Sammy to do his impression of Sinatra. He hesitated because he didn't know how the singer would react. But when Frank said, "Let's see it, Sam," he had no choice. Fortunately, Sinatra laughed and later asked to see Sammy's other impressions, which he thought were terrific. He also encouraged the kid to sing in his own voice. In fact, he chastised Sammy for wasting the Capitol exposure by just dancing. Sammy didn't want to tell him that he hadn't been permitted to expand the act's repertoire for lack of time.

After the last show, Sammy stopped by Frank's dressing room to say goodbye and to thank him for his advice. The singer waved away his expressions of gratitude, saying magnanimously, "Anything I can ever do for you—you've got a friend for life."

The Trio enjoyed a second major New York appearance in 1947, their first stint at Harlem's famous Apollo Theater.

Located on 125th Street near Seventh Avenue, the Apollo had opened in January 1934 in what was formerly Hurtig and Seamon's Burlesque. After about a year, the theater's owners, Sidney Cohen and Morris Sussman, sold out to a fierce competitor named Frank Schiffman. "Frank had no artistic taste at all," noted the new owner's friend, record producer John Hammond. Nevertheless, he managed to turn the Apollo into what author Mel Watkins has called "the most illustrious showplace for black entertainment ever to arise in Harlem or anyplace else." Indeed, the Apollo quickly became more than just a theater. It was a social and cultural beacon for an otherwise disenfranchised community. The bill, which changed every week, featured comics, big bands, singers, dancers, and other variety acts and included all of the major black entertainers of the day, from Louis Armstrong to Step'n'Fetchit to Ella Fitzgerald. Given their exposure to the best, Apollo audiences were notoriously intolerant of those who failed to meet their exacting standards.

As at the Capitol, Schiffman wouldn't let Sammy do his impressions, once again for lack of time. Nevertheless, the Trio scored with the Apollo audience. Sammy recalled, "There was no rush—like everybody rushing backstage saying you're great—like the stories you hear. It was just like we were accepted, and that already was talk enough. The stagehands told us, 'Yeah, you'll be back.'" They were right. Schiffman booked the Trio for a return engagement, even allowing Sammy to do his impressions this time.

Thereafter, the Trio became semiregulars at the Apollo, but the experience of performing at the fabled showplace never lost its allure. "It really was kind of special," Davis said. "There was a marvelous rapport. The audience talked back to the performer. The performer talked back to the audience. It wasn't heckling so much as we know it now. But the guy in the audience would say, 'You ain't doin' shit.' And the performer would say, 'Yes, I am!' right back at him." In time, the Trio would become Apollo headliners, going from an initial $650 a week to $1,500 to even more. At least two future stars, Leslie Uggams and Gregory Hines, have vivid memories of seeing a vibrant Sammy Davis, Jr., at the fabled showplace when they were youngsters. They were awed by his talent.

In July 1948, the Trio was again back on a New York stage, this time at the Strand. Headlining the bill were pianist Count Basie and his Orchestra and singer Billie Holiday.

The Trio was given a twenty-minute spot, ample time for Davis to include his impressions. But after opening night, Will was told to cut the act by eight minutes, which would restrict the Trio to dancing. Sammy insisted that they proceed with the full routine, and though he convinced his reluctant partners to go along with him, he kept this decision from the Strand's management. Fortunately, the second night the Trio was such a hit that when Sammy returned to the wings, Billie Holiday took his arm and said, "Come on, little man, you'd better carry me on or they'll never calm down."

The theater manager was furious that the Trio had disobeyed him, but he couldn't deny Sammy's audience appeal. When Will promised to comply with the original dictum thereafter, the manager said, "Keep the act as is and we'll cut eight minutes somewhere else."

Sammy considered the manager's decision an important object lesson. "What we just saw," he told his partners, "is how life is. If you 'make it,' you can have anything! But if you don't you can be the nicest guy in the world and they won't book you to play the men's room at intermission. Well, I'm gonna make it. And when I do what'll you bet they'll like me? They'll like me even if they hate my guts!" Finally realizing the full depth of Sammy's ambition, Sam and Will were too stunned to answer him. It was a moment of realization for Sammy, too. As he put it, "I think I was seeing me for the first time. And I liked it. I liked not 'taking it' and I liked winning."

Late in 1948, Sammy was afforded an important chance to heed Sinatra's advice—to sing in his own voice. A big band drummer named Jesse Price learned that Dave Dexter of Capitol Records was looking for new singers and recommended Davis. Price may have reinforced Dexter's own discovery, for musicologist Robin Callot maintained that the record company executive caught a late-night radio broadcast in 1948, a remote feed from a small club in South Central L.A. at which Sammy was singing. In any event, Dexter signed the entertainer.

In the late forties, Capitol was not yet the giant it would later become. Founded in 1942 by lyricist-singer Johnny Mercer, Los Angeles music store operator Glenn Wallichs, and film producer–songwriter Buddy

DeSylva, the burgeoning Hollywood-based company struggled during the war years when shellac, a major component in the manufacture of records, was in extremely short supply. Still, the company was so successful that in 1944 *Billboard* magazine could tell readers the upstart label was "crowding the big three," meaning Columbia, RCA, and Decca. Capitol was doing even better by decade's end, largely due to an impressive talent roster that included bandleaders Paul Whiteman and Stan Kenton and singers Peggy Lee, Jo Stafford, Margaret Whiting, and one of Davis' idols, Nat King Cole. So Sammy was thrilled to contract for twenty singles at $50 a side.

Because Davis was paid a flat fee instead of a percentage of each record sold, Will didn't think much of the deal. But Davis was more concerned about the opportunity than the money. "When I'm Bing Crosby," he told Mastin, "I'll ask for royalties."

Davis and Dave Dexter spent hours discussing appropriate material. Although Sammy couldn't read charts (a deficiency he never bothered to address), he was already a serious music aficionado with a broad range of tastes. The material he and the record producer selected covered an interesting gamut, from pop standards to rhythm and blues numbers to novelty tunes to a couple of original songs allegedly written by Davis himself. Dexter then brought Sammy together with one of Capitol's best conductor-arrangers, Dave Cavanaugh. Cavanaugh, who had overseen, or would oversee, LPs by Peggy Lee, Nancy Wilson, and Frank Sinatra, applied jazz and South American rhythms to several of the Davis offerings. Others were treated to lush string arrangements.

Sammy's first recording session took place in L.A. on January 13, 1949. He rendered four tunes that day, including a ballad by Buddy Johnson entitled "I Don't Care Who Knows" and the tender Jerome Kern–Dorothy Fields standard "The Way You Look Tonight," which became a vehicle for his impressions of Billy Eckstine, Al Jolson, Nat King Cole, Frankie Laine, and Vaughn Monroe (without identifying the singers on the track). These numbers hit the market in February as Sammy's first single. Despite efforts by Capitol's promotion department, the record went unnoticed by the buying public.

On February 22, Davis recorded four more tunes, and he returned to Capitol's studio for a pair of additional sessions in July. By then the label had released two more singles, which also went nowhere. Three more releases followed in the fall, two of which were attributed to "Charlie Green." Unfortunately, Sammy had no better luck under a pseudonym.

Davis returned to Capitol's studios one last time on December 9, 1949, the day after his twenty-fourth birthday. This session produced a rather strange and certainly eclectic mixture of material, including

"Wagon Wheels," a Western-style number that came complete with the sound of clopping horses, and "Laura," the haunting Raskins-Mercer theme from the 1944 film. "Wagon Wheels" was released in January 1950; "Laura" followed in April (with Jimmy Durante's signature tune "Inka Dinka Do" on the flip side). A final disk hit stores in May; it featured the dreamy Sammy Cahn–Saul Chaplin–Hy Zaret ballad "Dedicated to You" and "I'm Sorry Dear," a torch song previously recorded by Bing Crosby. By then, it was obvious that the public was not going for Davis' records under any circumstances, and he and Capitol parted company. Not one to take failure lightly, Sammy later blamed Dave Cavanaugh for his dismal performance.

As a struggling new label, Capitol wasn't in the best position to market its new singer. Moreover, the company's relatively small staff required Dave Dexter to spread himself too thin. Consequently, he couldn't adequately direct Davis' recording career. Finally, the best new songs that came Capitol's way went to its established artists.

Whatever Capitol's problems, some of the failure of the 1949 recordings must be attributed to Davis himself. One could argue that the broadly diversified material he recorded initially confused record buyers. Was Sammy Davis, Jr., a crooner like Sinatra? Or a jazz scatter? A legit singer in the mode of Alfred Drake or Gordon MacRae? A dancer, like Fred Astaire, who didn't take his warblings too seriously? Or a novelty performer doing musical impressions? In fact, he was all of the above.

The reason Davis displayed such disparate approaches to song was simple: in 1949, he was not yet ready to be a major recording star. He possessed the raw material—a pleasing vocal timber, impressive power, a range of several octaves, good instincts as an improviser and musical interpreter, and a wonderful sense of rhythm—but he lacked seasoning. At the time, he was more accustomed to singing in public for comic effect than singing in his own natural voice. He could identify and mimic the qualities that made others special, but he had no style of his own. Some would argue that as a vocalist he never stepped out of Sinatra's shadow, and, to a certain extent, that was so. In time, he would certainly gain confidence in his singing, maximizing the potential of his vocal instrument and utilizing his ability to dramatize a song.

Being dropped by Capitol just made Davis work that much harder. Like Ahab obsessed with the white whale, he fixed his mind on one thing: stardom. As he drove himself to do more and be better, the act became more about him and his versatility and less about a trio of flash dancers. With Sammy's impressions and the musical instruments he played, the occasional song rendered in his own voice, his displays of gunmanship, his solo spots as a dancer, and his banter with the audience, his aging partners became tangential to the act. They still displayed their solo specialties and all three men continued to dance in unison, but Will and Sam Sr. spent an increasing amount of stage time as backup performers. As time went on, they simply disappeared backstage after an opening routine to return for a rousing finale.

It wasn't just the many things Davis did onstage that altered the nature of the act. It was the way he did them: full out with growing poise and assurance and incredible energy. That anyone could be so diversified was astonishing enough, but when the possesser of all those gifts was a short, slim, boyish twenty-something, so seemingly innocent and eager to please, the result was irresistible.

Despite Sammy's dominance onstage, offstage Will remained the act's manager and his name continued to define the group. But, by the dawn of the fifties, Sammy's reputation was starting to spread and his hard work was garnering results. Consequently, the act became The Will Mastin Trio *featuring* Sammy Davis, Jr. (eventually becoming The Will Mastin Trio *starring* Sammy Davis, Jr.).

Nowhere was audience appreciation for Sammy more apparent than at the El Rancho Vegas, to which the Trio regularly returned. Somehow Davis convinced himself that this onstage approval would lead to a change and that he'd be allowed to go to the resort's bar, restaurant, and casino like the white entertainers. But it didn't happen.

Sammy had more fun on the rare occasions when another black entertainer was performing in Vegas at the same time. In 1949, singer Dorothy Dandridge appeared at a small club on the Strip called the Bingo. Davis knew Dandridge through her husband, Harold Nicholas, one half of the dancing Nicholas Brothers. The two entertainers arranged to meet whenever possible. One time, Sammy told Dorothy he'd come to the Bingo after her last performance and they'd hit the hot spots in the black section of town. As soon as she finished her last set, Dandridge rushed back to the small office that served as her dressing room, changed her clothes, and waited for Sammy to arrive. When he didn't appear, she called his rooming house but was told that he'd left some time earlier. Suspecting something amiss, she asked her pianist, William Roy, to look outside the club. Roy found Davis near the front door—where he'd been waiting for nearly an hour. The club management had refused to admit him or deliver a message to Dandridge for him, or even tell her she had a guest outside. When Dorothy saw Sammy, neither said anything about what had happened. By tacit agreement, they decided not to let their anger and frustration interfere with their plans. According to William Roy, they had a grand time that night.

CHAPTER 5

The Big Time

What made such humiliations endurable was Davis' absolute belief that playing towns like Vegas would eventually lead to his big break and that, when it came, the rules about where he could go and what he could do would crumble.

He moved closer to at least the first half of that dream in early 1951, when Arthur Silber booked the Trio into Ciro's, perhaps the hottest club in Los Angeles.* They would open for actress Janice Paige, a former Warner Bros. contract player who customarily played second leads, typically the star's best friend or rival. After leaving the studio in 1949, Paige had developed a nightclub act, initially with Jack Carson, her costar in numerous Warners features, and then on her own.

Herman Hover, Ciro's owner, was willing to book the Trio on the strength of its growing reputation. But he didn't want to pay more than $500 a week. Because this was $50 a week less than the Trio's standard asking price, Mastin rejected the offer. "We're not starving," he told Sammy. "No point taking a cut just to work a place." Davis was in shock. "He *wanted* to get into Ciro's," recalled Arthur Silber, Jr. "My God, that was a huge step. But Will said no, and Will was the boss. He may have been a very quiet man, but he had the strength of a bull. When he said something, that was it. You could argue with him, but you weren't going to win."

Fortunately, Silber's father went back to Hover, who agreed to meet Will's asking price. Later, Sammy learned that the agent had offered to pay the extra $50 a week himself. It was only then that Hover relented, saying, "If you believe in them that much I'll go for the $550."

After the contract was signed, the Trio had a month to prepare before opening night. "I went over the act piece by piece," Sammy recalled. "The construction was sound." Determined that the Trio look like win-

---

*Located on the Sunset Strip, the building that housed Ciro's is now home to the Comedy Club.

ners, Silber arranged for clothier Sy Devore to fashion new black mohair tuxedos for his clients. They all knew that a lot was riding on this appearance. But when it came to rehearsing at the club, Sammy downplayed everything, giving the house orchestra a mere taste of what he'd be doing, enough so that they could keep up, but no more. It was important, he felt, that everything remain in check for the big night, like a cork in a champagne bottle. When he finally pulled the stopper, everything would bubble to the top and flow like magic. Perhaps he also feared that if Hover knew how dynamic a performer he had become, the nightclub owner would find someone else to open for Janice Paige, who was less than a powerhouse herself. Sammy knew what he was doing, but his cavalier manner did nothing to reassure the nervous Hover. After one rehearsal, he told the Trio, "I still don't know what you boys do. I'll tell you what. You open the show, make it fast and take only one bow."

Finally, opening night arrived—March 23, 1951.* Ciro's had only one real dressing room, which went to Paige. So Sammy, his father, and Will had to make do with a corner of the attic, where, amid the extra tables and unused signage, Hover had set up a dressing table.

Sammy arrived at the club an hour before stage time. It was difficult to relax. With its French cuisine, station captains decked out in tails, and immaculately dressed movie stars at table after table, Ciro's reeked of elegance; it was unlike any place the Trio had ever played. As they moved downstairs from the attic, the three men had butterflies in their stomachs.

Then orchestra leader Dick Stabile announced, "Ladies and Gentlemen, Ciro's is proud to present . . . the Will Mastin Trio, featuring Sammy Davis, Jr." The band started to play their opening number, "Dancing Shoes," and it was time to put their nervous energy to work.

As usual, Sam Sr. and Will hit the stage first. Then Sammy joined them for their opening number. "We probably started faster than any act this crowd had ever seen," Davis recalled, "and we kept increasing the pace, trying as we never had before." At the end of "Dancing Shoes," they didn't even wait for the applause before they started hoofing again, offering a rotating round of spectacular individual turns. Finally, they paused. To enthusiastic applause, the older dancers stepped back, and Sammy went into his impressions. He wound up with Louis Armstrong, because it was hard to sing right after rendering the trumpeter's raspy voice. By "the time I finished Satchmo," Davis recalled, "they were pounding the tables so hard I could see the silverware jumping up and

---

*In his autobiography, Sammy would recall that his debut at Ciro's coincided with the Academy Award ceremonies and, as a consequence, the club offered only a midnight show that evening. In fact, the Oscars were awarded on March 29 that year.

down." Then he segued into the movie stars, including Edward G. Robinson, for which he used a gigantic cigar; the prop was a major crowd pleaser. These bits were even more successful, particularly as some of those Sammy imitated—Humphrey Bogart, for one—were in the room! By then, the audience was his, solely and completely. "They were reacting to everything," he said, "catching every inflection, every little move and gesture, concentrating, leaning in as though they wanted to push, to help. I was touching them. It was the most glorious moment I'd ever known—*I was really honest to God touching them.*" Then Will and his father rejoined him for another round of hoofing.

When the Trio finally concluded after forty minutes or so, the audience went wild. "It was as though they knew something big was happening to us," Sammy explained, "and they wanted to be part of it. They kept applauding and began beating on the tables with knives and forks and their fists, screaming for us to come back." Paige's contract precluded them from taking more than two bows, but Sammy insisted they return to the stage time and time again; he wasn't going to miss this moment for anyone. Even repeated bows weren't enough to quell the crowd, which began demanding an encore. Sammy was at a loss for what to do; he'd used up all of his standard impressions during the act. Then, in a flash of inspiration, he decided to try someone he'd never done before, Jerry Lewis, half of the hottest comedy team in the business, Martin and Lewis. Said Sammy, "The sight of a colored Jerry Lewis was an absolute topper. It was *over*. When I heard that scream I knew we'd had it. There was nothing we could do that would top that!"

Finally, after eight bows, the Trio left the stage. With tears streaming down his face, Sammy hugged his father and his mentor, the men who'd been with him since he was two and a half years old. Breathless, all three troupers realized that they'd been a part of something extraordinary, a moment in show business history that comes along once or twice in a generation. That, however, was an abstraction. On a personal level, Sammy knew that he'd finally achieved, totally and completely, the goal he'd set for himself: he'd connected with an audience exactly the way the big white stars did. Having found the key, he'd never lose it again.

Poor Janice Paige—to have to follow that act that night. Arthur Silber, Jr., had been standing next to her backstage, and, as he put it, "She was fuming mad: 'That little son-of-a-bitch, he's killing me. How can I follow this guy? All these gowns. I spent a fortune on these gowns, and put this [act] together.' . . . She wasn't so pissed at Sammy. She was pissed at how could she, as big as he was, go out there and try to top him? It wasn't going to happen."

And, indeed, it didn't. Paige "couldn't even get their attention," Sammy recalled. "It was strictly our night, there was a post-pandemonium atmosphere out there, and she was just one of the girls coming on to sing after three strong, hungry men had given the show of their lives. No one could have followed us then."

The next day, Paige—the headliner—went to Herman Hover and insisted he reverse the show's order. Her name would still be on top of the marquee out front, but she would open the show; Sammy and the Trio could close.

That night, Davis' second at Ciro's, the entertainer experienced something he'd never felt before: the thrill of performing in front of a presold audience. Because many in the showroom had heard or read about his triumph the previous night, they were predisposed to like him. What a difference! As he explained, "It's a lot easier to please the public when the experts have already said you're good." With nothing to prove, "knowing they belonged," as Sammy put it, the Trio took to the stage in complete confidence, giving, in his words, "an absolutely flawless performance."

Among those in the house that night was the object of Sammy's encore impression at the opener, Jerry Lewis. He and Davis had run into one another occasionally in the past, notably at the Club 500, a posh nightclub in Atlantic City where the duo Martin and Lewis was born. But Sammy and Jerry were hardly friends. Nor, in 1951, were they peers. They shared a somewhat common background, however. Slightly more than three months younger than Davis, Jerry was also the son of vaudevillians who occasionally performed in the family act as a kid and who cut short his education to become a full-time entertainer. Like Sammy, he'd known years of frustration, one-night stands, and stints of unemployment. But, in 1946, when he hooked up with another small-time entertainer, a suave, good-looking singer named Dean Martin, his luck changed dramatically. By the time Davis opened at Ciro's, Lewis was not only a top draw on the nightclub circuit, but he and Martin had become major movie stars.

Thus, when Jerry came backstage to see Sammy that evening, not only raving about the kid's talent but prepared to offer a critique of what he'd just seen, Davis was more than eager to listen.

Lewis offered several valuable tips, starting with the notion that Davis' remarks between numbers were too florid. "I know Englishmen who don't talk as good as you did onstage with such an accent," Jerry quipped. Sammy recognized that in his desire to prove he didn't talk like Amos and Andy, he had gone a bit overboard. Although he would try to tone down his patter, he would never totally succeed. Phrases like

"Ladies and gentlemen, with your kind permission" and "We hope you will indulge us" were simply too well ingrained to disappear entirely.

Lewis chastised Sammy for using Will and Sam Sr. to hand him and take away props—a hat, a cigar, his trumpet. This behavior, he said, demeaned the older men and made Sammy appear insensitive. "He was so right," Davis realized. "From the audience's point of view, it had to look like 'This kid's making his father and his uncle wait on him. What an ingrate!'"

Beyond the practical benefit of Jerry's suggestions, Sammy was touched at the far more successful entertainer's generosity and interest in him. As he put it, "Nobody else had ever done this for me. Nobody whose opinion I could respect above my own had ever sat in the audience with a pad on his knee and made notes trying to help me." Thereafter, Davis and Lewis became good friends. In fact, besides Frank Sinatra, there was probably no one in show business to whom Sammy felt closer. But his relationship with Frank was always one of younger man to older man, successful star to idol. There was a certain deference that Sammy paid to Frank, a reverential quality that allowed him to go only so far. He never wanted to look foolish with the great singer or confess to him his insecurities. He would much rather make him laugh. By contrast, though his bond with Lewis wasn't colored by awe, Sammy greatly respected Jerry's talent. The two men saw themselves as brothers, although Lewis, the younger in real life, would always play the role of the older, wiser, more worldly sibling to Davis' struggling but eager kid. Whenever Sammy had an important decision to make, he would invariably seek Jerry's counsel.

Sammy made several other important friends during his engagement at Ciro's. Movie stars Jeff Chandler and Tony Curtis caught the show with Byron Kane, a radio actor whom Sammy knew, and the quartet started to pal around together. "The four of us were constantly at Byron's apartment or at Jeff's house," said Sammy, "playing records and charades, sitting around the pool for hours talking movies, often daydreaming about Tony, Jeff and me doing one together." They were often joined by actress Janet Leigh, who was then engaged to Curtis (they would marry that year); she and Sammy would also become good friends.

Arthur Silber, Jr., was also part of the group. With Chandler and Curtis under contract to Universal and Leigh at MGM, they frequently made the rounds of these and other local film studios, chatting with their friends and meeting other actors, newcomers as well as established stars. Sammy and Arthur had become avid photography buffs, investing in a variety of cameras, lenses, and other equipment. Visiting Hollywood's dream factories gave them wonderful opportunities to make use of their hobby.

But they weren't solely interested in snapping the lords and ladies of film-dom. "For two young men it was the greatest thing in the world," said Silber, "to get chicks to come up to your room. 'Let me take some shots of you. Come up and pose for me.' That's the kind of a ruse that it was used for. The cameras weren't bought for that intention, don't misunderstand me, but it was a great way to get chicks to your room. By the way, some great pictures came out of that. Because as we got very good at it, as you develop a cameraman's eye, everything becomes a picture."

As Silber's recollection suggests, professional success helped Davis finally overcome his youthful fear of women, and he began to date with great regularity. White women, black women, one at a time, two at a time—as long as they were fun and attractive, he didn't care. Nor was it terribly important to him if they went with him because of his celebrity or for his inner qualities. He wasn't looking for anything permanent; he just wanted some kicks. Psychologists could no doubt argue that Davis' Don Juanism—a condition that would remain with him for the rest of his life—was a cover for deep-seated insecurities stemming from his feelings of being ugly and unlovable except onstage; this was probably the case, but he was nevertheless having a ball making up for lost time.

Finding obliging companions wasn't a problem. Although much has been made of how ugly Davis was, in person he radiated a perceptible physical appeal. For one thing, he kept his slim body in terrific shape, working out regularly long before it was fashionable. Moreover, his facial features, though far from regular or conventional, had character; he was interesting looking, particularly onstage. When he was in his element, he was transformed into someone almost handsome. Many women who saw him perform were drawn to his looks and sex appeal and wanted him, not for his fame, but for himself.

Perhaps for this reason, Sammy eventually became somewhat philosophical about his looks. In 1964 he said, "I know I'm dreadfully ugly, one of the ugliest men you could meet, but ugliness, like beauty, is something you must learn how to use. All my life I've resisted the temptation to be a little less ugly, to have my nose fixed, for example. My bone structure is good, my jaw line is good, my cheekbones are good, my body is well proportioned. Maybe if I'd had my nose fixed, I'd have become almost passable. But what does being passable make you? It makes you mediocre: neither ugly nor handsome. Complete ugliness, utter ugliness, like mine, though, is almost attractive. Yes, yes, I'm convinced that a really ugly man, in the end, seems attractive. A man who is so-so you don't even stop to look at, much less follow. A man like me you see, you stop and look at him, you follow him to go on looking at him, to assure yourself that he really is the ugliest thing you ever saw, and from looking at him so much, you know what happens? What happens is that you find something attractive about him, and you like him."

Around 1951, Sammy's base of operations had become the Sunset Colonial Hotel, a popular hostelry for show business folk on the Sunset Strip. With stores on the ground floor and the living quarters arranged around a central courtyard, the Spanish Mediterranean-style hotel was quite a change from the old Morris downtown. Recalled Arthur Silber, Jr., who eventually moved there as well, it "was close to all the action on the Sunset Strip." NBC's radio studio was nearby, and there were several swanky nightclubs, including Ciro's and Earl Carroll's, within walking distance, as well as the Garden of Allah, Schwab's Drug Store, and Dupar's ice cream parlor. Over the next few years, hanging out at these nightspots enabled Sammy to befriend quite a few of Hollywood's young Turks, including Marlon Brando, Elvis Presley, Diahann Carroll, and a then-unknown James Dean.

Sammy got a kick out of visiting movie studios and hanging around with stars. No one impressed him more than Frank Sinatra's close friend, Humphrey Bogart, who had been on hand for the Trio's opening at Ciro's with his wife, Lauren (Betty) Bacall. A few weeks later, Bogie invited Sammy to a party at his home in a posh area of L.A. known as Holmby Hills.

As stars went, Bogart was at the head of the A list. Although he'd made his reputation playing gangsters as a member of Warners' "Murderers' Row" (along with Cagney, Robinson, and George Raft), Bogie was, in fact, the prep school–educated son of a Manhattan society doctor. But, like the characters he portrayed, he hated snobs, stuffed shirts, and people who put on airs. Most of the time, he said exactly what he thought and enjoyed thumbing his nose at the establishment. What he respected was talent, which made Davis okay as far as he was concerned.

Intimidated by the other big names at the party, Sammy said little at Bogart's house that first time, and the fact that he drank Coke was somewhat disconcerting to the hard-drinking star. Nevertheless, the two men hit it off. "It was the start of a beautiful friendship," Davis noted. "In time I became a fringe member of the elite centered on the Bogart household which Betty had named The Holmby Hills Rat Pack." But to get along in such a fast crowd, Sammy found that he had to, as he put it, "extend my role as entertainer," meaning that he worked hard to be funny, engaging, and, in general, good company. Once established with the Holmby Hills crowd, this became his modus operandi whenever he was in the midst of bright, well-educated, or famous people, even when they were guests at his own home. "Whenever I was around Sammy," recalled actress Sally Struthers, "he was like Perle Mesta, the hostess with the mostest. He took it on as his personal responsibility to make sure that people were having a good time, and sometimes that meant him telling stories and sometimes that meant him being a great listener. That was as close to contemplative as I ever saw him, when he was listening." Television producer George Schlatter added, "Whatever Sammy did was always a performance. If you had lunch with Sammy it was a performance. And you left there almost exhausted because he gave you so much, so much of himself."

At the end of the Trio's original two-week engagement at Ciro's, Herman Hover extended their stay for a month. Now, as headliners, they were able to take over the star's dressing room, and their name was placed on top of the club's marquee. Befitting their new status, the Trio signed with the prestigious William Morris talent agency, and Arthur Silber became their manager. "Within a week, we were set for six months," Davis recalled.*

Immediately after Ciro's, the Trio returned to Vegas, moving to the Strip's fabulous hotel-casino, the Flamingo. They shared the bill with Sammy's old friend Mickey Rooney and singer-actress Frances Langford. Then they moved east, playing the Latin Casino in Philadelphia, among other venues.

While in Philly, Davis convinced Will Mastin to meet with Jess Rand, a young press agent Sammy had encountered a couple of times in New York. Six days older than Sammy, the Bronx-born showbiz devotee was then working for Ed Wiener, a press agent whose biggest claim to fame was his friendship with the powerful columnist Walter Winchell. Following a lengthy session at an all-night diner in Philadelphia, Will agreed to hire Rand and Wiener to promote the Trio's upcoming appearance at Bill Miller's Riviera, a posh nightspot in Ft. Lee, New Jersey, just across the Hudson from Manhattan.

The Riviera engagement came in July. Following the opening, *Variety* called Sammy "a superlative hoofer, a suave gabber, a solid vocalist and a standout mimic," and concluded, "The boy not only has a tour de force talent but a winning personality." Sammy was delighted, but he was even more impressed by the fact that Rand and Wiener got Winchell to see the show and to plug him in a column, because as far as his grandmother was concerned, an entertainer hadn't made it in show business until Winchell dropped his name. Davis also basked in the praise of the

---

*The trio remained with Arthur Silber until his death in February 1954. According to his son, Sammy, Sam, and Will continued to pay a commission to Silber's widow for many years thereafter, out of gratitude for the agent-manager's faith in them.

New York celebrities who caught his act, among them comics Jack E. Leonard, Red Buttons, and, most important, Milton Berle, who gave him some useful tips about how to phrase a joke. Berle, television's beloved "Uncle Miltie," became something of a mentor.

The Riviera engagement was significant for two other reasons. First, Sammy started spending more time with Jess Rand. As the two young men became friends, Sammy encouraged the press agent to leave Wiener, move to California, and open his own office, which Rand did. Among his first clients was the Will Mastin Trio. Although he didn't travel with the act on a full-time basis, he occasionally drove Sam Sr. from gig to gig (Sammy and Will preferred to take a train). Rand was thus the first outsider to become a member of Davis' entourage, joining Arthur Silber, Jr., who was now supervising the act's modest lighting and sound requirements, and Sam Sr.'s old friend, Nathan Crawford, who became the group's valet and driver. Rand, Silber, and Crawford were soon joined by a road manager, "Big" John Hopkins, a former Nat King Cole employee who remained with Sammy for many years.

In addition to Jess Rand, Davis forged another important relationship while performing at the Riviera. Morty Stevens was a rather quiet, sensitive, Juilliard-educated musician who played clarinet in the house band. One evening after listening to Morty noodle around on his horn, he asked the clarinetist if he would be interested in creating an arrangement for him. The song he had in mind was Henderson, DeSilva, and Brown's "The Birth of the Blues." Stevens was interested. Still insecure about his prowess as a vocalist, Sammy explained that what he wanted was an arrangement that would give him the freedom to put himself *into* the number, even dance a bit if he felt like it, not just stand in front of a mike and sing it. A few days later, Stevens returned with the arrangement and Davis was thrilled. As Sammy put it, "He'd taken my basic ideas of how I wanted to perform it and developed it with a complete understanding of my voice and my kind of performing, tailoring it for me so that I could really go with it."

Inspired, he told Will that he wanted to hire Morty as a permanent conductor-arranger. This would not only enable him to obtain other arrangements tailored to his special talents, but it would also give him the freedom to switch material around from show to show, as the tenor of a particular audience seemed to suggest. One couldn't take such risks with a house band.

But Will adamantly refused to take on the additional personnel. One could hardly blame him; it hadn't been that long since they'd had no idea where their next job was coming from. Now, in addition to their own needs, they had to worry about salaries for Silber and Crawford and

Rand's monthly retainer. Will reasonably felt they should savor their newfound success before burdening themselves with additional expenses. But, then, he didn't share Sammy's burning ambition.

The result was a full-blown argument between mentor and protégé. Eventually, Sammy stalked off, only to return and apologize. Not because he thought he was wrong, but out of respect for the old hoofer and what he'd given him over the years. Will apologized as well, telling Sammy that he sometimes forgot the boy was now a man and had a right to his own opinions. For the moment, they agreed to disagree, but it wouldn't be the last argument between them over the direction of the act.

From New Jersey, Sammy, Sam, and Will pressed on to other venues, now typically the top club in whatever town they played: the Chez Paree in Chicago, the Twin Coaches in Pittsburgh, Buffalo Bill's in Buffalo, the Chez Paree in Montreal, and the Beachcomber in Miami Beach.

Like Vegas, Miami Beach was a town that African American entertainers had to endure because it paid well. The owners of the Beachcomber, which included entertainers Sophie Tucker and Harry Richmond, tried to make the Trio feel comfortable, providing Sammy with a new red sports car and a suite at the Lord Calvert, the best hotel in the Negro section of Miami, but the working conditions remained oppressive. Because blacks were subject to a curfew in Miami Beach, Sammy had to carry a card indicating that he was performing locally; this was to protect him in case he was stopped by the police. Moreover, as in Vegas, Negroes weren't permitted inside nightclubs like the Beachcomber. Davis resented the fact that his own people couldn't attend his shows, not even the attractive African American women he met at the Calvert. At the end of the engagement, he told Will that he wouldn't return to the Florida playground until that policy changed. For once, he and Mastin were in accord.

At the end of 1951, the William Morris Agency purchased a full-page ad in *Variety* touting the Trio's accomplishments, with comments from a number of critics and columnists, including Blair Chotzinoff of the *New York Post,* who called the Trio "a brilliant new act" and Sammy "a triple threat entertainer." Hy Gardner of the *New York Herald Tribune* asserted, "If Sammy isn't the fastest and most breathtaking tap dancer I've seen, I'll retire, become an umpire, and have my eyes examined." *Variety* itself proclaimed Davis "a sure-fire talent . . . who excels in every department . . . with both polish and charm."

The Trio's success in nighteries was drawing the attention of a number of movers and shakers in another medium—television—sparking Davis' enduring affair with the tube. Over the course of the next thirty-plus years, he probably showed up on TV more frequently than any entertainer of his generation, except perhaps those with extremely long-running series. Game shows, talk shows, documentaries, sitcoms, drama series, Westerns, made-for-TV movies, soap operas, musical specials, telethons—whatever type of entertainment TV offered, Sammy Davis, Jr., wanted to be involved. According to one estimate, he made approximately one thousand television appearances during the course of his career, an average of about two a week.

In the early fifties, the new medium was rich in variety shows offering a combination of singers, dancers, comedians, and novelty acts, held together by an engaging emcee. In many cases, hosts themselves were entertainers, from singers Perry Como and Dinah Shore to comics Red Skelton and Red Buttons. These programs, which typically aired in front of studio or theater audiences, were tailor-made for nightclub entertainers. Not only did such performers have proven material to draw on, but they were accustomed to working live. Sammy's early appearances typically reflected in miniature the Trio's act at Ciro's or El Rancho Vegas. He was in the middle of doing an impression during a very early appearance on *The Toast of the Town,* the Sunday night variety show hosted on CBS by syndicated columnist Ed Sullivan, when, unbeknownst to Sammy, the coaxial cable that carried the broadcast signal into people's homes broke for what he called "the first time in television history." People could hear him but not see him. Some viewers, according to press accounts the following day, couldn't quite figure out if they were listening to one little black guy or if Sullivan had managed to corral appearances from James Cagney, Humphrey Bogart, and Edward G. Robinson. "It drew more attention," Davis concluded, "and caused more talk about us than there could possibly have been if everything had gone smoothly."

A few months later, on March 16, 1952, the Trio showed up on *The Colgate Comedy Hour.* The first variety show to originate from the West Coast, the program aired opposite Sullivan's show on NBC with several revolving hosts, including Martin and Lewis and Eddie Cantor. *Variety* paid tribute to the Trio's appearance on the show, noting that the act "lived up to the extravagant [advance] praise," and adding, "For fast foot work and mimicry there are few to match the Davis technique." Hosting that evening was Eddie Cantor. The irrepressible, bug-eyed radio and Broadway star was as taken with Sammy as *Variety*; when he learned at rehearsal that the show was running long, he decided to cut one of his own songs rather than reduce the Trio's airtime. He also held Sammy back after the act's spot for some on-camera banter, a mark of genuine approval.

Later, after the show, Cantor even gave the young entertainer a Jewish mezuzah, a gold capsule with a parchment prayer inside. He also arranged for the Trio to return to *The Colgate Comedy Hour* at the end of

September, while the act was in the midst of a record-breaking return engagement at Ciro's. At the time, Sammy told Marie Mesmer of the *Los Angeles Daily News* how kind Old Banjo Eyes had been, noting, "You know how most of these TV shows are. You do your stuff and get off. But Cantor interwove our routine into his show. He gave us a comedy writer. He spotted us just right. He made us seem not only like a great act, but made us feel great inside."

Davis was genuinely touched by this support. But one of his many gifts was his way of endearing himself to men like Cantor, William Morris' Abe Lastfogel, and Milton Berle. These seasoned veterans—all older, liberal, and Jewish—became Sammy's champions and looked for ways to help him scale the heights of show business.

Following Ciro's and *The Colgate Comedy Hour,* the Trio returned to the Flamingo Hotel in Vegas, then moved on to the Fairmont Hotel—the act's first booking at the prestigious San Francisco venue—and finally the Latin Casino in Philadelphia. As 1952 gave way to a new year, it was evident, even to Will, that the act was not merely a momentary sensation but had genuine staying power. Indeed, the Trio's weekly asking price had climbed well beyond the $1,000-a-week mark and, by the middle of 1953, would exceed five times that amount. Thus, Mastin agreed to take on Morty Stevens as a permanent arranger-conductor. He also engaged Sid Cullen, a writer well-known to industry insiders, to fashion new material for Sammy, including a specialty number called "It's Hard to Be Me" that critics and audiences adored.

Immediately following the Latin Casino gig, the Trio returned to Los Angeles for a tour of West Coast theaters with Jack Benny. After headlining the nation's premiere nightclubs, it might have seemed strange to become an opening act once more, but Sammy relished the opportunity to share the bill with the great radio and TV star. Watching the comedian from the wings taught Davis a great deal about comic timing and particularly comedic economy, for no one could get more laughs onstage by doing less than Jack Benny.

The admiration was mutual. Like Eddie Cantor, Abe Lastfogel, and Milton Berle, Benny became another Jewish liberal show business veteran who championed the rising African American entertainer. Whenever his celebrated friends came to see him during the tour, Benny made sure that Sammy met them as well. "These are the people you'll be dealing with soon," the comedian explained, "and I want you to know them as friends, first."

* * *

After the tour with Benny, the Trio returned to the nightclub circuit. One of their stops was the Fairmont Hotel, where they had become regulars. Sammy loved San Francisco. Like New York, the northern California city was lively and sophisticated, but it was freer, more open-minded, than Manhattan.

This time, Frisco offered something more: Eartha Kitt was in town. The previous year, the sultry, sexy black singer-actress had scored a triumph on Broadway in *New Faces of 1952* and had taken the show to the West Coast.

According to Davis, he and Kitt had met in New York, but Eartha didn't remember him, or so she claimed, when he stopped by the theater to say hello. Thinking he was a stagehand, she sent him out for coffee. And he went! By the time he returned, she'd learned who he was and, as she put it, "We all had a good laugh." Later, she caught his act and was suitably impressed. Thereafter, the two entertainers met several times for lunch, and, as Kitt was a far bigger star than Sammy, it was she, not he, who drew the attention of the other diners.

Not only was Eartha better known in 1953, but she was also more worldly and sophisticated. Although she was three years Sammy's junior and had grown up in Harlem, she was a graduate of the High School of the Performing Arts and had spent time in Europe, first as a member of Katherine Dunham's dance troupe and then on her own. Except for his gig in Hawaii in 1946, Davis had never been outside of North America. She disdainfully recalled visiting his hotel suite, which she found strewn with comic books, camera equipment, and LPs. "I thought Sammy was a great entertainer," she said, "but I wondered about his intelligence. What kind of mind did he have?" Once, they visited a friend of hers with a superb art collection. Fascinated, Sammy peppered the man with questions, although it was clear that he knew nothing about art. The next day, he showed up at Kitt's place with an armful of art books he had just purchased. Together, they savored the reproductions of great paintings, but Kitt encouraged him to investigate the accompanying texts as well. (Buying dozens of books on subjects of interest became a practice that Davis would follow throughout his adult life; some years later, for example, he sought out everything he could find about UFOs and alien encounters.)

Eartha enjoyed being with Sammy, but she found his high energy level exhausting. She was also somewhat mystified by his driving ambition. He seemed to want success so badly that it was, in her words, "haunting him." Moreover, he appeared threatened by her celebrity, for he continually reminded her that one day he would be equally famous, if not more so.

As far as Kitt was concerned, that was the end of the story. As she put it, she found Sammy "nice" and "amusing," but she had "no romantic interest" in him. At the time, she was in love with someone else, Arthur Loew, the movie theater mogul.

However, Sammy told *New York Post* reporter Jim Cook that he had proposed marriage to Eartha, giving her a seven-carat diamond ring, which she accepted. "The word was quickly broadcast that a marriage was in the mill," Cook added. "But a couple of days later Sammy had his ring back and it was all over." In the interim, the reporter said, the two entertainers had a fight over racial matters.

Kitt disputed Davis, saying through her agent, Virginia Wicks, that she had never expressed any interest in marrying Sammy. She had initially refused the ring he offered but, when he pressed the issue, she agreed to wear it as a token of their "friendship," provided that Sammy clearly understood that they were not engaged. When the press reported the story of their impending nuptials, Kitt sent the ring back, embarrassed by the publicity. "I like him," Eartha told her agent, "he's a sweet boy, but he gets mixed up."

Perhaps that was so. Nevertheless, Sammy's feelings for Eartha were apparently real. He told the readers of an *Ebony* magazine article in February 1956, "The closest I ever came to getting married was with Eartha Kitt. That was completely legit. It was not a publicity stunt." He maintained in this account, some three years after the fact, that her greater celebrity was the cause of the breakup. As he put it, if Eartha hadn't been so famous, "we would be married today."

Curiously, Sammy's friend, Arthur Silber, Jr., had little memory of the Kitt-Davis affair, although he was in San Francisco while Sammy was performing at the Fairmont. Neither he nor Burt Boyar took the relationship very seriously. Said Boyar, "I think he wanted to be with her, maybe marry her, because she was more glamorous in that moment in time. She was a bigger star than he was; she was probably more sophisticated. Sammy was always the kid outside, always wanting to be where the big people were, where it was happening, where the grownups were. Maybe Eartha Kitt was somebody he looked at as somebody who was already there. But I don't think there was any love especially. I don't think at that stage of his life he had time to be in love. He wanted to make it. There was no room for romance. Room to get laid, room to be with somebody important but, in the depth of his heart, it was only *Could this help me get where I'm going?* without ever plotting it out like that."

CHAPTER 6

A Crucial Year

Without question, 1954 was one of the most significant years—perhaps the single most important year—in Sammy Davis, Jr.'s life. During these twelve months, he would realize professional goals whose fulfillment had been unimaginable only a few years earlier.

The first milestone came right at the outset of the year, on January 11, when the Trio moved from the Flamingo to another resort on the Vegas Strip, the Last Frontier.

Slightly older than the Flamingo, the Last Frontier had opened on October 30, 1942, some seventeen months after the El Rancho Vegas. It was contained in a single rambling building, although its exterior resembled that of an Old West town. The frontier theme was maintained throughout the resort. Guests arriving by airplane were transported to the hotel by stagecoach. Even the swimming pool out front was surrounded by a corral.

Although Sammy was fascinated by Old West lore, what distinguished his move to the Last Frontier wasn't its museum or decor but the agreement the Trio struck with the resort's management. Not only would Sammy, his dad, and Will earn $7,500 a week while performing in the showroom—a new benchmark for the act—but they would also be allowed to stay in the Frontier's best suites, rent free, and enjoy the resort's amenities: casino, restaurants, and bar. Sammy could revel to all hours if he wished, gamble to his heart's content, and mingle with whomever he chose.

These concessions weren't simply gifts from some liberal-minded resort executives. They were granted because Davis, a savvy entertainer who knew he was getting hot, used them as bargaining chips—with the compliance of his dad and Will—and because the Frontier's management wanted to lure him and the gamblers who enjoyed his hip, swinging style from a rival establishment.

Of course, once the Trio had free run of the Frontier, other African American stars demanded like treatment at the Vegas venues they played. Thus, a major barrier in the history of show business in general and Nevada in particular came crumbling down—some three months before the U.S. Supreme Court reversed the notion of "separate but equal" in U.S. race relations through the landmark case *Brown v. the Board of Education*. When people speak reverentially of Sammy Davis, Jr., as a civil rights pioneer, his role in desegregating the Vegas Strip is one of the achievements to which they point, and rightly so.

The following month brought another major milestone: Sammy signed a contract with Decca Records. Given his prior experience at Capitol, the label's A&R executive, Mike Gabler, had to spend several months convincing him to sign. As Gabler put it, "He wasn't optimistic." Nevertheless, Davis recognized that Decca was far older and more established than its West Coast rival and could therefore offer emerging artists greater potential for success. In the three years since his last studio session, Sammy had matured as a singer, although he was still struggling to find a style of his own.

Gabler later asserted that Decca hadn't wanted to record Sammy's impressions of other entertainers, as had Capitol, arguing, "We felt they would identify him too much as a novelty singer." But, in fact, at his first session with the label, on June 7, Davis offered one of the mainstays of his nightclub act, Dudley Wilkinson and Arthur Hammerstein's "Because of You," complete with his standard repertoire of singers and actors—Nat King Cole, Billy Eckstine, Vaughn Monroe, James Cagney, Jimmy Stewart—plus a few additions, including Cary Grant, Jerry Lewis, and Dean Martin. Also at that session, he recorded, straight, numbers from two new Broadway shows: "And This Is My Beloved" from *Kismet* and the slightly more uptempo "Hey, There" from *The Pajama Game*. The latter had already been a hit for Rosemary Clooney, but Davis' version, which featured Sy Oliver and his Orchestra and a Morty Stevens arrangement, was distinguished by a beguine beat. On the vocal, Sammy demonstrated greater trust in the material than he had in most of his Capitol recordings. Although he wasn't a slave to the melody line, he was content to do the song without an excess of vocal tricks or bebop scat singing. The result was a pleasant and upbeat, though, in the long run, not particularly memorable rendering of the Richard Adler–Jerry Ross show tune.

Decca released both "Because of You" and "Hey, There" as singles. Not surprisingly, it was the latter that took off. In fact, by October, "Hey, There" had climbed to number one on *Cashbox*'s record charts, making it the first—and one of the few—Top 10 hits in Sammy's recording career.

* * *

By the time "Hey, There" was on its way to record stores, Sammy had scored another personal triumph, one about which he'd fantasized for years. In March, he, his dad, and Will debuted at the premiere cabaret in America, the Copacabana. The home of such headliners as Frank Sinatra, Martin and Lewis, Danny Thomas, and Jimmy Durante, this was the same Manhattan club that had drawn Sammy and his father to its 60th Street home in the downtrodden 1940s. Someday, he had then vowed, audiences would be coming to watch him. Now the dream was coming true.

Befitting such an occasion, Sammy determined to present himself with class and dignity. Accordingly, he told Will and his father that they shouldn't blast onto the stage with their usual burst of energy and the we'll-do-anything-to-please-you air. He wanted them to stroll on with finesse. Thus, he arranged for Morty Stevens to adapt a number from Kurt Weill's musical *Scene Scene* that offered just the right touch of elegance and sophistication.

Despite his preparations, Sammy was disappointed with the opening show. Afterward, he received the usual praise from backstage well-wishers, including several representatives from the William Morris Agency, but he knew that the audience had lacked the wild enthusiasm he'd enjoyed elsewhere. It wasn't for want of effort on his part. As he put it, "We'd stayed on for an hour and twenty minutes and I'd never tried harder in my life. I'd thrown everything I had at them." Later, he realized that the problem had been just that: he'd tried too hard. He had been so awed by the hallowed Copa, so determined to be the best entertainer anyone had ever seen that he hadn't been able to relax and be himself. As a result, he never really connected with the audience. Fortunately, he had another shot that evening, and traditionally the most important opinion makers would be present for the later set.

In the kitchen, before going on again, he shared a drink with the Copa's gruff but savvy manager, Jules Podell. When Sammy confessed that he was nervous, Podell growled, "What's there to be nervous about? You *got* the job. What do you think I hire? Amateurs? If you didn't belong here, you wouldn't be here."

Thus encouraged, Sammy hit the stage, and this time everything clicked. When the act came to an end, he looked out at the audience and saw, in his words, "a wall of people rising all around us; table by table they were getting to their feet, standing and applauding for us. I was unable to feel my feet on the floor or the fingers I knew I was digging into my palms, or hear anything except one vast, magnificent roar that went on and on and on. I looked at my father and Will and tears were pouring out of their eyes as they were from mine. After more than twenty years of performing together this was the climax, the ultimate payoff."

The next day, Davis celebrated, moving from the dingy America Hotel, which catered exclusively to Negroes, to the vastly more upscale Warwick. Then he went on a spending spree. From a tailor, he ordered a host of three-button suits with a center vent, paying overtime to have them ready in a few days. Elsewhere, he had himself fitted for silk pajamas and a robe. At Alfred Dunhill's, he purchased a variety of trinkets: silver lighters, pipes, cigarette boxes. Finally, at the Warwick Hotel's jewelry store, he acquired a diamond ring, a gold pen—for signing autographs—and a $900 Patek Phillipe watch.

Although Sammy had always been free with his money, this is the first recorded episode of his spending on such a massive scale. It would become a lifelong behavior pattern to celebrate by treating himself to a host of goodies. When he needed cheering up, he did likewise. And he did the same on days that were perfectly ordinary, neither outstanding nor terrible. Years later, in the mid-sixties, for example, a writer named Buz Kohan recalled walking twelve blocks with Sammy and Kohan's partner, Bill Angelos. En route, Sammy visited several establishments, including an electronics store, a men's shop, and a jewelry shop, and purchased a variety of items, including two television sets, several watches, and three overcoats, one for himself, one for Kohan, and one for Angelos. That walk, according to the writer, cost Davis about $60,000.

Around that time, Sammy offered an explanation for his behavior—already the subject of stories in the media—to writer Alex Haley. "That's my *pleasure*, man. Do you understand what I mean? I enjoy opening my closet door and saying, 'Oh, what suit should I wear?' So I have 20 suits too many! So I have too many tape recorders! And too many cars! I ain't *hurting* nobody! I didn't take a gun and stick somebody up and beat them over the head. I didn't rape nobody's daughter to get it! So I've got a lot of gold lighters; who did I *hurt* to get them? So I bought some gold watches at Cartier's; it gives me *pleasure*, is all."

Who did he hurt? Himself, of course—and, later, his family. By his own admission, he frittered away several fortunes during his lifetime. Had he not spent so prodigiously, he wouldn't have needed to work so hard in later decades, staying on the road when he might have pursued projects on stage or television that didn't pay as well but offered new creative challenges. And, of course, he could have bequeathed greater financial security to his loved ones. Over the years, at least one of his wives and many of his friends, as well as his agents and business associates, would try to curb his spending habits, all to no avail.

Perhaps the first to tackle this thankless task was Will Mastin, himself a model of modest living and a prodigious saver. Because Sammy was drawing against his salary and charging items to his hotel room, Mastin, who still supervised all aspects of the act's business, was well aware of his partner's binges. When he pointed out that during a single week of their Copa engagement, Sammy had gone through approximately $5,000, Davis replied, "So what? It's only a week's salary." The old hoofer countered, "It's five weeks' salary. Sure we're making $5,000 a week but we're splitting it three ways and we're *supposed* to only take a thousand a week apiece in salary and put the rest aside for agents and taxes and expenses."* Sammy promised he'd cut down when they went back on the road. Not entirely convinced, Will concluded with some sage advice: "You've got to start thinking about the future." But to Sammy, Will's notions were suspect. If he spent too liberally, his mentor's thrift was extreme as well. Davis disdained Mastin's unwillingness to open up his pocketbook and live a little, like the big-time entertainers they'd become. This was another indication of the fundamental difference between the two men, one expansive and liberal, the other cautious and conservative.

With landmark engagements at the Last Frontier and the Copa and a recording career that was at last on track, most entertainers would have been content. But not Sammy. Thus, he eagerly embraced an offer to star in a thirty-minute situation comedy for ABC.

The concept of the show, which was called *We Three*, was somewhat akin to the sitcom starring entertainer Danny Thomas, *Make Room for Daddy*, and to a lesser extent, the Lucille Ball–Desi Arnaz smash, *I Love Lucy*. As in real life, Sammy would play a nightclub performer who shared the stage with his father and uncle, hence the title. Naturally, Sam Sr. and Will would play their fictionalized selves, while an actress, Francis Taylor, was engaged to portray Sammy's girlfriend. A pilot episode was shot at the then-impressive cost of $200,000.

By October, the fall season had started, but without *We Three*. Part of the problem was that, although Sammy was a natural, his father and Will couldn't act; they could barely memorize lines. The main difficulty, however, was that, in 1954, the tab for virtually every show on television was picked up by a single corporate sponsor, and no one was interested in putting money into a show about the professional and personal life of an African American entertainer. Given the fare on television at the time, this was hardly surprising. Except for the demeaning *Amos and Andy*,

---

*Although the Last Frontier was paying the Trio $7,500 a week, the act was still drawing $5,000 elsewhere in 1954. That would soon change.

which was lifted from radio with black actors replacing the original white performers (who obviously could be heard but not seen), Negroes were virtually invisible as leading characters on television. They were restricted to playing menials and servants, like Jack Benny's Rochester, or to variety show appearances. The surprise isn't that *We Three* never aired but that ABC commissioned the pilot in the first place. Nevertheless, making the show represented an important moment for Davis. Having come so close, he would endeavor to return to character-driven television programming in the years to come.

In September, while awaiting word on the future of *We Three*, Sammy returned twice to Decca's recording studios. During these sessions, he recorded more than enough material for an LP, including such standards as "My Funny Valentine," "That Old Black Magic," and the first song that Morty Stevens arranged for him, "The Birth of the Blues."

November found Sammy, his dad, and Will back in Vegas for a second engagement at the Last Frontier. Normally, after his last show each evening, Sammy would party for hours. He was full of restless energy. As actor Dom DeLuise put it, "He was manic. He was always moving around and heading somewhere." Also, Davis hated to sleep. "He thought if he went to bed he was going to miss something," said George Schlatter. "And Sammy missed nothing."

On November 19, the entertainer varied his routine. He completed the late show at the Frontier to the usual cheers. Then he and his valet, Charlie Head, the latest member of the Trio's growing entourage, set out for Los Angeles in the brand new Cadillac convertible that Sammy's father and Will had recently given him in anticipation of his twenty-ninth birthday in December. Later that morning, Davis was expected at Universal's studio in the San Fernando Valley, where he was to record the title song for his pal Tony Curtis' latest picture, *Six Bridges to Cross*, an account of the infamous Brinks robbery in Boston. Henry Mancini had written the music for the song; the lyrics were by Sammy and Tony's buddy, Jeff Chandler. As soon as Sammy finished recording the number, he and Charlie were to return to Vegas in time for the Last Frontier's dinner show.

Charlie drove the first shift, so that Sammy, still pumped up from that night's performances, could relax in the back. About twenty miles outside of Vegas, the entertainer realized that he wasn't wearing his mezuzah. It was the first time he'd gone without the good luck charm since Eddie Cantor had given it to him. He and Charlie had driven too far to retrieve it, but he'd remember its curious absence later on.

After a few hours, Sammy took Charlie's place behind the wheel. Shortly before eight o'clock, with the sun rising behind him, he was traveling on Interstate 15 about sixty-five miles away from Los Angeles. In 1954, Interstate 15 ended just outside of San Bernardino. Cars traveling further west had two options: Route 66, which went slightly southwest to towns like Cucamonga and Azusa, and Interstate 10, which went further southwest to Los Angeles. The three roads, Interstates 15 and 10 and Route 66, met in a Y, with Interstate 15 the stem.

Sammy wanted Interstate 10. As he approached the Y, he saw a light green Chrysler Imperial ahead of him. The driver was a woman; he could tell by her hat. She had one passenger, also a woman, also wearing a hat. Just after the Chrysler entered Interstate 10, the driver slowed down. Realizing she wanted Route 66 and had taken the wrong road, she decided to rectify her error by crossing a dirt median separating the two thoroughfares. But, to get to the median, she had to back up. Doing so placed her directly in the path of Sammy's on-coming vehicle. Davis considered passing the car on the apron to the right of the highway, but his Caddy was too wide. And the eastbound lane had oncoming traffic. His only choice was to hit the breaks and hope for the best. He managed to reduce his speed, but not enough to avoid hitting the Chrysler. So he tried to at least minimize the impact by cutting the wheel and aiming for the car's rear fender. Upon impact, there was a sickening crash. The Caddy then careened off the Chrysler, carried Sammy into the eastbound lane where it miraculously slipped between two vehicles, and finally slammed to a stop against a concrete abutment. The force of the blow crushed in the front of the powerful vehicle. Sammy's forehead was thrust forward, and he plowed into the steering wheel.

Dazed and with blood streaming down his face, he opened his door, got out of the car, and sought to help Charlie out of the back seat where he'd been resting. A serviceman trying to hitch a ride in front of a nearby gas station saw the collision, rushed to Sammy's aid, and helped him get Charlie out of the car. "I saw his jaw hanging all loose," Sammy recalled, "blood running from his mouth." When Charlie looked at his boss, his face filled with shock and revulsion. In response, Sammy touched his cheek and felt his left eye dangling there, held in place by a thin string of muscle. He later learned that he had impaled the eye on a decorative cone-shaped protrusion in the center of the Caddy's steering wheel. He tried to, in his words, "stuff it back in," but failed. Then he went into shock, sagging to the ground. All he could think was that he'd worked so hard for so long and now, just at the moment when everything was clicking, it was going to be lost. "God, please don't let me go blind," he prayed. "God, please don't take it all away now." The serviceman returned to the gas station and phoned for an ambulance. Shortly thereafter, Sammy heard the sound of an approaching siren and a moment or two later felt himself being hoisted onto a stretcher and placed inside the vehicle, which then sped away.*

Meanwhile, the driver of the Imperial, Helen Ross, a seventy-two-year-old woman who lived in the Valley, and her sixty-nine-year-old companion, Bessie Roth, of Akron, Ohio, were recovering inside their car. At the point of impact, they had been thrust into the back seat with the front seat on top of them. Nevertheless, they sustained only minor injuries.[†] Charlie, by contrast, had a broken jaw and lost all of his teeth. But Sammy was in the worst shape. He'd bitten through his lower lip, his nose was broken yet again, and he sustained numerous cuts on his face (which were eventually removed by plastic surgery). But the biggest problem was his left eye.

At the Community Hospital in San Bernardino, where Davis was taken, the physicians who examined him initially thought his eye could be saved. To be certain, they called in an expert, Dr. Frederick Hull, who concurred with the staff doctors but noted that the damaged eye would never provide more than 10 percent vision. While that might seem better than nothing, the weak orb would depend heavily on the good eye and thus damage it over time. The result, a condition known as sympathetic blindness, could leave Davis with no vision at all. Accordingly, Hull recommended that the damaged eye be removed.

Meanwhile, Jess Rand and Jeff Chandler, who had been waiting for Sammy at Universal, had learned about the accident. They hopped in a car, reaching the hospital just as Dr. Hull was preparing to operate on Sammy's eye. Davis was unconscious, but the doctor assured Rand and Chandler that the entertainer would survive and that he would be able to resume his career.

While Sammy was in surgery, the press gathered en masse outside the hospital. Inside, messengers were delivering telegrams, flowers, and other gifts. And the phones were ringing nonstop, as well-wishers from all over, including Eddie Cantor and Jack Benny, called to express concern. David Dushoff, who owned the Latin Casino in Philadelphia and was enormously fond of Sammy, told Jess Rand, "Anything he needs, just send me the bill." The normally sleepy hospital in San Bernardino had never seen anything like this.

When Sammy awoke, he found himself lying in a bed with sheets that

---

*The source for this account of the accident, which differs somewhat from the version Sammy recounted in *Yes I Can* and elsewhere, came to this author from Arthur Silber, Jr., who, in turn, got it from the serviceman mentioned in the text.

[†]Shortly after the accident, the passenger in the Imperial, Bessie Roth, filed a $75,000 suit against Davis. On January 22, 1955, a federal jury held that he was not to blame for the crash or Mrs. Roth's minor injuries.

felt hot and sticky. His arms were tied to bars along the sides. He drew comfort from this: at least he still had his arms. He kicked out with his feet; he still had those too. But everything was in complete darkness, and he felt a terrible pressure around his head. He heard a nurse say, "Everything is all right, Mr. Davis." But he couldn't see. In a rush of panic, he asked the nurse if he was blind. She told him no, that his head was wrapped in bandages. He didn't know if he could believe her. Nevertheless, he promised not to disturb the dressing, so she untied his arms.

Shortly thereafter, Dr. Hull arrived and told him about the operation. "You're not blind," he added. "You're going to see. You'll be able to dance and sing and do everything you ever did." Eventually, Hull added, the eye socket would sufficiently heal for Sammy to be outfitted with a plastic eye; no one used glass anymore. After that, people looking at him wouldn't be able to tell the difference. In the meantime, the eyelid would droop, for the muscles holding it up had been destroyed. Accordingly, Hull suggested Sammy wear a patch. The physician concluded by saying, "I know it's a tremendous shock to find that you only have one eye, but the eye is lost and that cannot be changed. . . . Try not to think of what you've lost but of how much you still have."

After the doctor left, Sammy drifted off to sleep. When he awoke, his father, grandmother, and Will were at his bedside. So, too, were Janet Leigh and Tony Curtis. Leigh pressed a small Star of David into his hand (Sammy clung to the token so tightly it left a permanent mark on his palm). Then he drifted off again. When he regained consciousness once more, the room was filled with flowers, greeting cards, Bibles, and other tokens of affection, most of them from fans, people whom Sammy had never met. He was genuinely surprised and touched.

The next day, Dr. Hull removed the bandages from around Sammy's head, and he experienced a tremendous sense of relief as he discerned, first, light and dark, then shapes, and, finally, people, objects, and the world about him. Then Jess came in, congratulating him on his brilliant publicity stunt. Sammy was astounded to discover that he had been a front-page story in every major paper in the country for two days. Thanks to the press, virtually everyone in the United States and many people around the world now knew about the talented little black guy who was fighting valiantly for his life and his career—and they were rooting for him. "You're the hottest thing in the business," Rand told him.

Indeed, public interest was so keen, Will proudly announced the following day, that the Sands Hotel in Vegas was offering $25,000 a week for the Trio as soon as they were available, a huge jump from the $7,500 they were earning at the Last Frontier. Moreover, nightclubs all over the country were phoning the Morris office trying to line up dates.

Naturally, Davis was gratified by all of the interest. He was also relieved beyond words that his eye injury, though a terrible loss, didn't signal the end of his life or his career. In moments when he was alone, however, he worried that he'd never be the powerhouse on stage that he'd been before the accident.

Meanwhile, Will Mastin had his own devils to face. He knew that the act that bore his name derived its success from its youngest member. Now that the accident had made Sammy Davis, Jr., famous, he wondered how long it would be before his protégé would go out on his own, leaving him and Sam Sr. to fend for themselves. Mastin loved show business; it was all he knew. Even at roughly seventy-four, he wasn't ready to give it up; at the same time, he was too old to start over without the Trio's mainstay.

Will's fears weren't entirely unfounded. In the years since Sammy had become the breakout star of the act, friends and business associates had constantly encouraged him to leave the Trio. Indeed, there was something peculiar about watching two older men standing beyond this vital young-ster, snapping their fingers while he sang and disappearing entirely for much of the rest of the show. Even their flash dancing was decidedly old-fashioned compared with Davis' hip, modern material and style.

Will and Sam Sr. yearned for a bit of attention, even though they were proud of what Sammy had achieved. Sensitive to this, Jess Rand once managed to get Mastin's photo in one of the New York dailies, on some trumped-up story about the hoofer's many decades in show business. Will had tears in his eyes when he thanked the press agent. Then, the next day, Sam came to Rand's office, complaining, "You know, Will Mastin's name is up there, Sammy Davis, Jr.'s name is up there. There ain't no fucking word ever about Sam Davis, Sr., is there?" So Jess invented a story about Sammy dedicating an upcoming show to his father in honor of Sr.'s birth-day and managed to place it in a Brooklyn or Long Island publication. It wasn't a major New York paper, but Sammy's dad was pleased.

Of course, Sammy knew that he could manage just fine on his own. There were times when he resented how he'd been put to work at an early age and cheated out of a normal childhood. And, yes, there were moments when Will's stubbornness and conservatism irked him. But he loved the old man and his dad and was also deeply grateful to them. He probably wouldn't have put up a fight had they voluntarily decided to retire, but he wasn't about to push them out.

Will didn't know that, however. During the long days in the hospital, Sammy would occasionally look at his mentor in a moment of solitude and see the fear in the older man's eyes. Wanting to relieve his anxiety and restore his dignity, Sammy told him one day when the two of them were alone that now that they were getting so many offers, they should have a contract. As always, they would split everything three ways and Will would still be the boss. The only difference was that now it would be official. "We don't need a contract," Mastin protested. But Sammy insisted. In that instant, Will was transformed. "He walked to the side of the bed," said Davis, "and I saw the look of gratitude and relief from the tremendous fear that good man had been carrying. It flashed across his face and he turned away for a second. But now he was looking straight at me. He put out his hand and the touch of it, the feel of his strength, carried me back through all the years we'd been together."

Sammy was able to help ease his mentor's concerns, but he was less successful with his own. If there was one area in his life where he felt confident, it was his talent. But beyond his ability to get back on a stage lay issues that had underscored his behavior throughout his life: his hatred of his looks and stature, the intense need to be loved, the raging desire for the best of everything, and the realization that nothing was enough. Despite all he had accomplished, he wasn't fulfilled. He was lonely, often unhappy, and sometimes bitter. He was still a Negro in a world that too often hated blacks.

At the same time, he knew that he had been blessed with a rare and wonderful gift, his talent, and the employment of that gift had enabled him to experience life as few Negroes could at that moment in U.S. history. He didn't understand why he had been so lucky. And because of that, he feared that perhaps the accident had been some kind of payback, that he had been punished for taking his good fortune for granted.

As these thoughts consumed him in the hospital, he found himself wishing for some kind of spiritual comfort. "I was all mixed up," he said a few years later. "I was looking for something, but really didn't know what. I wanted something. Something morally intangible." Although his father and grandmother were Baptists and his mother Catholic, he'd had virtually no exposure to religion. Traveling around the country his entire life had left little time for church-going. Until this moment, he'd never felt the need.

Then one day, a rabbi from a nearby temple paid him a visit. He hadn't come to see Sammy per se; he just popped in as part of his hospital rounds. Catholic and Protestant clergymen had also stopped by, but Davis was particularly taken with this modern, athletic-looking man, so different from the rabbis with long beards, silk black coats, and broad-brimmed hats he remembered occasionally seeing as a kid in Harlem. Davis and the rabbi chatted for a while about secular matters—politics, show business, sports, and so forth. Then, Sammy turned to business. Why, he wanted to know, had he been blessed with so much talent? And did the accident, and the near loss of all he'd been given, indicate that he'd displeased God? Was he being told to shape up? "Sammy," the rabbi replied, "you look upon your accident as a warning or a threat. We don't believe that goodness should stem from threat of punishment. We worship God in love, not in fear." But, he added, the accident might be seen as a wakeup call; perhaps Sammy should start thinking about his life and its meaning. According to his faith, the rabbi explained, each person should strive to realize his or her potential. But also to *use* that potential for a larger purpose. As he put it, "The greatest use of life is to spend it on something which will out-last it."

Sammy and the rabbi left the discussion there, but in the months to come the entertainer would return to matters spiritual time and time again.

Davis was released from the hospital on November 27, one week after the eye surgery, but he had six weeks of recuperation ahead of him. He spent part of this time at the Palm Springs home of his good friend, Frank Sinatra.* In the desert, Davis concentrated on healing and regaining his strength. He also adjusted to viewing the world through one eye, which mostly meant doing without normal depth perception. As he later told Alex Haley, "I'd reach out for something and miss it [by] two, three inches. The first time I tried dancing again, I kept kicking myself in the other leg and tripping." But he was determined to compensate. Eventually, he reached a point where the vision in his one remaining eye was better than before. By the end of the year, Davis was restored to good physical health.

Recovering psychologically took much longer. In an interview with the *Boston Globe*'s Marian Christy shortly before his death, he con-fessed, "When I had the bad auto accident in November 1954, I was pleased just to be alive." But he added, "Then, over a two-year period, shock set in. I was depressed. I never spoke of my depression. I didn't turn to my father. I didn't turn to my friends. They didn't know what was going on inside me. I healed myself. I had always been a loner. So I iso-lated my feelings. I used work as a crutch. I ran away from depression by running on stage."

Not surprisingly, with only one eye, he also developed a fear of blind-ness that lasted for decades. Eventually this passed. As he said in 1976, "I've become fatalistic about it. If I go blind, I go blind."

---

*In *Yes I Can*, Davis described at length a visit that Sinatra paid to him while he was in the hospital. Jess Rand told this author that Frank never saw Sammy in San Bernardino, and Arthur Silber, Jr. supported Rand's recollection. Either way, there is no question that Davis benefited from Sinatra's support and encouragement in the wake of the accident and the loss of his left eye.

PART THREE

Top of the Heap

CHAPTER 7

The Return

Sammy finally recorded the title song from *Six Bridges to Cross* on December 2, 1954. But singing in a Universal Pictures recording studio was simple compared with getting onstage in a room full of people, with all of them wondering the same thing: Could he still cut it? Although the Vegas offers were tempting, Davis decided that he'd rather make his comeback at the site of his first triumph, Ciro's. Sinatra agreed with his decision. "The important thing is to start strong," he told Sammy, "and in L.A. you'll be home where you know you have friends around you. The Vegas money'll still be there."

After leaving Sinatra's Palm Springs estate, Davis readied himself at a home his father had rented in the Hollywood Hills. To help him, he hired an aspiring actor named Dave Landfield. (When Sammy returned to the road, Landfield would join his growing entourage as sort of a combination assistant and buddy.) Not content to simply get back in shape after the accident, Sammy perfected some new impressions—of Johnny Ray, Arthur Godfrey, and *both* of the stars of the Oscar-winning film *Going My Way*, Bing Crosby and Barry Fitzgerald. Singing more in his own voice, he also added new songs to his repertoire, including "That Old Black Magic," "Something's Got to Give," and "I Love All of You." As these numbers illustrate, he had settled comfortably into the popular middle-of-the-road material of the day, led by the standards of Porter, Berlin, the Gershwins, and Rodgers and Hart, and new songs in the tradition of these American masters. In his repertoire and in his style of singing, Davis placed himself amid the phalanx of vocalists, mostly Italian Americans and Jewish Americans, solidly behind Frank Sinatra: Dean Martin, Mel Torme, Perry Como, Tony Bennett, Julius LaRosa, Vic Damone, Eddie Fisher, and just a bit later on, Andy Williams, Steve Lawrence, and Jack Jones. In the early to mid-fifties, Sammy and his fellow troubadours, and their female counterparts, were the great champions of the airwaves. But, even as Davis readied himself for his comeback, the shadow of Elvis Presley was looming on the Memphis horizon.

The big night came on January 11, 1955. The day before, Sammy told Aline Mosby of the *New York Morning Telegraph* that he hoped people would come to watch him *perform*, "not to see if I look any different. The sentiment is great. But people coming to stare—this is what I resent." He added that he considered his return to Ciro's "the beginning of a new life."

When he arrived at the club, he saw a long line of people outside, hoping for a table. Inside, his dressing room looked like a florist's shop, with bouquets everywhere. There were also dozens of telegrams, and Sinatra was on hand backstage for moral support. "I just wanted to let you know that I'm going to introduce you out there," the crooner said. Gripping Sammy's shoulder, he added, "The patch is dramatic as hell," then left so his friend could collect himself.

Naturally, Sammy was nervous. He'd worked exhaustively in anticipation of this evening, so he wasn't terribly worried about his ability to perform—although, with the blind spot on his left side, there was always the unexpected. Mostly, he continued to be concerned about the audience. Could people relax and enjoy themselves with his eye patch serving as a constant reminder of what he'd been through?

When he hit the stage, he immediately discovered that they weren't going to forget, and they didn't want to. They reveled in the drama of the little guy who'd endured a horrible tragedy and had come back to face them. In a curious way, the loss of his eye had made him a hero.

Accordingly, every person in the audience rose to greet Sammy as he entered the showroom, cheering and applauding and, in a few cases, even crying. He peered out at the house, recognizing among the standing throng his friends Humphrey Bogart and Lauren Bacall and some of the other giants he liked to imitate—Cary Grant, Edward G. Robinson, James Cagney, Jimmy Stewart—plus many other celebrities, including the Spencer Tracys and Dick Powell and his wife, June Allyson. These were his own kind, and they were rooting him on.

Finally, Sammy raised his hands to quiet the well-wishers, and they slowly took their seats. Although he wanted to acknowledge the tremendous show of support, he felt that anything he said would sound like typical show business schmaltz, so, instead, he signaled Morty Stevens to start his opening number, "That Old Black Magic."

At the end of the song, he turned to bow to his conductor. But, without thinking, he had swiveled on his blind side and his head hit the microphone. The audience gasped at the loud crack and he felt a horrible shooting pain in his eye socket. With the quick wit that endeared him to people, then and later, he patted the mike and said, "Sorry, Frank. Didn't see you come in, baby." The audience roared its approval, and the awkward moment passed.

Finally, after more than two hours, Sammy brought the show to a close, prompting Ciro's owner, Herman Hover, to join him onstage with the club's entire staff—cooks, kitchen helpers, waiters, bus boys, hatcheck girls. Forming a circle around Davis, they burst into a chorus of "Auld Lang Syne."

"There'll never be another night like that," recalled television producer George Schlatter, then Hover's assistant. "I mean, standing ovation doesn't quite cover it. That night was love, admiration, respect, happiness, joy, appreciation, and surprise, and absolute delight—to see that, not only was he back, but with that burning ambition. And total lust to prove that he was, in every way, the fourth dimension in performing. So we just sat there. And we all knew that we were taking part in a very special moment."

Following his unforgettable return to Ciro's, Sammy, his dad, and Will took the act on the road, hitting many of the other posh clubs they'd headlined prior to the accident. These return engagements may have lacked the intense drama of Ciro's opening night, but they were still triumphs. At the Latin Quarter in Boston, for example, *Variety* noted that Sammy had "lost none of his zest or enthusiasm, for he dished out the slick type of entertainment that has long been his trademark." The trade paper also observed that Sammy was taking more and more of the spotlight himself. Will and Sam Sr. "have less to do each time around."

From Boston, the Trio went to New York for the capper of the tour, Sammy's return to the Copa. As at Ciro's, Davis enjoyed a celebrity-packed audience of sympathetic fans. The rooters included Eddie Fisher, Marilyn Monroe (whom Sammy had met the night of his return to Ciro's), the ice skating movie star Sonja Henie, producer Mike Todd with actress Evelyn Keyes, comics Jack E. Leonard and Sid Caesar, and actresses Debbie Reynolds and Anita Eckberg. "Sammy Jr.," crowed columnist Earl Wilson, "was so great that he overshadowed everybody." According to Frank Quinn of the *New York Mirror,* the entertainer left the "crowded room shouting for more." Quinn added, "Junior is also endowed with a winning personality, plus remarkable showmanship. Everything is polished to perfection but offered with a sort of friendly informality." Not surprisingly, the week before Sammy opened at the Copa, the newspaper editors and columnists who covered the nightclub scene had bestowed the Dinah award on the Trio for "the best variety act of the year."

But, just at the moment of Sammy's greatest triumph, *Confidential,* a monthly scandal magazine, made him the target of an exposé, gleefully reporting that he was romantically involved with a white movie star. Like the car outside of San Bernardino, he was again facing something that could destroy all he had achieved.

The star in question, Ava Gardner, had already divorced Mickey Rooney when Davis toured with him, but she and Sammy came to know one another after she married Frank Sinatra in 1951. In fact, she and Sinatra were still married at the time the *Confidential* story appeared in March 1955, although they had separated the previous year.

Four years older than Sammy, Gardner was something of a free spirit. Although she was one of the most beautiful women in the world, she didn't take herself, or her talent, very seriously. She was also completely devoid of race prejudice, despite her childhood in North Carolina, where her father had been a poor tenant farmer.

Thus, Gardner was a natural for Davis to approach in the fall of 1954, before the car crash. He'd been offered the cover of a national African American magazine entitled *One World,* providing he could find another star to appear in the photo with him. Would Ava do it? he wanted to know. Being Ava, she naturally said sure.

The photo session took place at Gardner's suite at the Drake Hotel in Manhattan. "It was a perfectly innocent thing," Sammy told readers of an *Ebony* article that appeared under his byline in 1956. He asserted that there were about fifteen or twenty people present, including the *One World* photographer, Ava's sister, and representatives from MGM, where Gardner was under contract. Because the issue of the magazine was scheduled for the end of the year, Sammy dressed up in a Santa Claus outfit, and, with the photographer snapping away, Ava leaned over him, as if she were telling him what she wanted for Christmas. "We made sure there was no physical contact in the photo," said Davis, "no hugging and looking at the camera."

After the session, Sammy told Ava that he collected photos of his celebrity friends and asked her if she had one for him. He wanted a large picture, 11 inches by 14 inches, so that it would look imposing framed and mounted on a wall. Ava didn't have any pictures that big, so Sammy asked the *One World* photographer if he'd snap a few shots of the two of them. After shooting a roll, the photographer agreed to let Gardner choose the pictures to be printed. It was understood that these would be for Sammy and Ava only; the rest of the exposures would be destroyed.

Instead, they wound up in *Confidential,* where they were given an entirely different context. In the accompanying text, a reporter named Horton Streete claimed that Gardner and Davis were in the throes of a passionate affair.

Things got even steamier, Streete added, when Ava joined Sammy for a night out in Harlem. This was around the time of the *One World* photo shoot and a concurrent Trio appearance at the Apollo Theater. After his final performance that night, the duo allegedly went to a club called the Shalimar, where she became intoxicated. Thereafter, Streete continued, they frequently saw one another at each other's hotels, to the apparent titillation of the staff in each venue. The story ended with a recitation of other "dark-skinned gents" seen in Gardner's company from time to time.

When *Confidential* hit the newsstands, Sammy and Ava panicked. Such a story could ruin careers in 1955, just as the civil rights movement was heating up. Fortunately, Gardner went to MGM's head of publicity, Howard Strickling, who wisely counseled doing nothing. "This is a rag that is published in a cellar somewhere," Strickling maintained. Suing, he added, would only serve to make it a major story in the legitimate press. He concluded, "The best thing we can do is ignore it completely." Garner took his advice, and the story soon faded away.

Nevertheless, there may have been some truth to what Streete wrote. Arthur Silber, Jr., told this author that Ava and Sammy did, in fact, share a bed on a few occasions. Such intimacy was not symptomatic of the major romance implied by *Confidential,* but simply the natural chemistry between two robust, sexually active people. Jess Rand, by contrast, maintained that nothing physical took place between the two stars.

In the long view of Sammy Davis, Jr.'s life, whether or not he had a fling with Ava Gardner is of relatively little consequence. Of greater significance is the fact that the *Confidential* article marked the moment when he started to become controversial. Before, the media and, by extension, the public tended to see Sammy as a modest, clean-cut, sweet young man, loaded with talent and determined to become a success with the help and guidance of his father and uncle. After the accident, he was widely regarded as a plucky entertainer who caught a terrible break but was undaunted in his climb to the top. In both instances, he was admirable and likable, hardly a threat to anyone, except perhaps to those with less talent.

By contrast, the *Confidential* article depicted Sammy Davis as someone to watch carefully: a cocky, swinging, fun-loving Negro who would stop at nothing to get what he wanted, even when his goal was a glamorous white movie star who had been married to his idol and friend. This posture went right to the heart of mainstream America's greatest fears about black men: their sexual potency and their desire to sleep with white women. The *Confidential* article didn't receive much attention in the establishment press, but it was a portent of things to come.

*   *   *

On April 3, while performing at the Copa, Sammy made a return appearance on Ed Sullivan's *Toast of the Town*. Eleven days later, *Time* magazine published a piece on the entertainer, asserting that, in the past four months, Sammy had become "one of the hottest acts in the nation's gaudier night clubs—Las Vegas' Last Frontier, Hollywood's Ciro's, Miami Beach's Copa City. Last week Davis was packing them in at Manhattan's Copacabana, and columnists were hurling exclamation points. *Variety*'s verdict: 'In the main, socko.'"

By April, Sammy had returned several times to Decca's recording studios, rendering, among other tunes, "Easy to Love," "Something's Gotta Give," and the title song from the Doris Day–James Cagney film, "Love Me or Leave Me." "Something's Gotta Give" became a hit single, as did "That Old Black Magic" and "The Birth of the Blues," which had been recorded before the accident. By the end of the year, Davis had not one but two LPs on the market, *Starring Sammy Davis, Jr.*, which was released on May 14, and *Just for Lovers*, released on October 15. Both were performing exceedingly well.

As 1955 wound down, he also appeared on several other television shows, notably Edward R. Murrow's lighthearted interview program, *Person to Person*, on November 4, and *The Milton Berle Show* four days later.* In addition, he enjoyed smash-hit engagements at the Last Frontier in May (where he opened with a specially written number, "Gee, It's Good to Be Home"), the 500 Club in Atlantic City in August, and the Chez Paree in Chicago in September. While there, he had started dating a beautiful African American model named Cordie King.

When he returned to L.A. near year's end, Sammy was still wearing an eye patch, even though he'd been fitted for a plastic orb months earlier. The patch had almost become a trademark. Not only did he have different colored swatches for different occasions, ranging from basic black to plaid, but he made jokes about his infirmity as part of the act. "So long, folks, gotta go do a Hathaway shirt ad" was one of his favorites. This reference to the clothier's dashing one-eyed symbol never failed to get a laugh. People loved the fact that Sammy could poke fun at himself, a knack that remained with him for the rest of his life. He peppered his act with jokes about his race, his stature, his spending habits, and, a bit later, his religion, and, later still, his jewelry. But, as 1955 drew to a close, he decided it was time to retire the patch. "It was Humphrey Bogart who convinced me to quit that," he later told Alex Haley. In his inimitable fashion, the tough-guy movie star bluntly asked his friend, "How long you gonna trade on the goddam

---

*In 1954, The Texaco Star Theater, recognizing the popularity of its host, changed its name.

patch? How long are you gonna keep using it for a crutch? You want people calling you 'Sammy Davis' or 'the kid with the eyepatch?'" That did it.

Putting the capper on this amazing year was a celebrity roast held by the Friars Club at the Beverly Hilton Hotel in Los Angeles on November 10. Not only was Sammy the first black entertainer to be honored by the Friars; he was the youngest. The speakers at the $1,000-a-ticket event included Sinatra, Berle, Bogart, Gary Cooper, George Burns, Pearl Bailey, Jerry Lewis, Tony Martin, Jeff Chandler, future U.S. president Ronald Reagan, and toastmaster Jack Benny. Afterward, Sammy described the evening as "a stamp you've arrived. It's acceptance by your own people, the people you love and work with."

Another sign of his arrival and his acceptance that year came with his decision to move from the Sunset Colonial Hotel to a home of his own. Finding a suitable place proved somewhat problematic, however. Naturally, Sammy wanted to live in one of the elegant parts of L.A., but, though he was embraced by the Hollywood community, the town's old establishment wasn't eager to have a Negro for a neighbor.

When he found a house he liked, George Schlatter volunteered to have the $75,000 mortgage put in his name. That way, no one would know a black man was moving in. It was a bold gesture on Schlatter's part. "At that point," the future television producer recalled, "I was making $200 a week [at Ciro's], and I must tell you, it makes your sphincter jump when you sign something like that. Because I knew Sammy didn't have any money. But that's how he got the house."

The home was at 8850 Evanview Drive, in the hills just behind Sunset Boulevard. Formerly owned by Judy Garland, the three-level Spanish Colonial–style structure boasted fourteen rooms, including five bedrooms, on an acre and a half of land. Although Sammy hoped that one day he'd enjoy it with a wife, he initially shared it with his family. He settled Rosa B., who'd been living in L.A. for some time, in an apartment of her own on the basement floor. There were semiprivate quarters as well for Sam Sr. and his girlfriend, a sweet, friendly nurse named Rita Wade, whom everyone called Pee Wee.* The upper floor of the house, which included a living room, bedroom, terrace, and guest room, was Sammy's domain, which he furnished with white rugs, mostly black furniture, and gigantic lamps. He also installed an oversized bed in the master suite, the equivalent of two regular double beds. "It's a fine house," the entertainer

---

*In the late forties or early fifties, when Rosa B. moved to California, Sammy bought her a house as well as a Chrysler automobile and hired a driver-helper, Rudy Duff. By the mid-fifties, however, she was getting too old to live by herself, so she moved in with her grandson. In the 1960s, Sam Sr. married Pee Wee and they adopted two girls, Suzette and Sandy, and moved into their own home in the L.A. area.

proudly told *Esquire* magazine's Thomas B. Morgan. "It means a lot to me. Someday, I'd like to arrange things so I can spend some time there."

As for the neighborhood, as Schlatter dryly put it, "You see, it's like anything else—the anticipation of it is so much more daunting than the realization. Sammy Davis was living next door to you, and the biggest stars in the world were dropping by your neighborhood. That made it a hell of a lot more acceptable, I'm sure."

Having his own home for the first time was wonderful. So, too, were the Friars Roast, the hit records, the television gigs, and his many sold-out nightclub engagements. But despite everything, Sammy remained troubled. He was still seeking peace of mind, the sort of spiritual comfort he'd found lacking when he was in the hospital.

Earlier in the year, while attending a benefit in San Francisco, he'd found himself seated on the dais next to a rabbi, Alvin Fine of Temple Emanu-El. Like the rabbi he'd met in San Bernardino, Fine exuded a combination of modernity and Old World wisdom that Sammy found compelling. He invited Fine to lunch, at which he shared his spiritual concerns with the clergyman. After Sammy voiced his growing interest in Judaism, the rabbi suggested several books on the subject and invited the entertainer to discuss them with him after he finished his reading.

Back in Los Angeles, Davis began studying the material Fine recommended. "At first, reading those books confused me," he later told Trudy B. Feldman of *Ebony*. "I would read a few pages, close the book, and try to figure out what the writer was saying. Little by little, I began to understand. That uncertain feeling that gnawed at my bones began to relax. Something was coming through and I wasn't confused any more. I began to understand . . . not only religion, but everything and everybody around me." One of the things that particularly struck him was the commonality between Jews and blacks, the fact that both groups had been enslaved and oppressed, had been, in his words, "despised" and "rejected," had both found the need to fight for "equality and human dignity."

The next time he was in San Francisco, Sammy again met with Fine. "It was one of the most wonderful afternoons I had ever spent talking to another person," he said. "We ran the gamut of Hollywood, down, up, and back again to Billy Graham." As with the hospital chaplain, Fine stressed the precept that good works resounded to the benefit of the benefactor, leaving Davis, himself a remarkably generous soul, to conclude that "when it comes to sharing, you suddenly find that you have much more than you thought you had in the first place."

Fine recommended that Sammy seek out a colleague in Hollywood, Rabbi Max Nussbaum. Born in Germany, with a Ph.D. from the Univer-

sity of Wurzburg, Nussbaum was a refugee from the Third Reich; he had
come to the United States in 1940. Hired by Los Angeles' Temple Israel
two years later, he was widely respected for his intellect and his passionate Zionism.

Davis felt an immediate connection with the man. As he put it, "His
warmth burst through and made me feel as if we were friends for years."
Over several months, Nussbaum added more reading material and met
frequently with Davis for follow-up discussions. By now, the entertainer
was strongly considering becoming a Jew himself. But Nussbaum
insisted that he proceed slowly, explaining, "We *cherish* converts, but we
neither seek nor rush them. We don't want today's enthusiasm to be
tomorrow's disappointment." So Sammy continued his studies. He also
visited temples in the cities where the Trio was performing, attending
services and chatting with other rabbis.

At about the beginning of 1956, he reached his decision: he wanted to
convert. Some of his friends, even those who were Jewish themselves,
thought he was crazy. One told him, "You have two strikes against you
already," referring to his race and his one eye. Others figured that he was
trying to ingratiate himself with Hollywood's elite, most of whom were
Jewish. Such notions persisted for the rest of Davis' life—and even after
his death. Indeed, more than one friend told this author that they
thought he'd converted either for the publicity or simply to feel closer to
his many Jewish pals.

Perhaps there is some truth in the notion that Davis wanted to bond
with his cronies. But it would seem that his kinship with Judaism also
sprang from a genuine need for spirituality. As he explained, "I found
something here that gave me a feeling of refreshing simplicity. It was
understanding of life all around me. It was an honesty you just can't
explain because it's a part of you deep inside." Putting it another way, he
said, "I wanted to be a Jew because I wanted to become part of a 5,000
year history and hold on to something not just material, which would
give me that inner strength to turn the other cheek. Jews have become
strong over their thousands of years of oppression and I wanted to
become part of that strength."

He later described his conversion as "the greatest thrill of my life."
He knew that his becoming a Jew would alienate some Christians and
even some Jews. He also expected some negative feedback from the
media, and, in fact, the news of his conversion did produce a strong
response from the press, not all of which was favorable. While he hoped
that people would respect his choice, he was willing to live with the consequences if they didn't. As he put it, "I've found something in Judaism,
and I'm not about to give it up."

Mr. Wonderful

Not only was Sammy's religious conversion big news. So, too, was his relationship with Cordie King. In early January 1956, he publicly acknowledged that he was serious about the attractive, five-foot-six, Mississippi-born model.

A few months older than Davis, King had grown up in Chicago and embarked on her career in 1949. Sammy first saw her on the August 1955 cover of the African American magazine *Jet*, where she was fetchingly decked out in a leopard skin swimsuit. He and Cordie met shortly thereafter in New York and again in September, while he was performing at the Chez Paree in Chicago. At that point, Davis invited King to be his guest for the Friars Club Roast in his honor in L.A., and she accepted. According to Vincent Tubbs, who wrote an article about the relationship in the February 1956 issue of *Jet*, Sammy bought Cordie a white fox stole while she was in California, and columnists "hinted about wedding bells."

There was only one problem: King was already married.

This was not something she kept secret—either from Sammy, who had gotten to know her husband, wine steward Melvin Brown, back in Chicago, or from the press. In fact, when asked in L.A. if she planned to marry Davis, Cordie replied simply, "I already have a husband" and described her trip to the coast as "a friendly visit."

But by then, Davis' competitive spirit had been aroused. Though it is doubtful that he was head over heels in love with Cordie King, he nevertheless decided he wanted her, married or not. In the weeks following King's trip to L.A., she and Sammy spoke frequently on the phone, and he brought her to several of the venues where he was appearing.

Sometime in late 1955 or very early 1956, he proposed. Flattered and somewhat confused, King said, "I don't think someone can just up and leave their husband because they're asked to." But Sammy continued to press, and her resistance finally crumbled. In mid-January, he brought

Cordie to Miami Beach, where the Trio was performing at a club called Ciro's, to meet his father and Sam Sr.'s girlfriend, Pee Wee. A few days later, Sammy told his nightclub audience that he and King were engaged. Back in Chicago, Cordie's husband, Melvin Brown, resigned himself to the situation, telling the press, "I want her to be happy, and if marrying Sammy Davis will make her happy, I won't stand in the way."

And he didn't. As the *New York Post*'s Jim Cook noted on March 15, 1956, "The chunky diamond ring soon went on her third finger, left hand—and Cordie's husband went out of their Chicago apartment." The ring, according to Vincent Tubbs, was a square-cut diamond with long baguettes on each side fashioned by one of Sammy's favorite jewelers, George Unger. The entertainer placed its value in the neighborhood of $15,000 to $20,000.

Shortly after Sammy's engagement to Cordie King, *Confidential* published a story about him and an attractive white, twenty-something actress named Meg Myles.

According to the writer, Matt Williams, Myles, who'd gained a modest following thanks to her role in the film *Phoenix City Confidential,* had met Sammy in October 1954 when she was an unknown starlet, singing in Los Angeles with a trio headed by Duke Mitchell, a friend of Sammy's. Williams asserted that after an evening out with Mitchell, Meg and Duke went to Sammy's room at the Sunset Colonial Hotel. There, Davis took some photos of the curvaceous actress, after which Mitchell took Myles home. She subsequently returned to Sammy's room, at his behest, and that's when the romance began. "In the next few weeks," Williams continued, "she often failed to show up at her own place the whole night long," adding that "residents and employees of the Colonial got used to spotting Meg arriving at Sammy's suite at one or two a.m. and slipping out hours later—in broad daylight—to whistle down a cruising cab." From time to time, Williams said, the duo was also seen at late dinners at eateries like the popular Hamburger Hamlet on the Sunset Strip, "where the two would moon at each other over cheeseburgers, medium rare. Meg was so wild about that Davis boy that she chose him to help her celebrate her birthday, November 13, 1954, and it was launched at the same ground beef palace." The affair allegedly came to an end after Sammy's auto accident, when he had more pressing matters on his mind.

In fact, Sammy was never romantically involved with Meg Myles. The actress told this author that she did meet the entertainer through Duke Mitchell, as Matt Williams alleged, that Sammy did take photos of her—"nice pictures, not pin-up pictures or anything," she pointed out—

and he did invite her to dinner for her birthday. But, on that occasion, as with most others, they were in the company of additional people. They also saw one another on a few subsequent occasions, including parties at Davis' grandmother's home. At one such gathering, Myles' roommate took a picture of the starlet with Sammy and several other people. Meg even visited the entertainer while he was in the hospital in San Bernardino.

But they were only friends. *Confidential* shaded its story with just enough truth, augmented by healthy doses of innuendo, that suing the rag would have been difficult and would only have given the allegations more attention in the mainstream press. So Myles did nothing. What made the story particularly damaging was an accompanying photo of Meg and Sammy cropped to remove the other people originally in the shot. The source of the photo—and the story—was Myles' former roommate.

When she saw the piece, the actress was stunned. As she pointed out, "In those days that was a terrible thing, to be put in that position of being accused of having a [romantic] relationship with a person of a different race." Worse, no one asked her if the story was true; everyone simply accepted its validity. As a consequence, her recording contract with Capitol Records was cancelled, as was a forthcoming appearance on *The Ed Sullivan Show*.

Moreover, the story ended her association with Davis. Looking back, Myles said, "What I resent so much about that was that I didn't have the intellectual strength to allow my friendship to exist in spite of things that people would say. . . . And that's sad." In the fall of 1959, she left California for New York, and, as she put it, "just started all over again," eventually forging an acting career in the theater.

The publication of the *Confidential* story had little or no impact on Sammy's relationship with Cordie King, for by the time the scandal magazine hit the newsstands, his engagement to the model was already falling apart.

Perhaps if the couple had been able to marry right away, the wedding would have taken place. But Sammy was just about to embark on a starring role in his first Broadway musical. Initially, he said that he hoped he and Cordie could wed sometime over the summer and honeymoon in Europe. Then he amended his plans. Because of his show, *Mr. Wonderful,* he told the press they'd settle for a week at a local resort; Europe would have to wait.

Instead, the relationship fell apart entirely. Cordie claimed that she grew weary of traveling to be with her fiancé, only to have him ignore her when she arrived. Apparently, Sammy simply lost interest in the model once the challenge of wooing her away from her husband disappeared. She was, in fact, rather shy and retiring, not really his type. Moreover, he relegated his love life to second place in the wake of his all-consuming efforts to make *Mr. Wonderful* a success. In any event, Cordie King was never even mentioned in Sammy's autobiography, *Yes I Can*. In the next few years, his relationships with other beautiful, accomplished women would eclipse her in the public memory—and, mostly likely, in his own as well.

The idea of bringing Sammy to Broadway originated with Jule Styne. Although the composer's best-remembered shows—*Bells Are Ringing, Gypsy, Funny Girl*—lay in the future, he was already a well-regarded veteran of the American musical theater, with the scores of *High Button Shoes* and *Gentlemen Prefer Blondes* to his credit, as well as numerous hit tunes written with lyricist Sammy Cahn, several of which were recorded by Cahn's good friend, Frank Sinatra.

Styne approached Davis about doing a Broadway show after seeing the Trio's act prior to Sammy's auto accident. Eager to prove himself in yet another medium, the theater, Davis immediately embraced the idea, even though starring in a musical was nowhere near as lucrative as touring on the nightclub circuit.

Far less enthusiastic was Will Mastin, who wanted to follow the money. The impasse produced another heated debate between mentor and protégé, made worse by Will's fear that if Sammy left the act for any reason, he'd never return. The solution—over Styne's objections—was for Will and Sam Sr. to appear in the musical as well, with the billing akin to that of their nightclub act. Thus, it became *Mr. Wonderful:* A New Musical Comedy with The Will Mastin Trio starring Sammy Davis, Jr., making for one of the more unusual marquees in the history of the Great White Way.

Aside from the casting of Will and Sam Sr., there were three other givens at the outset of the musical's gestation. First, because Davis had no acting experience outside the pilot of his unsold thirty-minute sitcom, Styne felt that he should play a character similar to himself, in other words, an entertainer. Second, Sammy insisted that the show be more than a collection of songs and jokes. He wanted it to carry a social message. Third, on the theory that theater audiences would be unhappy if they didn't catch some of Sammy's celebrated impressions, turns on musical instruments, and renderings of his hit songs, the second act would conclude with a portion of his nightclub routine. This was reminiscent of old-fashioned musicals, mindless crowd pleasers, with songs by an array of tunesmiths. By contrast, most fifties musicals followed the format established in 1943 by Rodgers and Hammerstein's *Oklahoma!* in which everything—song, dance, and story—was integrated to further the development of the characters or advance the plot.

Although the nightclub sequence would be a departure, the rest of *Mr. Wonderful* would follow the conventions of the day. Accordingly, once Sammy was onboard, Styne set out to hire a decent book writer. To his surprise, no one wanted the job. "Each writer made excuses," noted the composer's biographer, Theodore Taylor, "such as the impossibility of using the Will Mastin Trio within the framework of the show. It was apparent that none wanted to handle the 'black' theme. One writer, shocking Jule, said he could easily come up with a story that involved a black man raping a white woman. Broadway was loaded with closet bigots, much to Jule's surprise." Finally, Joseph Stein and Will Glickman, two young radio and television writers, agreed to tackle the assignment. They had recently written the book for a musical about the Pennsylvania Dutch country, *Plain and Fancy*.

What Stein and Glickman came up with was the tale of a young, talented, but essentially unknown entertainer named Charlie Welch who is discovered by a down-on-his-luck comic, Freddie Campbell. Eager to become the kid's manager, Campbell determines to make Charlie a star. Given Davis' insistence on some sort of social commentary, Stein and Glickman opened the musical at a small club in Paris, where the entertainer has settled to avoid the problems of Negroes back home. Thus, to risk stardom in America at Freddie's behest, he has to sacrifice the relative peace and security he enjoys abroad. In typical fashion, there was also a romance between Charlie and a girl, Ethel Pearson, whom he loves but is afraid to marry, and a secondary romance involving Freddie and his wife, Lil.

Prior commitments kept Styne from composing the score himself. He initially hired Stein and Glickman's *Plain and Fancy* collaborators, lyricist Arnold Horwitt and composer Albert Hague, but they were soon replaced by newcomer Jerry Bock and his partner, Larry Holofcener. In time, this duo became a trio, as Styne also brought in George Weiss, a more experienced writer of pop material. In the 1950s, a successful musical could spawn any number of popular hits, and creating such tunes was the goal of every Broadway hand. Two hit songs, in fact, emerged from *Mr. Wonderful*, the title song, which had three versions on *Billboard*'s charts in 1956, and "Too Close for Comfort," which became a hit for Eydie Gorme and inspired numerous other recordings, including several over the years by Davis himself.

As the creators of *Mr. Wonderful* readied the show, Styne and his

coproducer, a likable young man named George Gilbert, set about raising $225,000 to finance it. This proved as difficult as finding a good book
writer, and for the same reason: involvement with a black-themed show
headlined by a black star was risky in 1956. Ultimately, it took approximately two hundred investors, pledging in some cases no more than
$500 apiece, to capitalize the production.

Rehearsals started in late January 1956, after the Trio concluded its
engagement at Ciro's in Miami Beach. Like the show's creators and star,
most of the other principals were relative newcomers. Pat Marshall, who
played the manager's wife, Lil Campbell, was a veteran of two previous
New York shows, including *The Pajama Game,* but Juilliard graduate
Olga James made her Broadway debut as Charlie's girlfriend, Ethel.
Jack Carter, cast as Freddie Campbell, had taken over roles in *Call Me
Mister* and *Top Banana,* but *Mr. Wonderful* marked the first time that
he created a part. Like Davis, the droll comedian was well-known on the
nightclub circuit and to fans of television's myriad variety shows.

Another Broadway newcomer was Sammy's regular conductor, Morty
Stevens, who, with Ted Royal, arranged the score and who served as the
show's musical director. There was no choreographer at all. Although
Styne had wanted to hire a big name, such as Gene Kelly or Agnes
DeMille, Davis, who had never worked with a choreographer before,
convinced the producer to let him devise his own dance routines.* Even
Mr. Wonderful's director, Jack Donohue, had only one Broadway musical
to his credit, the Phil Silvers vehicle *Top Banana.* Although he'd been a
dancer in the *Ziegfeld Follies* in 1927 and worked in vaudeville during
the twenties and thirties, Donohue had more experience with film musicals than legit shows.[†]

Arguably the most noteworthy thing about the *Mr. Wonderful* company was that it featured, for perhaps the first time in Broadway history,
a truly integrated company of singers and dancers. This was no accident;
Davis had insisted on the hiring of a substantial number of African
Americans.

Two of them, Will Mastin and Sam Davis, were among Jule Styne's
biggest problems. The fact that neither could act considerably restricted
their performance opportunities in the show. Joseph Stein recalled that

---

*In all likelihood, Sammy received some help with his numbers from a featured cast
member, Hal Loman, who would work with the entertainer on projects in the future,
including his numbers in the film *Porgy and Bess.* Peter Gennaro labored without credit
on the dances for another of the show's featured players, Chita Rivera.

†Jack Donohue's film credits include five Shirley Temple pictures plus the Gene
Kelly–Frank Sinatra feature *Anchors Aweigh,* Sinatra's *It Happened in Brooklyn,* Doris
Day's *Calamity Jane,* and Esther Williams' aquatic musical, *Neptune's Daughter.*

at one point during rehearsals Sammy told him his father was unhappy about having so little to do. So Stein obligingly wrote a line or two in which Sr., playing Charlie's father, naturally, offers the kid a few encouraging words before his big nightclub debut. But Sam had so much trouble with the lines that Stein eventually reduced them to "Good luck" or "Break a leg" and, finally, to no words at all, just a supportive pat on the back.

As for Mastin, Stein asserted, "He was not very knowledgeable about Broadway musicals at all. And I remember one experience where Jule Styne and I and the director were in a room talking about some changes we wanted to make, and Will objected to something. And I remember Jule saying, 'Well, we had to do that because that's the way it works in the theater' and Will said, 'Don't tell me about the theater. We worked the Apollo for the last ten years.'" In other words, the hoofer saw no distinction between playing a variety palace and doing a legitimate Broadway show. On another occasion, Will objected to a line of Carter's in which Freddie bragged about teaching Charlie everything he knew. Mastin asserted that only *he* had the right to that claim. It was left to Styne to explain the difference between the real Davis and Sammy's onstage character.

In the fashion of the day, *Mr. Wonderful* was booked for an out-of-town engagement prior to its New York opening so that its creators could have an opportunity to gauge audience reaction to the material and make adjustments accordingly. It debuted at the Shubert Theater in Philadelphia for a four-week run starting on February 21, 1956.

The reviews were not good. The critics found the book dull and lacking in originality. The score was considered pleasant, but without the luster of the standards in the nightclub segment. In fact, the consensus was that Davis' cabaret act was the best part of the evening.

On that unpromising note, Davis met the following day with Styne and the musical's creators to figure out how to salvage the show. Two key decisions were made. The first was to cut back on the nightclub segment. Even though it had been the biggest hit of the evening, it so dominated the second act that everything else was thrown off balance. The important characters played by Jack Carter and Pat Marshall, for example, virtually disappeared. Eventually, Sammy's cabaret went on for about twenty minutes.

The creative team also decided to eliminate the show's message about race relations. Davis wasn't convinced that taking out every bit of social relevance was a good idea, but he accepted the consensus of the group. Accordingly, Charlie went from living in Paris to escape the stigma of being a Negro in the United States to being a small-time entertainer working at a club in Union City, New Jersey. In the process, he became simply a guy comfortable with being a large fish in a small pond, and his reluctance to try his hand at the big time turned rather muddy. As Davis put it, "Instead of a story about a sophisticated, sensitive guy who doesn't want to live with prejudice, Charlie Welch has become a schnook who doesn't have the guts to try for success. Why spend $300,000 to do a show about *that*?" By the time the company moved back to Manhattan, the star was acclimated to the change. So much so that, just before the New York opening, he told Don Ross of the *New York Herald Tribune,* "We're not trying to prove anything with this show. We're just trying to give two and a half hours of entertainment. We think we've got it all set now. We have a lot of laughs, a lot of good music."

On March 22, *Mr. Wonderful* opened at the Broadway Theater, which had a seating capacity of nineteen hundred. Bringing this piece of fluff to Broadway would have been risky in any event, but *Mr. Wonderful* opened a week after *My Fair Lady,* one of the best musicals of all time. Consequently, the critics were rather intolerant of Sammy's lightweight vehicle. Robert Coleman of the *New York Mirror* called the book "shoddy and tasteless" and the score "pedestrian." Walter Kerr noted what was lost when the racial element of the story was eliminated, telling readers of the *New York Herald Tribune,* "For a solid act and a half, Mr. Davis is pictured as a world-beater who just doesn't want to beat the world." Virtually all the critics recognized Davis' considerable talent, but most felt that it was misused in the present context.

As the reviews came in on opening night, Sammy grew more and more despondent. He blamed himself for the show's failure, for having put his career in the hands of others and allowing their judgments about what he should and shouldn't do to supersede his own. But depression soon gave way to resolve: he would turn the show into a success despite the reviews by appealing directly to average theatergoers, most of whom, he knew, were simply looking to have a pleasant evening out. Styne's coproducer, George Gilbert, who had become a friend of Sammy, told him he was foolish to think he could buck the critics, but Davis insisted on making the effort.

Despite their star's fighting spirit, Styne and Gilbert might have elected to close the show, except for one reality: *Mr. Wonderful* came into New York with a healthy $400,000 advance in ticket sales, built entirely on the strength of Davis' name. As very few of the ticket holders had asked for their money back, there was no reason not to run the show and see what happened.

The following night Sammy addressed the cast onstage before curtain time. He promised them that, if they put forth a 100 percent effort, he'd use all of his celebrity to promote the show. He would not only accept every single television and radio appearance and consent to every press interview that came his way, but he would go out and solicit others. As a consequence, he concluded, people would come to see him and the show would run. Picking up his enthusiasm, the chorus kids leaped to their feet, cheering. "It was straight out of an MGM musical," Davis said. Later that night, during the nightclub scene, a woman in the audience yelled, "The critics are crazy, Sammy. We love you." He blew her a kiss, saying, "So tell your friends." The audience cheered, prompting him to do an extra thirty minutes.

Davis kept his word. He promoted *Mr. Wonderful* everywhere he could. Amazingly, his campaign worked. People came, enjoyed themselves, and told their friends. Within a month or so, it was evident that the musical would go on. Sammy, who had a piece of the show and a one-year contract, settled comfortably into his room at the Gorham Hotel on West 55th Street.

While in New York, Sammy made room in his schedule for several sessions at Decca's recording studios. First came *Mr. Wonderful*'s original cast album. But he also recorded about twenty-five pop songs at sessions in February, March, August, November, and December. A number of these tunes became singles and several reached *Billboard*'s pop chart, but none climbed into the Top 10. In addition to the *Mr. Wonderful* LP, 1956 saw the release of Sammy's third solo offering, called *Here's Looking at You*. Finally, in January 1957, while *Mr. Wonderful* was still running, Davis joined jazz stylist Carmen McRae for eleven duets, and an album drawn from this collaboration, *Boy Meets Girl*, hit stores later that year.

Meanwhile, on June 24, three months into the run of *Mr. Wonderful*, Sammy, his father, and Will were guests on the premiere episode of *The Steve Allen Show*, which aired on NBC opposite Ed Sullivan's entrenched variety program. Sullivan had wanted only Sammy, not the Trio, for a return engagement, but Davis wouldn't abandon his father and Will. As an added bonus, Allen was offering $10,000, compared to Sullivan's $7,500, plus more airtime. The multitalented Allen clearly dug the multitalented Davis, and vice versa. Sammy and the Trio would return to the show numerous times over the next few years.

By the time *Mr. Wonderful* opened, Sammy had become pals not only with coproducer George Gilbert, but also with the show's stage manager, John Barry Ryan III, and Ryan's assistant, Michael Wettach, both of whom were from prominent New York families. And he was romantically involved with the musical's featured dancer, Chita Rivera. The twenty-three-year-old former ballerina was already a veteran of several Broadway and touring company productions, but her celebrated career would reach a new level the year after *Mr. Wonderful,* when she created the role of Anita in *West Side Story.** This quintet—Davis, Gilbert, Ryan, Wettach, and Rivera—would hang out after the final curtain, occasionally going to Danny's Hideaway or the Harwin, clubs where Sammy was welcome. But in the mid-fifties, many of New York's elite establishments, such as 21 and El Morocco, were still reluctant to have a Negro at ringside, even one starring in a hit Broadway show. After a few embarrassing incidents, Davis preferred to invite the gang to his suite at the Gorham, where they would gab, listen to records, play Monopoly or charades, eat, and drink. "It was his safe place," explained Burt Boyar. "Sammy's apartment was where he could just relax, and he didn't have to worry about someone yelling 'Nigger,' or saying, 'You can't come in here.' It was home and it was comfortable and so that's why we always went there."

It was shortly after *Mr. Wonderful* opened that Boyar entered Davis' inner circle. Like Sammy, he had been a show business kid. The son of a Broadway general manager (in fact, the celebrated Max Gordon's g.m.), Burt appeared in dozens of radio shows during the 1930s and 1940s and also played a small role in the Broadway show *Junior Miss.* As an adult, he quit acting and became, in time, a Broadway columnist. Boyar ran several items about Sammy while *Mr. Wonderful* was in Philadelphia, even though he and the entertainer had never met, so when the show came to New York, Davis invited the columnist to dinner. They became instant friends. Soon, the two men were not only dining together every evening before Sammy's show, but Burt and his attractive, stylish wife, Jane, would also hook up with Sammy and the *Mr. Wonderful* gang at the Gorham after the Boyars finished gathering items for the column at the town's hotspots.

Because Davis hated to sleep, he invariably outlasted most of his companions, in particular, George Gilbert, who had to go to Jule Styne's office during the daytime, and Chita Rivera, who often had morning dance classes. Burt and Jane were usually the last ones to leave. The columnist recalled more than one occasion when, after the others had left, Sammy would pull the bed out of the couch—he didn't have a separate bedroom—and lay down, fully dressed. "He often slept in his clothes," Boyar noted, "because he didn't want to go to sleep. He'd fall

*Rivera would go on to star in such Broadway shows as *Bye Bye Birdie, Chicago,* and *The Kiss of the Spider Woman.*

asleep out of exhaustion." When he finally drifted off, the Boyars would pull a blanket over him, take off his shoes, and then quietly slip out. Eventually, this routine became difficult even for Burt and Jane, because Boyar's column had to be written and filed by five or six in the morning.

Although Davis avoided New York's major nightclubs, he had no problem with the city's many fashionable stores. Despite the warnings of Will Mastin as well as his agents at the William Morris office, he spent money recklessly during the run of *Mr. Wonderful*. Once, at Gucci, he purchased more than a dozen pairs of shoes and a half dozen suitcases at a then-hefty $100 apiece. George Gilbert was shocked by his star's extravagance. "It's like letting Ray Milland loose in a distillery," he said, referring to the actor's Oscar-winning portrayal of an alcoholic. "You're doing *Lost Weekend*, but with money." On a more serious note, the producer added, "Look, I'm not trying to be a staff psychiatrist, but whatever your reasons are, you're only causing more trouble for yourself with all this." Sammy admitted that he knew Gilbert was right. "Then why do you keep doing it?" the producer asked. "I'm not looking to be right," Sammy told him. "I'm just looking to be happy."

As if his New York spending wasn't enough, Davis anticipated his return to Los Angeles after *Mr. Wonderful* closed, arranging to have a pool installed at his Evanview Drive house, along with an elaborate cabana-playhouse complete with a bar, movie projection room, and several bedrooms.

Sammy's need to be awake at all hours, constantly surrounded by friends, and his inability to curb his spending habits suggest that he remained a terribly unhappy person, one who was trying to fill his head and his time in order to avoid facing the root causes of his distress. In addition to the things he hated about himself—his looks, his height, and so forth—he had come to realize, with some despair, that celebrity was not going to be a panacea for all the slights he'd encountered when he was an unknown. He still felt unloved, except while onstage. He still needed constant approval. And he was still excluded from parties, posh restaurants, and ritzy clubs solely on the basis of his race. Sometimes, in social settings, he found himself being patronized by closet bigots, people who admired his talent but treated him like a pet or an exotic animal; such treatment was nearly as heinous as outright prejudice.

Moreover, he had started drawing fire from his own people. In early 1957, for example, shortly before *Mr. Wonderful* closed, he threw a party for the African American press as a thank you for the support he had received during the run of the show. But the gesture infuriated a prominent Negro columnist, Evelyn Cunningham, who castigated Sammy in print for segregating blacks from the rest of the working press.

Davis attributed the start of his problems in the African American media to the story of his alleged relationship with Ava Gardner. Before that, his professional accomplishments had been hailed as a credit to the race. Afterward, the focus shifted to the white women he dated, white men in his entourage (the most visible being his conductor, Mo Stevens), and his many white friends. All of which inevitably led to accusation that he wanted to be white himself. Once implied, this perception became accepted as fact and was repeated widely and often. The truth is, when it came to women, coworkers, and friends, Davis didn't think in terms of race. He thought in terms of good and bad—and he wanted to be around the best: women who were beautiful, sexy, and fun; friends who were bright, lively, and engaging; coworkers who were talented or skilled. Their color simply didn't matter.

Consequently, Davis resented the accusations hurled against him. He once noted that "it's a pain in the ass sometimes to be Sammy Davis, Jr., because I just can't make a right move racewise. . . . Every day becomes a challenge, to keep yourself level, to keep yourself from becoming embittered. Mind you, I'm proud to be black, but I don't want my blackness to be a burden to me. . . . It's unfair."

It wasn't just the white issue. In his dress, manner, and lifestyle, Sammy Davis, Jr., was too assertive for many black people. He wanted to live as he wished, which some found troubling. A few years later, for example, columnist Dick Schaap reported that Davis, appearing at a benefit in Harlem, got out of a chauffeur-driven limousine at 145th Street, decked out in a tuxedo, to buy a pack of cigarettes. A guy on the corner, taking note of this scene, turned to the entertainer and said, "Ease up on us, baby. You too strong." The columnist added, "It was a lovely line. . . . But Sammy Davis can't ease up." In public, Sammy tried to maintain a philosophical attitude toward his bad reputation within the black community. He told the *Saturday Evening Post*'s Pete Martin in 1960, "The most prejudiced people in the world are the oppressed. They have no other way to fight back, so they fight back with prejudice." But, deep down, he wanted the approval of "his people," just as he wanted the approval of whites. As he once told Tek Osborn of the *New York Courier,* "I believe—I've got to believe—that your people should appreciate you because you're an artist."

From the perspective of the early twenty-first century, it is perhaps difficult to understand what all the fuss was about. The battle for civil rights, advances in the portrayal of African Americans by Hollywood, and exposure over the years to public figures such as Little Richard, James Brown, Adam Clayton Powell, Jim Brown, Muhammad Ali, Malcolm X, Richard Pryor, Eddie Murphy, Michael Jackson, Darryl Strawberry, Dennis Rodman, Al Sharpton, and Sean "P. Diddy" Combs, to name a few, have dramatically altered expectations about the behavior of blacks, on the part of both whites *and* blacks. But, midway through the twentieth century, the relatively few African Americans who had become national celebrities—Joe Louis, Nat King Cole, Lena Horne, Eartha Kitt, Duke Ellington, Louis Armstrong, Jackie Robinson, Harry Belafonte, Sidney Poitier—were extremely circumspect in their public statements and behavior. They spoke carefully and acted with rectitude, as if they were walking on egg shells or carrying the future of the race on their shoulders. By contrast, Sammy Davis, Jr., went about his business as if he didn't care about breaking eggs or setting a good example for anyone. That was his choice. But the ambivalence he elicited from the black press and the larger African American community was the price he paid for that decision.

So he didn't sleep and he spent money lavishly. In early 1957, as the run of *Mr. Wonderful* was coming to an end, he finally had to deal at least with the latter—by reaching out to some folks in Chicago.

Since the 1920s, organized crime had played a major role in America's nightlife. During Prohibition, mobsters were primarily responsible for the importation of illegal alcoholic beverages into the United States and the speakeasies where such substances could be consumed. After the repeal of the Volstead Act, they remained a significant presence on the cabaret circuit, having either overt or behind-the-scenes interests in most of the major nightclubs around the country. Unlike Frank Sinatra, who was rather fascinated by the power and attendant violence of the Mafia dons, Davis simply saw mobsters as the people one had to do business with if one were to perform in places like the Copa (allegedly owned by Frank Costello) and Philadelphia's Latin Casino (supposedly Rocky Paladino's place). Some, like Chicago boss Sam Giancana, became pals, but Davis treated most of the wiseguys he encountered as friendly business acquaintances. They were particularly useful if he needed an advance against his salary for a future club engagement in order to meet his current expenses, which he regularly did. The club owners were perfectly willing to indulge him in this regard. Why not? It guaranteed that he'd continue to work for them. The problem, for Sammy, was that when those engagements arrived, he'd already been paid for them. What was he to do for money then? He created his own vicious cycle.

Of course, while appearing in *Mr. Wonderful*, he wasn't working nightclubs. His earnings from the show, although high by the Broadway standards of the day, represented a significant drop from his usual take. As a result, after nearly a year in New York, his finances were in total disarray. So, according to Jess Rand, as Sammy looked ahead to a new tour following the musical's close, he struck a deal with the boys in Chicago: they would pay off his outstanding debts and give him an interest-free loan for up to $100,000. In return, he would have to pay over 20 percent of his earnings for fifteen years. To ensure a proper accounting of his finances, a Chicago attorney, Joe Borenstein, was placed in charge of Sammy's affairs. According to Arthur Silber, Jr., the investors, in fact, got more than that fair share of Davis' money. However, in November 1960, Donald (Donjo) Medlevine (one of the owners of the Chez Paree) and another member of the group filed suit against Sammy in Los Angeles Superior Court to collect $91,000 as the unpaid balance on the loan.

There was one more element to the arrangement. A considerable sum would be paid to Sam Sr., who, in turn, would retire, thereby bringing an end to the Will Mastin Trio and, thus, enabling Sammy to finally go solo.

It was time. During the run of *Mr. Wonderful*, Will's behavior had grown more bizarre. As if to prove that he was still the boss of the act—and, by extension, Sammy—Mastin called weekly meetings of the Trio, even though the three men had nothing significant to discuss. Why, Sammy wondered, didn't the old man simply retire? But, as in the past, Sammy felt that such career decisions had to come from Mastin himself.

But the underlying feelings of discord continued. For his part, Sam Sr. shared Mastin's discontent, but by the time *Mr. Wonderful* had settled into its run, he no longer had the boss' will to press on. He had realized as far back as the Trio's opening at the Copa that his son's talent far exceeded his own, or Will's, and that they should get out of the way. But he couldn't make himself step down. After so many years of struggle and obscurity, he welcomed the limelight and the money that came with it. At last, however, he was ready to quit. For one thing, he had Pee Wee to help him forge a life outside of show business. Thus, when the offer came from the boys in Chicago, he grabbed it.

The last performance of *Mr. Wonderful* took place on February 23, 1957. then, the musical was in the black, having grossed well over $1 million, thanks entirely to Davis' Herculean efforts to keep it afloat. In fact, could have run longer. It closed solely because Sammy's contract was and he was ready to return to the nightclub circuit. Aside from the usical's producers and backers, perhaps the greatest beneficiaries of s drive to promote the show were the sponsors of the myriad charity enefits at which he performed while in New York. Over the year, he ent his name to at least several such events each week.

To mark the final curtain, Jule Styne and George Gilbert arranged a urprise for Sammy. They packed the onstage audience for the nightclub sequence with a host of celebrities, among them Walter Winchell, Jerry Lewis, Judy Holliday, Tony Bennett, and Shelley Winters. Gilbert himself took the role of the club's headwaiter. Edward G. Robinson, who was starring elsewhere on Broadway, arrived late, following his own show's curtain, to crack a joke or two with the kid who imitated him so effectively. Then Jerry Lewis started clowning around, and the scene descended into bedlam, much to the audience's delight. Shelley Winters managed to restore some order by taking the mike and reminding theatergoers how much Davis had accomplished, not only by turning a flop into a hit, but also by insisting on a fully integrated company. Thus, to a standing ovation and twelve curtain calls, *Mr. Wonderful* came to an end.

Sammy left the Great White Way somewhat wiser for the experience. As he told Tom Donnelly of the *New York World Telegram* at the time, "Oh, I've learned a lot. It's a fantastic business. My next show will have a good book, I guarantee you, because if it isn't a good book I won't do it."

Kim, Harry, and Loray

Sammy wasted no time returning to the nightclub circuit. As per his arrangement with the Chicago boys, he debuted at the Windy City's Chez Paree on February 24, 1957, mere days after *Mr. Wonderful* closed. Despite Sam Sr.'s retirement plans, he and Will were on hand for this gig, the decision having been made that it would be better if Sammy eased into a solo act.

Although some older favorites were featured in each show, Sammy brought quite a bit of new material with him, such as a specially written opening number, "Give Me a Saloon Every Time," a medley from *Mr. Wonderful,* Sammy's humorous discussion of television commercials, and a solid Elvis Presley impersonation.

The following month, the act moved on to Vegas. As the Trio's contract with the Last Frontier had expired, Sammy and his partners were free to take advantage of the whopping $25,000-a-week offer made by the Sands in the aftermath of Davis' automobile accident.

It was a big move, in ways beyond just the money.

Having opened in December 1952, the Sands was the fourth hotel-casino to debut on the Strip since the outset of the fifties. By the time the Will Mastin Trio opened there, five newer establishments had joined them, but the Sands quickly established itself as the coolest, classiest place in town.

In contrast to the pedestrian El Rancho Vegas and the Last Frontier, which looked to Nevada's past, the Sands was sleek and modern. The gigantic sign out front said it all. Over fifty feet high, the gleaming steel structure suggested the façade of a Mies Van der Rohe skyscraper, bisected by two horizontal rectangular marquees. The hotel's name was rendered in a bold art deco script, the "S" of which was more than thirty feet tall, followed by its slogan, A Place in the Sun, in sans serif caps. The principal interior featured cool woods and mood lighting, a dramatic departure from the glare and raucous atmosphere of the resort's neighbors, while the surrounding buildings on its sixty-five acres were sleek and low slung—and named after racetracks: Arlington Park, Belmont Park, Santa Anita, and the like. The main showroom, the Copa Room, which seated 450, boasted a Brazilian carnival motif and arguably the best Chinese food on the Strip.

Everything was well done, but, as Frank Rose pointed out in his history of the William Morris Agency, "It wasn't the facilities that would make the Sands the 'in' spot for Texas high rollers and New York and Hollywood sophisticates. It was Jack Entratter and the people he knew."

Described by Mel Torme as "a tall, slightly menacing character with the demeanor of an ex-boxer," Jack Entratter had started out as a bouncer at the Stork Club in Manhattan. In 1940, he became Jules Podell's assistant at the Copa. Entratter was no stranger to organized crime; his older brother had been part of the legendary Legs Diamond's outfit and was killed in a shoot-out. Unlike the gruff, aggressive Podell, however, Jack Entratter was smooth and courtly, and he genuinely liked the headliners who played the club, and let them know it.

With Entratter in charge of the entertainment, the Sands had no trouble booking top-name talent. In short order, the Copa Room was home to Frank Sinatra, Martin and Lewis, Danny Thomas, Tony Bennett, Nat King Cole, Red Skelton, Milton Berle, and Lena Horne. Horne described the Copa as "a beautifully run room, very classy," adding, "It was and is where the big money is for a cabaret entertainer."

It was also "the most blatantly run mob-place of all," to quote David Thomson, author of *In Nevada: The Land, the People, God, and Chance*. Unlike other Vegas resorts, which were controlled by one out-of-state criminal organization or another, the Sands had investors from outfits in Boston, New York, Chicago, Texas, Los Angeles, and elsewhere. The single largest shareholder at the time was Joseph "Doc" Stracher of New Jersey, although he had no official connection with the operation. On paper, the resort was owned by Entratter, Texas oilman Jake Freedman, the casino's operator Carl Cohen, and even Frank Sinatra, who, in a savvy public relations move, was allowed to purchase points.

Sammy never became an owner, but he liked Jack Entratter, and he liked the Sands. It was his kind of place: hip, smart, and elegant. And the Sands liked him. The resort would become Davis' home away from home for the next seventeen years.

Following Vegas, the Trio played the Copa in New York, where Sammy did sell-out business. He also managed to fit in two appearances on *The Steve Allen Show* on April 13 and 28. Then, it was on to other venues, including a return to Chicago's Chez Paree in July. Sammy packed the house.

Sam Sr. disappeared after the Chez Paree engagement; his absence was attributed to a heart attack. But, as Sammy moved on to the 500 Club in Atlantic City at the end of August and the El Morocco in Montreal in September, Will continued to join him onstage, albeit in a highly abbreviated fashion. Typically, the old hoofer, roughly seventy-eight years old in 1957, would open each show with a soft-shoe, then, as Sammy's mentor, present the younger man to the audience and vanish for the rest of the set. The critics and many in the audience were touched by the continuing presence of Davis' "uncle," but Sammy wasn't. He was disgusted by the way Mastin clung to the spotlight, selling his soft-shoe as if it were 1938 instead of twenty years later. Why couldn't the man accept the fact that it was time to go? His anger extended as well to his father, who'd simply bowed out without insisting that Mastin do likewise, thus leaving the mess in Sammy's hands. It was, as Davis later put it, the "one time I'd needed him to come through for me, [and] he'd come up empty."

As if this situation weren't stressful enough, Sammy's personal life had taken a dangerous and even more nerve-wracking turn. Once again, he'd gotten involved with a white actress, and, this time, people were willing to do him serious bodily harm if he persisted in seeing her.

Marilyn Pauline Novak, better known as Kim, was Columbia Pictures' biggest star and America's number one box office attraction when she happened to see Sammy Davis, Jr., at the Chez Paree during the Trio's second gig in 1957. The twenty-four-year-old sultry blonde actress was visiting her family in Aurora, a suburb of Chicago. Of Slavic descent, Novak, the daughter of a railroad man, had worked as an elevator operator and a dime store sales clerk before Harry Cohn, Columbia's combative production chief, tapped her to replace the studio's then-reigning queen, Rita Hayworth. The buxom, broad-shouldered Kim radiated an appealing mixture of regal aloofness and smoldering sexuality, but, when it came to acting, she was decidedly limited. Perhaps her insecurity over her talent led her to distance herself from the Hollywood set; in any event, she adopted a somewhat rebellious attitude toward the restrictions of stardom.

Kim and Sammy didn't really get acquainted in Chicago, but a few months later, they both attended a party at Tony Curtis' Los Angeles home. Curtis later said that he invited the actress on purpose, knowing of his friend's interest. "They both came over," Tony recalled, "and they spent the evening together—deep in thought, deep in talk. I could see right from the beginning that they were getting along in an intense way, and that was the beginning of the relationship." Davis remembered things differently. He told Alex Haley in 1966 that he and Novak were introduced that evening but nothing of consequence happened. "I doubt we exchanged 20 words," he said. "She was just one of the group."

Either way, someone at the party told Dorothy Kilgallen that Sammy and Kim looked smitten, prompting the syndicated columnist to write, "Which top female movie star (K.N.) is seriously dating which big-name entertainer (S.D.)?" Kilgallen followed this item two days later with "Studio bosses know about K.N.'s affair with S.D. and have turned *lavender* over their platinum blonde."

It is questionable that the executives at Columbia knew anything about a budding romance between their star and Davis at that stage because it was only after Kilgallen started spreading rumors about them that the duo began seeing one another. In fact, it was the columnist who brought them together. For, after the first tidbit appeared, Davis phoned Novak to assure her that he'd had nothing to do with planting it. "We can handle it any way you think best," he added. "I realize the position you're in with the studio." Seemingly unconcerned, Kim mentioned that she was cooking dinner and invited Sammy to join her. Naturally, he accepted. Afraid to leave his car where it could be seen, he asked Arthur Silber, Jr., to drive him to the actress' house.

Over meatballs and spaghetti, the two celebrities shared complaints about the constraints on their freedom. Sammy resented the way his race stigmatized him and Kim bemoaned Columbia's attempts to control her every move. Although they hadn't noticed any particular chemistry at Curtis' party, they suddenly felt like kindred spirits, two rebels eager to thumb their noses at the world's small-minded people.

Sammy left that evening at ten o'clock, the time he had asked Arthur to swing by Novak's house. He didn't know if members of the press or, for that matter, Columbia Pictures had the place staked out, but, to play it safe, he made a quick dash for the curb as the car pulled into view, leaping in before Silber even came to a stop, and they sped away.

No one caught Davis that night, but the lack of hard information didn't prevent Hedda Hopper, Louella Parsons, *Confidential*, several African American publications, and much of the rest of the press from speculating on what might be going on between Kim Novak and Sammy Davis, Jr. All the escapades of the past few years—Sammy's conversion to Judaism, the Ava story, his engagement to Cordie King, his alleged affair with Meg Myles—paled by comparison to this new controversy. If true, it would be, in the words of Associated Press columnist James Bacon, "the biggest Hollywood scandal in twenty years." Soon, Sammy and Kim were besieged with advice from well-meaning friends, virtually all of whom said the same thing: stop seeing one another. An entanglement between a Negro entertainer and a white movie queen would wreck both their careers.

Beyond the dire predictions, Davis took some ribbing as well. According to Sam Kashner, who wrote an article about the affair in a 1999 issue of *Vanity Fair,* when Milton Berle found himself at a urinal next to Sammy's in the men's room at Chasen's restaurant, the comedian reportedly pointed to his own penis and quipped, "Sammy, if Kim Novak ever sees this, you'll be back sleeping with Hattie McDaniel," a reference to the rotund black actress best known for playing Scarlett O'Hara's mammy in *Gone With the Wind.*

Beyond his friends and the nation's reigning gossip columnists, Sammy had one other group with which to contend, the African American media, and they found nothing funny in the story. As Davis later pointed out, the "Negro press started riding me harder than ever. Stuff like: 'Sammy Davis, Jr., once a pride to all Negroes, has become a never-ending source of embarrassment.'"

Despite these outside pressures, or perhaps because of them, Sammy and Kim continued to see one another, even though she was facing the most challenging assignment of her career, the twin roles of the doomed Madeleine and the vulnerable Judy in Alfred Hitchcock's psychological thriller *Vertigo.* She and Sammy made sure that they weren't spotted in public together, but they continued to meet for quiet, intimate dinners at Kim's house. As with their first get-together, Sammy enlisted Arthur Silber as chauffeur. Typically, Sammy would hide on the floor of Arthur's car, with a rug pulled over him to ensure that he wasn't spotted near Novak's home. When that grew tiresome, he rented a place in Malibu, using a third party for the lease so that his and Kim's trysting place couldn't be traced.

While Davis and Novak flirted with disaster, Columbia executive Max Arnow, the man who had discovered the actress, and the studio's publicity chief, Al Horwitz, did everything they could to quell the story, fueled by Kim's assurances that nothing was going on. Then, at Christmastime, matters escalated.

Kim, having finished *Vertigo,* returned to Chicago to be with her family for the holidays. Sammy had just opened at the Sands, where, according to Arthur Silber, Jr., he'd had a private telephone installed in his suite so that he could phone his girl without having to go through the hotel's switchboard. As it turned out, the phone was of no use: Novak's family had a party line, so Sammy was afraid to call.

Thwarted in his effort to communicate with the actress, Sammy begged Arthur to fly to Chicago for him. "He literally got down on his knees—tears were coming out of his eyes," Silber recalled. Arthur didn't want to go, but his friend was in such distress, he finally relented. Landing at O'Hare, he was met by Donjo Medlevine, one of the owners of the Chez Paree, a high-ranking member of the Chicago mob, and party to the loan advanced to Davis in 1957. Medlevine asked Arthur, "What the fuck has Sammy gotten himself into now?" What could Silber say? He didn't really understand what was going on himself. Apparently, what had started as a mutually shared rebellion between two figures in the limelight had turned into something else entirely. Silber's trip was indicative of, as he put it, "just how deep this affair went. I was sent to Chicago to go to Kim and say, 'Sammy loves you.'"

Even that didn't satisfy the entertainer. After days of begging and pleading, first with Jack Entratter and then by phone with Frank Sinatra, he arranged for the Sands to replace him with the Mills Brothers for several days so that he could fly east, meet Novak's family, and, according to several later reports, ask for her hand in marriage.

By this point, Harry Cohn was in New York for a variety of events—meetings with Columbia's East Coast executives, a banquet in honor of his brother Jack, and the opening of the studio's big-budget action-adventure drama, *The Bridge on the River Kwai*. When the mogul heard about Davis' plans, he went ballistic, as only Harry Cohn could. Popping nitroglycerine pills to quiet his damaged heart, he flew to Los Angeles the next day, determined to bring an end to the disaster.

Before Cohn could take matters in hand, they got worse. On January 1, 1958, Irv Kupcinet, columnist for the *Chicago Sun-Times*, broke the story wide open, reporting Davis' visit and his possible wedding plans. As she had done repeatedly in the past, Novak emphatically denied any romantic involvement with Sammy. But Kupcinet wasn't buying her protestations. Instead, he scoured the records of the courthouses of suburban Chicago, looking for an application for a marriage license, and he reportedly found the document he was seeking. "Although everyone involved emphatically denied it," Kupcinet said in 1985, "a marriage was definitely being planned." (Arthur Silber, who spent the holidays with Novak and Davis, insisted that the couple never took out a marriage license.)

In addition to Kupcinet, Dorothy Kilgallen continued to pursue the story, and on January 3, Walter Winchell joined the fray. But perhaps the most determined journalist was James Bacon. Four days after Kupcinet's January 1 column, Bacon managed to reach Kim's dad, Joe, on the phone from Hollywood. Mr. Novak told Bacon that Sammy had already returned to Vegas by plane and that his daughter was en route to Los

Angeles by train. When asked the big question—Was there any truth to the rumors of a marriage between Sammy and Kim?—the actress' father hesitated, then replied, "You better ask Kim about that."

Learning that Novak's train was due to stop in Las Vegas at 2:00 in the morning, well after Sammy's late show ended at the Sands, Bacon phoned a friend, asked him to stake out the station, and let him know if Davis showed up. The friend reported back that not only had Sammy met the train, but it left with him aboard. Certain that he could get the proof that had thus far eluded everyone, Bacon determined to meet the train when it arrived at Union Station later that morning.

Unbeknownst to the resourceful columnist, Sammy left the train at San Bernardino. Consequently, when Bacon arrived at the station, he found Kim exiting her car alone. "Where's Sammy?" he asked. "Sammy who?" she answered coolly. When pressed, she admitted that she'd seen Davis in Chicago, but only at a benefit where he'd been a performer. "But marriage to Sammy Davis?" she added. "You gotta be kidding." Bacon, in his words, "knew she was lying, but it's a game stars and the press play all the time. She denied it. And that was it. No story."

Sammy may have foiled James Bacon, but the unrelenting media scrutiny was taking its toll, as were his intense feelings for Novak, not to mention his financial woes and the ongoing situation with Will Mastin. "I felt like a man being pulled down into quicksand," he later told Alex Haley, "with mosquitoes buzzing around his head." He started drinking heavily for the first time in his life, tossing shots of whiskey into his usual Cokes, and gambling way over his head. On one occasion, he lost $39,000 at black jack during a single evening.

Then Harry Cohn entered the picture.

The man who kept a framed photo of his idol, Benito Mussolini, on his desk was not likely to sit idly by while someone he had nurtured from a nobody to stardom, an actress whose features had earned the studio more than $10 million over the past three years, threw everything away on some short, ugly black guy.

There is no doubt that Cohn planted himself firmly and decisively in the middle of the romance. But exactly *what* he did is a matter of debate. According to various accounts over the years, he reached out to Frank Sinatra; George Wood, a troubleshooter for the William Morris Agency, which represented Novak as well as Davis; the Chicago mob; an unnamed mob-related attorney; New York crime boss Frank Costello; and the West Coast racketeer Mickey Cohen. In the most colorful versions, a couple of hoods grabbed Davis at the Sands and drove him out to the desert, where they threatened to break his legs and put out his one good eye if he didn't stop seeing Kim.

Silber, who was sharing Davis' Vegas suite at the time, considered the story about the hoods and the desert highly improbable. If it happened, he never knew about it. He maintained that it was, in fact, Mickey Cohen who delivered the threat, but not in the way one might imagine. Cohen, who knew Sammy's father from the racetrack, warned Sam Sr. that Harry Cohn had asked him to intercede on behalf of the studio. He may or may not have taken on the job. (In his autobiography, Cohen said he refused to do anything to harm Sammy out of friendship for the Davis family.) But, either way, Cohen knew Davis was in danger and strongly suggested to Sam Sr. that his son quickly marry a black woman in order to squelch the rumors and thereby appease Harry Cohn.

Sam Sr. passed the mobster's warning on to Sammy, who was understandably terrified. Davis wasn't the bravest guy on the planet to begin with. "He was always afraid someone was going to hurt him," one friend told this author. That's one reason Sammy insisted that Arthur Silber, a young, big guy, always share his suite with him when he traveled.

Sammy had been on the receiving end of mob threats in the past. Once, when he was playing the Latin Casino in Philadelphia, he was yanked out of bed by two hoods, who burst into his hotel room while he was sleeping. They dragged him to the balcony outside his room and dangled him over the edge. His crime: dating a girl who was involved with one of the gang. Eventually, the hoods allowed him to make a phone call; he reached Donjo Medlevine, and the Chicago mobster bailed him out.

Another time, in Boston, Sammy was chatting in his suite with Arthur Silber and several others when his father burst in with a beautiful woman, who happened to be the girlfriend of a local mobster. Hot on Sam Sr.'s trail were several of the man's "friends." As Sammy charmed them in the living room, Arthur sneaked Sam and the girl out through the adjoining bedroom. "They wanted to shoot him on the spot," Silber recalled. "On the spot. I mean, guns were sticking out of everything. We just lucked out on that one. Oh, man, the close calls we had."

Given such experiences, Davis took Mickey Cohen's threat seriously.

His first thought was to ask for help from the mobster with whom he had the closest ties, Sam Giancana. But Giancana couldn't make this problem disappear. "We can protect you here in Chicago," he told Sammy, "or when you're in Vegas, but we can't do anything about Hollywood. Don't go back home unless you straighten things out with Harry Cohn."

That left Sammy with one choice: take Mickey Cohen's advice, find a black girl to marry, and get the Columbia mogul off his back.

Silber, who'd been out of the hotel when Cohen's warning came in, returned to the suite to find Sammy frantically thumbing through his address book. "What are you doing?" Arthur asked. "Looking for someone to marry," Sammy told him. "Oh, okay," Arthur replied, thinking his friend was kidding. Then, as he looked more closely, he realized this was no joke. Finally, Sammy stopped paging through the book. He'd found what he was looking for.

The woman Davis chose was a singer who was then appearing at a club in Vegas called the Silver Slipper.

Born in Texas in the early to mid-1930s, Loray White was the product of a broken home. Graduating from a Los Angeles high school, she quickly married and gave birth to a daughter, Debbie. But Loray was not cut out to be a housewife, so she divorced her husband and started laying the foundations for a career in show business. By the time she and Sammy got together in Vegas, she had managed to establish herself as a singer, earning roughly $350 a week on the nightclub circuit. She'd also enjoyed a small role in Cecil B. DeMille's 1956 epic, *The Ten Commandments*.

Loray was definitely Sammy's type. His longtime agent and business partner, Sy Marsh, described her as "a beautiful woman, bright, articulate, very well spoken." She and the entertainer initially met in 1955, while she was working at a club called the Bar O' Music on L.A.'s Sunset Strip. After dating for about eight months, they called it quits because, in Sammy's words, "she couldn't play it for laughs." Thereafter, Loray married a white record company executive named Frank Gallo, who she hoped would further her career. He didn't. Fortunately for Sammy, her second marriage was annulled shortly before he started wife hunting.

Given the delicacy of Davis' predicament, it's not surprising that when he and Loray recalled the circumstances surrounding their wedding—she in a June 1959 article for *Ebony,* he in his two autobiographies and a lengthy interview with Alex Haley for *Playboy* in 1966—they glossed over a few pertinent details. Harry Cohn had long since passed away; in fact, he died little more than a month after Sammy's nuptials. But most of the other principals in the Davis-Novak affair were still alive, including Mickey Cohen, Frank Costello, Sam Giancana, Jack Entratter, Frank Sinatra, and, of course, Kim Novak.

Loray was particularly circumspect. She maintained that one night while she was working at the Silver Slipper, Sammy showed up. They started spending time together, and a few days later, he proposed. At first she thought he was joking, but when she met him at the Sands later that night, he'd already told all of his pals that they were engaged. Thinking it was still a gag, she nevertheless decided to play along, maintaining the joke apparently all the way to the altar. She emphatically denied that the marriage was some kind of business arrangement. "Nor," she added discreetly, "was there any pressure from anyone, as far as I know, to get him to marry me."

For his part, Davis claimed in *Yes I Can* that the marriage was a reflection of his general despair at the time. Ending up drunk one night at the Silver Slipper, he saw Loray and, in a flash of inspiration, felt he could end his problems with the press, in particular the black press, if he married an African American. At the same time, he thought that perhaps he might find some stability and comfort if he had a wife to whom he could come home every night. So he proposed, and she accepted.

In *Why Me?*, published in 1989, twenty-four years after *Yes I Can* and fourteen years after the release of Mickey Cohen's autobiography, Sammy finally acknowledged that prior to hooking up with Loray, he'd been informed by a "friend" that Harry Cohn had asked some mobsters in L.A. to pressure him into dropping Kim. But no one had approached him, he added. He also noted that before the wedding, Sam Giancana phoned him to confirm that Cohn had seen the press stories about the engagement and was satisfied. As Giancana put it, "You can relax, kid, the pressure's off." Otherwise, this version of the engagement essentially followed Davis' earlier account.

What Sammy and Loray left out was the fact that the marriage was a business deal. According to Silber, the entertainer phoned Loray the day after he received the warning from Mickey Cohen and invited her to his hotel suite. When she arrived, he explained his situation and asked her to marry him. In return for saying "I do," he offered to pay her a substantial amount of money. How much is unclear. It may have been a lump sum, something on the order of $25,000, a significant amount in 1958. Or, it may have taken the form of a weekly expense allowance. In 1960, Gordon White of *Motion Picture* placed the figure at $250.

Either way, a payoff was definitely part of the arrangement. Loray went along with it for several reasons. First, the money was good. Second, she hoped the publicity would help her career. Third, she cared for Sammy and didn't want to see him hurt. She may have even loved him and secretly hoped that the marriage, despite its unconventional beginnings, would turn into the real thing. Silber subscribed to that theory.

As for Kim Novak, she simply disappeared from view on her return to Los Angeles. It is doubtful that Davis phoned her in the days leading up to his marriage. What could he have said? Your boss is threatening me with bodily harm unless I stop seeing you and marry someone of my own race, so that's what I'm going to do, but you're still the one I want? When she finally surfaced on January 12, the deed was done. At that point she told a UPI reporter, "Sammy and I are still very good friends, but we literally can't talk to each other now without people making something out of it. Cohn views me as a piece of property and has decreed that we can't see each other again—ever again."

The wedding took place on January 10 in the Emerald Room of the Sands. Earlier in the day, when Sammy and Loray signed their marriage license, he was so nervous a friend had to help steady his hand. Loray wasn't in much better shape. She spelled her first name "Leroy." She also showed up nearly an hour late for the ceremony, blaming her tardiness on the failure of her relatives to arrive in time to help her dress.

The ceremony was conducted by Justice of the Peace Arthur Olsen. Singer Harry Belafonte was Sammy's best man and Morty Stevens' wife, Ann, was Loray's matron of honor. Among those in attendance were comedian Joe E. Lewis, bandleader Harry James, dancer Donald O'Connor, stripper Candy Barr, and singers Dorothy Kirsten, Gordon MacRae, and Eydie Gorme. After the two-minute nuptials, Sammy proceeded to do his regular shows for the night, "singing love songs to the bride who sat at a table in the Copa Room," according to the *Los Angeles Mirror*. He also presented her with a $3,000 mink stole, in addition to an engagement ring composed of six baguette-cut diamonds and four rose-cut diamonds in a platinum setting and a diamond-and-platinum wedding band.

After the midnight show, while his friends partied, Sammy proceeded to get falling-down drunk. The more inebriated he became, the more angry he turned. Finally, he grabbed Loray by the throat and tried to strangle her. Then he burst into tears. She was crying as well.

Thus, Sammy Davis got married.

Kim Novak has consistently denied that she and Davis had an affair. In 1981, she said, "We were never lovers. Never. We were very good friends, but I didn't date him." To which she added in 1997, "I didn't really have an affair with him. I was a gentile raised in a Jewish neighborhood—always being shoved in the snow or having rotten pies pushed in my face—so I identified with him as a minority. I could tell he was in love with me as he was so nervous taking pictures of me that he forgot to take the lens cap off. It was so sweet, you know. 'Oh, you're a white girl and you talk to me.'—I knew how he felt."

Novak was right. Sammy probably was in love with her. Arthur Silber, Jr., certainly thought so. Burt Boyer disagreed, telling this author, "I don't believe he was ever in love with Kim Novak. He was attracted to her celebrity." But Boyar assumed they were intimate.

Assuming Davis and Novak slept together, it is probable that the relationship represented more than merely physical attraction. Asked about the actress decades later, Columbia executive Max Arnow said that he believed she and the entertainer shared a "serious love affair."

And it may not have ended, as most people assume, with Davis' marriage. Silber told this author that the entertainer and the actress continued to see one another for some time thereafter, "even though they were both scared silly." He added, "It had to finish. It had to come to an end—for both of them. It just didn't come to an end as fast as people thought it did."

Support for Silber's assertion can perhaps be found in Davis' 1980 book, *Hollywood in a Suitcase,* in which the entertainer told readers that he was "having a very deep and emotional affair with Kim Novak at the time" that he was acting in *Porgy and Bess*. Filming took place between September 22 and December 19, 1958, months after he had married Loray White. Perhaps he simply got his dates mixed up, but he seemed clear on the specifics, recalling that when he wasn't available to meet Novak for lunch or dinner, the film's director, Otto Preminger, who had directed her in *The Man with the Golden Arm,* would substitute for him. "You're going to get into a lot of trouble with this girl," the director allegedly told Sammy.

Whatever the nature and duration of the relationship between Davis and Novak, it found a fitting epilogue more than twenty years after its conclusion.

In 1979, one of Sammy's closest friends, Jack Haley, Jr., took Kim to the Oscar ceremonies, which he produced that year. Davis and his third wife, Altovise, accompanied Haley and Novak. Afterward, at the governor's ball, they dined together. Sammy invited Kim to dance, while Jack took Altovise to the floor. When the entertainer returned to the table, he was stunned. No one had snapped a picture of him and Novak. No one even noticed.

"That's how much things have changed," noted Haley. He was right.

CHAPTER 10

Big Screen, Little Screen

Sammy's nightmarish gig at the Sands ended on January 20. Ten days later, he made his first appearance in three years at a Los Angeles club. Instead of returning to Ciro's, he opted for the larger, and better-paying, Earl Carroll's Moulin Rouge, also on the Sunset Strip. Loray accompanied him to Los Angeles, but they didn't live together. He rented a house for her in the Hollywood hills, at $450 a month, while he returned to his home on Evanview Drive. Occasionally, he visited his wife, but he spent more time with Jerry Lewis, pouring out his longing for Kim Novak and lamenting his plight.

Despite Davis' rocky mental and physical condition, his opening at the Moulin Rouge was hailed as a triumph in *Variety*, which noted that he was doing fewer impressions and singing much more. This shouldn't have been surprising, as 1957 had seen the release of not only Davis' duet album with Carmen McRae, but also two more solo LPs, *Sammy Swings* and *It's All Over but the Swingin'*, both of which appeared to be inspired by Sinatra's popular theme albums for Capitol.

With Will Mastin still in tow, Sammy traveled from Los Angeles to an engagement at the Chez Paree in Chicago. Loray accompanied him as well. As she would tell *Tan's* Marc Crawford the following year, "You know, there were times when I felt I almost had him. Times when I was able to give him all of myself and felt that maybe he for the first time was about to let himself go, totally and completely." But, midway through the run, he sent her packing. "I don't know what happened," she said later. "Nobody can explain Sammy, not even himself."

In April, Davis and Mastin moved on to New York and Palm Springs for gigs at the Apollo Theater and the Chi Chi Club, respectively. On May 4, he returned to Manhattan for a concert at Town Hall, which Decca recorded and released as his first live LP the following year.

Loray again met with Sammy in the California desert. They got into a fight one night because he wanted to go without her to Sinatra's opening in Vegas; she returned to L.A. in a huff. That pretty much ended things. "There's no divorce in sight," Davis said at the time, but he added, "as for the future . . . I couldn't care less."

Business at these venues was great, the reviews enthusiastic. Meanwhile, Sammy was miserable. Thanks to the publicity surrounding his relationship with Kim Novak and his marriage to Loray White, he was convinced that people were coming to see him as an object of curiosity. He found the experience so "humiliating" and "degrading" that he dreaded going onstage for the first time in his life. To ease the pain, he drank heavily, starting as soon as he woke up. One night, when he'd been appearing at the Moulin Rouge, he became so depressed he even tried to kill himself, driving his car through the Hollywood hills at breakneck speed, looking for a familiar spot that boasted a sheer drop of several hundred feet. Before he could reach the location, his transmission snapped, bringing the car to a dead stop—and Sammy to his senses. "God had his arms around me again," he noted in *Yes I Can.* "Nothing else could have saved me."

Ironically, while the entertainer wallowed in misery, he was offered something he had desperately wanted for a long time: the opportunity to act in a feature film.

Anna Lucasta started as a comedy-drama about a Polish family in a Pennsylvania mill town. Written by Philip Yordan in 1936, it kicked around for years without finding a producer. Then, in June 1944, the American Negro Theatre performed the play at the public library in Harlem. The production was so successful that it moved to Broadway in August, where it ran for three years, grossing close to $400,000, an impressive amount in the mid-forties.

The play centered around the attempt by the title character, an aging prostitute, to turn her life around by marrying a dull but nice middle-class man named Rudolph, and the reactions of her various family members to her decision. A film version of the play, produced by Columbia and released in 1949, restored *Anna Lucasta* to its Caucasian roots, with Paulette Goddard in the title role. It was neither an artistic nor a commercial success.

By the late 1950s, Yordan, who had coauthored the original screenplay with Arthur Laurents, had written several more notable Hollywood features, including *Detective Story, Houdini, Johnny Guitar,* and *The Harder They Fall,* Humphrey Bogart's last picture. Thus, when Yordan decided to refilm his family drama, this time with a Negro cast, United Artists was willing to bankroll the effort, providing the costs were kept to a minimum. At the time, UA specialized in small-scale, thematically adventuresome films, typically made in partnership with independent producers.

Max Youngstein, the company's president, met with Davis while he was appearing at the Moulin Rouge to discuss his playing Anna's hip boyfriend, a sailor named Danny Johnson. Although Danny is in only a few scenes, disappears for a long stretch in the middle of the story, and loses the girl to the square country boy, Sammy was eager to play the part. He had already signed for a major role in Samuel Goldwyn's lavish film version of *Porgy and Bess*, but that wasn't scheduled to start production until the summer.

But there was a problem: Davis was slated for an engagement at the Sands while *Anna Lucasta* would be in production. He couldn't postpone the booking because he'd already borrowed against it to meet expenses. As the dates for principal photography couldn't be altered, he had no choice but to do both at the same time. Someone would drive him to L.A. following his late show, allowing him to sleep in the car. At the end of the day's shooting, he'd fly to Vegas in time for his dinner show. "The last thing in the world I wanted was to commute back and forth like a madman," he said later, "making my first picture without being able to devote myself to it." But there was no other option. His reckless spending had placed him in this predicament.

Before making the commitment to UA, he wanted the blessing of Eartha Kitt, who had been cast as Anna. As Davis told Will Mastin at the time, "God knows it's going to be tough enough without having *her* fighting me." First he sent her flowers; then he invited her to dinner, where he laid on the flattery, pointing out that she was an old hand at the picture business and he was a newcomer and would need her help. She was suitably impressed, and the deal was set.

Filming started around the beginning of May 1958 at the Goldwyn Studios in Hollywood under the direction of Arnold Laven, who had directed six previous features, starting with *Without Warning* in 1952. Laven was impressed with Sammy. "He came almost as an accomplished actor," the director said, "not as somebody who had not acted." However, as Laven noted, "He played it pretty much as himself, bringing his own persona to it."

Davis worked hard on his scenes, eager to master the technique of film acting, which he considered "a new adventure." Consequently, he sought advice from everyone on the set, including Eartha Kitt. The two got along in a professional manner during filming, although they didn't particularly like each other, in Laven's opinion, perhaps a reflection of the way their personal relationship had concluded five years earlier.

While in Los Angeles for principal photography, Sammy paid a few visits to Loray at the home he had rented for her, but by this point it was evident that the relationship was never going to work. As he put it, "It was doomed from the start."

Money had become a divisive issue between them. Loray resented the constraints Sammy placed on her spending, maintaining that she was given a fixed amount for groceries every week and all of her other purchases had to be approved by her husband or his designated representatives. For his part, Sammy complained that, restricted or not, Loray's spending was out of control. "That woman has broke me," he said the following year, "put me in hock up to my ears." He added, "Three times I went to her. 'Loray,' I said, 'it's a little rugged now, just hold the spending down a little bit, O.K.?' She opened more charge accounts."

But the Davises' dispute about money was a symptom, not a root cause, of their discord. The real problem was that Loray loved Sammy and he felt nothing in return for her. If anything, he resented his wife because she reminded him of why he'd needed to marry her in the first place.

Aside from his domestic problems, Davis' rigorous travel schedule began to take its toll as the making of *Anna Lucasta* progressed. Once, Sammy's limousine failed to pick him up after his late show at the Sands. He had to wait until 7:00 A.M. to catch the first flight to L.A. Too energized to sleep, he spent the night gambling. Then the plane developed engine trouble en route and had to return to the airport. He ended up chartering a private plane and arriving at the studio an hour and a half late, considerably poorer for his losses at the gaming tables, not to mention the charter fee.

Finally, one day Sammy collapsed on the set. "Just fell flat on the floor," noted Arnold Laven. "We called him a doctor, of course. . . . And the doctor said, 'It's very simple, the guy just ran out of energy.'" Laven called the William Morris Agency to see about getting Sammy the night off, but the management of the Sands was not inclined to be generous. He was expected for two shows that evening, and two shows he did.

Anna Lucasta debuted at the Victoria Theatre in New York on January 14, 1959, following openings in Los Angeles and Chicago the previous November. Although Arthur Knight, the esteemed critic for the *Saturday Review*, found it "a thoroughly engrossing film," most of Knight's colleagues were more stinting in their praise. Most vitriolic was the dean of critics, the *New York Times*' Bosley Crowther, who asserted, "If somebody dug down into the play-bin and brought up *Bertha the Sewing-Machine Girl*, they could probably turn it into a better movie than has been made by Philip Yordan of *Anna Lucasta*." Crowther also hated Eartha Kitt's posturing.

Davis fared somewhat better than his costar, as he brought a simple honesty to his portrayal. But his presence failed to help the picture at the box office. Most filmgoers skipped it entirely.

On August 25, roughly two months after *Anna Lucasta* wrapped, Sammy returned to a Hollywood sound stage, this time to star in his first dramatic role for television. An inveterate TV watcher, he was ecstatic. But the job hadn't come easily.

Ever since *Mr. Wonderful* closed, Davis had been after his agents to get him such an assignment. The size and nature of the role was of no great concern. But virtually nothing had changed since Sammy's aborted pilot; the networks weren't able to sell dramas or comedies that centered around African American characters. One agent was at least willing to try. Born in Brooklyn in 1919, Sy Marsh had started out as an entertainer himself, first as a teenager doing shows in the Catskills, then in the army, and finally as the cohost of a local L.A. television show. After five years, he decided to retire as a performer and go to work for the agency that had represented him, William Morris. In time, he became head of its television division.

Marsh decided that Davis' best bet lay with Harry Tugend, the producer of a thirty-minute anthology series called *General Electric Theater*. The show, which was hosted by Ronald Reagan, aired on Sunday evenings on CBS.

At first, Tugend was not the least bit interested in hiring Sammy Davis, Jr. But Marsh kept after him. Then, when Davis opened at the Moulin Rouge in January, the agent took the producer to a performance. The night that Tugend came, Sammy re-created a scene from *The Caine Mutiny*, imitated Laurence Olivier in *Hamlet*, and even performed one of the monologues from *Cyrano de Bergerac*. Tugend was suitably impressed.

Next came the matter of locating an appropriate vehicle. Eventually, Tugend found what he was seeking in a story by Kurt Vonnegut, which the author had developed into a teleplay with Valentine Davies. By a strange coincidence, Davies, who had won an Oscar for his story *Miracle on 34th Street* in 1947, wrote and directed *The Benny Goodman Story*, in which Sammy's father played bandleader-arranger Fletcher Henderson.

Like most of Davies' other work, his collaboration with Vonnegut, called *Operation Little Joe*, was a feel-good, family-oriented drama. Set in Germany shortly after the end of World War II, it focused on a lonely African American Signal Corps private, Robert Johnson, called Spider, who is befriended by a half-German, half-black orphan named Joe.

Spider wasn't exactly Othello, but the character was far more complex than Charlie Welch or the sailor in *Anna Lucasta*. Sammy had a mere five days to develop his role in rehearsal and put it on film, but he threw himself into the part. His director, John Brahm, was impressed, praising his ability to learn his lines quickly and deliver them flawlessly during each take.

Harry Tugend was pleased with the show, as were the executives at General Electric. Sammy was so delighted he started telling his night-club audiences to watch out for it. Then a problem arose: GE's advertising agency determined that a drama with a Negro in the lead could create problems because GE sold more than half of its products below the Mason-Dixon line. Better to be safe, the agency advised, and shelve the episode. The GE executives agreed.

When Sy Marsh learned of this decision, he became a man possessed. He knew that if *Operation Little Joe* didn't air, it would break Sammy's heart. Marsh told Alan Miller, the head of Revue, the company that produced the show, that, if GE didn't run it, he would call a press conference and explain why. Miller tried to get Marsh's boss, Abe Lastfogel, to rein in the obdurate agent, but Marsh told Lastfogel he would give up his job rather than let Sammy down. Impressed, Lastfogel backed Marsh, and shortly thereafter, GE agreed to air the show.

Sammy's dramatic debut, renamed *Auf Wiedersehen* (German for "goodbye"), took place on October 5, 1958, more than a month before *Anna Lucasta* debuted in select cities around the country. The entertainer acquitted himself well, portraying the self-contained, self-sufficient GI with an understated naturalness. GE needn't have worried. Its sales in the South remained solid, and the ratings were solid, too.

Auf Wiedersehen marked another door that Davis forced open. He wasn't the first Negro to star in a TV drama; Sidney Poitier had appeared in an episode of *Philco Television Playhouse* a season or two earlier. But Sammy's success made it somewhat easier for the next person.

By the time *Auf Wiedersehen* aired, Davis' marriage to Loray White was over. White would later tell the readers of *Ebony* that she found being Sammy's wife so nerve-wracking that, by the marriage's end, she was "just a shade of the relaxed, self-assured, confident person I once was." Curiously, she added, "If he wants to come home, I'll be there."

It's difficult to tell if the article under her byline was a fabrication cooked up for public consumption or the product of her own wishful thinking. Either way, there was no hope that Sammy would ever come home. He'd never been home with her in the first place. On September 20, 1958, she announced that she would seek a divorce. Early the following year, she filed in the Santa Monica Superior Court, on the grounds of mental cruelty. She wanted $2,000 a month in alimony and $15,000 in attorney's fees. Sammy refused to accept these demands, so her attorneys asked the court to appoint a receiver to take possession of his assets, which Loray estimated at $1 million.

California law mandated a year's waiting period between the approval of a divorce petition and final termination of a marital union. So White filed again, in Las Vegas, in March 1959, by which point she and Sammy had agreed to a settlement that called for her to receive $44,000. The divorce was granted by District Judge John Mowbray on April 23, some six months before the California decree would be final. Loray took home $10,000; the remaining $34,000 covered the payment of her debts. Sammy was not present in court.

In the fall of 1958, Sammy tackled two more acting assignments, one of which would remain a source of enormous pride for the rest of his life.

On November 8, he opened in his first dramatic play, *The Desperate Hours,* Joseph Hayes' 1955 thriller about three escaped convicts who take refuge in the home of a typical American family. This was essentially a do-it-yourself production devised by Sammy as an opportunity to demonstrate his ability to carry a straight dramatic role in the hope that it might lead to other work in films or television.

Aside from Sammy, the driving force behind the production was James Waters. Davis had met the tall, lanky actor through Waters' wife, Luddy, an actress who was Kim Novak's dialogue coach on *Vertigo.* When the Waters home burned in a fire, Sammy generously let Jim and Luddy move into a house he had rented but never used on St. Ives Drive. In an effort to repay this kindness, Jim, who had done office work in between acting jobs, volunteered to help Sammy with his correspondence. Before long, Waters had become Davis' office manager, replacing David Landfield, who wanted to return to his own acting career. In time, the extensive range of Sammy's activities and plans justified opening an office, managed by Waters. (For a time, Arthur Silber, Jr., had an office in the same building, where he ran Samart Enterprises, his and Sammy's joint venture to find projects that would engage their interests. Davis' woeful financial state forced him to withdraw from the company around 1965.)

According to Luddy Waters, *The Desperate Hours* appealed to Sammy because he relished the idea of tackling a role that his friend, Humphrey Bogart, had put on film, that of the leader of the convicts, Glenn Griffin.* Jim portrayed the other principal character, Dan Hilliard, the head of the

---

*The role of Glenn Griffin in *The Desperate Hours* was created on Broadway by Paul Newman.

family held hostage. That Davis would have to push around the six-foot-tall Waters gave the drama a different dimension from when Bogie faced down Fredric March as Hilliard, as did the fact that a Negro was portraying one of the bad guys. In fact, this was probably one of the first instances in Hollywood history when an African American played a role originally written for a white actor.* Davis' color-blind attitude in this regard marks another instance in which he served as a civil rights pioneer.

The drama, which played in the round for three weeks at the Hollywood Canteen Theater, drew mostly enthusiastic reviews, with Davis drawing the lion's share of the praise. Lee Kovner spoke for the majority, noting in the *Hollywood Reporter,* "There's no denying that he delivered a strong—at junctures, electrifying—performance."

Present in the house on opening night were a number of Sammy's friends: Tony Curtis and Janet Leigh, Sidney Poitier, Dorothy Dandridge, Barbara Rush, Tina Louise, and screenwriter Sy Bartlett. Aside from being old pals, Poitier and Dandridge were also starring with Davis in a concurrent, and far more important, project, *Porgy and Bess*.

The poignant drama of a lonely cripple and the loose woman he loves started as a novel, *Porgy,* published in 1925. Its author, DuBose Heyward, was inspired by the plight of a real-life crippled beggar named Sammy Smalls who shot a woman, Maggie Barnes, in a fit of jealous rage. Smalls and Barnes lived in Cabbage Row, the impoverished African American section of Heyward's native Charleston, South Carolina. This became the atmospheric setting of his novel, *Catfish Row*. Two years after the book's publication, Heyward and his wife, Dorothy, turned *Porgy* into a play, which ran for a noteworthy 217 performances on Broadway.

The celebrated composer George Gershwin discovered Heyward's novel prior to its dramatization. Certain that it would be the ideal vehicle for an opera he'd long been hoping to write, he convinced Heyward to contribute the lyrics to his music, along with George's most frequent partner, his talented brother Ira. Thanks primarily to the latter, the drug-dealing Sportin' Life, a relatively minor and one-dimensional figure in both the novel and the play, became a more significant and ominous presence. Ira was the lyricist for Sportin' Life's two principal solos, "It Ain't Necessarily So" and "There's a Boat Dat's Leavin' Soon for New York," while Heyward was largely responsible for more lyrical material, including Porgy's "I Got Plenty o' Nuthin'" and Bess' "I Loves You, Porgy." When completed, the unique score was operatic in form but imbued with a distinctively American sound, borrowing elements from folk music and the blues.

*The role of Dan Hilliard was created on Broadway by Karl Malden.

Under the auspices of Rouben Mamoulian, who had directed the play *Porgy*, the opera debuted to moderately enthusiastic reviews at New York's Alvin Theater in October 1935. Seven years later, producer Cheryl Crawford revived the show, reducing the size of the cast and orchestra and replacing the recitatives with dialogue, thereby transforming the opera into a musical. The revival ran more than twice as long as the original production.

Numerous American filmmakers had sought to acquire the film rights to the opera, but the Gershwin family had refused to sell (George Gershwin died in 1937). Finally, in October 1957, twenty-two years after the opera's Broadway debut, independent producer Samuel Goldwyn won the Gershwins' approval with an offer of $650,000 against 10 percent of the film's gross receipts. For the celebrated producer of *Dodsworth*, *Wuthering Heights*, *The Little Foxes*, *The Best Years of Our Lives*, and, most recently, the musical *Guys and Dolls*, making *Porgy and Bess* was a labor of love. He considered it the American musical theater's crowning achievement. He even hired Rouben Mamoulian once again to direct. He then brought in N. Richard Nash, author of the hit drama *The Rainmaker*, to write the screenplay. For reasons that aren't entirely clear, he also shifted the time of the drama from the turn of the century to 1910.

Unfortunately, many African Americans failed to share Goldwyn's reverence for *Porgy and Bess*. The opera's stereotypical characters and broad use of dialect were widely perceived as demeaning, as was a plot that included murder, drug addiction, and sex outside of marriage.

Harry Belafonte, who had several major films to his credit, including the male lead in 1955's all-black musical, *Carmen Jones*, was Goldwyn's first choice for Porgy. But Belafonte flatly refused the role. The producer then turned to Sidney Poitier. Although he was not yet the superstar he would become, the tall, handsome Bahamian-born actor was well respected, thanks to his work in such films as *Cry the Beloved Country*, *The Blackboard Jungle*, and *Something of Value*. After Goldwyn received a commitment for Poitier from Lillian Schary Small, whom he thought was the actor's agent, he announced the casting to the press. Then Goldwyn discovered that Small was simply the West Coast representative of the actor's actual New York–based agent, Martin Baum, and had no right to speak for Poitier. Worse, the actor didn't want the part. Feeling betrayed, Goldwyn essentially blackmailed Poitier into changing his mind, playing off his interest in another picture, Stanley Kramer's *The Defiant Ones*. When Kramer, who didn't want to offend the better-established, more powerful Goldwyn, hinted that he might not be able to use Poitier if the actor didn't take the role in the opera, Sidney gave in.

With Poitier on board, the producer was able to sign Belafonte's *Car-*

men Jones costar, Dorothy Dandridge, as Bess; Pearl Bailey for an important supporting role, Maria; Brock Peters, another *Carmen Jones* alumnus, as the villainous Crown; and Diahann Carroll as Clara, the young mother who sings "Summertime" at the outset of the drama.

That left the supporting character, Sportin' Life, the drug dealer who entices Bess to go with him to New York at the opera's conclusion. Sammy campaigned with all his might to win this pivotal role. "I don't mind admitting," he recalled, "I got all the pals I could muster—Sinatra, Jack Benny, George Burns, and guys like that—to root for me with Goldwyn. I nagged the William Morris Agency to make it a top priority."

But the producer wanted Cab Calloway, who'd played the role in a highly successful international touring production directed by Robert Breen. What finally did the trick for Sammy was his appearance at the Moulin Rouge. Davis treated Goldwyn's visit to the club as an audition, performing at an energy level that exceeded even his usual high-octane output. He even included a medley of tunes from *Porgy and Bess* for Goldwyn's benefit. The producer was knocked out, immediately agreeing to sign Sammy for the role. To show his appreciation, the entertainer gave the producer a watch that, in Frank Sinatra's words, "had everything on it except the planets and a couple of spaceships going by."

With an impressive budget of $7 million, *Porgy and Bess* was scheduled to start shooting right after the July 4 weekend. But on July 2, a fire erupted on Stage 8 of the Goldwyn Studios, where designer Oliver Smith had erected a gigantic set representing the environs of Catfish Row. The blaze gutted the sound stage, ruining not only the set but also many of the costumes and props. The cause of the fire, which resulted in damages estimated at $2.5 million, was never determined.

The disaster pushed back the start of filming by six weeks. During that interval, Goldwyn fired Rouben Mamoulian, replacing him with Otto Preminger. Although the heavy-handed Teutonic Preminger might seem a curious choice to direct an American folk opera, he had scored a resounding triumph with *Carmen Jones*. Before agreeing to the job, Preminger insisted on more rehearsal time, several script changes, and the right to shoot the film's extended picnic sequence on location. Goldwyn agreed.

The picnic sequence was, in fact, the starting point for the production. When the cameras finally rolled on September 19, the company was ensconced in Stockton, California, in the central part of the state. There Venice Island, a scruffy, rural outcropping in the San Joaquin River, stood in for the opera's Kittiwah Island, site of the outing staged by a group of wholesome churchgoers, including Bess. On the island, Sportin' Life taunts the revelers' religious convictions, pointing out the more fantastic stories in the Old Testament in the song "It Ain't Necessarily So." Hermes Pan was the film's choreographer, but Sammy worked out his own routine for the number, with the help of his *Mr. Wonderful* colleague, dancer Hal Loman.

Although Davis eschewed Pan's assistance, he got along extremely well with the celebrated choreographer, who was noted, in particular, for his long collaboration with Fred Astaire. In fact, when he wasn't working, Sammy frequently hung out with Pan and his ensemble of dancers. "He would do the dances with us," said a member of the troupe, Nichelle Nichols. "Just for fun. And he and Hermes would tap together, would do challenges. And they would fall all over each other laughing." As an added benefit, Sammy could become better acquainted with some of the attractive young ladies in the company, including Nichols, whom he briefly dated, although the relationship was more or less platonic.*

With Sammy, Dorothy Dandridge, and all of the churchgoers, Goldwyn had a gigantic ensemble of actors, singers, and dancers working in Stockton, plus a very large crew. Unfortunately, that year the Jewish High Holidays arrived while the company was on location. When Sammy told the producer he needed to be excused on Yom Kippur, the holiest day in the Jewish calendar, the producer was astonished, even though he was Jewish himself. When he realized that Davis was serious, he relented, although doing so cost him about $25,000 in salaries and expenses. As Goldwyn put it, "Directors I can fight. Fire on the set I can fight. Writers, even actors, I can fight. But a Jewish colored fellow? This I can't fight."

Sammy liked the elderly producer, who was well-known for his malapropisms. He also enjoyed a friendly relationship with Otto Preminger. "When everything settled down to its day-to-day routine," Davis recalled, "he and I started developing a repartee which kept the whole set giggling for days. When the cameras were whirring, I would give my very best, but between takes I played the comedian. It made the set a very happy place to work." The two men lunched together often, frequently hooking up after hours as well to hit some of L.A.'s more fashionable nightspots. When it came to working on his character, however, Davis was less dependent on his director than on Robert Breen, the man responsible for the long-touring stage production of *Porgy and Bess*. "Bobby spent an awful lot of time with me," Davis said, "helping me bring Sportin' Life to life. He helped me understand where the character was coming from." By the time they were through, Sportin' Life had

*Today, Nichols is best known for her portrayal of Uhura on the TV series *Star Trek* and the subsequent feature films based on the show.

become, in Sammy's words, "the epitome of evil," which "made the part a great challenge. People had to hate him, yet he had to be a little lovable as well." To achieve his goal, he gave the character a distinctive swagger and a reptilian manner, both of which set him apart immediately from the other, far earthier characters. He was decked out in a derby and cane with spats and high-button shoes. His flashy checkered suits were so tight, the costume designer, Irene Sharaff, wouldn't allow him to wear underwear beneath his trousers.

Shortly after filming began, Davis knew that things were clicking. After seeing some of the rushes, the film's musical director, Andre Previn, even whispered to him, "You're going to steal this picture." Playing the role didn't come without a price. During filming, Sammy suffered a heart attack. Although it was mild, causing him to miss only a couple of days of work, he was, at thirty-four, very young to suffer such a health problem. Doubtless, contributing factors were stress, heavy drinking, too little sleep, and the fact that he chain-smoked. Health problems aside, Sammy told Thomas B. Morgan of *Esquire,* "Let me tell you . . . that part was the gasser of my life."

Most of his costars, among them Poitier, Pearl Bailey, and Dorothy Dandridge, were nowhere near as delighted. Underscoring their initial concerns about the project was Preminger's heavy-handed directorial style. He was particularly cruel to Dandridge. Although she and the director had been lovers during the making of *Carmen Jones,* Preminger ragged her unmercifully while shooting *Porgy.* As Nichelle Nichols put it, "He would so denigrate her publicly, it was scandalous. She could not function. . . . It was terribly embarrassing to everyone, and everyone would walk away—didn't want to get fired, I guess. But you could not stand to see it, to watch it."

Finally, the other actors, including Davis and Poitier, insisted on a meeting with the director. They demanded that Preminger stop harassing Dorothy, and afterward he more or less complied.

Filming finally ended on December 11. Six months later, on June 24, 1959, *Porgy and Bess* debuted at the Warner Theatre in New York City. It was released as a road show engagement, meaning that it typically played in only one theater per city, with one matinee and one evening showing per day, and tickets were sold on a reserved-seat basis. This method of distribution was common for "event" pictures during the mid-fifties and the late sixties, when filmmakers sought ways to distinguish the significance of their offerings from the popular fare on television.

Shot in color in the widescreen format, Todd-A-O, using six-speaker stereo, *Porgy and Bess* could hardly have been mistaken for anything airing on TV. The vast majority of the critics raved about the production elements, from Leon Shamroy's photography to Oliver Smith's sets to Andre Previn's orchestrations, and warmly received the cast, although with some reservations about Dandridge. Overall, the picture was dubbed "a rich and devoted filming" by Paul V. Beckley of the *New York Herald Tribune*; "a handsome, intelligent and often gripping production" by *Variety*; and "a stunning, exciting and moving film, packed with human emotions and cheerful and mournful melodies" by Bosley Crowther of the *New York Times*.

But moviegoers never really warmed to the picture, and it performed only moderately well at the box office. Viewing it more than four decades later, one can see why. Though hardly bad, it has a studied quality that keeps it moribund. Preminger and Goldwyn were so awed by their source material that they were unable to inject the film with genuine life. Moreover, the gigantic Catfish Row set, while impressive, looks exactly like what it is, the re-creation of a village on a sound stage. The picnic sequence, shot in an authentic outdoor setting, only enhances the artificiality of the milieu. As for the acting, everyone tries hard, but the performances never take flight.

The sole exception is Davis, who is electric. Andre Previn was right: he steals the picture. But, then, he had certain advantages. To begin with, only he and Pearl Bailey were allowed to do their own singing. The other voices were all dubbed, including those of Dandridge and Diahann Carroll, both of whom were singers but not operatic vocalists. Because the musical soundtrack was recorded first, as is customary, the actors had to adjust their performances to match what they were hearing on tape, which is not an easy feat under any circumstance, for it inhibits any form of spontaneity, but is more difficult when the voice is not one's own.* Second, Sportin' Life has two of the show's best songs. Third, the character has a more urban sensibility than the opera's other, more pastoral characters. Modern audiences may not be rooting for him, but they can at least recognize and understand him better than the likes of Porgy or Crown.

Davis made the most of the role's advantages. As *Cue* noted on the picture's release, "Sammy Davis, Jr.—serpentine, acrobatic, evil incarnate— is the finest Sportin' Life yet; his rendering of 'It Ain't Necessarily So' is a classic of song and dance."

---

*Robert McFerrin, Adele Addison, and Loulie Jean Norman served as the singing voices of Poitier, Dandridge, and Carroll, respectively. Though Davis did his own vocals on the film, his recording contract with Decca precluded the use of his voice on the motion picture soundtrack album, which was released by Columbia. Thus, Cab Calloway rendered Sportin' Life's numbers on the LP. Decca, in return, released its own album, in which Davis and Carmen McRae did all the principal numbers from the opera.

Such was the strength of Sammy's performance that he might well have earned an Oscar nomination had he been eligible for consideration in the supporting actor category. But because he was billed above the title along with Poitier and Dandridge, the Academy ruled that he could qualify only for best actor. The role simply wasn't strong enough to support such a nomination. As it turned out, *Porgy and Bess* was acknowledged in only four categories—cinematography, costumes, sound, and scoring—winning only in the last.

No doubt, Sammy would have dearly coveted an Oscar nod, something he never received during his career. But he had no complaints about *Porgy and Bess*. Looking back years later, he said, "My finest piece of movie acting was Sportin' Life, and if I make nothing else, I'll let that stand on my record without a shadow of regret."

CHAPTER 11

Lovers and Friends

Sammy followed up his 1958 acting jobs with two more television roles the following year.

In late September, he went to work on an episode of *The Zane Grey Theatre*. With his love of all things Western, he had campaigned hard for a spot on the half-hour anthology series. Although the NBC drama was produced and hosted by actor Dick Powell, it was the show's principal writer, Aaron Spelling, who championed Davis' cause. What Spelling devised was an episode set in a typical frontier town, in which Sammy would play deputy to Powell's sheriff, saving his boss' life in a climactic shootout with the story's villain. After Powell approved the script, Spelling sent it to Davis, who loved it. Then, only days before the start of production, the show's sponsor refused to okay the episode. The reason: Davis' character kills a white outlaw, and a Negro simply could not be seen doing such a thing, not even to save another white man, in turbulent 1959.

Spelling threatened to quit the show. Then he was struck by an idea for a completely different story line, one that didn't involve white people. Rather, Spelling's new plot centered on a platoon of Negro cavalrymen, part of the Buffalo Soldiers who were once stationed at Davis' own Fort Warren. On a routine mission, escorting a Commanche chief to a peace conference, the troopers are waylaid by a band of renegade Apaches, forcing Davis' character, a corporal named Hopper, into a scheme that will enable his men and the chief to escape. As an added touch, Spelling had Sammy's character start out as a bigot, as prejudiced against Native Americans as many Caucasians are against blacks.

Within days, Spelling had the script in hand so that filming could begin on schedule. As with *Anna Lucasta*, Sammy was in the middle of an engagement at the Sands. Once again, he found himself commuting to Los Angeles in the wee hours of the morning and returning to Las Vegas after a hard day's work. Fortunately, filming lasted only three days, following a couple of rehearsal days.

The show, which Spelling called "Mission," aired on November 5, 1959. It was a taut little morality tale with a neat twist ending. Decked out in sideburns and a brush moustache, Sammy acquitted himself well as the black man who learns something about race prejudice. Even more important, he, Powell, and Aaron Spelling blazed new territory by featuring a Negro in a story of the Old West. At the time, few Americans had ever heard of the Buffalo Soldiers and would have scoffed at the idea of black cavalrymen or, for that matter, black cowboys or lawmen. *Variety* paid tribute to the drama's significance when it aired, noting that it broke "the racial barrier that has, up to now, existed in video's somewhat rigged version of the early American west."

A couple weeks after "Mission" wrapped, Sammy resumed his Las Vegas–Los Angeles commute on behalf of a return appearance on *G.E. Theater*. As with *Auf Wiedersehen*, he was again in uniform. This time he played the title character in *The Patsy*, an innocent farm boy who becomes the butt of his platoon's jokes during basic training. The episode was shot, in part, at Fort MacArthur in San Pedro. Originally scheduled to air in November, it was inexplicably held back until February 21, 1960, when, like *Auf Wiedersehen* and "Mission," it was well received.

Davis enjoyed acting for television, but, as he put it, "I'd like to do three or four of these things a year. Who wouldn't? They're fun and a challenge, but it sure isn't like playing a club. . . . [There] I get an immediate reaction from the audience. I get a terrific kick out of their reactions. Knowing if you're good enough, you can make people laugh and feel happy is a wonderful feeling."

Although he showed up on a few TV variety shows during 1959 and was even the mystery guest on the popular quiz program, *What's My Line?*, he returned to the nightclub circuit in a big way. He didn't even stop for more than one recording session with Decca during the year.

He hit many of the venues where he had appeared in the past, along with some new ones: Miami Beach's Eden Roc, the Mapes in Reno, and the Bellevue Casino in Montreal. In November, he returned to Chicago, this time for a four-day stand at the Roberts Show Club, on the southside, the city's equivalent to Harlem. He received special permission from the operators of the Chez Paree for this gig because he wanted to help the club's owner, Herman Roberts, who was experiencing financial problems.

What made these appearances particularly noteworthy was that Sammy Davis, Jr., was finally on his own, Will having retired on doctor's orders at the end of 1958. Mastin's absence from the act didn't mean that he simply disappeared. On the contrary. For about six or eight months, he continued traveling with Sammy as his manager, even though he didn't have much say in his protégé's affairs. According to Arthur Silber, Jr., Will would come to each venue Sammy played. There, Nathan Crawford would set out the old man's tuxedo and makeup in a dressing room of his own, just as if he were going to perform. Only he never did. He was simply "ready," as he put it, should Sammy ever need him. "It was so sad," Silber said. Furthermore, long after Will retired to California for good, the billing remained The Will Mastin Trio Starring Sammy Davis, Jr., and Sammy continued to split his earnings with Mastin and his father until 1969.

In addition to Will, Davis was, naturally, accompanied on the road by Arthur, Morty Stevens, his road manager-bodyguard Big John Hopkins, and, from time to time, Jess Rand and Jim Waters. In addition, there were three relative newcomers. The most recent was Sammy's valet, Murphy Bennett. A native of Chicago, Murphy had served in the army during World War II. After moving to Los Angeles in 1950, he became a waiter at the Garden of Allah, which is where he and Davis met. A sweet, gentle man, Bennett remained with Sammy for the rest of the entertainer's life. Davis noted in his 1989 autobiography *Why Me?*, "How can you figure life, or plan it? You need a dresser, someone to pack and unpack and look after your clothes, so you hire a man, the years go by, and he's your best friend, your confidant. He signs my autograph, carries my jewelry and my money. Nobody in the world knows who I want to talk to and what I want and don't want as well as Murphy."

In addition to Bennett, Sammy's entourage also included a rhythm section, the heart of any nightclub performer's orchestra, in the persons of drummer Michael Silva and pianist George Rhodes.

Silva soon became an audience favorite, largely because, in a special turn during Sammy's act, he would apply his drumsticks to every conceivable surface at hand—music stands, piano tops, the stage floor, and chairs. Davis also liked to turn everyday objects into rhythm instruments, so sometimes he would join Michael for a "drum" challenge, running around the room, alternating solos, and ending up in a duet.

Offstage, the entertainer enjoyed pulling pranks on Silva, who was slight like he was and easy to scare. The following year, after the release of the Hitchcock film *Psycho,* Davis took to hiding in Silva's shower and popping out when the drummer entered the bathroom. "And Michael would really jump out of his skin," Silber recalled. "Sammy would stand in there for an hour if he had to. That went on for a long time, months." Finally, Silva decided to pull the same trick on Davis. But before he could spring out and jolt the boss, Sammy pulled back the shower curtain, scaring Michael anew. "How the hell did you know I was there?" the disappointed drummer asked. "Man, don't ever put cologne on before you come into my room," Sammy told him.

Silva stayed with Davis for nearly a decade. Then, while the entertainer was performing in London, the drummer fell in love with a local girl and decided to stay in the U.K.

In contrast to Michael Silva, George Rhodes was soft-spoken and reserved. Like Murphy, he was a native of Chicago, where he had served as a pianist for blues singer Lil Green and subsequently performed with such jazz musicians as Red Allen and J. C. Higgenbotham. In 1947, he went to New York as part of the Arnett Cobb band. Later, he became an arranger for Apollo Records, as well as a player-arranger for Joe Thomas, Dinah Washington, and the Ravens. Originally hired for a short-term gig with Davis, Rhodes quickly became part of the inner circle. Like Morty, he was a solid musician. Indeed, a few years later, when Stevens left to join CBS, Rhodes took over as Sammy's conductor and principal arranger.

By the end of the fifties, Sammy's nightclub gigs featured more singing and less dancing than those in the past. His 1959 sets typically included a big number from *Porgy and Bess,* "I Got Plenty o' Nothin'" or "Where Is My Bess." He also featured a medley of Oscar-losing songs and either "The World Is Mine" or "When I Fall in Love" or both. Of course, Sammy still offered up some of his most popular numbers, such as "The Birth of the Blues," and a round of impressions (which now included the popular opera singer-turned-movie-star Mario Lanza). And he sometimes took a turn on the xylophone, the latest instrument he'd tackled, accompanied by Morty on the clarinet and Michael Silva banging away on a chair. This routine got the "heftiest palming of [the] evening" at Sammy's opening in Montreal, to quote the local *Variety* stringer.

In *Yes I Can,* Davis discussed at length his feelings of dissatisfaction with his performances during this period. He maintained that anger and frustration over the continued slights and hurts in his personal life, mostly racial in nature, and the direction of some aspects of his professional life—the struggle to get dramatic roles on TV, for example—had fostered a rather listless and phony persona on stage. Perhaps this was so, but there were certainly no complaints at the time from his audiences or critics.

His reviews were great and he was a hit wherever he went, but he continued to stir up controversy along the way. While on the road in 1959, he managed to give the media two stories to savor.

The first came early in the year. While performing in Chicago, he appeared on *The Jack Eigen Show,* a late-night radio program on NBC that originated from the Chez Paree. During the conversation, Eigen noted that when it came to the public, Frank Sinatra was not always the most tolerant celebrity. To which Davis replied, "I love Frank and he was the kindest man in the world to me when I lost my eye in an auto accident and wanted to kill myself. But there are many things he does that there are no excuses for. Talent is not an excuse for bad manners . . . it does not give you the right to step on people and treat them rotten. This is what he does occasionally." Sammy also asserted that Sinatra was not the top vocalist in the country. Egging him on, Eigen asked, "You think you're bigger than Frank?" and Sammy answered, "Yes."

Why would he say these things? Most celebrities know better than to criticize their friends in public, and Sammy was no exception, particularly when the person under discussion is as thin-skinned as Frank Sinatra. Some have argued that Davis was speaking out of anger and frustration, that his relationship with the crooner had a decided downside. And there is some truth in this assertion. For one thing, Frank sometimes demeaned Sammy in front of others. Once, for example, both entertainers were present at a large dinner party at an expensive restaurant. At the conclusion of the meal, Sammy reached for the tab, but Frank preempted him, saying, "Give me the check, Sammy. I have much more going for me than you have," a reference to the fact that Sinatra's record albums were bigger sellers and he was a far greater film star. Frank "often made Sammy feel like the mascot," asserted Rat Pack chroniclers Lawrence J. Quirk and William Schoell, "the house Negro." Dom DeLuise shared this assessment, saying, "It was very clearly established that the king was Frank and the court jester was Sammy." Once, in Vegas, DeLuise recalled that Davis was eating a meal when he was told that Sinatra wanted to see him. Sammy left immediately to answer the summons. Quirk and Schoell also asserted that Sammy "was tired of feeling as if he owed everything to Frank. For one thing, Sinatra never seemed to acknowledge the fact that Sammy was a genius in his own right, a brilliant performer every bit as talented as Frank if not more so."

There is no question that Sinatra had a cruel streak, as Sammy no doubt knew from firsthand experience. And Davis *was* sometimes treated as a junior member of Frank's inner circle. But, clearly, Sinatra respected Davis' talents. For his part, Sammy adored Frank and was awed by him. Sinatra was the yardstick by which he measured true stardom, including his own. He was also enormously grateful for his friend's many kindnesses, such as introducing him on his return to Ciro's following his auto accident. But he certainly didn't "owe everything to him." Outside of the gig at the Capitol Theater in 1947, Sinatra had done relatively little to help Sammy professionally at that stage of their relationship, although that would soon change. If anything, he served, like any good friend, primarily as a booster and ringside cheerleader. It is much more likely that the things Davis told Jack Eigen were simply a matter of Sammy talking off the top of his head without thinking. Perhaps he was tired after his shows at the Chez Paree that night. Maybe he'd had too much to drink.

Whatever prompted his utterances, there is no doubt about their impact: they infuriated Sinatra. He was particularly vexed, people have since asserted, because Sammy's remarks were made in Chicago, where Frank had so many "friends." Embarrassing him in front of "Momo" Giancana and the boys was damn near unforgivable.

Unfortunately for Sammy, this was a particularly bad time to incur Sinatra's wrath. In the years since his Oscar-winning role in *From Here to Eternity,* the crooner had become a major player in Hollywood, with films such as *Guys and Dolls, The Man with the Golden Arm, High Society, The Joker Is Wild,* and *A Hole in the Head* to go with his solid gold records for his current label, Capitol. He was just about to star in an MGM picture called *Never So Few,* in which he managed to secure a supporting role for Sammy over the objections of the Metro brass. In the wake of *The Jack Eigen Show,* Frank insisted that Davis be dropped from the World War II melodrama, even though his friend had already signed a contract with the studio. Sammy was replaced by Steve McQueen.*

The loss of the role was heartbreaking, as was the loss of the $75,000 salary. But, even more, Sammy was devastated by Frank's fury. Given all the slights, real and perceived, that he had endured in his own life, he hated hurting anyone. But to be seen as a cruel ingrate by the man he esteemed above all others was almost more than he could bear. He tried time and again to phone his friend and apologize, but Sinatra refused to take his calls. He even went to Peter Lawford, a more recent member of Frank's inner circle, to intercede for him, but Lawford had no luck. Once he sensed the extent of Sinatra's ire, the polished British actor feared pushing the issue out of concern for his own role in the MGM picture. Thus, Sammy continued dangling. "You wanna talk destroyed," said Lawford's manager, Milt Ebbins. "Sammy Davis cried from morning to night."

Matters worsened in March when Davis moved on to the Eden Roc in Miami Beach, while Sinatra was practically next door, performing at the Fountainebleu. Sammy was sure that if he could see Frank in person, he could straighten everything out, but Sinatra instructed the hotel's personnel that if his former friend showed up, he was not to be admitted to

*In his 1980 book *Hollywood in a Suitcase,* Davis maintained that he gave up the role in *Never So Few* because he and Frank had different opinions about how it should be played. Given Davis' ongoing need for money and his eagerness to work in features, not to mention his enthusiasm for hanging out on a movie set with Frank, it is difficult to imagine him voluntarily giving up the assignment. Somewhat later, he admitted to Randy Taraborrelli, author of a biography of Sinatra, that Frank "cut me out of a film. I was sorry, so sorry."

his show. The feud became the talk of the town. Earl Wilson even heard about it in New York, telling readers of his column on March 5 "that Sammy was ready to hurl himself prostrate on the stage to ask Frank's forgiveness. One report to Sammy was: 'It wouldn't help you.'"

In May, while Davis was at the Moulin Rouge in L.A., Sinatra, apparently feeling that the upstart had suffered enough and after hearing Sammy make another public apology, agreed to take the entertainer's call. Following a second, private apology, the feud was over. Shortly thereafter, Davis and Sinatra were performing at a benefit for SHARE (Share Happily and Reap Endlessly), a Los Angeles charity composed of show business wives, including Jeff Chandler's ex, Marge, and Dean Martin's Jeannie. All Hollywood cheered at the sight of the duo hugging as they joined together for a rendition of "The Lady Is a Tramp."

Sammy barely had time to recuperate from the Sinatra fiasco before he was back in the news again. This time, the stories focused on his romantic relationship with yet another white woman.

It was in October 1959, while he was performing in Montreal, that he encountered a blonde, twenty-three-year-old dancer named Joan Stuart. Stuart had joined several cast members of *Up Tempo,* the revue in which she was appearing, to catch Sammy's act at the Bellevue. He knew a member of Stuart's party, who introduced him to the dancer. They "kind of hit it off right away," said Stuart.

After that evening, Sammy and Joan began to spend time together, mostly during the afternoon and early evening hours. In her words, they "went to coffee shops mostly and just sat and talked. We found we had lots in common." The fact that Joan looked remarkably like Kim Novak may have had some bearing on Davis' feelings, but he also found himself charmed by her rather sedate, simple approach to life. She had few boyfriends, focused on her dancing, and spent a lot of time reading and taking long walks. In this she was rather different from the worldly women who typically came his way. Moreover, he felt that he could relax and be himself with her. "When I began to talk to Joan," he said, "I felt like a different person. I found that this was the first time I ever sat with a girl and was myself as I really am, not as Sammy Davis, Jr., night club star. . . . I didn't have to be flip or cute. It was a wonderful feeling."

According to *Jet,* which ran an article about the romance in its February 11, 1960 issue, Sammy proposed to Joan on their fifth date, and she accepted. He later explained his haste by citing an old adage: "When you meet the right girl, marry her."

For the moment, they decided to keep the news to themselves. When Sammy returned to the States, they continued their courtship by phone.

Then Joan joined him during his stint at the Sands, where, on November 6, they announced their plans. "I'm riding on cloud nine," she said. Sammy added, "I'm thrilled" and said they intended to marry shortly after Christmas.

But December came and went with no nuptials. One obstacle was Sammy's intense work schedule, which then included the filming of his two television dramas in L.A. A far more serious problem was the opposition of Stuart's parents, whom Davis had never met.

"Naturally, we don't approve," Stuart's mother told the Associated Press after the engagement was announced. "It's ridiculous." She added that Joan had never before had a steady boyfriend. "I don't know what happened this time," she said. "She's only known him about 10 days." Her father, a department store night watchman, echoed his wife's dismay.

In mid-December, Sammy moved on to the Copa in New York, and Joan joined him for his opening. Although the press wasn't allowed to photograph the engaged couple, Allan Morrison reported in *Jet* that Sammy "bounced buoyantly through his opening night shows." But shortly thereafter, his mood took a downward spiral, and he told the journalist on December 30, "I got troubles and problems, man." He also hinted that he might have a story for Morrison the following day, but the reporter heard nothing further. At roughly the same time, Sammy told Hy Gardner, a columnist for the *Beverly Hills Citizen*, that the engagement was off. Gardner even wrote a column to that effect, but held it back because Davis wanted to be a gentleman and let Stuart break the news to the media.

No such announcement was forthcoming. Then, on January 8, 1960, Sammy flew to Toronto for a brief gig at the Barclay Hotel. Stuart wasn't there to greet him, work having kept her in Montreal. Consequently, Sammy was moody and nervous.

The next day, she showed up, and, as Allan Morrison put it, "Once again he was the happy song-and-dance man, the incarnation of charm." This certainly suggests that the romance was back on track. So does Sammy's visit to Joan's family in Montreal the following day. During a long, frequently trying afternoon, he managed to win them over. "They all loved him," Joan said later. Suddenly, Mrs. Stuart was telling the press, "I like Sammy, he's a wonderful chap." That night, the entertainer informed his Barclay Hotel audience that he had just returned from the "Big Four Summit Conference." The audience roared. On a roll, he added that if he weren't in the best of singing voices, it was because he'd "been doing some talking" that afternoon. After the show, he told reporters that the meeting with Joan's parents had gone well but that the couple would refrain from tying the knot until the ailing Mr. Stuart felt well enough to attend the ceremony.

Little else was heard on the subject for several months. Then in April, Hy Gardner filed the column he'd written in December. The engagement was off. Sammy told Gardner that the issue wasn't race. "We knew and realized that our marriage would invite criticism and hostility," said the entertainer. "We were aware of the tall mountains we'd have to climb and the weight of the cross we'd have to bear, she more than I. But we had such great rapport we didn't care what people said or thought. I'd love her if she were white, green, yellow, or polka-dotted." What brought an end to the relationship, rather, was a combination of his heavy schedule and his indebtedness, both of which made marriage to anyone inadvisable, and her desire to continue working as a dancer. Regarding the latter, Sammy said, "I didn't want to play second fiddle to my wife's career." Of course, her income could have helped alleviate his financial stress, but, in all likelihood, neither reason was correct. Most probably, the relationship, which had escalated so quickly, simply withered away with the passage of time. It is impossible to know what motivated Stuart, but, in Sammy's case, it is fair to assume that the insecure entertainer, no longer a kid at age thirty-four, was desperate to be loved. As with Cordie King, he was quick to fall head over heels with a beautiful, sweet woman who responded to his advances, and was just as quick to become disillusioned when he delved beneath the surface of his initial infatuation.

In public at least, he put the best possible face on his latest romantic debacle, saying, "Our decision makes both of us unhappy. But we're young and vital and smart enough, I think, to know that it is more adult to prevent a mistake than to learn by making one." Then he moved on to other conquests.

In fact, he moved on very quickly. Almost immediately upon his return home from Canada, he met someone else, another beautiful white woman, and was, again, instantly captivated.

May Britt was not a typical Hollywood star.* Born Maybritt Wilkens in Lidingo, Sweden, in 1933, she was discovered by Italian producer Carlo Ponti when she was nineteen, working as a photo lab assistant in Stockholm en route to a career as a photographer. Seeking a new face for his films, Ponti was struck by Britt's fresh-scrubbed Nordic looks, including her shoulder-length blonde hair and the sprinkle of freckles across her nose. The producer took her to Rome, where she made her film debut in *Le Infideli* in 1952. After five more Italian pictures and numerous TV appearances, 20th Century Fox brought her to the United States, where

---

*Initially, Britt spelled her name Mai and later changed it to May. For the sake of continuity, it consistently appears here as May. Either way, her name is pronounced "My."

she costarred in *The Young Lions,* playing the flirtatious wife of a German officer opposite Marlon Brando as her husband's dashing aide. She made such a striking impression that Fox signed her to a seven-year contract. In 1958, she married a UCLA college student named Edwin Gregson, the son of a wealthy Los Angeles stockbroker. But the marriage lasted a mere nineteen months, with Britt filing for divorce in September 1959. Although she appeared sultry and sexy, she was somewhat shy, unusually direct and honest, robustly athletic, and aloof from the Hollywood scene. *Life* magazine even dubbed her a "Star with a New Style" when it featured her on the cover of its August 17, 1959 issue. Despite the first flush of stardom, May didn't take herself or the movie industry very seriously; she'd never sought celebrity or a career in acting. She just happened to be in the right place at the right time when Ponti came upon her.

She was attempting to fill Marlene Dietrich's rather sizable shoes in a remake of *The Blue Angel* when she caught Sammy's eye. He was having lunch in the Fox commissary with an old friend, Barbara Luna, when Britt walked in. He had seen May in *The Young Lions* but found her even more striking in person. Luna, who was playing one of Britt's backup singers in *The Blue Angel,* told him to forget about her. "She's a nice girl," Luna conceded, "but she doesn't do anything but work. She goes nowhere with nobody!" Shortly thereafter, Davis was lunching with friends Jay and Judy Kanter. They knew Britt and echoed Luna's sentiments. "She's so straight," Jay asserted, "that nobody even goes over to say hello to her. And the best have tried. She's not interested in dating, parties, nothing! She's strictly work. She's getting a divorce from some kid who's got millions and she won't take a nickel from him."

His friends' discouraging words simply strengthened Davis' resolve to meet this gorgeous iceberg. He took to phoning Luna at regular intervals, asking her to invite May to one of the informal get-togethers he regularly held at his home. As she put it, "He became the crazy Sammy that we've all seen—the hysterical stamping-his-little-feet ten-year-old. 'I want what I want when I want.' And just nagged me and drove me crazy."

But Luna refused to play matchmaker. It wasn't just May's reclusive nature that concerned her. The Filipino actress was reluctant to get in the middle of an interracial relationship out of concern for both parties. Finally, Sammy arranged an outing at the Cloisters to mark singer Dinah Washington's closing night at the club. Luna's and Britt's mothers were in town at the time, and Barbara thought the occasion innocuous enough to invite May and their mothers to join her and the rest of Sammy's party. May consented to go, but at the last moment, her mother felt too tired to attend, so she invited a friend, film producer George Englund.

During the evening, Sammy danced with Luna and Dinah Washington, but he remained focused on Britt. He wanted to dance with her but was afraid to ask. For one thing, he didn't know what Englund's presence meant. Later, he invited May, and her date, to join him and his friends for a nightcap at the Playhouse, the name he'd given the poolhouse–guest house–movie screening room at his house, but she declined.

Clearly, the evening hadn't gone as Sammy had planned. What he didn't know was that May was not as oblivious to his presence as she appeared. In fact, she was pleased by his pursuit. As she told this author, "I became interested in him the minute I met him, I think. You see, when Sammy put on his charm, there was nobody as charming in the world."

Unaware of May's interest but determined to persevere nonetheless, Sammy phoned her a few days later. "I'm having some friends up to the house tonight," he said, "running a few movies—would you like to come by?" She said she was sorry but she had dinner plans. "Well, how about after dinner?" he pressed. She told him to give her his number and she'd phone when she was through eating. By midnight, she still hadn't called. Then, finally, the phone rang and she said, "Hello there. I'm coming over now. Will that be all right?" He told her that was fine.

Fifteen minutes later, she arrived—alone. Although she wasn't much of a drinker, she agreed to try some orange brandy because she liked oranges. Enjoying the taste, she agreed to another. Instead of loosening her up, the liquor made her sick. Noticing her pallor, which was even paler than usual, Sammy offered to drive her home. When they arrived at her door, he shook her hand and said rather formally, "Thank you very much for coming tonight. I hope you feel better." Then he told her he was going to Las Vegas in a couple of days and asked if he could call her from Nevada. "I'd like that very much," she replied. The moonlight shone down on her, making him feel weak. As he put it, "I felt a shimmering glow within me like nothing I'd ever experienced, as though by looking at her I'd become transfused with her warmth and serenity. The moment was something apart from all moments through all the years of my life."

Much as Sammy wanted to stay in Los Angeles and see what developed with May, he had to be in Vegas. He wasn't going for pleasure. He, Frank, and some other guys—a group they were calling the Rat Pack—were going to make a movie together and perform onstage at the same time. It was work, but it also promised to be fun. It turned out to be a gasser!

CHAPTER 12

The Rat Pack

The Rat Pack had its origins in the group that coalesced around Humphrey Bogart and his young wife, Lauren Bacall, at their Holmby Hills home in the early fifties. In addition to Sinatra, its members had included David and Hjordis Niven; Judy Garland and her husband, Sid Luft; restaurateur Mike Romanoff; agent Swifty Lazar; writer Nathaniel Benchley; and composer Jimmy Van Heusen. Also on hand from time to time were the likes of director-screenwriter-actor John Huston, writer John O'Hara, cartoonist Charles Addams, singer-writer Kay Thompson, and Sammy. What this merry band had in common, aside from success in their chosen professions, was a marked irreverence for the establishment, a liberal political outlook, and a fondness for spirited conversation, good humor, and booze. As Kay Thompson put it, "We were all terribly young and terribly witty and terribly rich." Although their politics aroused the ire of Hollywood's more conservative set, people such as John Wayne and William Holden, the Holmby Hills Rat Packers were far from hard-core rebels. For the most part, they dressed, talked, and behaved like most other members of the industry.

In the wake of Bogie's death, his widow fell in love with Sinatra, and the two nearly married. Although the relationship disintegrated, Frank fell heir to the Rat Pack tradition. But the group that he headed was decidedly different from the original crowd. The new members enjoyed each other's company, but they didn't spend a great deal of time hanging out together when they were home in L.A. For one thing, several had wives and families that required their attention; others, like Sinatra himself, were single. Also, most of them were entertainers, unlike Bogart's crew, which covered a variety of creative disciplines. Frank and his pals were constantly taking off for various parts of the world, so the occasions when they were all at home at the same time were few and far between. That they were all entertainers is largely what made them a pack. Unlike Bogie's group, which was strictly social, Sinatra's Clan, as the group was also sometimes called, performed together live, in movies, and ultimately on records. It was first and foremost a professional association.

At its center was Frank Sinatra. He was not only the leader and the glue that held the group together, but he was also the living incarnation of the Rat Pack. He defined the guys' swinging style, manner of dress (shiny sharkskin suits, crisp white shirts, thin dark ties), drink of choice (Jack Daniels), and colorful lingo (calling people "Charley," penises "birds," and women "broads," to cite a few examples). He decided where and what the group would do, be it a film, a TV special, a joint recording venture, or a personal appearance. And, of course, he determined who was in the Pack in the first place.

His right-hand man was Dean Martin. Although many observers predicted Martin's demise in the wake of his celebrated breakup with Jerry Lewis in 1956, the singer had, in fact, become more popular than ever. Not only did his records sell well, thanks to a laid-back, syrupy style that made even Crosby sound energetic, but Martin was on his way to a solid solo career in motion pictures, as per his work in *The Young Lions, Rio Bravo, Some Came Running,* and *Bells Are Ringing.*

It was, in fact, while Martin was making *Some Came Running* in 1958 that his friendship with Sinatra, the top-billed star of the picture, blossomed. The two crooners had known each other for years, of course, but being together for two months on location in Madison, Indiana, population 10,500, took their relationship to a new level. They even rented a house together while the rest of the company stayed in a hotel. There, they played host to other members of Frank's inner circle, notably songwriter Jimmy Van Heusen, Sam Giancana, and their costar Shirley MacLaine. They enjoyed playing poker, drinking, smoking, and telling jokes, and, when that got boring, Frank, Dean, and Shirley took off for the gaming parlors in Cincinnati.

Sinatra and Martin discovered they had much in common. They were both from blue-collar Italian families. Frank hailed from Hoboken, New Jersey; Dean (born Dino Crocetti) came from Steubenville, Ohio. They also shared similar tastes in clothes, booze, music, and, to a certain extent, people. And, as singers on the cabaret circuit, they had a wealth of common experiences and acquaintances. But where Frank, the elder by about a year and a half, was intense, easy to anger, and needed to be surrounded by people, Dean was friendly but not too friendly and kept his feelings to himself. Shirley MacLaine described him as a *menefreghista,* Italian for, in her words, "one who does not give a fuck," and the description was apt. Although he'd earned a reputation as a womanizer and a boozer, Dean, at least by the early sixties, was perfectly content to play golf during the day and watch cowboy shows on TV at night. He even considered Frank's Rat Pack idea so much bullshit. But, if it pleased his pal, what the hell, he'd play along. Frank admired Dean's aloofness. Here was someone who went his own way, someone he couldn't push around. Moreover, Dean was taller than Frank, better looking than Frank (thanks, in part, to a splendid nose job), and funnier than Frank.

By the time the Clan gathered in Vegas in January 1960, Sinatra's life was bound to Martin's in ways apart from those of his other pals, including Davis. Frank had already joined Dean on stage at several of the latter's nightclub appearances. They both had points in the Sands. They were directors of Hancock Raceways in Massachusetts, thanks to a joint stock purchase. And they were both under contract to Capitol Records. In 1959, Sinatra even conducted the orchestra for one of Dean's albums, *Sleep Warm*.

Frank genuinely enjoyed Dean's company, but he was less enamored of another Rat Packer, Peter Lawford. The singer had met the handsome British actor in the late 1940s, when they were both under contract to MGM. Over the ensuing years, they shared an occasional evening out, bar-hopping or playing cards with other members of the Hollywood set. They also costarred in the 1947 film *It Happened in Brooklyn*.

Unlike Dean and Frank, Sinatra and Lawford came from radically different milieus. Peter, some eight years younger, was born in London, the son of a knighted World War I general who fell in love with the future star's mother while each of them was married to someone else. Because of the scandal, the senior Lawfords moved to France, where Peter spent his early years. Educated in private schools, he became a child movie actor, first in Britain and then in the United States. His big break came during the war years. Unable to serve in the military because of a childhood injury, he was suddenly a hot property, and MGM snapped him up. For several years he enjoyed success at the box office, but his urbane charm ran counter to the earthy realism of pictures in the postwar years, prompting MGM to release him in 1952. Drifting into TV, Lawford starred in a couple of series, including one based on MGM's own *Thin Man*, but by the end of the fifties, his career was in the doldrums.

His relationship with Sinatra went through an extremely rocky patch as well. In 1953, Louella Parsons told her readers that Peter had been out on the town with Frank's ex, Ava Gardner. Even though Lawford protested his innocence, the singer would have nothing to do with him for five full years. Then, in August 1958, mutual friends Gary and Rocky Cooper staged a dinner party to bring the two back together. By then, Peter had married Patricia Kennedy, a member of the glittering, fabulously wealthy family headed by former U.S. Ambassador to the Court of St. James Joseph P. Kennedy. A week after the party at the Coopers, Pat Lawford invited Sinatra to dinner, after which Peter was back in the crooner's good graces. But the alliance remained awkward. Sinatra tolerated Lawford; he was even willing to toss him the occasional career bone. But mostly he considered the actor a useful conduit to his more appealing brother-in-law, the junior U.S. senator from Massachusetts, Jack Kennedy.

Perhaps the least likely member of Frank's Pack was a tall, thin, dour-faced Jewish comedian from Philadelphia named Joey Bishop, three years Sinatra's junior. The singer caught Bishop's act at the Latin Quarter in the early fifties, liked what he saw, and arranged for the comedian to open for him when he appeared at Bill Miller's Riviera in 1952. The friendship developed from there.

Bishop's humor was dry, inoffensive, and designed to appeal to a broad base. But he *was* funny and a terrific ad-libber. Once, when he was appearing at the Copa in New York, Marilyn Monroe arrived late. All eyes shifted to the blonde bombshell, leaving Bishop to figure out how to regain his audience's attention. Without missing a beat, he turned to Monroe and said, "Honey, didn't I tell you to wait in the truck?" He was witty offstage as well. As Sinatra put it, "The guy's always good for a laugh, fun to be with. Somebody who can bring you up if you need it. He never fails me on that score." Like Dean Martin, Joey was not a late-night carouser. For one thing, he drank very little; for another, he wasn't interested in cheating on his wife. But that was okay with Frank. Bishop was the court jester. He wasn't a babe magnet like Dino.

Besides, Sinatra had plenty of other people with whom he could hang out after hours, ex-officio Rat Packers like Sammy Cahn, Jimmy Van Housen, Robert Wagner and his wife, Natalie Wood, and Tony Curtis and Janet Leigh. The latter couple was also close to Sammy, as well as to Dean and Jeannie Martin.

And then there was Sammy. He was ready to party whenever Frank beckoned. Like Peter, he'd do whatever the leader asked. Like Joey, he was good fun and affable. And like Dean, he knew his way around a nightclub stage. Even Sinatra had to respect Davis' talent, for Sammy could do things—tap dance, play musical instruments, render impeccable imitations—that none of the others could hope to tackle, while singing and clowning with the best of them as well.

But, of course, Sammy was short, had one eye, was Jewish and black. Sinatra, as well as the others, never let him forget those differences. There were constant references to his unique qualities. Even his nickname, "Smokey," called attention to his race—not, as some would have it, to his penchant for cigarettes (after all, Frank, Dean, and Peter smoked, too). As if this appellation weren't enough, when the fellows got together in the early evening at the Sands' steam room, they donned robes bearing their names, which rested on pegs on a wall. All the robes were white, except for Sammy's. His was black.

This, then, was Sinatra's group—as they might put it, two dago singers, a Limey swell, a kike comic, and a short, colored, multifaceted entertainer. Together, they would take Vegas by storm, and the town would never be quite the same again.

But it was a movie that brought the quintet together in the first place. *Ocean's Eleven* had its origins in real life. During World War II, a group of GIs stationed in Germany had gotten their hands on some valuable radio equipment, dismantled it, and transported it out of the country bit by bit. The film story by George Clayton Johnson and Jack Golden Russell turned the GIs into former commandos, now struggling civilians. Instead of smuggling Nazi radio parts, they would steal millions of dollars from five of the Vegas Strip's biggest hotel-casinos.

For years, a B-film director named Gilbert Kay had peddled the idea without success, hoping to direct the project himself, with perhaps William Holden as the leader of the gang. Finally, in 1958, Kay sold the project for $5,000 to Lawford. He, in turn, took it to Sinatra, as Frank had a multipicture deal with Warner Bros. through his company, Dorchester Productions. When Jack Warner heard the plot, he reportedly quipped, "Let's forget the picture and pull the job." Nevertheless, he gave Sinatra permission to press ahead. Frank, in turn, promised Peter a starring role in the picture as well as a back-end percentage of the profits.

The screenplay went through several hands before it wound up with Harry Brown and Charles Lederer, the only writers to receive credit for the result. By the time they finished, what had started as a traditional caper film, emphasizing the gang's detailed planning sessions and the heist itself, had become something much milder, more like a buddy picture long before Hollywood had a name for such a genre. There were an unusual number of jokes, a couple of songs, and several scenes with various gang members simply hanging around chatting. The caper itself, coming well in the second half of the film, would consume only a few minutes of screen time.

But Sinatra wasn't interested in making a substantial crime drama, or any other kind of drama, for that matter. As he told Sammy, "The idea is to hang out together, find fun with the broads, and have a great time. We gotta make pictures that people enjoy. Entertainment, period. We gotta have laughs." In this he was so successful that a friend of Lawford's dubbed the film "a ten-million dollar home movie." In fact, it cost only around $2.2 million, but the point was well taken.

Aside from its light tone, *Ocean's Eleven* was tailored to fit the personas of the Rat Pack members in the cast: Frank as Danny Ocean, the outfit's ring-a-ding leader; Dean, his laid-back lieutenant, Sam Herman, the most independent member of the group; and Peter as Jimmy Foster, suave, always in need of money, and not too well liked by some of his colleagues, notably Martin (who wasn't particularly fond of Lawford in real life).

Beyond Frank, Dean, and Peter, the script's best developed parts went to Cesar Romero as a slick mobster engaged to Jimmy Foster's mother; Akim Tamiroff as the hypertense financier of the caper and the frequent butt of Danny Ocean's jokes; and Richard Conte as the gang's electrician, a devoted single dad dying of cancer. The roles of other, less colorful gang members were parceled out to such Sinatra cronies as Henry Silva and Buddy Lester, and even Shirley MacLaine was on hand for a cameo as a drunken New Year's Eve reveler. For Danny's estranged wife, Sammy recommended sultry Angie Dickinson, and Frank liked the idea.

In contrast to the roles of their fellow Rat Packers, Sammy's Josh Howard and Joey's Mushy O'Connor were rather inconsequential and poorly developed. In Sammy's case, the part was that of a lowly garbage collector. While his friends dashed about in well-tailored slacks, sport coats, and brightly colored cashmere sweaters, Davis spent much of the picture in a green one-piece jumpsuit with a white turtleneck, albeit clean and neatly pressed. Some have argued that Josh's profession was Sinatra's final payback for Sammy's ill-considered remarks about him on *The Jack Eigen Show*.

But Sammy's role had its compensations. He was given one of the two songs written for the picture by Cahn and Van Heusen ("Ee-O-Eleven"), although he had to perform it in a parking lot surrounded by his fellow sanitation workers, while Dean sang the other song, "Ain't That a Kick in the Head," on a nightclub stage with several adoring beauties looking on. Moreover, Sammy's salary was a hefty $125,000 and he was third-billed above the title—ahead of Peter—while Joey was buried in the credits among the supporting cast. For these reasons, as well as his friendship with Sinatra, Sammy threw in with Frank and the Pack rather than with John Wayne, who offered him the role of a heroic slave in his production, *The Alamo*, filming concurrently in Texas. As the entertainer later put it, "I saw my movie breakthrough coming with the Clan pictures rather than playing a small part in a very big Wayne film."

Filming began on January 26, 1961 at the Riviera, one of the five operations targeted by Ocean's mob. During the twenty-four days of location work, the company would also shoot at the Desert Inn, the Flamingo, the Sahara, and, of course, the Sands. As this was the first major feature to be shot in Vegas, businessmen "broke their backs to co-operate," reported Colin McKinlay, the local correspondent for the *Los Angeles Mirror*, "and the production crews from Warner Bros. were wined and dined during the filming."

When the supporting players were on call, they observed a normal shooting schedule. The day typically began with makeup at around 6:30 or 7:00 A.M., and the first set-up was called at about 8:00. The Rat Packers mostly worked in the afternoons and for brief periods of time, typically about three hours a day each. Their favorite window was between 3:00 and 6:00 P.M., after which they took a steam and got ready for their evening shows at the Sands. The entire quintet showed up for filming only once during the three and a half weeks in Vegas.

But when the Rat Packers worked, they worked quickly. Sinatra was famous for doing only one take, fearing that he'd lose his freshness and spontaneity if forced to repeat the same lines over and over. Dean and Sammy shared his feelings. All three refused to endure the usual movie set routine of hurry up and wait. The crew was on notice to ready set-ups on time and without error. The guys weren't even too keen to learn their lines. Every location was littered with cue cards.

They even took time away from their own project to fit in cameos for another film. George Sidney's rambling, unfunny comedy, *Pepe,* starring the Mexican actor Cantinflas, Dan Dailey, and Shirley Jones, was set partly in Vegas. Like Mike Todd's Oscar-winning *Around the World in 80 Days, Pepe* was replete with cameos—thirty-five in all, including the Rat Packers and two other members of the *Ocean's Eleven* cast, Richard Conte and Cesar Romero.

The task of maintaining order under such trying circumstances fell to the director of *Ocean's Eleven,* Lewis Milestone. Fortunately, Milly, as he was called, had been making movies for decades. His credits included several notable war pictures, among them *All's Quiet on the Western Front,* for which he won an Oscar. Having started in the business as an editor, he could more or less cut a film in his head while shooting. He also story-boarded every shot, so he and his crew knew precisely what each set-up entailed before they got to it. E. B. Radcliffe of the *Cincinnati Enquirer* visited the set and reported, "I've never seen so much work done under such difficulties with so little fuss and furor." In Joey Bishop's opinion, "It would have taken a great director to have been able to take this gang of people and get a good picture out of them. He had to be as *little* a director as possible and still get his points across when the time came."

While Milestone remained relatively philosophical about the way principal photography unfolded, other members of the company were sometimes irked. "Ah, that movie!" recalled Akim Tamiroff. "I waited and waited and waited for them to show up to do one little scene and Milestone keeps telling me, 'Be patient, be patient, they're coming, they're coming.' I said, 'When will we shoot the scene, at two in the morning?' When they finally show up it's more like a party than a film set. I've never worked like that." Angie Dickinson added that "you'd have to look hard to find a camera to prove to you that they weren't playing. They really had fun together." Even Tamiroff, frustrated though he was, had to admit that making the movie was sort of a kick.

But the real laughs came at night. That's when the boys hit the Copa Room stage.

It was Frank's idea—naturally—that he, Dean, Sammy, Peter, and Joey perform live at the Sands while making the picture. He even came up with the name for the event. After reading in the papers about a conclave involving the Western world's most important heads of state—Eisenhower (U.S.), Khrushchev (U.S.S.R.), MacMillan (Great Britain), and de Gaulle (France)—he joked, "We'll have our own little Summit meeting."

"Within a week after our 'Summit' was announced," Sammy recalled, "there wasn't a room to be had in any hotel in town. People flew in from Chicago, Los Angeles, New York—from all over the country—weeks before we got there, to be sure their rooms weren't sold out from under them. We'd been in Vegas for a week, and still plane, train, and busloads of people were pouring into town, arriving without hotel reservations, sleeping in lobbies, cars, anywhere, hoping to get rooms. All of Vegas was affected by it, but The Sands was the hub and you could hardly push your way through the lobby and casino. Hundreds of people crowded the entrance to the Copa Room, fighting for tables with money, connections, or both." Countless members of the Hollywood set made the trek to the desert, from Milton Berle and Jack Benny to Kirk Douglas and Lucille Ball.

Of course, Sammy, Frank, and Dean were big individual draws in Vegas, so the idea of seeing all three together, plus Joey Bishop and Peter Lawford, made for a special event indeed. It was a classic case of the right performers being in exactly the right place at exactly the right time. To understand this phenomenon, one must remember that the early sixties represented the final gasp of a world before teens and twenty-somethings replaced middle-aged adults as the arbiters of popular taste.

No place reflected adult fun better than the Vegas Strip, a sea of bright lights and flashing neon that had grown to proportions unimaginable even when the Will Mastin Trio first played there in 1947. New York and San Francisco were culturally richer; Chicago and Los Angeles were bigger, with more to offer. But Las Vegas represented a single idea: nightlife—food, booze, entertainment, and, above all, gambling. Gambling was what made all the rest of it possible. The rooms were inexpensive; so were the shows (a seat for the Summit cost $5.95, including dinner!). Hotels offered buffets groaning with food at ridiculously low prices, sometimes even for free. Why? To entice people to drop their money at a game of chance. The more you lost, the better you were treated.

Many other popular singers performed in Nevada, of course. People loved Tony Bennett, Mel Torme, Nat King Cole, Perry Como, and Bing Crosby. But these guys were simply vocalists. With Frank, Dean, and Sammy, on the other hand, the voice was part of a larger package, an image, an entire way of life. These guys were hip. They were cool. They were talented and rich, but they came from the streets, so they were a little rough around the edges. They knew their way around booze and broads. And they were outrageous, perhaps even a little dangerous—with even more dangerous friends. Alone, each was potent enough. Together, they were like some exotic club for gifted bad boys. Every guy wished he could join and every woman wanted to know its members a whole lot better. That they looked down on the "clydes" and the "dullsville" places many of them came from just made them that much more appealing.

There was no guarantee that all five Rat Packers would be on hand for every show. Sinatra promised Jack Entratter one of the quintet for each set, with the others joining in if they felt like it. But, although occasionally someone stayed away, most of the time audiences got the full Pack. The guys were having so much fun grooving with each other and the audience, they just naturally gravitated toward the Copa Room each evening.

Joey Bishop was the emcee, the ringmaster. Typically, he'd start by introducing one of the three singers, who'd render a number or two. Then the others would drift on, and the mayhem, some of it scripted, some ad lib, would begin. Early into the set, a couple of the guys, usually Frank and Dean, would wheel on a cart filled with glasses and bottles of booze, prompting Joey Bishop to quip, "Here they are, Haig and Vague." Dean, who'd perfected the art of appearing drunk while cold sober, would usually look around with a dazed expression and ask, "How did all these people get in my room?" He also liked to render a few lines of "When You're Smiling," but with a twist in the lyrics: "When you're drinking/When you're drinking/The whole world drinks with you." At some point, Sammy could be counted on to add, "You can get swacked just watching this show." The high point of the set was when all three singers came together to sing "The Lady Is a Tramp" or "The Oldest Established Permanent Floating Crap Game" or Sammy's signature song, "The Birth of the Blues." Rarely, however, did they manage to finish a number without cracking up or cracking wise.

Being a perfectionist, Davis was the most determined to give audiences at least a few numbers, and perhaps even a tap dance, without the usual hijinx, but doing so wasn't easy. A microphone was set up backstage, so fellows taking a break could make derogatory remarks while the other guys were performing. They took full advantage of this, particularly Dean. In addition, everybody wandered on and off the stage at will. One time, while Martin was singing, Sammy, Peter, and Joey strolled behind him wearing tuxedo jackets and boxer shorts—with their pants folded over their arms. The bit had no point whatsoever, but it drew a huge laugh.

Of course, they all teased one another, and naturally, many of the jokes played off the Rat Packers' ethnicities. There were Jewish jokes and Italian jokes. In keeping with the latter, Joey liked to say to Frank, "Stop singing and tell the people about all the good work the Mafia is doing." But Sammy was the brunt of most of the ethnic humor. "Hurry up, Sam, the watermelon's getting warm" was a typical retort, as was, "Smile, Sam, so the folks can see you." Once, when Sammy managed to get through a particularly swinging number, Dean said over the backstage mike, "I don't care what anybody says, anybody who sings that good has got to be colored." Moreover, in virtually every show, Dean would pick Sammy up, turn to the audience, and say, "I'd like to thank the NAACP for this award." It always got a huge laugh.*

Sometimes, Davis managed to get a bit of his own back. Once, Bishop said to him when he arrived onstage, "Okay, Sam, you're free now to do anything you like." "What do you mean, I'm free?" Sammy replied, bristling boldly. "All of a sudden, *you're* gonna do it? Lincoln freed me." Then Bishop chimed in with, "Moses freed us, you idiot." A standard part of the repertoire featured Sammy and Peter doing a soft-shoe to the tune of "Shall We Dance." As a lead-in, Peter would suggest they do a number together, as if it had just occurred to him, prompting Sammy to say, "Are you serious? Do you really want to dance with me—one of the great Jewish Mau-Mau dancers of all time?" "Sure, Sam," Lawford would reply, "I'm not prejudiced. I'll dance with you." Sammy would retort, laughing, "I know your kind. You'll dance with me, but you won't go to school with me." As something of a variation on this bit, Sammy

---

*Joey Bishop, who claimed credit for writing that bit, said it was originally supposed to be "I want to thank the B'nai B'rith for this award," a reference to Sammy's conversion to Judaism. "But," said Bishop, "Dean couldn't remember the words B'nai B'rith. He blew it every night until he finally changed it to NAACP" (Taraborrelli/B).

might drape his hand on Dean's shoulder, prompting the latter to state emphatically, 'I'll dance wit ya, I'll sing wit ya, I'll swim wit ya, I'll cut the lawn wit ya, I'll go to bar mitzvahs wit ya. But don't touch me."

Of the racial jokes, Sammy said in 1963, "We do it because we can do it—for a point; to show the public that there's nothing we can't do on the stage. There's no star system with us." To which Frank's daughter Tina added years later, "It was always clear to me that the Summit's ethnic humor—however incorrect by today's standards—was meant to poke fun at bigotry, not endorse it. In real life, Dad was offended by racial jokes and epithets, and wouldn't stand for anyone using them in his presence." There is no question that Sinatra did much to support the cause of civil rights in the United States. Some have even argued that Sammy's presence as a charter member of the Rat Pack was itself a statement about racial equality, and there is validity to this assertion, for he *was* standing toe to toe on the same stage and in the same films with the likes of Sinatra and Martin. But, even in the context of the early sixties, the racial quips were often crude and hurtful. Later, Sammy acknowledged this, saying, "For the times, yeah, the jokes were offensive. But, man, look at the company I was keeping. I had to put up with it. I loved those guys, and I knew they loved me. But, yeah, it wasn't right. I didn't like it a lot of the time. Sometimes I had to wonder, Are these cats for real or what? I had to bite my tongue a lot."

The Copa Room was a swinging place that winter. George Schlatter compared being in the audience to "watching some beautiful children in a very elegant playpen. It was a romp." Shirley MacLaine noted that the shows were filled with "an energy there that has never been duplicated since," and Milton Berle dubbed the Rat Pack "the greatest comedy act in history."

For the boys, showtime was only the start of the merriment. After the final set, they were too keyed up to sleep, so they'd move out into the casino to do a bit of gambling. Occasionally, Frank or Dean would take over for one of the dealers. The gamblers loved that. No one lost when Sinatra or Martin held the cards. Sometimes, they'd repair to an upstairs suite and party with some of the showgirls. One of them, Betty Rose Lehman, recalled, "Sammy was the one who really recruited girls for the Rat Pack. He would have someone in his organization call up all of the hotels and say, 'Send me your best showgirls. The fellas are lookin' for some fun.' All of us girls from all the hotels, would all go to the Sands and wait in a private lounge for the guys to get offstage. They always had terrific food and lots of booze. Then, when they were ready, we would go off with them—three with Dean, three with Sammy, and so on. Frank sometimes ended up with four or five."

Despite the nightly partying, Sammy managed to take at least a weekend off to be with May Britt, whom he invited to be his guest at the Sands. To his surprise, she brought her mother with her. Naturally, on her first night in town, she and Mrs. Wilkens came to see the show. Sammy, not wanting grief from the press, let it be known that she was Sinatra's guest—with Frank's blessing, of course. He had the following day free, so he escorted May and her mother around town. That evening, she dined in her room, then caught the boys' second show, this time alone. When she joined Sammy in the dressing room afterward, he finally got up the nerve to kiss her. As she was taller than he, he asked her to remove her shoes, and she laughingly complied. By now, May was definitely smitten. "I thought he was a very kind person," she said. "He was a very generous person, he was a very thoughtful person. When I say generous, I don't mean presents. I mean generous in his mind. And very intelligent. And I thought he was very, very handsome."

For Sammy, May's visit was wonderful, an important milestone in their relationship. But for the Rat Pack as a whole, the high point of the Vegas adventure came on February 7, when John F. Kennedy showed up. Only weeks earlier, the Massachusetts senator had formally announced his candidacy for his party's nomination for president, and he was in town ostensibly lining up votes from Nevada's Democrats.

Sinatra, in particular, was taken with Kennedy. He admired the senator's vigor, good looks, charm, and dynamism as a public speaker. At the time a supporter of liberal Democrats, Frank wanted to do all he could to ensure Kennedy's nomination and election. And he liked the guy. Kennedy was as interested in broads and partying as he was. Accordingly, after the show, Frank invited JFK to join him and his pals upstairs. According to several subsequent accounts, it was at this post-show bash that Sinatra introduced Kennedy to Judith Campbell, a twenty-five-year-old beauty whom the crooner had briefly dated himself. This would mark the start of a two-year affair between the future president and the brunette party girl, who was simultaneously seeing Frank's other good friend, Sam Giancana.

When Kennedy left for Oregon the next day, he took with him more than the sweet memory of Judy Campbell. His brother-in-law, Peter Lawford, told Sammy that the Vegas hotel operators had contributed $1 million—in cash—to the senator's campaign.

A week later, on February 16, the curtain rang down on the Summit. It had been a blast and highly profitable for all concerned. But it was time to return to the real world. For one thing, the guys still had a movie to finish.

CHAPTER 13

May

Work on *Ocean's Eleven* resumed on February 18 at the Warner Bros. studio in Burbank, but the Rat Packers hardly settled into a humdrum routine, even with Jack Warner and his minions on hand to monitor their progress. They were continually pulling gags on the set: throwing cherry bombs, squirting each other with seltzer bottles, engaging in water pistol duels, with Sinatra's one-take edict remaining in force. Even the sound of planes flying overhead failed to change the crooner's outlook. In addition, he disappeared for a few days to cut a record album, Dean took off for a solo gig at the Sands, and Peter flew to Israel for a role in Otto Preminger's *Exodus*.

Sammy spent most of his off-hours with May Britt. When he got a ten-day hiatus from filming, he rented a yacht, and the two cruised to Mexico, along with a few of Sammy's close friends, including Arthur Silber, Jr., and George Rhodes and their wives. The trip ended with Davis and Britt deeply in love.

On March 18, when *Ocean's Eleven* wrapped, the Rat Pack's fun continued. Davis and the gang immediately flew to Miami to join Frank for a mini-Summit during his gig at the Fountainebleu. Because Sammy was under contract to the Eden Roc, Sinatra cleared his friend's appearance by agreeing to dine there—and to bring his buddies. The Eden Roc was content with the resultant publicity.

The stage shows were a ball, but the guys—sans Dean, who had to return to L.A.—were really in Florida to shoot a one-hour Frank Sinatra special for television designed to capitalize on Elvis Presley's return from the army. Putting Presley, the current teen idol, together with Sinatra, the teen idol of the forties, seemed a curious business, particularly as Frank hated rock and roll, but the combination worked. When the show aired on May 12, it drew the highest ratings of any Sinatra special to that point. Presley was on only briefly, however. The rest of the time, Frank kibitzed with Joey and joined Sammy for a medley of recent pop hits.

Davis and Lawford also re-created their "Shall We Dance" number from the Summit.

By the time Sammy returned home, May had gone to New York to film scenes for her latest picture, *Murder, Incorporated*. Hoping to avoid the intense press scrutiny that had plagued his affairs with Kim Novak and Joan Stuart (to whom he was still technically engaged), Sammy adopted a code name when phoning May at her hotel. Because they both liked Charles Schulz's comic strip, *Peanuts,* he chose "Charlie Brown." With Britt's Swedish accent, it became "Sharlie Brown," her pet name for him thereafter.

By this point, Sammy was once again thinking seriously of marriage, but he didn't know how May would feel about having a black husband, particularly as her acting career might suffer from such a union. Still, he missed her terribly while she was away. Consequently, one night when they were talking on the phone, he said wistfully, "Wouldn't it be great to be married?" He hadn't planned on saying it; it just popped out. Fearing her reaction, he quickly added, "Listen, at these prices on the phone two could live cheaper than one." But she picked up on the sincerity behind the banter and indicated that the idea of marriage had its charms. Stunned, Sammy quickly broke off the conversation so that he could gather his thoughts. Had she been serious? he wondered. Could someone as beautiful, sweet, and talented actually be interested in someone like him?

After about an hour, he called her back. He started on a light note, then eased back into the subject weighing on his mind. Again, May's responses were all up, all positive. Clearly, she had no concerns about an interracial relationship. Having grown up in Scandinavia, a region free of racial prejudice, she considered all people basically the same. Though she no doubt had some awareness of the civil rights movement in the United States, it was probably fragmentary, as was her understanding of its root causes. That people might hate her for marrying a Negro was not something she could imagine. Nor could she conceive that such a marriage might jeopardize her career.

But knowing would have made little difference. Britt was a woman of substance, with a strong character, not the kind to let the opinions of others, threats to her stardom, or even the risk of physical injury sway her from her chosen path.

Given the gravity of the conversation, Sammy decided to fly to New York to talk things over with May in person. By the time his plane landed, an energetic reporter for the *New York Journal American* had learned that the actress and the entertainer were an item. On April 17, the story broke in the press. May was blithely unconcerned, but Sammy, having been down this road before, expressed caution. As her divorce from Ed Gregson wouldn't be final until September, he felt that they should maintain a low profile, perhaps not even see one another, until fall. May found that idea totally unacceptable. She was in love. She knew that Sammy loved her. And she was convinced that together, as husband and wife, they could meet whatever problems might arise. For the moment, Sammy allowed himself to be swayed by her optimism and to revel in his newfound love.

By the end of April, Davis was in Chicago for a three-week stint at the Chez Paree. May, having finished work on *Murder, Incorporated,* joined him there. By now they were no longer attempting to hide from the public. Thus, the *Chicago Defender* ran a front-page article about the duo on April 30 under the headline "Is Sammy Falling for Swedish Lass?" In mid-June, May, then on a promotional tour for Fox, admitted to a black Detroit paper, the *Defender,* "I love Sammy Davis, Jr., very deeply and completely." Asked if she would marry him, she said, "It depends on Sammy's decision," but she asked back, "If I love a man, don't you think I'd marry him?"

While May wrestled with the press on her tour, Sammy was in London, where on May 7 he had opened a twenty-five-day, forty-seven-show engagement at the Club Pigalle. He was understandably nervous about performing in the British capital for the first time. After his opening night, *Variety* reported, "He was clearly feeling his way and getting to sense the type of audience he was due to face," but added, "He shows tremendous versatility and so obviously enjoys entertaining that the feeling of delight is swiftly communicated to the audience."

A week later, Sammy was on the bill for a Command Performance. He likened the charitable gala to "a gigantic Ed Sullivan show, with the biggest stars of two continents." He was given nine minutes in the spot next to closing. Pianist Liberace would follow him with a single song.

Performing under such rarified circumstances, with the Queen herself in attendance, is intimidating, no matter how experienced the performer. In his dressing room before the show, Sammy calmed his nerves by imbibing scotch—not his normal beverage of choice—with Nat King Cole, who would close the gala's first half. The liquor didn't do much good. "I ain't *never* been this scared before!" Davis told Cole. Seeing his distress, Nat generously assured him that the audience was waiting for him, eager to be knocked out by his vitality and talent. Thus encouraged, Sammy delivered one of the best performances of his career. Such was the furor in the house that he was called back to the stage for several extra bows, a virtually unprecedented accolade at a Command Performance.

Sammy had a blast in London. Staying at the Mayfair Hotel, one of the world's great hostelries, was itself a thrill, and he spent money lavishly. He also visited the notorious Tower of London and the Hammer Film Studio, where his favorite horror pictures were made. Hammer's two principal stars, Peter Cushing and Christopher Lee, became great pals. Perhaps best, all the Brits he encountered seemed oblivious to his race. As a result, he was able, for the first time since his youth, to go anywhere he liked without feeling self-conscious about being a Negro. Such was his feeling of liberation that he considered settling permanently in England; the greater career options back home were all that precluded his move. Although his future lay in the States, he nevertheless became a tremendous Anglophile. As his friend, British songwriter Leslie Bricusse put it, "Sammy became more English than any Englishman you've ever met. He really did. He wanted to be David Niven and Ronald Coleman and Rex Harrison all rolled up into one." As proof, he took to sporting a bowler hat and a rolled umbrella and talking like an Oxford don.

Although London was a kick, Sammy still missed May. Finally, her promotional tour ended and she joined him. She also arranged for her father to fly in from Sweden so that he and Sammy could meet. Naturally, the entertainer worried about Hugo Wilkens' reaction to their wedding plans, but Wilkens assured him that he and his wife would be proud to have Sammy for a son-in-law. He added that he knew about America's racial conflicts but felt that if two people loved each other enough, they would be fine.

Encouraged, Sammy announced their engagement at a press conference on June 6, 1960. He acknowledged the difficulties that no doubt lay ahead, but he added, "I can't let a lot of people living in glass houses to deprive me of my right to a full life and pleasure with the woman I love."

By now, May clearly understood what she was facing in marrying an African American. Before announcing the engagement, Sammy sat down with her for a serious talk. Thus, she told the press, "It is possible we may happen to find hotels where we are not allowed to stay as husband and wife. There may be some states in America where we will not be received in the families. There may be public places where we will be obliged to part due to the different colors of our skins. Well, let it be so. We will avoid staying at these hotels and places, and not visiting these 'friends' will not be a great sacrifice to either of us."

The American press played the story to the hilt. A friend of May's told *Motion Picture* magazine that Britt was the kind of woman who needed "to lift her marriage above the ordinary, to give it a great purpose, a deep meaning, a kind of brave significance." Meanwhile, one of Davis' so-called pals reiterated the old Sammy's-only-interested-in-white-women theme, asserting that the entertainer's entire "life has been on the search for the white goddess who will relieve him of the torment he suffers as a Negro. Sammy will deny it, but I believe that it was always his intention, a dream so vital to him, that he would die without it."

True, he had been involved with Kim Novak and Joan Stuart, but he had also married Loray White, proposed to Eartha Kitt and Cordie King, and dated several other black women. Davis himself said a few months after his union with May, "I'm not trying to prove anything and I'm not trying to deny what I am, for I need only look in the mirror to know this."

African Americans were divided on the issue of Sammy's impending nuptials. In an article devoted to the subject on June 25, the *Pittsburgh Courier* quoted a reader from Brooklyn, who wanted to know, "Why doesn't he stay in his own race?" and another from Atlanta, who asserted, "It seems that all of our most eligible Negro men run to white women as soon as they get to the top." But a Philadelphia woman stated, "So what if he does marry a white woman? . . . After all, isn't ours a fight for integration? If we can't accept an interracial marriage, we certainly are not ready for all the benefits of being accepted as first-class citizens."

Gordon White, the author of the *Motion Picture* story, predicted that Sammy and May were "about to become the most controversial husband and wife in the history of Hollywood. Already, their plans to marry have aroused the sympathy, rage, understanding, respect and contempt of a world half-startled by their courage, half-dismayed at their madness. Is their love the ultimate folly? Can their relationship ever be accepted— or will the world punish them with social banishment?"

Twentieth Century Fox, for one, wasn't going to wait around to find out. May's employer announced on June 21 that the actress' option would not be renewed when her contract expired in 1961. The studio cited the poor reception accorded *The Blue Angel* and the fact that May had turned down several projects. But no one was fooled. Britt was furious. Not because the studio decided to drop her, but because no one from Fox had the courtesy to let her know before informing the press. A couple of days later, Fox's production chief, Buddy Adler, rescinded the announcement, but, when the time came, Fox did, in fact, let May go.

The reaction back home was to be expected, but Sammy was stunned when Sir Oswald Mosley, the leader of the British Fascist Party and the head of a "Keep Britain White" campaign, staged a demonstration outside the Club Pigalle. A group of Mosley's uniformed, swastika-laden followers, about thirty in number, carried banners with slogans like "Go home, Nigger" and "Sammy, Back to the Trees," and called May a "slag," a derogatory term for a white woman who consorts with black men. With tears in his eyes, Sammy called the demonstration "the most savage racial attack I have ever come across."

Mosley's demonstration both infuriated and frightened Sammy. He'd realized before announcing the engagement that May was putting her film career at risk, but for the first time he began to fear for his own future as well. As he later said, "I really expected to lose some of my club dates. I was putting my career on the chopping block. It even occurred to me that I might never work again." He was relieved in the days following the demonstration when thousands of supportive letters and telegrams flooded in from people all over Britain and the lines outside the Club Pigalle grew even longer.

His final night in London came on June 10. He'd enjoyed sell-out performances throughout the run, but on that evening, the Club Pigalle was so crowded that the owners had to put extra tables on the stage. Sammy did two full hours, closing with "We'll Meet Again," which brought him, as well as many in the house, to tears. Indeed, it was a sad farewell. The Brits had embraced Davis as they had no other American entertainer in recent memory, except Danny Kaye, who took the Palladium by storm in 1949. As Leslie Bricusse put it, "We had never seen anybody that brilliant on a nightclub or theater stage ever. He was just phenomenal." If the Brits loved Sammy, he loved them right back. He would return to London many times over the ensuing decades and the city never failed to charm him. But that first engagement would always remain memorable.

The following day, May went off to Sweden and Sammy set out for Brazil, where he performed for two weeks. On June 25, ABC aired a sixty-minute special shot while he was in London. Called *Sammy Davis Jr. Meets the British,* the program featured a bit of location footage but was primarily an extended excerpt of Sammy's act at the Pigalle. The special marked the first time that a major network had given Sammy an hour of airtime.

When the Democrats gathered in Los Angeles for their national nominating convention, Sammy flew home from Boston to attend the opening session on July 11. Closing in on a first-ballot victory, John F. Kennedy had arranged for Sammy, Frank Sinatra, Peter Lawford, Tony Curtis, Janet Leigh, and several other members of his Hollywood contingent to lead the delegates in a rendition of "The Star Spangled Banner." Sammy was particularly delighted to participate, hoping his presence would send a message to those who had seen civil rights protests on TV, acknowledging that blacks were also engaged in the mainstream political process. When he was introduced to the audience, he proudly stepped forward. The applause was loud and strong, but there was also a discernable chorus of boos coming from the Mississippi delegation. Sinatra leaned over and whispered, "Those dirty sons of bitches! Don't let 'em get you, Charley." Sammy tried to heed the advice and concentrate on the national anthem, but, as the familiar lyrics came from his mouth, tears fell from his eyes. Backstage, reporters clustered around him, but he refused to respond to their questions. Although he'd been planning on visiting May before flying back east, he was so humiliated that he proceeded immediately to the airport.

Two days later, Sammy's opening at the Lotus Club in Washington, D.C. occasioned a virulent racist demonstration like the one in London, this time at the hands of George Lincoln Rockwell and the American Nazi Party. Again, there were uniformed protestors, with swastikas on their armbands, bearing placards with sentiments like "What's the Matter, Sammy? Can't You Find a Colored Girl?" and "Go Back to the Congo, You Kosher Coon." In their midst was a small black dog with a sign attached to its back that read, "I'm Black Too, Sammy, But I'm Not a Jew." Again, Sammy was in shock. His only consolation was that May wasn't present to witness the hatred of his fellow Americans.

A much more pleasant experience awaited him when he returned to Las Vegas on August 3. About sixty journalists had been imported for the world premiere of *Ocean's Eleven,* along with a host of celebrities. The evening included a cocktail party for the press and a reprise of the Rat Pack's Summit hijinx in the Copa Room. Finally, around midnight, before a crowd of about ten thousand cheering fans, they entered the Fremont Theater for the screening of the film.

The following week, on August 10, the picture opened at the Capitol Theater in New York. Instead of cheering fans, it encountered lukewarm critics, most of whom considered the picture a major disappointment. They found the lead-up to the heist overly long and tedious, the script riddled with too many "in" jokes, and the stars essentially playing themselves. But they knew they would carry little weight with the public; the picture was a box office smash.

Although the gang would go on to make other films together, *Ocean's Eleven* remains the quintessential Rat Pack movie. The fact that the picture is set in Beverly Hills and Vegas, their milieus, adds to the allure. Moreover, Cahn and Van Heusen's two songs are engaging, and the climax is genuinely funny. If it is hardly a work of art with nowhere near the high-tech suspense of the 2001 remake, *Ocean's Eleven* is nevertheless a pretty picture postcard of a more innocent time and the ring-a-ding crew that embodied this era.

* * *

As summer gave way to fall, Sammy continued on the nightclub circuit. For the first time in a decade he was without Morty Stevens, who had left to become the head of CBS-TV's West Coast music division. For a time, George Rhodes did double duty, conducting the orchestra while continuing to serve as Sammy's pianist. Eventually, he settled in as the entertainer's permanent musical director and principal arranger, holding the baton until his death in 1986.

From Nevada, Sammy returned to Los Angeles, where he shot an episode of the thirty-minute television series *Lawman*. On October 26, shortly after the episode wrapped, Sammy opened a one-man show at L.A.'s Huntington Hartford Theater. Given a legitimate setting, he tried something a little different. During the show's first half, the orchestra was in the pit and he received backing from a group of ten dancers assembled by his friend, Hal Loman. His repertoire included a dramatic rendition of "Ol Man River" from *Show Boat* and "Trouble," the tricky patter song from *The Music Man*, which he pantomimed to the recorded vocal by Robert Preston, the musical's star. During the show's second half, the dancers disappeared, the band was behind Davis on the stage, and his performance took on the trappings of his traditional nightclub fare.

He also found time for several recording sessions during the second half of 1960. The material covered the now familiar range of pop standards, such as "The Lady Is a Tramp," "I Gotta Right to Sing the Blues," "Mountain Greenery," and "Fascinating Rhythm." There were also numerous Broadway show tunes, including several dramatic character songs, "Gesticulate" (*Kismet*) and "Where Is the Life That Late I Led?" (*Kiss Me Kate*), not normally heard on pop LPs. He also recorded a dozen or so Oscar-nominated (but losing) numbers, arranged and conducted by Morty and by Buddy Bregman, for a theme album, *Sammy Awards*. The other material was sufficient for three more LPs: *I Gotta Right to Swing!*, *Mr. Entertainment*, and *Forget-Me-Nots for First Nighters*.

With nearly a dozen solo albums behind him, Davis had matured into a confident and vibrant recording artist. Comparing his work on his later tracks for Decca with his early output for the label, one can hear tremendous growth. Not so schizophrenic as his Capitol disks, the material from 1954 through 1957 still contained hints of a singer with control problems. Where his high notes had a crystalline clarity, his lower baritone register occasionally descended into a distinctive growl. Moreover, he sometimes sang too loudly for a medium that values intimacy, as if he wanted to overwhelm rather than embrace his listeners. And he relied so often on his bag of tricks—bending notes, improvising off the melody, adding words or altering lyrics to personalize the material, and some scatting—that the point of the songs occasionally got lost. By the end of the 1950s, he was much more willing to be an interpretive artist, putting his warm tonal quality and superb sense of rhythm to work in the service of the material. A case in point is the Irving Berlin number "Change Partners" from *Sammy Awards*, which is rendered relatively simply and makes magnificent use of his tenor range.

No doubt, the executives at Decca were pleased with Sammy's development and the maturation of his style. But the 1960 tracks marked the end of his relationship with the label. Not surprisingly, he had elected to sign with Frank Sinatra's new company, Reprise.

Whenever possible that fall, Sammy fit in appearances in support of John Kennedy's run for the presidency against the Republican candidate, Vice President Richard M. Nixon. Indeed, the whole Rat Pack labored vigorously on Jack's behalf, marking the first time that a major group of celebrities lobbied so visibly for one particular presidential candidate. Today the practice is common, but during Hollywood's Golden Age, stars under long-term studio contracts were forbidden by their bosses from engaging in partisan politics, although expressions of patriotism were encouraged, particularly during World War II. By 1960, the studio system was virtually over, but celebrities had yet to realize their power with voters. The Rat Pack served as pioneers in this regard.

Sinatra was, by far, the most committed to the cause (outside of Peter, the candidate's brother-in-law). Dean failed to grasp Kennedy's charms, but occasionally went along out of his friendship with Sinatra. Sammy didn't know JFK very well, but he hoped that the handsome, bright young man would champion the cause of civil rights. Moreover, Sammy liked being part of the Kennedy in-crowd. As he later noted, "There were always groups huddling, planning activities, and it was exciting to be there, everybody knew you and you knew everybody and you were all giving yourselves something in which you deeply believed. It was like belonging to a club."

Accordingly, wherever he performed, he'd check in with the local Kennedy coordinator and arrange drop-bys at rallies and cocktail party fund-raisers. Not surprisingly, his efforts were targeted toward black, Jewish, and Hispanic voters. As these votes were likely to go to JFK anyway, there were some in the campaign hierarchy who would have preferred that Sammy, with the May Britt controversy swirling around him, simply disappear. Besides, who needed the kind of jokes the pundits were making? To wit: If elected, Kennedy would have to decide whether to make Sammy ambassador to Israel or to the Congo. But who was going to tell Frank to cut Davis lose?

Matters escalated in October. May's divorce had become final at the end of September, and she and Sammy had planned to wed shortly thereafter, with Sinatra as best man. Since Davis had been booed at the convention, picketed in the nation's capital, and greeted with a bomb threat on his opening at the Huntington Hartford, he had tried to downplay his engagement, avoiding appearances with May where reporters or photographers could spot them. But even though they were keeping a low profile, their relationship remained the subject of gossip columns and news articles all over the country.

As the wedding day drew near, the race between Kennedy and Nixon tightened dramatically. Sammy feared that the publicity from the wedding might cost Jack enough votes to give the Republicans the win, particularly as Sinatra, his best man, was so closely identified with the senator's cause. Accordingly, he decided to postpone the wedding until after the election. His publicists, Rogers and Cowan (who had recently replaced Jess Rand), blamed the nuptials' delay on technical difficulties stemming from May's divorce.

One positive thing to emerge from this interval was that it enabled Sammy to reconnect with Will Mastin. Meeting with the old man, still ostensibly his manager, to coordinate his schedule with his wedding plans, Davis found Will surprisingly sympathetic. Both men ruefully acknowledged that success had blinded them to the love that had underscored their many years together. Finally, Sammy walked across the room and embraced his mentor. "Whatever the reason," he said later, "or whoever was at fault, I was glad to have that warmth and friendship again."

On November 8, John Kennedy edged out Richard Nixon in one of the closest elections in U.S. history to become the thirty-fifth president of the United States. Five days later, Sammy Davis, Jr., married May Britt. The twenty-minute ceremony, held at Sammy's home before about thirty invited guests, was conducted by Rabbi William M. Kramer, May having converted to Judaism the previous month. Frank Sinatra was, indeed, the best man, Peter Lawford was an usher, and Shirley Rhodes, George Rhodes' wife, served as matron of honor. Afterward, Sammy joined about two hundred friends for a reception at the Beverly Hilton Hotel. May, who had contracted the flu a few days earlier, remained at the house on Evanview Drive. This was now her home as well as his. In fact, she had used the months leading up to her marriage to put her own stamp on the house's principal rooms: the master bedroom, kitchen, and living room. Despite Sammy's initial protests, she paid for the redecoration as a wedding present. Rosa B. remained in her ground-floor apartment, but Sammy's dad and Pee Wee moved into a house of their own so that the newlyweds would have some privacy.

Sammy stayed only an hour at the reception, then rushed home to his bride. He wasn't about to let May's illness cast a shadow over the festivities. Throughout his life, he'd been looking for love. That near-desperate search had led him down numerous, very public blind alleys over the years, including a sham marriage, two broken engagements, and several heart-wrenching affairs. But he had at last found someone to love who loved him in return, loved him enough, in fact, to wreck her own career in order to be with him. And, if that weren't enough, she was beautiful, kind, intelligent, and strong.

The following day, Davis left for an engagement in San Francisco, but May's illness kept her in L.A. Even after her recuperation, she stayed at home at Sammy's insistence because of bomb threats coming into the theater where he was performing his one-man show. He returned home each weekend, following his Saturday night show, and remained with his wife until late Monday afternoon. While in San Francisco, he kept his lodging place a secret for security reasons and added another bodyguard to his team, a private detective named Paul Newer. The threats continued when he moved on to the Copacabana in New York in December. Arriving at the club on opening night, he found a horde of people standing outside, along with a platoon of policemen and FBI agents. "We got word, Mr. Davis, that you're going to be killed tonight," the authorities told him. The threat didn't affect his showmanship, however. *Variety* argued that he could "do no wrong" that evening, praising his "exuberance" and "warmth," and adding, "There's an electric quality about the whole performance."

Indeed, Sammy was exhibiting greater confidence onstage than ever before. Later, he credited the change to age and experience. As he put it, "I wasn't 'the kid' anymore. I was working just as hard, but not as wildly, not wasting anything as I used to. I made everything count." He continued to devote ever more time to his singing and his comic routines—with an increasing injection of racially directed humor, timely now, thanks to the civil rights movement. But these developments came at the expense of his dancing. That was a loss, for he was pure magic on his feet. Having started hoofing at the age of three, he had enjoyed a thirty-year run, which is as much as most dancers could expect. At thirty-five, he had no choice but to cut back.

Among those who came to the Copa was Evelyn Cunningham, the African American columnist who had chastised Sammy in print for throwing a party for the Negro press in 1957 and had remained on his case thereafter. After the show, she told him that she'd love to meet his wife and invited both of them to her apartment the following week. In

Davis' opinion, Cunningham's visit meant that people were finally starting to come to terms with his marriage. As he put it, "The same person who'd battered me bloody in her column for as long as I could remember seemed to have been trying to let me know, 'I don't care who you married as long as it's on the level.' Certainly, not all of the white or Negro people believed in what I had done, the only logical answer was that they respected the honesty of it and, at least, *my* right to believe in it."

It was a relief to get out from under the controversy, but Sammy was still nervous about appearing in public with May. There were isolated pockets of bigots who sent death threats and otherwise disrupted his life. May did fly to New York to see her husband's show at the Copa and to meet Evelyn Cunningham, but the sight of her at ringside made him extremely uncomfortable. When she confided shortly thereafter that she was pregnant, he wanted to take her on a shopping spree. What better place to find maternity clothes and trinkets for the baby than New York? But he stifled the temptation out of fear for their safety. She was not afraid to join him in public. She wanted to, in fact, but she complied with his wishes. "The first year will be the toughest," he told her. "If we can survive that, then I think we'll have it made."

CHAPTER 14

"A One-man Band"

Sammy's efforts on behalf of Kennedy's victory earned him an invitation to the president's inauguration on January 20, 1961. Davis reveled in the idea that he, an uneducated black man from Harlem, could participate in such a pivotal moment in his nation's history. In addition, Sinatra was staging a gala the night before the swearing-in ceremony to help the Democrats wipe out their $2 million campaign debt, and, naturally, Sammy was among the scheduled performers. Although he was slated to appear at the Latin Casino near Philadelphia in mid-January, he arranged for several evenings off to attend the festivities. He bought a new tuxedo as well as a suit to wear to the inaugural, plus several outfits, including a ball gown for May.

Then, three days before Sammy's planned departure for the capital, he received a phone call from Evelyn Lincoln, the president-elect's secretary, asking him not to attend the ceremonies. The reason was purely political: JFK, who had been elected by the slimmest of margins, would need the help of the Southern Democrats in Congress to achieve his legislative agenda, and the sight of Sammy and his white wife at the new administration's inauguration would hamper this effort.

Davis was devastated. First, because he would miss a once-in-a-lifetime opportunity. Second, because all of his friends would be there, and his absence would definitely be noticed. Third, because he would have to tell the owners of the Latin Casino that he wouldn't need a few days off after all. That was humiliating enough. But, worst of all, he would have to tell May.

She wasn't with him. She was at home in California, spending most of her first trimester in bed at the urging of her obstetrician, Dr. Paul Steinberg. When Sammy broke the news, she was upset, but not for herself. "Oh, Sammy," she cried, "they must have broken your heart." Although he appreciated the fact that she didn't make light of this terrible slight, he tried to put the best possible face on the situation.

Then he went back to work, telling the press that the Latin Casino couldn't afford to give him the time off and that he didn't want to disappoint the audience. When the night of the gala came, he acted as though nothing were wrong, but he couldn't help wondering what people were thinking, knowing that his friends were very visible in Washington. As he put it, "It hurt like a motherfucker."

In *Yes I Can*, he maintained his 1961 cover story. Because the book was published less than two years after Kennedy's assassination, Sammy wanted to avoid casting aspersions on the slain president's memory. But he was more forthcoming in his second autobiography, *Why Me?*, published twenty-four years later. By then, the world had learned much about Kennedy that was unknown at the time of his murder: his myriad sexual liaisons, his medical condition, his family's links to organized crime. That he had accepted Davis' help during the campaign and then turned his back on him in the flush of victory suggested a remarkable insensitivity and a deplorable lack of courage on Kennedy's part.

A week after the inauguration, on January 27, Sammy was present for a mini–Rat Pack reunion as Frank and Dean joined him and comic Jan Murray (substituting for Joey Bishop) at New York's Carnegie Hall in a concert Davis organized to benefit Martin Luther King's Southern Christian Leadership Conference. Sammy was delighted to help the cause.

The concert represented his most overt act to date in support of the civil rights movement. Most of the sit-ins, marches, and demonstrations were taking place in the South, and he was afraid to appear below the Mason-Dixon line, except for Miami Beach, which differed from the rest of the region. So he had confined his civil rights activities to sizable donations, contributions he could ill afford in light of his spending habits. He also refused to appear at clubs that catered exclusively to whites, a practice he had begun in the mid-fifties, and he brought pressure on the club owners to create more job opportunities for African Americans. This was particularly true of the Sands in the still racially divided city of Las Vegas. In March 1960, the NAACP had forced the town to officially desegregate its public places, but the hotel-casino operators implemented the changes as slowly as possible. Fed up, Davis told Jack Entratter that he should lead the way. As the entertainer put it, "Things are changing, Jack. Even Mississippi's getting ready to change." A few years later, when blacks threatened to picket Vegas' resorts, Sammy threatened to carry a placard himself unless Entratter complied with the protesters' demands in advance. Jack did so, and, as a consequence, no one marched outside the Sands, the only hotel thus spared.

* * *

February 1961 found Sammy back home and hard at work on his first LP for Reprise. "It's a gas," he said of his association with Sinatra's new label. "A real constructive thing. Frank is letting each artist buy stock in the company—a sort of share-the-profits deal, real crazy." Reprise also contracted for its artists' recordings for a relatively brief window, after which the master tapes would revert back to their creators. Sammy, with his ever-present need for money, was in no position to take advantage of this potential opportunity. He sold his future recording rights back to the company.

Davis' album, titled *The Wham of Sam*, helped launch the label in March. As with Sammy's Decca output, Morty Stevens did some of the arranging and conducting, half of the material in this instance. The other half was handled by Marty Paich. Six months older than Davis, the Oakland-born musician had a master's degree from the Los Angeles Conservatory of Music and had worked on LPs with a host of jazz artists—Art Pepper, Shelley Manne, and Stan Kenton, to name a few— and several pop vocalists, most notably Mel Torme.

Stevens' work on *The Wham of Sam*, which featured a full orchestra including strings, was first rate. Particularly notable was Billy Strayhorn's "Lush Life," with its distinctive riffs by guitarist Tony Rizzi. But Paich's efforts were exceptional. Songs like the Gershwins' "Soon" and Rodgers and Hart's "Thou Swell," usually rendered at a moderate pace, were given uptempo jolts, enabling Sammy to swing without ever going too far. And the bluesy "Bye Bye Blackbird," with just bass and percussion on the first verse, highlighted his impeccable sense of pitch and, in the final chorus, his improvisational skill.

According to Will Friedwald, author of *Jazz Singing* as well as the CD liner notes for *The Wham of Sam*, Davis specifically asked for Paich because he admired the musician's work with Mel Torme. Clearly, Sammy knew what he was doing. "The one time when Davis emerged from Sinatra's shadow on record," asserted Friedwald, "with a sound that was really his own, was when he teamed up with Marty Paich." And the arranger-conductor's use of a ten-piece jazz band brought out Sammy's jazz instincts, instincts that had been nurtured for decades as he listened to recordings by Basie, Ellington, Charlie Parker, Miles Davis, and others.

Although *The Wham of Sam* is widely regarded as one of Sammy's best albums, it was somewhat overshadowed by the simultaneous release of Sinatra's own Reprise LP, *Ring-a-Ding-Ding!*, which was named for a new Cahn–Van Heusen song, a paean to the Rat Pack ethos. Of course, as Chairman of the Board, Sinatra got first crack at everything, including the best new tunes. But it must also be said that Frank paid meticulous attention to every detail of his recordings. Sammy never attempted to match his idol in this regard.

By the time *The Wham of Sam* was in record stores, Davis was back on tour, at the Fountainebleu in Miami Beach in mid-February (his contract with the Eden Roc having expired) and Harrah's in Lake Tahoe, Nevada in March (his debut with the resort-casino). Then, on April 20, he set off for a month of appearances in Brazil and Argentina. He was stopped by the immigration authorities because his passport had expired but, fortunately, he knew people in the White House, and an emergency renewal was issued.

Sammy flew back to Los Angeles on May 19, but a few days later, he left home again, this time for Kenab, Utah. He was needed for the second Rat Pack film.

Sergeants 3 was based on Rudyard Kipling's poem *Gunga Din* and the 1939 MGM movie of the same name. Set in nineteenth-century India, the rousing adventure dealt with the British Army's efforts to quell the fanatical Thugs. The focus was on three fun-loving noncoms, one of whom decides to leave the military in order to marry, much to the dismay of his chums.

In the hands of screenwriter W. R. Burnett, the action in *Sergeants 3* moved to the Old West, where a band of diehard Native American Ghost Dancers create problems for a trio of U.S. Cavalry troopers: Michael "Mike" Merry, Charles "Chip" Deal, and Lawrence "Larry" Bayer (played by Sinatra, Martin, and Lawford, respectively). The water boy was transformed into an ex-slave named Jonah Williams, played, of course, by Sammy. Joey Bishop was given the part of a fourth sergeant, a stuffed shirt who makes life difficult for the merry triumvirate.

Kenab, the location of numerous Hollywood Westerns, was rich in picturesque landscapes, but it offered none of the off-hour diversions the Clan had enjoyed during the making of *Ocean's Eleven*. Among the town's biggest attractions was a Dairy Queen that stayed open until eleven o'clock. "My advice to everybody," quipped Joey Bishop, "was to get two scoops because after that there wasn't a goddamn thing to do."

But the Rat Packers made their own fun. Prior to their arrival in Kenab, Frank had arranged for their hotel to renovate their top-floor rooms so they could reach one another—and play pranks on one another—by means of connecting interior doors. Sammy's room was the sole exception. As a joke, he was forced to stay at the opposite end of the corridor from the other guys, and all the rooms near his were purposely kept vacant. The nights were filled with screenings of Laurel and Hardy films, energetic poker games, drinking sessions, and, from time to time, trysts with call girls imported from Vegas.

"There was one prevailing mood with those guys," said pretty, perky Ruta Lee, cast as Larry's fiancée, Amelia, "and it was laughter." Lawford took his fare share of ribbing because he showed up about thirty pounds overweight. When Frank started calling him "Fatty," Peter went on a crash diet.

But Sammy remained the favorite target. He was so easy to pick on and seemed to enjoy the humor so much. He wasn't quite as amused as he appeared, but he understood his role in the Clan pecking order. As Ruta Lee put it, he was "the windup toy. He was the pet. He was like a loving, wonderful adoring puppy that got into your lap and into your heart and you would never be able to shake loose of the dearness and the sweetness and the fun that he brought to life."

The light-hearted mood that colored the evenings prevailed on the set as well. As with *Ocean's Eleven,* the Rat Packers didn't start work until late, usually around 11:00 A.M., although the other cast members, which again included Henry Silva and Buddy Lester, were expected to be at work at 8:00. Sammy went out to the locations more frequently than the others, showing up even on days when he wasn't called.

By contrast, Sinatra never hung around if he wasn't needed, and he still refused to do retakes. But the energy he conserved in this regard was spent, for several weeks, at least, in nighttime performances at the Sands, where he and Dean were booked as a duo. Sammy and the rest of the gang went to see their friends work. They made several other trips to the Strip as well, cheering on the headliners at the various showrooms and occasionally taking the stage themselves to re-create bits from the Summit.

None of this activity made director John Sturges' task easy. He was perfectly at home with Westerns, having directed *Gunfight at the O.K. Corral, Last Train from Gun Hill,* and *The Magnificent Seven,* and he had worked with Sinatra before, on *Never So Few,* so he had some idea of what to expect. But the presence of the entire Rat Pack made for greater merriment than Sturges had experienced on *Never So Few,* which had involved only Frank and Peter. As Ruta Lee put it, Sturges "had his hands full with this crew, let's face it. I think he tried every day to make it slightly more meaningful and more serious. And he did. He did some beautiful work. He got some beautiful shots. But nobody could take this picture too seriously."

After two months in Utah, the company returned to L.A., where principal photography continued at the Goldwyn Studios, whose facilities

were rented by United Artists, Frank's producing partner in the enterprise. It marked Sammy's first return to the studio since *Porgy and Bess*.

May, nearing the end of her pregnancy and no longer confined to bed,
would occasionally come to the lot. Ruta Lee noticed that she "didn't
mean for this to happen, but it was like suddenly a wet blanket would
come on the hilarity that was going on. We had to behave ourselves
because May was on the set and May was so shy that maybe she wouldn't
laugh at the crazy, dirty humor that was going around or the jokes that
were being said—or she wouldn't understand them. She was very sweet
but very reticent about joining in on the hilarity."

Britt *was* shy and reserved, but she also resented the way Frank,
Dean, and the others treated her husband. In addition, she had begun to
realize that marriage was not going to alter Sammy's lifestyle; he had
continued to hang out with his friends while they were dating, and his
behavior hadn't changed. His constant need for a host of people was
something she was not, in her words, "crazy about."

Sergeants 3 was still in production on July 5 when May went into
labor—three weeks early. The previous night she had joined Sammy in a
spirited pillow fight that took them all over the house, laughing and giggling like kids. They later assumed that their playing around contributed
to the early delivery.

Sammy rushed from the studio to Cedars of Lebanon Hospital, where
he greeted Burt and Jane Boyar, his houseguests at the time. He arrived
just moments before his wife gave birth to a baby girl, 7 pounds, 14
ounces. Sammy called the set to give Sinatra the news, and Frank then
told the press. When asked how the new father was doing, Frank replied,
"He's too nervous to talk about anything." Later, Davis posed for photos
at the hospital boasting a button that read, "It's a Girl." He and May
named her Tracey Hillevi (after actor Spencer Tracy, whom Sammy
admired, and May's mother's maiden name).

Seeing his little girl for the first time was a profoundly moving experience for Sammy. He looked down at her tiny light brown arms and legs
and couldn't help hoping that, as he put it, "she would live in a world of
people who would not notice or care about a layer of skin." Then he visited his wife. She was asleep when he entered her room, but he took her
hand and promised her that he would "build something good and strong
and wonderful" for their family and that he would never let her down.

Seven months later, on February 10, 1962, *Sergeants 3* opened in New
York. Although Davis later considered it the best of the Rat Pack movies,
calling it "a good story with a lot of fine points" and packed "with action,"
the critics much preferred the earlier film version of *Gunga Din* starring

Cary Grant, Douglas Fairbanks, Jr., and Victor McLaglen. Although the Monument Valley landscapes made for an attractive backdrop, even the action sequences in *Sergeants 3* were routine, shockingly below John Sturges' previous efforts. Andrew H. Weiler spoke for the vast majority of his colleagues, asserting in the *New York Times* that the "principal cast members give the strange impression in *Sergeants 3* of having never left a Las Vegas nightclub."

One might argue that a Western was simply not the best genre to capitalize on what made the Rat Pack tick. None of the stars made the slightest concession to the story's setting and time period. But whatever the shortcomings of the Clan members, Sammy arguably fared the worst. If his garbage man in *Ocean's Eleven* placed him below the others on a socioeconomic level, he was even more subservient here, in the part of a former slave who wants more than anything to be what the other guys already are—a soldier. From his first moment on camera—playing the trumpet and tap dancing on a saloon bar, egged on by a bunch of cowboys, one of whom has a gun on him—he is forced into the kind of Step'n'Fetchit mode that was so prevalent in the films of the 1930s and 1940s, that of a grinning, high-voiced, naïve Uncle Tom. He responded to criticism by saying, "*Sergeants* wasn't to be taken seriously. It was a fun-type show that people could enjoy without getting all wrapped up in morals and points. That was one of the big reasons I took the part, disregarding my love and affection for Frank. I have never done or said anything in my professional life that I thought was a hindrance to my race."

Sammy was now a father, but he wasn't about to let that slow him down.

After *Sergeants 3* wrapped, he devoted several days in July to laying down tracks for future Reprise LPs. Then, in August, slightly more than a month after Tracey's birth, he was off to Monaco for a gala benefit, followed later in the month by the start of a seven-week return engagement in London.

While in the British capital, Sammy made friends with Anthony Newley and Leslie Bricusse, whose first musical, *Stop the World—I Want to Get Off,* was then a smash hit at the Queens Theatre, just up the road from the Prince of Wales, where Davis was performing. "We used to have supper after the shows every night," recalled Bricusse, "and we became instant friends." Sammy's suite at the Mayfair served as a major hangout, as did the White Elephant, a restaurant popular with show people.

Davis and Newley formed a mutual admiration society. "They were both unique theater talents," explained Bricusse, "and they were both multitalented. Sammy admired the fact that Newley had not only written *Stop the World* and directed it, but starred in it in a very unusual way,

Sammy Davis, Jr., was born in Harlem on December 8, 1925. By then, the community in Upper Manhattan had become a magnet for blacks from all over the world. (Schomberg Center for Research in Black Culture, New York Public Library)

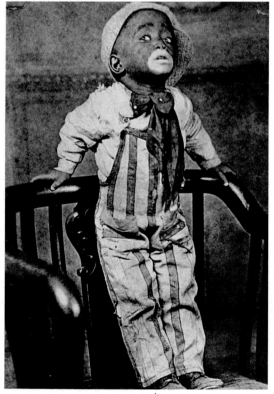

Around age three, Sammy hit the road with his father, a professional dancer. They performed in several large-scale musicals produced by an African American impresario named Will Mastin. (Photofest)

In 1933, eight-year-old Sammy sang and danced as the title character in the Vitaphone short *Rufus Jones for President*. Broadway star Ethel Waters played his mother. (Movie Star News)

Forced to abandon his large-cast productions during the Great Depression, Will Mastin *(right)* formed a flash dance act with Sam Davis and Sammy. (Photofest)

By the late forties, Sammy dominated the Will Mastin Trio with his comic impressions, turns on musical instruments, and the occasional song. White middle-class audiences couldn't believe that such a slight, sweet, ingratiating young man could possess so much talent. (Photofest)

Numerous show business veterans helped propel Davis to stardom, among them the irrepressible Eddie Cantor. Cantor frequently invited the Will Mastin Trio to appear on his popular variety show, *The Colgate Comedy Hour*, sharing bits with Sammy after the act's regular performances. (Photofest)

Sammy's first close friend was Arthur Silber, Jr., the son of the Trio's manager. After graduating from high school, Silber went on the road with Davis, serving as a combination confidant, bodyguard, and lighting technician. (Arthur Silber, Jr., Collection)

Davis refused to let a horrific automobile accident in November 1954 derail his career. Although he lost his left eye, he was soon back onstage, making his patch a trademark as well as the source of numerous jokes. (Photofest)

In an unusual career decision, Davis temporarily abandoned his highly lucrative nightclub career in 1956 for a starring role in a Broadway musical, *Mr. Wonderful*. He is seen here with Olga James, who played his girlfriend. (The Billy Rose Theater Collection, Lincoln Center Library for the Performing Arts, New York Public Library)

Hired as Davis' pianist shortly after *Mr. Wonderful* closed, George Rhodes eventually became the entertainer's highly valued conductor and principal arranger. Rhodes remained with Sammy until his death in December 1985. (Shirley Rhodes Collection)

Faced with threats against his life as a result of his love affair with movie star Kim Novak, Sammy married singer Loray White in a brief ceremony at the Sands Hotel on January 10, 1958. (Sands Hotel Collection, University of Nevada, Las Vegas Library)

More than anything, Davis wanted to be a movie star like his friend and idol Frank Sinatra. Arguably his best screen role came in his second feature, Samuel Goldwyn's lavish production of the American folk opera *Porgy and Bess,* in which Sammy portrayed the serpentine drug dealer Sportin' Life. (Photofest)

In January 1960, Sammy joined his pals *(left to right)* Dean Martin, Peter Lawford, Frank Sinatra, and Joey Bishop for a nightly romp onstage at Vegas' Sands Hotel. The Rat Pack, as the gang was called, created a sensation. (Sands Hotel Collection, University of Nevada, Las Vegas Library)

While performing in Vegas at night, the Rat Pack was also making a movie by day. The caper film, *Ocean's Eleven*, featured third-billed Sammy as a sanitation worker, Josh Howard. (Photofest)

On November 13, 1960, Sammy married movie star May Britt in a Jewish ceremony at his home in Beverly Hills. News of their relationship sparked demonstrations at numerous clubs where Davis performed and ruined Britt's film career. (Corbis)

In 1961, Sammy left his recording company, Decca, to join Frank Sinatra's new label, Reprise. Here the ebullient entertainer celebrates the release of his first album for Reprise, the highly regarded *Wham of Sam*. (Corbis)

As the Civil Rights movement gained momentum in the early sixties, Davis became a familiar presence at rallies staged by the Southern Christian Leadership Conference. Here the organization's leader, the Rev. Martin Luther King, Jr. *(second from left)*, observes Sammy clowning for the camera. (Corbis)

The final Rat Pack movie, 1964's *Robin and the 7 Hoods,* was a musical takeoff on the Robin Hood legend with Frank, Sammy, and Dean as gangsters in 1920s Chicago. On the outs with Sinatra, Peter Lawford and Joey Bishop were not among the featured players. (Photofest)

Davis returned to Broadway in October 1964 as the ambitious boxer in *Golden Boy.* Despite difficulties out of town, the musical remake of Clifford Odets' play was a smash hit. (The Billy Rose Theater Collection, Lincoln Center Library for the Performing Arts, New York Public Library)

While Sammy was performing in *Golden Boy,* his autobiography, *Yes I Can,* was published. He and May celebrated its release with his coauthors, Burt and Jane Boyar. (Burt Boyar Collection)

During *Golden Boy*'s lengthy run, Davis astounded industry observers by also starring in *A Man Called Adam,* a feature film about a troubled jazz trumpeter . . . (Photofest)

. . . and by hosting a weekly television variety series, *The Sammy Davis, Jr. Show*. Among the short-lived program's most memorable episodes were the two featuring Davis' friend Judy Garland. (Photofest)

Following the close of *Golden Boy* and the demise of his TV series, Davis triumphantly returned to the nightclub circuit. He is seen here at the Copa Room of the Sands Hotel in 1966. (Sands Hotel Collection, University of Nevada, Las Vegas Library)

Playing off his emerging image as a "groovy" sixties hipster, Sammy portrayed Big Daddy, a jargon-spouting jazz musician–cum–religious guru in the 1969 movie musical *Sweet Charity*, starring John McMartin and Shirley MacLaine. (Photofest)

On May 11, 1970, Davis married Altovise Gore, a dancer some twenty years his junior. The private ceremony, held at the municipal courthouse in Philadelphia, surprised many of his friends and enraged his three children. (Photofest)

There were plenty of laughs when Sammy met the bigoted Queens cabdriver Archie Bunker (Carroll O'Connor) on the February 19, 1972, episode of *All in the Family*. *TV Guide* ranked the show 13th among the greatest television episodes of all time. (Photofest)

A lifelong Democrat, Davis alienated many of his friends and fans when he joined the administration of Richard Nixon. They were even more incensed by this photo of him hugging the president at a rally during the 1972 Republican National Convention in Miami. (Corbis)

Davis' weekly syndicated talk show, *Sammy & Company,* which debuted in 1975, helped cement his image as a glitzy, showbiz phony who laughed too hard at unfunny jokes—as he demonstrates here with guest Flip Wilson. (Photofest)

Despite his developing dependence on cocaine and alcohol during the 1970s, Davis remained a powerhouse entertainer. (Las Vegas News Bureau/LVCVA)

By the 1980s, the closest members of Davis' inner circle were his personal manager Shirley Rhodes and his valet Murphy Bennett (*behind* Sammy). Joining them on the occasion of Davis' re-signing with the William Morris Talent Agency were agent Marty Klein (*upper right*), Davis' attorney John Climaco (*lower right*), and Climaco's young son, John. (John Climaco Collection)

Among Davis' more unusual roles was that of the Caterpillar in Irwin Allen's large-budget musical remake of *Alice in Wonderland*, which debuted on CBS in December 1985. (Photofest)

In 1987, Sammy shared the bill at Bally's with his old friend Jerry Lewis. "We re-created the old type of Las Vegas show business, and it has worked wonderfully," Davis said. The duo made several other joint appearances thereafter. (Las Vegas News Bureau/LVCVA)

In 1988, Davis joined Dean Martin and Frank Sinatra for the highly touted "Together Again Tour." After Martin dropped out, Liza Minnelli became the third superstar in the package, which was then redubbed "The Ultimate Event." (Photofest)

Sammy's final movie role was that of an elderly dancer in *Tap*. The film, released in February 1989, augured well for Davis' future as a character actor, but his career was cut short by cancer. (Photofest)

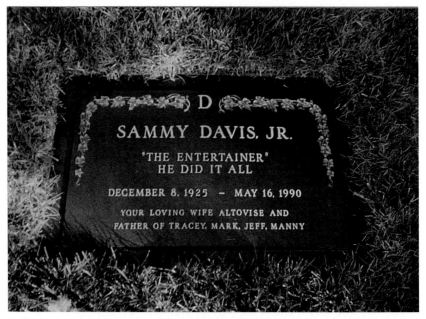

Felled by lung cancer at age sixty-four, Sammy Davis, Jr., was buried at Forest Lawn in May 1990. He rests near the graves of his father, paternal grandmother, and Will Mastin. (Courtesy of www.findadeath.com)

using a box full of talents that only Newley had. Nobody else was like him. And, similarly, Sammy could do everything on a stage. . . . They almost wanted to be one another. It was very interesting."

Davis so loved the Newley-Bricusse musical that he would record four numbers from its score: "Gonna Build a Mountain," "Someone Nice Like You," "Once in a Lifetime," and "What Kind of Fool Am I?" The latter, released as a single on September 1, 1962, would become one of his biggest hits, climbing to number 17 on *Billboard*'s pop chart and continuing in the Top 100 for fifteen weeks. This marked the start of a lifelong working arrangement among Sammy and Newley and Bricusse. During his career, he sang roughly sixty of their tunes, including numbers written by Bricusse alone.

Sammy's closing night at the Prince of Wales took place during the first week in October. After his second performance, he offered "a midnight matinee," a set exclusively for people in the business, particularly the singers and dancers in the other West End shows, who couldn't have seen him otherwise. He started shortly after 12:00 P.M., and, incredibly, didn't leave the stage for five hours. "It was the greatest one-man marathon tour-de-force I ever wish to see," Bricusse recalled. "It was just sensational."

Back in L.A., Sammy barely had time to kiss May and cuddle with Tracey before he was off to the Sands for one of his regular engagements. When he returned home, he went to work at the Cocoanut Grove, the glamorous showroom in the Ambassador Hotel. Army Archerd observed in *Variety* that Sammy "seems to be entering a golden era. With added success, he's added a new-found humility and finesse, but retains his authority and audience rapport as before."

Twice during his three-week gig Sammy took off for special appearances. On November 6, he flew back to London for his second Royal Variety Gala, becoming the first American to entertain at two Command Performances in a row. Angus Hall of the *Daily Sketch* described him as "more than a mere star. He is unique. He is a troupe of acrobats. He is a team of dancers. He is a one-man band. He is a hit parade of singers. He is show business." After the final curtain, Queen Elizabeth greeted the performers backstage. "I didn't know what to say," Sammy joked a couple weeks later. "You know, I ain't no Frank Sinatra, but he ain't no queen. Man, talk about scared."

On November 12, Davis again left Los Angeles to perform at the Folsom State Penitentiary near Sacramento. His show for the prison's two thousand inmates came as a result of his role in an Allied Artists film then called *Reprieve,* that was being shot, in part, on the grounds.

Sammy's two scenes for the picture were not filmed at Folsom; they were both set in a cell re-created on a sound stage in Hollywood. As an illiterate convict named Wino, he was one of a number of guest stars hired to spark interest in the rather downbeat drama. But the thrust of the story was carried by Stuart Whitman as an ambitious but sympathetic guard (later warden) and relative newcomer Ben Gazzara as John Resko, an embittered convict who became a talented artist.

As Resko's first cellmate, Davis interacted solely with Gazzara. Trained at the Actors Studio and the star of two major Broadway dramas, *A Hatful of Rain* and *Cat on a Hot Tin Roof,* Gazzara respected Sammy's commitment to the project. "He was letter perfect," the actor recalled. "He was prepared. He was very disciplined, and he took it seriously." He liked Davis as well. "He was nice to people," Gazzara said, "he was kind. I never saw him bitchy. I never saw him put anyone down. Actually, I never heard a sardonic word come out of Sammy's mouth."

The $1 million production took a mere six weeks to shoot, of which about two weeks were spent at Folsom. But it wasn't released until nearly a year after the start of principal photography. One reason was the July 18, 1962 opening of a competing prison drama, United Artists' *Birdman of Alcatraz.* When *Reprieve* finally debuted in New York as *Convicts 4* on October 3 (following openings in Los Angeles and other select cities on September 25), comparisons with *Birdman* were inevitable—to its disadvantage.

After *Convicts 4* wrapped in December 1961, Sammy's calendar continued to be filled with a dizzying round of nightclub engagements, studio recording sessions, guest shots on television shows, and even a featured role in a movie musical.

His personal appearances included his traditional December–January stand at the Copa, always a high spot. Other gigs in 1962 included his regular appearances at the Sands, a six-day stint at Larry Steel's Club Harlem in Atlantic City in July, and a concert on August 11 at Forest Hills Stadium in Queens, New York, where he played to a near standing- room crowd of 12,500. *Variety* took this occasion to dub him "one of the superior performers of this era." Sammy himself felt he was working at the top of his game. "Right now things couldn't be better," he joyfully proclaimed. "I'm meeting with more acceptance than I have ever before in my life. This year around the circuit has been my biggest year. It's the great American dream of the underdog who makes good. And in my case I had a hundred guys waiting for me to fall down and mess my marriage up. Somewhere along the line, God helped me."

A week after Sammy's appearance in Queens, he re-created his role in *The Desperate Hours* at the Mineola Playhouse in Mineola, Long Island, once again alongside his office manager, James Waters, and character actor Roy Glenn. The production, directed by the esteemed Lloyd Richards (whose Broadway credits included Lorraine Hansberry's *A Raisin in the Sun*), won the approval of the *New York Post*'s Jerry Tellimer, who called it "real and terrifying."

Finally, in October, Sammy returned to the Cocoanut Grove. Reprise recorded his opening-night performance and a two-album set the following year. On the album, there are ample opportunities along the way to sample Davis' humor and audience repartee, including his warning fairly early on: "I hope you have no place to go for the next hour or so. I do a long time on stage. . . . I am what is commonly known as a ham."

Meanwhile, Davis' career as a television actor was taking off. He was the guest on six dramatic shows in 1962, including three Westerns, a new series, *Frontier Circus*, on January 4, and two episodes of *The Rifleman* (February 19 and November 26). He donned more modern dress for his January 29 visit to Jackie Cooper's *Hennessy*, his April 3 cameo on another new series, *Cain's Hundred*, and his June 29 role in the hip detective drama, *77 Sunset Strip*. But his most memorable appearance of the season came on the February 20 episode of the sixty-minute anthology series *The Dick Powell Show*. As ex-boxer Gabe Masters, the title character in "The Legend," he joined forces with a hard-drinking but dogged reporter played by Powell to bring down a ruthless racketeer. The chemistry between Davis and Powell underscored the taut drama.

Davis' frequent television appearances were no accident. He and his agent at William Morris, Sy Marsh, actively courted the producers of the top-notch shows. Although things had opened up a bit, virtually no one was writing leading parts for Negroes in 1962. More often than not, an episode had to be scripted specifically for Sammy, once he let his interest in a program be known. Sometimes he looked for roles that invariably went to white actors, like the gunfighters he portrayed on *The Rifleman*, to force the realization that, historically, African Americans had held such occupations. At the same time, he didn't want his color to always be a factor in his work. As he put it, "I want people to stop thinking Negro actor and just think actor."

Because virtually all of Sammy's TV roles were hand-tailored for him, they typically fell into one of two distinctive categories: either he was a soft-tempered little guy who shows real character when it counts, as in *The Dick Powell Show*, or he was a hard-edged loner with a vulnerable core, as in *The Rifleman*. He had played variations of both types in the past and would again in the future. Indeed, these broadly defined characters, together with his patented "hep cat," served as the basis for virtually all of his future dramatic work.

In between his live engagements and TV gigs, Sammy supported his recording career, spending two days in the studio in February 1962. He was once again teamed with the inventive Marty Paich for an LP devoted to Broadway material. Surrounding the four songs from *Stop the World* were a controlled but electric version of "I've Got a Lot of Livin' to Do" from *Bye Bye Birdie*, "Something's Coming" from *West Side Story*, and a very clever bongo-driven treatment of Cole Porter's "Begin the Beguine." Released later in the year, the LP *What Kind of Fool Am I?—And Other Show-Stoppers* was a solid follow-up to *The Wham of Sam*, earning a Grammy nomination for album of the year. Sammy's single of "What Kind of Fool Am I?" was also nominated for record of the year, but it lost to Tony Bennett's rendition of "I Left My Heart in San Francisco."

In late 1962, Davis was cast in the big-screen adaptation of *The Three-penny Opera*, based on the 1928 musical drama, *Die Dreigroschenopera*, by Berthold Brecht and Kurt Weill. The tale of Macheath, a gentleman criminal also known as Mac the Knife, whose assorted relationships with women cause his downfall, had been filmed once before, by G. W. Pabst in 1931. The remake starred Curt Jurgens as Macheath, Hildegard Knef as Jenny, the double-dealing prostitute, and Gert Frobe as Macheath's nemesis, Mr. Peachum, the prince of the beggars (Frobe would soon gain fame as the title character in the James Bond film *Goldfinger*). Sammy, the only American in the cast, was the narrator–ballad singer, who renders the show's biggest hit, "Mac the Knife," at the outset of the piece. According to George E. Pitts of the *New York Courier*, he earned $30,000 for this role, which probably required no more than a couple of days to shoot.

Principal photography took place in Berlin during the latter part of 1962. The film's producer, Kurt Ulrich, was under enormous pressure to wrap the picture because he had promised the heirs of Weill's and Brecht's estates that he would finish by the end of the year. If he didn't, the rights reverted back to the original owners.

Ulrich's haste may well have contributed to the result, which was dreadful. Under the direction of Wolfgang Staudte, the film was plodding and clumsily staged, and the sets and costumes were uninspired, despite a hefty budget, one of the largest for a postwar German production. Davis' scenes, shot in the United States without Staudte's involvement, bear no relationship to the rest of the movie. When he appears from time to time to introduce the principal characters or to comment on the action, he is either before a backdrop, which looks completely artificial in contrast to the naturalistic settings of the rest of the picture, or he is inserted into the action by means of process photography, which is just as jarring.* Not surprisingly, his best moment comes at the beginning, with "Mac the Knife." His version isn't as uptempo as the famous pop single by Bobby Darin, but it is livelier than the droning pace at which "Mac the Knife" is traditionally sung in the context of the show.

The film premiered in Munich in February 1963 but it wasn't seen in the United States until November 1964. In addition to its other flaws, the English dubbing was laughable. Audiences in a Memphis theater were so outraged that it was pulled after only two days.

Sammy's work on the film was succeeded by another round of personal engagements, the climax of which came in April 1963, when he launched a five-week engagement at the London Palladium. The *New York Post* called it the "greatest triumph of them all." On May 21, Sammy hopped over to Paris for a one-night benefit concert at the Olympia Music Hall, marking his first appearance in the French capital.

While in London, he also starred in a BBC-TV special called *Meet Sammy Davis,* a one-man show featuring his wide variety of talents, including his skill with a six-shooter. One segment of the show found him conducting the orchestra while singing "I've Got a Lot of Livin' to Do" in a British accent. This was followed by a charming soft-shoe routine of "Me and My Shadow," which Sammy rendered with just a gentle piano and Michael Silva's drums behind him. Throughout, Davis was completely at ease in front of the camera. When the show aired in the United States, *Variety* called it "one of the most impactful shows of its kind for many a moon . . . a well-nigh faultless program." The following year, Sammy reteamed with the show's producer-director, Dennis Main Wilson, for *Meet Sammy Davis, Jr., Part 2,* which was every bit as engaging.

Back in the United States, Davis opened at Harrah's in Lake Tahoe in mid-July 1963, followed by a three-week gig in August at Atlantic City's Club 500. But he took time on August 5 to join Johnny Mathis, Ray Charles, Marian Anderson, Joe Louis, James Baldwin, and the Rev. Martin Luther King, Jr., for a rally in Birmingham, Alabama to raise funds for

---

*A process shot involves inserting one element, in this case, Davis, into previously filmed footage, in this case, material shot at the studio in Berlin. The latter was projected behind the entertainer through a transparent screen in what is called "rear projection" as the new footage was being shot, thereby creating a blend of both.

the city's contingent to the August 28 March on Washington. Davis knew King, having staged the benefit for the civil rights leader's Southern Christian Leadership Conference at Carnegie Hall in January 1961. On that occasion, he told Dr. King he'd be happy to help him raise money but would never appear in the South. "We'll get you down there," King prophesied. It took more than two and a half years, but there Sammy was.

Davis was also present for the March itself. On that momentous occasion, he joined 250,000 other Americans, black and white, in the nation's capital for a nationally televised celebration of the civil rights movement, even though Attorney General Robert Kennedy had warned him that his name was on the White Citizens Council's "Ten Most Wanted" list. Remembering the demonstrations against him when he performed at the Lotus Club in 1960, Sammy was nervous as he joined the other celebrities on the steps of the Lincoln Memorial. But actress Ruby Dee, who chatted with him, found him "well informed and genuinely concerned" about the cause.

Davis' fears were not unfounded. Numerous groups had threatened to disrupt the March. But the demonstration, climaxed by King's electrifying "I Have a Dream" speech, remained peaceful. Indeed, it became a joyous celebration, beyond the wildest expectations of its organizers. As Davis recalled, "Everybody had love in their hearts and on their faces and it was wonderful, happy-making." Indeed, the March on Washington was a galvanizing event in U.S. history. As King noted, "Millions of white Americans, for the first time, had a clear, long look at Negroes engaged in a serious occupation. For the first time millions listened to the informed and thoughtful words of Negro spokesmen, from all walks of life. Their stereotype of the Negro suffered a heavy blow."

For Sammy, the March was not a wake-up call, but it did stimulate him to consider greater participation in the movement. He wasn't comfortable with some of the more radical elements, such as Malcolm X and the Black Muslims. In this, he was hardly alone; most Americans considered the Muslims extremists in 1963. But he strongly supported the nonviolent, integrationist approach advocated by King's SCLC and the NAACP. With regard to the latter, he told the African American newspaper the *New York Courier* a full year before the gathering in Washington, "I'll work for the NAACP any time, any place—not to help the guys that are trying to take advantage of a situation, but to help that 'cat' that gets into trouble. Nobody cares about him. Maybe the NAACP does 'bug' people, but it gets justice. Why should a kid have to stay in jail without counsel or anything just because he's a 'colored cat'? The NAACP sees that this doesn't happen. They get things going."

Sammy was even more impressed by King. Two months before the

March on Washington, he said, "We only need about 25 more men like Martin Luther King, on both sides of the color spectrum, and this thing would be over. . . . Just to talk to Martin Luther King is a thrill. He's the Gandhi of the Negro race."

The March notwithstanding, the biggest event of the summer of 1963 for Sammy came on June 4, when he and May finalized their adoption of a three-year-old boy, whom they named Mark Sidney. May's pregnancy with Tracey had been difficult, but the adoption was not a reflection on her ability to bear more children. She and Sammy had, in fact, discussed adoption even before their marriage; they wanted to do something to help in the face of so many homeless kids.

Not surprisingly, Sammy was on the road when Mark joined the family. Accordingly, it fell to May and Tracey to make the boy feel welcome and ease his adjustment into the Davis household.

CHAPTER 15

Pallies

Shortly after the March on Washington, Sammy set off on a tour of Australia, Hong Kong, and Japan. As with most everywhere else he played, the Australian press quizzed him about the Rat Pack and his relationship with Sinatra, who was not popular with the media Down Under. The world remained fascinated by the antics of the successful, swinging stars who were so pleased with themselves and one another. Shortly after Sammy's return from the Pacific Rim, he set out for Chicago for a third picture with the gang. This gathering marked the culmination of a string of Clan events that had run throughout 1962 and 1963.

Back in August 1962, Davis had joined forces with Sinatra and Martin for a three-night stand at the Club 500 in Atlantic City. This appearance was a gesture of support for the club's owner, Skinny D'Amato, who was experiencing a financial downturn. All three singers were close to D'Amato. The team of Martin and Lewis was born at the Club 500 and Skinny had hired Frank in the early fifties, when no one else wanted him.

That fall, Sammy hooked up with the other two members of the Clan for a Rat Pack movie of sorts. Neither Sinatra nor Martin were involved, but *Johnny Cool* was the first feature for Peter Lawford's production company, Chrislaw (named for Peter's son, Christopher). Sammy and Joey Bishop appeared in supporting roles, and the title tune, sung by Sammy, was written by honorary Rat Packers Cahn and Van Heusen. It also starred Henry Silva, who had appeared in both *Ocean's Eleven* and *Sergeants 3*.

Actually, by the time *Johnny Cool* went into production, Peter had been banished from the Pack. Frank, never too fond of Lawford, had fallen out with the actor the previous February over President Kennedy's visit to Palm Springs. Originally, JFK had planned on staying with Sinatra. In anticipation of the visit, Frank had undertaken an extensive building program on his estate. Then Jack decided to stay with Bing Crosby instead. The official reason was that Crosby's home was easier for the Secret Service to secure, but the president's decision probably had more to do with his need to distance himself from Frank and his underworld friends than any issue of physical safety. Sinatra felt humiliated. It was bad enough that he had labored long and hard on Kennedy's behalf and that Crosby had done nothing in that regard, but Bing wasn't even a Democrat. Frank had to blame someone, and Peter, who'd delivered the bad news, was the natural fall guy. Kennedy's decision wasn't Lawford's fault, but Sinatra never spoke to the actor again.

That Bishop and Davis would lend their names to Peter's film project in the face of Sinatra's fury with Lawford reflected some courage on their part. The appeal certainly couldn't have been the roles they were offered. Joey played a used-car salesman and Sammy was an enigmatic gambler named "Educated." Neither was on the screen for more than a few minutes.

Opening in October 1963, *Johnny Cool* drew some favorable reviews, notably from the *New York Daily News* and the *Los Angeles Herald Examiner*, but *Newsweek* more accurately described it as a "woeful, dreary, stupid, jerry-built messy fraud of a picture."

While Lawford's film was in production, Sammy joined Frank and Dean in Reprise's recording studio. Martin and Davis shared a duet on "Sam's Song," which had been a hit for Bing Crosby and his son Gary in 1949, while Frank and Sammy joined forces on the old chestnut "Me and My Shadow." The latter featured a clever contrapuntal melody by the song's arranger, Billy May, and played charmingly off the singers' real-life relationship. Both duets were released as singles and made *Billboard*'s pop chart, but the Frank-Sammy collaboration was the more successful of the two, climbing to number 64 and hanging on to a spot in the Top 100 for six weeks.

In addition to the duets, Sammy, Frank, and Dean were part of an ambitious four-album series conceived by Sinatra for Reprise. It featured major pop singers re-creating the scores of four hit Broadway musicals—*Finian's Rainbow, Guys and Dolls, South Pacific,* and *Kiss Me Kate*—with new arrangements created especially for the LPs. Other participants included Rosemary Clooney, Bing Crosby, Debbie Reynolds, the McGuire Sisters, Dinah Shore, Jo Stafford, and Keely Smith. Highlights of Davis' contributions include "Too Darn Hot" and "Sit Down You're Rocking the Boat" on the *Kiss Me Kate* and *Guys and Dolls* albums, respectively.

In November 1962, the three pallies were together again at the Villa

Venice in Northbrook, Illinois, a small town outside of Chicago. The club was owned by Sam Giancana, although his name didn't appear on any deeds or licenses connected with the property. After spending $25,000 on a massive redecoration project designed to turn the facility into a showplace, Giancana established a lavish gambling den in a nondescript Quonset hut two blocks away. His idea, based on the Las Vegas model, was to introduce entertainment into the supper club as a means of attracting sophisticates to the nearby gaming parlor, with a shuttle service provided to take them from one venue to the other.

The new Villa Venice was a classy place. Patrons arriving at the club boarded gondolas, which transported them on a small, winding "river" to the main showroom. There they were seated at tables dressed with fine linen cloths and bouquets of flowers. The food was Italian, but dinner cost extra. The cover charge alone was $100 a person.

Eddie Fisher presided over the club's grand reopening on October 31. According to FBI wiretap reports, the singer performed without a fee, as did the Rat Packers, who followed him in late November. Frank's daughter Tina maintained that her father agreed to this gratis engagement to repay Momo for his "help" during the 1960 presidential election, even though, by November 1962, Frank and JFK were no longer pals. Dean and Sammy were there for Frank.

One concession Sinatra obtained from Giancana was the right to record the Rat Pack's stint at the club, which he planned to release as an LP on Reprise. Frank expected to make $500,000 from this endeavor, but for reasons that aren't entirely clear, no album was released until 2001, long after Sinatra sold the label and all three of the performers were dead.

The CD indicates how in sync the entertainers were with one another. Between the original Summit at the Sands and their subsequent get-togethers in Miami and Atlantic City, plus the informal sessions at one another's solo gigs, they had the patented Rat Pack bits down cold. But there was always room for a few new wrinkles. One evening at the Villa Venice, for example, Frank asked for a stool and someone threw one to him. "I thought you owned some of this," Dean said with mock indignation. "And that's how they treat you." Later, he pointed toward a table and told the others, "Hold the noise down, there's a gangster sleeping up there."

The mobsters, and everyone else in the house, loved the ribbing. As a consequence, the trio's stand at the Villa Venice was a smashing success—and Giancana's Quonset hut casino was, too. People may have enjoyed themselves, but a visit to the mobster's little Las Vegas cost most patrons a fortune. Peter Lawford described the setup as "a sucker trap . . . plain and simple," adding with barely concealed disgust that "Frank lent himself and Dean and Sammy and Eddie Fisher as bait to bring in the high rollers while Sam [Giancana] and the boys fleeced them." But Lawford also noted, "I guess it was either that or die."

For their trouble, the entertainers were subjected to interviews in their digs at the Ambassador East Hotel by FBI agents, who, not surprisingly, were intrigued by all the activity surrounding the Villa Venice. Sinatra said that he was performing as a favor to the club's owner, Leo Olsen. Dean basically stonewalled his interrogators. And Sammy, the most hospitable of the three, quipped, "Baby, let me say this. I got one eye, and that one eye sees a lot things that my brain tells me I shouldn't talk about. Because my brain says that, if I do, my one eye might not be seeing after a while."

Whatever their motivations, the entertainers helped Giancana and his associates take in more than $3 million by the end of November. Satisfied, Momo suspended the Villa Venice's entertainment policy as soon as the Rat Pack engagement ended on December 2. He shut down the Quonset hut gambling parlor altogether.

As for Sammy, Frank, and Dean, on January 23, they were back at the Sands for another three-week Summit. Eight months later, to the day, they returned to Vegas for another two-week stand, and at the end of the following month, they joined forces for a charity benefit at the Polo Lounge of the Beverly Hills Hotel. It wasn't a singing occasion; they just offered some chit-chat and a few comic bits and answered audience questions. Typical of the fare, Frank at one point said to Dean, "I want to talk about your drinking." To which Dean answered, "What's the matter? Did I miss a round?" With that as a warm-up, the trio went back to Chicago at the end of October to start work on their third picture together.

Like *Ocean's Eleven* and *Sergeants 3, Robin and the 7 Hoods* was a Frank Sinatra production, part of a deal the "Leader" made with Warner Bros., which also included the merger of his Reprise Records with the studio's own label. The new film was designed, like the first Clan feature, to place Sinatra and his pals where they felt most comfortable, in a twentieth-century urban setting and on the wrong side of the law. But like *Sergeants 3*, the screenwriter, David R. Schwartz, adapted a classic story, in this case the tale of Robin Hood and his Merry Men. The result was a lively, Damon Runyanesque account of Prohibition Chicago with Frank as Robbo, the head of an independent mob that runs afoul of a newly formed syndicate headed by Guy Gisborne (Peter Falk). Gisborne has more muscle and a corrupt deputy sheriff (Victor Buono) in his pocket, but Robbo has the support of the people after he gives $50,000 in unearned payoff money to charity. Between them stands the beautiful and well-bred but ruthless daughter (Barbara Rush) of the former crime boss (Edward G. Robinson in a cameo).

In keeping with the Robin Hood metaphor, Dean was Robbo's right-hand man, Little John, and Sammy was Robbo's driver, Will. Peter Lawford was to have played Allan A. Dale, a square former orphan who makes Robbo famous and then takes charge of his philanthropies. But after the JFK debacle in Palm Springs, the role went to—of all people—Bing Crosby. Joey Bishop, who had signed a contract to play one of the other hoods, also had a falling out with Frank, and he, too, was kicked off the film.

Ocean's Eleven had featured two musical numbers, but with the addition of Crosby, Sinatra decided to make *Robin and the 7 Hoods* a full-blown musical with eight original Cahn and Van Heusen tunes. That decision having been made, he turned the directing assignment over to his friend Gene Kelly, with whom he had costarred in *Anchors Aweigh* and *On the Town*. Kelly had choreographed and/or codirected a number of his own pictures, plus the Broadway production of Rodgers and Hammerstein's *Flower Drum Song* and Jackie Gleason's poignant film drama, *Gigot*. He agreed to produce as well as direct Frank's gangster picture, but the arrangement fell apart three weeks before the beginning of principal photography. According to one source, Sinatra thought Kelly was putting too much dancing into the production and ordered him to cut back. When Gene objected to Frank's tone, he was fired. Kelly maintained that he left of his own accord. Either way, he was clearly unhappy with the project's evolution. "If you're the producer, you're supposed to make the decisions," he told a *New York Post* reporter. "I wasn't making any decisions. I was taking orders. Quietly, I like the boys, but friendship isn't always everything in this business."

Scrambling quickly to avoid a delay in filming, Sinatra brought in Howard W. Koch, the producer of *Sergeants 3*, and Gordon Douglas, the director of Frank's 1955 tearjerker, *Young at Heart*. Douglas had no experience with musicals, but he was a reliable craftsman who knew how to deliver a project on time and on budget. And, indeed, he brought *Robin and the 7 Hoods* to a swift conclusion without mishap.

That didn't mean, of course, that filming proceeded in an orderly fashion. Chubby character actor Victor Buono likened principal photography to "being in a Vegas nightclub. Frank and Dean and their friends turned every place they went into a Vegas club." Sammy was working in a real Vegas club, the Copa Room at the Sands, during part of principal photography. Thus, once the company returned to Los Angeles, he was back to commuting to and from Nevada, as he had done so often in the past. As he didn't get to spend much time with May, who stayed home with the kids, he invited her to visit the set. But she refused, saying, "Frankly, I can't stand your relationship with Frank, the way he treats you, the jokes, the way you kowtow to him."

The most notable event during the making of the musical occurred on the morning of November 22. The cast and crew were at work on the Warner's lot in Burbank when they learned that President Kennedy had been shot and killed in Dallas. In his autobiography, *Why Me?*, Davis recalled that he and his costars were shooting the scene in which the mobsters bury their former leader when they learned the news from Texas. But according to the call sheets for the picture, only Frank was working that day. Although Sinatra was devastated, he and the crew continued working until nearly 3:00 P.M. Then Sinatra returned home and went into deep seclusion for days. (For what it's worth, Sammy's version included Joey Bishop among those on the set that terrible morning; Bishop wasn't even in the picture, and Sammy himself wasn't in the burial scene.)

Wherever he was when he heard the news, Davis, like the rest of the country, was in shock, even though JFK was hardly a friend. Not only had the president banished him from the inauguration, he had tried to remove Sammy and May from a White House guest list the previous February, when about a thousand prominent African Americans were invited for a reception in honor of Abraham Lincoln's birthday. Unknown to Kennedy, one of his assistants had reinstated Davis' name. Shocked to see Sammy and his Caucasian wife in the receiving line, JFK made sure that no photos were taken of the couple that evening. The entertainer was probably unaware of JFK's reaction to his White House invitation, but he knew Kennedy was no friend. Still, he resolved to take flowers to the president's gravesite the next time he was in Washington—as thanks for Kennedy's stand on civil rights.

Robin and the 7 Hoods opened in Los Angeles on July 29, 1964 and in New York on August 5. The critics were evenly divided as to its merits, with Bosley Crowther of the *New York Times* calling it "an artless and obvious film" and his colleague on the *Daily News*, Dorothy Masters, dubbing it "a zinging, swinging spoof." In truth, it fell somewhere in between. A poor man's *Guys and Dolls*, it certainly broke no new ground, was overly long, and fell apart at the end. But it did offer a picture-stealing performance by Peter Falk and several delightful Cahn–Van Heusen songs, including "Style" and "My Kind of Town."

For the most part, audiences enjoyed *Robin and the 7 Hoods*. It certainly made money. The following year, Frank and Dean would join forces for a modern comedy, *Marriage on the Rocks*, and two years after that they hit the trail for *Texas across the River*. The latter even featured Joey Bishop, who'd managed to regain Frank's favor (he played, oddly enough, an Indian). But *Robin and the 7 Hoods* marked the end of the Rat Pack pictures per se. Sammy would be tied up with a Broadway musical, *Golden Boy*, for several years. And Dean was busy with his own projects, which, in 1965, included the launch of his Matt Helm features—a spy series in the James Bond tradition—and the start of his long-running variety show on TV. Sinatra had plenty to do that year as well, such as a big World War II thriller, *Von Ryan's Express*, and, in 1966, he married the much younger Mia Farrow.

Looking back in 1967, Sammy told the *Los Angeles Times'* Sally Marks, "The Clan thing was a simply marvelous period in our lives, but we all have to move on. It's like the Marx Brothers pictures. . . . Let me not knock it. I'm not saying that if the climate was right, it wouldn't be marvelous to do another *Ocean's 11*. . . . It really made it for me, those pictures I did with Frank and Dean and Peter."

He exaggerated a bit, but the Rat Pack association, despite its somewhat demeaning elements, did enhance Davis' stature in certain quarters where he was not well established. For one thing, it brought him into the Hollywood mainstream. All of his previous pictures except *Porgy and Bess* had been small-budget independent pictures with limited audience appeal or, in the case of *The Threepenny Opera*, a foreign film. Even *Porgy* was an anomaly, being an opera with an all-black cast. Davis, always eager to be part of the in crowd, appreciated Frank's letting him participate in three first-tier, highly commercial ventures. But his entry into the big-time world of Hollywood proved more of a psychological boost than a door-opening career move. With the sole exception of 1969's *Sweet Charity*, in which he had a relatively minor role, Sammy would not be part of a big, mainstream Hollywood film again until the 1980s, when, perhaps by coincidence, he was again teamed with Dean and, later, Dean and Frank.

The Rat Pack connection unquestionably boosted Davis' standing with the American public. By the time *Ocean's Eleven* debuted, Sammy was a widely celebrated entertainer and a popular recording artist, but most of the time he came off as a sweet, eager-to-please, clean-shaven, eyeglass-wearing kid. With the Rat Pack, he became cool. He even looked better, growing a moustache and sometimes a goatee and often ditching the black hornrims. He also borrowed Frank and Dean's ring-a-ding manner, mixing in his own brand of African American jazz-based hipness, with a touch of *Amos and Andy* tossed in for good measure. Davis' transformation was enhanced by the Clan's live appearances, but millions more people saw him in the Rat Pack films than saw them on stage. He may not have had as much to do on screen as Frank or Dean, but he was there, and he was swinging with the rest of them, one black guy with some pretty heavy white dudes. For the many minions who were charmed by the idea of these cool cats grooving with each other, the image stuck.

The reputation was Sammy's to keep or to lose. First he did one, then the other.

Golden Boy

Debuting on Broadway on November 4, 1937, *Golden Boy* was the biggest hit in Clifford Odets' distinguished career. Like the playwright's previous works, *Awake and Sing* and *Waiting for Lefty*, the drama was rooted in the urban American experience and tinged with the playwright's leftist social ideas. But it also reflected his conflicted feelings about his financial success, the result of a stint as a screenwriter in Hollywood. The central figure in his drama was Joe Bonaparte, a boy from an Italian American family who risks his career as a concert violinist by boxing, partly to make money but mostly because he wants to be a "somebody." Luther Adler created the role, with Frances Farmer as Lorna Moon, the hard-edged New Jersey girl caught between Joe and his manager, Tom Moody. *Golden Boy* became a film in 1939, with Barbara Stanwyck and William Holden (in his first starring role); it returned to Broadway in a 1952 revival headed by John Garfield, a member of the original cast.

It was a thirty-four-year-old producer named Hillard Elkins who thought of transforming the drama into a musical with a Negro protagonist instead of an Italian American. In the years since *Golden Boy*'s debut, the fight game had come to be dominated by African American boxers, so Elkins' idea seemed a natural. But it didn't gel until he caught Sammy's "midnight matinee" at the Prince of Wales in London in 1961.

After that show, the young producer shared his notion with Davis. Sammy was captivated by the idea of transferring the Italian American immigrant experience to the environs of Harlem. Particularly intriguing was the idea of keeping Joe's romantic interest, Lorna Moon, white. A racially integrated love story, while echoing Sammy's real-life marriage, was a daring notion at the time in any medium—theater, film, or television. It was a major selling point, for Sammy had vowed after *Mr. Wonderful* that he would return to Broadway only in a vehicle of substance. He also thought that a bravura performance might open more doors for him in Hollywood; beyond anything, he wanted to be a movie star, like his friend Frank Sinatra.

Still, Sammy's participation in the musical came with several conditions. First, he insisted on a racially integrated cast. "Absolutely," Elkins agreed. "Fifty-fifty." Sammy also wanted his musical director, George Rhodes, to conduct the show, which was acceptable as well. In return, Sammy gave the producer a three-year commitment, an unusually long time for any star but particularly astonishing in light of his far more lucrative career in nightclubs. A long run would cut into his earnings, but it would offer him one advantage: he could get off the road and settle down for a while.

In return for his long-term commitment, Sammy was awarded 10 percent of the musical's weekly box office gross, 15 percent of the profits, and a sizable expense account. Collectively, this amounted to about $20,000 a week, the highest amount ever earned by a Broadway performer to that point. Of course, Sammy was still splitting his earnings with Will Mastin and his father, so he saw only a third of the total.

With a firm commitment from Davis, Elkins engaged Odets to adapt his play; he hired composer Charles Strouse and lyricist Lee Adams to create the score. Strouse and Adams were best known for their first Broadway outing, *Bye Bye Birdie*, a spoof of the Elvis Presley craze. Elkins, who'd produced only one previous Broadway production, also set out to raise the money for the musical, a laborious job as it was capitalized at a then hefty $465,000 (roughly half eventually came from Capitol Records, which earned the rights to the cast album as part of its investment).

Meanwhile, Sammy returned to the nightclub circuit, with gigs at Harrah's Lake Tahoe, the Olympia Music House in Paris, and, of course, the Sands.

While in Vegas, he also played a small role in an independent feature film called *Nightmare in the Sun*. Directed by character actor Marc Lawrence, it told the rather shoddy story of a hitchhiker (John Derek) accused of a murder he didn't commit. Davis played a hearing-impaired truck driver who picks up the hitchhiker near the picture's beginning. *Nightmare in the Sun* was screened in Los Angeles in December 1964, but it quickly vanished, doomed by an overly melodramatic script, poor acting, and lethargic directing.

After Vegas, Sammy traveled to New York for a memorable two weeks at the Copa starting on April 30. Thanks in part to his Rat Pack association, Davis was as hot as an entertainer could be. Consequently, people stood outside the club every evening throughout the engagement, hoping someone would cancel a reservation. Jules Podell tried to accommodate as many patrons as possible. Noted the *Times'* Robert Alden, "In its 24-year history, the Copacabana has never had more patrons or taken in more money as it has during Mr. Davis's present turn at the club."

While Sammy spun his magic onstage, the creators of *Golden Boy* tried to inject new life into a twenty-seven-year-old warhorse.

The score developed readily, with jazzy uptempo numbers and poignant ballads, ideally suited not only to Sammy's voice but also to that of the suave African American singer Billy Daniels, who had signed on to play Eddie Satin, the gangster who takes charge of the boxer's career. Standouts included "Night Song," a number in which Joe (now called Wellington) expresses his ambitions and frustrations; a lush title-song ballad for Lorna; and "Don't Forget 127th Street," a lively production number.

Unlike Strouse and Adams, Odets was struggling. He didn't know enough about the African American experience to effect the adaptation. His close friend and protégé, playwright William Gibson, thought Odets would have eventually succeeded, but he was felled by cancer in August 1963. By then he had completed two drafts of the adaptation, but a great deal of work remained. Elkins brought in several play doctors, but none of them found the key to the book. Finally, he decided that he, Strouse, and Adams would have to rewrite the text as they went along, in conjunction with the show's director, Peter Coe. How much help Coe could offer remained to be seen. An Englishman, he had been hired largely on the basis of his recent success with another adaptation, *Oliver!*, the musical based on Dickens' *Oliver Twist*.

Rehearsals began at the Ethel Barrymore Theatre on May 15, a couple of days after Sammy's closing at the Copa. Besides Billy Daniels, his costars included his *Desperate Hours* colleague, Roy Glenn, a then-unknown Louis Gossett, Jr., and rotund Johnny Brown as Joe's father, brother, and brother-in-law, respectively, and Hollywood character actor Kenneth Tobey as fight manager Tom Moody. The all-important role of Lorna Moon had gone to Paula Wayne, a sultry blonde with a sexy, whiskey-soaked voice. Born in Oklahoma, Wayne had made her Broadway debut in the 1957 edition of the *Ziegfeld Follies* with Beatrice Lillie. Excited about getting underway, Sammy told the press that *Golden Boy* was something special. By contrast, "*Mr. Wonderful* was just a series of jokes and songs, very much a revue. It certainly wasn't anything like Odets."

On June 26, the cast and crew moved to Philadelphia for a five-week run at the Shubert Theater. Engagements were also booked in Boston and Detroit, making for a road tour of fourteen weeks in total. Before leaving New York, Sammy justified this unusually long tryout period, saying, "I don't go for the unfairness of all those last-minute switches in shows. It's not going to happen to me; that's why I'm doing 14 weeks on the road. Thank God, everybody concerned feels the same way. Oh, I'm not saying there ain't gonna be problems. I'm just saying you've gotta give yourself enough time to straighten out your problems."

He had no idea what he was in for.

The Philadelphia critics were kind and every performance at the Shubert was selling out, thanks to Sammy's drawing power, but the creators of the show knew things weren't right. With the book still wobbly, all of the other elements in the production lacked clarity and purpose and, as a result, nothing sparkled. In a search for that elusive cohesiveness, Sammy and the entire creative team spent their off-hours rewriting scenes and bits of dialogue. One change called for making Joe a pianist rather than a violinist. How many black violinists were there? they asked themselves. Later, they turned him into a surgeon.

The strain of working on and performing the show simultaneously began to grate on Davis. May and the kids came with him to Philadelphia, but he had no time to spend with them. He worked his voice so hard he developed laryngitis. Worst of all, he was not getting along with Peter Coe. According to Charles Strouse, the director's "tendency was to make stage pictures. He couldn't care less who the star was." As the musical's principal drawing card, with his name in lights above the title on the marquee, Sammy rightly felt that the focus should be on him. The two men became so hostile toward one another that they actually came to blows, according to a subsequent report in *Life* magazine.

The situation worsened when the company moved on to Boston. The critics there were far from enthusiastic. If anything, the unfocused tinkering by so many hands may have actually made the show worse. Elkins realized that his only hope lay in hiring an experienced scriptwriter. Consequently, he invited two celebrated professionals to view the production. The first was Paddy Chayefsky, the author of *Marty* and numerous other award-winning films and TV dramas. The second was William Gibson, Odets' close friend and the author of such well-regarded plays as *Two for the Seesaw* and *The Miracle Worker*. Chayefsky advised Elkins to close the show, but Gibson was more deliberative. Motivated, in part, by his desire to help Odets' family, who could earn a significant amount of money from a hit Broadway musical, he told the producer and

Sammy that he wanted to think about what he'd seen. He promised nothing, but he left for his Cape Cod summer home with a copy of the musical's script and score.

There Gibson began to realize that the show's problem was that it didn't go far enough to bring the African American experience onto the stage. The musical was set in Harlem, but it didn't ring true. He recalled one scene in which Joe meets Lorna at an inner-city park. Coe had added a few kids on swings to give the setting some atmosphere. But, in Gibson's words, it was like "a Jimmy Stewart movie in the middle of Ohio City. It had nothing to do with the reality of the day."

Also clouding the issue, in Gibson's opinion, was Joe's career conflict. Given the civil rights element, it became unnecessary baggage. There was enough of a conflict in the boxer's desire to escape the confines of a white-dominated society and achieve the kind of success that was unavailable to most members of his race, particularly as the race issue was compounded by Joe's growing love for Lorna. Elkins had set something important in motion when he decided at the outset to keep the woman white, but the implications of that decision had been subordinated to Joe's career struggle. Cut that and focus on the romance, Gibson thought, and perhaps the story would come alive.

With these ideas in mind, he started to write, and after only five days he had the first act sketched out. Returning to Boston, he read what he had written to Sammy, Hilly Elkins, and the show's creators. They were extremely enthusiastic. Thus inspired, Gibson went home and drafted the second act. About three or four days later, he read the act in Boston and received the same warm response.

The only dissenting voice came from Peter Coe, who had been summoned to Boston from London, where he was enjoying a three-week vacation. Coe liked the show the way it was, which left Elkins with a fundamental choice: embrace the new concept and replace Peter Coe or retain Coe and keep tinkering. He chose the former.

There was no question about who should take over. Arthur Penn was William Gibson's first and only choice. He and the director were close friends who had shared a highly rewarding collaboration on *Two for the Seesaw* and *The Miracle Worker*. Penn enjoyed a successful career in films as well.

After watching the show, Penn was far from enthusiastic. But he agreed to take on the project, primarily as a favor to Gibson. With the new director on board, Elkins then had to decide how to rehearse and develop what amounted to a new show while performing another one at night. It was a daunting task.

On August 25, the company moved on to Detroit, setting up shop at the Fisher Theater. Not only was the city sweltering in the summer heat, but it was in the midst of a race riot. If Gibson wanted topicality, it was practically on his doorstep. Moreover, the newspapers were on strike, so there were no reviews. That was probably just as well, for, as new material was ready for testing it was added incrementally into the show. For several weeks, the cast performed parts of one version and parts of another, with the balance between the two constantly changing. Consequently, as Charles Strouse put it, "People didn't know what the hell was happening, but they still kept buying tickets."

Once again, Sammy lost his voice, the result of singing full-out during daytime rehearsals and then in performance at night. He didn't know any other way to sing. A throat specialist advised him to take a month off and rest his throat, but shutting down the show even for a few days was impossible. So Sammy simply carried on. Never one to accept failure, he was determined that the musical would be a hit even if it killed him. During his few free hours, he was either memorizing new material or working with Strouse and Adams on new songs or sharing his experiences and feelings with Bill Gibson in order to fill the book with the greatest possible verisimilitude. "Sammy essentially ran the company," said Arthur Penn. "The actors, the dancers, all were beholden to him and in awe of him and he was a powerful figure in this show. He sort of said to Bill and me, 'You take care of getting the book and the music and the numbers together. I'll take care of the company, the kids in the company, the feeling.' They were splendid dancers and splendid singers, but many of them were unfamiliar with the theater or Broadway, and Sammy did offer a kind of beacon of performance expectation that was really quite remarkable."

Elkins also labored admirably to keep the company intact. When new sets and costumes were mandated by changes in the book or score, he financed the expenses with his American Express card. When he was maxed out, he raised additional capital. By the time the show opened on Broadway, the producer estimated the overage at $250,000, an incredible amount in 1964.

Gibson and Penn labored to refine the book. These changes, in turn, mandated changes in the score, although Gibson tried whenever possible to work with the existing material, moving it around as needed. To stage the new musical numbers, including a wonderfully energetic, percussion-driven opener showing a variety of boxers in training, Penn brought in the well-regarded director-choreographer Herbert Ross, who worked without credit.

Perhaps Penn's most significant contribution lay in his efforts to help Sammy and Paula Wayne take Joe and Lorna from typical musical comedy cardboard figures to believable, flesh-and-blood human beings. He talked with them about their characters, but he also taught them sensory and preparatory exercises, the kind of techniques used by members of the Actors Studio to achieve realism on stage and on screen.

"Arthur brought a wonderful sense of human relationships amongst the characters of the play," said Gibson. "A lot of it was keeping Sammy from bursting out into theatrical blubberings when he wanted to show he was suffering and stuff. He'd do something that was very unattractive and also not very skillful technically." Even Penn was impressed by the change in his star, saying, "Sammy had a lot of emotion available to him, more, in fact, than Paula had, and he was more able to draw on it. Where it may have lacked elegance, it had a kind of brilliance of another sort behind it."

Thus, as the run in Detroit wound down, everything started to come together. The new book was in place, albeit with rewrites continuing. The score was largely set, although here, too, there were changes. The main characters were taking on greater depth, both in the way they were written and in the way they were performed. There were even alterations in the sets, the costumes, and the dances. "For the first time in months, we felt that we were on the right track," Elkins asserted. Audience members were leaving the theater clearly moved by what they had seen. Some even wept during the show's final moments. "It was really incredible that we were able to get anywhere," said Penn. "But we did. And it was a great willingness on everybody's part once we had committed to it to get it as good as we could possibly get it."

The company took up residence at the Majestic Theatre in New York in mid-September. The opening was scheduled for the 28th, but Elkins pushed it back three weeks so that work on the production could continue. Sammy had originally planned on taking a week's leave of absence from the show to appear in a film, *The Sandpiper,* with his friends Elizabeth Taylor and Richard Burton. Realizing that leaving the musical at this point could badly damage its momentum, he reluctantly bowed out of the picture.

By now, the company was exhausted from months of nearly round-the-clock work. Again, they found preview audiences warming to the show, although some bigots were so upset by the interracial love story that they threw rocks through the theater windows. Said Elkins, "Sammy was very concerned, as were we all, for his safety."

Opening night was set for Tuesday, October 20. On the 16th, Sammy learned that more changes would be instituted over the weekend, requiring additional rehearsals in between the two evening shows and the Saturday matinee. With his throat still shot, he couldn't take any more. He'd finally reached the end of his strength. Realizing this, Elkins asked Penn to cancel rehearsals, but the director refused, insisting that the work was necessary. In an act of self-preservation, Sammy simply disappeared. Shortly before curtain time on Saturday afternoon, May called the Majestic to tell Elkins that her husband wouldn't be coming. She asserted that she didn't know where he was, although that was probably not true. The producer had no choice but to cancel the matinee. Sammy's understudy, Lamont Washington, went on that evening, but 70 percent of the audience walked out.

Elkins didn't know when or even if his star was planning on returning to the show. He, Penn, and the others were furious. And frightened. If Sammy quit, where would they be? The show totally revolved around him. He was onstage for all but twenty of the show's 125 minutes, dancing in four numbers and singing ten songs. There was no other African American star at the time who could possibly have taken his place. Finally, early Sunday morning, Hilly got word—perhaps from Sammy directly, perhaps from someone else (accounts vary)—that his star was not deserting him.

Indeed, following this bit of rest, Davis resumed his killing pace, rehearsing on Sunday until early Monday morning. He returned later on Monday for more work. The following day he attended a luncheon of the National Conference of Christians and Jews, which had honored him with its Brotherhood Award. Then, instead of relaxing at home, he went to the theater and rehearsed all afternoon, putting additional strain on his aching throat. When he finally stopped at about 6 P.M., he repaired to his dressing room, ate some pasta, and watched the news on TV. He also glanced at the many telegrams and floral bouquets from friends and fans. The well-wishers included Laurence Olivier and Robert Kennedy, then running for a U.S. Senate seat from New York, but Sammy was disappointed to find nothing from Sinatra. "Maybe Frank didn't send one on purpose," he said wistfully. "Maybe he wanted to make me mad and provoke me into a better performance."

As was customary with Broadway openings, the show had an early curtain that night, 7:00 P.M., so that the critics could make their filing deadlines. Sammy started a bit rocky. His opening number clearly reflected the wretched condition of his throat, but, after that, he dug into that incredible wellspring of energy and drive, and his performance took off. Particularly impressive was his work in the dramatic scenes, thanks to the hours he had worked with Penn. When the final curtain rang down, the crowd leaped to its feet, giving him the kind of ovation that every Broadway actor dreams about. But Davis knew the house was packed with the company's friends and family and wasn't necessarily indicative of the all-important reaction from the critics. Fearing the worst, he donned a tuxedo and repaired to Danny's Hideaway to wait for the reviews.

Finally, the agony was over. Someone phoned the nightclub with Walter Kerr's review in the *New York Herald Tribune*. It wasn't a total rave but it was close. Sammy's raspy voice notwithstanding, the critic found his performance "serious, expert, affecting." He also praised Tony Walton's sets and costumes and Tharon Musser's lighting and considered the book so strong that it could virtually stand alone as a straight play again. What a remarkable comment in light of where the production had started.

The *Times'* Howard Taubman, dean of the New York critics, was somewhat less enthusiastic than Kerr, maintaining that the story failed to become emotionally engaging. Still, he loved the musical's "snap, speed and professionalism." He also felt the book's "swift, keen-edged lines about the Negro condition" had "bite and integrity." Best of all, he concluded on a positive note, asserting, "So much is vibrant, colorful and well-founded in background, pungent comment and sheer theater that even a *Golden Boy* with a lost heart can be a rewarding evening's companion."

Some of the other critics were less positive, but overall the show was considered, if not perfect, superior to most Broadway offerings. They could live with that. There was no question that *Golden Boy* would settle into the Majestic for a long, long run.

No one was happier than the show's star. He had finally earned the respect he'd been seeking for so long outside the narrow world of nightclubs and showrooms. And how wonderful it felt. Prancing around the crowded tables at Danny's, he hugged everyone in sight, loudly proclaiming, "I'm ten feet tall! I'm a Broadway star! We've got a hit!"

CHAPTER 17

"On the Seventh Day, He Works"

While Sammy was in Detroit, May lived with the kids in an apartment she rented in Manhattan. Although she was now a full-time homemaker, she had help around the house in the person of Lessie Lee Jackson, a combination nanny, maid, and cook extraordinaire. Also nearby was Sammy's grandmother, Rosa B., who had traveled east with the family. But Sammy's rambunctious children made his household too enervating for the elderly woman, so she returned to California, where she died in 1966.

The apartment, on Second Avenue in the Eighties, was fine, but Sammy wanted something that would look like the home of a star. Although May was more interested in a home than a showplace for outsiders, she deferred to her husband's wishes. Once *Golden Boy* was up and running, the Davises moved into a spacious two-floor duplex in a brownstone on East 93rd Street, just off Fifth Avenue.

Wanting to travel to the Majestic in comfort, Sammy bought a navy-blue Cadillac limousine, complete with a bar, telephone, and television. Typically, he would arrive at the theater an hour or so before curtain and retire to his dressing room, which Hillard Elkins had renovated to the tune of about $10,000. It featured wall-to-wall carpeting, custom-built furniture, and an entertainment system with color TV, stereo, and tape-recording equipment. Liberally scattered throughout the room were photos of Davis and his famous "friends," including Queen Elizabeth, JFK, and Audrey Hepburn, and the more than two hundred telegrams he had received on opening night.

Eight performances a week kept Davis alert. As he put it at the time, "I love doing *Golden Boy*. It's a great show, it's tremendous exercise." Just his concluding fight scene with Jamie Rogers required tremendous concentration and skill. If the timing were off even a little bit, one of the participants could get hurt—and Sammy did on several occasions. Demanding, too, was a choreographed rumble in Act One that pitted Joe against several street toughs. On the evening of June 30, 1965 one of the dancers accidentally delivered a knee blow to Sammy's chest during this sequence, and it landed right above his heart. Visibly shaken, he was helped off the stage and rushed to a hospital. His understudy, Lamont Washington, finished the performance that evening and stood in for the star for several nights thereafter. Given such mishaps, it is not surprising that Davis said on the show's closing, "I never worked so hard in my life. It got to a point that doing a movie or a benefit or a night club was a pleasure."

And he did an amazing number of such things.

During the first year of the show's run, he performed at a variety of charitable affairs and made several trips to the Reprise recording studio, thereby enabling the label to release the LPs *Sammy Davis Jr. Salutes the Stars of the London Palladium* and *The Shelter of Your Arms* in 1964 and *Sammy's Back on Broadway* in 1965. He even managed a couple of nightclub appearances. In February 1965, for example, he flew to San Juan on a Sunday, his day off, did two shows at the Hotel El San Juan, and then flew back to Manhattan. On June 20, he joined Frank, Dean, Trini Lopez, Count Basie, master of ceremonies Johnny Carson (substituting for an ailing Joey Bishop), and several other notables for a gala at Kiel Auditorium in St. Louis. The evening, organized by Sinatra to benefit a halfway house for ex-convicts, was beamed live via closed-circuit television to several other venues, including the El Morocco in New York.* And in mid-August, Sammy appeared for two shows, at midnight and 2:30 A.M., at the Club Harlem in Atlantic City, to help out the cabaret's owner, Larry Steele. Although the nightspot's patrons would have been delighted with sixty minutes, Davis did an hour and a half during the first show and more than two and a half hours at the second.

He also made numerous TV appearances that year. Not only was he a guest on *The Tonight Show Starring Johnny Carson* eight times between October 1964 and October 1965, but he also hosted the show on November 23.† In addition, he hosted *Hullabaloo*, an NBC variety show devoted to popular music, on February 23, 1965 and, on March 3, he played himself in an episode of *The Patty Duke Show*, an ABC sitcom produced by Peter Lawford that featured the Oscar-winning actress as identical teenage cousins. In September, he returned to host *Hullabaloo* again,

---

*A kinescope of this concert was discovered in 1997 and shown with great fanfare at the Museum of Television and Radio in New York. Although it doesn't present Sammy, Frank, and Dean at their Clanish best, it remains the most complete audiovideo record of a Rat Pack engagement.

†At this point, *The Tonight Show* originated from New York.

joined Sinatra for the usual pie-throwing mayhem on *The Soupy Sales Show,* and served as the New York emcee for the *17th Annual Emmy Awards* (which Danny Thomas cohosted from the Hollywood Palladium).

He even found time for two TV specials of his own. The first, which aired on February 18, was a highly successful sixty-minute show produced by the New York affiliate of ABC. Called *The Swinging World of Sammy Davis,* it featured Peter Lawford, Sammy's *Golden Boy* costar Billy Daniels, and Lola Falana, a member of the musical's ensemble who was becoming something of a Davis protégé.

The following November 21, ABC, inspired by its New York affiliate, nationally aired *Sammy Davis and the Wonderful World of Children.* Sammy was the only adult in the hour, which featured a host of talented youngsters. On the whole, it was not well received; the *New York Herald Tribune* called it "a strange and repelling hour."

When not otherwise engaged, Sammy could often be found at the nightclub openings of other entertainers or at some bash or party. Less than a decade had passed since he'd opened in *Mr. Wonderful,* but, thanks to the civil rights movement, he no longer had to hide out in his private digs, fearing rejection, scorn, or the back-door racism of closet bigots if he ventured forth to the best nightspots or parties. Now he was welcomed everywhere.

Although Sammy would often plug his musical at his public and televised appearances, Hillard Elkins was not entirely happy with the extent to which his star exerted himself. Occasionally he would talk to Sammy about slowing down, but, as he put it, "Knowing the nature of the beast, it was pointless to try to do something that wasn't going to get done."

But Elkins fully supported Sammy's decision to take a night off in March 1965 to participate in a civil rights march in Alabama. In fact, Elkins was instrumental in securing Sammy's presence for this occasion.

The march was organized by Martin Luther King, Jr., and the Southern Christian Leadership Conference. Wishing to bolster the registration of Negro voters in the South, the organization focused its efforts on the small town of Selma, Alabama. Dallas County, of which Selma was the seat, had 15,000 eligible African American voters but only 350 were registered. The local white officials were doing everything in their power to keep their black neighbors disenfranchised, instituting a literacy test so difficult King said that even "Chief Justice [Earl] Warren might fail to answer some of the questions." Most Negroes in the county never even got to take the test. Some were discouraged from doing so through beatings administered by the local sheriff, Jim Clark, and his deputies; others were fired from their jobs if they indicated a desire to register.

To focus national attention on the situation, King and his followers decided to stage a protest march, covering the fifty miles from Selma to the state capital in Montgomery to present a petition to Governor George Wallace.

The march began on March 7. Late in the afternoon, the demonstrators reached the Edmund Pettis Bridge on the outskirts of Selma, where they were met by fifty helmeted state troopers and Jim Clark's deputies. After a ninety-second warning, the officials charged the group, freely wielding billy clubs, bullwhips, and tear gas. Seventy of the six hundred marchers were hospitalized on what came to be known as "Bloody Sunday."

Legal issues prevented a resumption of the demonstration until March 21, when King and his followers finally marched out of Selma. They planned to camp out at several select spots along the route and arrive in the Alabama capital five days later.

To give added weight to the final leg of the journey, Harry Belafonte organized a group of celebrities to join the protesters outside of Montgomery on the evening of the 24th and to enter the capital with them the following day. These celebrities included Tony Bennett, Billy Eckstine, Leonard Bernstein, Shelly Winters, Betty Comden, and Adolph Green. Belafonte wanted Davis to participate as well. Rather than reach out to Sammy directly, the singer called Hillard Elkins, and the producer, in turn, relayed the invitation. Although Sammy had performed at a fundraising concert in Alabama and had joined the March on Washington, his fear of hardcore protests in the deep South hadn't abated, and this one promised to be dangerous indeed. He asked his producer to tell Belafonte that he, Hilly, couldn't afford to close *Golden Boy* for a night in order for Sammy to make the trip. But Elkins told Harry the truth. Belafonte responded by saying, "Tell him I bought the night." When Elkins relayed the news, Sammy knew he was trapped.

Thus, on March 24, he set out with Elkins and the producer's girlfriend, Murphy Bennett, a former New York City Deputy Police Commissioner named William Rowe, and two security men recently added to Sammy's payroll, Joe Grant and Herb Seeger. They flew into Birmingham, where they were greeted by the notoriously racist chief of police, Bull Connor. Also present was Charles Evers, the brother of slain civil rights leader Medgar Evers, who drove the group to the protesters' camp site. "The first thing we see [along the way]," recalled Elkins, "is a huge billboard, red, white and blue, saying, 'Help keep the U.S. out of the UN.' And the first thing we hear is, 'This is ABC, the white news.' It was not conducive to relaxing. For any of us."

That night, Sammy took part in an improvised show in the middle of a clearing. The group had no stage so they performed on wooden coffins loaned for that purpose by a local mortician, with lighting equipment provided by the U.S. Air Force. The following morning, the entertainer and the rest of the marchers—some fifty thousand of them—set off for Montgomery. As they gave forth with the movement's anthem, "We Shall Overcome," they sensed that, to quote King, the "smell of victory was in the air."

Behind the barricades that lined the streets, Sammy could see hundreds of furious local citizens "glaring at us, resenting us, angry, fear in their eyes. There were no jeers, no insults, they watched us in silence, despising us." As King put it, "We were reminded that this was not a march to the capital of a civilized nation, as was the March on Washington. We had marched through a swamp of poverty, ignorance, race hatred, and sadism."

The presence of the National Guard, ostensibly there to protect the marchers, provided no comfort. Consequently, Sammy was nervous and agitated. "My stomach, my arms trembled," he recalled. "My legs were weakened and I walked heavily." But he drew comfort from the sight beyond the guardsmen and the locals: dozens of photographers, journalists, and cameramen, all recording the moment for history and for newspapers, radio stations, and TV news programs around the country. Millions of people would be exposed to this effort to enfranchise Negro citizens, he realized. Emboldened by the media's presence, he marched on, proud that he had come. Elkins called it "a very, very important moment for all of us," while King equated the demonstration to Mahatma Gandhi's celebrated March to the Sea in India. Shortly thereafter, the U.S. Congress enacted the Voting Rights Act of 1965.

As soon as the march concluded, Davis, Elkins, and their group quickly left Alabama. But the memory of that brief sojourn would always remain with Sammy.

Most things Davis did during his first year in New York were neither as momentous nor as frightening as the civil rights march. But the sheer range and number of his activities, all undertaken while he was giving a maximum effort eight times a week on the stage at the Majestic Theatre—astonished both his friends and members of the press. "Some people think Davis has a God complex," Dick Schaap wrote, tongue in cheek, in the *New York Herald Tribune,* "but this is absurd. On the seventh day, he works."

Sammy's explanation for his incredible drive was simple: "As a jack of all trades, master of none, I can't let the grass grow under my feet. I've got to keep developing in every medium—night clubs, TV, theater, records, everything." The key, he said, lay in his approach: "When I work, I work. When I relax, I'm all relaxation—total. I stop all the molecules, it's a form of yoga, I guess." Others saw his awesome regimen in a different light. One acquaintance asserted, "Sammy's trying to kill himself. It's a death wish. He has all the talent in the world but he still can't believe he's any good."

This assessment was wrong. The *only* facet in his life where Sammy felt genuinely confident was his ability as a performer. But his need for love, approval, and respect was bottomless, since, at root, he felt woefully lacking in all three. Later in his life, he came close to acknowledging this, saying, "I wanted to prove the world wrong [for abusing him]. Maybe that's why I strived so hard for success. I thought success could insulate me. All my life I had heard: 'They say you can't succeed.' My answer was, 'Who are they?'"

Despite his overweening ambition and nearly boundless energy, he still had physical limits—and he reached them in September 1965. On the afternoon of the 23rd, he collapsed in his apartment. May immediately summoned a physician, John Holloman, and when he arrived, Davis told him, "I'm very tired. I feel terrible. I'm just exhausted." After examining his patient, Holloman gave him some tranquilizers, then advised May, "Get him out of here. I don't want him doing a thing for two weeks."

For once, Sammy followed his doctor's orders, immediately booking a flight for Honolulu. The next day he left, with only Murphy Bennett for companionship. "It was absolutely marvelous," Davis said shortly thereafter. "No one knew we were coming. So there was none of that nonsense of the 17 leis around your neck when you get off the plane. I played 18 and sometimes 27 holes [of golf] a day. It was the first time in my life that I'd ever arrived in a town when I didn't have to ask first, 'Where is rehearsal?' and second, 'When does the first show go on?'"

Meanwhile, back home, Hedda Hopper was telling her readers that the "Sammy Davis, Jr., musical *Golden Boy* closed Thursday night in New York City when the star was found to be on the verge of a nervous breakdown from overwork." Uninformed of Sammy's departure in advance, Elkins was stunned when he learned that his star had left town. But he was aware of the extent to which Sammy had been pushing himself and couldn't really begrudge him a brief respite. He decided to reopen the show the following night, with Sammy's understudy, Lamont Washington, filling in. But, of course, business fell off dramatically during the star's absence.

Although the reasons for Davis' exhaustion were perfectly evident, his departure for Hawaii without his family sparked divorce rumors in the press. "That's what they say every time he exits the door," May responded. "I'm disgusted with those divorce rumors. They're ridiculous."

As her comment suggests, this wasn't the first time the media had speculated about problems in the Davis household. As recently as that summer, when May vacationed without her husband in Lake Tahoe, some journalists had raised the specter of a legal separation. Sammy said at that time, "I respect my wife and I love her more now than when I first met her. I'm not going to lie. Every married couple has arguments and disagreements. We've had our share. But we are not separated and I doubt that we ever will be."

In truth, the marriage was in deep trouble.

Sammy wasn't lying when he said he loved his wife. And she loved him. But they were fundamentally different people. Where he was constantly on the go, never wanting to be alone, focused on making a big impression with his manner of dress, lifestyle, and spending habits, May was essentially a homebody whose world centered almost entirely on her family. She was satisfied with the fundamentals of life; he was entranced by its trappings.

Although May's lack of conceit was admirable, in a strange way it was a problem, too. At least for Sammy. When they met, she was a celebrated movie star. He reveled in the idea that they were both glamorous, popular public figures. When they arrived at a function, the flashbulbs would pop and people would turn to look as they emerged from their limo, each of them dressed to the nines. Davis loved that. By contrast, the simply clad, sometimes even frumpy little woman now waiting for him at home was a turn-off.

For her part, May, while understanding her husband's insatiable ambition and drive, wanted her man to occasionally join her world, to sometimes put her and the children ahead of his career, his friends, and his public. When Sammy first broached the subject of doing the musical, she had embraced their stay in New York as a time of family togetherness, something they'd never been able to enjoy in the past. She imagined them snuggling up on the couch, watching TV after he returned from the theater, or sharing quiet afternoons before he went off to work. She also envisioned Sammy accompanying the kids to nearby Central Park, taking an interest in their projects at home, sharing quality time. But most of that never happened. Part of the problem was that Sammy had no idea how to be a husband or a father to young children. He'd never seen his own parents together as a couple during his childhood, nor had his own dad ever played ball with him, taken him to the circus, or done the other things that parents typically do with their kids. So he had no role model.

Aside from that, he wasn't cut out for fatherhood by temperament. Nearly a kid himself, he knew how to have fun with Mark, Tracey, and Jeff, a three-year-old he and May adopted during the run of *Golden Boy* and named for Jeff Chandler. But his needs and wants always came first. Hitting the nightspots and partying with friends were not activities that went hand-in-hand with being a reliable dad, nor was doing charity benefits, nightclub gigs, and guest shots on TV. For one thing, when he was home, he needed to sleep. Most of the time, he wasn't prepared to sacrifice any of his passions in the name of family togetherness. Thus, as Sammy's daughter, Tracey, noted in her 1996 memoir, *Sammy Davis Jr., My Father,* "We seldom saw our father."

There were numerous occasions, however, when Sammy agreed to try harder—to please May or, sometimes, just to get her off his back. But something else usually intruded, causing him to break his promise. For example, one Friday night, early in the run of *Golden Boy,* May had planned a quiet dinner at home after his performance, Friday evening being the start of the Jewish Sabbath. Instead, Sammy enticed her to join Hilly Elkins and Hilly's companion at fashionable 21, promising they would share a quiet dinner at home the following Friday night. But when the appointed evening came, he had to attend a photo session for *Life,* which was devoting a large spread to him and the show. May was furious because he hadn't warned her in advance. It wasn't an oversight; Sammy hadn't wanted to disappoint her. Why risk a fight, he reasoned, when the photo session might be cancelled? To make matters worse, he then told her *Life* wanted to send a photographer to the apartment on Sunday for shots of the family. May hated the idea, saying, "But the article is about you and *Golden Boy.* The children and I have nothing to do with it. And I don't believe that kids should be brought up seeing their faces in magazines and getting the idea they're something they're not." Sammy countered with a rather different point of view: "We have a good life because people are interested in me. I don't have the moral right to say, 'Sorry, fellas, this is my home, no press,' ignoring the fact that they have a job to do and that by doing their job through the years they've done me a lot of good." Sammy won that round.

One shouldn't think that May's attitude meant that she wanted to chain her husband to the bed—or herself either. "I didn't sit home all the time," she asserted. "There were many times I was with him, for benefits and whatnot. But I can't say that I ever enjoyed it very much. Once in a while I did. When there was a normal amount of it. But there was so much of it."

What she wanted was balance. The time out with other people should be met with occasions when she and Sammy could be alone together. Compared with most couples, they had barely seen one another since their wedding four years earlier.

Subordinate issues involved Sammy's spending, which was far in excess of what she felt was appropriate or desirable, and Sammy's relationships with other women. He had warned her about these issues before their wedding, but he lacked the willpower to do anything about them. May tried to control his spending activities where possible, but her influence was relatively limited. Obviously, she was even less of a factor when it came to his romantic escapades. She knew that his one-night stands and brief flings were essentially meaningless. But his philandering was nonetheless hurtful. Perhaps worst of all, they kept Sammy away from home as well.

More threatening perhaps was his relationship with Lola Falana. The stunning, sexy African American singer-dancer was born in Camden, New Jersey in 1941, making her some sixteen years younger than Sammy and eight years younger than May. Although she had started performing in her preteens, she was a complete unknown when she auditioned for the *Golden Boy* company. But, as Elkins put it, "She was extraordinarily attractive, and a hell of a singer." Although Falana was only a member of the ensemble, she was decked out in a distinctive pair of skin-tight, gold-colored stretch pants. People who caught the show were soon talking about "the girl in the gold pants." With Sammy as her mentor, her career as an entertainer began to take off outside the confines of Broadway. By the time *Golden Boy* moved on to London in 1968, Falana and Davis were romantically involved. But their affair may have started when they were in New York.

As Sammy's round of outside activities continued to escalate, matters at home turned worse. Under pressure from May, he again promised that he would try to slow down, and, for about a month or six weeks, he was true to his pledge. But this had a negative impact at work. His absence at functions attended by other members of the *Golden Boy* company gave some of the singers and dancers the feeling that he was taking them for granted. Maintaining morale is vitally important when people have to do the same show night after night. When the company's head cheerleader is AWOL during the fun times, it is a downer. Moreover, Elkins complained that by cutting back on his availability to the press, Sammy was hurting business. Zero Mostel and Robert Preston, who were respectively starring in *Fiddler on the Roof* and *I Do, I Do* at the same time as Sammy's run in *Golden Boy,* were picking up the slack with journalists, and the show's ticket sales dipped as a result. "The producer and backers had a right to expect me to use all my weight to make it as profitable as I could," Sammy later explained. "And for the last month and a half they hadn't been getting all that they were buying."

Soon he was back to the old routine.

CHAPTER 18

A Book, a Film, and a TV Series

Sammy's outside activities during *Golden Boy*'s first year were myriad but scattered. As the musical entered its second autumn in New York, his projects became more focused. He even opened an office in Midtown and convinced George Rhodes' wife, Shirley, to run the Manhattan operation.

The first project of note was the publication of Sammy's autobiography, *Yes I Can*, in October 1965.

The book's origins dated back to early 1957. On the closing night of *Mr. Wonderful*, Sammy and Burt and Jane Boyar had impulsively decided to leave the cast party at the Harwyn and go to El Morocco, one of the swankiest clubs in New York. They were admitted—very coolly—by Angelo, the usually effusive maitre d', and taken to a table at the far side of the room. Burt, who regularly covered the club for his column, was seething. He knew that they had been placed in the least desirable part of the club rather than in the area typically reserved for stars of Davis' magnitude. When Boyar told Sammy this, the entertainer said little but was clearly upset, having once again come up against the same subtle, but nonetheless real prejudice that he'd experienced so often in the past. The hurt was profound.

Davis and his friends quickly finished their drinks and left the club. On the way home, Sammy said, "We should write a book about how it feels like to be treated this way," and *Yes I Can* was born.

For several years after the El Morocco incident, Sammy or the Boyars would bring up the book idea, but other things always intruded. In addition to writing for the *Morning Telegraph*, Burt was also contributing a weekly column and numerous features to *TV Guide*. Sammy was busy with his many projects. Finally, in 1961, the Boyars decided the time had come. They started traveling with Sammy and visiting him at his home in L.A. when he was doing a film or TV show or was between gigs. Whenever he had some free time, they would talk to him about his life. Of course, as close friends, they already knew a great deal about him. He had filled many a late-night hour with reminiscences back in New York, when they hung out together during the run of *Mr. Wonderful*.

"When we were together, having fun, he could talk all night," said Boyar. "He'd talk about the old days, talk about this, talk about that. But as soon as it was work, no. He'd worked enough all day. I remember once in Canada, he was doing this show and we were waiting for him at this motel we were all staying at. And he never showed. So we called over to the club, and they said, 'Oh, he's playing poker with the girls.' . . . I was so angry. So you could be with him a month, and you'd work two days. But those two days would accumulate into what became a book."

Initially, Boyar tried writing his column on the road, purposely joining Sammy at venues that lent themselves to this purpose, such as Miami Beach and Chicago. But finding the right sort of material for a Broadway column was just too difficult, so he arranged a leave of absence. As things turned out, he never went back to the paper.

As the interviews with Sammy progressed, the Boyars discovered that they were more productive if they came prepared with inquiries that could jog his memory. So they began interviewing his friends and relatives as well, including his father, grandmother, Will Mastin, May, George and Shirley Rhodes, and Arthur Silber, Jr.—about one hundred people. Davis later likened the result to "a gigantic jigsaw puzzle. Bang! In go the pieces," adding that the Boyars "told me things I didn't remember. I'd be in tears and run out of the room. It was really like being analyzed."

The publication rights were ultimately sold to Farrar, Straus and Giroux. The Boyars' arrangement with Sammy called for them to split all of the earnings from the book equally, and, on Burt's advice, Davis used his share of the royalties to set up a trust fund for his kids.

After about a year, the research phase ended, and the Boyars started to write. In most instances, Burt did the initial drafting; his work was then reviewed by Jane, who made changes and suggestions. The choice of a title derived from a Strouse-Adams song cut from *Golden Boy* prior to its opening. Sammy had recorded it for his Reprise LP *If I Ruled the World*, issued a few months before the book's publication. Like the song's lyrics, Sammy's story seemed to Burt and Jane to reflect, above all else, the entertainer's sense of undeniability.

Beyond the choice of title, Sammy left to the Boyars the decisions about how to organize the material and what to include, although he would eventually review the entire text and could reject anything he wished. Ultimately, they made three important stylistic choices: they would rely heavily on dialogue, which would obviously have to be invented to simulate actual conversations; memories of incidents derived from others would be given to Sammy, whether he actually remembered them or not, for the book would unfold from his own, first-person perspective; and, above all, they would endow the book with a strong narrative drive, not worrying about dates or a certain level of detail. As Burt later explained, "I ignored everything I felt was boring and just told the story I felt was the most fun to tell. And it excluded all the stuff you get in good biographies, which is where people were born, where they came from, who their parents were, when they got married. All this data that should be there, I didn't do that."

If the book was short on details, it resonated with what Boyar called "emotional truth." Above all else, *Yes I Can* vividly captured what it meant to be, first, a black man, and, second, a black entertainer in America during the 1930s, 1940s, and 1950s. Although the civil rights struggle dominated the news in 1965, most whites had devoted little thought to the everyday realities of Negro life in the modern era. In this sense, *Yes I Can*, which was published virtually concurrently with such other landmark memoirs as *The Autobiography of Malcolm X* and *Manchild in the Promised Land*, was eye-opening, even shocking.

When Sammy finally reviewed the manuscript, he made virtually no changes. Burt said this was because he knew the entertainer so well he could write in his friend's voice. As he put it, "I just felt like I was Sammy. If you're with him long enough and you have a certain theatrical flair, which I probably have, having been an actor—and also admiring him so much—it became possible to think like him. I could just talk right out of his mouth."

According to Silber, the book's initial draft ran to more than double the final length and included some of Davis' encounters with members of organized crime, such as the fellow who held him over a balcony in Philadelphia when he was dating the mobster's girlfriend. "If they'd printed it then," Silber said laughing, "we would all have been dead." Even in its final, printed form, the book ran to 630 pages, with no index or appendixes, much longer than the average celebrity memoir at the time—or now, for that matter.

The process of cutting, trimming, and shaping the material took a long time and involved several editors, none of whom seemed ideally suited to the task. Finally, the head of the publishing house, Roger Straus, took over the manuscript himself. According to Boyar, Straus hadn't personally edited a book since *The Lost Weekend* in 1944. But once he became involved, said Boyar, "everything went swimmingly."

Yes I Can hit America's bookstores strong. It had an initial printing of fifty thousand copies, a very large run for its day. It was also a selection of the Literary Guild book club and had been excerpted prior to publication in both *The Ladies' Home Journal* and *Harper's*. Most of the reviews were at least moderately enthusiastic. Maurice Dolbier of the *New York Herald Tribune* called the book "one of the most candid, engrossing and important American autobiographies of our time," predicting that it would have "a long and influential life."

And, indeed, it did. With Sammy plugging the book wherever possible, including an appearance on the *Today* show for its launch on September 20, it received plenty of press, backed by an advertising budget of $25,000, a significant amount in 1965 when books such as *Yes I Can* retailed for $6.95. It became a *New York Times* best seller, chalking up sales of more than ninety thousand copies and remaining on the list for roughly six months, an unusually long time.

To his credit, Sammy never tried to claim the success of *Yes I Can* for himself, always acknowledging Burt and Jane Boyar. As he told *Newsweek* at the time, "I did not type a letter. I did not put one syllable on a piece of paper. It's my experience, but it's their talent."

In late November, roughly a month after the publication of *Yes I Can*, Sammy launched another major project, this one a feature film.

A Man Called Adam told the story of Adam Johnson, a gifted but self-destructive jazz singer-trumpeter, loosely modeled on the great Miles Davis. The screenplay by Les Pine and Tina Rome had originally belonged to Nat King Cole. When Cole died, it reverted to his associate, Ike Jones, who brought it to Sammy. Sammy not only agreed to play the title character but also decided to coproduce the picture with Jones and Joseph E. Levine. Not to be outdone by Frank, Dean, Peter, and Jerry, all of whom had their own production companies, Sammy had formed Trace-Mark Productions (named for his first two kids) back in January 1963. He had acquired several properties, but *A Man Called Adam* was his first venture to reach the production stage. Sammy brought Jim Waters east to represent him in the producer's chair. Waters would share the credit with Jones, and Levine was billed as the executive producer.

To direct, Sammy reached out to Leon Penn (father of Sean), with whom he had worked on an episode of the TV medical series *Ben Casey* in the fall of 1963.* Formerly an actor himself, Penn had directed

---

*In the episode, Sammy played a baseball player named Allie who is wounded in one eye during a crucial game. *The Hollywood Reporter* asserted that he gave "insight and analytical emotion to his solid performance" (Reed Porter, *Hollywood Reporter,* October 4, 1963). When *A Man Called Adam* was in production, Sammy called the *Ben Casey* episode "the very best thing I ever did on TV," adding that he and Penn "speak the same language" (Thompson, H., 11/26/65/P).

numerous other shows for television, including episodes of *Breaking Point, Slattery's People,* and *Dr. Kildare,* but *A Man Called Adam* was his first feature.

Penn, Davis, Jones, and Waters put together an interesting, eclectic cast, a mix of black and white actors, including Cicely Tyson as Adam's girlfriend, in her first starring role in a feature film; Louis Armstrong as her musician grandfather; Frank Sinatra, Jr., in his film debut as a young but talented trumpeter; Peter Lawford as a ruthless band booker; and Ossie Davis as Adam's more emotionally stable brother, Nelson. Ossie, like Sammy, was also appearing in a Broadway show at the time.

Budgeted at $700,000 (and costing $100,000 less), *A Man Called Adam* was shot over a six-week period starting on November 22, 1965. Some of the work took place on a sound stage at the Movietown Manhattan Film Center on West 54th Street, but Penn also utilized a variety of New York area locations, including the Gorham Hotel, where Sammy had stayed during the run of *Mr. Wonderful;* Small's Paradise, a celebrated Harlem nightclub; the Fulton Fish Market, now part of South Street Seaport; and a cottage in nearby Westchester County. "We took the camera out onto the streets," Sammy said in 1980, "most unheard of in those days. We let them run on authentic backgrounds, with believable people and real traffic noises, daring and experimental for its time."

The acting reflected the same approach toward verisimilitude, with an emphasis on improvisation. Adding to the open atmosphere was a sign at the studio proclaiming "Everybody Welcome." Naturally, this included Sammy's entourage: Murphy, Shirley Rhodes, his bodyguards Joe Grant and Herbie Seeger. During free moments, they would sometimes join the star in his dressing room for a game of whist. "This is the best part of the day," Davis told Dick Schaap, who wrote a feature article about the picture for the *New York Herald Tribune.* "It's my only chance to relax. In here, I can be as colored as I want. I don't have to talk right and I can eat pork chop sandwiches."

The one member of Sammy's inner circle who was not often present was May, who saw the movie as just one more impediment to a normal home life. Sammy recalled that, after the first day of filming, he rushed back to the apartment to change clothes before going to the theater for his evening performance of *Golden Boy.* He wanted to tell his wife about how well the day had gone, but he didn't. "I had the sudden realization that she would find my enthusiasm offensive," he recalled.

It was on one of May's rare visits to the studio that Sammy collapsed in his dressing room, shivering and feverish with a virus. After examining him, a doctor predicted that he would be unable to work for a few days, but three hours later, he was on stage at the Majestic.

Sammy, who turned forty during principal photography, remained simply irrepressible. Nowhere was that more evident than on the Manhattan Film Studio sound stage. For the only time in his film career, he was the picture's producer and played its main character. Bernard Weintraub, who covered the production for the *New York Times,* noted, "On the movie set, Davis is definitely The Star. He starts singing and then yells, 'cut, cut, cut, let's do it over.' A member of the crew drops a prop and Davis points to him and exclaims: 'Circle his name. He's off my Hanukkah list.' Everyone laughs. Davis is the focus of attention at all times."

Davis also took his acting seriously. Adam was the most complicated character he had ever tackled on film—sweet and lovable one minute, irrational and violent the next—and he worked hard to get the character right. Leo Penn was a great help. Said Davis, "We literally bounced off each other—one inspiring the other. We functioned almost as an entity." Penn was equally complimentary, describing Sammy as "a very creative, spontaneous performer," who occasionally inspired him to "get a fresh slant" on a scene or a bit of business; he considered directing Davis "a sheer joy."

The result of this collaboration was evident on the screen when *A Man Called Adam* was released on August 3, 1966. Although a few critics found Davis a bit over the top, most agreed with Howard Thompson, who praised the "savage intensity and deep feeling" the entertainer brought to his role. But the downbeat, melodramatic, cliché-riddled script and the picture's lethargic pace could not be overcome. As a result, most of America missed Sammy Davis' most significant screen role and his best work as a leading man outside of his performance in *Golden Boy.*

Typically, Davis would stick around the theater after his final bows in *Golden Boy* and chat with the audience. On an evening in mid-October 1965, he told them that he "was getting something he had long wanted and hoped for—a regularly scheduled network television show." Although he had starred in a special for ABC the previous year and was working on another for the network, it was NBC, not ABC, that offered him a weekly series, which it planned to introduce as a midseason replacement in January. *Convoy,* a documentary-style drama about the navy in World War II, was getting mauled in its Friday evening time slot by two CBS comedies, *Hogan's Heroes* and *Gomer Pyle, U.S.M.C.* Perhaps a variety show with a hip black host would do better, or so the thinking went at NBC. Most stars would have preferred to wait until fall, when the networks roll out their new shows with considerable fanfare, but Sammy seized the opportunity.

"I'd have walked over dead bodies to do it," he explained. "It was a great opportunity for my people. I'm the first Negro to have an hour-long show in prime time. I couldn't turn that down."*

May was nowhere near as effusive. "You might as well live in a hotel between the studio and the theater," she told him, tears streaming down her cheeks. Then, she added, "Sammy, I can't take this lifestyle anymore" and threatened to go back to California—with the kids. Her attitude sickened him; he didn't want to lose her or his family. At first, he agreed to pass on the NBC deal, but he couldn't maintain his resolve. By then, May had adjusted somewhat to the idea. At least she didn't leave town.

The contract was signed on October 27. In addition to hosting the series, Sammy would be its executive producer; this title gave him control over the show's personnel and budget. Trusting Sammy with money was clearly a mistake. First, he used $30,000 to order eighty-four suits from his favorite tailor, Sy Devore, telling the press that he intended to wear four different outfits per episode, without repeating a single suit between the show's premiere and the end of the season in May.

Sammy then decided that the company could save money if he built a rehearsal hall in his Midtown suite of offices. He devoted a large space to this purpose, arranging for the installation of a beautiful wood floor, with mirrors and balancing bars affixed to the walls. The only problem was that the rehearsing performers made so much noise that the attorneys who occupied the suite beneath them threatened to sue. Thus, the rehearsal hall became a very expensive storage space.

Overall responsibility for *The Sammy Davis, Jr. Show* was given to Joe Hamilton. A client of the William Morris Agency, like Sammy, Hamilton had done extremely well with the popular, inventive *Garry Moore Show,* which he helped launch in 1958. He had also married the breakout star of that program, Carol Burnett, for whom he'd also produced several well-regarded specials. Hamilton was already at work on Davis' upcoming ABC special. So, too, were the series' principal writers, Bill Angelos and Buz Kohan.

"Rather than a variety show, ours will be a show with variety," Hamilton told the press. "We hope to have an air of spontaneity and freshness about it." He noted that the "NBC Television Network bought Sammy Davis. We intend to give them and the viewers all the Sammy possible within the framework of a one-hour show."

---

*Sammy was referring to variety shows. Bill Cosby had already broken the color barrier for weekly dramatic programming when he costarred with Robert Culp in *I, Spy,* which had debuted in fall 1965. For those keeping score, NBC had initiated a weekly variety show starring Nat King Cole in 1956, but each episode ran only fifteen minutes (later expanded to a half hour).

By then, Davis was starring in his feature film as well as his Broadway musical. He didn't have time to absorb much in the way of new material for a weekly TV program—extensive comedy sketches, for example—at least not until his other projects wrapped. Accordingly, the series would have to revolve around his extant repertoire. Fortunately, after decades of nightclub performances and recording sessions, he had a lot of material at his command. As most of it was unfamiliar to his production team, he took a couple of days in November, booked himself into the Fountainebleu in Miami Beach, brought Hamilton and the writers down as his guests, and ran through his entire bag of tricks—all of the songs, dances, impressions, and specialty bits that he'd done since 1945. He did two shows a night, and each show was entirely different. Hamilton, Angelos, and Kohan were astonished at the range and depth of his talent. Thereafter, the team flew back to New York and started culling items for the shows. That George Rhodes would be wielding the conductor's baton for the series made things somewhat easier.

In a sense, the limits on Davis' time gave the show a distinctive quality. It would have to be more like a weekly musical special, spotlighting the individual talents of the host and his guests, rather than the typical variety show mix of songs, banter, and comedy sketches. Its physical setting was also unusual. Rather than taping in a theater with a proscenium stage and the audience out front, each episode would be staged in a studio, with the audience arranged into several seating units called pods. These units carved the floor into several distinct playing areas.

NBC appointed Alan Ebert to be the show's publicist. In a revealing two-part series of articles published in *TV Guide* after the program's demise, Ebert recalled that his first job was to organize a photo shoot with the star. He also needed to interview him so that he could send out press releases to promote the program. Given Davis' busy schedule, neither task was easy.

Although Ebert was unsympathetic at first, he and Sammy began to bond. So much so that, after a meeting on December 6, Davis took his publicist aside and said, "Listen, baby. Few people around me ever tell me the truth. I have a feeling you will. So if you ever see me doing something you think is wrong, tell me. I may get mad. I may even holler, I might even ignore you. But, baby, you better believe I'll be thinking about what you said, and if you're right, I'll know it and I'll tell you."

Sammy started work on the show's first episode in Burbank on December 19, a Sunday. Normally, the program would originate from NBC's studios in Brooklyn, but to accommodate his special guests for the premiere, Elizabeth Taylor and Richard Burton, the entertainer flew to California following his performance of *Golden Boy* on Saturday night.

Getting the Burtons was a major coup. They were the most intriguing couple since Jack and Jackie Kennedy. Once they had been offered a whopping $500,000 for a single television appearance and turned it down. But they agreed to do Sammy's show, out of friendship, for a mere $50,000—and they donated that to charity.

Burton, who had starred in Lerner and Loewe's *Camelot* on Broadway, could carry a tune. But what to do with Liz? She wanted to sing, too, although she had a tiny, girlish voice. She selected a Welsh miner's song—in honor of her husband's native land—as well as "What Do the Simple Folk Do?" from the Lerner and Loewe musical. She warbled the latter with Dick and Sammy. The three friends engaged in some meaningless banter, and Burton rendered the *Camelot* finale. According to the show's cowriter, Buz Kohan, Dick and Liz "were drinking champagne backstage and by the time they got around to shooting the show they were not exactly as sober as you would have liked." Worse, Sammy was so in awe of his movie star friends that he fawned over them on camera. "That is wrong," Kohan explained. "When you're coming out as the star of the show, you should be the star of the show. You shouldn't have to play that game with your guests."

The taping session didn't end until 1 A.M.; Sammy missed his plane back to New York. Finally, flying out at 8 o'clock Monday morning, he arrived back in Manhattan several hours late for his call for *A Man Called Adam*. There was also a performance of *Golden Boy* that night.

The rest of the premiere episode was shot in New York. The other guests were singer Nancy Wilson and the dance team Augie and Margo, which had frequently opened for Sammy on the nightclub circuit. But when it came to putting the show together, Davis threw all the weight to the Burtons.

When the show premiered on January 7, 1966, Sammy opened with his usual verve, singing "Nothing Can Stop Me Now" from Anthony Newley and Leslie Bricusse's second musical, *The Roar of the Greasepaint—The Smell of the Crowd*, with special lyrics to suit the occasion. So far so good. Then, after a commercial, Richard Burton appeared, reading a dictionary definition of friendship, his voice full of import and a blank expression on his face. From there on, the program was plodding and, at times, even embarrassing. TV critic Jack Gould caught the essence of the problem, telling readers of the *New York Times*, "The dynamic personality of Sammy Davis never had a chance to emerge last night in the spiritless and static debut of his own program over the network of the National Broadcasting Company. How in the world it would be possible to throttle such vitality is hard to conceive, but the opening

216

hour was totally lackluster and a keen disappointment." *Time* magazine called it "a shambles."

But the ratings were spectacular, though most who watched the show were as disappointed as the critics. If Sammy had any chance of keeping his audience for another outing, he needed to rebound quickly. And that he could not do. ABC, miffed that he had signed with a rival network after it had given him two hour-long specials, decided to air its latest project with the entertainer, *Sammy Davis, Jr. and His Friends,* on February 1. In so doing, the network invoked a clause in Davis' contract that precluded his appearance on any other television program for twenty-one days before and eight days after the show's debut. This meant that, following his series' premiere, Sammy had to absent himself from his own show for four consecutive weeks.*

How does one do *The Sammy Davis, Jr. Show* without Sammy Davis, Jr.? NBC and Joe Hamilton did the best they could, getting Johnny Carson, Sean Connery, and Jerry Lewis as substitute hosts. The interim shows weren't bad. But, despite their popularity, neither Lewis nor Carson nor Connery could keep the ratings from dipping.

During his hiatus, Sammy worked to streamline the show's format, insisting on a breakneck pace, a minimal amount of guest-host banter, and a maximum amount of entertainment. He was so manic that he started to anger people inside the program's production office and in NBC's executive suite. When Ebert warned him about his behavior, Sammy expressed genuine surprise. But he appreciated the heads-up, telling Murphy to give Ebert both his and Murphy's phone number, so that the publicist could reach him whenever necessary. "From now on, baby," Sammy said, "you're it. You handle the entire magila. If you can't reach me, call Murphy. He knows where I can be reached at all times. If you call with something you think I should do, I'll do it. One last thing— tell those guys at NBC I ain't difficult." To prove his point, he agreed readily when Ebert asked him to meet with various members of the press to let them know that he would return in a new and improved program. By January 21, he had done nineteen such interviews and had six more scheduled.

As for the ABC special, *Sammy Davis, Jr. and His Friends,* it was, in the words of *Variety,* "light, fast-moving and withal provided a solid hour of entertainment." The "friends" in the title included Frank Sinatra and

---

*In an effort to avoid this scheduling debacle, Davis tried to convince ABC to air its special in December. When that failed, he tried to buy the show outright but was refused.

Count Basie, with whom Davis had recorded an album, *Our Shining Hour,* the previous year. The fact that the special was written and produced by the same people as the series made its success that much more poignant, as did the fact that it was directed by Clark Jones, who had worked on the premiere episode of *The Sammy Davis, Jr. Show* and shared directing duties throughout the rest of the season with Mack Bing, the program's associate producer.

On Sunday, January 23, Davis taped the episode of his show that would mark his return. After each number, he ran over to Ebert to get the publicist's opinion, and Ebert kept telling him, "Great." He wasn't lying to the star. He considered the outing, in his words, "one of the best variety shows I've ever seen. Sammy kills himself in it."

The hard work was clearly evident when the episode aired on February 11. It opened with Sammy emerging from a package marked "Do Not Open Until February 11, 1966." Backed by six female dancers, the entertainer burst into "Back in Your Own Backyard," with clever special lyrics acknowledging his four-week enforced vacation. After the commercial break, he went into a medley of several of his best-loved songs. So far, he had barely spoken a word. Finally, he told the audience, "Glad you could make it tonight," and added jokingly, "Glad *I* could make it tonight." He then gave way to his guests: singer Trini Lopez, his *Golden Boy* costar Paula Wayne, and comedian Corbett Monica. Also on hand from *Golden Boy* were Johnny Brown and the show's chorus. Unlike Burton and Taylor, these people knew how to work in a variety show setting, so they all came off well. Late in the program, Davis returned with his popular lip sync routine to Robert Preston's "Trouble" from *The Music Man,* and he brought the hour to a conclusion with "I've Got a Woman," which started as a duet between him and Lopez and eventually expanded to include the entire *Golden Boy* company. It was a rocking conclusion to an extremely well-done show.

Davis and Ebert decided to treat this new episode as though it were the premiere, screening it for the press at an invitation-only cocktail party. "The screening and party were a smash," Ebert recalled. So, too, were the reviews. "Whatever had been seriously amiss in the mid-season premiere of *The Sammy Davis, Jr. Show,*" intoned *Variety,* "was more than corrected in this return."

The show was electric, but the ratings were dismal. In the weeks that followed the taping of the second episode, the production team maintained an unusually high level of quality. But, as Alan Ebert noted, by then Davis was "having trouble getting really big names for the show." Where, the publicist wondered, "are Sam's so-called big friends? Why hasn't Sinatra, Dean Martin, or Joey Bishop made an appearance?"

It is unlikely that even their presence could have made much of a difference. The ratings remained in the doldrums, and by mid-March no one expected them to improve. As the numbers flattened out, dissent grew within the production team, with Davis on one side, Joe Hamilton on the other, and the writers caught between the two camps. Sammy had what Buz Kohan described as a "seat of the pants" approach to production. He liked to leave his options open until the last minute. Hamilton, by contrast, favored what Kohan called "a very organized, disciplined show, where you had a rundown and you had a schedule and you knew where everybody was going to be at each moment."

An example of Davis' approach came with the show that was taped on February 27 and aired on March 18. His primary guest was Judy Garland, a friend since the days of Humphrey Bogart's Holmby Hill Rat Pack. Kohan and Angelos put together a killer medley for Garland that ran something like twelve minutes. But she was not physically up to the challenge. Ebert said she "looked so awful that when she walked right by me, I didn't recognize her. She looks 20 years older than her age." She was also, in his words, "suffering with extreme laryngitis and a severe case of nerves." Hamilton was sufficiently concerned about her ability to perform that he made sure the dress rehearsal was taped. When Garland successfully finished the run-through, Sammy was so relieved he told her she didn't have to come back and do the routine for the real show; they could use the dress rehearsal tape. But she wanted to take another shot at the medley, convinced she could do it better. And, during the actual show, she did. As Kohan put it, "She went out that night and just killed. I mean, we were on the floor. Tears were just streaming down my face. It was just such an emotional evening." Instead of sighing with relief at having dodged a potential disaster, Sammy, on the spur of the moment—and on camera—invited Judy to come back the following week. So they had to go through the same anguish all over again.

A week after the taping of the Judy Garland episode of Sammy's show, *Golden Boy* ended its run. The problem didn't lie with the box office. The musical was selling out on a regular basis, but Sammy couldn't take the routine any longer. As he put it, "I needed to get back into my own world of different shows every night, in different cities, to different people." His contract with Hillard Elkins wouldn't expire until May 1967, some fifteen months away, but Elkins realized his star was unhappy. So he offered Sammy a deal: he would close the show on Broadway if Davis would agree to star in a London production at some point in the future. Sammy agreed.

The final curtain fell on March 5. After 569 performances, not including the many weeks of tryouts and previews, Sammy may have had his fill of Joe Wellington, but it was only a momentary sensation. "Outside of my wife and three youngsters," he had said a few months earlier, "the greatest thing that has ever happened to me was my doing *Golden Boy* on Broadway. And if I may be excused for blowing a few personal notes of satisfaction, it took a fellow who felt he was successful in night clubs, movies and television—plus records—and made him almost as well known as Dean Martin." He also pointed out, "I needed Broadway and so should every performer worth his salt." He vowed to return to Broadway at some point in the future. "I'm going to go back," he told Alex Haley a few weeks after the show closed, "and I'm going to keep going back until I learn it."

Immediately after the final performance, Sammy took a week's vacation in Hawaii. Before he left, NBC announced its preliminary fall schedule, and *The Sammy Davis, Jr. Show* was not among the returnees. Davis hoped that the network would reconsider, so, when he returned to New York, he worked even harder on the remaining episodes. Ebert, for one, was amazed. "Here's a guy who's won countless awards," wrote the publicist, "is a world-wide star and he's in panicsville, because his show may be cancelled. He can't accept defeat. He also can't accept, I fear, the knowledge that the whole world doesn't rush to tune in his show."

This was the sad reality; by mid-March, the cancellation was official. On April 3, the NAACP announced plans to picket the network in protest. Ebert tried to convince Davis to stop the demonstration. But Sammy refused, saying, "They're my people and they want to further the Negro cause by doing something through me. I'm not going to interfere." He and Ebert parted angrily, although they later patched up their differences. The demonstration, of course, had no impact on the outcome. The show was cancelled not for racial reasons but for lack of ratings.

Sammy decided to go out in style, making his final episode a one-man tour de force. He opened with a smashing medley that included "Lonesome Road," "Gonna Build a Mountain," and "Yes I Can." He then proceeded to display his gunmanship, his range of impressions to the tune of "Rock a Bye Your Baby with a Dixie Melody," and his still magical gifts as a dancer, donning his tap shoes and a straw boater (given to him by Maurice Chevalier) for a memorable turn on "Put on a Happy Face." After singing "There's a Boat Dat's Leavin' Soon for New York" as Sportin' Life and the dramatic "Soliloquy" from *Carousel* and reprising the "Trouble" number from *The Music Man*, he brought the performance to a close, dressed as a clown, with "What Kind of Fool Am I?"

When he finished, he removed his fright wig and gloves and placed them on a stool. Then, quietly suggesting he would be back someday to claim them, he left the stage.

Throughout the taping, Sammy had maintained a brave front, joking with and entertaining the staff, crew, and his entourage. When the performance was finished, he repaired to his dressing room to change for the cast party. Before leaving for the bash, Buz Kohan decided to pay his respects and to say goodbye in a more private setting than the party. When he entered the star's dressing room, he saw Sammy sobbing, cradled in the arms of his bodyguard, Joe Grant. The sight was startling. Embarrassed, Kohan quietly retreated, closing the door behind him. "Ten minutes later," the writer recalled, "he comes down, he's Charley Charm as if nothing happened. But that moment. It looked like the Pietà. That picture just sticks in my mind."

Indeed, few things in his professional life hit Sammy harder than the cancellation of his show. It was his first major career failure since the end of his recording contract with Capitol Records in 1949.

After the airing of the final episode on April 22, Robert Lewis Shayon wrote in the *Saturday Review*, "The promise to return was more than acting; it was real. Sammy Davis, Jr., was patently telling viewers he'd be back on television as the star of his own weekly program, despite the failure of his initial effort. It was a quixotic, winning gesture. But there is no place for sentiment in the economics of television. 'No, Sammy, it's not in the cards,' one was tempted to mutter. 'You've had your chance and it didn't work. Some other Negro entertainer will have to make the big breakthrough in television.'"

Shayon was right. It would be left to comic Flip Wilson, whose show debuted in 1970, also on NBC, to succeed where Sammy had failed. Davis would never again star in his own weekly variety series. He told Alex Haley shortly thereafter, "I've got no cop-out. It was nobody's fault but mine," adding, "We never got over that bad beginning—even when we started to swing those last six or seven shows. But it was a ball to be on for the 16 weeks it ran."

CHAPTER 19

That's All!

The demise of *The Sammy Davis, Jr. Show* did little to tarnish Davis' reputation. It had not been a ratings success, but it was a noteworthy effort. Likewise *A Man Called Adam*. Meanwhile, he had scored impressively with *Golden Boy* and *Yes I Can*. Indeed, one could argue that he was at the top of his game in the years between 1964 and 1966. Looking back, Gerald Early, editor of a 2001 compilation of writings by and about the entertainer, asserted that in the mid-sixties, Sammy was "arguably the most famous black man in the United States, his only possible rivals being Martin Luther King and Muhammad Ali."

But as Davis' career was cresting, his personal life wasn't. May was as unhappy as ever. Thoughts of divorce were more frequent, but as Sammy's time in New York drew to an end, she wasn't yet ready for such a drastic move. A few weeks before *Golden Boy* closed, she took the kids and returned to California to find a place for the family to live, because Sammy had sold the house on Evanview Drive while living in the East.

Curiously, May chose a very grand place, the former home of movie mogul David O. Selznick, for which Sammy paid approximately $320,000 (according to his daughter, Tracey, it is now worth in excess of $6.5 million). Located on Summit Drive in the hills off Benedict Canyon, the Georgian-style brick edifice had four bedrooms, a study, a large family room with Dutch doors leading to a generous backyard, a den, a breakfast room, a huge kitchen, a sauna, and an office. "I still remember the first day I saw that grand and wonderful house," Tracey noted in her 1996 memoir. "It was like being in a fairy tale."

Sammy joined the family after taping his final show at the end of March. But he barely had time to settle into his new digs when he was off again for an engagement at the Sands in early May. To mark his first appearance in the Copa Room in two years, he brought along a team of five dancers headed by Lola Falana.

Davis was delighted to be back in the element he knew best and in the showroom where he had enjoyed twenty-nine previous engagements. "A performer realizes the first day here that he has everything going for him," he said at the time, "the best bands, the best lighting. If people come to see you, they come to be entertained. It's a definite plus factor for an entertainer."

Present on opening night, *Variety* noted that Sammy gave "the audience a show to remember." Thanks to Reprise, listeners at home were able to get a good sense of what transpired in Vegas that spring; producer Jimmy Bowen had recorded six shows during the run. The result was a two-album set called *Sammy Davis, Jr.: That's All!*, which was released in January 1967.

As far as the material was concerned, *Sammy Davis, Jr.: That's All!* didn't contain many surprises. Davis stayed with his usual mix of pop standards and recent Broadway fare ("As Long As She Needs Me" from *Oliver!*, "Sweet Beginnings" from Newley-Bricusse's *Roar of the Greasepaint*, and "I Want to Be with You" from *Golden Boy*). Several of his biggest hits—"The Birth of the Blues" and "What Kind of Fool Am I?"— were on prominent display as well.

If Sammy's repertoire was not terribly novel, his interpretations were both engaging and delightfully original. He drew from the same bag of tricks that had served him since the late 1940s, but he employed them with such imagination and brio and backed them with such power and range that such old familiar tunes as "Chicago," "The Lady Is a Tramp," and his opener, "With a Song in My Heart," seemed somehow new.

The set also revealed how wonderfully playful and confident a comic Davis had become. As Sally Struthers observed, "He didn't just stand there and sing. He told stories, and the audience loved him for it. I think his humor was one of his greatest assets."

Sometimes, in the *That's All!* disks, Sammy's humor showed up in the music. When the audience laughed at his quips, he ad-libbed, "If you wanna hear me sing serious, you're gonna hafta buy my records." Of course, his impressions were humorous and he trucked them out during the set, with "One for My Baby" as the vehicle. But, at the heart of his shtick were his racial bits, which alternated between self-deprecation and braggadocio. These showed up most engagingly in a ten-minute monologue that Davis rendered with the panache of a stand-up comedian. He started by poking mild fun at the squares who come to Vegas and immediately turn into swingers, then he segued into observations about racial and ethnic stereotyping, noting that as he was both black and Jewish, he had his choice of two. "Can you imagine each morning getting out of bed," he asked the audience, "never knowing how you want to spend the day? Whether you want to be shiftless and lazy or smart and stingy? And you ain't lived 'til you've tried kosher water-melon." He concluded by advising the audience, "I love to have fun this way. I make jokes about it on stage. However, after the show, if you want to march anyplace, I'll be with you. Last two years, I marched so much, I marched one day with the White Citizens Council. Didn't even know it. Can't afford to miss any of them marches, baby."

Partly the racial humor reflected Davis' inability to put aside his own race consciousness. But it was also designed to ease the minds of white middle-class audiences at a time when Black Power groups and sum-mertime urban riots were making many whites very nervous. Davis even hoped he might change a few minds through humor. As he told Alex Haley that year, "It's a little romantic to say it, but I like to think that after every audience I have, two or three people will walk out feeling differ-ently about colored people generally, and me, in particular."

With the jokes, the soaring musical numbers, and the surprise bits here and there, *Sammy Davis, Jr.: That's All!* perfectly captured and pre-served that moment in time when the entertainer was relishing his return to the nightclub circuit and was at the very top of his game. The two-disk set serves as the best commercially available example of what made Davis such a peerless live performer when he was in his prime.

In late June, Sammy joined another civil rights demonstration in the Deep South, this time in Mississippi. Like the Selma March the previ-ous year, this protest was designed to foster black voter registration. Among those spearheading the effort was James Meredith, who in 1962 became the first African American to register at the University of Mis-sissippi (Ole Miss), over the intense opposition of the state's governor, Ross Barnett. The demonstrators' plan was to march from Tougaloo, the home of an African American college, to the state capital in Jackson. Sammy was part of a contingent from Hollywood that would participate in a rally in Tougaloo to kick off the campaign. He'd arranged to borrow Frank Sinatra's plane to transport him, Marlon Brando, TV star Anthony Franciosa, and the Olympic decathlon champion Rafer Johnson. Before leaving, however, Davis received word from Bobby Kennedy, then a U.S. senator, that his life would be in danger if he showed up in Missis-sippi. "Don't go down there," Kennedy warned. "They're out to get you and I can't protect you." Sammy knew the situation in Tougaloo was serious. James Meredith had already been badly wounded by a shotgun-wielding racist. But he felt he had to go. As he told the *New York Times* just before his departure, "I'm not going down there to get shot. But we can't all sit around Beverly Hills talking about it. Somebody has to do something." In the meantime, Kennedy promised to have the Justice

Department make the FBI agents in Tougaloo aware of the entertainer's presence and to closely monitor his movements.

At the rally, attended by some ten thousand protesters, Sammy sang a few songs and then introduced Martin Luther King, Jr., who spoke. Also on the bill were soul singer James Brown and comedian Dick Gregory. "The program went off without a hitch," said Davis, "no thanks to the police who were standing there listlessly. We had only a few dozen black security people without weapons, college kids who were giving their bodies in service."

Afterward, King tried to convince Davis to spend the night, but Sammy could not be persuaded. He felt he'd done his bit for the cause; now it was time to leave while he was still in one piece. Brando stayed but the others in Sammy's party departed with him, happy that, in Rafer Johnson's words, they "had lent support to those who bravely stood up for justice."

Sammy spent much of the rest of 1966 on the road, revisiting many of his favorite nightclubs and showrooms, with Lola Falana joining him from time to time as a featured attraction. These included a gig at the Fountainebleu in Miami in early July and a seventeen-show stand at the Club Harlem. While in Atlantic City, Sammy astounded patrons, the press, and the Club Harlem's owner, Larry Steele, by telling a Friday night audience that he didn't think he'd given a good show and picking up the tab for the entire house, some nine hundred people. This gesture cost him an estimated $4,000.

At the end of the month, he was on to the El San Juan in Puerto Rico and then, in August, Harrah's Lake Tahoe, for the first engagement in a record-breaking, three-year, $1 million deal that he'd signed with the hotel-casino (it included bookings at Harrah's Reno as well as Tahoe). In October, he surfaced in Chicago for a stand at the Chez Paree as well as several charity events; mid-November found him in London for his third Royal Variety Show; and, in the usual fashion, he ended the year and welcomed in 1967 at the Copa in New York.

As 1966 gave way to a new year, the road show continued. The highlight of 1967 came on July 1, when Sammy launched a three-week engagement at the Olympic Music Hall in Paris. The opening night, a $100-a-ticket benefit for the United Jewish Charities Fund, brought out a host of luminaries, including Mr. and Mrs. Andre Dubonnet, couturier Pierre Cardin, actor Alain Delon, singer Charles Aznavour, and, to quote the *New York Times*, "a large assemblage of Rothschilds."

Also present in the audience that evening was the beautiful Austrian actress Romy Schneider, whom Davis subsequently met through international playboy Porfirio Rubirosa, with whom he became extremely close during his Paris engagement. Sammy enjoyed a brief but passionate relationship with Schneider. "Those three weeks with Romy were irreplaceable," he recalled. "I felt like we were living inside a marvelous romantic movie in which I was a duke or a prince and the world was mine. We were together at other times, in other places, but it was never so good."

Following the City of Lights, Davis embarked on a tour of Europe that included concerts in Amsterdam, Copenhagen, Stockholm, Rome, and several other venues. Footage from these shows, plus musical numbers staged at select locations (like the Eiffel Tower), formed the basis for a TV special produced by a German company, Bavaria Atelier Gesellschaft. (The special didn't air in the United States until December 1969, when it was syndicated by Multimedia Entertainment.)

Davis also made his first visit to Israel. From the moment he landed in Tel Aviv, where he was serenaded by hundreds of uniformed Israeli soldiers, he found the experience incredibly moving. It went beyond the fact that he was a converted Jew visiting the Jewish homeland. He felt that, as he put it, he "had come to the land of the unwanted, as *I* had so often been, and they were reaching out to me." A particularly magical moment came when he performed at the Mann Auditorium in a benefit for the families who lost loved ones during the recent Six-Day War. He concluded with "Exodus," the theme from the Otto Preminger film, which was not part of his usual repertoire. "I don't know where my voice came from," Sammy recalled. "I sang like a cantor in a temple. And because Israel was not just a physical place to me, but something spiritual which had permeated my being, despite my throat being constricted, despite my soul sobbing, a majestic voice that I cannot call my own rang through the hall."

Backstage after the show, he enjoyed a different kind of thrill, exchanging eye patches with the celebrated, one-eyed hero of the Six-Day War, Moshe Dayan. By the time Davis left Israel, he'd received several lucrative offers for future concerts, but he accepted none of them. "I would return to Israel as often as I could be useful," he said later, "but I would not take money."

Between his live engagements during 1966 and 1967, Davis managed several appearances on *The Tonight Show* and guest shots on some of TV's hottest series, including *Batman* on October 12, 1966, *The Wild, Wild West* on October 14 (the episode also featured Peter Lawford), and *I Dream of Jeannie* on February 27, 1967. One of his best TV roles was his appearance on *The Danny Thomas Hour* on November 20, 1967. The sixty-minute anthology series was produced and hosted by Thomas, who had formed a highly successful TV production company with Dick Powell's former writer-producer, Aaron Spelling. Both Thomas and Spelling were friends of Davis.

In something of a throwback to *Auf Wiedersehen,* Sammy played Jessie "Chris" Christianson, a GI stationed in Europe during the waning days of World War II. Like Spider Johnson, his character was a loner, in this case a crack radio repairman assigned to an all-white Signal Corps, who befriends a corporal who might be a German spy.

Based on a true story, "The Enemy," as the episode was called, was a crisp, well-written tale. Davis shaved off his moustache in keeping with the story's time period, but he also sported a decidedly un-1940s Afro. The persona he projected was familiar, that of a mild-mannered soul with more smarts and guts than surface appearances would indicate. While noting the role's resemblance to those in Davis' past, *Variety* called his "display of dramatic intensity . . . the apogee" of his career as a dramatic actor. But anthology shows had become passé, and the ratings for the program were poor.

He ended 1967 with Frank and Dean on an NBC special hosted by Sinatra's daughter Nancy, who had become a popular recording artist in her own right. The special, *Movin' with Nancy,* aired on December 11 and was produced and directed by Jack Haley, Jr., who would become one of Sammy's best friends.

Davis enjoyed his television assignments, but he had his heart set on becoming a movie star. As his dramatic work in *A Man Called Adam* hadn't led to much, he decided to try a comedy, *Salt and Pepper,* for his next venture.

Like *Ocean's Eleven,* the project originated with Peter Lawford. Looking for a way to revitalize his lifeless career, the actor had hired Michael Pertwee, a British screenwriter who had been dashing off comedies since the late 1930s, to develop a lighthearted romp in the mode of the Rat Pack flicks: start with a couple of pals, toss in a few girls and some danger, and mix it up with mild jokes and bits of business.

Pertwee's solution was a tale of two London nightclub owners, Charlie Salt (Davis) and Christopher Pepper (Lawford), who become embroiled in the plot of a mad colonel who is in possession of a nuclear bomb. Along the way, Salt and Pepper are dogged by a curmudgeonly Scotland Yard Inspector (Michael Bates).

Lawford won the backing of United Artists, producers of the smash James Bond films. The venture would fall under the joint auspices of Peter and Sammy's production companies, Chrislaw and Trace-Mark, with Milt Ebbins, Lawford's former agent, serving as the producer.

Filming took place in London during summer 1967, with Sammy balancing his work on the picture with his European concert engagements. Ebbins had originally hoped to film the London street scenes in Soho, but the thoroughfares became so clogged with fans that the setting had to be re-created on the backlot at Shepperton Studios in Boreham. This unanticipated expenditure added an extra $144,000 to the film's cost.

Sammy and Peter had a ball in London. Only half a dozen years had passed since Davis' triumph at the Palladium, but the city had changed dramatically. Rock bands, led by the Beatles and the Rolling Stones, had made England the music center of the world, while Mary Quant and her Mod look had become a fashion sensation. The Brits were redefining pop culture, and stately London had become a very swinging place indeed. No two people were more eager to partake of the city's pleasures than Davis and Lawford. And, as May had stayed home with the kids, there was nothing to stop Sammy from giving full rein to his desires.

Adopting the latest fashions—bellbottom pants, love beads, and Nehru jackets—the two stars let their hair grow long, added muttonchop sideburns, and began spewing the latest buzz words: groovy, far out, and peace and love. During their off hours, they liked to hop on their twin motorbikes and head over to Alvaro's, a disco on King's Road in Chelsea that catered primarily to youngsters half their age. When they weren't at Alvaro's, they could often be found in their suites at the Mayfair, hosting parties that overflowed with booze and drugs, notably marijuana, hash, and LSD.

Although there were women aplenty, Davis had fallen for one in particular, a white model. Then he discovered that she was sleeping with Peter, too. This resulted in such a major falling out between the stars that work on *Salt and Pepper* came to a complete halt for several days. Sammy and Peter met to iron out their differences, but, high on booze or drugs or both, they nearly came to blows. Finally, Davis called Lawford "a motherfucker," plaintively asking his friend why he did such a thing to him, knowing that he was in love with the girl. "Well then I did you a favor," Lawford replied, coolly. "She's a tramp." At that point, they both started laughing, and the battle was over. So was Sammy's relationship with the model.

Trying to make a picture with all the outside distractions wasn't easy. The thankless task of keeping things moving fell to Richard Donner, who had directed Sammy and Peter in their *Wild, Wild West* episode. Although the Brit would go on to enjoy a major feature film career, directing such blockbusters as *The Omen, Superman,* and the *Lethal Weapon* series, to date he had worked primarily in episodic television.

Eager to escape the confines of TV for the greener pastures of features, Donner became more than a little frustrated as principal photography progressed. "Sammy and Peter were very undisciplined," he recalled, "and there was a lot of cutting up. We'd have an eight o'clock call and they'd show up at noon, hung over from whatever it was they had ingested the night before. It was terrible for me, and I had no way of controlling them because they were the producers. What was I going to do, fire them?" Much of the time, the stars would wind up improvising dialogue and comic bits, most of which were not funny and bore little relationship to the story at hand. But Donner let them do what they wanted. He figured he could eliminate "all that extraneous stuff" in the editing room.

Instead, he was fired shortly after the picture wrapped. According to Milt Ebbins, he was dismissed because he did a bad job of shaping the picture. "It cost us fifty thousand dollars to fix it," Ebbins asserted.

But, in a real sense, there was no fixing *Salt and Pepper*. Although a few critics found the film mildly amusing on its opening in July 1968, Archer Winston spoke for the majority, writing in the *New York Post*, "Both stars should be ashamed of themselves for lending their names, fames and talents to this kind of short-changing the public."

The realities of family life awaited Sammy when he returned home. And they boiled down to this: his marriage was over. May had finally had enough. There was no precipitating incident, no final, irrevocable fight, just the sad realization that after seven years she and her husband were fundamentally incompatible. They loved one another, but they wanted different things out of life. And nothing could bring either of them around to the other's way of thinking.

May broke the news to Sammy in November, but where he was at the time isn't clear. According to Earl Wilson, he was at their home on Summit Drive. Shortly thereafter, he left for Vegas and his latest opening at the Sands. Leo Guild maintained in the *National Enquirer* in January 1968 that Davis was already in Vegas when May phoned to say she wanted out. In fact, Guild asserted, he was in the room with Davis at the time. "Sammy's shock wasn't an act," Guild wrote. "I heard him say he didn't think he could go on stage. Silent tears coursed down his cheeks." In the end, Guild asserted, he pulled himself together and, in the best show business tradition, gave his regular performances that night. But afterward, in his dressing room, he fell apart again.

By November 25, the break was official. The *New York Daily News* trumpeted the story with "MAY TO SAMMY: IT'S ALL OVER." The subhead was "They Follow Rat Pack Leader," a reference to the fact that Sinatra had announced his separation from Mia Farrow two days earlier. On

December 19, May appeared at the courthouse in Santa Monica, testifying on behalf of her petition for divorce. "There was no family life to speak of," she told the judge. Granting her petition, he awarded her $3,000 a month in alimony and child support. But under California law the decree wouldn't be final until December 1968.

After the separation, Davis moved out of the house on Summit Drive. But the place was really too large to suit May, so he bought her another house, nearby on Angelo Drive, and he returned to the former Selznick estate. Then, about a year after the divorce became final, May and the kids left L.A. and moved to Lake Tahoe. Of course, they knew the Nevada town from Sammy's numerous engagements at Harrah's. In fact, it reminded May of her native Sweden with, as she put it, "the lake and the pine trees and all that." By contrast to smog-riddled L.A., the mountainous Nevada air was pristine and, if the local African American population was tiny, the community was at least relatively free of prejudice. More important, Tahoe lacked the intense racial climate that had pervaded southern California by the late sixties. (In 1965, while the Davises were in New York, a race riot had erupted in Watts, an African American section of Los Angeles, that resulted in thirty-five deaths, four thousand arrests, and $40 million in property damages.) The fact that Sammy performed at Harrah's several times a year meant that he would be able to see the kids. And, of course, they could visit him in L.A. whenever possible.

Sammy accepted the situation gracefully. By then, he and May had settled into a warm friendship, born by the fact that they still genuinely loved one another. She would try to involve him in all major parenting decisions, and he tried to participate to the extent that his personality and long-distance phone calls permitted.

But the loss of one's wife and family is a terrible blow, particularly for one such as Davis, who had an all-consuming need to be loved and was so lacking in confidence outside of the public arena. He never blamed May for leaving him. He blamed himself. Many years later, he told TV talk show host Sally Jessy Raphaël that he still considered his former wife "a very, very special lady" and their years together "a very special time in my life." He added, "I wish I had the, as one would say in my religion, the *sachel* to know what I know now. Because she gave me such happiness and I was not able to deal with it. Because I had show business dead center in my mind. To be the have-all, be-all. And I was able, for whatever reasons there were—and they were certainly negative—to ignore her needs, my children's needs, and to go on with my own personal needs."

Six months after the divorce, he told a reporter for a London paper, the *Daily Mail,* "I have loved twice in my life and both times have failed [presumably, the first love was Kim Novak]. Now I no longer want to love or be loved. Love is fickle. Love is intangible. Love can disappear overnight. In this phony theatrical business, they all say, 'I love you.' Every girl you meet says it, and it means nothing, nothing at all." He added with some bitterness, "I am very much like something that lies at the bottom of the sea—things attach themselves to me and I become involved with the attachments. But I have to be involved even when I make mistakes. Life ain't pretty all the time. You can't always be the winner. I know I am not a winner any more. A winner is a man who can walk tall with his head held high. Unashamed, unafraid and unsupported. I walk haltingly with each step. And it is horrible."

What his life would have been like had he and May remained together is impossible to say, but perhaps some of his subsequent problems—his substance abuse issues, for example—might not have happened. She might also have helped him keep a clearer perspective on himself, for she was nothing if not honest. But it was not to be, and, over the ensuing years, he went down several bad roads in her absence.

One might also wonder what his future would have held had he not enjoyed an extended stay in London during the summer of 1967, a time of such dramatic change in terms of lifestyle and popular culture. Sammy was in the right town to experience the new wave, but the era and the man were no longer in sync. The youth movement, by definition, didn't work for someone in his forties, and Davis was forty-one and a half during the summer of 1967. As the movement swept the United States and ultimately the world, many members of Sammy's generation, including Frank Sinatra and Dean Martin, remained true to who and what they were. But Davis and Peter Lawford were not as comfortable in their skins as their Rat Pack pallies. They chose to adopt the trappings of the new era—the hairstyles, the clothing, the lingo—along with the drugs and sexual experimentation, and make them their own.

In so doing, Sammy, for once, was following the parade, not leading it. Moreover, it wasn't a parade he really understood. He didn't seem to realize that, beyond the clothes and the slogans and the long hair lay hardcore issues that the kids were raising to protest the world they were inheriting from their elders. They condemned, for starters, the kind of conspicuous consumption for which Davis was the poster boy. Because he didn't get the movement's underpinnings, he thought the outer dimensions were an end in themselves. Consequently, he was like the shell without the substance and, when Americans realized it, he stopped being cool and started to become a joke, the epitome of the worst elements of showbiz glitz.

In all likelihood, Sammy would have reached the same point whether he'd been in London during the summer of '67 or not. As the sixties progressed, the youth movement became pervasive and unavoidable. But, having been there, he became caught up in the new scene that much sooner. And it did him little good.

PART FOUR

An Aging Hipster from La-La Land

CHAPTER 20

Sad Times
and Swinging Times

Some two and a half months after Sammy's divorce became final, he went to work on the biggest-budget film of his career. Universal's $10 million musical, *Sweet Charity,* was the screen adaptation of the 1966 Broadway hit about a hapless dancehall hostess, Charity Hope Valentine, whose good heart and trusting nature always seem to get her into trouble with men. Based on the Fellini film *The Nights of Cabiria,* the musical featured a book by Neil Simon with music and lyrics by Cy Coleman and Dorothy Fields. Sammy's friend Shirley MacLaine was tapped to star in the film version, replacing the show's original headliner, Gwen Verdon. Verdon's husband and the show's director-choreographer, Bob Fosse, was retained to head up the picture, marking the start of his heralded film career.

As Big Daddy, a jazz musician turned spiritual guru, Sammy had only one scene.* It came in the film's second half, when Charity and her tightly wound boyfriend, Oscar (John McMartin), attend one of Big Daddy's unorthodox religious services. The scene is primarily an excuse for a big production number called "The Rhythm of Life."

Principal photography started on January 29, 1969 and ended around mid-June, but Davis' scene was shot over three days in March. The setting was a garage, and one of Universal's largest sound stages was utilized to create a three-story structure. Its centerpiece was Big Daddy's wheels, a 1927 Buick, painted from hood to trunk in a psychedelic montage. Sammy's costume was the perfect complement to the car. Created by Edith Head, it consisted of a pink dashiki and black leather pants. The eight rings on his fingers and the pounds of love beads around his neck came from his own, growing jewelry collection.

*The character Davis played was known as Daddy Johann Sebastian Brubeck when Arnold Soboloff created the role on the stage.

When not otherwise engaged, Davis was busy snapping pictures behind the scenes at Universal. At the time, Sammy owned more than five hundred cameras. His love of photography was so great that he even opened a camera store and became a member of the Association of Magazine and Newspaper Photographers. His work appeared in several publications, including *Playboy,* and graced the covers of numerous record albums other than his own.

The world premiere of *Sweet Charity* was in Boston on February 11, 1969, followed by its opening in New York on April 1. It was initially shown on a roadshow basis, with reserved seats, two screenings a day, and an intermission. Its initial running time of 157 minutes was shortened to 133 minutes when it went into general release.

Film musicals were a popular genre in the sixties, sparked by the tremendous critical and commercial success of *West Side Story, My Fair Lady,* and *The Sound of Music,* but *Sweet Charity* failed to capture the hearts of moviegoers. Despite an engaging performance by MacLaine and Fosse's innovative choreography, the picture was too long, pointlessly bloated, and not particularly funny, even with an original book by Broadway's hottest jokemeister, Neil Simon. Sammy's performance was unmemorable, as well. Fosse's choreography for "The Rhythm of Life" failed to showcase Davis' unique gifts, and his stoned-out, jargon-spouting, love bead–laden preacher played into many of the worst elements of his evolving persona. Most critics failed to even address his presence in their reviews of the picture.

Shirley MacLaine recalled in her 1991 memoir, *Dance While You Can,* that she and Sammy had long, deep discussions about the meaning of life on the set of *Sweet Charity.* "Soon after that," she added, "he began his search into different religions."

Davis' search led him down a rather dark and potentially dangerous road. It started one evening after a visit with his kids at May's home on Angelo Drive. As usual, his attempt at fatherhood hadn't gone very well. Depressed, he didn't want to return to his empty house, so he decided to drop by the Factory, a disco that he, Peter Lawford, and several others had established in Hollywood. There he ran into some actors he knew, and one of them invited him to go with them to a party.

When he got to the bash, he found that all the guests were wearing hoods or masks and each of them sported a single red-painted fingernail. Spying a naked woman chained to an altar decked out in red velvet, Sammy asked what was going on and was told the guests were members of a Satanic coven. He wasn't impressed. As he put it, "I'd read enough about it to know that they weren't Satanists, they were bullshit artists and they'd found an exotic way they could ball each other and have an orgy. And get stoned. It was all fun and games and dungeons and dragons and debauchery and as long as the chick was happy and wasn't really going to get anything sharper than a dildo stuck into her, I wasn't going to walk away from it." Later, one of the guests lifted his hood and revealed himself to Sammy. It was Jay Sebring, his hairstylist. Davis wasn't surprised. "I'd always known Jay was a little weird," he said.

But so was Davis. He was intrigued by his friends' flirtation with the dark side. "Evil fascinated me," he said later. "I felt it lying in wait for me. And I wanted to taste it. I was ready to accept the wildness, the rolling in the gutter, and having to get up the next morning and wash myself clean."

Shortly thereafter, he had an engagement in San Francisco. While he was there, he met Anton LeVey, the head of the Church of Satan, who warned him, "Don't get involved with this unless you really want to commit yourself to something." Sammy wasn't deterred. If anything, LeVey's admonition just whetted his interest. By the time he came back home, he, too, was sporting a red fingernail. Most people, including those who caught his nightclub act, had no idea that this meant anything; it just seemed to go with his tinted aviator glasses, Nehru jackets, love beads, and other affectations.

Indeed, the red fingernail didn't mean much more than that to Sammy. He liked the sense of living on the edge and flirting with danger—other than confronting gun-wielding bigots down South—but he certainly didn't take the Satanism thing seriously. What appealed to him about cult membership was that it was, in his words, "bodacious and shocking." He wanted to see how much he could get away with. He also liked the coven's kinky approach to group sex. But, within a relatively short time, he realized that membership wasn't all fun and games. After a "meeting" at which the sadomasochistic group sex went too far, he found some nail polish remover and quietly resigned.

Concurrent with Sammy's work on *Sweet Charity* came his appearance on a new NBC variety show, which would further his image as a late-sixties hipster.

Created and produced by George Schlatter, Sammy's old pal from Ciro's, *Rowan and Martin's Laugh-In* offered an hour of fast-paced, irreverent humor. As a gaggle of fresh, talented, mostly unknown comics—Goldie Hawn, Ruth Buzzie, Arte Johnson, Jo Anne Whorley, Henry Gibson, Judy Carne, and, a bit later, Lily Tomlin—whizzed through a series of one-liners, sight gags, and short sketches, they created a host of odd but memorable characters. These quickly entered the popular consciousness, along with a series of silly catch phrases, from

"Sock it to me" to "You bet your bippy." Although the hosts, Dan Rowan and Dick Martin, were older and more established than the rest of the cast, their breezy approach perfectly suited the show.

Laugh-In enjoyed high ratings when it debuted as a special on September 9, 1967, but no one expected much from the series on its midseason launch on January 22, 1968. In fact, it was slated for only a fourteen-week run, after which it was to be replaced by another, already scheduled program. Schlatter credited Davis' guest appearance on March 28 with helping to make *Laugh-In* must-see TV.

According to the producer, Sammy's involvement with the show came about rather innocently. He and Davis were schmoozing in Schlatter's office one day when they started reminiscing about old burlesque comedians they admired: Billy Zoot Reed, Redd Foxx, Moms Mabley. "Remember Pigmeat? Pigmeat Markham?" Sammy asked. Schlatter, in fact, recalled the black comic, and soon they were both doing Pigmeat Markham bits, one of which featured the pithy jingle, "Judge is good/Judge is fine/Everybody gonna do some time/Cause here come da judge." Davis started riffing on the theme, making up limericks of his own. "And in the office we were hysterical," Schlatter said. He told Sammy, "You've got to come on the show and do that."

Davis was willing. He decided to add to the bit by sporting not only a black robe, but also a British judicial wig, powdered white in the customary fashion. He and the show's writers made up corny bits of shtick to go with the punch line.

The night they taped the episode, Schlatter recalled, numerous cast and crew members left the Burbank studio chanting, "Here come da judge, Here come da judge." Thinking they might be onto something, he put the episode on the air as fast as possible, and, indeed, the slogan soon swept the country.

Thereafter, numerous other celebrities, even prominent political figures—including, of all people, staid Richard Nixon—were clamoring to make cameo appearances on *Laugh-In*. Instead of yanking the show at the end of fourteen weeks, NBC kept it on the air through 1972.

While Sammy was cavorting at the studios of Universal and NBC and living on the edge in Los Angeles, momentous events were taking place around the country, primarily as a result of the war in Vietnam.

America's presence in the tiny country in Southeast Asia had risen dramatically since the death of President Kennedy. In November 1963, the United States had sixteen thousand men serving as "military advisors" to the forces of the beleaguered South. By 1968, there were half a million Americans engaged in the conflict; more than thirty thousand soldiers had come home in body bags. Demonstrations against the war took place in cities around the country in 1967. Borrowing the nonviolent posture and many of the tactics of the civil rights movement, the dissidents had, to some extent, co-opted the ongoing struggle for racial equality, with Martin Luther King himself leading antiwar rallies. Meanwhile, the formerly cohesive civil rights struggle had splintered into a variety of factions. New groups like the Black Panthers and emerging leaders, like Stokely Carmichael, Eldridge Cleaver, H. Rap Brown, and Angela Davis, were advocating a more militant approach to change and articulating an antiwhite bias that alienated former Caucasian supporters.

Despite his problems, LBJ, who had been elected by the largest majority in history in 1964, looked like a formidable candidate for reelection at the outset of 1968. Leaders in the left wing of the Democratic Party had urged Robert Kennedy, who was opposed to the war, to challenge the president for the nomination, but Kennedy declined. In his stead, Eugene McCarthy, the relatively unknown and somewhat mystical senator from Minnesota, entered the fray. When McCarthy came within a few points of defeating Johnson in the New Hampshire primary, the equation changed dramatically. On March 18, Kennedy decided to enter the race after all. Less than two weeks later, Johnson announced his withdrawal from the race. Five days after that, on April 4, Martin Luther King, Jr., was assassinated in Memphis.

Like everyone else in America, Sammy had a hard time keeping pace with these tumultuous events, but the loss of Dr. King, whom he considered a friend, was particularly horrific. He was in New York at the time, rehearsing for an upcoming revival of *Golden Boy* in Chicago and London. Feeling compelled to speak out in the wake of the tragedy, particularly because he feared that riots would erupt across the country—and they did in more than one hundred cities—he went on the *Tonight Show* that evening to remind Americans of King's dream of change through nonviolence. He made similar statements, urging restraint, on the other two networks. Then he flew to Atlanta for the funeral.

When he returned to New York, he met with Bobby Kennedy's brother-in-law, Sargent Shriver, to discuss ways he could contribute to the battle for the Democratic Party nomination. Sammy had never blamed Jack's brother for the debacle over the inauguration in 1961; Peter Lawford told him that Bobby had argued vigorously in favor of his attendance. During the intervening years, the two men had established a personal relationship that far exceeded Sammy's casual acquaintance with Jack. He spent several occasions at the Kennedy home, Hickory Hill, in McLean, Virginia, and, at least once, visited Bobby at the family compound in Hyannis Port. Bobby's wife, Ethel, recalled how, on that visit, Sammy gamely joined her on her sailboat for a regatta, trying without much success to mask his fear of water, a reflection of his lack of swimming skills. Bobby genuinely liked Davis, and the feeling was mutual. As Sammy put it, "I loved being with him and with Ethel. They were affectionate to each other, like two comfortable shoes together, not only demonstrative but you knew this was as solid as rock. I also enjoyed being with them because Bobby was a marvelous listener."

He noted in his second autobiography, *Why Me?*, that he participated in Kennedy's 1964 run for a U.S. Senate seat from New York, although it is difficult to see how he could have been much of a factor during that campaign. He was in Detroit, trying out *Golden Boy*, when Bobby announced his candidacy, and was consumed with the musical nearly round the clock until its opening on October 20, only a couple of weeks before the election.

But he was eager to do what he could for RFK during the rough-and-tumble primary season in 1968. Particularly after King's assassination. As he put it, "Now Bobby was hope. If I were not already committed to a producer, investors, a large cast, and theaters in England and Chicago, I would have taken a few months off from performing and joined the Kennedy campaign full time." In fact, Bobby needed all the help he could get, because McCarthy refused to leave the race after Kennedy tossed his hat in the ring. The Minnesota senator felt with justification that he'd earned the right to be the antiwar candidate since he'd taken on the entrenched president when the cause appeared all but hopeless. Moreover, LBJ's vice president, Hubert Humphrey, had also entered the race, and he clearly had the support of much of the Party establishment. In 1968, presidential primaries didn't carry the weight of later years. While McCarthy and Kennedy faced off in Indiana, Nebraska, Oregon, and, finally, California, Humphrey was busy lining up delegates in states where delegates were chosen by other means.

While in New York, Sammy devoted as much attention to the campaign as possible, attending numerous rallies and fund-raisers. The more time he spent with the senator, the more invigorated he became, saying later, "I, like everyone around him, was moved by his idealism to the point where I heard the drums, I heard the bugles, I saw the flag flying, and I believed—as I had never before believed in any political person—that marvelous things were coming, that Robert Kennedy was going to lead America into a new age in which all Americans would be free and rich and love each other."

A couple of weeks after King's funeral, the *Golden Boy* company moved on to Chicago for a tryout engagement prior to the show's debut in Lon-

don. Many members of the ensemble had returned from the original production, including Lola Falana, but the principals were all new, with
Gloria De Haven, Mark Dawson, John Bassette, and Al Kirk taking the
place of Paula Wayne, Kenneth Tobey, Johnny Brown, and Louis Gossett,
Jr., respectively. Hilly Elkins had persuaded William Gibson to make
some adjustments to the book, primarily to update the topical references in light of the changes that had occurred since 1964. Perhaps the
most dramatic alteration was that Joe's dad, originally played by Roy
Glenn, was transformed into the boxer's mother, with Hilda Haynes in
the role. The lineup of songs was also altered, as four numbers from the
original production, including the haunting title tune and Eddie Satin's
"While the City Sleeps," were dropped in favor of three songs that had
been cut earlier, among them Sammy's personal anthem, "Yes I Can." The
direction was handled by the show's original stage manager, Michael
Thoma, who re-created Penn's staging with an assist from Sammy.

The musical was well received in Chicago, even though the city was
in the midst of a race riot at the time. It sold out at most performances,
but not everyone in the audience was a Sammy Davis, Jr., fan. "I was
thoroughly included in the hatred felt in Chicago for the blacks," said
the entertainer. "During the show, sometimes I got booed from the audience and in the scene where the white girl refused me people would
applaud. I had four security men, one private and three black Chicago
Police Department officers, who were always assigned to me."

Aware of the intense feelings dividing the city, Sammy wanted to
reach out to members of the African American community, including its
more radical elements. First, he arranged a tour of the black ghetto.
When he was barred from an area reserved for the Black Panthers and
other militant organizations, he realized with some astonishment that
they considered him an Uncle Tom.

Refusing to accept this situation quietly, Davis put out the word that
he wanted to meet with some of the local militants, adding, "Not the
leaders. I want to meet the kids on the street." Consequently, four young
men came to his dressing room one day after a performance. Saying he
wanted to help, Sammy asked what they were trying to accomplish and
what they needed. He offered money, but they said they could always
steal money. Rather, they needed his commitment—on a day-to-day
basis. He said they had that, itemizing the civil rights marches he'd
attended. They were demonstrably unimpressed. "Don't mean shit
today," they told him. "This is '68."

Unable to connect with the kids, he tried again with the leaders of a
radical group called the Commandos. But he found them extremely hostile as well. "We don't need no nigguh lives with whitey," one of them

told him flatly. Refusing to rise to the bait, he tried to remain civil, and, little by little, the Commando leaders opened up. As they did, he began to realize that their lives consisted of nothing but problems. "They had no homes," he said, "few jobs, and they had a major alienation between them and the white power structure even before the riots had begun. It was the cause of the riots." His solution was to bring the militants together with people who could effect change, namely, members of Mayor Richard Daley's administration, but they refused. They wouldn't even meet with the publisher of Chicago's major African American newspaper. The publisher was black, but a member of the established elite; thus, he, too, was suspect.

The attitude of the Commandos and the street kids was a genuine wake-up call for Davis. "There was a time," he said later, "when you joined the NAACP and you paid $100 to be a Life Member and that was your commitment to race." Now, suddenly, the rules had changed. He wanted to help. More than that, he wanted to be part of the in group now that black was beautiful. But he didn't know how. It wasn't so much a race thing as an age thing. The militants would have treated Martin Luther King in much the same fashion.

Sammy's meetings with the radicals in Chicago left him feeling, in his words, "weakened by their sadness" and stung by his own "impotence." The best thing he could do, he decided, was to maintain his present course, helping Bobby Kennedy become president. He realized that this reflected a "Let Charley do it" mentality, but he truly believed that RFK could be a positive agent for change. Thus, whenever he could, he traveled to nearby Indiana, where, on May 7, Kennedy faced his first primary against Eugene McCarthy (Kennedy won). Davis also tried to shore up delegate support for his candidate in Illinois. "Almost every afternoon," he recalled, "I campaigned somewhere in Illinois and Indiana. I went out to universities and talked about Bobby. I drew large crowds because my popularity was high and there was a known association with the Kennedys. The new young black voters were very receptive to Bobby; his image with the ethnic groups in general was much stronger than John's had been; he had a deeper emotional key to the black people."

Davis desperately wanted to help as the campaign shifted to Oregon and California, but the Chicago run of *Golden Boy* had come to an end and it was time to move on to London. The day he left for England, he phoned Kennedy to express his regrets and to wish the candidate luck. "I'm sorry you can't be with us to the end," Bobby told him. "If we're lucky enough to win, it won't seem right you not being there." Sammy promised to phone and to keep in touch through Peter Lawford as well.

* * *

Golden Boy debuted at the London Palladium on June 5 for a limited, twelve-week run. As in New York, the critics were captivated by the show's energy, its lively choreography, and Tony Walton's imaginative sets. But, if anything, they were even less enamored of the book than their American counterparts. In a repeat of the Manhattan premiere, Sammy experienced problems with his throat on opening night, a fact noted by many of the critics in their reviews. But none of it mattered. The entire engagement was sold out prior to the opening, making *Golden Boy*, according to the *Hollywood Reporter*, "the first such SRO in Palladium history."

Sammy barely had time to savor the thrill of his London theatrical debut and the smashing cast party afterward when he learned that Robert Kennedy had been shot. The senator was leaving a ballroom in the Ambassador Hotel in Los Angeles on the evening of June 6, following his remarks to supporters in the wake of his victory in the California primary, when he was shot by a Jordanian immigrant, Sirhan Sirhan. Although Davis was devastated, he tried to go on with the show that night, but he couldn't. Before the start of the second act, he came onstage and told the audience his laryngitis was simply too severe for him to continue. "But this is providential," he added, "as I really did not want to appear tonight. For once my heart is not in the theater. It is many miles away in America." Then he asked the audience to pray for his fallen friend.

Later, in his penthouse suite atop the Playboy Club, loaned to him for the run of *Golden Boy* by Hugh Hefner, Sammy told a reporter for the London *Evening News*, "At times like this there doesn't seem much point in talking. There doesn't appear to be any message of hope. It looks like there are no good people left in the world." He added, "It was a marvelous feeling to have a man like him running for office. He was one of the few white men left who could walk the streets of Watts and Harlem. Now to see him wasted away." But he also gave voice to a concern shared by millions of other Americans, now as well as then, passionately asserting, "What has to be done immediately is something about the violence. Calling an inquiry isn't enough. We have got to make it impossible for people to buy guns unless they are responsible human beings. The gun laws of America are ridiculous and everyone knows that they are. People get slaughtered and annihilated. And not only the nation's leaders. We find people shot down from a tower as they walk the streets. Do you know that a 12-year-old kid can buy a machine-gun through mail order? No questions are asked. This has got to be stopped immediately. A group of us must accept responsibility for the future and people have got to commit themselves. It's like watching a weed grow and doing nothing about it."

He returned to the show the following night. Ticket holders that evening, and at every other performance during the musical's run, were thrilled by his presence. As Hollywood columnist Sheila Graham noted, "I attended a performance and the audience went wild. It wouldn't let him go. I was told it happened every night." One of her New York colleagues found the same thing, adding, "I've seen nothing like it since the Beatles."

Sammy again immersed himself in the social whirl of swinging London. He hobnobbed with his posh pals, like Tony Newley, Leslie Bricusse, and Laurence Olivier, at their favorite hangout, the White Elephant. But he also partied with a new group, including young rock stars Jimi Hendrix and Cass Elliot (of the Mamas and the Papas), who were into drugs and sexual experimentation. "They were the wild scene in London," Davis said later, "and we cooked." Rat Pack chroniclers Lawrence J. Quirk and William Schoell asserted that, in the spirit of the age, Davis sometimes took "two or three girls with him to bed at one time, holding all-night orgies in his hotel suite, occasionally engaging in quickie homosexual acts just to see what it was like. He bragged endlessly about the women he had—as if trying to prove he was the epitome of the stereotypical Negro stallion—but mostly kept mum about the times he had sex with men (including a brief interlude with Peter Lawford).* Most of this activity was done under the influence of drugs—pot, speed, mescaline, LSD, anything and everything that was verboten and trendy. He wanted to soak up every single sensation that he could, do everything that was possible to do in this world. Most of all, he wanted to keep loneliness at bay."

Aside from his one-night stands and quickies, Sammy was also seeing Lola Falana, perhaps even seriously. "They were really close," said Sammy's assistant–office manager, Shirley Rhodes. "She was a sexy, good-looking girl. And very talented. And they made an attractive cou-

*This author spoke to several of Davis' close friends and associates about his alleged homosexual relationship with Peter Lawford and found no one who could validate Quirk and Schoell's assertion. However, Arthur Silber, Jr., said, "I wasn't there but I know for a fact that Sammy experimented bisexually. But only experimented, and it didn't work for him. That was during the drug period. I guarantee you it never happened before that." Burt Boyar considered such homosexual experimentation unlikely, but admitted that Sammy "wanted to experience everything. If he could have been pregnant, he would have." Late in his life, Davis himself told Linda Witt of *People* magazine, "The truth is I'm not a homosexual, but I'm not ashamed to say I had a homosexual experience. And it was like drugs, which I've tried too. You make a choice" (Witt/P). But he indicated that his experience came while he was in the army.

ple. I thought eventually they may get married. But Altovise came along and said that wasn't going to be."

Born in Brooklyn, Altovise Gore was roughly eighteen years younger than Sammy. The daughter of a subway conductor, she had attended the New York High School for the Performing Arts. As a senior, she managed to land a dancing job in *Kwamina,* a short-lived Adler-Ross musical set in a fictional West African nation. This was followed by work in two other unsuccessful musicals: *High Spirits,* an adaptation of Noel Coward's *Blithe Spirits* that starred Tammy Grimes and Beatrice Lillie, and *Mata Hari,* based on the life of the World War I spy.

Like Lola Falana, Altovise was a member of the London cast of *Golden Boy.* She portrayed Joe's homemaker sister, Anna, the role created on Broadway by Jeannette DuBois. As the character dressed in rather dowdy housedresses and Altovise favored jeans and leotards at rehearsals, Sammy paid little attention to her in New York and Chicago. Then she showed up at the opening night party in London decked out in a long white evening dress cut low in the back, and he suddenly realized that this tall, slim African American woman was stunning. She also had a bubbly, upbeat, relatively uncomplicated personality.

Sammy and Altovise started hanging out together. He even convinced Lola Falana to share her suite, two floors below his own, with Gore, thereby enabling Alto, as her friends called her, to move from her cramped London boarding house across town. He and Alto flirted with one another, but nothing more. She had a boyfriend back home, an aspiring doctor, while he had Lola and, in his words, "a whole lot of London chicks who'd been waiting for me since the last time." So they kept their relationship platonic. Still, she was delighted to be in his company. "My first impression," she recalled in a 1978 article in the magazine *Sepia,* "was, 'Wow, he's really bright, and look who I am talking to. This is the greatest entertainer in the world.' I was thrilled to death." As she got to know him better, she found him to be something more: "genuine and down to earth," in her words. She was particularly impressed with his kindness toward the *Golden Boy* chorus kids. As she put it, "That did it for me."

As was his habit throughout his drug-using years, Sammy kept his older, "straight" pals separate from his "hip" young friends, knowing that the behavior of the latter would discomfort the former—and perhaps provoke their approbation as well. Most of his long-standing buddies had no idea what he was doing when they weren't together. As Leslie Bricusse explained, "It wasn't obvious that Sammy was into anything in particular. It really wasn't. He drank a lot, but we all drank quite a bit in those days. So I don't think there were any markers. And, again, if you were not part of the drug scene, you were not aware of it. You either were in it or you weren't in it. We were never a part of it."

Hand in hand with his growing use of illegal substances, Davis' spending habits exceeded even prior levels. By his own later admission, he owed so much money to London merchants that a process server tendered him a summons to settle his affairs in court while he was in the middle of a performance of *Golden Boy*. Sammy's valet, Murphy Bennett, became so concerned for his boss that he even offered to take a substantial pay cut. Davis' solution to this mess was to arrange a substantial loan from the giant department store, Harrod's.

Despite his generally self-destructive behavior, the entertainer tried to do something positive by reaching out to his children while he was in London. As the show was running during the summer and they were out of school, he asked May if they could come over for a vacation. She thought Jeff, then about five, was too young, but she was all in favor of Tracey and Mark spending time with their dad.

The vacation started poorly. The night the kids arrived, Sammy drank too much and consequently slept until noon the next day, thereby wrecking their sightseeing plans. The following night, he cut back on the booze, but was unable to sleep as a result. So he invited Alto and Lola to come up to his suite. Tracey happened to wake up while they were there. When she came into the living room and saw the three of them together, she ran back to her bed. Sammy tried to comfort her, but the tearful seven-year-old told him that she wanted to go home. "You've got no time for me," she declared. "Well, if you want to go back," he responded angrily, "then go back." The next day, he apologetically tried to convince her to change her mind, but to no avail.

This incident was emblematic of Sammy's relationship with his daughter for many years to come. When they were together, he would invariably do something to anger Tracey, who grew into a headstrong, rather intolerant teenager. Even though he was often at fault, he didn't mean any harm by his behavior; he was who he was. But Tracey's ire would, in turn, anger him, so their times together would often descend into an argument. Matters were less strenuous with Mark, who, at eight, was a more easygoing personality. He, too, was hurt by Sammy's neglect, but, where Tracey let her feelings explode, he tended to keep them to himself. Mark had been willing to stay in London, for example, but he didn't think Tracey should travel by herself, so he left with her.

In the wake of this debacle, Sammy began spending even more time with his rock friends, getting, as he put it, "deeply into drinking and partying." He increased his drug intake as well. Most of the get-togethers occurred at his penthouse suite, where he and his young "friends" would strip naked and sit around in the buff, talking or watching movies. Partner switching and group sex were also part of the scene, and Sammy enjoyed his share, but, for him, these occasions were less about fun and more about escape. Still mourning the death of his marriage, his credo became "Anything not to feel anything."

The only time he really came alive was onstage at the Palladium. *Golden Boy* had originally been scheduled to close on August 28, but it was such a smashing success that he agreed to extend the run for several weeks, with the final performance coming on September 14.

Immediately thereafter, Davis embarked on a multicity tour of West Germany that lasted until October 2. He was accompanied by Lola Falana as well as five members of the *Golden Boy* ensemble, billed as the Lester Wilson Dancers. Among them was Altovise Gore, who acted as a sort of mistress of ceremonies, introducing Sammy and appearing at various points during the act to light his cigarettes and hand him drinks. "From the audience," Sammy said, "it looked like I was traveling with my personal harem. When we got back to the States the girls continued traveling with me; it was a new look to the act and the raised eyebrows were good for business."

His first gig back home was at the Sherman House in Chicago, which started on October 9. He did capacity business during the eighteen-day outing. In fact, the lines outside the club were so long that its owner, Jerry Kaufman, had to hire extra security guards for crowd control.

Davis' ability to pack in the people continued when he moved on to Harrah's Lake Tahoe in early November, prompting a local critic to marvel at his ability to fill the resort's showroom during the lull between Labor Day and the Christmas holidays. No one marveled, however, when Davis traveled from Tahoe to Vegas for his first engagement at the Sands in a year; his reputation as one of the town's biggest draws was well established by then.

Sammy was happy to be in demand, but the frenzy that greeted his live appearances only increased his continuing ennui when he was not onstage. Offstage, he was miserable. Consequently, he started doing longer sets, to the point where club managers would have to ask him to cut back. He would try to be accommodating, but, as he said later, "There were nights I couldn't bring myself to break away from all that love coming at me."

During his off hours, he persisted in finding ways to escape reality. He used booze to sink into a state where he felt numb and could blot out feelings altogether. Conversely, drugs enabled him to experience heightened, hallucinogenic sensations having nothing to do with his daily life.

Sex continued to be another palliative. He recalled seeing three different showgirls during his engagement at the Sands. One night, all four of them wound up in his suite together, prompting him to suggest that they make their quartet a permanent thing, and they agreed. Each member of the foursome, including Sammy, pledged fidelity to the others. He recalled in *Why Me?*, "On our first night 'at home' after our shows I said, 'Hey, why don't you chicks ball and I'll just sit here and watch.'" They complied. At first, observing the girls' lovemaking was wildly stimulating, but, after a while, Sammy wanted to join in the fun. He waited to be invited, but the entreaty never came. Finally, he went off to bed alone, jealous over the frenzied activity continuing in the living room. After that night, he grew increasingly disenchanted with the arrangement, and it soon ended.

When he played Vegas, Tahoe, or Reno, Sammy also tried to gamble away his unhappiness, dropping between $5,000 and $10,000 a day on Keno. When he learned that the head of 20th Century Fox, Kirk Kerkorian, wanted to get rid of his jet, a Lockheed Lodestar, Sammy decided to lease it. The weekly operating costs alone were $5,000, but he deluded himself into thinking he could afford the plane by simply dispensing with Keno. Moreover, he convinced himself he'd be saving a fortune on first-class tickets, although they cost nowhere near the price of renting a private jet and full-time crew. The bottom line is that he liked the idea of playing the bigshot, of being able to tell friends and family members, including May, that he'd send the jet for them when they wanted to visit. As he put it, "I overdosed on every excess that fame or money could provide."

The tumultuous year 1968 ended on one bright note. In November, Reprise released a new Davis LP entitled *I've Gotta Be Me*. The title track, a ballad from the failed Broadway musical *Golden Rainbow* starring Steve Lawrence, provided Sammy with an equivalent to Sinatra's concurrent anthem "My Way." Each song combined a highly dramatic melody line and arrangement with a defiant statement of individuality. On December 14, Reprise released his version of "I've Gotta Be Me" as a single and it climbed to number 11 on *Billboard*'s pop chart, where it remained for sixteen weeks, making it Sammy's biggest hit of the decade, surpassing even "What Kind of Fool Am I?" It remained a staple of his act for many years to come.

CHAPTER 21

Altovise

Sammy started 1969 in Las Vegas, filming his first big-screen Western since *Sergeants 3*. But *Man with a Load of Mischief* bore no resemblance to a Rat Pack picture. It was more akin to the revisionist shoot-em-ups that Sergio Leone made with Clint Eastwood, pitting a sullen loner against an array of corrupt and venal opponents, all of whom deserve the violent deaths he metes out.

In this case, the loner, Jedidiah Kelsey, was played by James Caan. Caan's comely costar was Stephanie Powers, portraying a half Indian–half Spanish outcast who aids Jedidiah in his battle against a local lawman (Aldo Ray). Sammy was cast as a sadistic gunman, Kid Dandy, who is aligned with Kelsey's enemies.

The exteriors were shot in the scenic Valley of Fire, outside of Las Vegas, where a typical frontier main street was erected. The interiors, including the saloon where the bulk of Davis' scenes occurred, were filmed at the Colorvision Studio in L.A.

Although Sammy loved decking himself out in an all-black leather outfit and displaying his proficiency with a six-shooter, *Man with a Load of Mischief* was a total disaster. As James Caan put it, "The script was just ridiculous. It was just stupid. It had no plot or anything. Four days into it, I go, 'What the fuck are they doing?'" Stephanie Powers felt the same way.

Worse, executive producer Samuel Ray Calabrese couldn't afford to pay the company members their full salaries, prompting Caan to file suit against the production. The upshot of this legal action, he maintained, was that the Cinerama Company was prohibited from releasing the picture. Indeed, it sat on the shelf for about five years. Then, around 1975, the footage was acquired by a new company, International CineFilm Corp., which renamed it *Gone with the West* and attempted to market it at the annual film festival in Cannes, with no apparent success.

* * *

Sammy had better luck on the small screen. On March 17, 1969, he returned to *Laugh-In,* marking the one-year anniversary of his initial appearance on the show. The following week, he showed up on ABC's police drama, *The Mod Squad,* in his first dramatic role for television since *The Danny Thomas Hour* aired in November 1967.

In a sense, *The Mod Squad* was to drama what *Laugh-In* was to comedy. Both programs embraced the fashions, attitudes, and issues of the day—from a liberal perspective—and were carried primarily by bright, hip, attractive youngsters. In the case of the Thomas-Spelling drama, the stars, Peter Cole, Peggy Lipton, and Clarence Williams III, played typically troubled, rebellious young adults who form a special undercover squad within the Los Angeles Police Department. Although the concept was far-fetched, the show was a hit.

Sammy's episode, called "Keep the Faith, Baby," featured the entertainer as a Catholic priest named John Banks, whose civil rights activism causes his suspension from the church. Banks is also being stalked by a murderer (played by Robert Duvall), who confessed his crime to Banks in a moment of weakness and now fears the priest will testify at his trial. The Mod Squad is assigned to protect Banks from the killer. Although Davis' dialogue was liberally spiced with the lingo of the day—"I can dig it," "Peace," "Groovy"—he tackled his role in a clean, simple fashion, letting the man's sincerity and dedication override his hipness. "Although there are several flaws in the script by Harve Bennett," wrote Bill Ornstein of the *Hollywood Reporter,* "Sammy Davis, Jr., comes through with an outstanding dramatic performance."

On March 30, five days after Sammy portrayed a dedicated priest, his own sense of dedication was the subject of a tribute in New York City as the NAACP honored him with its prestigious Springarn Award. Established in 1914 by J. E. Springarn, then chairman of the organization's board of directors, it was presented annually to someone whose contributions to civil rights and/or the image of African Americans was particularly noteworthy. Previous winners included Thurgood Marshall, J. Philip Randolph, Martin Luther King, Jr., and Ralph Bunche, as well as such performing artists as Duke Ellington, Paul Robeson, Leontine Pryce, and Marian Anderson.

Roy Wilkins, executive director of the NAACP, presented the award. "You know, you never have to be ashamed of Sammy Davis," he told the distinguished assemblage. "He will never let you down. . . . He is a devotee of excellence." Wilkins then read from the award citation, which praised Davis' "superb and multi-faceted talent which has earned him a prominent place in American entertainment." It also recognized him as a "peerless worker in the vineyards of freedom."

The entertainer responded by speaking—without a prepared text—about the state of the civil rights movement at the end of the sixties. He acknowledged the disenchantment of the younger generation, conceding that "we have come up empty for them." But he also pointed out that, without his efforts and those of the people in the audience, these youngsters wouldn't have enjoyed the freedom to "make the signs and to do the protests that they're undertaking." As he spoke, one could almost feel his own inner struggle. On the one hand, he was proud of the impressive gains achieved through King's nonviolent integrationist approach, but, on the other, he saw validity in the less accommodating demands of the era's newer, more radical leaders. If he seemed ambivalent about the movement's future direction, he was more confident when it came to such core issues as love of country and the treatment of people as individuals, not members of a particular race. As he said by way of conclusion, "I thank the young people for making me aware of the fact that I am of African descent. But America is my home. And I'm going to do everything I can to make it a place worthy of the word democracy."

Always sensitive to how he was perceived by the Negro community, Davis was clearly touched by the honor the NAACP had bestowed on him. Years later, he cited the Springarn as one of the two awards that carried the most significance for him (the other being his Kennedy Center honor).

The following month, Sammy took a rare and well-deserved vacation. The idea for the trip, a ten-day cruise of the Caribbean, came from Sidney Poitier, who was convinced that his friend badly needed a rest. Joining them would be Poitier's girlfriend, Joanna Shimkus; Quincy Jones, a friend of Davis since the late 1940s; Jones' wife, Ulla; another friend of Poitier, Terry McNeely; and McNeely's girlfriend, Dolores.

Sammy was given clear instructions by Poitier: he could bring a date, but he had to leave behind his entourage and his usual twenty pieces of luggage. Not knowing whom to invite, Davis chose Peggy Lipton, the gorgeous blonde star of *The Mod Squad*. They didn't know each other well, having worked together only on the recent episode of her show. Moreover, Lipton was in the midst of an on/off relationship with record producer Lou Adler. But she agreed to go on the cruise. Then, on the flight from New York, she began to feel that she'd made a mistake. Her discomfort grew more acute the following day in Nassau, where twin yachts awaited the vacationers. Finally, she made her apologies and fled, leaving Sammy embarrassed and without female companionship.*

Then Joanna Shimkus suggested he call Altovise. Sammy and the dancer had kept their relationship platonic since the London run of *Golden Boy,* but everyone around them saw definite signs of romantic interest—on both sides—as they toured the country for Sammy's nightclub gigs.

Agreeable to the idea, Davis phoned Shirley Rhodes in New York and asked her to call Alto and invite her to fly down to Nassau. But the dancer couldn't be located. Poitier and his guests decided to delay their departure until the following day in the hope that she could be found, but when morning came with no word from New York, they departed. Still hoping for a happy outcome, Sammy left reservations at the airport for a seaplane to transport Alto to his yacht, should she arrive. Indeed, late that afternoon, she did. "When Altovise Gore stepped out of that tiny seaplane into the little dinghy we sent to pick her up," Poitier wrote in his 1980 memoir, *This Life,* "passengers and crew from both boats broke into applause. First of all, the girls were happy that Altovise, no stranger to any of them, had joined us. Quincy, Terry, and I were happy that Sammy had company. But listen to me when I tell you that Sammy Davis, Jr., was the happiest person in the fleet. Altovise Gore was a special kind of special. She made the difference, and it showed on Sammy's face."

As the cruise progressed, Sammy grew even happier about his choice to replace Peggy Lipton. Seeing Altovise away from the rigors of show business was a revelation. He liked the fact that she wasn't jaded or terribly sophisticated, and that she delighted at being in the presence of celebrities like Poitier and Jones. As he put it, "She didn't have May's 'I couldn't care less' attitude." Moreover, after years of playing around, he found in Alto someone with whom he could share things. It was a welcome change from the kind of short-term, impersonal affairs to which he had resigned himself. When the cruise ended, neither knew exactly where the relationship was headed. But they both realized they weren't just friends any more.

Two months after his Caribbean idyll, Sammy was back in London, where he and Peter Lawford joined forces to reprise their roles from *Salt and Pepper*. The sequel, originally called *Here We Go Again* and released as *One More Time,* found the intrepid nightclub owners in pursuit of a ring of diamond smugglers, following the murder of Chris' twin brother, Lord Pepper (also played by Lawford).

*By a strange coincidence, Quincy Jones married Peggy Lipton four years later.

Rather than rehire Richard Donner, Davis, Lawford, and producer Milton Ebbins brought in Sammy's old pal, Jerry Lewis. Lewis had forged a successful career as the star, director, producer, and, often, screenwriter of a series of slapstick films, among them *The Ladies Man* and *The Nutty Professor*. *One More Time* would mark his first foray as a director outside of his own vehicles.

Sammy loved working with Jerry. He considered his friend "a brilliant director" who "did all his homework meticulously and knew exactly what he wanted before he reached the set." The entertainer's enthusiasm stemmed, at least in part, from the attention Lewis lavished on his scenes, giving him all sorts of extra shtick. There was a natural synergy between the two men. Not only did they share a similar brand of humor, but Davis' screen persona was not that far from Lewis' own, particularly in the *Salt and Pepper* pictures, where Sammy played something like Lou Costello to Peter Lawford's Bud Abbott. On the picture's release on June 10, 1970, Richard Cuskelly of the *Los Angeles Herald Examiner* praised the star-director collaboration and noted that Lewis allowed "Davis to display his full—and rather amazing—comedic range."

Less enthusiastic was Milt Ebbins, who blamed Jerry for excessive cost overruns during filming. He also hated the director's cut of the film, as did United Artists' Herb Jaffe. As a consequence, Ebbins spent three weeks reediting the footage.

The new version satisfied Jaffe but woefully disappointed Sammy. "It was a crying shame," he said, "to see what happened to the film after it left" Lewis' control. In his opinion, Ebbins and Jaffe "cut all our throats along with the celluloid."

There is no way to know how *One More Time* would have played had Lewis had his way, but the version of the film that debuted on June 10, 1970 was dreadful. Howard Thompson stated the majority position in the *New York Times*, writing, "Let's fervently hope that *One More Time* wraps it up forever for the team of Sammy Davis, Jr., and Peter Lawford. . . . The picture proceeds to die on its feet, even with Davis hysterically imitating his director."

Thompson got his wish.

While Davis was in London during principal photography, he took time to meet with a Black Muslim leader named Michael X. "My interest in Michael X was not necessarily to endorse his views," he said, "but merely to find out what was happening to the black movement in London." At the time, Michael was at least as controversial in the U.K. as Malcolm X had been in the United States four or five years earlier. Indeed, the British Muslim leader went further than his American counterpart, talking from time to time about "killing Whitey." Sammy was unaware of Michael's more extremist views and certainly didn't share them. Still, his association with the man prompted FBI director J. Edgar Hoover to label the entertainer a "black nationalist" and to order his agents to place Davis under surveillance. Unaware of such scrutiny, Sammy came to feel enormously fond of Michael X, such that he called his visits with the Black Power leader "one of the great pluses of getting to" London.

Another plus was performing for the British public. On the day *One More Time* wrapped, Davis opened at one of the city's leading cabarets, Talk of the Town. The club called for its headliners to do no more (or less) than sixty minutes, and Sammy vowed to comply with the house rules. But on opening night, he started at 11:00 P.M. and reluctantly left the stage at 1:30 A.M. "Even then he looked good for another hour," observed *Variety*. Sammy supplemented his Talk of the Town engagement with several late-night cabaret performances at the Playboy Club and a benefit at the Lyceum Ballroom for starving children in Biafra and Nigeria.

In August 1969, while Sammy was still in London, actress Sharon Tate was murdered by members of the Charles Manson cult in Beverly Hills. Davis knew Tate and her husband, Roman Polanski. Among the other victims was his hairdresser and one-time fellow Satanist, Jay Sebring. Their deaths, and the drug overdose of Jimi Hendrix shortly thereafter, caused Davis to reexamine his hedonistic lifestyle. As he put it, "I knew that I had been pushing my luck at everything, stretching the rubber-band financially, drugs, debauchery. . . . I was almost forty-five years old. I had more clothes than I had closets, more cars than garage space, more jewelry, more everything if it could be bought on credit . . . but no money."

His solution was to ask Sy Marsh to leave the William Morris Agency and become his partner in a company they would own jointly, splitting all profits fifty-fifty. The timing worked because Jim Waters had decided to resign as Sammy's office manager to devote more attention to his family. Marsh was intrigued by the idea of becoming Sammy's partner, but his career at William Morris was flourishing. He was the head of the television division, boasted an impressive list of clients, and was assured by his superiors, notably Abe Lastfogel, that he was being groomed for even greater things. At the same time, Marsh keenly felt responsible for keeping his clients working, and the stress was getting to him. Also, he had a child and hoped for another, and wanted to spend more time at home. He saw Davis' offer as an opportunity to slow down a bit. He also thought it offered exciting earnings potential for them both. But, as Sammy's agent of many years, he knew about his client's reckless spending habits. Building a business couldn't work unless Davis moderated his style of living.

When Sammy promised that he wouldn't borrow money or undertake any major expenditures without first consulting Marsh, the agent accepted his offer. Opening an office on Sunset Boulevard, they called their new venture Syni, short for "Sy and I" and pronounced like the mountaintop where Moses received the Ten Commandments from God. "Can you think of a better name for two Jews?" Sammy quipped.

There was a clear division of labor within the company. Davis would handle the performing while Sy would concentrate on business matters. In this capacity, he would arrange the entertainer's tours and handle his film, TV, and recording deals. Sammy also expected Marsh to expand their mutual earnings potential by seeking out businesses that they could establish or acquire.

The search for business ventures wasn't a new concept for the entertainer. He'd demonstrated his entrepreneurial proclivities numerous times in the past, starting with Samart Enterprises, the joint venture he had formed with Arthur Silber, Jr., in 1958. At Silber's behest, they had explored a variety of opportunities, including the establishment of a line of men's sportswear, but Sammy lacked the capital to move forward. Two years later, in 1960, Davis and his Chicago attorney, Joseph Borenstein, had formed a film and video production company, Esquire Films. They announced three projects, including a biopic about an ex-con, and a TV sitcom in which Sammy and Peter Lawford would play former army men turned nightclub operators. None of these projects came to pass either, although the sitcom served as the starting point for *Salt and Pepper*. Three years later, when Davis formed Trace-Mark, he unveiled an ambitious production program. But nothing besides *A Man Called Adam* and Sammy's two joint ventures with Lawford ever emerged from this endeavor.

Why the interest in business, a field for which he was so clearly unsuited? Like many performers, Sammy wanted to assert greater control over his creative destiny; that's why so many of his ventures were related to the performing arts. Then, too, sheltering income from the IRS was always attractive to someone in his tax bracket. But he was also captivated by the idea of being a big-time wheeler-dealer like Frank Sinatra. He loved the idea of coming to an office with his name on the door, plopping his feet on his desk, and considering matters of gravity. Indicative of his attitude was the way he decked out his offices in New York during the run of *Golden Boy*. According to writer Buz Kohan, "He had an applause sign on his desk that lit up when he said something funny. And everybody in the office was equipped with things they would never use. You'd have a large tape recorder and a small tape recorder and a three-speed phonograph and an intercom and a typewriter and anything that was a gadget."

As Sy Marsh saw it, his first responsibility was to get Davis' finances in order so that his earnings could be used in a mutually productive fashion. As he delved into Sammy's records, he was astonished to find that the level of indebtedness was even greater than he had imagined, exceeding several hundred thousand dollars, significant money at that time. He also failed to realize the extent to which Sammy had drawn advances against his earnings from myriad venues on his future touring schedule. In addition, he had invested between $20,000 and $30,000 in a liquor store with the Commandos in Chicago, and it wasn't turning a profit. "Sweetheart," Sy told him, "anybody who can lose that kind of money in a liquor store is a genius." He insisted Sammy get out of the deal. He also told him to abandon the jet he was leasing from Kirk Kerkorian. The plane was costing him $250,000 a year. As Kerkorian had refurbished the interior to the entertainer's specifications, he was reluctant to let Sammy off the hook. Appeasing Kerkorian cost something on the order of $1 million, according to Marsh.

With Davis overdrawn at so many of the places he was scheduled to perform, Marsh felt the only way the entertainer could see significant income within a relatively short period of time was for Marsh to go to the operators of these venues and demand an immediate 100 percent increase in booking fees. So he hit the phones. "I lost a couple of fringe accounts," he said, "but in a year I doubled his salary. He went from $1.5 million to $3 million." One operator who resisted Marsh's efforts was Jack Entratter. Sy wouldn't be able to renegotiate Sammy's Vegas appearances until his contract with the Sands expired in 1974.

While Marsh played tough guy, Sammy tried to do his part for the cause. "Staying out of the shops wasn't easy," he said, "they were my natural playgrounds, but every time I felt like I needed a new watch I called Sy and he told me the right time."

After several years of hard work, Marsh finally reached a point where he could tell his partner, "You're completely out of debt. You don't owe a penny to anyone." Sammy couldn't believe it. He also couldn't make it last.

Davis had made two feature films in 1969, and he was tired of the movie business. "I think acting is the way for me to go," he said in November of that year. "Acting in television, not movies. The way they make movies with all that wasted time drives me up the wall. With television, you get in there and do it." And, as the sixties waned, his chances for film stardom were as remote as ever, so he increasingly looked for television opportunities. He was particularly hoping that a ninety-minute made-for-TV movie, *The Pigeon*, would develop into a weekly series.

The project, another in Davis' association with Danny Thomas and

Aaron Spelling, featured Sammy as Larry Miller, a former Vietnam vet who decides not to follow in the footsteps of his father, an LAPD police lieutenant (Sammy's *Desperate Hours/Golden Boy* costar, Roy Glenn). He opts instead to open a detective agency with his former army sergeant (Pat Boone). The plot centered on the good-hearted but struggling detective's determination to help an old college friend (Victoria Vetri) and her mother (Dorothy Malone), who are being hounded by a ruthless crime boss (Ricardo Montalban).

When *The Pigeon* aired on ABC on November 4, 1969, it turned out to be a rather lackluster affair. Perhaps as a sixty-minute series it could have become sharper and tighter. And the idea of an African American gumshoe offered some promise, particularly as there was only one private eye of any color (Mannix) on the air at the time. But none of the networks warmed to the premise. Over the next few years, Davis and Aaron Spelling would continue searching for the right vehicle for him.

Thanks to Sy Marsh, Sammy was now earning much more money from his live appearances, but the venues available to him were rapidly changing. Americans were no longer eager to don suits and fancy dresses and go to a downtown club for an evening out, and most urban centers weren't considered safe after dark. Furthermore, the newer singing sensations were rock musicians who could earn more in a single concert hall or stadium performance than one could garner in a week of nightclub appearances. Consequently, Ciro's, the Chez Paree, the Latin Quarter, and the other cabarets around the country found themselves faced with twin problems: the unavailability of popular acts to book and the waning support of patrons. As a consequence, they began to close; all that remained of Sammy's regular venues by the start of the 1970s were the showrooms in resort towns where swanky nightlife was still part of the allure: Las Vegas, Tahoe, Reno, Miami Beach, and San Juan. When he played America's major urban centers from then on, it was at New Jersey's Garden State Arts Center, the Music Hall in Boston, the Hollywood Bowl in Los Angeles, the Westbury Music Fair on Long Island, and the Musicarnival in Cleveland. One of the few nightclubs that continued to occupy a regular place on his calendar was the Copa, which managed to hang on until the death of Jules Podell in 1973.*

---

*Curiously, one of the first commercial ventures of Sammy and Sy Marsh's new company was a grand reopening of the Cocoanut Grove, the posh Los Angeles nightclub located in the Ambassador Hotel. They undertook the project in association with the hotel's president, Hugh Wiley. Following a $1.5 renovation, the club reopened on April 20, 1970, with Sammy as the headliner. Davis stayed with the operation as entertainment director for several years, but, according to Marsh, it was never a financial success.

Sammy's act changed noticeably as the new decade dawned. He'd stopped dancing almost entirely, rarely picked up a trumpet or a pair of drumsticks, and relegated his impressions to, at most, an isolated few moments in a show of sixty minutes or longer. Middle age had something to do with his diminished range, particularly when it came to hoofing. But he was also following the changing nature of popular entertainment. Dance acts, novelty acts, and magic acts had long since fallen from favor, whereas singers and comedians flourished. So Sammy focused on the skills that were in vogue.

As a further concession to changing tastes, Davis looked for material other than old standards and Broadway fare. Several Blood, Sweat & Tears songs—"Spinning Wheel," "You Make Me So Very Happy," and "When I Die"—became part of his repertoire, as did Jim Webb's "Wichita Lineman" and Mac Davis' "In the Ghetto." Sammy actually got first crack at the latter. Jimmy Bowen, one of Reprise's hottest producers, arranged for Sammy to record the tune shortly after it was written, but the entertainer blew the session, arriving several hours late and unprepared. "He couldn't get the melody," the producer asserted. Instead, "In the Ghetto" became a big hit for Elvis Presley. According to Bowen, this session was typical of Davis' late sixties recording career. The conflicting demands on his time and the inevitable presence of a large entourage distracted him at song conferences and recording sessions.

Sammy altered his onstage appearance as well as his repertoire. Instead of sleek tuxedos and fitted suits, he began wearing glittering versions of his personal attire: headbands, Nehru jackets (covered by a mink cape, which he'd remove after his entrance), see-through blouses, checkered pants, and pounds of jewelry—huge rings on most of his fingers, heavy medallions, and gold chains. Not everyone was charmed by his new look, but Davis liked being outrageous. As early as fall 1965, he told journalist Haskel Frankel, "I'm a performer. I'm expected to be a little larger than life." As for the jewelry, it wasn't something planned. Slowly, he started sporting more and more rings and other decorative items until they became part of his shtick. Pretty soon he was offering jokes like "I don't know what Washington, D.C.'s doing for the old folks but I've got *my* social security" and "When you grow up in a tough neighborhood, you learn to take everything of value with you."

But even with all these alterations, the fundamentals of his act remained constant. He kept the energy level high and adapted each set to suit that particular house. With regard to the latter, Burt Boyar observed, "He had the most amazing ability to read an audience. He'd come out with two numbers planned and by the time he finished those two he knew exactly what they wanted and he gave them what they wanted." Sammy couldn't explain the source of this sixth sense. He chalked it up to osmosis, "a feeling, almost spiritual. . . . Sometimes you've got a jazz audience, they want it to cook. Or you've got a show audience, a talk audience, or an audience that involves all of those things. How I recognize them is uncanny. Blindfolded. I hit it ninety-nine percent of the time."

Sammy wanted to please his fans, but he varied the act to engage himself as well as his audience. This practice was due, in part, to his desire to stay fresh. But he also continued to feel the need to push himself, to test the limits of what he could do. "If you don't give yourself some stretching room," he explained, "some freedom, you'll never find anything. You don't know you have the ability to be funny unless you try a line, you don't know if you can ad-lib if you're going to do the same jokes every night. There are lines I know are going to get a belly laugh but after a few shows I get sick of hearing myself say them and so I drop them. I forget them for three or four engagements, then when I bring them back in they're fresh for me."

Whatever a given show's content, the constant was the entertainer himself: who he was, what he did, what he thought and felt. "He completely shared himself," said actress Sally Struthers. "He let you know exactly who he was. He was an imp. He was an elf. He was funny. He was crazy. He was overly energetic. He was wild. He was loud. If you saw an hour and a half of him onstage, you knew just about everything there was to know about Sammy Davis, except whether or not he had an appendix scar."

And if, by chance, he found an audience that wasn't up to his usual expectations, he would, in the words of Mel Torme, "pull out all the stops" until he won them over, employing "every trick, every nuance, every ounce of showmanship he had learned in a lifetime of performing in front of audiences." At this, he was a master.

As the seventies began, Sammy still had his group of backup dancers with him, with Altovise Gore the featured member of the troupe. But, since the Bahamas cruise, he saw her socially as well as professionally. They enjoyed one another's company. Being with Alto was a lot of laughs. But Sammy also saw in her the possibility for hope, for change, the first time he'd experienced that sensation since his breakup with May. As he put it, "I had the feeling that with her I could get myself on the road to a straighter, more productive life." Thus, his thoughts, and Alto's, started turning toward marriage.

There were negatives, of course. Alto wanted children of her own, and Sammy, recognizing his severe limitations as a father, felt he'd done enough damage to the three kids he already had. And, of course, Altovise was much younger than he.

Probably the biggest concern was the almost total lack of empathy between Sammy's girlfriend and Mark, Tracey, and Jeff. In her 1996 memoir, Tracey described in painful detail how she and her brothers first met Gore. The encounter took place at a dinner at Sammy's house on Summit Drive. Dinner at home with their dad was unusual in and of itself; Sammy usually took the kids to restaurants. But the bigger surprise was the presence of the dancer. The sight of a stranger very much at home in the house where they had formerly lived—and where their mother had lived—did not make for a warm first impression. Neither did Alto's attempts at dinner conversation. She tried hard to be friendly, telling the kids about herself and asking them about their schooling, but the youngsters were not responsive. Tracey and Mark were particularly sullen, answering her questions in monosyllables. Tracey left that evening thinking that to accept Altovise would be to betray her mother. In her view, "This was war."

Then Sammy confessed that he wanted to marry Alto, and matters turned even worse. Tracey, for one, was completely mystified by this decision. How, she wondered, could he spare the time for some woman when he never had any for his kids? She blamed her mother for not giving her some advance warning about her father's plans, so that she could emotionally prepare herself for the announcement. She didn't learn until later that Sammy had failed to consult May beforehand. "Only my father would spring something like this on his children," she maintained, "without first telling their mother so they would have some sort of moral support." When May did find out, she was stunned, perhaps even a little heartsick, as she still loved Sammy. Then she pulled herself together and assured the kids that whatever else happened, their father would always be their father. If they needed him, he would be there. Later, she gave her ex-husband hell for the way he broke the news to his children.

Confronting his family, and the children's reaction to Altovise, had been extremely unpleasant, but Sammy felt that the pluses in his relationship with the young woman far outweighed the minuses. Thus, on May 11, 1970, he and Gore tied the knot. Instead of a lavish ceremony in Los Angeles attended by family members and friends, like Sammy's wedding to May in 1960, or even a Vegas bash, like his 1958 nuptials to Loray White, he chose to marry Altovise in a quiet civil ceremony. It took place in the municipal courthouse chambers of Judge Joseph Gold in Philadelphia, where, earlier that day, Sammy had taped an appearance on *The Mike Douglas Show*.

According to singer-actress Leslie Uggams, most of Sammy's friends were "shocked" when they learned of the wedding. So were Tracey, her brothers, and their mom. Not only weren't they invited to the wedding; they weren't even advised of the nuptials in advance. Tracey learned about her father's marriage on television. She was furious.

The fact that Sammy and Altovise tied the knot so quickly and quietly and so far from home gives one pause. Burt Boyar maintained that this wasn't simply a spontaneous gesture on Sammy's part. "He went and got married in secret," asserted Boyar, "because he knew that all of his friends would have disapproved. Not of Altovise, but of his marrying somebody. He was not somebody who should be married." Davis' office manager and close friend Shirley Rhodes particularly opposed the idea. According to Boyar, she told Sammy, "Buy her an apartment, take care of her. But don't marry anybody."

Among their concerns was the fact that Davis couldn't remain sexually faithful to a spouse. But Sammy knew that as well as they. He told Altovise before they wed that if she wanted a permanent relationship with him, she would have to give him the freedom to be with other women from time to time. She wasn't against an open marriage, as long as Sammy agreed to keep his affairs inconsequential—and didn't expect her to sit at home while he had his fun.

That she was willing to marry him in the face of his obvious drawbacks as husband and father, and breadwinner, suggests that she either loved him very much or that love wasn't her paramount concern. It was the latter, according to Peter Lawford. He maintained that Altovise was less interested in the man than "in what Sammy could do for her career." Lawford added, "I think Altovise grew to care for Sammy a great deal, but that marriage was more about two people having uses for each other than anything else."

What "use" had Sammy for Altovise? Sy Marsh believed that having spent most of his career currying favor with the white world, Davis wanted to win over African Americans now that black was chic. "That's the reason he married Altovise Gore," Marsh said. "She was a black woman. It would open up more doors to his being accepted."

That may have been the goal, but no matter whom Sammy married, he would never be the African American community's entertainer of choice. Many blacks took pride in his accomplishments, while more or less resenting his lifestyle, but his music—redolent with the tunes of Newley-Bricusse, Porter, Gershwin, and Rodgers and Hart—was not the sound of the inner city. His humor, for all the black references and Amos and Andy dialect, worked better with Caucasians than with "his people."

In any event, Davis admitted to talk show hostess Sally Jessy Raphaël late in his life that he was simply attracted to Altovise at the time they wed, but he was not in love with her. He added that he fell in love with her later on, but not everyone who knew Davis buys into that; some argue that Sammy *never* loved his third wife.

Whatever the circumstances, Sammy and Alto were married. After the ceremony, they strolled hand in hand through old, picturesque Philadelphia. When they reached Rittenhouse Square, they found an elegant shop, where Sammy bought his bride a long black-diamond mink coat. Back at the hotel, he told her that the fur was emblematic of the future he envisioned for them. He wanted a wife who would share his lavish and outlandish lifestyle but who would forge her own identity, become a personality in her own right. When they went someplace in public, he wanted people buzzing, not just about him, but about both of them.

It was a lot to ask of a twenty-something chorus girl who wasn't particularly worldly or well educated and whose talents were rather limited. But Altovise Gore Davis was determined to rise to the challenge.

CHAPTER 22

Entering the Seventies

In the year following the disappointing airing of *The Pigeon*, Sammy maintained a steady stream of TV appearances. He was on *The Tonight Show* and *Laugh-In* several times and was a guest on Dean Martin's highly successful NBC variety show. He showed up on three sitcoms: *The Beverly Hillbillies*, Lucille Ball's *Here's Lucy*, and Danny Thomas' *Make Room for Grandaddy*. He also hosted an NBC special called *The Klowns*, a tribute to the venerable circus performers. He honed his skills as a dramatic actor as well, with two roles on *The Mod Squad*. On February 10, 1970, he portrayed an ex-junkie-turned-director of a halfway house for addicts; on October 20, he returned as a tormented entertainer.

But his two most memorable TV appearances from late 1969 to the end of 1970 were a ninety-minute, one-on-one conversation with British journalist David Frost and a two-part, three-hour outing on *The Name of the Game*. The latter, called "I Love You, Billy Baker," aired on NBC on November 20 and 27, and featured Sammy as the title character, a beloved soul singer whose life is falling apart, as journalist Jeff Dillon (Anthony Franciosa) discovers when he attempts to do a feature story on Baker for his magazine, *People*.* Most of the episodes were shot in and around Las Vegas in August 1970, which allowed for cameo appearances by Ray Charles, Joey Bishop, Jack Carter, Norm Crosby, Redd Foxx, Marilyn Michaels, Ike and Tina Turner, and Dionne Warwick.

Billy Baker was not intended to be Sammy Davis. To make the point, Sammy was decked out in an awful Sonny Bono–style wig and sang more hard-edged songs than his usual repertoire. The character's mental distress, far worse than Sammy's hangups, offered the entertainer a gen-

---

*Franciosa was one of the three regular stars of *The Name of the Game*. His episodes rotated with those of Robert Stack, who played a tough investigative reporter, and Gene Barry, who portrayed the head of the publishing empire for which Franciosa and Stack's characters worked.

uine acting challenge, particularly at the end of the second half, when Billy falls apart completely. But the singer's super-mod outfits (such as a red jumpsuit with long white fringe at the midriff), the large entourage always partying in his hotel suite, and his fondness for jargon helped cement the phony, overly hip image Davis was inadvertently fostering.

In contrast, Sammy gave Americans a glimpse of his real self when his *David Frost Show* appearance aired on March 13, 1970. He sang, talked about his feelings about his race and his childhood in vaudeville, explained how he developed his impressions of Bogart and Olivier and Mel Torme, even demonstrated a bullfighter's technique, and did some hoofing.

Davis knew and trusted Frost. Given his comfort level with his host, Frost's skill as an interviewer, and the fact that Sammy was the sole guest for ninety minutes, the entertainer was able to come across in a much more engaging fashion than, for example, in his many appearances on *The Tonight Show,* where he struck many as the epitome of phony glitz. By contrast, he seemed a thoughtful, interesting, and genuine person with Frost. As Harriet Van Horne told readers of the *New York Post,* "Well, he was marvelous. . . . His conversation has wit and style and pace. He is articulate, choosing his words with nice precision and underscoring his points with sudden thrusts of caricature."

The following year, 1971, proceeded in a similar vein, as Davis mixed live performances—at the El San Juan Hotel, the Sands, the Deauville, the Now Grove, Carnegie Hall, Cleveland's Musicarnival, Harrah's Lake Tahoe, and many others—with guest appearances on several TV talk shows and a Bob Hope special. He even did a week's stint on a popular game show, *The Hollywood Squares*. In place of *The Name of the Game,* he ended the year with a made-for-TV Western called *The Trackers*.

As with *The Pigeon, The Trackers* was produced by Aaron Spelling, who had disbanded his partnership with Danny Thomas for a company of his own. Like Spelling and Davis' previous telefilm, *The Trackers* was also a pilot for a projected weekly series. Gerald Gaiser's teleplay essentially transported *The Pigeon*'s soft-spoken, dedicated gumshoe to a frontier setting, in this case, in the role of Deputy U.S. Marshal Ezekiel Smith, an expert tracker, gunman, and outdoor survivalist. The Western depicted a bit of racial consciousness, borne by Smith's conflict with a bigoted rancher (Ernest Borgnine) who grudgingly accepts the marshal's help in the wake of his son's murder and his daughter-in-law's kidnapping. The two men end up forming deep bonds of respect and affection through the exigency of their situation.

When the show aired on December 14, 1971, it drew enthusiastic reviews, but, once again, the networks failed to pick up Sammy's pilot for a series.

*   *   *

While Davis played a U.S. lawman on television, he explored ways he might serve the federal government for real.

Sammy had met Richard Nixon, who succeeded Lyndon Johnson on January 20, 1969, on a couple of occasions. Notably, Nixon and his wife, Pat, had caught a performance of the Will Mastin Trio at the Copa during the late 1950s and visited with its youngest member afterward. But the two men were hardly friends.

Davis' involvement with the Republican president came at the behest of a North Carolina public relations and marketing consultant, Robert Brown. Although Brown had served as a board member for the Southern Christian Leadership Conference, he and Sammy barely knew one another prior to 1969. Then they shared an evening in New York, shortly after Nixon appointed the businessman as a special advisor for domestic affairs, making him the highest-ranking African American in the White House. Brought together by a mutual friend, Davis and Brown started chatting over drinks. The occasion was primarily social, but the conversation inevitably turned to the new administration, with Davis eagerly interrogating the special advisor on his agenda for blacks.

As both Brown and Davis well knew, Nixon had never been popular among Negro voters. In 1960, African Americans supported Kennedy by an overwhelming majority. In 1968, Nixon won narrowly over Hubert Humphrey by appealing to the states of the Old Confederacy through what was dubbed the Southern Strategy; once in the White House, he could hardly distance himself from this power base. Nevertheless, as Brown told Davis, the president was more sympathetic toward the nation's disenfranchised than many people supposed. He was particularly interested in seeing minorities obtain greater economic control over their future by enabling them to establish their own businesses. Thus, in the first year of Nixon's stewardship, the Office of Minority Business Enterprise was created.

Brown tried to convince Sammy of the president's good intentions. Their first conversation led to other talks, and the more they got to know one another, the more Brown came to realize that "Sammy could be a fantastic ally for what I was trying to do. He was a very smart man, he was articulate, and he had some depth to his thinking." It was obvious that Davis desired to be a force for change. So Brown encouraged the entertainer to visit him in Washington. "I'll take you around," he promised, "introduce you to people and so forth, so you'll know exactly what's going on yourself." After that, he added, "I'll keep you informed. I will send you material. I will call you. I will have other people call you. I will have people meet with you and brief you."

Sammy accepted Brown's offer, but he remained somewhat concerned about allying himself with the president. Few politicians were
more intensely disliked by their opponents. Brown understood Davis'
concern, but he scored points when he asked, "Look, do you think you
can help most by being out there, kicking Nixon in the teeth, or do you
think you can help most by being here on the inside, trying to make
whatever is wrong right?"

The truth is that Sammy didn't need much convincing to forge an
alliance with the administration. Having been treated as an embarrassment by Kennedy and virtually ignored by Johnson, he liked being
courted by the White House for a change. The idea that he could hobnob with Beltway movers and shakers, even get to know the president
personally, had enormous appeal for someone who craved stature and
status as he did. Moreover, Brown and some of the people delegated to
visit Sammy in L.A. broadly hinted that, should the entertainer ever
decide to retire from show business, an ambassadorship might not be
out of the question. Sammy later denied this, but David Steinberg, his
friend and press agent at the time, said, "I was there. It happened."*
Regardless of what benefits might derive to him personally, however,
Davis was primarily drawn to Nixon by his desire to be of service to others. Later, the entertainer said bitterly, "Maybe that was a dream that
was too goddamn big for me. But I thought I could help."

Finally, he accepted a seat on the National Advisory Council on Economic Opportunity. The council, with twenty-one members—businesspeople, social scientists, professionals from a variety of fields—met
several times a year to advise the director of the Office of Economic
Opportunity, Donald Rumsfeld, on the financial concerns of the poor,
minorities, and others in need, from whites in Appalachia to Native
Americans to blacks and Hispanics.

On July 2, 1971, Nixon formally announced Davis' appointment in a
ceremony at the White House. Afterward, Sammy spent about half an
hour in private conversation with the president. Concerned that he was
taking up too much of Nixon's time, he tried to leave, but the chief executive insisted he stay until the members of his cabinet arrived for a meet-

---

*Born and raised in Milwaukee, David Steinberg came to California after, by his own
admission, twice flunking out of college. A cousin of Sy Marsh's wife Molly, he got a job,
with Sy's help, in the mailroom of Jay Bernstein's thriving public relations company.
Around the fall of 1968, Steinberg worked his way up to press rep and was assigned
Sammy as a client. Although David was more than twenty years Davis' junior, the two
men became instant pals: they drank together, bedded women together, did drugs
together, traveled together. With Sammy's encouragement, Steinberg eventually formed
his own P.R. firm, with Davis as his first client. Today, he serves as the manager for Billy
Crystal and Robin Williams.

ing. "I met the whole Cabinet," Davis told James Bacon a few months later, "and then one of them came out with the autograph pad. 'My 16-year-old daughter thinks you're neat,' he said. Well, here I am signing an autograph while the President of the United States and the whole Cabinet is waiting in the White House."

Following his appointment, Davis reached out to his socially conscious friends, including Harry Belafonte, Sidney Poitier, and Ethel Kennedy, eager for their advice on the issues he should raise in council meetings and the objectives he should stress. None of them would accept or return his calls. He was considered a traitor for aligning himself with the hated Republican. As he put it, "I lost a lot of friends because of my support for the President—and that's forever, man."

Although he'd been concerned beforehand, the reaction still wounded him. Why couldn't his friends realize that he simply wanted to help his people, and Nixon was the man who could make something happen? What his friends realized, as he apparently did not, was that his association with the administration validated the president, gave him greater credibility within the African American community at a time when, contrary to his campaign pledge in 1968, he was not ending the Vietnam War and was compiling enemies lists of dissidents at home. Davis' friends considered Sammy an easy mark: he let the administration put him on a relatively powerless advisory council, gave him a little face time with the president, offered him a photo op or two with the chief executive—and then used his celebrity to curry favor with voters who should have been casting their ballots elsewhere.

Who's to say who was right, Sammy or his liberal friends? Either way, he refused to be cowed. Rather, in the wake of his appointment, he traveled frequently to Washington, not only to attend council meetings, but also to visit Bob Brown. A warm friendship developed between the two men. In all likelihood, Davis accomplished more through his many one-on-one chats with Nixon's closest black advisor than he did through his more formal government service. To begin with, he took copious notes at meetings of the National Advisory Council on Economic Opportunity. Afterward, he'd review what had transpired with Brown, offering his own opinions on the topics at hand.

In addition, a curious bond emerged between Sammy and Nixon. In some respects, the two men had vastly different personalities. The entertainer was brash, exuberant, and such an extrovert he couldn't stand to be alone for a minute. By contrast, the president was something of a loner, an introvert, and more comfortable with ideas than with people. But they had both known impoverished youths, were unusually sensitive to criticism, and were more than a little controversial. Perhaps for these reasons, they felt like kindred spirits. In any event, Brown asserted, "Nixon liked Sammy Davis, Jr., very much. He really admired and respected Sammy, and he wanted Sammy to know that. So much so that Sammy could call and get through to Nixon. I mean, there weren't a lot of people who could do that."

Some months after Davis' appointment to the Council, Nixon made him a member of a similar advisory body on drug abuse. Given his own predilection for illegal substances, Davis' involvement on such a council would seem hypocritical indeed. But at that point his usage was restricted to nonaddictive narcotics, notably marijuana and hash, and to hallucinogens like LSD. The council's primary concern—and Sammy's—was the increasing dependence on hard, addictive drugs, notably heroin and cocaine, in America's harsh inner cities, where they were ruining the lives of countless minority youths.

A secondary concern involved the American soldiers in Vietnam, whose drug use had reached alarming levels. Sammy said later, "Of all the GIs over there in the drug rehab hospitals, the majority were black. It was out of kilter. Blacks are a minority." He also felt these soldiers were being unfairly treated, asserting that "black kids were getting bad discharges for minor [drug] abuse, while whites who'd been caught with the same thing were getting off clean. It was causing riots on military bases and on ships." Davis asked Brown how much Nixon knew about the situation. After speaking with his boss, Brown phoned back and said, "The president asks if you'll go to Vietnam for him, be his eyes and ears and report back to him."

Sammy agreed to make the trip. While he took his mission to Southeast Asia seriously, he was also eager to perform for the African Americans stationed there. He felt that most other entertainers who had made the trek, notably Bob Hope, directed their talent rosters toward middle-class whites, keeping at least one eye on the home audience for the TV specials derived from their visits.

The trip was scheduled for late September 1971. Davis was in Las Vegas on September 18, when he became ill following a performance at the Sands. Rushed to the Sunrise Hospital, he was found to be suffering from an enlarged and misaligned liver, which was extremely painful and dangerous. His doctors wanted him to rest for at least a month, which meant the Vietnam trip would have to be postponed. They also told him he had to stop drinking or he'd be dead inside of three years. "Anyone who drinks as hard as I did for fifteen years might have expected something like this," Davis told the press the following month. "I would get up on the set and start drinking before breakfast. I used to put away more than Dean Martin spills."

For a while, Sammy was true to his pledge; then he resumed his drinking. Fortunately, his doctors were wrong about its short-term impact. More than a decade would pass before he would have to confront the consequences of his further alcohol consumption.

Davis bounced back from his illness with renewed vigor. During the first half of 1972, he played his own Now Grove in L.A. in February, the Sands in March, the Westbury Music Fair in April, the Elmwood Casino in Windsor, Ontario in May, and Harrah's Lake Tahoe in June. These live performances remained the lifeblood of his career, but his most important contributions in 1972 came in other arenas: TV, records, and politics.

On February 19, he made a guest appearance on CBS's top-rated situation comedy, *All in the Family*. Like *Laugh-In*, *All in the Family* had been a midseason replacement. When it debuted on January 12, 1971, few knew what to make of it. The central character, Archie Bunker (Carroll O'Connor), was a loud-mouthed, opinionated taxi driver who hated all ethnic and racial minorities, bullied his sweet but not-too-bright wife, Edith (Jean Stapleton), and had little tolerance for his liberal son-in-law, Mike Stivic (Rob Reiner). Despite Bunker's constant carping, Stivic and his wife, Gloria (Sally Struthers), lived with Archie and Edith in their modest, two-story home in Queens. Beneath the discord, the family members loved one another, which took the edge off the raw, sometimes offensive material. Although it was different from other TV fare, *All in the Family* slowly gained popular acceptance. By its second season, it was a hit.

One of the show's biggest fans was Sammy Davis, Jr., and he wanted to be part of it. Although he informed the show's cocreator and producer, Norman Lear, of his interest, Lear was reluctant to book him. Unlike other shows, *All in the Family* eschewed celebrity guests for fear that the presence of overly familiar faces would distract from the verisimilitude of the episodes.

Not one to be deterred, Sammy kept up the pressure for months until finally Lear came to an important realization: Davis' presence would only be distracting if he played a fictional character. Not so if he portrayed himself. Indeed, it might be interesting to see how a bigot like Archie Bunker would react to such a renowned African American.

From there, the episode was relatively simple to devise. The premise found Sammy as a passenger in Archie's cab, giving the two a logical forum in which to banter. Having the entertainer accidentally leave his briefcase in the back seat provided an acceptable excuse for him to make a subsequent trip to the Bunker home.

Sammy was so eager to get cracking on the episode that he woke up at 7:00 A.M. on his first day of rehearsal, even though he wasn't on call at

CBS until 11:00. Sally Struthers recalled that when he arrived at the studio, he "stormed into the room, so excited to be on our show that he didn't even want to hear about how excited we were that he was there. And every day he would show up with new gifts. He brought us all gold necklaces. He brought so much joy to that rehearsal hall. We'd never had a guest star on before, so this was very exciting for us."

It was also exciting because the setup was perfect. Audiences were accustomed to seeing Bunker's insensitivity to his next-door neighbor, a young African American, Lionel Jefferson (Mike Evans), whose smart retorts went over his head. But the black-white interaction took on an added dimension when the black guy was a star. One of the show's funniest bits played off Archie's awe of the celebrated entertainer. Before Davis' arrival in Queens, he gravely cautions Edith to avoid references to Sammy's glass eye. Then, nervous in the star's presence, he makes the gaff himself: when Edith serves coffee, he asks Sammy if he would like cream or sugar in his eye.

Though he admires Davis, Archie can't forget that the entertainer is a Negro, and Sammy quickly recognizes this. The writer of the episode, Bill Dana, used the duality to wonderful effect, with Archie unwittingly proffering one stereotypical observation and insult after another and Sammy following with double-edged zingers that elude Archie's grasp. The climax of this interaction came just before the entertainer's departure, when he agrees to pose for a snapshot with Archie, and then surprises him with a peck on the cheek just as the shutter clicks. That kiss and Carroll O'Connor's reaction to it produced what is widely regarded as the longest sustained laugh in TV history.

While the kiss was the episode's climactic moment, the whole show was a gem. In fact, it is difficult to recall any other celebrity guest appearance that was used more creatively on a sitcom. Such was the quality of Sammy's shot on *All in the Family* that, in 1997, *TV Guide* ranked it thirteenth among the greatest episodes in television history. As an outgrowth of his work on the show, he would form enduring friendships with Carroll O'Connor and Sally Struthers. In 1980, eight years after his appearance on *All in the Family*, the entertainer renewed his acquaintance with the Queens bigot, visiting the show's successor, *Archie Bunker's Place*.

A week after Davis' stint on *All in the Family*, Sammy left for Vietnam, fulfilling the commitment he had made to Bob Brown and the Pentagon the previous fall.

"We flew in an Army C-50 with no windows," he recalled, "a heavy transport that usually carried jeeps, like an empty garage, with benches along the sides, no insulation, eating TV dinners on a rough and rainy night." Accompanying Davis was a group of about twenty people, including Altovise, George and Shirley Rhodes, his musicians and backup dancers, an army colonel, a nurse, and two physicians from Nixon's drug commission. Also on board were members of a government photography unit, which would record his visit for a public service film promoting the U.S. government's antidrug program. Sammy made clear to the American press before leaving the States that he had no plans to turn his performances or encounters with the GIs into a commercial TV special, such as those put together by Bob Hope.

They arrived in Saigon on February 23, and the following day, Davis toured the U.S. Army's detoxification center, which, to his amazement, looked like a POW camp, with barbed wire around its perimeter and watchtowers manned by armed guards. Flanked by members of his own party and a group of local officers, he entered the facility, where he was treated with deep suspicion by the forty or fifty patients he encountered, the majority of whom were black. They warmed up slightly after Sammy asserted that he wanted to help and that if they gave him a chance and found out he was a phony, they hadn't lost anything but a bit of time. He also made reference to his own army experience, which he rightfully described as "lousy." That, at least, won their attention.

"What do you want?" one guy finally asked. "I want to understand what's going on," Sammy replied. And slowly, a dialogue began. Along the way, he shared his perspective on drug use, admitting that he, too, had considerable experience with illegal substances. Before he left the facility, he promised that he'd try to have the barbed wire fence and guarded watchtowers removed from their compound.

Sammy's first show came in Long Binh, where he performed for more than twelve thousand GIs. It "wasn't an all-black show," he explained in a June 1972 article for *Ebony,* "because that isn't the way I work." Aside from his dancers—two blacks, two whites, and one Asian American—he brought a black singer, Blinky Williams, and a white singer, Lynn Kellogg (who favored country music), and an African American comic, Timmie Rogers. "Timmie Rogers is just funny, period," Davis asserted. "He does black humor and white humor and the whole audience related to him." Sammy did a few other large stage shows, in Da Nang and elsewhere, but the majority of his gigs were more intimate. "Mostly I was performing near fire bases," he said, "a hundred, two hundred soldiers, sometimes only fifty or seventy-five. I'd take four or five people with me and we'd get there and an NCO would say, 'You do the show here, in this round area,' and he'd point to a few square yards of ground, my stage. A few hundred yards away the enemy was fighting. A cat would warn me,

'Don't sing too loud. Charlie can hear you.' Often I'd take only a guitar player with me and there'd be only ten or twenty guys and I'd sit on the ground and sing to them and then we'd rap for a while before the shooting started." It was dangerous indeed. "There was no way of getting away from the fact that we were in a war zone," Davis said. "I was in one spot just the day before U.S. forces suffered two dozen casualties, including six deaths."

Everywhere he went, he stayed on army bases, departing each morning at five or six o'clock for that day's round of visits. Invariably, officers turned out to greet him, but he insisted on having an African American private on hand as well, someone who could "pull my coat to what was happening in that particular locale." Whenever possible, he'd get together with a group of enlisted men for a "rap session"—no officers, just him and the guys and one of the civilian physicians from home. It took time and patience to gain the soldiers' trust, but eventually they opened up.

On his departure after ten days, Sammy felt he had a clear picture of the situation, which came down to this: because the enemy was a determined, entrenched force, impossible to distinguish from local friends, most of the U.S. soldiers never felt safe and couldn't trust anyone but themselves, and, worst of all, many of them had no idea why they were fighting and dying. Drugs provided the only relief from the nightmare. Getting the stuff was neither difficult nor expensive. The couriers tended to be Vietnamese women, servants known as *mamasans,* who couldn't be searched by the U.S. military police. "They'd sell little vials for five dollars," Davis said. "Pure. You'd twist the tobacco out of a cigarette and pour the hit in there, twist it and light it. The cats would get stoned on that. And with pure cocaine! Hooked."

Sammy was troubled by what he had seen, but he was deeply moved as well. Winning over the men had taken hard work, and he had also connected with the soldiers through his shows, large and small. "In all my 45 years in show business," he noted in *Ebony,* "I have probably given no more rewarding performance than the 18 I gave during a 10-day period this spring in Vietnam."

Shortly after his return home, he submitted a list of twenty recommendations to Nixon, and the president effected half of them very quickly. "The most vital one as far as I was concerned," Davis said, "was that he changed the detoxification center immediately back into a hospital. Only a week later they pulled down the barbed wire, opened the place up, and flew in a professional medical team to deal with the situation. People who went over there later told me there wasn't a guard in sight. The drug problem began to be seen in Washington for what it really was—a dreadful symptom of a dreadful war."

CHAPTER 23

The Candy Man and the Man in the White House

A few days after Davis' return from Vietnam, U.S. radio stations began to play a relatively simple Newley-Bricusse tune, written originally for the 1971 film musical *Willy Wonka and the Chocolate Factory*. Neither Newley nor Bricusse nor the artist who recorded it, Sammy Davis, Jr., expected the song to become a worldwide sensation. But MGM Records and "The Candy Man" gave him the biggest single of his career.

This surprising turn of events had its origins in the winter of 1970, when Davis decided to leave Reprise. During his decade with the label, he had produced twenty-five well-regarded solo LPs, but in those days, the talent roster had included the likes of Jo Stafford, Rosemary Clooney, Count Basie, Duke Ellington, the Four Lads, the McGuire Sisters, Dinah Shore, and Debbie Reynolds, plus, of course, Frank Sinatra and Dean Martin. By the end of the sixties, Reprise and its parent company, Warner Music, had dropped most of those artists in favor of younger, more contemporary talent: the Kinks, Sonny & Cher, the Electric Prunes, Joni Mitchell, Jethro Tull, the Fugs, Arlo Guthrie, Jimi Hendrix, the Association, the Grateful Dead, Petula Clark, the Doors, Black Sabbath, Doug Kershaw, Gordon Lightfoot, James Taylor, Fleetwood Mac, and Deep Purple. For those who had known Reprise in its early days, the transition was amazing. Quincy Jones likened it to "walking into a whole different planet."

There was little enthusiasm in this new universe for Sammy's middle-of-the-road material. Even the entertainer felt the need to change with the times. Around 1968, he told Jimmy Bowen, one of Reprise's ablest producers, that he wanted to do an R&B album to prove to members of the African American community that he was, indeed, a brother. But R&B wasn't Davis' kind of music. Uncomfortable with the genre, he laid down tracks that were stilted. He knew the numbers weren't working, but he persevered anyway. Seeing Sammy's frustration, Bowen assigned the project to a hot young producer, Mike Post. Bowen thought the former guitarist, a blues and R&B aficionado since childhood, might inspire the entertainer. But even Post couldn't turn Sammy into a soul singer. Davis became so frustrated during the recording sessions for the LP that at one point he broke down in tears, slamming his fist into a wall, crying, "Oh, fuck it, fuck it, fuck it." He told Post, who was white, "You're blacker than I am." The tracks sat on the shelf for a while but were finally released in 1970 under the title *Sammy Steps Out*. It marked the entertainer's last LP for the label.

Given Davis' apparent inability to carve a niche for himself in the changing world of pop music, Mo Ostin, Reprise's general manager, didn't put up much of a struggle when Sy Marsh announced that Davis wanted to leave the label. But, in doing so, Marsh made a significant error: he failed to negotiate a contract for Sammy elsewhere beforehand. When he tried to locate a new home for his partner, he was met with considerable disinterest. Electronic music in all of its guises—psychedelic rock, folk rock, British rock, and soul—so dominated record sales that few A&R execs wanted to sign anything else.

One guy was different.

Berry Gordy, Jr., a former record store owner turned R&B songwriter, had built his Motown empire by discovering, molding, and shaping young, vibrant African American artists in his native Detroit. Starting with Jackie Wilson in 1957, he created hit after hit with the likes of Smokey Robinson and the Miracles, Mary Wells, Martha and the Vandellas, Stevie Wonder, the Temptations, the Supremes, Marvin Gaye, the Four Tops, Gladys Knight and the Pips, and the Jackson Five. Gordy turned all of these unknowns into stars, but, by the end of the sixties, the record mogul, two years younger than Davis, wanted more. He wanted to be part of the entertainment mainstream, to mix with his peers in Hollywood, to branch out into films and other media, and to represent, not just kids for whom he played Svengali, but established artists, respected stars.

The combination of Berry Gordy and Sammy Davis, Jr., seemed made in heaven. Sy Marsh may have been unaware of Gordy's larger ambitions, but he couldn't have tailored his appeal better. Phoning Gordy, Marsh said, "Berry, just think about this: wouldn't it be great to be able to announce that the world's number one record producer, Berry Gordy, who's black, has signed the world's greatest entertainer, Sammy Davis, Jr., who's also black?" Gordy was so excited about the concept, said Marsh, he started screaming on the phone.

Gordy and Davis signed their contract in mid-April 1970 at the Ambassador Hotel before a full contingent of journalists. As part of the agreement, Sammy was to be given his own label, Ecology, under the Motown umbrella.

The following month, the partnership's first album, *Something for Everyone*, hit the marketplace. It included a broad range of material, the contemporary stuff Davis had been featuring in his act as well as "My Way," and "For Once in My Life." All of the tracks had, in fact, been recorded at Reprise prior to Davis' departure, and he took the masters with him when he signed with Motown. Gregg Geller, a former Reprise executive and producer of the posthumous CD box set, *Yes I Can! The Sammy Davis, Jr. Story,* described the album as "an ill-advised attempt to appeal to the 'youth' market, circa 1969. It's pretty embarrassing, as I recall."

In February 1970, Deke Richards, the Motown producer who shepherded *Something for Everyone* through the label's system, recorded two Davis concerts at Carnegie Hall. Sammy also participated in several recording sessions at Motown's L.A. studio, some of which were produced by Marvin Gaye. Although he laid down more than enough material for another album—tunes primarily, if not exclusively, in the Motown pop-soul tradition—no LP was forthcoming, neither a live album derived from the Carnegie Hall gigs nor a studio disk. Finally, Marsh asked Gordy to explain the delay, and Gordy told him, "Well, my men out in the field don't think he's got the Motown sound." That couldn't have come as much of a surprise to Davis in light of his R&B cuts at Reprise. As a consequence, Gordy declined to authorize the LP's pressing. A personality clash between Sammy and Berry may have been a factor as well. As Deke Richards saw it, the relationship had devolved into "this ego thing between the two guys. Both of them had tremendous egos, just different kinds of egos. Sammy was used to having a lot of people around. He was used to being thought of as being in a class by himself, this whole aura. Berry had his own ego, but his was very cool." An example of the deteriorating relationship came with one of Sammy's openings at the Now Grove. When Davis arranged for Gordy to be seated at a less than ideal table, the mogul stalked out of the club, leaving Richards to explain his abrupt departure.

Clearly, there was no point in continuing the relationship. Given the fanfare that had accompanied Sammy's signing, neither he nor Gordy wanted to call attention to the swift demise of their collaboration, so both parties agreed to go their separate ways quietly, without notifying the press. Marsh also convinced Gordy to give him the masters from Davis' Motown sessions, worth some $250,000.

* * *

Once again, Sammy was without a recording contract. Having made the rounds the previous year, Marsh now didn't know where to turn. Then he thought of a relatively new player in the field, Mike Curb. Putting out feelers, Marsh learned that the record executive would be delighted to have Sammy under contract. The only problem was Sammy. "Mike Curb?" he asked Marsh dubiously. "Do you think that's right for me?"

Born in Georgia in 1944 but raised in southern California, Curb had started writing jingles for commercials, including Honda's "You Meet the Nicest People" campaign. This led to a hit single, "Little Honda," penned by the Beach Boys' Brian Wilson and performed by a group Curb had assembled, the Hondells. Following several years of compiling rock music for feature film soundtracks, such as *Wild in the Streets,* he took over MGM Records—at the age of twenty-five. There, the politically and socially conservative executive championed soft rock as performed by, among others, a chorus of young people known as the Mike Curb Congregation.

Where Berry Gordy's great talent lay in sanitizing R&B enough to attract mainstream white youths without alienating the genre's traditional black constituency, Mike Curb focused on making contemporary sounds acceptable to older audiences while not entirely losing more conservative young listeners. A case in point came in 1971 with the Top 40 single by the Mike Curb Congregation, "Burning Bridges," the theme song from the Clint Eastwood film, *Kelly's Heroes.* Although Curb and Gordy were miles apart at first glance, they were both in the business of delivering feel-good music to a broad constituency.

Marsh won Davis over with an irrefutable argument: Curb wanted them and no one else was beating down their doors. But, this time, Sammy signed his contract without the glare of a big media circus.

He and Sy hoped Curb would make an album from the Motown sessions, but the tracks were no more appealing to Curb than they were to Gordy. The search for material started anew. The MGM executive knew that Davis wanted to change the direction of his recording career. Being in the forefront musically was important to Sammy. With this in mind, Curb hired Isaac Hayes to write a vocal for his instrumental title theme for the hit blaxploitation film, *Shaft.* This number, called "John Shaft," would figure prominently on Davis' first MGM LP.

But Curb had another tune in mind as well. He had recorded Newley and Bricusse's "The Candy Man" as the Mike Curb Congregation's follow-up to "Burning Bridges." Even though he was pleased with the result, the song wasn't getting any airplay. Then one night, it hit him: "The Candy Man" was somewhat akin to "High Hopes," a big hit that had brought Frank Sinatra together with a chorus of young kids in the late fifties.* So he decided to ask Sammy if he would be willing to bring the same kind of verve to "The Candy Man."

In point of fact, Davis was *not* willing. Although he loved the work of Newley and Bricusse, he hated their innocuous little song from *Willy Wonka*, which he called "timmy-two-shoes," "white bread," "cutems," "Blechhh!" He wasn't wrong. With lyrics that asserted the Candy Man mixed his confections "with love" and made "the world taste good," the tune was about as corny as a song could get. Even Newley and Bricusse weren't too fond of it.

Davis also felt it was ill-suited to his image. He asked Marsh, "Can you imagine me, a swinger, a cat that's done everything ninety-two times around the pike, and I'm going to sing to kids? Like I'm Julie Andrews? Who's gonna buy this? It's stupid." Marsh reminded him that they were trying to develop a relationship with MGM. Rejecting one of Mike Curb's first ideas, particularly in the face of the producer's tremendous enthusiasm for it, didn't seem the best way to cement their new partnership.

So Sammy agreed to stop by the MGM recording studio and do one take. If that didn't work out, too bad. Curb was agreeable. After all, he didn't need to book an orchestra or bring in the kids. He just had to add Davis' vocal onto the existing tracks.

Davis "walked in the studio and he knew every word," said Curb. "He didn't even have a sheet in front of him with it. But he meant what he said: he was going to do one take. And he did one take. There was just one slight problem with the lyric, but I didn't want to say that, so I said, 'Sammy, we made a little technical error in here, could you give us one more take?'" At first Davis told him no, but, after listening to the playback, he relented. "And he went back in," Curb continued, "and he just nailed it. It was one of the most magnificent performances. He just knocked it right out of the ballpark."

According to the MGM executive, the master was remixed that very night and the disks were quickly pressed and shipped. Sammy jetted off to Vietnam, still dubious about the record's potential.

The single was released on March 11. Unlike the Congregation version, it got airplay and before long it made *Billboard*'s Hot 100, where it remained for twenty-one weeks. But it didn't reach the number one spot until June 17. As Leslie Bricusse observed, "It clambered up the charts like someone climbing Mt. Everest. It took weeks and weeks to get

---

*Written for Sinatra's 1959 film *A Hole in the Head*, the tune "High Hopes" by Cahn and Van Heusen won an Oscar for best song. By a strange coincidence, *A Hole in the Head* served as the basis for the musical *Golden Rainbow*, whose score included Davis' hit, "I've Gotta Be Me." Thus, in a roundabout way, two of Sammy's most popular recordings owed their origins to this Frank Capra comedy.

there. None of us could believe it." Just as surprising, the recording earned Sammy a long-wished-for Grammy for best male pop vocalist. He bested Harry Nilsson for "Without You," Mac Davis for "Baby, Don't Get Hooked on Me," Don McLean for "American Pie," and Gilbert O'Sullivan for "Alone Again (Naturally)."

Was "The Candy Man" worth all the fuss? Not really. Like "Mersey Doats" and "How Much Is That Doggie in the Window?" it was a novelty song that momentarily captured the public fancy. There are those who attribute its success, at least in part, to the suspicion that it was really about a drug pusher, candy being slang for narcotics, particularly cocaine. But druggies would have hated the song's soft rock arrangement and jocular kids' chorus. Perhaps the best that can be said of it is that "The Candy Man" was a product of its time, an era in which a few record producers and songwriters tried to apply electronic music to material in the Tin Pan Alley tradition in an effort to reach audiences that were not interested in, or ready for, the more hard-edged forms of rock.

Sammy certainly felt a greater personal affinity for the Newley-Bricusse tunes from *Stop the World* and *Roar of the Greasepaint,* but this was the one that worked best. Ultimately, as far as he was concerned, that was all that mattered. For the rest of his life, he would be grateful for his one and only number one hit, particularly as it earned him something on the order of $500,000 for a few minutes' work. Beyond the money, the disk added, to quote Curb, "a completeness to his career. It was at a point in his career when he was older than most artists who were having hits at the time. So it meant a lot to him."

The album that featured "The Candy Man" was also a tremendous success. Released in April 1972 under the title *Sammy Davis, Jr. Now,* it reached number 11 on the charts. In addition to the Newley-Bricusse tune and "John Shaft," its tracks ranged from "I Want to Be Happy" from the 1920s musical *No, No, Nanette,* then enjoying a highly successful Broadway revival, to Jim Webb's "MacArthur Park," which had been a big hit for Richard Harris.

On the theory of striking while the iron was hot, a follow-up LP, *Portrait of Sammy Davis, Jr.,* was released a mere seven months later. It included another song in the "Candy Man" mode called "The People Tree," which again paired Sammy with the Mike Curb Congregation on a Newley-Bricusse number. Released as a single, "The People Tree" enjoyed a five-week run on *Billboard*'s pop chart, but it reached no higher than 92.

More memorable musically was the album's inclusion of a Jerry Jeff Walker ballad about a down-and-out song-and-dance man named "Mr. Bojangles" (not to be confused with Bill "Bojangles" Robinson). Originally recorded by Walker in 1968, "Mr. Bojangles" became a breakout hit for a country-folk group, the Nitty Gritty Dirt Band, two years later. Sammy resisted "Mr. Bojangles" for a long time because he feared that he would end up like the title character himself one day, a rather startling notion when one realizes that Davis earned $50,000 a week in Vegas and millions of dollars a year. Finally, he put it in his act, where his interpretation proved extremely effective, one of the centerpieces of his live engagements. But the recording was not a breakout hit. Lacking the pull of a hot single, *Portrait of Sammy Davis, Jr.* climbed no higher than 128 on the charts, suggesting that the push Davis got from "The Candy Man" was already starting to wane.

The magic was definitely gone with Sammy's two subsequent LPs, *Sammy Davis, Jr.: The Original TV Soundtrack* and *That's Entertainment,* released in September 1973 and August 1974, respectively. The former, the soundtrack from a GE-sponsored television special, *Sammy,* which aired on November 16, 1973, included fare in the standard Davis tradition, such as "This Dream" from *Roar of the Greasepaint,* "Over the Rainbow" from *The Wizard of Oz,* a *Porgy and Bess* medley, and "The Birth of the Blues." With *That's Entertainment,* Davis offered a retrospective of numbers from the MGM songbook, a tie-in of sorts to the studio's feature film of the same name, which paid tribute to its musical motion pictures.

Not surprisingly, neither of these disks broke the Top 100, and the relationship between Davis and MGM came to a quiet conclusion. A couple more albums lay in his future, including a recording of country music songs released as *Closest of Friends* by Applause Records in 1982. But essentially, 1974 brought Davis' active years as a recording artist to a close, a surprising end to the high he enjoyed only two years earlier.

Business matters occupied Davis' attention during 1972. On February 18, before his trip to Vietnam, he unveiled his plans to coproduce and star in a series of modestly budgeted feature films. He had already optioned the first three projects, but none was ever made.

Shortly thereafter, Sy Marsh announced that he and Sammy had acquired three arena-stage theaters, one near Chicago, one in southern California, and one in Houston. "Theatre-in-the-round concerts are the top money-makers for superstars today," Marsh told the press. "This is a definite trend." Beyond booking other artists, Davis planned to tour his theaters in 1973 with a revival of the musical *A Tree Grows in Brooklyn* (based on the Betty Smith novel) and then head for Broadway. As with the films, this venture never came to pass.

But the most important business opportunity, certainly the most meaningful one to Davis, came from a Minnesota banker named Deil Gustafson. Gustafson was the head of a consortium that had recently taken control of a Las Vegas hotel-casino, the Tropicana.

Over the years, several resorts had attempted to woo Sammy away from the Sands. He wasn't the only target: Sinatra had departed for Caesars Palace, and Dean Martin had moved on to the Riviera. But Davis remained in the Copa Room out of loyalty to the Sands in general and Jack Entratter in particular. But the resort took on an impersonal air after it was acquired by Howard Hughes in 1967. So, after Entratter died in March 1971, Sammy decided to move on.

Deil Gustafson couldn't have played Sammy better. Not only was he willing to dramatically increase the entertainer's fee as a performer, but he also offered to make Davis a partner and vice president in the operation and to let him run a new showroom, to be called the Superstar Room, along the lines of his management of the Now Grove in Los Angeles. Once Sammy purchased a share of the Trop, he would become the first African American to hold an interest in a major Vegas hotel-casino. He simply loved the idea.

Not as old as the Sands and far younger than the El Rancho Vegas and the Last Frontier, the Tropicana had been a fixture on the Strip since it opened its doors on April 4, 1957. About a mile past what was then the heart of the action, it featured three hundred rooms on thirty-four lovingly tended acres. In 1960, it opened its stellar attraction, the Folies Bergiere, which would continue in its own theater while the Trop's headliners held sway in the Superstar Room.

Davis wouldn't be free to perform at the Tropicana until his contract with the Sands expired in 1974. But there was nothing to prevent him from having a financial interest in another operation. Thus, on August 29, he announced the acquisition, an $800,000 investment in Hotel Conquistador, Inc., doing business as the Tropicana Hotel and Country Club at 3801 Las Vegas Boulevard. He applied for his license with the Nevada Gaming Control Board in Carson City the following day.

For Davis, the idea of having a share in a major Vegas enterprise had profound social and psychological significance, signaling that he had arrived—like Frank and Dean. Considering that twenty-five years earlier, he hadn't even been allowed *inside* most Vegas establishments, his deal with the Tropicana was an amazing testament to how far he, and African Americans in general, had come in a quarter century.

It is ironic that this, one of the proudest moments of Sammy's life, should come only a week after the start of one of the most frustrating, humiliating, and hurtful periods he ever experienced.

* * *

After three and a half years in office, Richard Nixon had been unable to end the war in Vietnam. He was vilified again and again at protests and rallies around the country. Moreover, in June 1972, a band of burglars with connections to the White House had been arrested for attempting to break into the offices of Democratic Party Chairman Larry O'Brien at the Watergate hotel and office complex in Washington, D.C. But none of that mattered to the delegates who gathered in Miami in August for their presidential nominating convention. The previous month, the Democrats, also meeting in Miami, had selected a little-known, uncharismatic, far too liberal senator, George McGovern, as their standardbearer, thus assuring Nixon's reelection by a wide margin. The Republicans had much to celebrate, and they were doing it with unabashed glee.

Looking around at the assemblage happily chanting "Four more years, four more years" at every opportunity, one saw impeccably dressed fat cats, middle-aged middle Americans clad in polyester, rosy-cheeked teens and twenty-somethings with Pepsodent-white teeth and razor-cut hair. "These were clean neat people," Theodore H. White observed in his book, *The Making of the President 1972.* Unlike the Democrats, who had embraced inclusion at their convention, there was a startling absence of black, Asian, and Hispanic faces at the Republican convention. White noticed one African American delegate placed conspicuously on an aisle in the hope that she would draw the networks' TV cameras.

Up in the visitors' gallery the first night, in the section reserved for VIP guests, there was another black face, that of Sammy Davis, Jr. Standing out in his brown, broadly checked suit with wide lapels and love beads, he proudly told the *New York Post,* "It's a marvelous feeling here. The people are warm and friendly. Frankly, I didn't know what the reaction was going to be."

He took center stage at a show at Marine Stadium on Tuesday, August 22, the night before the president's formal nomination. The event was billed as a rally for Young Voters for Nixon. Thanks to a constitutional amendment, people between the ages of eighteen and twenty-one would be able to cast ballots for the first time in the November election, and the Republicans wanted to capture their share of this voting bloc. The kids made a loud, joyful audience.

Although Nixon had not been scheduled to attend the rally, he showed up at its conclusion. The surprised audience went ballistic, and the president responded with his own brand of effusiveness. Praising those who performed that night—Davis, in particular—he noted that he'd been watching TV the previous evening when a network commentator asked Sammy, who was sitting in the presidential box with Mrs.

Nixon, about the charge that he'd sold out his liberal convictions in order to be invited to the White House. "Well, let me give you the answer," Nixon told the crowd. "You aren't going to buy Sammy Davis, Jr., by inviting him to the White House. You buy him by doing something for America." Standing nearby, Davis, so badly hurt by the attacks from his friends on the left, was overwhelmed. That the president, despite the weighty affairs of state, thought enough of him to address this issue was almost more than he could bear. Following his naturally effusive instincts, he walked up behind Nixon, put his arms around him, and gave him a hug. Then he stepped back, to the applause of the audience, while the president continued with his remarks.

No one present thought much about the embrace. Certainly not Nixon or Bob Brown, who had accompanied the president, or, for that matter, Sammy. It just seemed to evolve naturally out of the spirit of the moment.

But they were forced to reconsider after a still photograph capturing the embrace appeared on that evening's late-night news broadcasts and ran on the front pages of newspapers around the country the following day. It was also prominently featured in the September 1 issue of *Life*. The reaction was anything but understanding. Rather, Sammy suddenly found himself at the center of a storm of controversy. "More than a few people felt that I, a black man, had done a bad thing by hugging the President of the United States," he observed in *Why Me?* "The White House was receiving calls from Republican campaign fund supporters threatening cutoffs. Nobody liked it. The Democrats who had seen me with Bobby and John were angry all along that I had gone to a Republican, and the hug was a catalyst. Bill Gibson's wife wrote me a scathing letter telling me she never wanted to see me again, that I was an embarrassment. The black press excoriated me. 'Sammy sold us out.'" Ironically, in light of the trouble it was causing, the White House sent Sammy a 17 by 20 copy of the photograph, signed by Nixon with the inscription, "To Sammy Davis, Jr., With grateful appreciation for helping to make the 1972 convention a great success."

For months thereafter, Davis received hostile letters, telegrams, and phone calls. He was even booed in some places, including a concert on behalf of Jesse Jackson's Operation PUSH, which was part of the Black Expo held in Chicago shortly after the convention. Of the reaction at the concert, Davis said, "Nothing in my life ever hurt me that much. My accident when I lost my eye didn't hurt me that much. I thought it was unfair. I thought I had something in the bank account, something I could draw on that would make people say we ought to hear the cat before we condemn him. All right, you screwed up, bad choice, whatever. But to have people come down on you without hearing your side of the story—nothing hurt me that much. That will live with me the rest of my life."*

The incident refused to die, and the longer it went on, the more hurtful it became. Even for someone as accustomed to controversy as Sammy Davis, Jr., the outrage over what, to him, was a reflex action was shocking. He felt, with some justification, that the photo of the hug, presented by itself, absent the president's precipitating remarks, distorted what had transpired. Devoid of the moment's context, he came across as, in his words, a "lackey" and an "ass-kisser."

It seemed so unfair. Davis told Dorothy Gilliam of the *New York Post* some nine months later, "They're really trying to infer that I don't care about my people. I'll match my caring with anybody: Emotional, spiritual, financial. Say you don't agree, that you'd like me, but don't say I don't care."

Then he added, "I'd like to know where all these mothers were when, say, after Juan [*sic*] Carlos gave the black power symbol at the Olympics, I went on the air and gave the sign for peace, love and togetherness, and then did this"—he demonstrated the Black Power salute, a raised arm topped by a clenched fist.† In making this remark, Sammy departed from the issue of whether he had a right, as a black man, to embrace a white president—or even whether, by doing so, he had made himself into an Uncle Tom—and moved into much murkier territory. Rather shockingly, he seemed to draw a parallel between his putting his arms around a conservative Republican president and his support of several athletes' use of the Black Power gesture at the Olympics. Nixon, the embodiment of the white establishment, had nothing in common with such militants.

Gilliam, who caught the dichotomy, described Davis as a "political enigma." But she missed the ultimate point. "Political enigma" implies that Sammy had an agenda, elusive to an outsider. This wasn't so. He was simply so eager to be loved, to do good, to be perceived by the public as a caring, thoughtful human being that, by 1972, he was skittering about like the Road Runner, unable to identify individuals and causes that merited his

---

*Sammy's appearance at the Chicago concert was captured in a feature film documentary on the 1972 Operation PUSH Black Expo, along with performances by Marvin Gaye, the Staple Sisters, the Temptations, Isaac Hayes, the Cannonball Adderly Quintet, Curtis Mayfield, Roberta Flack, Quincy Jones, Gladys Knight and the Pips, and many others. Called *Save the Children*, the film debuted at the Apollo and several other New York theaters on September 19, 1973.

†After taking the gold and bronze medals in the 200 meter race at the 1968 Olympics in Mexico City, Tommie Smith and John Carlos stood on the winner's platform, bowing their heads as the national anthem played while they raised their gloved fists to protest racism in the United States. As a result of this controversial demonstration, Smith and Carlos were ejected from the Olympic village.

support and those that did not. He hadn't had to confront such choices in the early days of the civil rights struggle. Then, Dr. King, the NAACP, white liberals, and everyone else on the side of change spoke, more or less, in unity. But the United States was far more fragmented in 1972. Nothing was clear-cut; there were shades of gray everywhere. And Davis couldn't navigate successfully in this changing environment.

The hugging incident became the symbol of his confusion and the confusion he engendered in others. Which was the real Sammy? one might reasonably have asked at the time: the guy who consorted with Michael X, attended benefits for Angela Davis, sported fashions that suggested a modern sensibility, peppered his conversation with "in" gestures and slogans, and showed up on hip TV shows like *Laugh-In* and *The Mod Squad*? Or the guy who warbled white-bread songs like "The Candy Man," bought points in Vegas hotel-casinos, embraced a conservative Republican president, and, as Davis did the following year, lent his name to that most establishment of games: golf?* The answer is neither. In this sense, there was no real Sammy. Occasionally, he would feel something so strongly—his conversion to Judaism, his marriage to May—that he persevered regardless of what others thought. But, more often than not, he was, in the words of his friend, Meg Myles, a "chameleon." He derived so much of his sense of self from what he saw reflected back at him from friends and fans that he became whatever people wanted him to be. Because that differed from group to group, the result was an ill-formed polyglot. Moreover, he bought into everything that seemed attractive, now, in. Writer Carl Gottlieb, who got to know Sammy around this time said, "He'd give you the peace sign and the Black Power sign in one. And you'd go, 'Excuse me, Sammy, but those are like very different cultures and symbols.' But not in his mind. Because everybody was doing them, he figured, 'Okay, if I can combine the two, then I satisfy everybody.' He'd go, 'Peace, love, and togetherness.' And, on togetherness, he would clench his fist. Well, that's kind of a misreading of the Black Power salute. But, in his mind . . . He sang a Randy Newman song called 'Sail Away,' which is about slavery. But he misreads the lyrics. I mean, he sings the lyrics as written, but he sings it without any trace of irony. There was a lyric about 'sweet watermelon and the buckwheat cake.' He sings it like it's a lyric about good food

*In July 1973, a lesser stop on the PGA tour, the Greater Hartford Open in Hartford, Connecticut, became the Sammy Davis Jr. Greater Hartford Open. With his usual race consciousness, Davis said at the time, "I'm proud to be the first black man to have a tournament of the PGA tour named after me" (AP, *New York Times*, December 29, 1972). He continued his association with the Hartford Open through 1988.

when, in actuality, it is a song about slave food and slave treatment. You've got to hear Randy Newman's version of 'Sail Away' and Sammy's version and you can compare the two and you realize how he has misread the lyrics and misread all the irony contained therein. Because he just didn't get that. If it had hostility in it and new revolution, I don't think he could understand that."

If anything, Davis' intense desire for love and respect made the outpouring of vituperation he received in 1972 all the more sad. It was like kicking a dog after he fetches your slippers. Moreover, it went on and on. Bob Brown, who, after all, had brought Davis into the administration, was deeply stung by the reaction as well. What infuriated him, in particular, was the fact that people seeking assistance from the Nixon administration for various pet projects still tried to elicit Davis' support while publicly vilifying him. "To my mind," Brown said, "it was a low point for black leadership and white leadership and everybody else in this country."

Those who considered Nixon, in Bob Brown's words, "a reincarnation of the devil" may have felt it was a case of TV mirroring real life when Sammy turned up as a hapless minion of Lucifer on the February 14, 1973 episode of NBC's *Wednesday Mystery Movie*. The teleplay, entitled *Poor Devil*, found Davis in a high-tech, ultra-modern version of Hell, with Satan (Christopher Lee) akin to the CEO of a thriving megacorporation. *Poor Devil* represented yet another in Sammy's ongoing attempts to land a weekly series; this time he thought he had it nailed. A month before the pilot aired, he told an audience while performing in Cincinnati that he was "104% sure" he would have a sitcom on NBC in the fall. Once again, he was disappointed. Although *Poor Devil*'s format—an impish devil involved in the plights of ordinary mortals—offered some promise, it was poorly executed, lacking any sense of wit or style.

Though NBC passed on *Poor Devil*, the network was intrigued by a variety special it aired six days prior to the supernatural comedy. Called *NBC's Follies*, it featured, in addition to Davis, Mickey Rooney, Connie Stevens, Andy Griffith, and John Davidson. The brainchild of John Hamblin, NBC's vice president for live nighttime programming, the show was an attempt to capture the glamour and panache of big-time vaudeville, with headliners, old burlesque-type sketches, and beautifully costumed chorus girls. It was performed with a live audience in a theater whose proscenium stage was outlined in lights. An interesting innovation for TV variety was the absence of a traditional host. *Variety* praised the special's "good pace" and the skits that featured those two old vaudevillians, Davis and Rooney. Still, the trade paper expressed doubts about the show's chances in a weekly setting.

Variety's concerns notwithstanding, *NBC's Follies* did well in the ratings, fostering the show's placement on the network's fall schedule, with Sammy and Mickey as regulars. To secure Davis' services, NBC signed an exclusive five-year, $3 million contract with the entertainer. In addition to the variety show, he would be a guest on other network programs and star in specials and made-for-TV films, some of which he would also help create.

The show, subtly renamed *NBC Follies,* debuted on September 13 with, in addition to Davis and Rooney, Diahann Carroll, Jerry Lewis, the Smothers Brothers, and the Weavers. Critic John J. O'Connor in the *New York Times* found the program "pleasantly and attractively entertaining," but audiences never warmed to it; its last episode aired December 27. Aside from a couple of specials broadcast in the fall of 1973, including *Sammy,* an excellent one-man show produced by Gary Smith and directed by Dwight Hemion, nothing else of substance emerged from the contractual relationship between Davis and the peacock network.*

In May 1973, some four months after Richard Nixon's second inauguration, the president decided the time had come to give Davis some payback for his terribly painful support. Accordingly, he invited Sammy to entertain at the White House and to be his guest overnight in the residence. Before an audience that included members of the cabinet and Senate and the *Apollo 17* astronauts, Davis sang "The Candy Man," "I've Gotta Be Me," and "Mr. Bojangles," earning a standing ovation at the conclusion. Then he joined Altovise and the Nixons in a receiving line and, later, during the post-show festivities, danced with the First Lady while the president took the floor with his wife.

The glittering Washington evening was exciting enough, but staying in the White House was truly momentous. Sammy was fully aware that he was the first African American guest to ever sleep in the executive mansion.† "It was the greatest thrill of my life," he told *Ebony* shortly thereafter. "I will always remember that day and how I was so happy, I couldn't

---

*Taped in London, Sammy did feature one guest star, Sam Davis, Sr., who spent a segment of the show reminiscing with his namesake. The father-son reunion was a highlight in a special filled with memorable moments.

†President Theodore Roosevelt entertained Booker T. Washington at the White House, but the head of the Tuskegee Institute didn't spend the night. During the administration of Franklin D. Roosevelt, William V. S. Tuban and Edwin James Barclay, respectively the former and current president of Liberia, became the first Negroes to sleep in the White House, and Emperor Haile Selassie of Ethiopia was an overnight guest of President Eisenhower. But, of course, these distinguished gentlemen were not Americans.

even fall asleep in the Queen's Room." The following morning, he and Altovise met the Nixons for coffee, after which the First Lady breakfasted with Sammy's wife in her quarters while Davis shared a private meal with the president. The entertainer pushed a serious agenda with Nixon that morning: increased support for black-owned businesses, better public education in urban schools, and grants for the Negro College Fund and black universities in general. "I asked for funding wherever possible," he recalled, "but also for the administration's arm-around-the-shoulder to facilitate network public service announcements, which the FCC could do, so that private donors would be encouraged to make endowments. The President was inquisitive, and there was a constant exchange." Later, Bob Brown told him how much Nixon had enjoyed their conversation. "Sammy," the special advisor said, "you are as close to Nixon, in terms of being able to influence his thoughts, as any black man has ever been to a President. I can't think of any man he holds in higher esteem, white or black. We stood there for about five minutes just talking about you."

But Nixon's days and nights would soon be consumed with his efforts to survive in office. Around the time of the Davis visit, the Senate launched its televised hearings into the host of illegal administration activities and dirty tricks known as Watergate. In October, Nixon's vice president, Spiro Agnew, resigned, the center of a separate scandal. That same month, the first serious cries for Nixon's impeachment were raised, the result of the president's having fired the special Watergate prosecutor, Archibald Cox, along with the concurrent resignation of Nixon's attorney general, Eliot Richardson, and the firing of Richardson's deputy, William Ruckleshaus, all of which became known as the "Saturday Night Massacre." As 1973 turned into 1974, Nixon's problems worsened, with his taped conversations in the Oval Office proving to be his ultimate downfall. Finally, on August 8, 1974, he resigned from office.

Ever the loyalist, Davis stood by the president as the breadth of the scandal emerged. In July 1973, for example, he told the press, "My support of the man continues unchanged. . . . I'm not gonna run scared and go the other way just because of Watergate. I admire that man very much." But, after the Saturday Night Massacre, he realized that Nixon's presidency was crippled, leaving him unable to follow through on Sammy's domestic agenda. "Nothing's being done," he complained to Robert A. DeLeon of *Jet*, "and that's the frustrating part. That's what drives you crazy because none of the things I asked for were controversial . . . they were middle of the road." Three months later, he finally broke with the president, saying, "Nixon is not to be explained, he is not to be rationalized at all. . . . I disagree with everything that's being done, totally. . . . In a year, the man is wiped out, his top advisors are all being indicted. . . . They have been falling by the wayside, they are dropping like goddamned flies. All people that I knew, all people that I respected."

In later years, Davis looked back with considerable bitterness on his association with Richard Nixon. It had cost him some good friends and much credibility within the liberal and African American communities. As he told Lerone Bennett, Jr., of *Ebony* in 1980, "My egomania told me I could change the man. Obviously, I was wrong and made a bad choice."

Thereafter, even when Frank Sinatra came out in support of Ronald Reagan, Sammy kept his politics to himself.

CHAPTER 24

An Open Marriage

In December 1973, as Sammy turned forty-eight, he and Altovise moved into a new home, also on Summit Drive, but this one had more land, nearly two acres. Built in 1938, the two-story house measured 10,900 square feet and had previously belonged to two couples in Sammy's circle of friends, Tony Curtis and Janet Leigh and Anthony Newley and Joan Collins. It was valued at approximately $900,000 (when it was placed on the market in 1990, following Sammy's death, the asking price was $4.25 million).

The Davises renovated extensively. When the work was finished, the house included seven bedrooms, a billiard room, a media room, guest and children's wings, and a two-floor master suite with a separate living room and office. There was also a pool house with two bedrooms and three baths. Later, after Sammy took up cooking as a hobby, he had a separate structure built that included a state-of-the-art kitchen and dining room; it cost $95,000.

The main house had twenty-two rooms. "Though none of the rooms has any stylistic connection with any of the others, the overall effect is that of a Las Vegas hotel lobby," Paul Slansky told readers of the *New York Daily News* in 1981. The large, off-white living room probably saw the most action. It featured an S-shaped bar with comfortable easy chairs, a music area complete with piano, a movie screen served by a projection room behind the opposite wall, and a spacious sunken conversation area, known as "the Pit."

Scattered throughout the mansion were displays of Davis' various collections: cameras, walking sticks, belt buckles, and guns. A Plexiglas case housed his treasured movie memorabilia. Dubbed "the vault" by Sammy's friend, James Caan, it included a pair of Marilyn Monroe's high heels, a suit worn by Fred Astaire in *The Band Wagon*, James Dean's red jacket from *Rebel Without a Cause*, a John Wayne Stetson, and a ruby slipper worn by Judy Garland in *The Wizard of Oz*.* The garage housed the entertainer's extensive array of cars, including a Mercedes, Rolls Royce, Jaguar, Ferrari, Dusenberg, DeLorean, a rare Cadillac station wagon, and a gold custom-made Stutz Bearcat.

Perhaps the home's dominant features were the myriad testaments to its owner's celebrity, from a framed photo of Sammy as a boy, which shared the entranceway with a LeRoy Neiman painting of him, to dozens of photos of Davis with the rich and famous. Present, too, were framed magazine covers featuring his likeness, a *Golden Boy* playbill, the book jacket for *Yes I Can,* his record album jackets, the *Billboard* Hot 100 chart for June 17, 1972—the week "The Candy Man" hit number one—and even a degree in "Hamburgerology" from "McDonald's University." "There's a lot of memorabilia here," Davis conceded, "but I would like to think it doesn't overpower the house." On the front door, a placard read, "This home welcomes all colors and races and religions, as long as they have peace and love in their hearts. The Davises."

One might reasonably assume that having spent nearly $1 million for their new estate, plus the cost of renovations, the Davises had settled into a blissful married life by the end of 1973. But in the two and a half years since their wedding, Sammy and Alto had each come to realize that life with the other wasn't exactly perfect.

For Altovise's part, being Sammy's wife didn't mean building a life with her husband, but fitting herself into the world he had already established. To begin with, she had to cope with Sammy's children, who still resented her, calling her the "Wicked Step" and "Alpo," a popular brand of dog food. She also had to contend with her mother-in-law. Elvera wasn't an ever-present factor in her son's life, but still, the tension was annoying.

Then she had to win the acceptance of those in Sammy's inner circle, notably his security people, Murphy Bennett, Shirley and George Rhodes, Sy Marsh and his wife, Molly, and Lessie Lee Jackson. Each wielded considerable influence over and enjoyed easy access to Davis. None saw any reason to yield any power to a newcomer.

Of course, Davis could have insisted that they respect Altovise's role; at the beginning, he did to some extent. Burt Boyar recalled a time when

---

*Possessing a more jaundiced view of Hollywood than Sammy, Caan jokingly presented the entertainer with the tap shoes he wore in the 1982 movie, *Kiss Me Goodbye*. He signed them in white ink, "Jimmy (Taps) Caan." "Well, do you know they opened that fuckin' vault and they were in there," Caan said, laughing. "So it was Bojangles, Fred Astaire, and Jimmy (Taps) Caan. It was like one of his treasures. He put them right in the shrine."

Shirley Rhodes was with the Davises and Altovise was snapping gum. "She tried to be very diplomatic," Boyar said. "She wanted to say, 'You don't chew gum at all. Jack Benny and Mary Livingston will not think highly of you if you're chewing gum.' She didn't say that, but she thought the snapping was an opportunity to say something, and Sammy said, 'She can do whatever she wants. She's Mrs. Sammy Davis, Jr.'" More often than not, though, Davis stayed on the sidelines and let his wife negotiate these relationships.

Then there were his friends and the Hollywood set in general. As Leslie Uggams put it, "Sammy ran with kings and queens and all kinds of people. And it took a certain kind of woman to be his wife, because you had to be able to communicate with all those people. And I'm sure it was extremely intimidating for her. I mean, all of a sudden you're Sammy's wife and you're sitting with Mr. Sinatra and those types of people. Or you're in England having tea with the queen. . . . Now, how you handle that fear . . . You either say, 'Okay, I'm going to do this,' or you start using something to help it from being so scary. And I guess that wound up happening."

Burt Boyar shared Uggams' assessment. "It's a hard job, being Altovise, coming into his world," he explained. "Just imagine: you've been a fan of this guy, he married you . . . he says, 'Okay, now, we're going to meet some people. This is Jack Benny. And this is Lucille Ball.' And Lucille Ball says, 'Darling, come to my house tomorrow.' This is very tough on a girl. And I call her a girl because she was only in her early twenties, so she was young. And here she is with the absolute heavy hitters of Hollywood. Her acceptability was as Sammy's wife, and they loved Sammy."

Shortly after the Davises moved into the Ambassador Hotel, Mary and Jack Benny invited them over for dinner. Among the other guests were Milton Berle, George Burns and Gracie Allen, Swifty Lazar and his wife, the David Nivens, the Ricardo Montalbans, Loretta Young, and Lucille Ball and her husband, Gary Morton. Lucille Ball approached them as soon as they came in, embraced Altovise, and said, "We're going to be friends, I hope."

Davis asked several black women, people to whom he felt close, like Leslie Uggams and Dionne Warwick, to help Alto ease into the Hollywood scene, and they did what they could. Said Uggams, "We'd been doing this a long time, so he wanted us to take her in hand, which we did. She was kind of scrutinized at the beginning because, you know, she was Mrs. Sammy Davis. So what you wear, where you go to get your hair done, where you go to get your nails done mattered, and he knew that we knew where to go because we'd lived out there [in L.A.], and also because we were ladies who were in the limelight."

Sammy also took a hand in the education and training of Altovise Davis, but most of his teaching served her poorly: how to drink, how to do drugs, and how to spend money. Later, he would have cause to regret playing Pygmalion to her Galatea.

Sammy also arranged for Alto to join a prestigious charity for mentally challenged children, SHARE (Share Happily and Reap Endlessly). It was the pet project of a group of socially prominent members of the Hollywood community, including Gloria Franks (the former wife of Sammy Cahn), Jeannie Martin (Dean's spouse), Shielah MacRae, Janet Leigh, and Joy Orr (Jack Warner's stepdaughter). Each year, the SHARE ladies threw a gala show and auction which drew the cream of the entertainment industry. Some of the guests, including Sammy, Dean, and Frank, also performed in the shows, as did the SHARE ladies themselves. One didn't simply join SHARE; the organization had a long waiting list of women seeking membership, and, to get in, one had to be nominated by a member of the group and seconded by another. Nevertheless, Sammy quickly arranged for Alto's membership. "He certainly wanted Altovise to be part of the group," said Gloria Franks. "And we knew that. Some of the girls knew her. Not everybody, but some of them did. So it was just a question of speaking out for that person."

But Davis didn't stop there. As he told Altovise on their wedding night, he wanted her to establish her own identity, to become a celebrity in her own right. He did what he could in that regard, mentioning her frequently on *The Tonight Show* and other television appearances, being photographed with her for newspaper and magazine articles, having her continue to tour with him as part of his act during the early days of their marriage. "I never discussed it with him," said Boyar, "as to why, but I guess I could figure it out: it made her more of a person to create chemistry with. It made it a better package. It's just something he wanted to do. It was also the Daddy Warbucks syndrome: 'I'll give her a Rolls Royce, I'll make her famous.' I know he enjoyed that, being Daddy Warbucks."

Alto was young, vivacious, and attractive. These qualities helped her do and be what Sammy wanted. Robert Culp, for one, liked her enormously. "Altovise was, in many ways, like Sammy," he said. "She was modern and hip and smart and sharp and black and matched him. And had tremendous joie d'vivre and spirit. I thought for the longest time that she was the best thing that could have happened to Sam. And that may have been so until they hit hard times. That's true of a lot of marriages. They hit hard times and personalities change."

Despite Alto's natural gifts, doing what Sammy wanted wasn't easy— and he could be a demanding taskmaster. Even Tracey Davis, hardly her stepmother's biggest champion, conceded, "Pop was very hard on Altovise and demanded a lot from her, probably more than she was able to handle. It was difficult for her. And with people like me there to make sure that everything bad or out of line was magnified, she didn't stand a chance."

For Sammy's part, marriage to Alto, a seemingly attractive alternative to the loneliness and desperation he had experienced in the wake of his divorce from May, turned out to be something of a drag. Those of his friends and colleagues, like Shirley Rhodes, who told him he should never remarry weren't wrong. He really wasn't cut out for married life and lost interest somewhat quickly. "He wasn't madly in love with her," asserted Arthur Silber, Jr. "Maybe at the beginning. . . . You start out that way. But all through the rest of the years, it was just for show." Boyar maintained that, after about a year, Sammy was contemplating divorce. The idea continued to weigh on him after he and Alto moved into their new home. "I think they were in Chicago," Boyar said, "and he had a lawyer go to the hotel room and tell her to go back to Los Angeles. I don't know if he would have sent her back to the house, because the house . . . meant a great deal to him. But she refused. She would not be divorced. And, in order for him to divorce her, because of the [California community] property law, the fifty-fifty, he would have to sell his house. And that house had tremendous meaning for Sammy. For him to sell that house, which was two acres in Beverly Hills, it would be like giving away everything he worked for. And he wouldn't do it. So he determined to coexist."

Writer Carl Gottlieb, who spent some time at the Davis home during this period, saw much the same thing as Boyar.* "Sammy was talking about divorce and assets and fooling around and girls," Gottlieb recalled, "and he said, 'Of course, if I do that, I got to give her half, so I don't do that.' So in that moment he was speaking of his relationship in purely economic terms. . . . It was cheaper to keep her, is what he was saying."

In fact, the Davises did separate in 1974. "Oh yeah, we had a crucial point in our marriage," Altovise noted four years later, "and we were separated for just a little time. We re-evaluated ourselves. We were apart a month and then we got together again."

In the early days, she traveled with Sammy, but eventually that came to an end. Thereafter, each spouse became more independent of the

---

*Born in 1938, Gottlieb first established himself with the San Francisco improv group the Committee. He went on to write for *The Bob Newhart Show*, *The Odd Couple*, and *The Smothers Brothers Comedy Hour*. He would become acquainted with Davis at the end of 1974, when he became a writer for Sammy's talk show, *Sammy and Company*. Gottlieb would go on to coauthor the screenplays for *Jaws* and *The Jerk* and David Crosby's autobiography, *Long Time Gone*.

other. Speaking of Davis' syndicated talk show, *Sammy & Company*, which started airing in 1975, Gottlieb said, "I don't think I ever saw her at a taping. She may have come to the premiere show and the wrap party and she was at the house once when I was in the house, but she was off in another wing. In the time, the three or four months I spent with him, she wasn't part of his life. I never saw her participate meaningfully in anything." Harrah's Holmes Hendricksen added, "Alto's life was Rodeo Drive and Beverly Hills, being at all the premieres and the parties, being on that A-list, being seen, that's what she loved. Sammy's life was hotel rooms and being on the road. Sitting in a hotel room waiting to go do a show. That was his life 90 percent of the time. After a while, and I don't know when that happened, Alto wasn't part of that life. They were together when Sammy was in Beverly Hills. Her life in Beverly Hills, that was a constant. And the line was that Sammy was out, working his ass off, doing two shows a night, and Alto's down in Beverly Hills, going up and down Rodeo spending it. Should Sammy have made his life Rodeo Drive and Beverly Hills? Or should Alto have given up Rodeo Drive and Beverly Hills and gone on the road? I can't answer."

Of course, Davis wasn't spending his nights alone when he was out of town. One of his alleged girlfriends during this period was a half black–half white Vegas showgirl named Kathy McKee, whom he'd started seeing in 1968, around the time he first met Altovise.

"I'll never forget that first night," McKee wrote in an article for *Penthouse* in 1991, "because I met two other members of the famous Rat Pack. When the two of us walked into Sammy's dressing room, Frank Sinatra was there." Sammy left for a few minutes, and Sinatra told her that Dean Martin would be arriving shortly. As a joke, he asked her to strip down to her underwear to greet him. "I was hesitant at first," said McKee. "But I thought I was being put to a test to see if I could play in the big leagues. So I slipped out of my black-and-white polka-dot jumpsuit and greeted Dean Martin wearing my black bra, matching bikini panties, and white go-go boots." Martin was not amused; Sammy was also incensed when he heard about the gag a few days later.

According to McKee, she and Davis continued to see one another on a regular basis for several years thereafter, but their relationship remained platonic. "Meanwhile, I grew increasingly fond of him," she wrote, "and eventually began to wish he *would* make a move. But I knew he had plenty of girlfriends." Then, in 1970, McKee moved to Los Angeles to try her hand at acting. One night, Sammy invited her to his home for dinner. "Nothing would ever be the same in my life again," she asserted.

That evening, Davis asked McKee to join his act, replacing Alto as the lead dancer in his backup group. She quickly accepted. "For the first few months," she said, "Sammy kept his distance from me. I heard rumors that he was having affairs with showgirls from various casinos. It seemed that everyone close to him knew that he liked one or more women at a time after his shows. Why, I wonder, wasn't I one of them?"

Finally, after about six months, they became lovers. Shortly after that, he dropped the dancers from his act, but McKee stayed on, as mistress of ceremonies, introducing him and undertaking the sorts of little bits Altovise had once performed. Between gigs, Sammy was with his wife and McKee could do as she wished. In fact, she had a boyfriend in Los Angeles. But on the road they were inseparable. "I always had my own hotel room," she explained, "but I would only go to it early in the morning, after Sammy and I had had sex." Perhaps because of the differences in their heights—McKee was 7 inches taller—Sammy preferred oral relations with the showgirl to intercourse. "Getting three or four blowjobs a day from me was routine," she freely told her *Penthouse* readers. "I think if he hadn't had other demands on his schedule, he would have asked for twice as many. In hotel rooms, in dressing rooms, in movie theaters, backstage, in limousines, aboard airplanes, it didn't matter—if I was willing he was ready."

As with his brief foursome in London in 1969, Sammy used McKee to exercise his fascination with lesbian encounters and group sex, encouraging her to submit to the advances of an attractive blonde woman, a former showgirl, whom they met in Miami; then he joined them for a threesome. Several more such encounters ensued, in Los Angeles and elsewhere. But, finally, they ceased, because, as McKee put it, "He could tell that my heart wasn't in it."

The affair came to an end, she asserted, when Sammy became interested in Satanism. "Lovemaking became a ritual tied into the worship of the occult in ways I didn't want to understand," McKee wrote. When he began watching X-rated movies with a sadomasochistic bent, she fled back to Los Angeles. She noted, "Sammy and I stayed in touch, of course, and I should have known his fascination with devil worship was simply a phase he quickly outgrew. Our friendship resumed, though we saw each other less frequently."

Given Sammy's earlier flirtation with devil worship, his return to Satanism seems unlikely. But his interest in X-rated movies, sadomasochistic or otherwise, was another matter. "He had a notorious porn collection," said Carl Gottlieb, "and a notorious bootleg tape and film collection. In those days prints were hard to come by. They weren't sold, there were no tapes or videos. It was as tightly controlled as the studios could control them. People who collected films had to go out of their way. Most of the stuff was stolen. He had it, he had a lot of stuff."

Gottlieb asserted that Davis also had video equipment, which he used to record group sexual encounters. "But," the writer said, "it took so much dope to get everyone stoned to the point where they would be uninhibited and ignore the camera, there was no one left to work the camera. So the resulting footage was always blurry or grainy or out of focus or not framed correctly. You never got any details."

Far from being ashamed or secretive about his interest in porn, Davis talked about it freely with his straight friends. When *Deep Throat,* one of the most famous of all X-rated films, opened at a sleazy Los Angeles theater called the Pussycat, he even bought the house for a night and invited a group of his pals to join him for a screening, carrying them to and from the movie house's unsavory neighborhood in rented limos. One can only imagine what Davis' guests—Lucille Ball and Gary Morton, Milton and Ruth Berle, the Dick Martins, and other members of the Hollywood establishment—thought of the film, whose title derived from the main character's special gifts when it came to oral sex. Shortly thereafter, Sammy managed to acquire a bootleg copy of *Deep Throat* for his personal collection and, according to Kathy McKee, she watched it with him almost a hundred times.

Not content with simply viewing porn, Sammy wanted to get to know the stars of these X-rated epics as well. He became friendly enough with Marilyn Chambers, best known for the film *Behind the Green Door,* for her to ask him to be the best man at her wedding. But he established a special relationship with the star of *Deep Throat,* Linda Lovelace. Indeed, for a time, she and her unsavory husband, Chuck Traynor, became part of Sammy's inner circle of friends. As one might imagine, the entertainer was less intrigued by the porn star's conversation than by her other skills. As McKee put it, "The main event for Sammy was watching Linda swallow his cock—just as she'd done for the camera while filming *Deep Throat.*"

Lovelace, who detailed her relationship with Davis in her 1980 memoir, *Ordeal,* asserted that once she and Sammy got together, they had sex almost every evening—in his home, while her husband and Altovise made love, or, alternatively, watched movies in the den. Before or after the lovemaking, Davis would talk to Lovelace about his life and would play some of his recordings for her. Not surprisingly, he also expressed interest in her career. "For a time he seemed intrigued by the thought of my becoming part of his show," she said, "but that never came about. He did suggest that I put together a big Las Vegas act."

While Davis was usually kind and attentive to Lovelace, she, like

McKee, occasionally saw his dark side. "When he was talking with me," she asserted, "he would often describe things that he wanted to do to me. He would like to tie me down on a bed, then have other women come in and make love to me while he watched. That other side of Sammy could be scary." She added, "Only occasionally did Sammy's far-out ideas become reality. There were times when the two men had Altovise and myself go through a 'scene' together while they watched." On one occasion, Lovelace asserted, Davis even gave vent to his curiosity about what it felt like to "deep throat" someone by giving a blow job to her distinctly uncomfortable husband.

According to Lovelace, things changed when she and Traynor accompanied Sammy and Altovise on a four-day vacation in Honolulu in July 1973. Columnist James Bacon took the occasion to report, "Sammy has become Linda's biggest fan—even has prints of the movie which he has screened in Beverly Hills and London." What the columnist didn't know was that, one night at a private party, Davis told Lovelace, or so she asserted, that he was falling in love with her. Altovise happened to overhear his remarks and fled the party, despite her husband's efforts to calm her down. Lovelace encouraged Sammy to follow Alto to their hotel, but he told Linda, "No, I'm right where I should be, right where I want to be." Thereafter, she said, he fantasized from time to time about leaving his wife and marrying her.

Whatever Sammy's feelings for Lovelace, she was clearly not in love with him. If anything, she saw him as a buffer between her and her sadistic husband. But she liked the entertainer. By contrast, she was mystified by Altovise. As far as she could tell, Sammy's wife didn't share his passion for mate swapping or group sex, "scenes," in the parlance of the day. Nevertheless, said the porn star, Alto had occasional sexual relations with Traynor, whom she didn't even like. "And while all this was going on around her," Lovelace added, "she remained silent. She never really participated in the conversation. She was just there. I could see that Altovise wasn't into scenes any more than I was. She went along with it because that was what Sammy wanted. I always felt a kinship with Altovise. We were alike in many ways but not alike in motivation. She did things to keep her man happy; I did things to keep my man from killing me."

In the end, Sammy didn't leave Altovise for Linda Lovelace. Instead, Lovelace left her despicable husband. In so doing, she also put the entire freaky L.A. scene behind her, including her relationship with Sammy Davis, Jr.

What is one to make of Davis' kinky sexual relationships with the likes of Kathy McKee and Linda Lovelace? Clearly, much as he liked hobnobbing with the elite, from presidents to movie stars to European royalty, he was drawn to lowlifes and sleazoids as well. One must remember what Sammy said when he started his flirtation with Satanism: "Evil fascinated me. I felt it lying in wait for me. And I wanted to taste it. I was ready to accept the wildness, the rolling in the gutter, and having to get up the next morning and wash myself clean."

He tried to keep his two worlds separate. "Dionne and I would have a laugh," recalled Leslie Uggams. "Whenever we were invited to the house, it was all the nice people. You know, drug-free. The wild and swinging parties, we were never invited to—which we were happy about. He had his one group of friends and then he had his other group of friends. A couple of times when we were up there, there were a couple of people, we would say, 'Uh-huh. They're not looking too correct, and they're not talking too correct. They must have got their nights mixed up.' So we were the square friends. And Sammy respected us for that, and loved us for that."

Occasionally, however, the groups overlapped. Leslie Bricusse, who saw Linda Lovelace and Chuck Traynor at Sammy's house, thought, "It was bizarre, the group he moved into." But, like virtually all of the entertainer's straight pals, Bricusse and his wife, Evie, looked the other way. "Sammy's friends stayed very loyal to him," the songwriter noted, "as indeed we did."

An exception was Frank Sinatra. He had no problem with Davis' extramarital affairs or his interest in lowlifes; Sinatra played around himself and had several pals from the wrong side of the tracks. But he was old school when it came to the use of illegal substances. Booze was fine, but, as a band singer, he'd seen too many musicians destroy their lives by smoking reefer and shooting up. When he heard about Sammy's drug abuse, he dispatched his friend, restaurateur Jilly Rizzo, to convey his disappointment. On the surface, Davis breezily dismissed the warning. "I was trying to act like a big shot with Jilly," he recalled, "but I was dying inside. I loved Frank Sinatra. To know that he was pissed off at me, well, that was tough." For several years thereafter, contact between the old friends was minimal. When they happened to bump into one another at an industry affair or social gathering, they'd exchange curt greetings and then move on. Hurt, Davis would console himself by doing more drugs.

As Sinatra no doubt knew, Sammy had graduated by this point from marijuana, hash, and acid to the new substances of choice: cocaine and amyl nitrate. These were particularly important adjuncts to his sex life. "Sex was always preceded by cocaine," said Kathy McKee. "And sex without popping capsules of amyl nitrate wasn't really sex to Sammy. He luxuriated in the brief, hot, soaring high the amyl nitrate gave as I sucked him. He'd groan and clutch my head as the drug made him flush. His hips would arch upward and he'd sometimes moan, 'Oh, baby, oh, baby, get it! Get it!'"

But, for Sammy, coke and the other drugs were not just about enhancing his sexual experiences. They were about staying hip. They were the in thing, what the kids were doing, so that's what he wanted to do, too. He eagerly showed that he was "with it" in the company of such younger men as Rob Reiner and Carl Gottlieb. If he encountered them at a party or restaurant, he would offer samples of his stash, proud that he was able to score quality drugs. "He obviously knew about drugs," said Gottlieb. "He wasn't a novice. You could tell from his coke etiquette. He'd take a sniff and offer it. Whatever the coke etiquette was, he had it. Among my peers, it was a surprise that people didn't do drugs. But, with his generation, it was a surprise that people did."

Given his excessive personality, Sammy naturally went for all the trappings of the drug scene: the little gold spoon worn around the neck, the bowl of white powder conspicuously sitting in the den. He didn't just invite people over for a hit or two occasionally. Virtually every night was open house at Sammy's place in those days. "I started going to Sammy's house every night to party," recalled Lorna Luft, Judy Garland's daughter and an emerging singer in her own right, "and when [her half-sister] Liza [Minnelli] and [Liza's husband] Jack [Haley, Jr.] were in town, they'd go, too. There would always be a crowd there—Sammy, his wife Altovise, and a whole host of managers, agents, and assorted Hollywood types. Most of us would be up all night doing cocaine and partying our brains out. I loved it. . . . Sammy's house became my home away from home."

Luft also noted, "When he was working out of town, Sammy would often fly his friends down to wherever he was playing so we could party there. A sort of moveable feast." Of course, this meant adding to the amazing array of personal belongings that already traveled with him—clothes, shoes, hats, and outerwear for every conceivable occasion, jewelry by the ton, books, record albums and stereo player, movie projector and films, and so forth. Now, he also toted a vanity-type case, "inside of which," to quote McKee, "was a vast amount of cocaine and amyl nitrate. I always thought this gave a new meaning to Sammy's reputation as 'the Candy Man.'"

In addition to the drugs, Davis had escalated his consumption of alcohol since he had attempted to quit in 1971. Booze was ultimately more important to him than drugs. "I was with Sammy a lot when cocaine was around," said David Steinberg, who became Davis' pal as well as his press agent during the late sixties. "We were both doing it, and I'm sure we were doing more than we should have. All over the world. But Sammy was never a big druggie. He certainly dabbled, but it was more the show of it—having it around to attract other people. It was the booze [that really got to him]." Davis said much the same thing himself, telling readers of *Why Me?* that "for feeling good I preferred booze, from the taste and effect down to just the pleasure of holding the glass in my hand."

There is no question that the drinking, the drugging, and the partying brought Sammy pleasure. He knew how to have a good time, drunk, stoned, or sober. But behind the wild times lay a frightened, unhappy man. To begin with, he was nearing fifty. "This was a hard time," he said later. "Man, getting old in show business—it ain't easy. You fall into certain traps trying to keep your youth, trying to be hip." On another occasion, he said, "I hated the sight of fifty. I had this carved-in-granite image: the finger-snapping, perpetual motion, tight-pants swinger. But was there anything more depressing than an aging swinger? And how could there be an old Sammy Davis, Jr.?"

Even worse, he was running away from who he was. In addition to the old issues about his looks, identity, and lack of self-worth, he felt trapped by the Superfly persona he had been fostering since the late sixties. As he put it, "I didn't like what I had created and what I had become, and I had to face that. . . . It was more like the Billy Crystal imitation.* A certain amount of that theatricality is wonderful. That's what they pay you for. And I definitely have never been the boy next door. But I went too far. You can go too far over the edge." As a result, he told Fred Bruning of *Newsday,* he had "created a lifestyle that was no good for me. My life was empty. I had drugs, booze and broads, and I had nothing."

Lorna Luft, who opened for Davis at an engagement in Reno, maintained that his substance abuse didn't impact his performances, and, to some extent, this was so. His personal appearances between 1973 and 1977, the years of his heaviest drug and alcohol use, included highly successful engagements at the Valley Music Theatre in Los Angeles, the Nanuet Theatre Go-Round in Nanuet, New Jersey, the Kennedy Center in Washington, D.C., Harrah's Tahoe, the Diplomat Hotel in Hollywood, Florida, the Masonic Auditorium in Detroit, the Deauville in Miami Beach, and the Greek Theatre in Los Angeles. Looking at his reviews

---

*During the 1980s, Crystal started doing an impression of Davis as a running bit on *Saturday Night Live,* with fellow regular Joe Piscipo as Sinatra. The dead-on impression played to the worst elements of Davis' persona, making him look like a shallow, sycophantic, overly glitzy, oh-so-hip clown. According to David Steinberg, Crystal adored Davis and considered the bits good clean fun. But they left a very negative impression of the entertainer with those who caught them.

during these gigs, one sees a solid array of positive comments. He even drew enthusiastic notices from the notoriously tough New York theater critics when he opened for two weeks in April 1974 at a legitimate Broadway house, the Uris, doing essentially his club act.

But, regardless of what others thought, Sammy knew that drugs and booze were affecting his work. "My performances were mediocre at best," he said later, "and I was using tricks and gimmicks to get an audience response. People were still buying it, but I knew inside that I was letting myself slip." Sometimes, he would, indeed, lose control. Once, he said, he came out, did two or three songs, thought he'd been on for an hour, thanked the audience, and left the stage. Another time, he told the same joke twice without realizing he'd done so. On a third occasion, he announced after a couple of songs, "Well, folks, some nights I have it and some nights I don't have it. Tonight I don't have it." Refusing to continue, he instead picked up everyone's tab.

Occasionally, one critic or another would notice something amiss. One noted in 1974, "Davis' habit of losing control and laughing at himself has a certain charm, but this went on five minutes on the night covered and grew very tiresome indeed." Another asserted two years later, "In previous appearances, Sammy Davis, Jr., seemed tired and distracted," while a third observed some five months after that, "Davis . . . was so loose and informal that at times his performance was self-defeating."

His health sometimes suffered along with his work output. In February 1974, for example, while appearing at the Diplomat Hotel in Miami Beach, he was rushed to St. Francis Hospital, complaining of chest pains. He was later transferred to Mt. Sinai in L.A. for further tests, causing him to miss several performances at the Diplomat and forcing him to delay his subsequent gig at the Sands in Vegas. On his opening night at the Uris in New York, he was suffering from a high fever. And, in September 1975, while performing in Vegas, he experienced severe pains in his arms and legs, resulting in a week's hospitalization.

Of course, his employers were aware of his problems. "There was a period there when he was undependable," recalled Harrah's Holmes Hendricksen, "and we didn't know whether he was going to work. Most of the time he did, but once in a while we'd have to cancel a show. . . . He'd have to take a day or two to get his health back. That wasn't a continuous thing, but it happened occasionally." Such was Sammy's deteriorating reputation among industry insiders that Joyce Haber reported in the *Los Angeles Times* in July 1973 that the manager of an unnamed Puerto Rican venue told her, "The gamblers are taking odds on whether he'll appear or not, if so how late and whether he'll finish without berating the microphone or the management."

Haber also reported that Sammy had agreed to sing "Ol' Man River" in an all-star television tribute to lyricist Oscar Hammerstein II. He made numerous demands on the producers of the special, Paramount-TV, including insistence on a full orchestral accompaniment. Every demand was met. Then, on the day of the taping, Paramount was informed by a member of Sammy's entourage that the entertainer would not appear. No amount of pleading could change his mind. Finally, John Raitt was brought in as a last-minute substitute.

"I'd had a similar example of Sammy's erraticism three years ago," Haber told her readers. "We had an appointment for a luncheon interview at Sam's house in Benedict Canyon. Just as I was leaving to meet him, his press agent called to ask if I'd meet him at the Ambassador Hotel—which is some 30 minutes away—instead. Sam was involved in revamping the Cocoanut Grove and he wanted the interview taped for publicity purposes. Indignantly, I refused. In the end, we met at Sammy's house, some 45 minutes after the intended time—and Sam was so besieged by his cordon of followers that the interview was a disaster. I never ran it."

One simply didn't behave in such a way with an important industry observer like Haber. But that didn't stop Sammy. He dished out the same kind of treatment to a European princess. Indeed, the former Grace Kelly experienced the full force of Davis' erratic behavior when he came to Monaco in June 1974.

The occasion was the opening of a new gambling casino in Monte Carlo, for which a gala benefit had been arranged for some twelve hundred invited guests. As was always the case with charitable events, Sammy agreed to headline the show without a fee. In return, the sponsor was expected to cover his expenses, which would customarily include first-class round-trip airfare and accommodations for himself and his party. Naturally, Princess Grace and Prince Ranier agreed to do this. Sammy also asked for the loan of the Grimaldis' yacht and crew for five days, so that he could make a bit of a vacation out of the trip. When they assented, the deal was struck.

Asking for the yacht was aggressive enough, but then, according to David Steinberg, Sammy aggravated the situation by doubling the number of people in his entourage. So, instead of covering airfare and hotel rooms for roughly a dozen people—Sammy, Altovise, Sy and Molly Marsh, David Steinberg, and the personnel needed for Sammy's show—the Grimaldis found themselves paying for twice that number. Ten or so more first-class round-trip tickets and hotel accommodations for a couple of nights would represent a significant amount of money. To their credit, the royal family raised no objections to these unanticipated expenditures.

Sammy, Altovise, and the Marshes decided to travel by way of Paris so they could do some shopping. When they reached Monaco, something happened to infuriate Sammy. Accounts differ over what the something was.

According to Sy, Davis learned that the gala, which was to start around 6:00 P.M., would include a presentation by the architects who had designed the casino and a fashion show, plus several other performers. As a result of these extras, he wouldn't go on until at least 11:00. He tried, said Marsh, to get the event planners to streamline the show, but they refused.

As Steinberg remembers it, what infuriated Sammy was the fact that Princess Grace had not placed Altovise at the head table during the festivities, which he felt was, first, an affront to him as the show's headliner, and, second, a form of racial discrimination.

Whatever the specific cause, the result was the same: Sammy started to drink. And the more he did, the angrier he became. As he ranted and raved, the members of his party began egging him on. Their comments, according to Steinberg, were along the lines of, "Yeah, Sammy, they're treating you like shit. Fuck them. Don't perform." Steinberg and Davis' bodyguard, Joe Grant, saw the situation differently. "Sammy, you've got to work," David told the entertainer. "You're getting paid." "No, I'm not," Davis replied. "I'm doing this for free." "No, you got twenty-five or whatever it is round-trip first-class tickets," Steinberg reminded him. "You've got hotel rooms for twenty-five people. You've got a yacht." But Sammy couldn't be swayed. "Fuck 'em," he told his friend, "I'm not going. They can't treat me like this.'"

When word of his decision reached Princess Grace on the afternoon of the gala, she was apoplectic. In an effort to salvage the evening, she dispatched one of her trusted officials to reason with Sammy. But by then, Davis was drunk and ready to kill. Steinberg maintained that had the official agreed to seat Altovise at Grace's table, the situation might have been resolved. But the offer was never made. Instead, the official told Sammy that he and his wife could join the Grimaldis at their table *after* he finished performing. "So," he told the official, "it's like then the fuckin' organ grinder lets the monkey sit at the table." "No, no, monsieur, it's not like that," the official replied, trying to be accommodating. But Sammy wasn't buying. "My wife isn't good enough to sit at that fuckin' table 'til I show up," he insisted. "That's exactly what it is."

"It was the back-of-the-bus syndrome," Steinberg explained. "The reality is that Sammy was a paid performer and nothing more to them.

There's nothing wrong with that, it just is, okay? But Sammy gets fucking nuts. He thinks it's a whole racial thing."

Frustrated, the official gave up. Finally, Princess Grace attempted to save the day by phoning a member of Sammy's party herself (Sy or David, depending on who is telling the story). By then, however, she was so angry she made matters worse. And Sammy was so drunk, he probably couldn't have performed no matter what she said. The end result is that he and Altovise made their way down to the dock, along with Sy and Molly Marsh and perhaps one or two others, and sailed away—on the Grimaldis' yacht! One hour before the show was to start!

The gala went on as scheduled, with several performers, including Bill Cosby, Desi Arnaz, Jr., and Burt Bacharach covering for Sammy.

"The next morning, when we woke up," Sy recalled, "We were greeted by newspapers running the story on the front page—'Sammy Davis Too Drunk to Perform.'" He and Davis simply ignored the flap and continued using the yacht for the allotted time. Then they flew home as originally planned.

Eventually, the Grimaldis sent Marsh a bill for something like $300,000 for the use of the yacht. "Now I wasn't too thrilled about this because we didn't have $300,000 to just throw away," he asserted. He decided to tell the royal family that unless they reached an accommodation with him regarding the expense, he would call a press conference, attribute Sammy's walkout to their failure to invite him to a cocktail party the night before the gala, and blame the oversight on racism (none of which he thought was true). "So I sent this wire back," he said, chuckling, "and we never heard from them again."

Assuming Marsh's version of events is correct, Sammy may have gotten a free five-day vacation, but this hardly compensated for the negative publicity. The press covered both sides of the story, but, for the most part, he came across as a petulant baby.

CHAPTER 25

A New Showroom, a New Show, and an Old Musical

Free at last from his contract with the Sands, Sammy opened at another Vegas resort in November 1974. But, surprisingly, his new home was not the Tropicana. It was Caesars Palace.

Everything had gone according to plan the previous year. In July 1973, the Trop's new 1,150-seat Superstar Room, designed to Davis' specifications, had opened with Mitzi Gaynor as the headliner. Two months later, Sammy's license was approved by the Nevada Gaming Board. And two months after that, he proudly told *Jet* magazine, "There will be a lot of changes in terms of the attitude of the club, who works there and this and that because I'm involved and I've got to have *my* people in the joint."

But, in the end, what Deil Gustafson and his associates offered was not an equity interest in the resort but profit points. When Sammy's attorneys scrutinized the contract, they advised that he turn the deal down. So many conditions would have to be met, they asserted, before a profit would be declared, that the points were meaningless; Sammy would never see any money out of the deal. So he and the Tropicana parted ways.

Not wanting to return to the Sands, Davis needed a new place in which to perform. "The guys at Caesar's [*sic*] offered me anything I wanted," he said. Which boiled down to $175,000 a week—for two shows a night, six nights a week. That represented top dollar at the time.

At the behest of its founder, Jay Sarno, the resort had set a new standard for opulence in a town known for it. Opening in 1966 at a cost of $10.6 million (borrowed from the Teamsters' Central States Pension Fund), Caesars was more than just another expensive venue on the Strip. It drew its inspiration from Imperial Rome, and everything, from the copy of the Louvre's Winged Victory of Samothrace out front to the toga-like costumes of the staff to the parchment-style stationery, contributed to the concept. So outrageously grand was the execution of its theme that Caesars Palace became an attraction in its own right.

Everything there operated on a grand scale, including its showroom, the Circus Maximus, which seated nearly double the number of the Sands' Copa Room. Sammy found the size of the place a little intimidating at first. Nevertheless, he maneuvered around the stage with his usual brio.

He had more or less returned to the standard material for which he was known. "I went through my super black period," he said at the time, "and a period showing how erudite I could be, and now I'm trying for the informality of what a good nightclub show is." As *Variety* noted, his act, consisting almost entirely of songs and patter, was "free and easy," highly entertaining but lacking the explosive energy and versatility on which he had built his reputation. Sammy attempted a seven- or eight-minute tap routine on his opening night, but, halfway through the number, he found his breath so ragged and his legs so weak that he had to switch to a soft-shoe. The audience was impressed by his dexterity, but he knew better. As he put it, "You can't be my kind of an entertainer, at my age, and run yourself stupid partying and boozing and drugging. I used to be able to do it. But I couldn't anymore."

Driven to be the best, living on superlatives and standing ovations, he couldn't stand what was happening to him. In his mind, he was "a dancer who couldn't dance anymore, an aging legend of youth and motion." He was still drawing big crowds at top-drawer places like Caesars, but he feared that one day soon his diminishing talents would become widely recognized and people would no longer want to pay money to see him. Cutting out the boozing, drugging, and partying would certainly have helped, but fear of what was happening to him onstage drove him to push the envelope even further. As he later put it, "What I was really saying was, 'Will somebody help me, please? I'm losing it.'"

In the opinion of many, including some of Davis' closest friends, he made matters worse by lending himself to a ninety-minute syndicated talk show that went into production some two months after his Caesars opening.

In all likelihood, the idea of Sammy Davis, Jr., hosting a regular TV chat fest originated with the series' executive producer, Pierre Cossette, best known as the producer of the annual Grammy telecast, a position he has held since the award show first started airing in 1971.

Sammy brought several attributes to the venture. First, he was a major star. Second, he was experienced, having taken over for Johnny

Carson on several occasions; he also was a cohost of *The Mike Douglas Show* numerous times. Third, his versatility as an entertainer offered possibilities for breaks in the usual talk show routine, in addition, of course, to the talents of his guests. Fourth, he had a lot of friends in the industry who could be expected to appear on his program.

The interest in high-powered talent speaks to the state of the genre in the early to mid-seventies. Outside of Tom Snyder, the new prince of late late night, and Phil Donahue, whose daytime show went national in 1970, Sammy's competitors—Mike Douglas, Virginia Graham, Dinah Shore, Dr. Joyce Brothers, Merv Griffin, and, of course, Carson—primarily offered gossipy, amusing chit-chat featuring "scintillating" celebrity guests, most of whom were on hand to promote a project of their own. Occasionally, a song or stand-up routine would offer a break from the chatter.

No one was planning any major departures from the standard premise with *Sammy & Company*, except that, in addition to the host and his sidekick, New York radio personality William B. Williams, the show would feature a group of comic actors, including Avery Schreiber, Joyce Jillson, and Sammy's *Golden Boy* costar, Johnny Brown, to perform a couple of sketches on each outing. Carl Gottlieb was brought in to write their material, as was a tall, nice-looking Canadian, Alan Thicke, who would go on to host his own talk show and star in a popular family sitcom, *Growing Pains*.

That Sammy wasn't integrated into the sketches spoke less about his comic talents than his availability. The routines required rehearsal and time to memorize lines. He had no interest in doing either. Nor was he planning to prepare for each week's interviews or read the books written by his guest authors. He wanted the show to be lively and fun, but he wasn't out to be the best talk show host ever. His primary reason for doing the series was to earn extra, badly needed income. In deference to the other demands of his schedule, the show's producer, Eric Lieber, formerly of *The Mike Douglas Show*, would spoon-feed Sammy background information for the interviews, draw on his extensive repertoire of songs for airtime material, and tape several episodes back to back. While the show would be based at the Hollywood studio of TransAmerica Video (TAV), episodes would be recorded in venues at which Sammy was performing at night, notably Vegas, Reno, and Tahoe. A string of programs would even be shot poolside at a hotel in Acapulco, Mexico.

After two and a half months of taping, *Sammy & Company* debuted the first week of April 1975 in forty markets around the country. Its unenviable time slot in the all-important New York and West Coast markets was 11:30 P.M. on Sunday evenings.

Typically, each episode featured three guests, with singer Ray Charles on hand for the premiere, along with the stars of two current TV sitcoms, Freddie Prinz (*Chico and the Man*) and Suzanne Pleshette (*The Bob Newhart Show*). In the succeeding weeks, several of Sammy's celebrated pals showed up—Shirley MacLaine, Steve Lawrence, Sarah Vaughn, Bill Cosby, and Carmen MacRae—plus such hot TV luminaries as Jean Stapleton (*All in the Family*) and Alan Alda (*M*A*S*H*). A number of Davis' talk show colleagues—Dinah Shore, Merv Griffin, and Mike Douglas—also stopped by, to pay him back for his visits to their shows. But the show's unfortunate time period in the two most important markets no doubt served to discourage some heavy-hitters. As Carl Gottlieb put it, "I think we were happy to get whoever we got."

But Davis always treated his guests with the utmost respect. "Of all the people that I've worked with in talk shows," said Eric Lieber, "I had never seen anybody of his magnitude—and he was a big star—be as gracious to other performers. I mean, genuinely gracious. And some of those people didn't warrant that attention."

In the opinion of Lieber and others, Sammy sometimes went too far in his efforts to be a good host. He was so eager to put people at ease he came across as obsequious. And his propensity for laughing long and hard at unfunny or moderately funny remarks turned into an industry joke. "He would open his mouth," recalled Dom DeLouise, "and then he'd lean forward and then he'd fall on the floor. I always thought, 'What the hell is he on?'" Actually, Sammy was simply trying to be polite. As Ed McMahon explained, "He laughed, in part, so that people trying to be funny wouldn't be embarrassed by something falling flat. There's a real honest courtesy to the man, that concern for others." McMahon was right, but to the world at large, Davis was perceived not as kind but as phony.

Otherwise, Eric Lieber did his best to ensure that his star made a favorable impression. "I was protective toward him," the producer said. "He knew that, aside from trying to do some good shows, I would watch out for his interests and I would keep him within the parameters of what he could do."

Lieber soon realized that Sammy, lacking time to prepare for interviews, performed best when dealing with show business guests and industry chatter. Accordingly, the producer stopped seeking book authors, sports figures, and celebrities in other fields and focused primarily on actors and entertainers. After several weeks, it also became obvious that without Sammy's participation in the sketches, they felt disconnected from the rest of the show, and so, after several months, they were dropped.

With musical guests, the tendency was to pair the singer and Sammy—

without rehearsal. Artists like Davis, Ray Charles, Steve Lawrence, and Sarah Vaughn could usually pull off an unprepared duet. But such was not the case when the singer was less adept. When Roy Clark made an appearance, for example, Lieber tried to get Sammy to rehearse with the country music star, but Sammy was certain that he and Clark could wing something together. "And it was a disaster," Lieber recalled. "I mean, Roy couldn't keep up with Sammy. We probably threw it out."

Although *Sammy & Company* was neither a ratings champion nor a critics' darling, it was inexpensive to produce, so it was renewed for the 1976–77 season and then again for 1977–78. In all, fifty-five episodes aired during the three-year period, making *Sammy & Company* far and away Davis' longest-running and most financially successful television outing. The host earned a tidy sum, but he frittered away a significant percentage of it by purchasing, in December 1975, the show's home, TAV's studio and production facility. He immediately allocated more than $500,000, a large amount of money in 1970 dollars, to upgrade and renovate the plant, but he lacked the capital to sustain the operation. In short order, he had to sell the facility to Merv Griffin, whose late-night talk show was also taped at TAV.

Financial considerations aside, *Sammy & Company* did little to benefit Davis. Not surprisingly, Lieber said, "For the kind of show he did, for the kind of show that it eventually evolved into, he was fine. But, you know, he was Sammy. Given the fickleness of the American viewing public, I think it's something of a tribute to him that that show ran for three years."

Carl Gottlieb offered a more sober appraisal. "He was okay," the writer said. "But even in the world of talk show hosts, the successful ones are authentic. Carson was Carson, Jack Paar was Jack Paar. Phil Donahue was very authentic. Sammy . . . brought to it the same surface glitter he brought to everything."

Leslie Bricusse, who caught the shows taped in Acapulco, where he had a home at the time, shared Gottlieb's assessment. "I felt then that he was scraping the barrel a bit," the songwriter asserted, "doing that kind of work . . . because that does not enhance your star status. It makes you too available every day to everybody." David Steinberg went so far as to label Davis' involvement with the show "as dumb a move as Sammy has ever made." He added, "Sammy Davis, Jr., had a lot of talents—a great singer, a great dancer, a great impressionist. A fascinating interviewer he was not. And with that laugh of his? How much of that can you watch? I think when you take artists and put them in businesses outside of what they do, you're making a mistake. I think people should grow, but you weren't getting Sammy Davis to grow. I think it was a silly decision."

Years later, Davis viewed some of the tapes of his show and came to share Steinberg's assessment. "I watched myself doing phony breakups," he said, "laughing too hard at things that weren't that funny, and laughing at things that weren't funny at all. . . . People looked at each other. 'Why is he laughing?' I watched myself introducing guests. 'My dear friend . . . a great talent . . .' I remembered reading that my introductions were too flowery. It was my vaudeville upbringing of giving another performer all the courtesy possible, verbally 'carrying them on,' but I belabored it. I'd resented reading it, but they'd been right."

His other television appearances during the *Sammy & Company* years were restricted by his lack of time, but few of them served to counterbalance the impression created by the talk show. During the first season, for example, he played himself on Freddie Prinze's NBC sitcom *Chico and the Man* and on CBS's daytime soap opera *Love of Life* (he was a fan of this and several other afternoon soaps). Even his guest shot on Carol Burnett's popular, well-written variety show on September 20, 1975 failed to showcase him well.

Sammy fared somewhat better the following season. On December 7, 1976, he played dual roles on an episode of Aaron Spelling's latest hit for ABC, *Charlie's Angels*. As himself, he hired the three beautiful detectives played by Kate Jackson, Jaclyn Smith, and Cheryl Ladd to protect him from the threat of kidnapping in the wake of several aborted attempts. He also got to portray a prickly Sammy Davis, Jr., lookalike in the person of liquor store tycoon Herbert Brubaker III. "As himself for real, Davis doesn't have a lot to do except be nice to everybody," noted *Daily Variety*. "But every time he becomes the other character, the screen comes alive." Joining him in the episode was his wife, Altovise, who played herself.

Two nights after the *Charlie's Angels* episode aired, Sammy was among the featured performers on a star-studded, critically acclaimed Gary Smith–Dwight Hemion special for CBS entitled *America Salutes Richard Rodgers: The Sound of His Music*. The following August 22, he joined his friends Steve Lawrence and Eydie Gorme and Carol Burnett for another Smith-Hemion special, *Steve & Eydie Celebrate Irving Berlin*. Even more elegant than its predecessor, the ninety-minute show featured its quartet of stars in a stunning opening medley. But arguably the most memorable number found Davis tracing the history of song and dance through "Alexander's Ragtime Band," starting with vaudeville and the great Bert Williams, whom Sammy impressively impersonated, and concluding with the popular disco style. The show won an Emmy for best outstanding comedy-variety or music program.

Roughly two weeks after the Irving Berlin special, Sammy showed up at the Sahara Hotel in Vegas for a show that was 180 degrees away from the elegance of a Smith-Hemion special, the annual Jerry Lewis telethon in support of the Muscular Dystrophy Association.

The idea of featuring a host of performers on a national network hookup for nearly twenty-four hours, supported by periodic locally sponsored segments, for the purpose of enticing people to phone in pledge donations to the MDA had originated in 1965, when the show, based in New York, raised $1 million. By 1973, when the telethon relocated to Vegas, contributions rose to $12.4 million. Two years later, earnings were nearly $19 million and the telethon was carried on 195 stations around the country. By then, it was an eagerly anticipated Labor Day event in many American households.

The telethon was, in a way, a perfect vehicle for Davis. He got to hang out with Jerry Lewis, he drew pleasure from helping the kids who were the focus of the MDA's activities, he was treated like a prince by the telethon organizers, and he got to perform for an extended period of time before an adoring audience.

After 1978, Sammy would cement his relationship with the MDA, becoming a fixture on every telethon until the year of his death. Sometimes he was a featured headliner, sometimes he hosted from a "remote" location—Atlantic City in 1980, 1981, and 1985 and New York in 1989. He also served as the MDA's national vice president from 1984 to 1989. "He never said 'no' to any requests our President, Bob Ross, asked of him," said Gerald C. Weinberg, the organization's senior vice president and director of field organization. "He always stood ready to help the MDA in every way possible."

Doing TV reached more people, but Sammy's bread and butter rested with his personal appearances. Setting up Sammy & Company to accommodate his live engagements turned out to be wise, because his need for money mandated that he perform whenever and wherever high-paying gigs presented themselves. In 1976, for example, he supplemented his regular appearances in Vegas, Tahoe, Reno, and Miami with a stint at the London Palladium in September. He followed this with an extensive European tour that included stops in Amsterdam, Copenhagen, Brussels, Antwerp, Paris, Vienna, and four cities in West Germany. Some six months later, he embarked on a tour of Australia. "In fine voice," noted Variety on his opening in Melbourne, "he chatted and ad-libbed with the audience in the three-quarters filled hall, inviting those with cameras to come to stage edge for better pix."

In the long run, Davis' most important personal appearance during the Sammy & Company period came in January 1978, near the end of the show's airing, when he followed Frank Sinatra into Caesars Palace. The significance of this event was that it facilitated a get-together between the two old friends arranged by their wives after several years of non-communication.

Meeting in the hotel's Bacchanal Room with no one else present, Sammy and Alto and Frank and his wife, Barbara, exchanged pleasantries for a few awkward moments. Then the men repaired to a booth of their own, where the older entertainer proceeded to vent his feelings about Sammy's drug use. "Look," Sinatra said, "God put you here for a lot of reasons that you and I don't even know about. He gave you a talent, and you're abusing it. And I'm watching my friend go down the tubes. I loved you when you were nothing. I'll love you when you go back to being nothing. But you're cheating yourself. You're cheating your friends, and you're cheating your public! So long as you're going to do that, then I don't want to be around you."

Other friends had delivered similar, albeit more gentle, messages over the years, but to no avail. This time it was different. Somehow Sinatra got through; Sammy heard Frank's message. He promised to quit doing drugs, and he kept his word.

Getting clean came just in time, for a few months after meeting with Sinatra, Davis embarked on the third, and final, stage musical of his career, one that would place as many demands on his talent and stamina as had *Mr. Wonderful* and *Golden Boy*. Perhaps he could have met the challenge anyway, but how much better it was to tackle such an ambitious project clean, if not always sober.

When *Stop the World—I Want to Get Off* first opened in London in 1961, it offered a marked contrast to most American musicals of the period. In the United States, shows still tended to focus on lifelike characters in lifelike situations and settings. By contrast, *Stop the World* was allegorical, presenting prototypical human beings in a nonrealistic environment in order to make comments, satiric and otherwise, about the human condition.

Specifically, the show traced the development of a British Everyman called Littlechap from birth to death, detailing his rise in business and politics and his concurrent inability to commit to the women in his life—from his understanding wife, Evie, to his various mistresses—until old age, when it's too late. In addition to writing the book and score with Leslie Bricusse, Anthony Newley directed the production and also created the role of Littlechap, donning white clown-like makeup for the role and making extensive use of his talent for mime, à la Marcel Marceau. Anna Quayle portrayed Evie (named for Bricusse's wife but also evoking the first woman, Eve). In addition, she appeared as the females of various nationalities—German, Russian, American—with whom Littlechap dallies, thereby suggesting that, without knowing it, he sought his wife in each romantic interlude. In keeping with the show's symbolic underpinnings, the set was simple, evoking a circus tent with several rows of semicircular bleachers. Beyond the two leads, the cast consisted of two young women, who served as Littlechap's daughters, and a tiny Greek chorus of seven.

When the show transferred to Broadway in October 1962, with Newley and Quayle reprising their roles, it failed to stir the New York critics or, for that matter, average Broadway theatergoers, who were mystified by its flagrant departures from the familiar musical conventions of the day. Still, *Stop the World* managed to run for about sixteen months at the Shubert Theatre, largely on the strength of its melodic score, which included "Gonna Build a Mountain," "Once in a Lifetime," "Someone Nice Like You," and "What Kind of Fool Am I?"—all of which were, of course, successfully recorded by Sammy Davis, Jr. A national tour starred Joel Grey, and in 1966, Bill Sargent, a producer who specialized in filming stage productions, brought *Stop the World* to the silver screen. Newley declined to be involved, so Tony Tanner, his replacement in the London production, played Littlechap, with Millicent Martin as the women in his life.

Obviously, Davis loved *Stop the World*'s score, but he adored the show as well, seeing himself in Littlechap's rise from poverty to wealth and fame. From the moment he saw the musical on his second trip to London, he vowed to do it someday. Finally, thanks to Hillard Elkins, his moment arrived in the spring of 1978. By then, Sammy was not only ready to meet the challenge of portraying Littlechap, but he was eager to return to the Broadway stage, saying, "I wanna grow some more as a performer." He also recognized that he had taken less than full advantage of his opportunity with *Golden Boy*, diluting his focus with his many outside activities. "Ok, I was an ass," he told Jay Carr of the *New York Times*. "Now I can do it. My head's better placed."

He knew better than to submit to another three-year contract and limited his commitment to twenty-two weeks, roughly the amount of time that *Golden Boy* had spent in rehearsal and tryouts. He also negotiated a three-way split of the profits with Hilly Elkins and Newley-Bricusse. According to the *Los Angeles Times*, sell-outs in some venues would yield Davis as much as $70,000 a week, an impressive sum but less than half his weekly salary at Caesars Palace.

Stop the World was an anomaly in its day, but American musicals had changed considerably by 1978. In place of tightly structured plot- and character-driven shows in the Rodgers and Hammerstein tradition, there were, on the one hand, loose, youth-oriented pieces with contemporary music, like *Hair, Jesus Christ Superstar,* and *Two Gentlemen of Verona.* On the other hand, there were shows in which stylistic and/or thematic concerns dominated everything, from Stephen Sondheim's *Company* and *Follies* to Kander and Ebb's *Chicago* to Stephen Schwartz's *Pippin* (the latter two were spearheaded by Sammy's *Sweet Charity* director, Bob Fosse).

How Davis' *Stop the World* would fit into this new theatrical universe was determined primarily by the decision to hire Mel Shapiro as the show's director. Shapiro was best known for his collaborations with playwright John Guare on Guare's 1970 hit play *House of Blue Leaves* as well as his hip, exuberant adaptation of *Two Gentleman of Verona.* The surprising Tony Award–winning musical of 1971 featured a score by *Hair's* Galt MacDermott. At the time Sammy's *Stop the World* was being launched, Shapiro was working with Leslie Bricusse on a new musical in London called *Kings and Clowns.*

According to Shapiro, Davis was planning on playing Littlechap as Newley had done, in clown makeup. "I don't understand why you want to wear white face," Shapiro told him. "What kind of comment does this make for a black man to wear white face? I mean, are you making a comment on white people? It makes it so complicated." In all likelihood, Sammy was so enamored of Newley's interpretation of the role that he couldn't see doing it any other way. But the director's observation struck a responsive chord. From then on, Sammy trusted Shapiro, as he had Arthur Penn during *Golden Boy.*

The elimination of the clown makeup marked the first in a series of decisions that moved the revival away from the style of the original production. Out with the white face would also go Newley's frequent use of mime, more suited to his talents than Sammy's. An important secondary character, Littlechap's boss and father-in-law, who had been invisible in the Newley version became apparent in the form of a giant hand holding a cigar. Bill Byers and Joseph Lipman were hired to reorchestrate the score in a more modern vein. And set and costume designer Santo Loquasto replaced the basic circus tent environment with a very colorful, graffiti-laden structure, part of which was placed on a turntable so that it could be moved and shifted to suggest different locales. It was larger and more imposing than the original setting and more urban in its sensibility. Bricusse likened it to the paintings of Dutch artist Karel Appel, but it also resembled the fun, funky creations of the American artist Red Grooms. Furthermore, the cast included a much larger chorus of racially mixed young men and women, clad in vibrantly colored unisex jumpsuits. All these elements brought the show closer to the feeling and attitude of Shapiro's *Two Gentlemen of Verona*.

Another major change was the seemingly obvious decision to make Littlechap an African American negotiating the strata of race-conscious America instead of a Cockney upstart determined to rise in an extremely class-conscious Britain. At first glance, making this transition work without losing the essence of the show seemed insurmountable, as the original book and score had been steeped in English culture and mores and made broad use of Cockney slang. But Newley and Bricusse, having spent many years in America, were able to make the alterations themselves. Perhaps because the work remained in the hands of its creators, it made the transition from early sixties England to late seventies America with relative ease.

A final change saw the inclusion of a new Newley-Bricusse song, "Life Is a Woman" for the first act finale. This addition reflected the creators' desire to bring something musically fresh to the production, a wish no doubt shared by Sammy.

Taken individually, none of the changes in the production's content or style was overwhelming, but their cumulative weight resulted in a major rethinking of the show.

When rehearsals began in Los Angeles on April 24, 1978, Sammy threw himself into his role. Although he identified with Littlechap, he didn't want to just play himself. His goal was to personalize the character while retaining its symbolic universality. He also had to find ways to subtly move from youth to old age as the show progressed. Finally, he needed to reinvestigate the show's major ballads, seeing them in the context of a theater piece as opposed to material for a nightclub act. "He was truly magnificent to work with," recalled Shapiro. "He and I had a great time, because he loved being directed and was very willing to try anything. And things he didn't want to try—things he didn't think would work—he would try anyway, and when they worked onstage he was very happy and complimentary." "Mel had a wonderful effect on Sammy," said Marian Mercer, the tall blonde Tony Award–winning actress cast as Evie and Littlechap's other women. "He was helpful to him because Mel is a real theater director. In the wrong hands, this show can be terrible."

Mercer found Davis a pleasure to work with as well. "He's terrifically generous with people," she recalled. "He made the whole thing wonderful for the kids, the dancers. With gifts all over the place. It was just a wonderful, wonderful experience."

What emerged from Sammy's character work was something quite different from Newley's creation. His Littlechap was more of a cross between Stan Laurel, Charlie Chaplin, Jerry Lewis, and the Kingfish. At select moments, Davis plumbed his own inner feelings to evoke the everyman's emotional highs and lows; at other times, he opted for shtick and bits of business. But his main problem was that he couldn't memorize his lines and the lyrics to the patter songs. "I mean, it was like a television show," recalled Shapiro. "We had cue cards all over the rehearsal hall and assistants holding up cards with the lyrics on it." As a last-ditch effort, Davis moved out of the house on Summit Drive, renting a hotel apartment for himself and one security man. There, he finally committed his part to memory. To relax, he prepared meals for himself in his kitchen, having taken up cooking as a hobby about two years earlier.

The show premiered in San Diego on May 19. During the eight-day run, the company recorded the cast album, which was produced by Sammy's former associate, Mike Curb, for Warner/Curb Records. Then the show moved to the Shubert Theater in Los Angeles, where, according to Hilly Elkins, tickets for the entire three-week run sold out in a matter of hours. The local reviews were enthusiastic, with Dan Sullivan of the *Los Angeles Times* particularly effusive in his praise of both Davis and the production.

Although things were going well onstage and at the box office, a major problem had developed behind the scenes. Sammy had insisted that his personal conductor, George Rhodes, be hired as the show's musical director, and Elkins had agreed. But Bricusse and Newley didn't care for the conductor's work. In L.A., they insisted that he be replaced by their longtime associate, Ian Frazer. Under pressure, Davis relented. As a consequence, Rhodes was fired and Frazer took over when the show debuted at the Shubert. What no one anticipated was that George's wife, Shirley, would quit as Sammy's office manager to protest her husband's firing. In the wake of Shirley's departure, Sammy reconsidered the situation and demanded that Rhodes be rehired, refusing to perform until his friend was back in the pit. Without Davis, there was no show. So Ian was out and George was back in. And Shirley returned to Sammy's employ.

From Los Angeles, *Stop the World* moved on to the Aerie Crown in Chicago, the O'Keefe in Toronto, and, finally, Lincoln Center's New York State Theater, where it opened on August 3. All three facilities were huge. The New York State Theater, for example, seated 2,755, an appropriate capacity perhaps for its regular tenants, the New York City Ballet and the New York City Opera, but too large really for such an intimate musical. Elkins regretted selecting the facility. "If I had the choice over again," he said, "I would certainly have gone for a smaller venue. I think the show was a bit lost in the theater it was in."

It is doubtful, however, that a more intimate setting would have altered the musical's critical reception: the New York reviewers positively hated it. The *Post*'s Clive Barnes called it "a sort of disaster on wheels that overplays everything that was bad in the original, and neglects everything that was good." Douglas Watt at the *Daily News* described it as "an intolerably cute show, as well as an almost utterly senseless and lifeless one." The *New Yorker*'s Brendan Gill disliked it so much he didn't even stay for act two.

Given the show's limited run and Sammy's popularity, *Stop the World* performed well at the box office during its three weeks at Lincoln Center. But the original plan had been to reopen the show at a commercial Midtown venue in January, after Davis fulfilled several long-standing personal engagements, and to stay there through May. In light of the show's abysmal critical reception, this plan was abandoned, and *Stop the World* ended its run on August 27.

But the following month, the cast was reassembled at the behest of Bill Sargent. The man who had brought the original stage production of the musical to movie theaters was determined to do the same with the Davis version. No one on the production team shared Sargent's enthusiasm, but according to Elkins, the filmmaker kept upping his offer until neither Hilly nor Sammy felt they could turn him down.

As with all of Sargent's ventures, this was to be a filmed version of a stage production. Because the show was no longer running, Elkins booked the Terrace Theatre in Long Beach, California, where cinematographer David Myers captured the action live before an invited audience. Four months later, Sargent previewed the result under the title *Sammy Stops the World* at L.A.'s RKO Cinerama.

The response to the picture was so negative Sargent withdrew it and reedited the footage. In September 1979, a year after filming, the revised feature, cut by about an hour, debuted at the Charles Theater in Atlantic City. The 104-minute version played no better than the film's previous incarnation.

CHAPTER 26

Difficult Adjustments

After *Stop the World* closed, Sammy went back to his usual round of personal appearances, enlivened by the occasional TV gig. On April 9, 1979, he joined Steve Lawrence on the annual Oscar telecast, singing an eight-minute medley of songs overlooked by Academy voters. Four months later, he guest-starred for five episodes on one of his favorite soap operas, *One Life to Live*.

Of course, Davis made his usual stops in Vegas, Tahoe, and Reno as the seventies wound down. But, in November 1978, he also teamed with an old pal, drummer Buddy Rich, and Rich's orchestra for a half dozen concerts at the London Palladium, where, as always, he found a receptive audience. When Sammy played a week at the Westbury Music Fair the following May, he also received a warm reception, prompting *Newsday*'s Bill Kaufman to write, "Davis, 52, still has it. He put on his usual, predictably solid show with all the usual, predictable songs that everyone paid their money to hear."

Yes, he was still a draw. Yes, he still put on a good show. But gone was the flash, the incredible diversity, the unbelievable energy. This was a performer fully confident in his talent, bent on giving his audience, primarily fans of long standing, the set pieces they loved. The shows were slick and professional and enjoyable, but they weren't fresh or energetic. As the Vegas *Variety* stringer observed on Sammy's opening at Caesars in March 1979, "Sammy Davis, Jr., at 53 is now one of the most matured performers and growing blander by the month."

As the decade came to an end, Sammy's maturation showed in ways beyond his onstage repertoire. He still boasted a formidable array of rings, but gone was his outrageous manner of dress. In his opening set at the Westbury Music Fair, for example, he was decked out in a gray suit. He was still sporting a modified Afro, but that would soon give way to his former straight, slicked-down hairstyle. Sammy sheepishly confessed to

Burt Boyar that he needed longer, straight locks so that he could comb them over a bald spot on his crown.

Offstage, he was slowing down as well. "At one time I used to think that if you didn't go fingerpoppin' until 4 A.M. you were out of it," he said in mid-1978. "I go to Vegas now and cook in my room. I had room service come up one time." When he was working, he had to conserve his energy.

Reminders of younger, if not better, days came with two events at the end of the seventies. First, in December 1978, Sammy marked the twenty-fifth anniversary of his conversion to Judaism by celebrating Hanukkah with Rabbi William Berkowitz and a congregation of five thousand at B'Nai Jeshurun in New York.

Then, some two and a half months later, on March 1, 1979, Will Mastin was found dead in his Hollywood apartment. At nearly one hundred, the old hoofer had died from natural causes. At the funeral, Sammy cast his mind over the many moments he had shared with his "uncle," from his earliest years in vaudeville through his first major triumph at Ciro's, the auto accident, the opening at the Copa, and so forth. He chose to remember the good times rather than their sad final days together. "Will did not give me my talent," he said later, "or understand what to do with it, but he started me on the road and he taught me everything he could, which was a lot. If there had not been a Will Mastin, there might never have been a Sammy Davis, Jr."

By the end of the seventies, Davis had earned in excess of $50 million and was taking in more than $3 million a year. But he had frittered away the solvency Sy Marsh had managed to establish for him earlier in the decade. Part of the problem was his large payroll, which included his regular musicians and conductor, technicians and roadies, bodyguards, and office personnel. The fact that he was splitting his income fifty-fifty with Sy had to be a contributing factor as well.

But the biggest problem remained Sammy's excessive spending habits. He was fond of saying, "I love to live a particular life-style and I really don't give a damn, because I'm not going to wait until I'm 70 years old and decide to go on a vacation 'now that I've got all the money.' There will be no $5 million left to a cat. I'm gonna spend it all. Good times, except for what it takes to take care of the family for the rest of their lives. What am I gonna do, try to impress somebody by getting a 30-foot Chris Craft when I really want a 140-footer with six in the crew and a cook? Well, if you're gonna do it, *do it*. If you ain't gonna do it, don't do it."

Sammy's outrageous spending habits were well-known within the

Hollywood community and to the world at large. But when he heard Phyllis Diller quip on TV at the end of the decade that "Sammy has earned his success. He just hasn't paid for it," he decided he needed to prove to his friends that he was flush. His vehicle for doing so was a lavish dinner party to ring in the 1980s.

His ally in this project was Altovise. "The whole country's going to hear that we're broke," she told her husband after catching Diller's remark. By this point, Altovise cared every bit as much as Sammy about their public image.

In her mid-thirties, Altovise Gore had certainly grown into the role of Mrs. Davis. She could still be charming when she wished, but she could also play the Beverly Hills grand dame to a fare-thee-well, alienating many of Sammy's closest friends and colleagues. "I resented her because she was a user," said Sy Marsh. "She used him." One time when he and his wife, Molly, were in Mexico City with the Davises, they hooked up with the old mobster Sam Giancana, who had moved there to escape his problems back home. Giancana offered to show the two women some of the better shops in town. At a dress salon, Momo encouraged Molly and Alto to pick out anything they liked and he would foot the bill. Molly demurred, but finally selected something relatively inexpensive because Giancana simply wouldn't take no for an answer. "Altovise," Marsh said, "psshew. Took one, two, three, she loaded up."

Another of Davis' colleagues called the entertainer's wife "bad news," adding, "I have no respect for her at all." She also alienated one of Sammy's oldest friends, Arthur Silber, Jr., who, after years on his own, rejoined Davis' road staff for a tour of Australia in 1979. "The nicest thing I can say about her," Silber said, "is that she is the biggest cunt I ever met in my life, and that's about as dirty as I think I can get. She was high. She had affairs with all of her masseuses that came over. She was fucking everybody she could. Sammy didn't give a shit by then."

As Silber pointed out, Davis may have gotten off drugs, but Alto wasn't so fortunate. She had also developed an addiction to alcohol. "I feel bad for her," Mark Davis told this author. "She did get caught up in the lifestyle. You can't just completely blame her."

According to Lorna Luft, Alto's friends tried to help her get straight, arranging an intervention. "It was set up by some very good friends of Sam's," Luft recalled. "Sam knew about it. I knew about it. And it worked. The intervention worked. She went off and she did what she had to do. But then she bullshitted her way out of it." Tracey Davis maintained that Alto spent time at the Betty Ford Center and other rehab facilities, but each time returned to her former lifestyle.

Privately, Sammy acknowledged his role in Altovise's problems. According to Burt Boyar, "He said, 'I'm totally responsible. I married this nice, sweet girl. She was a good dancer. She came from a nice, wholesome family. I married her, I gave her a Rolls Royce with her name on the license plate. I began making a celebrity out of her. I'd go on television and bring on Altovise. I made her a personality, so she'd walk down the street and they'd say, "Hi, Altovise." ' And he said, 'I also introduced her to the dark side of life. I taught her the drinking and the drugging and the partying. I could walk away from all that, but she couldn't. I'm responsible.'"

In an effort to build on the career foundation Sammy provided, Alto managed to land supporting roles in two feature films, a low-budget sci-fi thriller, *Kingdom of the Spiders,* starring William Shatner, which was released in September 1977, and a 1980 musical called *Can't Stop the Music,* which also featured Valerie Perrine, Bruce Jenner, and the Village People. Allan Carr, a friend of Altovise, produced the latter. But, after *Can't Stop the Music,* her career stalled.

Tracey Davis, who turned eighteen in 1979, thought that part of her stepmother's motivation for trying to establish an independent career was her jealousy over her predecessor, May, who had been a successful movie star before marrying Sammy. In any event, Alto wanted to be taken seriously as an actress. Tracey remembered one evening when Altovise asked Sammy how one joined the Academy of Motion Picture Arts and Sciences; clearly, she was hoping she could become a member. Sammy told her that she needed to have a body of work, perhaps four or five films, to establish her validity with the prestigious body. Alto mentioned her features, to which her husband replied, "Yes, dear, but they have to be of some merit." At that point, he, Tracey, and whoever else was present started to laugh.

As the foregoing illustrates, Sammy could be terribly cruel to Alto, as could the members of his inner circle. "It got to be overwhelming," Leslie Uggams asserted. "And you make your decisions in life. You either stay or you go. And she tried to stay, but it was eating her up." Sally Struthers also sympathized with Alto's plight. "I absolutely adored her," the actress said, "but now that I look back I realize she was not very happy. I think it was not very easy being married to Sammy. It was not an easy marriage to someone who so compartmentalized his life."

As the years went by and they forged their own lives, Sam and Alto spent less and less time together. She told Chris Make of *Black Stars* in October 1980, "Sammy and I spend the holidays together—that certainly is important. I . . . have learned that in this business you cannot always be under each other's feet. It's good to get away."

Mel Shapiro, who only knew Sammy through *Stop the World*, was rather mystified by the entertainer's relationship with his wife. "I couldn't figure it out," the director said. "He went his way and I think she went her way. He fucked who he wanted, when he wanted. And they were sort of together and there was a show of some marital something or other, but she was very removed from the whole process."

As Shapiro asserted, Sammy's public pronouncements about Alto and his marriage remained positive. "My relationship with my wife cannot be touched," the entertainer told Jason Winters of *Black Stars* magazine in July 1978. "We have our arguments, oh yeah, some of them have been beauties, but there ain't going to be *no* divorce. I can tell you that."

His wife was sometimes a little more forthcoming. When she left Sammy to film *Kingdom of the Spiders* in Camp Verde, Arizona, thereby fueling rumors that her marriage was over, she conceded to the *National Enquirer* that there was, in the words of the tabloid's Barry Dillon, a definite "lack of communication between her and Sammy." Dillon added, "Altovise said it's tough to get through to her husband because of all the hangers-on who surround the dynamic entertainer."

Alto's relationship with Sammy's children contributed to her unhappiness. As Mark Davis put it, "We weren't so cordial to her. We did not give her any respect." He added jokingly, "She's the wicked step, so that's what you do. You're a kid. That's my job." Sammy's daughter, Tracey, went beyond a lack of cordiality. In her memoir, she admitted, "I once told Alto that she should never make Pop choose between her and me because she wouldn't win. After all, I was the only thing that ever came from him. . . . I was the only thing he ever made. There was a special bond there, a father-daughter bond, an unbreakable link."

Altovise struck back at Tracey occasionally and, to a lesser extent, Mark and Jeff, who were not as overtly hostile. Tracey cited the interval during the summer of 1978 when Sammy and Alto were staying at the Essex House in New York and he was taping his appearances on *One Life to Live*. Tracey and her brothers went east to visit their dad, all of them staying in the same suite. One day, Tracey went down to the hotel lobby without her room key. In the lobby, she saw Altovise heading for an elevator. Altovise gave her stepdaughter a blank look, boarded the elevator, and closed the door before the girl could join her. Catching another elevator, Tracey knocked on the door to the suite, but Altovise refused to answer, forcing Tracey to return to the lobby to get a spare key. When she asked her stepmother why she hadn't opened the door, Alto, a blank expression on her face, claimed she had no idea Tracey had been knocking.

Tracey cited another instance a few years later when Alto, who did Sammy's Christmas shopping, sent each of his children a piece of used clothing: a worn dungaree vest for Jeff, a dirty polo shirt for Mark, and a pair of used jeans for her. Her father had no knowledge of the bizarre gifts, and when he saw them, he shook his head in disbelief. Was this some kind of gag? he asked his daughter. Could there be jewelry or money or something stashed in the pockets? No, Tracey told him, there was nothing hidden inside the vest, shirt, or pants. Feeling terrible, he apologized. According to Tracey, Sammy and Altovise later had a major fight over this incident, resulting in Alto's eviction from their home for several weeks. Tracey never learned why Altovise had sent the bizarre gifts but attributed her behavior to the "pressures of being with a super-star, especially one who was rarely home."

For whatever reasons, there were many elements in her marriage to Sammy that left Altovise unfulfilled. That was between her and her hus-band. Then there was the way they and their marriage were viewed by the Hollywood community and the world at large. For reasons that even his closest friends didn't always understand, Sammy consistently went out of his way to praise Altovise to the media and affirm his abiding love for her. Shirley Rhodes explained his public posture by saying, "What is he going to do? Say that I married a drunk and a stupid woman? Or a loose woman? That makes him look bad." But, she added that when she saw him on TV, talking about her in glowing terms, "I used to throw up almost every time."

When it came to this, their public image, Sammy and Alto were united. Each believed in the importance of maintaining a positive impression, superficial though it may be.

Perhaps it was such a concern that led husband and wife to renew their wedding vows in a ceremony performed at the Bistro in Beverly Hills in September 1977. In contrast to their original wedding, held in Philadelphia with no friends or relatives in attendance, the Davises pledged their love the second time before a host of celebrity pals, including Lucille Ball, Sally Struthers, James Farrentino and his wife, Michelle Lee, George Hamilton, David Janssen, Danny Thomas, and Dick Martin. Rev. Jesse Jackson officiated.

Most certainly, public appearances were on Sammy and Alto's minds when they launched what came to be known as the Decade Party.

It started out as a sit-down dinner for twenty-five couples. But it soon grew to a major shindig for virtually everyone Sammy and Alto knew. Some four hundred people were invited in total. The Davises never expected everyone on the guest list to come, but they were wrong. The acceptances poured in from everywhere—New York, London, Paris. Suddenly faced with a major event, Sammy and Alto shrugged their shoulders and went with the flow, hiring two catering companies, two bands, a florist, and valets for parking. They purchased a new red silk Fabrice dress for Alto and overhauled the public rooms of their house. In case of rain, they also rented a tent supported by steel girders. By the time they were finished, they had spent roughly $75,000.

Not since the Academy Awards had Hollywood seen such a gathering, which included Liza Minnelli and her husband, Jack Haley, Jr.; Zsa Zsa Gabor; Rita Hayworth; O. J. Simpson; Kenny Rogers; Robert Culp; David Janssen; Robert Blake; Muhammad Ali; Dick Van Patten; Jack Albertson; Greg Morris; Fred MacMurray and his wife, June Haver; and Ricardo Montalban. As Sammy later said, "The cross section of faces was astonishing—directors, producers, the sporting world people, and the superstars, the Old Guard and the new hot kids, obscure white and black actors, the main meat-and-potatoes television people."

"It was extravagant beyond belief," recalled Lorna Luft, one of the guests. "Everything had to be the most expensive, the biggest, the best, whatever." Sammy tried to enjoy himself, but the outrageous cost of it all was never far from his mind. The following day, the guests compared notes about the sumptuous gathering on the phone while local columnists rehashed the bash in gushing detail for their readers, some labeling it "the party of the century." Thank you bouquets and telegrams flooded the house for days. Sammy was happy that everyone had such a good time, but, for once, he was embarrassed by his own ostentatiousness. He knew full well there were people of real wealth in Hollywood who could afford to throw such a gala, but he wasn't one of those fat cats. When he needed every dime he could get, he had instead spent a fortune to prove to strangers that he wasn't strapped for money.

Aside from Davis himself, no one was more sickened by the irony than Sy Marsh. "It was a wild party," Marsh told his partner. "Except the hangover's going to last a year."

As it turned out, the "hangover" lasted for the rest of Sammy's life because readers of the society pages weren't the only ones to peruse the stories about the Decade Party. The bash came to the attention of the Internal Revenue Service as well.

Davis had been on the agency's radar screen for some time. In 1966, he had, in fact, been tendered a bill for $227,483 after the IRS disallowed deductions from his returns dating back to the end of the fifties and early sixties. But the situation in 1980 was far more serious, for Sammy and Sy had invested hundreds of thousands of dollars in several tax shelter schemes, including one with John DeLorean and another with Geo Dynamics Oil and Gas Company of Jenkintown, Pennsylvania. These deductions were disallowed in the mid-seventies.

On the advice of their attorneys, Marsh and Davis decided to contest the decision, but the problem was dragging on and on. Meanwhile, the interest penalties on the nonpaid debt continued to accrue. Shortly after the Decade Party, the IRS informed Marsh of plans to seize his Beverly Hills estate as well as Sammy's. "The lawyers can't hold them off anymore," Sy told his partner, who was performing at Harrah's Tahoe at the time. "They're threatening to put a lock on your house, and mine, and then sell them at a public auction if we don't come up with a million four and fast."

When they hung up, Sammy was sick. Gripped with panic, he called his partner back and told him, "I'm finished, Sy. It's over. Atlas can't hold up the fuckin' world anymore. I'm disappearing. I'm getting out of the business. I've worked too long and I've failed." He dashed out of the hotel, determined not to do his show that night. His friend Doug Bushausen, vice president of entertainment for Harrah's, chased after him. "He caught up with me," Sammy recalled, "and I threw my arms around him and I cried all the water of the dry tears I'd been shedding for weeks, months." Together they walked back to the hotel, and he went ahead with his scheduled performances.

As if Sammy's problem with the IRS weren't bad enough, he was named in a $23 million lawsuit at roughly the same time. The suit stemmed from his and Sy's involvement in Daniel Boone Chicken Farms, a start-up operation of fast-food restaurants intended to compete with Kentucky Fried Chicken. The venture failed to get off the ground, resulting in a total loss for its investors, who then sued the company's principals. Sammy was named a defendant because the plaintiffs' attorneys argued that his involvement in the venture led some people to invest who might not have done so otherwise. Representing him in this matter was a Cleveland attorney named John Climaco, whom Davis had met through their mutual association with the Highway Safety Foundation. After successfully adjudicating the case on Sammy's behalf, Climaco became a close friend as well as Sammy's regular attorney.

In fact, the IRS didn't exercise its threat to seize the Marsh and Davis houses—at least, not then. But the near-miss made it evident that Syni was no longer working. So, too, did the partners' investment in TAV, the Daniel Boone Chicken Farms, their disastrous involvement in a quail breeding farm in Grapevine, Texas, and other failed ventures. Through Climaco, Davis negotiated a termination of the partnership and, on February 20, Sammy and Sy formally ended their business relationship.

In the wake of Sy's departure, Sammy returned to the William Morris Agency to handle his professional opportunities. He looked inward, to Shirley Rhodes, to manage his personal finances and day-to-day business affairs. Rhodes was already running his office and was among his closest confidants, having emerged as the single most important member of the entertainer's inner circle, outside of Murphy Bennett. Although she'd had no business experience prior to her association with Sammy, she possessed a sharp mind, good common sense, a willingness to learn, and an uncompromising honesty—with Sammy and with everyone else. Those skills, and her deep, abiding love for her boss, enabled her to serve him well for the rest of his life, after which she took on the thankless task of being executrix of his estate.

As for Sammy's problems with the IRS, he later indicated that he met with agents Charles Callahan and Bill Byron in the wake of the agency's threat to take his home and worked out an initial good-faith payment of between $50,000 and $100,000, followed by six months' worth of installments on the balance. Thereafter, he arranged an advance from Harrah's that enabled him to make a down payment of $200,000. He also promised himself that he would cut down on his personal spending. But his problems with the government persisted for the rest of his life.

Despite his short-term promise to control his spending habits, one thing was clear: Sammy was totally incapable of maintaining his pledge for long. As his friend Sally Struthers put it, "He was his own worst enemy with money. He couldn't go through it fast enough. It wasn't just for things for himself. It was for things for other people. Absolute strangers, people he just met, his dear friends, his wife, his children, his house staff, his cronies." Sy Marsh also acknowledged Sammy's generosity, saying, "There is no single human being that is kinder, nicer, more considerate than Sammy Davis. To a fault. If he ran into somebody he knew who was down-and-out, a little busted, and they said, 'Sam, I could use a little money,' he'd say, 'Let me call Sy,' and he'd call me and say, 'There's so and so here, give him $5,000 or give her $5,000.' He could never turn anybody away." His largesse extended to institutions as well as individuals, with civil rights and Jewish organizations at the forefront of his generosity. The result was that no matter how much Sammy was earning, regardless of who was managing his finances, he was always waiting for the next big check to arrive. "I remember once when he got sick," Leslie Bricusse noted, "the only time as a performer when I knew he got sick. Altovise called me on the second day and said, 'What are we going to do for money?' And that's when I looked at the five hundred gold watches. He had no financial stability whatsoever."

PART FIVE

"Now I Like Me"

CHAPTER 27

"I've Never Felt Better"

Three months after the breakup of Sammy's partnership with Sy Marsh, the entertainer was reunited with another old friend, Dean Martin. What brought the former Rat Packers together was a big-budget, star-studded chase picture, Sammy's first major feature since *Sweet Charity* in 1968.

The Cannonball Run was inspired by a real-life cross-country race, the Cannonball Sea-to-Shining-Sea Memorial Trophy Dash. The race extended from New York to California, with the participants, bound by no rules, freely mixing with ordinary travelers on public thoroughfares. Named for Erwin "Cannonball" Baker, a daredevil endurance driver of the 1920s and 1930s, the highly illegal contest had been held sporadically five times between its inception in 1971 and the point when filming commenced.

With the encouragement of his friend director Hal Needham, the race's founder, writer Brock Yates, turned the anything-goes race into the basis of a screenplay, a loose amalgam of gags, stunts, and romance, with the action frequently shifting among the contest's fun-loving, glory-driven speedsters.

The Cannonball Run starred Burt Reynolds. Then the hottest star in America, Reynolds was known for his good-ole-boy roles in *Smokey and the Bandit* and *Hooper*, both directed by Needham. His friend and frequent costar, Dom DeLuise, was cast as his sidekick, with Farrah Fawcett as his love interest. Sammy and Dean were paired as two Vegas hustlers who enter the race disguised as priests, a gambit apparently employed in real life during one of the Cannonball runs.

Filming began in Georgia in mid-May 1980 and continued in Vegas and the greater Los Angeles area. For actors like Sammy and Dean, who hated multiple takes, Hal Needham was the ideal director. Using multiple cameras for each sequence, the former stunt coordinator eliminated many of the redundancies of shooting movies, including separate setups for individual close-ups. Moreover, he encouraged his players to ad-lib and to enjoy themselves while the cameras turned; he figured, if the actors were having fun, audiences would enjoy themselves, too. Said the picture's first assistant director, Bill Coker, "This was one of the most cooperative and incident-free projects that I've ever been associated with in thirty years in the business. The stars could do no wrong. Basically, they all came out and did shtick."

Between setups, the stars tended to gather in Martin's trailer; during the off hours, they typically met in Burt Reynolds' hotel suite, with, in Reynolds' words, "everyone pretty well lubricated, trading stories until about three a.m." It was in the wee hours of the morning, the star added, that "Sammy really got going, as if he was about to do the first of two shows that night, which prompted Dean to say, 'Oh, da little guy's going to sing again. Oh shit. I'm going to bed now.'"

A few years later, Davis told Roderick Mann of the *Los Angeles Times* that doing *The Cannonball Run* was the most fun he'd had since the Rat Pack pictures.

Of course, working with Dean was particularly fun. His and Sammy's roles were no more demanding than those in *Ocean's Eleven*, *Sergeants 3*, or *Robin and the 7 Hoods*, and Dean, who was not in particularly good health at the time, hadn't made a film in six years. Being reunited with his pallie brought out the best in him. "They were cracking each other up all the time," said Bill Coker. "The characters they played were a reflection of their relationship."

The picture wrapped in early July, debuting the following June on a record 1,682 movie screens. For the most part, the critics hated the often tasteless, crash-laden, stunt-riddled gagfest, but audiences found it perfect mindless summer fare. By October, *The Cannonball Run* had taken in more than $62 million domestically. Eventually, it would gross a like amount in other outlets around the world, making it far and away the most financially successful film in Sammy's career.

In September, William Morrow and Company published Sammy's valentine to the motion picture industry, *Hollywood in a Suitcase*. The Boyars had moved to Spain, so Sammy hired a British ghost writer, Simon Regan, to work with him on the project. The thirty-eight-year-old Regan brought with him eight years of experience as an investigative reporter with a British publication, *News of the World*.*

*Later in life, Regan turned himself into a muckraker-cum-conspiracy theorist, turning out poorly received books about various members of the royal family, including Prince Charles, and founding a scandal sheet called *Scallywag*. He died on August 8, 2000.

To gather material for their book, Regan traveled with Sammy off and on for a couple of years, drawing on his insights about a broad spectrum of cinema lore and history. He collected stories of the greats with whom Sammy had worked and socialized, and behind-the-scenes anecdotes from Davis' own checkered film career. Much of the text was autobiographical, but, in contrast to *Yes I Can,* Davis saw this book as light entertainment. He wasn't interested in delving too deeply into his own psyche or his emotional upheavals. In a chapter on the Rat Pack, for example, he mentioned the 1960 Democratic presidential convention but glossed over the boos that assailed him during the singing of the national anthem. The only departure from his airy approach came in the chapter called "Black Cats," a major portion of which was devoted to his 1972 trip to Vietnam. As this instance suggests, not all of the book's material was film-related, but what held the loosely organized chapters together was the author's passion for the big screen. The title derived from his willingness to carry reels of film with him on his travels in the days before home videos so that he would never be without some of his favorites.

Most literary critics greeted *Hollywood in a Suitcase* with some disdain. The *L.A. Times'* Jack Slater, for one, described it as "Prosaic, superficial . . . a baggage of names that never rises above name-dropping." Nevertheless, the book was a success; it sold out its first printing of seventy-five thousand copies and went back to press, later enjoying a second life as a mass-market paperback.

Appropriately, the publication of Sammy's tribute to movies came during his fiftieth year in show business. He marked the occasion with several events in 1980. On June 12, for example, he was the guest of honor at a benefit at the Century Plaza Hotel in Los Angeles to launch the Sammy Davis, Jr. Freedom from Hunger Fund, sponsored by the Friends of Tel Aviv University. More than fifteen hundred guests paid $200 apiece to see an impressive roster of entertainers and speakers: Shecky Greene, Bea Arthur, Danny Thomas, Jack Carter, Redd Foxx, Sean Connery, Henry Mancini, James Farentino, and mistress of ceremonies Dionne Warwick. Following a short film retrospective of Sammy's career put together by Jack Haley, Jr., the entertainer received an honorary fellow degree from the university. He then thanked his guests by singing "With a Song in My Heart," "New York, New York," and "Mr. Bojangles."

Some two months later, Sammy offered a one-night, fiftieth anniversary concert at the Music Center in downtown Los Angeles, his first appearance in the Dorothy Chandler Pavilion. Once again, the occasion was a benefit, this time on behalf of Pasadena's Therapeutic Living Center for the Blind; the event raised more than $50,000 for the center.

Finally, on November 25, the Friars Club took note of Sammy's fiftieth anniversary, presenting him with its Life Achievement Award at a gala dinner for more than one thousand in the International Room at the Beverly Hilton Hotel. The speakers included Jimmy Stewart, Johnny Carson, Jack Lemmon, Ben Vereen, Henny Youngman, Dick Shawn, Burt Reynolds, Don Rickles, Slappy White, Diahann Carroll, and mayor Tom Bradley, with Milton Berle serving as toastmaster. Many of the speakers took humorous potshots at the guest of honor. Carson, for one, quipped, "We've been celebrating Sammy Davis' 50th year in show business for about 8 years now and we're all a little sick of it." Berle called Sammy "the illegitimate love child of Menachem Begin and Pearl Bailey." When Sammy finally responded, he chose not to make light of the occasion, saying instead, "I never thought I'd live to see a day I would be so honored like tonight. As I look around this room, I see no one who is a stranger to me. I see only friends. I see people who came and said, 'Hey, I love you.'"

Of course, most entertainers who manage to sustain fifty-year careers are in their seventies when their golden moment arrives. Davis, having started at roughly three, was merely middle-aged. He may have lost the incredible vigor of his youth, but he showed no signs of retiring as he entered his second half-century as a performer. For one thing, he couldn't afford to retire. For another, he still lived for the moments when he could look out from center stage and see hordes of people loving him, applauding him, showering him with approval.

He found that his effort to eliminate drugs was having a decidedly positive effect on his work and on his attitude. "I've never felt better," he told the *Los Angeles Herald Examiner* in October 1980. "I've never sounded better, and I've never cared more about the business and what I'm doing. Performing is fun for me again."

Davis held onto his 1980 momentum over the next several years, combining his regular appearances at Caesars, Lake Tahoe, Reno, and elsewhere with a variety of interesting new venues.

On March 10, 1981, for example, he headlined a gala at the Atlanta Civic Center to show his support for the city in the wake of the murder or disappearance of twenty-one African American children. The sold-out event, which was Davis' idea, raised more than $148,000 to help Mayor Maynard Jackson finance the police investigation into the crimes. Frank Sinatra was also on hand for the gala.

In June, Sammy played two nights at the Melody Fair in North

Tonawanda, New York, his first appearance in the Buffalo area in seven years. A few weeks later, he did a series of seven shows at the Apollo-Victoria Theatre in London, then hopped over to Paris to sing at a benefit at the Lido. As his visit coincided with the Paris opening of *The Cannonball Run,* he also participated in the premiere festivities. He brought 1981 to a close with a two-week stint at the Hilton in Sydney, where the top ticket price for the dinner show, $54, set a house record. Taking note of this, Sammy promised the opening night audience, "You're gonna get your money's worth."

In April 1982, Davis played Heinz Hall in Pittsburgh, his first engagement in the Pennsylvania city in fifteen years. Sharing the bill with Leslie Uggams, he tap danced more than he had in years, on the venerable tune from *No, No, Nanette,* "Tea for Two." He also devoted more time to his impressions, which he introduced in "As Time Goes By." Although they remained crowd pleasers with the older set, Sammy curiously stuck to the same stars he'd been doing for decades—Bogie, Cagney, and Stewart—as if he were unaware of impressionists like Rich Little, who mimicked contemporary stars. A week later in Lake Tahoe, Sammy put even more dancing into the act and took a turn on several musical instruments. A surprised Ruth Robinson told readers of the *Hollywood Reporter,* "I've seen him 30 or 40 times over the years and have never seen some of the things he did this night. Admitting to 57 years, he donned a pair of tap shoes and cut loose with some razzle-dazzle tapping that would have done a 20-year-old Sammy proud." On the bill with Davis at Harrah's was jazz great Count Basie and his Orchestra.

July found Sammy on a brief tour of Israel, which he called "my religious homeland." A guest of the Israeli Association for Soldiers' Welfare, he toured several hospitals, chatting with and entertaining men and women wounded in the fighting with Lebanon. He also visited strife-torn Beirut. In an act of incredible generosity, he took the names and phone numbers of Los Angeles area relatives of the soldiers he encountered and, with no fanfare or publicity, called them when he returned home. His trip climaxed in a meeting with Prime Minister Menachem Begin, which Sammy called "the greatest experience of my life."

Davis was almost as effusive about his participation in Macy's annual Thanksgiving Day parade three months later. As he told the *New York Daily News,* his ride on one of the floats down Broadway to Herald Square reminded him of his Harlem youth, when he didn't have enough money for subway fare. Then, in a revealing comment, he added, "All my life I've been accepted by an audience, but today I really made it. I was accepted by my people, the people of New York, and I wasn't singing or dancing or acting to an audience that was responding to me. This is different. I was frozen up there in the cold wind, but I got warm because of the warmth of the people."

He warmed himself up the following month, vacationing in Hawaii. This respite came after a week of benefit performances at the Fairmont Hotel in San Francisco, Sammy's Christmas gift to those in need, with a different charity the beneficiary each night. He ended 1982 with a New Year's Eve performance at the Hawaiian Village Hotel.

Concurrent with Sammy's personal appearances during the 1982 holiday season came his first, and only, big-screen animated feature, which debuted in theaters on November 19.

Based on *Heidi,* Johanna Spyri's popular 1880 novel about an enchanting orphan, *Heidi's Song* was a labor of love for its producers, William Hanna and Joseph Barbera. Best known for their TV cartoon series, including *The Flintstones, The Huckleberry Hound Show,* and *Scooby Doo, Where Are You?,* Hanna-Barbera had previously produced a few low-budget, minimal quality features, based on their popular TV characters, Yogi Bear and the Flintstones, and E. B. White's *Charlotte's Web.* But, with *Heidi's Song,* they aimed for something better. Accordingly, they budgeted the production at $8 million and paired lyricist Sammy Cahn with Burton Lane, the composer of the musicals *Finian's Rainbow* and *On a Clear Day You Can See Forever,* for a Broadway-style score.

The result, which took more than eight years and involved seventeen full-time animators, was disappointing. Some critics found the film saccharine in the extreme. Others considered it simply another extension of the producers' Saturday morning television fare. No one saw it as a worthy complement to animated features produced elsewhere.

Davis was the single stand-out among the cast members, playing, of all things, the ringleader of a gang of rats. Like Fagin in Lionel Bart's *Oliver!,* the Head Ratte instructs his gang in the art of thievery, a musical sequence that found him and his band sporting hats and waving their tails and high-stepping in unison like the Rockettes. According to Richard Gertner of *Motion Picture Product Digest,* Sammy stole "the show, upstaging the main plot."

Sammy had been able to maintain his frenzied schedule during the early eighties because his health permitted him to do so. After the illnesses of the mid- to late-1970s, he seemed back on track physically. But this changed on March 13, 1983, when he was rushed to the intensive care unit of the Washoe Medical Center in Reno, Nevada. "He had been working with the flu and developed pneumonia," said Arnold Lipsam, David Steinberg's partner, who had taken over as Davis' publicist. He was released from the hospital after nearly a week. But this wouldn't bring an end to his physical problems that year.

The following month, on April 9, 1983, he appeared on an episode of Aaron Spelling's latest hit series, *Fantasy Island*. Outside of his annual stints on the *Jerry Lewis Telethon* and two or three visits to *The Tonight Show* each year, Sammy had kept a relatively low profile on television during the early eighties. In March 1980, he reprised his role of ex-con Chip Warren on *One Life to Live* and appeared the following month on Redd Foxx's NBC sitcom, *Sanford and Son*. He returned to the ABC soap a third time in May 1981, his only major television engagement that year. In October 1982, he joined the cast of another of his favorite daytime serials, *General Hospital*, playing the recovering alcoholic father of the character portrayed by series regular Bryan Phillips. But that was the sum total of his TV acting during a three-year period.

Davis' infrequent small-screen appearances didn't reflect a waning interest in television but were indicative of changes in the medium. Variety shows were virtually a thing of the past. Sitcoms were hot, as were glitzy prime-time soaps and police dramas, but the target markets for these programs were the age groups with the greatest buying power, teens to thirty-somethings. At fifty-plus, Davis didn't have the right demographics.

Occasionally, through, a show came along that appealed to older audience members, and then he was a welcome guest. Such was the case with *Fantasy Island*. The sixty-minute drama, which had debuted on ABC in January 1978, was set at a plush resort on a remote tropical paradise. Each week, the resort played host to several guests whose lives are somehow unfulfilled. Sammy's episode, entitled "Edward," cast him as a mogul who places business success over family throughout his life, something to which Davis could relate, and longs to capture what he missed in his personal relationships.*

Like his *Fantasy Island* character, Sammy sought a rather dramatic change in his life, albeit in the professional arena. In April 1983, after nearly eight years with Caesars Palace, he left the prestigious Vegas resort for the far less imposing Aladdin.

"Playing Caesars was a mistake," the entertainer said a few years later. "The room was too big. I was a hero for filling the place, but it couldn't last, and then it would be 'Sammy isn't making it.' To fill that room six days a week, two shows a night, with fourteen hundred people, you need

---

*Davis would make a second guest appearance on *Fantasy Island* on May 12, 1984. The episode, entitled "Bojangles and the Dancer," was set in the 1930s and told the story of a would-be dancer who wants to meet the legendary hoofer, played by Davis.

a hot record or a TV series. Or you should have a major divorce. Or be a man just turned into a girl. But a performer like myself should play small rooms. Five hundred seats. Fill that twice a night at $25 per head for two drinks and you're not exactly out of the business."

After nearly four decades as a Vegas headliner, Sammy knew all the tricks for filling a showroom. A lavish tipper, he ensured that every bellhop, car attendant, dealer, and bartender in whatever resort he was playing would sing his praises to the guests. In addition, he would typically throw a sumptuous party for the local cab drivers whenever he hit town, knowing that, in return, they'd recommend his act to passengers seeking an evening's entertainment.

But even with such help, putting paying customers in the seats night after night was becoming harder to do. Like prime-time TV, Vegas was changing. The days when the town served as a magnet for high rollers and East Coast sophisticates were rapidly drawing to a close, thanks in large part to the legalization of casino-style gambling in Atlantic City in 1976, plus the rising popularity of state-sponsored lotteries around the country. "Atlantic City had a real impact on Las Vegas," asserted film historian David Thomson in his 1999 book on Nevada. "Although gambling revenue built Vegas, in the early eighties the rate of increase was slowing. There were so many other ways and places for Americans to gamble. Las Vegas was having to compete with theme parks, foreign travel, and the extensive American leisure industry. Moreover, the town had become safer and more earnest, there were those who said it was duller. The great entertainers of the fifties and sixties were less and less evident. Instead, Las Vegas had become the home or refuge of entertainers like Wayne Newton, Paul Anka, and Don Rickles, who seemed to play fewer places outside Nevada."

To replace the diminishing lure of the gaming tables, the town increasingly sought to draw entire families to the desert, offering recreational amenities for everyone, with a special emphasis on the youngsters. In this, Circus Circus pointed the way toward the future. When it opened in October 1968, it featured within its circus-tent-shaped environs not just the usual slots, roulette wheels, and craps tables, but also midway-style rides and activities for kids. The casino was so successful its owners added a hotel to the site in 1973.

The next stage in this trend—gigantic full-family theme resorts—was still a few years away. For the moment, Sammy was content to abandon the gigantic Circus Maximus. The Aladdin had opened in 1966, four months earlier than Jay Sarno's paean to ancient Rome, but its Baghdad Theatre could hold no more than 850 patrons when pushed to the absolute limits. Davis was invigorated by the move.

Immediately following his debut at the Aladdin, Sammy opened at the Wilshire Theatre in Los Angeles, marking his first one-man show in his hometown in eight years. "Do you realize how much I'll save in room charges alone?" he jokingly asked Johnny Carson when he dropped by *The Tonight Show* during the run.* In contrast to Davis' usually favorable notices, his stint at the Wilshire Theatre drew some serious objections from the *Los Angeles Times*' Dennis Hunt, who found the show's pace a bit "languid," would have preferred more dancing, and was annoyed that Sammy restricted his impressions to celebrities who were either dead or long since retired. Otherwise, he found the ninety-minute outing "a pleasant, low-key affair."

That summer, Sammy took a few weeks off from his round of live performances to join Dean Martin, Burt Reynolds, and much of the original *Cannonball Run* gang for a sequel. Hal Needham was back as director, so the same joie de vivre that had prevailed three years earlier colored the atmosphere in Tucson, where the entirety of *Cannonball Run II* was shot.

Newcomers to the cast included Henry Silva and Shirley MacLaine. For Sammy, being with Silva, Shirley, *and* Dean was like having a mini–Rat Pack reunion. After hours, Reynolds and the others did their best to fill in for Peter, Joey, and Buddy Lester, but no one could take Frank's place. So, around July 20, the Chairman of the Board himself showed up, to film a scene in which he comes to the aid of the Cannonballers after a gang of mobsters kidnap one of their own.

For the rest of the cast and crew, working with a legend like Frank Sinatra was nerve-wracking, although Sinatra, in good spirits, tried to put his colleagues at ease. As for Sammy and Dean, they were just happy to spend a day hanging out with their friend, as was Shirley MacLaine.

In deference to Toho-Towa, a Japanese film importer and one of the picture's financial backers, *Cannonball Run II* had its world premiere in Tokyo in December 1983. When the sequel opened in the United States six months later, it failed to rouse either the critics, who hated it even more than the original, or the moviegoing public. As a consequence, the $20 million caper grossed a mere $62 million, roughly half of its predecessor's take. This disappointing return put an end to any possibility of a *Cannonball Run III*.

* * *

*The Tonight Show moved permanently from New York to Los Angeles in 1972. Ed McMahon told this author that Davis generously gave McMahon the use of his Summit Avenue home during the transition, free of charge, enabling Carson's sidekick to take his time finding a permanent place to live.

As soon as Davis finished his scenes, he was back on the road, starting with a concert at the Meadow Brook Festival in Rochester, Michigan on August 3, 1983. On that occasion, as with numerous others in the eighties, he shared the bill with the manic comic Rip Taylor. In keeping with the practice he'd established several years earlier, Sammy came out at the top of the show, with no introduction. After performing for an hour, he brought on Taylor for a half hour. After an intermission, Davis returned for another ninety minutes. This approach served two purposes: first, it freed Taylor from having to cope with audience anticipation for the headliner. Second, it allowed Sammy to perform at a peak energy level by breaking his set in two, with a breather in between.

From Michigan, Davis went on to Harrah's new resort-casino in Atlantic City and then, in September, he returned to the Aladdin, where *Variety* found him "in top form." On November 2, he was back on Broadway for a two-week limited engagement at the Gershwin Theater. In contrast to his solo appearance in the same venue nearly a decade earlier (when it was called the Uris), Davis shared the marquee with another high-powered performer, Bill Cosby.

Sammy first met the popular stand-up comedian, twelve years his junior, in the 1960s, when Cosby was a hit on America's coffeehouse circuit. But they started to become friends after they did a benefit together around 1980. By then, Cosby had broken TV's color barrier, becoming the first African American to costar in a regular weekly drama, *I, Spy.* He'd gone on to his own sitcom, the short-lived *Bill Cosby Show,* and seven feature films, including two with Sidney Poitier, *Uptown Saturday Night* and *Let's Do It Again* and Neil Simon's *California Suite.*

In the case of *Two Friends,* the show at the Gershwin, Cosby came on first, but Sammy joined him after only a few minutes. Following a bit of banter, some of which was ad-libbed, Davis again yielded the stage to the comedian, returning in the second half for his own turn. Typically, Cosby would show up to wreak havoc with Sammy's rendition of "Mr. Bojangles."

As most of the critics observed, the program consisted of little more than the entertainers' regular acts plus a bit of chatter. The *Times'* Mel Gussow found the evening "overlong" but also noted that it gave "New Yorkers a chance to see Mr. Davis on Broadway again and to catch up with Mr. Cosby, a genuine humorist and archetypal family man."

Early the following year, Davis and Cosby would take their show to Harrah's Lake Tahoe and Caesars Palace. By then, they'd become fast friends. Sammy enjoyed his onstage chemistry with the comedian, but he valued the Coz's support behind the scenes even more. Although he'd been drug-free for a number of years, Sammy was still wrestling with his alcohol problem during their appearance in New York. He later described himself as 150 degrees into a 360-degree lifestyle change. "And Bill was there for me," he said, "and he was supportive. Never dictatorial. . . . He knew what I was going through, and we never discussed it until I had made the complete 360 on my own. And then he said to me, 'I'm so proud of you.'"

By the end of 1983, Sammy had completed the turn, but it took a dramatic wake-up call to effect the change.

The transition started immediately following his Broadway show with Cosby, when Davis was booked into Harrah's Tahoe. He loved playing the mountainous Nevada resort, but somehow he couldn't get energized for this engagement. He attributed part of his problem to poor dieting. Self-conscious about a small paunch emerging around his middle, he was trying to lose weight by restricting himself to a single meal a day, but this regimen left him somewhat listless and tired. He was also drinking too many vodka and Cokes.

One evening, nothing seemed to work. "I couldn't lift the show off the ground," he recalled. "I was trying with every trick I knew, everything that had ever worked for me, but I just couldn't excite them. . . . I was functioning at thirty percent. . . . I was embarrassed to be performing like this." After about forty-five minutes, he quit trying. Apologizing to the audience for performing so poorly, he left the stage—after picking up everyone's tab, an act of generosity that cost him roughly $17,000.

In December, when he opened at Harrah's in Reno, he still felt out of sorts. In fact, he was in worse shape because he'd tripped one night while removing his clothes for bed and injured his ribs on an end table. For a week or so, he tried to ignore the pain in his side, but finally it became so excruciating he asked Murphy to take him to the emergency room at Reno's Warsaw Medical Center. There, an internist told him he had "a touch of jaundice, with overt signs of liver damage."

Postponing his Reno engagement, Sammy returned to L.A., where he checked himself into Cedars Sinai Hospital. There, his physician, Gerald Blankfort, informed him that his problem stemmed from his liver, which had become so swollen that excess fluid had entered his stomach. Lancing his stomach produced three and a half quarts of fluid. Fortunately, the discharge was nontoxic, but Sammy's liver was so damaged he had to stop drinking immediately or he would die.

He was capable of stopping. As Blankfort reminded him, he had gone without alcohol during his hospitalization and not suffered any physical effects from the withdrawal, thereby indicating that his addiction was mental, not physical. As Blankfort put it, "All you have is a lifetime habit. But you can beat that."

The problem was that Sammy loved to drink. Liquor was such a part of his life that from the moment he woke up, a drink was by his side. A sip here, a sip there, and, by most nights, he had a nice buzz on. He would miss that, but he took his predicament to heart. As he told Alto-vise shortly thereafter, "I'll miss booze. I'll miss it a lot. But as soon as you see a gallon of liquid drained out of your stomach you stop. I'm not ready to die. I can't afford it." Thereafter, a soft drink, Strawberry Crush, became his libation of choice.

Sammy was extremely proud of his decision to get off the sauce. But David Steinberg told this author that despite the entertainer's public pro-nouncements about being clean and sober after 1983, he never cut out booze entirely. At the very least, Davis moderated his intake enough that he lived another seven and a half years without further liver problems.

One of his biggest concerns at the outset was how the absence of booze would fit in with his swinging image. He casually introduced the subject onstage when he returned to Reno at the very end of December 1983, poking fun at himself for drinking soda pop. When he got a sur-prising round of applause, he added, "Frankly, I'm enjoying being straight. It's fun to wake up and know what I did the night before." When that earned him another hand, he went with the flow, offering a few more jokes about his age and his drinking. The response continued to be warm and enthusiastic.

Later, back in his room, he decided that perhaps the time had come to accept his age. He'd certainly fought against it for long enough. Even better, it seemed that his fans were prepared to see him in a new guise, maybe even preferred an honest fifty-plus performer to a never-say-die but over-the-hill swinger. As Davis put it later, "We were friends grow-ing older together. They wanted what I *am*, not an imitation of what I'd been."

CHAPTER 28

Turning Sixty

Six months after the premiere of *Cannonball Run II,* Sammy was back on America's movie screens. MGM's *That's Dancing* paid tribute to stellar hoofing on film, from the silent era to the MTV videos of Michael Jackson. Unlike its predecessors, 1974's *That's Entertainment!* and 1976's *That's Entertainment, Part II,* whose clips were drawn solely from MGM's own archives, *That's Dancing* featured footage from a wide range of sources. These were divided into thematic segments, each hosted by an appropriate celebrity: Gene Kelly, Mikhail Baryshnikov, Ray Bolger, Liza Minnelli, and Davis. Sammy's portion considered legendary hoofers of the thirties, including Bolger, Fred Astaire and Ginger Rogers, Bill Robinson and Shirley Temple, and Eleanor Powell.

Sammy shot his sequence for *That's Dancing* in October 1983, but the film's producers Kip Niven and Davis' good friend Jack Haley, Jr., took more than a year to winnow their selection of clips. Finally, the picture was released on January 15, 1985.

Although the documentary's narrative was a bit syrupy and pretentious, the vintage footage was full of gems. Unfortunately, fans of movie musicals were a diminishing breed by 1985. Consequently, *That's Dancing* performed poorly at the box office. MGM would wait nearly a decade before releasing a fourth and final compilation, *That's Entertainment III,* put together by the associate producer and film editor of *That's Dancing,* Bud Friedgen and Michael J. Sheridan.

Two months after the premiere of *That's Dancing,* Sammy was back in Vegas at a new home, the Crystal Room of the Desert Inn.

Far older than either the Aladdin or Caesars Palace or, for that matter, the Sands, the Desert Inn opened in April 1950, three years after Sammy's debut at the El Rancho Vegas. Only the fifth resort on the Strip, it was launched by gambler Wilber Clark but completed—when Clark ran out of money—by Moe Dalitz and the Cleveland mob. By the time of Davis' debut, the Inn was owned by Howard Hughes' Summa Corporation and almost nothing of its original structures remained. (Summa would, in turn, sell the property to Kirk Kerkorian in 1986.)

To switch venues, Sammy had to take a drop in pay—to $100,000 per week—and had to commit to bookings four weeks in length (he was accustomed to stints half to three-quarters of that duration). He accepted these conditions because the Inn attracted mostly long-standing Vegas habitués, Sammy's kind of people, and its main showroom, like the Aladdin's, was relatively small, seating roughly seven hundred. "I had a good feeling about the Desert Inn," he said later, "that I could create some excitement there."

Shirley Rhodes was worried about Sammy's ability to sustain two shows a night for four straight weeks, but, since he quit drinking, he felt newly energized. So much so that he told his manager he wanted to go all out, do a one-man show, without an opening act. "Have them put that money into more musicians," he instructed her. "I want a concert-sized orchestra." Once committed, he felt a few fleeting pangs of concern. Was he really up to the strain? And, if so, why put the added pressure on himself?

As it turned out, he made the right decision. Following his opening on March 11, *Variety* found him "up to the task" of captivating a major Las Vegas showroom all by himself. Not only was he, in the critic's opinion, "in better voice . . . than in earlier appearances within the last five years," but he was dancing up a storm.

Sammy was thrilled by the booking. "I was in concert with a sixty-piece orchestra," he said, "in my best shape ever, and from opening night it was pure excitement." No longer trying to act the young hipster, he focused instead on keeping his act fresh. Not only did he reinvigorate songs he'd been doing for decades, but he risked new yarns and ad-libs, turning his daily routine and lifestyle into the grist for humor.

Such was the excitement about Davis' show that patrons were returning to see him two or three times a week. Even Sinatra, performing at the Golden Nugget at the same time, told him, "The word is out on you. You're having a renaissance. I couldn't be fucking happier."

Sammy returned home after the Desert Inn gig to start work on his first made-for-TV movie since 1973's *Poor Devil*.

In addition to Walt Disney's famous 1951 animated feature, *Alice in Wonderland* had given rise to numerous film and TV adaptations, including a 1966 animated version by Hanna-Barbera that featured a score by Davis' *Golden Boy* colleagues, Charles Strouse and Lee Adams, and starred Sammy as the voice of the Cheshire Cat (his song, "What's a

Nice Girl Like You Doing in a Place Like This?", was the best number in the show).

But no one had imagined a production quite like the one envisioned by Irwin Allen. Best known for his big-screen, star-studded disaster films, notably *The Poseiden Adventure* and *The Towering Inferno,* Allen planned on bringing the same epic scale to his production of *Alice.* Budgeted at a then awesome $14 million, the adaptation would also draw from Carroll's *Through the Looking-Glass,* run four hours (with commercials), include nineteen songs by Steve Allen, and feature several major special effects, including a twelve-foot version of Carroll's firebreathing Jabberwocky.

In keeping with the rest of his grand concept, Allen assembled a cast of some thirty-five stars, among them Red Buttons, Sid Caesar, Sherman Hemsely, Roddy McDowall, Jayne Meadows, Anthony Newley, Donald O'Connor, Ringo Starr, Beau Bridges, Carol Channing, and Jonathan Winters. For the all-important title role, the producer decided not to cast a young woman, in the traditional manner, but to use a real girl. After looking at more than six hundred youngsters, he chose a Los Angeles elementary school student, Natalie Gregory. Gregory had appeared on numerous TV series, including *Magnum, P.I., Highway to Heaven,* and *Cagney and Lacey.*

Davis was cast in duel roles. As the Caterpiller, he was encased in a long blue costume that inhibited any lower-body movement but allowed his features to be seen, in contrast to the outfits of most of the other stars, whose well-known faces were buried behind pounds of makeup, prosthetics, feathers, fur, and masks. His second role, that of Father William, found him decked out in typical eighteenth-century garb, including tricorn hat and powdered wig. The character derived from the poem "You Are Old, Father William" that Alice recites at the Caterpiller's command. It served as the basis for a song-and-dance duet between Sammy and Natalie Gregory that evoked the spirit of Bill Robinson's turns with Shirley Temple in the 1930s.

Before filming, Sammy rehearsed the number for several days with the show's choreographer, Jillian Linn. One day, as he executed a turn, he felt a sharp pain in his hip. Ignoring the discomfort, he continued with the rehearsal but afterward soaked in a tub of very hot water. "What I needed was about four fingers of vodka," he said. "But that was out." His hip still throbbed the next day, but he kept rehearsing. Finally, after several days of continuing pain, he consulted an orthopedic surgeon, Eugene Harris, who told him that his hip socket was disintegrating, a common occurrence among dancers and athletes.

Harris gave Davis two alternatives: he could replace the hip joint with one made of metal or plastic, a complicated procedure but the one that offered the greatest return in terms of mobility and freedom from pain. Or Harris could reconstruct the hip. This was a less invasive procedure, but still required about two months of rest and recuperation. "If successful," Harris warned, "you'll get a year or a year and a half out of it, maybe two at best. But eventually you'll have to have a hip replacement."

For the moment, Sammy did nothing; he couldn't afford to be out of commission for eight weeks. To begin with, he had to film his sequence in *Alice in Wonderland,* which took several days. The show's director, Harry Harris, an Emmy winner with more than four hundred hours of TV to his credit, was unaware of Sammy's hip problem but could tell that he was weak and tired. The "Father William" number required numerous retakes; sometimes Natalie Gregory, who was not a dancer, made a mistake in the hoofing or the lip-syncing was off. But, despite his pain, Davis refused to quit until the sequence was flawless. "He was a major trouper," Harris said, "I would say to him, 'Sammy, if you don't want to do anymore, I can make it work.' But he was a perfectionist. He wanted to do it right. A very terrific guy."

It took about sixty days in total to film *Alice in Wonderland,* roughly a third longer than it would typically require to shoot four hours of TV. Still, when the show debuted on CBS on December 9 and 10, 1985, the critics found it shoddy, despite its lavish budget, and ponderous, deserving of three hours of airtime at the very most. Its lethargic pace was made worse by Gregory, who was adorable but lacked the spunk to drive the production. Davis wasn't particularly memorable as the Caterpillar, but he fared better than most of his costars, some of whom delivered performances so campy and over the top that they were excruciating to watch. Kay Gardella, the esteemed TV critic for the *New York Daily News,* advised readers, "If you have any Christmas shopping to do, this would be a good time to get it done." Viewers must have taken her advice because *Alice in Wonderland* made a surprisingly poor showing in the ratings.

After completing his work for Irwin Allen, Sammy moved on to several long-scheduled appearances at, among others, Harrah's in Atlantic City. But he remained in tremendous pain. During his off-hours, he used a cane to get around and frequently soaked his aching joints in hot tubs. Onstage, he carried on as if nothing were wrong. But occasionally, he'd take a wrong turn or bend in such a way as to send a hot, searing flash rushing to his head. At such moments, he'd turn his obvious discomfort into a joke, telling the audience, "Damn, if I'd known I was gonna live this long I'd have taken better care of myself."

Although he was in agony, he was so terrified of surgery that he refused to take action. Finally, in November, he simply couldn't stand the pain any longer. He instructed Shirley Rhodes to cancel or postpone several upcoming gigs, with an estimated loss of more than $1 million in income, and entered Cedars Sinai Hospital, where, on November 11, Dr. Harris performed reconstructive hip surgery.

Harris thought the operation went well, but he would need a month before he could determine its success for certain. Such an interval would have been difficult for anyone to endure, but for someone as focused on immediate gratification as Davis, it was torture. So were the seemingly endless days of sitting around at home, doing nothing. "I had no buffers," he recalled, "no drugs, no whiskey, just reality. And reality is fear of the unknown waiting around the bend."

As the weeks went by, he grew more and more depressed, refusing to see visitors and taking his frustrations out on anyone close at hand—Altovise, Murphy, Shirley, George, even pals who phoned, like Jack Haley, Jr., and Shirley MacLaine. Normally fastidious about his grooming, he grew a beard and left his hair uncombed. Then one day he snapped out of his funk. Telling himself, "Enough! Nobody ever said that life is supposed to be a smooth road," he shaved his beard and straightened his hair. He got up, got dressed, took his meals in the dining room, and opened his door to friends. Joining him on December 8, his sixtieth birthday, were his father, Milton Berle, Clint Eastwood, Danny Thomas, Jack Haley, Jr., and Steve Lawrence and Eydie Gorme. To mark the occasion, Altovise arranged for a birthday cake in the shape of Sammy's autobiography, *Yes I Can.*

A few days later, Harris pronounced the operation a success. "In another month you'll be walking without the crutches," he told his patient, "but use a cane when you're in a crowd."

Davis was elated. He couldn't wait to get back to work. Never in his entire adulthood had he gone two months without performing. Even his auto accident in 1954 put him out of commission for only six weeks. Looking ahead to 1986, he saw a tour of Australia scheduled for January. This seemed the perfect place to mark his postoperative return to the stage.

A few weeks later, his tour was thrown into question by a grave personal loss. On Christmas day, George Rhodes, Sammy's musical director of nearly three decades, died of a heart attack at the age of sixty-six. Sammy had grown to love and depend enormously on the one-time pianist. On a personal level, he may have been closer to Murphy or even George's wife, Shirley, but no one had served a more vital role in his act. Without George's ability to keep the musicians alert at venue after venue, Sammy couldn't have moved at will through his vast repertoire of material during each show, an essential element of his performance style. He also benefited from dozens of classy George Rhodes arrangements and from the conductor's gentle, soft-spoken, calm demeanor. "I'd never felt the pain of loss like that," Davis said later.

In the wake of George's death, Sammy had second thoughts about the Australian tour, but, in the end, decided to honor the commitment. As he told Shirley, "I've got to find out if I can make it. I can't lay in this fuckin' bed looking at ghosts much longer. And I don't mean just George. I mean the ghost of me." He wanted his manager to stay at home and focus on herself for a change, but she insisted on joining him as usual. "I've got to go everywhere we were together," she told the entertainer. "I've got to see him there, and not see him there, and then maybe I'll be able to let him go." Instead of hiring a new conductor, Sammy had his regular trumpeter, Fip Recard, perform dual roles during the tour. Thereafter, Morty Stevens would return to the fold, the only conductor besides George who could read Sammy's intentions and bail him out if he got stuck.

Davis' opening night at the Sydney Hilton was a disaster. The problem wasn't Recard's conducting or even Sammy's hip; it was his voice. As soon as he said, "Good evening, ladies and gentlemen," his throat closed and he could barely speak. He didn't know what to do. As he said later, "I couldn't dance and I couldn't sing. Though I could be amusing I had no delusions of being Milton Berle. I was helpless."

Out of desperation, he just started talking, initially about what was happening to him physically at that moment and then branching out to whatever other subjects crossed his mind. Drawing on his innate sense of humor and decades of show business experience, he managed to turn his embarrassment and acute discomfort into a routine, with the sympathetic audience lending its support. As he talked, his voice returned enough for him to try a few songs. They were painful to the ear—at least he thought so—but, again, the house stayed with him. So much so that when he left the stage after sixty minutes, he got a rousing ovation. "I'd sung horribly," he confessed. "I wasn't that funny, I'd done a poor show. But they knew that I hadn't lost it partying, that it was legitimate, and how hard it was." The following day, he earned press accolades for his consummate showmanship.

Meanwhile, Dr. John Tonkin, a vocal specialist, told him there was nothing wrong with him physically. Rather, he was suffering from an emotional reaction to his hip surgery and to George's death. "When you get the confidence back," Tonkin said, "and when God decides you can sing again, you'll sing." In the interim, Davis struggled through the rest of the Sydney run, avoiding the more vocally demanding songs in his repertoire and doing his best with rhythmically driven tunes like "The Birth of the Blues."

At the next venue, Adelaide, his voice began to improve and, by the time he moved on to Melbourne, he was almost back to normal. Sammy wallowed in the sensation. "I sang everything I knew," he said, "going for the high notes and taking them from above, not crawling up to them in hope, no, I attacked them from the sky and I never missed and to me it was like church bells ringing."

Back home, he resumed his normal schedule, which included a stint at the Hotel Diplomat in Hollywood, Florida in early spring. He also spent several days working on a low-budget, independent feature film, for which the hotel's owner, Marge Cowan, served as associate producer.

Called *The Perils of P.K.,* the comedy was the pet project of Naura Hayden, an actress who appeared in several B-pictures during the 1950s and was a guest on such TV series as *Gunsmoke, Bonanza,* and *77 Sunset Strip.* Budgeted at a modest $1.5 million, her film was a wacky Hollywood spoof centering on the title character, a former movie queen who yearns to return to the big time. Hayden not only wrote, produced, and edited the picture, she also starred as P.K. Her husband, Joseph Green, served as her director.

Davis appeared in only one sequence, a fantasy in which P.K. imagines herself making a movie. He is her director, of all things, a Swede named Ingmar Ibsen.

It is highly unlikely that Sammy held out serious hopes for *The Perils of P.K.* He took the role as a favor to Marge Cowan and for fun.

A few months after the Florida filming, Hayden previewed the comedy at the Oak Park Plaza Theatre in Kansas City. For reasons that aren't clear, a *Variety* stringer attended the screening and submitted a review to the trade paper, which ran it on June 17. Among other things, the critic stated that the cast has "some fun visualizing a string of tired jokes, but . . . the vaudeville-like gags and punchlines do not have the makings of a marketable film." According to Hayden, the *Variety* critic "had no right to be there. The picture wasn't finished. It didn't have the sound effects in, it didn't have a lot of things in. The thing was about two and a half hours long at that point. I was very upset that this guy was there, whoever he was."

After the Kansas City screening, Hayden continued to edit, eventually cutting the picture to ninety minutes. To date, it has not been released. Part of the problem, she maintained, was that Dick Shawn, who played P.K.'s psychiatrist, died before he could supply the intended voice-over narration. In 2002, she resumed work on the project, whose title she shortened to *P.K.*, hoping to have it completed in the near future. If so, fans may have one final Sammy Davis, Jr., performance awaiting them on the big screen.

In early June, Davis returned to the Desert Inn, his first Vegas appearance since his hip operation. He was determined to show both the media and the paying customers that he could still execute a time step or two, and they responded with delight.

Early in his Desert Inn stint, Sammy received a visit from his daughter, Tracey, then almost twenty-five and engaged to Guy Garner, an Italian American college basketball player and aspiring actor, whom she had met when they were both students at Santa Rosa College in Santa Rosa, California.

Sammy's relationship with his daughter had been strained throughout the years. As a teenager, she had tried to inure herself to her father's neglect. But, deep down, she ached at the way everything in his life—his work, friends, hobbies, women—seemed to take precedence over her and her brothers, that is, until they did something of which he disapproved; then he'd turn severe. Sammy was furious, for example, when Tracey dropped out of Santa Rosa College to be with Garner after he transferred to California State University, Northridge. Davis was so angry that he refused to let his daughter stay with him temporarily while she searched for a place of her own near the college's San Fernando Valley location.

When Tracey entered Cal State herself, eventually earning a B.A. in public relations with a minor in sociology, Sammy missed her graduation. He phoned Tracey from New York a few days before the ceremony and told her that if it was important to her, he'd be there, but if she didn't mind he'd rather not charter a plane. Hurt, she told him not to come. In fact, she longed for him to see her graduate. What daughter wouldn't? Sammy should have realized that, and he should have *wanted* to be there. After all, Tracey was the first member of his family to go to college, let alone earn a degree.

At least on the surface, Davis' sons, Mark and Jeff, accepted his distant attitude with greater equanimity. "I think Tracey took it much harder," said their mother, May Britt. "As far as I know. The boys, I think, took it as more natural that Daddy's always busy. I think Tracey was more sensitive to it."

In fact, Mark was more than a little upset by Sammy's lack of attention. Looking back, he said, "I ran the full gamut of emotions. Yeah, of course, I was angry and whatever. Since he was not there, I did not have that father figure to rely on. It was frustrating. It was very difficult. You don't know who you are. Especially if you are a boy. You look up to your father. Now you've got your mom. My mom's great. I love my mom to death. But, being a guy, you can't draw everything you need off of a woman. So that I missed."

Mark so longed for Sammy's companionship that he took up golf at around age thirteen. Their hours together on the links meant a great deal to the boy, but even playing golf was an activity that had to be planned. "You had to call," Mark explained. "You had to schedule it. And sometimes it was difficult to spend time with him because of his schedule."

Perhaps in his effort to be like his father, Mark started drinking heavily during his senior year in high school. He also started experimenting with Quaaludes and cocaine. After graduating, he decided not to go to college. Instead, he became one of his father's roadies, eventually becoming an assistant stage manager. Traveling with Sammy enabled him to see the old man in a new light. They became colleagues more than parent and child. As Mark put it, "We didn't have depth. We didn't put ourselves in that position to get deep into each other's lives. It was kind of like an unsaid understanding. I was okay with it, but it wasn't what I really wanted. Because I would rather have had my father in my business and stopping me when I was being stupid, you know, than to not have him do it."

Offstage, Sammy may have had a laissez-faire attitude toward his son's behavior, but, when it came to the act, he was a tough taskmaster. If anyone, including Mark, screwed up during a performance, the entertainer would make light of the mishap in front of his audience but would hold a serious discussion with the offender after the show. According to Tracey, Mark's substance abuse problems made him so unreliable he was eventually fired. He returned home, but May told him he couldn't just hang around the house; he had to either enroll in college or find a job. So Mark left Lake Tahoe. He bummed around for a long time, his sister noted, endured a lot of bad years. Eventually, he straightened himself out, but before doing so, he married several times, starting at age twenty-one. In 1985, he and his wife Jane gave birth to a son, Andrew, making Sammy a grandfather for the first time.

Jeff was the least troubled of the three kids. Shirley Rhodes described the boy as "always happy, always up. A sweet guy." Rather than question or resent his father's relative lack of involvement in his life, he simply accepted, and was grateful for, whatever Sammy *did* offer. Shirley maintained that, of the three children, Jeff was the only one who was readily available for phone calls and visits whenever the entertainer played Tahoe. He didn't become intransigent or develop a chip on his shoulder like Tracey, and he avoided the alcohol and drug problems that beleaguered Mark. Like his brother, Jeff graduated from high school but decided not to go to college. He ended up working in the Beverly Hills Library and married some years after Sammy's death.

In contrast to Mark and Jeff, Tracey felt the need for some sort of emotional showdown with her father. As her wedding approached in June 1986, she decided the appropriate occasion had finally arrived. Hence her visit to Las Vegas.

It took a bit of time to work up the courage to say what she wanted to say. On her arrival in town with her friend Julie Clark she caught her father's show at the Desert Inn, then went to visit with "Uncle" Frank Sinatra at the Golden Nugget. Finally, in the early hours of the morning, she was ready to confront Sammy in his suite. Not knowing how to start, she bumbled around for a moment, then blurted out, "I love you, Pop, but I've never really liked you." Sammy, drawing on a cigarette, came over to her and said, "Yeah, well, I have news for you, Trace. I've never really liked you much either." He spoke calmly and without rancor, but his honesty stunned her.

Deep down, Tracey had to acknowledge that to a certain extent she deserved her father's resentment. Over the years, she had displayed her animosity toward Sammy—and Altovise—at every opportunity, spoiling any number of dinners and family outings. Now, at last, she was prepared to let that anger go, willing to share her hurts and disappointments rather than mask her feelings behind a hostile veneer. Although caught offguard, Sammy appeared willing to do the same. Slowly, he sat next to Tracey on a sofa, and they began to talk, looking back on the years, trying to figure out where they'd both gone wrong so that they could move forward in a new spirit. Using her college graduation as an example, Tracey told her father how hurtful his absence had been, that he shouldn't have asked if she wanted him to come, he should have just been there. Sammy admitted that he'd made a big mistake, but also pointed out that if his presence was that important to her, she should have insisted he be present.

After several hours of painfully honest communication, father and daughter were in tears and hugging one another, feeling they'd finally broken through to a new understanding. Just before Tracey went to bed, Sammy did something he'd never done before: he asked for his daughter's phone number. Later, in her bedroom, Tracey looked back on that moment, a big grin plastered on her face. She felt that she had a father at last.

Having cleared the air, Sammy and Tracey enjoyed themselves enormously at her wedding a few weeks later. The ceremony, held at Sammy's home, took place on the evening of June 28. According to

Tracey, her dad watched *Father of the Bride,* the classic MGM film starring Spencer Tracy, three times to prepare for his role.

After the ceremony, performed by Jesse Jackson, the proud father sank into a chair and cried. Then he, the rest of the wedding party, and the small group of family members and friends in attendance joined a much larger gathering at Nicky Blair's restaurant, where a sumptuous party took place. Sammy's contingent included Aaron Spelling and his wife; Lola Falana; Jack Haley, Jr.; Steve Lawrence and Eydie Gorme; Danny Thomas and his wife; and the Robert Culps. Before the cutting of the wedding cake, which was topped off by a black bride and a white groom, the father of the bride made a toast in which he expressed his love for the happy couple and those assembled to share the moment with them. No doubt, as he looked out at the people smiling back at him, Sammy's thoughts drifted back to the day he married Tracey's mother nearly twenty-six years earlier. How happy he had been then, so full of love and hope for the future. But fearful, too. He knew full well that a black man didn't wed a white woman in 1960 without consequences. Now his daughter, half-black, was marrying a white man, and most people accepted the union readily. How the world had changed in a quarter century. It was amazing, really. Thus, when he raised his glass, he could say to the beaming couple, "Tracey and Guy, this is your world. May it always be reflected, as it is this evening, by people who love you very much." Then, being Sammy, he ended with a joke: "Now cut the cake. I want to find out which chick is going to jump out!"

"*The Alternative Is Something Else Again*"

Roughly six weeks after Tracey's wedding, Sammy was at the Hollywood Bowl. Nearly fourteen thousand people turned out to see what the *Los Angeles Times*' Leonard Feather described as "a new and mellower man."

Having passed age sixty, Davis was finally putting some of his demons to rest. He had little left to prove—to the world or to himself. He may have failed to engage the younger generation, but he retained a tight hold on the affections of their parents and grandparents, many of whom regarded him as a peerless entertainer. He still did what he could to help his fellow human beings. In the wake of his liver problems, he established the Sammy Davis Jr. National Liver Institute and, each year since 1983, hosted a Variety Club telethon in St. Louis to establish a pediatric intensive care wing at a local hospital (for which he had raised some $12 million by 1989).

Best of all, perhaps, Sammy had come to terms with himself. Gone was the self-hatred that had driven him for so long. "Now I *like* me!" he proudly told Lerone Bennett, Jr., of *Ebony*. "I like me because I think I'm a genuinely good person. I'm no better than anybody else—I'm talking about as a human being—and no worse. I have my failings. I have my fears. I have my frustrations. I have problems I still have to work on, but, boy, do I like me—and I couldn't have said that ten years ago." In fact, he looked back on the Sammy Davis, Jr., of the early to mid-seventies with considerable discomfort. As he told an audience at Harrah's Reno, "That person you saw 10 years ago wasn't me. It was a caricature, gone by the wayside."

Newsweek looked back on this period a few years later and asserted, "Slowly—and somewhat painfully—Davis moved into a role as a kind of senior statesman of show business. He drank strawberry soda instead of vodka, wrapped his hands around Pac-Man machines instead of beautiful women, took off some of the gold chains, stopped wearing hot pants and lamé jump suits at his concerts, and toned down the sycophancy he once, acknowledging a particularly devastating impersonation, referred to as 'that early Billy Crystal stuff.'"

He even began to give some thought to retiring. As he told Lerone Barrett, "Yes, I want to go out at the top of my form. I don't want to stay on so long that people will be whispering in the wings and saying what I've heard them say about other performers. 'He's lost it. For God's sake, get him off the stage.'"

No one was even close to suggesting such a thing about him in 1986. Handled properly, as at the Hollywood Bowl, solo concerts could be energizing and financially rewarding. And Sammy had proven himself up to the task, hip reconstruction and all. But it was nice, he found by the mid-eighties, to occasionally share the workload with someone else. Thus, the following year, he joined forces with two old pals. First, in May, he and Jerry Lewis launched a joint appearance at Bally's Grand Hotel in Las Vegas.

As with Cosby, Sammy and Jerry each had their solo turns, but they also kibitzed, sang, and even tap danced together. "We represent the end of an era," Davis told *Newsweek*'s Charles Leershen at the time. "Our act is the last hurrah for a certain type of show business." Indeed, he and Jerry were different from the attractions elsewhere in town, acts that ranged from country artists (Willie Nelson), R&B groups (Kool and the Gang), and sitcom stars (Suzanne Somers) to glitzy revues like the Hacienda's *Fire and Ice*, the Stardust's *Lido de Paris*, and the Riviera's *An Evening at La Cage*.

Three months after his gig with Jerry, Sammy joined Frank Sinatra for a three-night stint at the Greek Theater in Los Angeles. "The two stylists did their decades proud," proclaimed *Variety*, "waxing grandiose, comic and kitchy in manners worn smooth and slick with experience." Rather than mixing it up in the old Rat Pack tradition, the entertainers were now content to render cut-down versions of their individual acts, first Sammy, then Frank. But they did end the show together, with a rousing medley from *Guys and Dolls*.

Shortly thereafter, Sammy spent about a week in the tiny Brazilian mining town of Ouro Preto ("Black Gold" in Portuguese), playing himself in *Moon over Parador*, director-screenwriter Paul Mazursky's spoof about New York actors and South American politics. The feature starred Richard Dreyfuss as the dictator of a fictional country and the despot's double, a struggling American thespian. Sammy appeared as the grand marshal of a Carnival parade, perched atop a gigantic float gaily singing "Begin the Beguine." He returned near the end of the picture, as witness to the dictator's assassination. When the picture opened on September 9, 1988, Michael Wilmington of the *Los Angeles Times* took note of Davis' bit, calling it "a wry self-parody."

Back home, Sammy embarked on return engagements with Sinatra and Lewis during the second half of 1987. Then, in early December, he, Altovise, and his kids flew to Washington, D.C. for one of the greatest accolades a performing artist can receive, the Kennedy Center honor. Presented every year since 1978 by the John F. Kennedy Center for the Performing Arts, the award honors a virtual Who's Who of U.S. performing artists over the past fifty or sixty years, from composers and musicians to dancers and choreographers to actors, singers, directors, and dramatists. Sharing the accolades with Sammy in 1987 were Perry Como, Bette Davis, choreographer Alwin Nikolais, and violinist Nathan Milstein.

The ceremony was a two-day affair. On December 5, the formal medal presentations were made at the State Department under the purview of Secretary George Schultz. The chairman of the Kennedy Center, Roger L. Stevens, draped the medals around the recipients' necks as actors Hume Cronyn and Jessica Tandy read each inscription. The following evening, Sammy returned to the White House for the first time since the Nixon administration, attending a reception for the medalists hosted by President and Mrs. Ronald Reagan. Later that evening, at the gala itself, Lucille Ball, a 1986 Kennedy Center honoree, hosted the portion of the program devoted to Sammy. In her introduction, she told the distinguished assemblage, "Sometimes I think his first words were 'Let me entertain you.' And entertain us he does. . . . There's only one Sammy Davis, the little giant of entertainment." After a brief film highlighting the honoree's achievements, he and the audience were treated to a tap dance bonanza by the Nicholas Brothers, Sandman Sims, Chuck Green, and Jimmy Slide, followed by 1986 honoree Ray Charles' rendition of "The Birth of the Blues."

Like virtually everyone seated in the place of honor, Sammy was deeply touched by the tribute and the award. As he told Cynthia Gorney of the *Washington Post*, "It was like someone saying, 'You're accepted. We love you. We're giving you this for the bulk of your work. But we're also saluting a kind of show business that perhaps when you and a few others quit, or pass on, there ain't going to be no more. And if that don't make you feel warm, and forget a lot of the rancor that you might feel, I don't know what does." The gala, hosted by Walter Cronkite, was broadcast on CBS at the end of the month.

* * *

Five days after the gala, Sammy was in the hospital.

Dr. Harris had been right about the entertainer's hip reconstruction; it had represented only a short-term solution. Thus, just over two years after the first operation, he underwent the more complicated replacement procedure. Because of his small stature, a special artificial socket had to be constructed. This time, the recuperation period was twelve weeks, but Davis wasn't as frightened or depressed as he'd been in 1985. His upbeat attitude seemed in keeping with his more philosophical approach to life in general. As he told the *New York Post* shortly before the procedure, "Well, the alternative is something else again, so I'm very happy about it!"

Davis returned to action at the end of February 1988, with a relatively sedate appearance on *The Tonight Show*. In early March, he opened at Harrah's Reno. Then, immediately after the Nevada gig, he joined Frank Sinatra and Dean Martin for the kickoff of one of the biggest—and most ballyhooed—events on the concert circuit, a multicity, cross-country engagement appropriately billed as the *Together Again Tour*.

Naturally, the idea originated with Frank, who found the notion of performing with Sammy and Dean more than twenty years after the last Rat Pack film appealing on several levels. First, the singer was worried about Martin, who had lost his son, Dean Paul, in a plane crash the previous year. Even before the accident, Dean, then nearly seventy, had become increasingly reclusive, content to golf by day and watch TV at night. After the devastating death of his namesake, he withdrew from the world almost entirely. Sinatra told Sammy a tour would "be great for Dean. Get him out. For that alone it would be worth doing."

Then, there were the financial benefits. "Frank designed the tour so that we'd make four years' salary in one," Sammy said. Sinatra knew that Davis was increasingly interested in retiring but couldn't afford to do so. He figured the tour would set up his friend for the rest of his life. Accordingly, Sinatra privately dubbed the tour "the Pension Fund."

Best of all, from Sinatra's perspective, the tour offered a chance for him and his pals to recapture the glory years when they could party all night, drink, gamble, and sleep around. Frank was seventy-two at the time and had been married to his third wife, Barbara, for nearly twelve years, but he was still eager to play.

Sammy immediately embraced the tour. As usual, anything Frank wanted was okay with him. But Dean took some convincing. "I didn't want to do it," he said years later. "Hell no, I didn't. Who the hell needed it? We were old. I was done. My best days were behind me. I was working here, working there, you know, just to keep myself going, somethin' to do. But this? I knew that this was gonna be a lot of work." In the end, he came onboard because he could see that Frank and Sammy were enthralled by the idea and he didn't want to let them down.

Instead of simply sending out a press release to announce their plans, Frank, Dean, and Sammy held a press conference at Chasen's restaurant on December 1, 1987, a few days before the Kennedy Center honors. Signaling their view of the tour as a return to Rat Pack class, they met the journalists decked out in tuxedos. "We'd expected a good turnout," Sammy recalled, "but the crowd awaiting us was like for a major news event, all wire services, local newspapers, all TV networks and radio, major magazines, and the foreign press." Once the press conference was underway, the three pals displayed the same sort of good-natured ribbing with which they'd delighted audiences at the Sands in 1960. Early on, Dean quipped, "Is there any way we can call this whole thing off?" He was making a joke, but there was an undercurrent of true feeling behind the crack as well.

Show business had changed dramatically since the sixties. Instead of performing at clubs and showrooms, Frank, Sammy, and Dean were now booked into giant concert halls and indoor stadiums, venues that seated tens of thousands of people. Such settings often required the entertainers to work on a portable stage with the audience placed on all four sides. Dean appeared ill at ease with this format during rehearsals, forgetting to turn frequently so that all of the patrons could get an equal view of him. He also seemed tentative with "Volare" and "That's Amore," songs that he'd been doing for decades, even though the lyrics were displayed in front of him on TelePrompTers.

As the rehearsals progressed, Sinatra and Davis became increasingly worried about their friend. When a sound technician named Joseph Wilson asked Sammy, "You think he'll last the tour?" the entertainer replied, "Fuck man, I'll be amazed if he lasts through the rehearsals." Then he added, "But I pray to God he does. Jesus, I don't know what we're gonna do if he doesn't." Martin was aware of the concern. He later quipped, "Frank and Sam were ready to replace me after the first rehearsal; I knew that. I didn't know who they could get, though. I couldn't think of anyone old enough."

By the time March rolled around, Dean and Frank's managers, Mort Viner and Eliot Weisman, who were producing the tour, had put together some ten or twelve venues throughout the United States and Canada, with more to be added later. The idea was for the guys to perform for a couple of months, take the summer off to rest and meet their obligations in Vegas and elsewhere, and then reteam for a second round of play dates in September and October. Advance ticket sales were phenomenal. In every city where they were booked, the concerts sold out within hours. Moreover, theater operators in Paris and London began pleading for a European leg. Frank told Sammy, "The accountants say you should come out of this with from six to eight million dollars."

The tour kicked off at the sixteen thousand–seat Oakland Coliseum on March 13. Looking around the vast, empty arena a few hours before showtime, Sammy felt a pang of concern. "I had never played to that large a crowd in my life except military bases," he said, "never to a paying audience." To him, stadiums were "rock-'n-roll country." He also worried that he, Frank, and Dean would fail to live up to expectations. Many of the ticket buyers knew the entertainers as three 1960s swingers but would find instead a trio of senior citizens. In case anyone missed the point, the concert would be peppered with age-related jokes. Even Frank was nervous, or at least keyed up. Just before show time, he reminded his pals of the frenzy that had accompanied the Summit at the Sands in 1960. Then he added, "Tonight we will entertain more people in one show than we did during that entire run in Vegas."

The format was simple. Dean would go on first, do about a half hour, followed by Sammy, who would also perform for about thirty minutes. After intermission, it would be Sinatra's turn. Then all three entertainers would conclude the program with an extended medley, kicked off by "Side by Side," for which Sammy Cahn had written special lyrics equating the stars' high spirits with the tour's vast earnings potential.

Sammy's fears about the audience's reaction were unfounded. Everyone loved the show. Like Elvis and the Beatles, Frank, Sammy, and Dean evoked very personal memories of a particular era in America, and those who lived through that era were delighted to see them united once more.

But not everything was roses in Oakland. As Dennis McDougal told readers of the *Los Angeles Times,* Dean performed his set with a "detectable loss of vitality." On numerous occasions, members of the audience shouted out, "We can't hear you!" Moreover, Dean struggled with the lyrics to several songs and at one point, he mistakenly flicked a lit cigarette into the audience. One of his standard bits was to shoot a butt stage right, then put his fingers in his ears as if it were going to explode. He simply forgot he was working in the round and misjudged where the cigarette would go. But the gesture was disconcerting. Finally, he seemed lost at several points during the trio's medley, prompting Sinatra to tell the audience, "Don't worry, he'll catch up to us."

After the show, Frank chastised Dean for the cigarette incident. But most unforgivable was Dean's refusal to go out drinking with him. This was Sinatra's primary motivation for the whole tour. "When'd you get so goddamn old?" Frank asked in disgust, knocking over the chair in which Martin was sitting and sending his friend plunging to the floor. Later, settling for a late spaghetti meal at the hotel, Sinatra started in on Dean again, saying, "I wanna go out, Dean. C'mon, pallie. You're making me feel old." "You *are* old," Dean replied. At that, Frank took Dean's plate of spaghetti and dumped it on his head. Frank laughed uproariously, but Dean just stared at him with sauce dripping down his face. At that point, Sinatra realized the tour was going to be less than the barrel of laughs he had imagined.

From Oakland, the guys moved on to the Pacific Coliseum in Vancouver and then the Seattle Center Coliseum. Then it was on to Chicago for several shows. By this point, Sinatra's nerves were starting to fray, and he had a fit when he learned that he, Sammy, and Dean weren't staying on the same floor at the Omni Ambassador Hotel. He finally negotiated a change in rooms, but Dean, content to remain where he was, refused to move. Then Frank complained to Mort Viner about the quality of Dean's singing, although what really angered him was his friend's continuing refusal to party. In fact, his frustration had begun to seep into the show, in the form of several cutting remarks. Martin didn't try to defend himself when Frank became nasty, or turn the comments into quips. He just took them; but he didn't like them.

By the last night in Chicago, Dean had had enough. After the show, he simply packed his bags and flew home. Said Mort Viner, "He didn't say goodbye to anybody, and nobody knew he was leaving. . . . Frank was disappointed. But that all went by the boards. They stayed friends." The press was told that the singer withdrew from the tour because of a serious kidney problem, one that required his immediate hospitalization.

There has been much speculation about Martin's sudden departure. A few months after the fact, Stephen Williams of *Newsday* wrote, "The story making the rounds is that Dean had finally tired of being the butt of Sinatra's jokes." In her 1995 book, *My Lucky Stars: A Hollywood Memoir*, Shirley MacLaine, who was also Mort Viner's client, asserted that Dean left because he was simply fed up with Frank and with the tour. She added, "Mort arranged for a private plane to take Dean back to California, where he checked Dean into a hospital to make it look good. Dean needed some rest anyway."

Viner, however, maintained that Martin's hospitalization was genuine. He told this author, "I was on the airplane with Dean when we came home. We went from Chicago to the airport to the hospital. I had already called the hospital and they were prepared to check him in. Dean's doctor had arranged all that."

Perhaps Martin was in genuine physical distress. But even Viner conceded that his client wasn't happy on the tour, and his health problem provided a way for him to get out of an extremely unpleasant situation.

After Dean's departure, Sammy and Frank carried on as a duo, performing at the Metro Center Arena in Bloomington, Minnesota and then moving on to Radio City Music Hall, where they played to standing room only from April 6 to 10. The *New York Times'* Stephen Holden called the opening show "a night of triumph for Mr. Davis, whose performance earned him a standing ovation." To which Bob Harrington of the *Post* added, "So powerful was Davis' performance that Sinatra's entrance after intermission would have been anti-climactic if he'd been anyone but Sinatra."

The reviews and ovations were great, but as far as Frank and Sammy were concerned, the tour was pointless without Dean. There could be no Rat Pack reunion with only two Rats. HBO agreed, scrapping its plan to tape the April 6 show at Radio City for airing on its premium cable channel. Still, the massive sell-out crowds—and the extremely lucrative box office receipts—were hard to give up. Frank and Sammy wanted to carry on somehow, providing they could find another headliner, a third powerhouse entertainer. They considered MacLaine and Steve and Eydie, but ultimately chose someone far younger, Liza Minnelli, who signed up on April 15, five days after Frank and Sammy's Radio City gig ended. As it would take time to retool the show, Eliot Weisman cancelled the few remaining spring bookings, and Davis and Sinatra went their separate ways, agreeing to meet up again in the fall, as originally planned. In the meantime, Sammy had a feature film commitment to honor.

The idea of making a contemporary movie about tap dancers originated with screenwriter-director Nick Castle, Jr. Although Castle's previous features—*TAG: The Assassination Game, The Last Starfighter,* and *The Boy Who Could Fly*—were aimed directly at the powerful youth market, he was thoroughly familiar with the popular film musicals of the thirties, forties, and fifties. His father, Nick Castle, Sr., had choreographed quite a few of them. Castle wanted to create a vehicle that would feature contemporary music and his own modern style of filmmaking and also Hollywood's great dance tradition. The result, which he called "a kind of urban fantasy," centered around Max, a former tap dance sensation–turned–cat burglar, who is confronted with two options on his return to New York following his release from prison: join his former gang for a big heist or go straight as a dancer. Pushing him toward the latter are his love for a beautiful dance teacher named Amy, Amy's wise-ass son, and her father, Big Mo, a one-time vaudevillian who has an idea for making tap dance relevant for a modern audience.

Castle's project, simply dubbed *Tap*, jelled when Gregory Hines agreed to play Max. The forty-two-year-old Hines had much in common with Davis. He, too, came from Harlem, was multitalented, and, as the son of a dancer, became a professional performer as a child. But, unlike Sammy, Hines was appearing on Broadway at age nine. As an adult, he starred in several notable stage musicals, including *Eubie* and *Sophisticated Ladies*, but he was better known for his roles in such films as *Wolfen*, *The Cotton Club*, *White Nights*, and *Running Scared*. Hines credited Davis' unprecedented success with easing his own path to the top. For that, he worshipped Sammy; he was also awed by the older entertainer's talent. As far as he was concerned, Davis was the only person to play Little Mo. The film's producers, Gary Adelson and Richard Vane, wanted to consider other choices, but Castle agreed with Hines. As he put it, "They had a good relationship and they wanted to work together and what other movie is going to come along like this? So it made a lot of sense."

Realizing that Big Mo was his best film role in years, Sammy went all out to capture the old down-on-his-luck ex-vaudevillian, willingly shedding any remaining vestiges of glamour. Decked out in a worn gray cardigan sweater and baggy pants, adding a slow shuffle to his walk, and sporting a bandana around his head (replaced later by a crushed hat with a pushed-up brim), he resembled a senior citizen one might see on any Harlem thoroughfare. As Frazier Moore noted in the *New York Post* on the film's release, "It's a startling moment in his film *Tap* when Sammy Davis, Jr., is first glimpsed. Frail, bent, leaning on a cane, this is a man, to put it mildly, slowing down." But he was full of life when it came to one of the film's highlights, a "challenge" tap number that he performed with a group of veterans, including Sandman Sims, Bunny Briggs, Jimmy Slyde, and Harold Nicholas.

Part of the picture's importance for Sammy lay in its depiction of these old-time vaudevillians, the kind of performer he'd known so well in his youth. "These were the kinds of guys who never made it big," he explained, "but their enthusiasms contributed so much, not only to tap dance, but to the business in general." Among them was his father, Sam Sr., on whom, in large measure, he based Little Mo.

Ironically, on May 21, while Sammy was making *Tap*, the elder Davis died at the age of eighty-seven; the entertainer was in New York for location sequences when he got the news. It wasn't entirely surprising. Sam Sr. had had several heart attacks and wore a pacemaker; he had developed Parkinson's disease as well. Still, Sammy was devastated by the loss. "He wasn't crying or doing any of that," said Shirley Rhodes, "but he was very low and very down. He was very close to his father. He was crazy about his dad."

Sammy delivered the eulogy two days after his father's death at Forest Lawn's Wee Kirk o' the Heather. Recalling his early days on the road with his dad, he told the assemblage, "This is a recognition of the man. We gather, not out of sadness. He wouldn't want us to do that. He left strict instructions. Make sure you play 'Butter on the Table.' Play a lot of Count Basie. And don't have a lot of them words bein' said over me." The mourners, including Steve Lawrence and Eydie Gorme, Janet Leigh, Danny Thomas, Jack Haley, Jr., and Milton Berle, listened as their friend described his father as "a man who never thought he was going to be more than a good performer. He lived the good life. If I have any class, it's from watching him." But, in a somewhat revealing remark, he added that his dad and Will Mastin "set me up so I'd be ready as a human being and a performer. It took me a long time to take my hat off in true appreciation." After the funeral, Sammy held a reception for friends and family at his home. The following day, he returned to New York to finish his work on the picture.

Released on February 10, 1989, *Tap* was not a success. Given its story line and the ages of its principal characters, there was little to attract the sort of youngsters who had flocked to *Flashdance* and *Footloose* earlier in the decade. Older moviegoers tended to be discouraged by the critics, who mostly praised the musical sequences but found the plot hackneyed and overly melodramatic.

Sammy was happy with *Tap* despite its reception. As he said at the time, "I've only done a couple of pictures that I've been proud of—for one reason or another—and this is certainly one of them. And if I don't do another picture for 10 more years, I'll be happy."

As it turned out, he didn't have another ten years. *Tap* became his final feature film.

On September 17, *The Ultimate Event,* as the Frank-Sammy-Liza tour was called, kicked off with a concert at the Summit Arena in Houston. From Texas, the show traveled to Phoenix, Atlanta, Miami, Philadelphia, the greater New York metropolitan area, Worchester, Massachusetts, Chicago, and finally Los Angeles in time for Thanksgiving. The format was much the same as the *Together Again* tour except that Sammy opened the show, followed by Liza. Obviously, the closing medley was altered to accommodate the change in personnel. The fact that Sinatra and Minnelli both had hits with "New York, New York" became a running bit in the newly fashioned finale.

The new tour lacked the nostalgic appeal of the Frank-Dean-Sammy teaming, but the opportunity to catch three powerhouse stars made it a blockbuster event of a different sort. At forty-two, Liza had two decades on Sammy and three on Frank, and clearly neither man could match her vibrancy. Indeed, Sinatra, his voice nearly shot, struggled mightily at each performance, but few cared; he was still Frank. By contrast, Davis' voice was as powerful as ever, as evidenced by his closing number, the intensely dramatic "Music of the Night" from *Phantom of the Opera*. Later, Sammy told Shirley MacLaine that he sang full out on every song at every concert. The reason was simple: he was sharing the bill with Frank. Old or not, Sinatra was still the best as far as Davis was concerned, and he always would be.

Minnelli also inspired Davis. "Sammy and Liza had a very competitive thing," said George Schlatter, who produced and directed the televised version of *The Ultimate Event.* "They'd be backstage and Liza would walk to the wings with Sammy and she'd say, 'All right, go get 'em' and he'd say, 'Just wait. You try to top this.'"

Though he missed Dean, Davis was delighted to be working with Liza, the daughter of Judy Garland and Vincente Minnelli; he'd known her since she was a little girl. He recalled in *Hollywood in a Suitcase* how the two of them would play hide-and-seek whenever he'd visit her mother's home. "I really do feel like an uncle to that girl," he wrote.

It is no wonder that they felt like kindred spirits. They shared a similar background, temperament, and outlook. Both were children of entertainers. Both entered the business themselves as youngsters. And both were high-energy performers who would do anything to please an audience. In addition, each had struggled with drugs and alcohol and could empathize with one another.

Of course, Frank had also known Liza her whole life. He loved her, but, for him, the tour had become drudgery. As a consequence, he tended to keep to himself after hours. Said Liza's sister, Lorna Luft, who traveled with the stars during part of the tour, "The three of them never hung out, trust me. It was always Liza and Sammy. Frank was up there somewhere. You didn't want to be in the man's way in case he wasn't in a great mood."

After Thanksgiving, the tour resumed, with a two-night stop in Detroit, where George Schlatter filmed both concerts for pay-for-view television, followed by a return to Miami in conjunction with the Super Bowl.* Unlike the original Frank-Sammy-Dean outing, which had only a domestic agenda, the trio then embarked for Japan, Australia, and finally

---

Frank, Sammy, Liza: The Ultimate Event initially aired on February 8, 1989, on Showtime Event Television (SET). Those who wished to order the ninety-minute concert paid an average of $10 to $15 per household. It was also released on videotape, selling at $29.95. In July 1990, a few months after Sammy's death, the program was carried on Showtime's regular premium channel, and in August 1995, it aired on PBS.

Europe, where the schedule included concerts in London, Munich, Helsinki, and Stockholm. Sans Frank, Liza and Sammy even performed in Monaco, where, presumably, Davis' walkout on the prince and princess in 1974 was considered ancient history.

At the end of May 1989, Davis returned to the States, exhilarated by the experience. As he told *Daily Variety,* "It was like the most beautiful thing. Frank could not have been better on stage and off. We had fun. We giggled. We laughed—and the audience loved us."

"I Don't Think This Is the Way I'm Supposed to Go Out"

The Cosby Show was one of the most successful sitcoms in TV history. From the program's inception in September 1984, Americans heartily embraced the Huxtables of Brooklyn: physician Cliff (Bill Cosby), attorney Claire (Phylicia Rashad), and their five children. The well-written scripts, engaging cast, and a warm, gentle brand of humor kept the show in the Neilsen top twenty for eight seasons in a row, three in the number one spot.

Given Sammy's friendship with Bill Cosby, it is somewhat surprising that he didn't appear on the sitcom until the middle of its fifth season. When he finally showed up, he delivered a memorable performance, playing a one-time boxer named Ray Palomino. Estranged from his family for years, Palomino is summoned by Cliff, who is caring for the ex-pugilist's pregnant granddaughter. As the young woman is not married and has no other relatives, Huxtable hopes Ray can see her through a difficult time. His problem lies in convincing the old man he's up to the task. A secondary story line concerns Claire's growing realization that Palomino is illiterate.

The episode, which aired on February 6, 1989, while Sammy was touring with Frank and Liza, reflected the entertainer's continuing maturation as a character actor, a logical outgrowth of his work in *Tap*. As with Big Mo, he submerged his own persona in favor of portraying another down-and-outer. His scenes with Cosby crackled with the sort of banter that enlivened their two-person stage shows—clearly, the men enjoyed working together—while his initial meeting with Ray's granddaughter had poignancy.

Not as memorable perhaps as Sammy's visit to *All in the Family*, his appearance on *The Cosby Show* was far more satisfying than his seemingly endless turns as himself on sitcom after sitcom. Unfortunately, time ran out before he could further extend his portrayals in the genre. *The Cosby Show* wasn't his final TV appearance, but it did mark his last guest shot on a regular weekly series.

Sometimes life has a funny way of mirroring art. In *The Cosby Show*, the backstory for Sammy's Ray Palomino—his inability to read and write—came close to echoing the entertainer's own lack of education. Even more so was his character's reaction to the news of his granddaughter's pregnancy. "I don't understand you, man," Ray says to Dr. Huxtable. "Man brings me into his office and lays a baby on me. You can't drop a bomb on people's heads like that."

The irony is that Altovise did almost the same thing to Sammy in real life.

Davis had made it perfectly clear at the time he proposed to her that he had no interest in having any more children. At the time, Altovise said she understood. But as the years went by, her maternal instinct grew more acute, and in 1989, she and Sammy adopted a child, Manny.

According to Shirley Rhodes, the boy, roughly ten years old at the time of the adoption, initially appeared about a year earlier. "I think we were up in Lake Tahoe working," she said, "and Altovise showed up with this little boy. At first, I think she was calling him Sammy. And Sammy must have raised hell about it, and he became Manny." Even Shirley isn't entirely sure how Manny became part of the Davis family. She told this author, "The story I heard, and I have no idea if it's accurate or not, is that Altovise's mother's hairdresser, somebody in that beauty shop, had this little boy. And Altovise's mother became friendly with the little boy and used to take him home with her sometimes. And that's how it all came about."

Later, the press would speculate about the boy's parentage. According to the *Star*, admittedly not the most reliable source, Altovise told a London paper, the *Mail*, that Manny was her natural child and had been raised by her parents prior to his adoption. The *Star* also quoted an unnamed friend to the effect that Manny was Sammy's birth baby. "None of the above is true," said Rhodes. "The only child Sammy had is Tracey. That's his only natural child." And, she added, Altovise had had a hysterectomy and, therefore, couldn't have been Manny's birth mother.

Whatever the boy's origins, after his first appearance with Alto, he started showing up in her company from time to time. "Well, I had a long talk with Sammy about this little boy," Rhodes said, "asking him why and where he came from and stuff, and he didn't know very much about him. Except that she wanted to adopt him. And I said, 'Sammy, how can you do that? You've got three kids here that you don't see or have a really close relationship with.' So he said, 'I'm not doing it. I don't want any more kids. It's too late in my life.'"

In the meantime, Manny was traveling back and forth between the Davis home and New York, where, presumably, he lived with his birth mother. Then finally, one day in September or October 1989, one of Sammy's security people, Brian Dellow, phoned Shirley to say, "Mr. D. wanted me to tell you what happened." "What happened?" she asked. "They adopted Manny." Not surprisingly, Sammy couldn't bring himself to tell Shirley on his own.

Rhodes was not the only one unaware of Davis' plans in advance. He didn't inform his children either. Tracey wrote in her memoir that she learned about the adoption on television, when Sammy appeared on some program and announced it. She was enraged.

When she finally reached her father on the phone, she asked how he could do such a thing. At first, he thought she was concerned about his money, so he promised her that Manny wouldn't impact her inheritance. But that wasn't what bothered her. She was upset that she had learned about this momentous event at the same time as the rest of the country. Moreover, she failed to understand why her father would want to adopt another child when he lacked time for the three he already had. Sammy tried to calm her by saying the announcement had just slipped out; he hadn't planned on revealing anything. With regard to the adoption itself, he said he did it in the hope that a child might help Altovise get off booze. Tracey astutely pointed out that one should sober up before tackling motherhood.

As it turned out, Manny didn't have much time with his stepfather. As a consequence, he remained a mystery to most of those close to the entertainer. "I'd see him," said Shirley. "You know, if he came on the road a couple of times, I'd see him. I mostly said, 'Hi, how are you?', that sort of thing. He was a little kid. I remember one time I saw his clothes all over the floor, and I said, 'Pick up your clothes.' It didn't go over too well with his mother, I guess." Likewise, Tracey asserted that she encountered the boy about three times in total and exchanged only a few words with him on those occasions.

Manny's involvement with the Davis family came too late to be included in Sammy's second autobiography, *Why Me? The Sammy Davis, Jr. Story*, which arrived in bookstores around May 1989. Like *Yes I Can*, it was published by Farrar, Straus and Giroux and coauthored by Burt and Jane Boyar.

After the tremendous success of his first memoir, Sammy figured he'd get around to a second volume at some point. As he neared his sixtieth year, he decided the moment had finally come. Although the Boyars were still living in Spain, they made numerous extended trips to the United States to work on the project. The process of putting together the book mirrored the first collaboration: Burt and Jane compiled lists of questions and then grabbed Sammy for long conversations whenever possible. He wanted the project to succeed, but he wasn't always eager to dredge up the past. Sammy said that he found looking backward "very painful. The guy from 25 years ago doesn't exist anymore. The guy from 10 years ago doesn't exist anymore. And I hope 10 years from now I'll be able to say that this guy doesn't exist anymore. He's a better human being, a more caring person."

Thus, it was up to the Boyars to get their friend to talk. "We would be with him for a month," Burt recalled, "and get maybe three sessions of work, because he'd change the plans. He'd say, 'Hey, we've got to watch the ballgame today, and then I've got to do the show'; 'C'mon, babe, I'm tired'; or 'Frank's in town.' He would do anything to get out of talking about himself. That didn't mean he didn't want to do it, but he just couldn't bring himself to do it." As a consequence, the interview process took roughly a year.

Talking with Sammy's relatives, friends, and colleagues was somewhat easier. "Sammy opened all the doors," said Boyar. "Everybody knew they could speak to us. His instruction to everybody was, 'Tell them everything, don't hold back anything.'"

Sammy didn't hold much back, either. By the time they finished the research, the Boyars had a tale that included Davis' alcohol and drug problems, his passing interest in Satanism and fascination with pornography, his open marriage with Altovise and myriad sexual encounters, his never-ending money problems, and his involvement with the Nixon administration, plus insights into his deep-seated insecurities and other psychological hangups. Turning such intense material into a book proved easier the second time. "By then, we knew better how to do it," said Burt.

Once again, the authors let anecdote and emotion drive their story, with frequent extended passages of dialogue for dramatic effect. And, of course, anything they learned from others was put into Sammy's mouth. After conferring with their editor, Roger Straus, the Boyars condensed the 630 pages of *Yes I Can* into 134 pages for *Why Me?* so that readers who had missed the first book could learn about Sammy's first thirty-six years. The Boyars added some new material to these passages, including the story of his first dramatic TV role on *General Electric Theatre* and President Kennedy's request that he absent himself from the inaugural, the book's most stunning revelation, in the opinion of some critics.

Where the first volume derived its title from a song written for *Golden Boy,* its successor, which concluded with the Oakland opening of the *Together Again* tour, reflected Davis' wonderment that God had blessed him with his multiple talents, the source of virtually everything else in his life.

Why Me? failed to live up to the success of *Yes I Can;* by 1989, times had changed and celebrity autobiographies no longer had the same cachet. Moreover, numerous other books about the black experience had been published in the interim, so that those portions of *Why Me?* dealing with race relations were less resonant. Still, the autobiography met with moderate success, thanks in part to Davis' promotional efforts. It performed even better abroad.

Four months after the publication of *Why Me?,* Sammy was in Florida, appearing at a private concert for the leading executives of General Motors. During his stay, he and Shirley Rhodes met with Eliot Weisman, who was then handling his bookings, and his attorney, John Climaco. The discussion concerned Davis' ongoing problem with the Internal Revenue Service. Final disposition of the matter was pending in tax court, but it was clear that Sammy would owe the government a significant sum. The purpose of the meeting was to work out a general payment plan so that they could proceed when the final bill came due. Climaco was confident that they could negotiate successfully with the IRS. He had also worked out a plan whereby Sammy's other outstanding debts could be retired by the following year. Best of all, he and Weisman had arranged bookings over the next three years that would put several million dollars in Davis' bank account. "There is light at the end of the tunnel," Climaco proudly told his client as the meeting adjourned. Sadly, these plans went unrealized.

Davis enjoyed performing for the GM execs, an appreciative audience. But he was having a problem with his throat, and after the first performance, he asked Shirley to make an appointment with an ear, nose, and throat specialist. "I want to see him when we get home," he told her.

He visited the doctor almost immediately upon his return to Los Angeles, assuming he had strep throat or something similar. But the diagnosis was much, much worse: it was throat cancer. Five decades of heavy cigarette smoking had finally caught up with him.

Davis was faced with two treatment options. First, his oncologist, Dr. Joseph Sugarman, could surgically remove the tumor. This choice offered by far the highest potential for success, but, in all likelihood, Sugarman would also have to remove part of his larynx. Even though Sammy was contemplating retirement, he couldn't bear the idea of not being able to sing again, much less communicating through an electronic speech device. So surgery was out. That left radiation therapy, bombarding the tumor with high-energy X-rays in the hope of killing the cancer cells. Not only did this approach offer a much lower survival rate—two cases in ten—but the daily exposure to radiation would damage Sammy's nearby healthy cells as well. Most likely, he was told, he'd suffer such side effects as fatigue, eating problems, hair loss, skin reactions, and intestinal disorders.

Sammy postponed the start of treatment for a week so that he could fulfill a booking at Harrah's Lake Tahoe. On September 14, his publicist, Arnold Lipsman, gave the story to the press. The following day, papers around the country delivered the terrible, unexpected news. In the *New York Post*, the report was carried on the front page under the banner headline "SAMMY DAVIS FIGHTS CANCER." The good news, the journalists were told, was that Davis' condition was "localized." As a consequence, Sugarman predicted "a full and complete recovery following treatment." In the meantime, however, Sammy would be unable to participate in a third round of *Ultimate Event* concerts scheduled in October for Toronto, Washington, D.C., Boston, and Charlotte, North Carolina. Sinatra and Minnelli performed most of these concerts as a duo.

Davis' performances in Lake Tahoe were not among his best, but he tried to maintain a brave front. He told one Harrah's audience he fully expected to be back. To *Variety*'s Army Archerd, he said, "If it had to happen—at least it did at a time when my head is in the right place and I can cope with this. I'm straight and clean. Everything is right with me personally and professionally. I have the total support of my family about me. I have no 'double paranoia.' Like my hip surgery, we'll take this— one step at a time. It's nice for me to know at this stage of my life how many people care for me as a person, not as a performer." Naturally, Sammy was terrified, but, even among friends, he tried to remain optimistic. As he told Shirley Rhodes, "I don't think this is the way I'm supposed to go out."

The treatments began on September 18, 1989 and lasted roughly ten weeks. They were extremely debilitating and his weight dropped from 110 pounds to 92. "Everything he ate had to be a shake or puree," said Altovise. Once, when her husband was thoroughly disgusted with everything placed before him, she tried putting a steak and fries in the blender. "But he took one bite and that was it," she said. "It looked terrible."

On November 13, near the end of the ordeal, Shirley arranged for Sammy to skip a day of treatment. He needed his strength for a very special gala that evening, a star-studded event in honor of his sixtieth year in show business.

*   *   *

Davis and George Schlatter had been planning the celebration for some time, long before the entertainer fell ill. Technically, Sammy's sixtieth anniversary in show business had arrived in 1988, but, between the *Together Again* tour and *The Ultimate Event,* he had been too busy to give the milestone the attention it deserved. Now, he and his old friend were making up for this omission with a benefit for the United Negro College Fund at the six thousand–seat Shrine Auditorium near downtown Los Angeles with an amazing roster of celebrities drawn from the worlds of entertainment, politics, and sports. Even Bob Hope told *People* magazine, "I've never seen a turnout like this for one performer."

Hosted by Eddie Murphy, the festivities began, appropriately, with Frank Sinatra, who prefaced his rendition of "Where or When" by telling Sammy, "You're my brother and you're the greatest." Whitney Houston sang "One Moment in Time," and Stevie Wonder, Anita Baker, Nell Carter, and Lola Falana performed songs associated with the honoree. Michael Jackson, who hated to do TV, nevertheless showed up to offer a special number that he created with Buz Kohan, one of the writers of Davis' old variety series. Called "You Were There," the song acknowledged Sammy's unprecedented role in paving the way for African Americans in show business.

Paying tribute as well were Jesse Jackson, Clint Eastwood, Mike Tyson, Goldie Hawn, Diahann Carroll, Richard Pryor, Shirley MacLaine, Ella Fitzgerald, Magic Johnson, Gregory Peck, and, in a taped appearance, President George Bush. In a humorous monologue, Bill Cosby told the audience about Sammy's penchant for traveling with everything he owned, including a "thousand pounds of camera equipment—for a man with one eye" and "framed pictures of anyone he's ever met."

As the glittering evening unfolded, the object of all this attention was seated in an enclosed area off to one side of the stage, where he was joined by Altovise, his mother, and other members of his family. For the most part, he watched wistfully and with enormous pride as friends and colleagues honored him. Then came a very special part of the show.

Schlatter had arranged for Sammy's tap shoes to be close at hand. During his song and dance number, Gregory Hines was to go over to Davis and invite the entertainer to join him on the stage for a tap challenge. Seeing Sammy's frail, weakened state, Hines was afraid to do so, but Schlatter insisted. He knew that his friend would rise to the occasion. And he was right.

When Davis reached for the shoes, the audience exploded. On their way back to the stage, Sammy summoned up his old bravado and whispered to his *Tap* costar, twenty-one years his junior, "Make it easy on yourself." In the customary protocol of a dance challenge, Hines started things off with a set of moves. He then paused while Sammy answered with some steps of his own. When Davis finished, Greg introduced a new routine. Thus they proceeded, trading steps, for several rounds. Finally, Davis executed some particularly nifty moves. Hines started to take his turn but, instead, looked over at the frail older man, shook his head in disbelief, and broke into a huge grin. He then bent down and kissed his idol's shoe. The six thousand people in the house leaped to their feet, whistling, applauding, crying. The sight of this young, vibrant dancer humbling himself before the aging master was among the most emotionally transfixing moments in modern show business history.

A few days later, journalist Paul Green set the gala in its proper context. "Mention the name Sammy Davis, Jr., to someone under 30," he told readers of the *Los Angles Times,* "and the first image will probably be of a slick Las Vegas type loaded down with gold chains and oozing show-biz platitudes. Picture Billy Crystal's wickedly funny impression. That's why the all-star salute to Davis at the Shrine Auditorium on Monday was so valuable. It put the spotlight back on Davis' exceptional talents as an all-around entertainer . . . and on his historical importance as one of the first black performers to achieve mainstream popular acceptance." Green added, "The best thing about the salute . . . was its integrity and sense of purpose."

George Schlatter put the gala in a more personal context, saying, "There have been other evenings and there have been other performances and there have been other emotional events and there have been other times when there were a lot of stars on stage. But I don't think there ever was a time when everybody on the show had a personal, passionate reason to be there. They had something to say to Sammy. Nobody was there just because they were an important artist. They were there because they had had a relationship with Sammy and they meant something to him, and he sure meant something to them. I know it never happened before and I don't think that it will ever happen again, where there was that kind of outpouring of love. Everybody who had ever worked with him wanted to be there. I could have done a twelve-hour show." Schlatter taped the gala for ABC, which aired the two-and-a-half-hour special on February 4, 1990.

As for Sammy, he called the tribute, which raised $250,000 for the United Negro College Fund, the "happiest day of my life." And that wasn't all. Backstage, he gleefully whispered to all who would listen, "I got some good news today. Four or five weeks of recovery and I'll be back screaming and hollering again."

* * *

371

Two weeks after the evening at the Shrine Auditorium, Sammy was on hand as grand marshal for the fifty-eighth annual Hollywood Christmas parade. Roughly two weeks after that, he was honored at the twenty-second annual NAACP Image Awards. Introduced by Sidney Poitier, who called him "the quintessential performer of the 20th Century," Sammy received a two-minute standing ovation from an audience of twenty-two hundred as he collected his Hall of Fame award.

By the night of the NAACP affair, the entertainer was sure his health problems were behind him. "They can't keep me away from the lights," he boasted. "Now that my radiation treatments are over, I'm going to rest four weeks, then I'm back in business. I'll do a show in Atlantic City, Tahoe or Reno. I can't wait." He made plans to get his voice back in shape by working with a highly individualistic "voice builder" named Gary Catona. Best known for helping Jack Klugman after Klugman's cancer therapy, Catona also worked with Shirley MacLaine when the actress returned to live performances. They couldn't start immediately; Davis' throat was still too raw from the radiation. But they planned to get together during the early part of 1990. In the meantime, Sammy signed to act in a made-for-TV movie, which began filming in Chicago in January.

The Kid Who Loved Christmas had the distinction of being the first Christmas-themed television film with an all-black cast. The plot centered on the attempt of jazz musician Tony Parks (Michael Warren) to adopt an orphan named Reggie (Trent Cameron) after the death of the musician's wife (Vanessa Williams), despite the opposition of the head of the local social service agency (Esther Rolle). Sammy played Sideman, a retired pianist and one of Tony's close friends. Like *Tap*'s Big Mo, the musician has weathered life's bitter blows, emerging wiser in the ways of the world. He gladly passes that wisdom on to Tony. Particularly memorable is a scene between Davis and Warren in which the old man talks about the importance of children in one's life.

Although Sammy was tired and run down during filming and working conditions were tough, thanks to Chicago's bitter winter weather, the entertainer gave his all to the project. "When he was doing a scene," said the film's director, Arthur Allen Seidelman, "he was really there. I mean, he wasn't an actor coasting on his name. He gave me everything he had and, in doing so, he had to overcome intense, immediate pain. But he did that—fully, fully, fully and in the moment."

The director also noticed the extent to which the other members of the cast revered Sammy. As he put it, "They recognized the pioneering role he had had in terms of black performers, black actors. And so there was not just a genuine warmth for him as a person—because, you know, he had an effervescent and warm personality that one responded to— but it went beyond that. There was a recognition of his importance and value to them, culturally and racially. And it wasn't an incidental thing. It was very important to them to let him know. And particularly, I think, because they knew that he was ill. And so there was a particular effort to reach out to him and to let him know what he meant to them."

Sammy spent about three weeks in Chicago. Shortly after he returned home, he checked into Cedars Sinai for treatment of a yeast infection in his gums, a by-product of his radiation therapy, and learned that the cancer had returned.

As Sammy started a program of chemotherapy, old friends rushed to his bedside, including Frank Sinatra, Steve Lawrence, and Liza Minnelli. May Britt, who had maintained a warm friendship with her ex-husband through the years, visited several times. These occasions were particularly meaningful to Sammy, who still loved the former movie star. Dean Martin, who was in Cedars Sinai at the same time, stopped by on the day of his release, even though Martin hated visiting sick friends and rarely even attended funerals. "It was just horrible," recalled Mort Viner, who accompanied Dean. "Sammy looked like this little thing in bed and he had tubes coming out of him—his mouth, his nose. He had IVs in his hands. He was just filled with that stuff." Ever the wit, Martin took a look at his friend and quipped, "Sammy, why are you wearing all your jewelry in the hospital?" It broke Sammy up, but he had to force himself to stop laughing because the strain on his throat was extremely painful. Perhaps the most poignant of all was a visit from Davis' old flame, Kim Novak. Wanting to look his best for the occasion, Sammy sent home for a favorite silk robe and silk pajamas.

Though in pain, Sammy remained optimistic. On Valentine's Day, he advised the press, "I'll be back. As long as people keep praying for me, I'll make it." *Entertainment Tonight,* for one, heeded the call, sponsoring a 900 telephone line whereby fans could leave Davis a get-well message; roughly twenty-five thousand were logged in a two-week period.

Privately, friends and colleagues were more than a little concerned. Hollywood is a small community; before long, the word around town was that this time the entertainer wouldn't bounce back, that his days were numbered. "Those stories are not true," Altovise asserted. "He's not dying. Just the opposite. He's beaten the throat cancer. In fact, he's talking. His voice has come back. It's raspy, but it's back."

Perhaps Sammy's wife was putting on a brave front for the media and the fans or was exercising wish fulfillment, but the sad rumors were true.

The chemotherapy was not working; it was a matter of too little too late. With nothing left to do medically except keep the patient as comfortable as possible, Cedars Sinai released Sammy on March 13. As those closest to him knew, he was going home to die.

All had been made ready at the mansion on Summit Drive. Sammy's gigantic bed was replaced by a hospital bed, and the door to his bedroom was locked at all times; no one was admitted without Shirley's permission. She and Murphy Bennett stationed themselves in the office on the floor below the bedroom. There they monitored Sammy's business affairs and entertained friends waiting to see him. This regimen was difficult for both of them, particular Murphy, who was not in the best of health himself, having undergone a quintuple bypass operation the previous July. On the landing between the floors, a nurse's station had been created, with an array of drugs, life-saving equipment, and other medical devices.

According to Tracey, Altovise was drunk when her father arrived home. This was not the first time Sammy's wife had turned to alcohol as a way of getting through a crisis. According to one friend, she was rarely sober. One day, when her stepmother had turned up at the hospital in a state of inebriation, Tracey, who was pregnant at the time, became so angry she screamed, "If you take one day, one hour, one minute off my father's life because of your drinking and the stress it causes, I will come up here and I will *kill* you."

Mark, who moved into his father's house on Sammy's return from Cedars Sinai, was more tolerant; Altovise's solution was his own. "Yes, I was drinking," he said. "I was drinking just so I could get in there, just so I could get in his bedroom." Lorna Luft maintained that the situation was pretty bad. "When Sam was sick," she said, "Altovise was way out of control, way out of control. And it was awful. What was sad was that, as sick as he was, he knew that he had no wife. I mean, there were nights that we'd go over there and there was no food and no this and no that. She didn't know what was going on. And there he was, lying there with tubes in him."

Sammy was in no position to cope with his wife's condition. Consequently, when he returned home, he opted to reside in the master bedroom alone. "Not only didn't he want to be bothered with her," his daughter asserted, "but he was scared to death that she would stumble in drunk. 'You know,' he said, 'fall on top of me and kill me because I won't have the strength to peel her off.'" "That's true," one of Sammy's pals told this author. "He was afraid of her. Because she would be drunk, and he was very fragile at that point."

Once he was home, even more friends wanted to visit. But Sammy had limited physical and emotional resources and would see only those who were particularly close. David Steinberg stopped by every morning to watch reruns of *The Golden Girls* with him. Frank Sinatra was a frequent caller, but he had to steel himself for his visits and always left in a daze, his head bowed, unable to look anyone in the eye. Liza Minnelli was even worse; she could handle only one trip to Summit Drive. Even then, she spent an hour with Tracey and Tracey's husband preparing herself emotionally for what cancer had done to her "Uncle" Sammy.

By then, his condition had become difficult to face for even the most stoic. In addition to a dramatic weight loss, Davis could barely whisper. The pain was too great. More often than not, he made his wishes known by scrawling on a pad of paper. The tumor, about the size of a softball, was clearly visible under his neck, and it gave off an unpleasant odor.

On April 20, the patient was able to briefly forget his illness, as Tracey, some ten days overdue, finally gave birth to a boy, named Sam Michael. When Tracey brought the infant into Sammy's room, he insisted on holding his namesake in his arms, weak as he was. Looking down at the little smiling face, he whispered, "Poor thing looks just like me." Said one of his associates, "It was really a pick-me-up for him. . . . And the sight of this tiny little infant rejuvenated him for a while."

As April gave way to May, the list of visitors became even more restricted. Harrah's Doug Bushausen and Holmes Hendricksen flew down from Nevada. Lola Falana stopped by. "I was told when I went in he might not respond," she said, "and not to be upset. But he turned his head and looked up and gave me the prettiest smile. That smile was a gift I will carry the rest of my life." After his brief visit, a tearful Jerry Lewis told the press, "I felt totally helpless, but I had to see him. It was heartbreaking. I was shocked to see him so weak. I had prepared myself mentally, but I was still shocked." When Bob Brown arrived, Sammy was asleep. "I just stood there for a while," the former Nixon aide said, "and just talked, talked to him about how much I loved him and how much I appreciated everything he had done for me as an individual and that I thought he had made a major impact on so many lives and on this country and, indeed, on the world and that people would never forget him, ever. That he was a great, great human being." Brown wasn't sure if Sammy heard him or not, but he thought so. As he put it, "His eyes were working."

Nancy Sinatra came with Jack Haley, Jr. As with Bob Brown, Sammy was sleeping when she entered his room, so she pulled a chair next to the bed and sat beside him. "After a little while," she recalled, "he opened his eyes and recognized me. He reached out for my hand, and I got down on my knees on the floor next to him, taking his hand in both of mine. I rested my forehead on his arm—very gently because he was so frail and thin—and we stayed like that for a little while. As the minutes passed, my heart went back through all of the wonderful times we had shared. I was able to recall very special images of him looking fit and full of energy, and those memories sustain me to his day. After a time, I felt him stir, so I pulled back a bit, still holding his hand. He weakly pulled it away and seeing the tears in my eyes, slowly waved me away. I knew he didn't want me to see him like that, because he was a proud man, so I stood up to go. He reached for me once more. I took his hand and kissed it and whispered, 'I love you, Sam.' He was unable to speak, so he squeezed my hand as if to say, 'I love you, too.' Then he rested his hand at his side and closed his eyes, and I left."

In addition to friends, the fans remembered Sammy, too. The Davis household was brimming with flowers and candy, plus thousands of get-well letters and telegrams. The missives came from admirers across the country and around the world. The man who'd been afraid of dying alone and forgotten, like Mr. Bojangles, was comforted to know that there were legions of people out there pulling for him. He'd never met them, but they cared, and they wanted him to know it.

Finally, Altovise sent for Rabbi Allen Freehling. "By that point he was deathly ill and pretty much comatose," Freehling recalled, "but we were able to communicate a little bit. It was certainly clear that death was drawing near. He was aware of it, certainly the family was aware of it, and, while he was being made comfortable physically and my sense was emotionally as well, that was certainly a troubling time. Especially for Altovise, who, on the one hand, was prepared to let him go because she certainly didn't want him to suffer any more, but on the other hand, certainly was not comforted by the fact that she was losing her husband."

All his life, Sammy had been a fighter, and that was his instinct now: to push, to drive, to carry on. He simply didn't know how to give up. His drive had taken him to places he'd never imagined, allowed him to hobnob with the rich and famous on several continents and to live like a multimillionaire. Having done so much, the man who hated to sleep could at last rest. Finally and forever. The time had come. Tracey, by his bedside, whispered, "Pop, if you want to die, I understand. You can just let go and I'll be all right and make sure everybody else is all right. You can let go. You'll always be with us. You're a part of me and you're a part of Sam, and I'll always be a part of you. It's all right."

And so it was.

On Wednesday, May 16, 1990, Sammy Davis, Jr., died. He was sixty-four years old.

Epilogue

The world soon learned of the entertainer's death. Jim Henson, creator of the Muppets, also died on May 16, but this tragic loss didn't detract from the extensive media attention devoted to Sammy Davis' demise. America's newspaper of record, the *New York Times*, called him "a durable fixture in the firmament of American life," adding, "He was an incandescent figure. And the glow survives." The *Chicago Sun-Times'* Vernon Jarrett described him as "*the* consummate entertainer of our time," praising not only Davis' great and diverse talents, but also the skill that enabled him to overcome "the destructive external pressures of society" and "those of human weakness inside himself." "Although he gained fame with credits in stage, film and records," Fred Schuster told readers of the *Los Angeles Daily News,* "Davis was almost as well-known for his pioneering efforts at breaking the color barrier in Hollywood and for his flashy lifestyle. A survivor of the vaudeville tradition, he exerted an influence on several generations of entertainers. Elements of Davis' stage savvy and stylish dancing can be seen in the work of Michael Jackson, as well as that of numerous other musical performers."

Entertainment Tonight devoted an entire telecast to Davis and Henson. In New York, WNEW radio dropped all of its regularly scheduled programming, giving itself instead to Sammy's extensive work on vinyl, supplemented by phone conversations with his friends and colleagues. In Las Vegas, all the hotel-casinos on the Strip dimmed their exterior lights for ten minutes to honor the town's favorite performer, and on Hollywood Boulevard in Los Angeles, tap dancers shared steps around Sammy's star on the Walk of Fame. Benjamin Hooks, executive director of the NAACP, proclaimed, "The world has not only lost an irreplaceable talent, but a humanitarian whose heart was so big, so filled with caring for others, that it dwarfed his fame."

The funeral took place at Forest Lawn Memorial Park in the Hollywood Hills on May 18. An overflow crowd of more than twenty-five hundred mourners were present to say farewell, among them Frank Sinatra, Dean Martin, Shirley MacLaine, Jerry Lewis, Robert Goulet, Janet Leigh, Liza Minnelli, Michael Jackson, Bill Cosby, Stevie Wonder, Carroll O'Connor, Ben Vereen, Billy Crystal, Tony Danza, Angie Dickinson, Robert Guillaume, Robert Culp, Ricardo Montalban, Burt Reynolds, Milton Berle, and hundreds of fans. Those unable to find seats in Forest Lawn's Liberty Hall gathered in an open-air courtyard, following the proceedings by means of portable loudspeakers.

Rabbi Freehling conducted the service and Jesse Jackson delivered the eulogy. Jackson told the assemblage, "He's not the last of a kind. There was no Sammy before Sammy. Sammy was the *only* of a kind." Other speakers included Gregory Hines, who recalled seeing Sammy at the Apollo when he was a kid, noting, "It was a moment in my life that affected me in every aspect of what I did and how I carried myself—and for six years after that, I was Sammy Davis, Jr." Led to the podium by California State Assembly Speaker Willie Brown, Altovise thanked everyone for coming. "The outpouring of love that we've felt from you during these last few months meant so much to him," she said softly, "and has meant so much to my family. How lucky we all were to have Sammy in our lives." At this point, she paused, her voice broken as tears streamed down her cheeks. Then she added, "And how dearly I will miss him."

After nearly two hours, the service concluded with Sammy's recording of "Mr. Bojangles." Thereafter, his bronze casket, blanketed with yellow orchids and white roses, was carried to a hearse for the two-mile drive to his final resting place, Forest Lawn's Glendale Cemetery. The cortege, composed of some three hundred cars, was quietly greeted by scores of mourners lining the streets along the route, some bearing signs with sentiments like "Sammy, We Love You." During the twenty-minute graveside service, Jesse Jackson said quietly, "Sammy lives in us. He lives in our hearts, in our dancing feet, in our song." The reverend then broke into applause, shouting, "Let the heavens rejoice! Let the heavens rejoice!" Those around him joined in the ovation.

And then it was over. The tearful mourners departed, and Sammy Davis, Jr., was left to share the peace and quiet with his father, grandmother Rosa B, and Will Mastin, who were buried nearby.

Seven months later, *The Kid Who Loved Christmas* aired in syndication on independent television stations around the country. In general, the TV critics praised the engaging, though somewhat syrupy, Yuletide drama. Sammy's role was too tangential to make a truly significant impact, but, for many, the heartwarming story was made that much more poignant by his presence so soon after his death. As Irv Letosky observed in the *Los Angeles Times,* "While his last role was a cameo, his few scenes serve his memory warmly."

If *The Kid Who Loved Christmas* represented Davis' final gift to his fans (save perhaps for *The Perils of P.K.*), his legacy to his family was more tangible and infinitely more complex. Contrary to a widely held belief, he did not die penniless, nor did he leave Altovise and his children wanting. On the contrary. His estate was valued at approximately $4 million: $2 million in personal property and $2 million in real estate. Altovise was the principal beneficiary of these holdings. She was also the beneficiary on insurance policies totaling $2 million. Tracey, Mark, and Jeff were each named on policies worth $500,000. In addition, Sammy had established trusts for each of them decades earlier.

The problem was that Sammy's indebtedness exceeded his assets. The largest claimant by far was the Internal Revenue Service. When the final tab on the disallowed deductions was totaled, it came to $5.2 million. Davis owed another $16,000 to a variety of individual claimants, from the jewelry shop at the Riviera Hotel in Vegas to Nate and Al's, a popular delicatessen in Beverly Hills, to Von's, a supermarket chain. And there was an outstanding balance of $140,000 on a mortgage on a shopping center in Virginia.

The insurance payoffs were exempt from claims against the estate, but because Sammy and Altovise filed joint tax returns, her inheritance was fair game. For about fifteen months, Altovise's attorney, Vasillios Choulos, attempted to negotiate a settlement with the U.S. government, in conjunction with the attorney for Sammy's estate, Herbert D. Sturman, and the executors of the estate, Shirley Rhodes and John Climaco. As negotiations proceeded, the interest and penalties on the debt continued to mount. Ultimately, the total exceeded $7 million.

Finally, in 1991, the tax court ordered the sale of Sammy's holdings to satisfy the debt. The first to go was his gun collection, even though the entertainer had bequeathed one piece, a pistol used by Gary Cooper, to Clint Eastwood and the balance of his collection to the Gene Autry Western Heritage Museum in L.A. Sold at auction in San Francisco on August 2, the collection netted about $30,000.

The following month, on September 22, Butterfield & Butterfield sold some five hundred pieces of jewelry, clothes, and memorabilia in a highly publicized auction held at the Davis home on Summit Drive. The items, valued at about $250,000, ranged from Sammy's collection of canes, belt buckles, and movie memorabilia to his gold record for "The Candy Man" to scrapbooks, photos, and articles from his personal wardrobe. Far exceeding expectations, the sale brought in approximately $439,000, but the spectacle saddened many fans and shocked industry observers. "I wouldn't feel right buying anything," said one of the twelve hundred or so people who were present at the auction. "It's like the guy's whole life is out here on the floor. It's not right." Another agreed, saying, "After all the time he spent entertaining us and all that he gave to us, it's hard to see all his stuff auctioned off like he was nothing."

On October 24, Butterfield & Butterfield held a separate auction of

Sammy's paintings and other works of art, a collection valued at about $250,000. Finally, at the end of the year, Altovise divested herself of the house on Summit Avenue for just over $2.7 million. That money went to the government as well. Thereafter, she foolishly used some of her insurance payments to purchase another home in Beverly Hills. As a tangible asset, it became a target, and the court ordered its sale as well. By that point, everything of value was gone, but millions of dollars of indebtedness remained.

The attendant publicity from all of this activity did much to destroy the positive assessment of Sammy's life and career that had accompanied his death. As John Tayman and Doris Bacon told readers of *People* magazine a few weeks later, "The debt has cast a shadow on Sammy's memory, touched off debate about how he handled his money and has thrown suspicion on recent actions by his widow Altovise."

As Tayman and Bacon observed, Mrs. Davis' behavior contributed to the negative publicity surrounding the shocking situation. After pleading unsuccessfully with the tax court to let her retain some of her husband's possessions, including several paintings and numerous pieces of jewelry, she hid items marked for sale, including a valuable Campbell's soup can painting by Andy Warhol. Nancene Cohen, a paralegal in Sturman's office, said in a sworn affidavit, "We were shocked to find that 185 items of Mr. Davis' jewelry were missing" prior to the auction. Also gone were five fur coats and the portrait of Sammy by LeRoy Neiman. Altovise was ordered to appear before a judge to explain why items listed in the insurance inventory had not been made available for sale. "Some of the questions were answered, some were not answered," Sturman told the press.

The Warhol painting was eventually returned; other missing items apparently were not. One Harrah's executive told this author, "After Sammy died, a lot of things that we had given him, we being Harrah's, all of a sudden disappeared from his home. I know that we gave him a painting that used to hang over his bar and as soon as he passed away, the painting was gone. It didn't exist any more. I also know that there were two people who helped Altovise haul a lot of stuff and store it out to the Valley." The cache to which the executive referred was discovered in a Burbank storage locker at the end of 1991, a few months after the art auction. The police told Aaron Curtiss and Paul Lieberman of the *Los Angeles Times* that the locker had been rented by someone who worked for Altovise, but it was listed under the name of Matias Hoenczyk, an unrelated individual whose driver's license had been stolen shortly before the rental commenced. When Hoenczyk received a $365 bill, he complained to the manager of the storage facility that he'd never rented anything at the place. The manager, in turn, contacted the police. Presumably, if Altovise's employee had kept up the payments without having to be billed, the cache would never have been found.

One can readily sympathize with the widow's plight. Losing her husband was horrendous enough, but being totally uprooted from her home, her possessions, and her memories turned her grief into an ongoing nightmare. The way she chose to respond to the situation, however, made her an object of pity and derision and, by extension, further tarnished her husband's memory in some quarters.

Altovise's claims of poverty also aggravated the situation. Her apparent duress reached such a point that friends took to contacting other friends to raise money on her behalf. One of those solicited was Sally Struthers, who did write Altovise a check. "And then," Struthers said, "I never ever heard from her again." Another pal who helped Alto financially was Jack Haley, Jr. Instead of gratitude, Sammy's widow turned on Haley, showing up at his home and demanding the return of some personal items—tapes, films, and videos—that Davis had given his friend prior to his death. Tracey, whose tolerance for her stepmother didn't improve upon her father's demise, told the press, "I'm sick of all the complaining Altovise has been doing about the financial mess she says my father left her. These are problems [with the estate], but they can be solved."

Finally, in 1997, Altovise and her attorney, Sonny Murry, reached a settlement with the IRS for just $300,000, a fraction of the outstanding debt. By then, Sammy's widow was living in a small town in Pennsylvania. Returning for a visit to Los Angeles around the same time, she told *Variety*'s Army Archerd that she had been in rehab and had held a variety of jobs, including one in a restaurant and one in a women's clothing store. She has since returned to New York, but according to several informed sources, she hasn't finished wrestling with her substance abuse problems. In the meantime, she has devoted herself to launching a foundation named for her late husband and, in 2002, established a Vegas-style gaming Web site in Sammy's memory.

As for other members of the family, Alto's son, Manny, now in his twenties, became a pianist, according to journalist Walter Scott. Mark Davis managed to free himself from his drug and alcohol problems, fathering a second son, Ryan, in 1998. Tracey gave birth to a daughter, Montana, in 1993, and a third child about eight years later. By then, she had divorced Guy and remarried and was freelancing as a producer of commercials. Her mother, May, also remarried, to attorney Lennert Ringquist. They live quietly in the San Fernando Valley, where the one-time movie star has forged a second career as a painter.

On April 7, 1993, nearly three years after Sammy's death, Murphy Bennett died at the age of seventy. Four years later, Jane Boyar passed away. Morty Stevens is also gone, as is Sammy's sister, Ramona. Their mother, Elvera, outlived them both. She died on September 2, 2000 at the age of ninety-five.

Dean Martin survived Sammy by five years. Then, in May 1998, the world lost Frank Sinatra. As Peter Lawford had died before Sammy, at the end of 1984, Joey Bishop was the only living member of the celebrated Rat Pack as of early 2003. But the memory of the gang's halcyon days lives on. A few months after Sinatra's death, HBO debuted a semi-accurate docudrama entitled *The Rat Pack,* with Ray Liotta as Frank and Joe Mantegna as Dean. Don Cheadle, perhaps best known to TV viewers as the prosecuting attorney on *Picket Fences,* won an Emmy for his portrayal of Sammy. The remake of *Ocean's Eleven* starring George Clooney, Brad Pitt, Matt Damon, and, again, Don Cheadle, at the end of 2001 prompted a major revival of interest in the Clan, inspiring, among other things, the release of several CDs of their joint live appearances and a two-part four-hour documentary on the entertainers on A&E's *Biography.* For Davis fans, the records served to supplement a comprehensive four-CD box set issued by Rhino Entertainment in 1999.

In 2000, Burt Boyar celebrated what would have been Davis' seventieth birthday with the publication of a single-volume trade paperback called *Sammy: An Autobiography.* Published by Farrar, Straus and Giroux, it was a compilation of *Yes I Can* and *Why Me?* plus a bit of additional information. After the death of his beloved wife, Boyar moved back to the United States, settling in Los Angeles. As of early 2003, he was working with Leslie Bricusse on two projects based on his books with Sammy, a Broadway musical and a biopic. He remains in close touch with most of the surviving members of the entertainer's inner circle, including Shirley Rhodes, one of his best friends.

Afterword

What, then, is Sammy Davis, Jr.'s legacy? How should he be viewed in the early years of the twenty-first century, more than a decade after his death? If one uses the same yardstick he invariably applied to measure himself—Francis Albert Sinatra—he initially appears wanting.

To begin with, Sinatra was the premier vocalist of his era, arguably the greatest popular singer of all time. He perfected a style of rendering a tune that no one had ever attempted before, inspiring dozens of imitators as a consequence. He launched at least a dozen songs that endure, many of which were written specifically for him by his pals Sammy Cahn and Jimmy Van Heusen. Moreover, he lavished endless care on his recordings. As a result, his talent as a vocalist is beautifully preserved on vinyl, from his days as a band singer with Harry James and Tommy Dorsey to his final pairings with other singers on a couple of highly successful duet albums. Moreover, Sinatra excelled as a motion picture actor, with an Oscar for best supporting actor and a half dozen notable films to his credit, including *On the Town, From Here to Eternity, Guys and Dolls, The Man with the Golden Arm, High Society*, and *The Manchurian Candidate*.

By contrast, Sammy could boast no in-house songwriters like Cahn and Van Heusen. He was closely aligned with Leslie Bricusse and Anthony Newley, but they never wrote a song specifically for him. And, unlike Frank, he lacked two qualities a great recording artist requires: patience and time. The pressures of his live engagements, stemming from his never-ending need for cash, greatly limited the hours he could devote to laying down tracks. As for film work, nothing would have given Davis greater joy than to be a movie star of Sinatra's stature. But his race and physicality severely narrowed the options available to him in this regard. Unfortunately, that one great role in that one great picture never came his way. He shined in *Porgy and Bess* and suitably acquitted himself as a dramatic actor in *A Man Called Adam*, but in general these films were badly flawed. Although Davis appeared in some fifteen features (excluding cameos), not one truly stands the test of time.

Records and films aside, Sinatra appeared from time to time on TV, even starring in his own variety show during the fifties. But he picked his shots carefully. Sammy showed up anywhere and everywhere. Arguably, his numerous game show appearances and soap opera roles diminished his long-term stature, as did his many guest shots as himself on sitcom after sitcom. His stint on *All in the Family* became a TV classic, but that is because the basis for genuine humor, not forced merriment, lay in putting an African American superstar together with the series' bigoted protagonist. For the most part, however, Sammy simply showed up too often on too many shows that were unworthy of his presence and did himself little good in the process. The biggest case in point was his own syndicated talk show.

In addition, Sinatra demonstrated sound political instincts in his alignments with John F. Kennedy and, decades later, Ronald Reagan. At the very least, his involvement with these political figures did his public image no harm. By contrast, Davis' association with Richard Nixon touched off a storm of controversy, forever alienating many former boosters.

Finally, Sinatra had, or least appeared to have, a firm sense of self and maintained it during the good times and the bad and from decade to decade. If one liked him, great. If not, too bad. Sammy, on the other hand, was desperate to please everyone, to be loved by everyone, and to be in the forefront of whatever was in vogue at any given moment. If Frank was a rock, Sammy was a chameleon. People sensed this and lost respect for him as a result, particularly in the late sixties and seventies, when social and political change was coming fast and furious in the United States and around the world. Sammy tried to ride the wave but didn't skim beneath the surface. He embraced the outer manifestations of what was happening as if they were ends in themselves, appearing hollow and phony as a consequence. Added to this were the other excesses that marked his life: a flamboyant display of conspicuous consumption; an overuse of pop words and phrases; an overindulgence in booze, drugs, and cigarettes; and an insatiable need to be seen, which accounted for so many TV appearances. The upshot was that he became a figure of derision, the inspiration for the deadly and damaging impression by Billy Crystal on *Saturday Night Live*.

Ironically, the same excesses that detracted from Davis' reputation accounted for his incredible success as well. The need for universal acceptance and love and the desire to do more, be better, top every facet of the entertainment industry—including Broadway, which Sinatra never attempted—propelled him to go well past any conventional definition of accomplishment. A less driven individual would never have succeeded in his time and place with his drawbacks. Any one of these obstacles— being short, black, or poor, possessing unconventional facial features, losing an eye along the way—would have deterred most people. But not Sammy. He was simply undeniable.

When he worked, he didn't just perform in the customary manner. He threw himself into everything, as if his life depended on doing well—

because, in a fundamental sense, it did. That intense ferocity had rarely been seen before, and audiences were awed by it.

Even more were they awed by the fact that this slight, diminutive guy could dance, sing, do impressions, tell jokes, and play musical instruments. And that he could do each of these things with consummate skill. No entertainer before or since—no, not even Frank—had ever displayed such amazing diversity. This, again, derived from that same drive, that excess. He didn't just *become* a singer, an impressionist, a trumpeter, a pianist, a drummer. He had to learn each of these skills. He kept at one until it was mastered, then looked around for the next challenge.

The problem, in terms of Davis' long-term legacy, is that one had to *see* him do all of these things in order to understand what made him such a phenomenon. His unique qualities as a performer couldn't be captured on records, where one simply heard the voice, or on film or television. Even a variety show appearance could only begin to suggest the full force of his gifts. Not only were his stints on TV relatively short, but television is a cool medium. Sammy was a hot performer. The small screen reduced him as a matter of course. No, to fully appreciate his breadth, depth, and intensity, one had to spend an hour or two with him—live. Thus, only those who were there—in the nightclubs, the showrooms, the concerts— were truly in the know. What remains—the recordings, films, TV appearances—are merely the echoes, the shadows of what could not be captured in any permanent way.

Moreover, one had to see him live between the late forties and midsixties. After that, age, substance abuse, and the changing nature of show business caused a diminution in his remarkable range until, finally, the general public knew him primarily as a singer. Or, God help us, a personality, someone who is famous for being famous.

So, tragically, the essence of Sammy Davis, Jr., came and went, along with that special time in entertainment history when his unique magic and public taste coalesced perfectly. Then the moment was lost forever, along with other memorable live performances. One can read the reviews. One can listen to those who were there. But one can't see it for oneself.

Still, *something* does remain in terms of a legacy, and it exists in the best sense of the word. Go to the movies, watch TV, see who's hot in music, look at the ads in magazines. There are no more racial barriers. African Americans are everywhere. Talent is now the sole yardstick for success. And that, in large measure, is thanks to the little guy who kept saying "Yes, I can" when almost everyone else said no.

He was present for major demonstrations in Alabama and Mississippi as well as in Washington, D.C. But he was also in Las Vegas, agitating for the rights of African Americans on the Strip. He was in Hollywood, pushing for major dramatic roles for blacks on television. He was in New York, insisting on integrated ensembles in Broadway musicals. He was at nightclubs and concert halls around the country and on the nation's movie screens palling around with some very popular white stars. He was the voice of calm in the wake of Martin Luther King, Jr.'s assassination and an advocate for black soldiers who had abused drugs in Vietnam. He served as the memory bank for a generation, sharing the pain and humiliation of racism in a searing autobiography. And in the way he conducted his own life, he became a major force for equal treatment in every facet of the American scene.

To him, race mattered only because other people made it matter. As far as he was concerned, the world would be just fine with no color distinctions at all. So he made none. He took a lot of heat from various segments of American society for his choices in this regard, including many in the African American community, but, in this facet of his being, there was no pandering for popular acceptance. He decided early on that he was going to be and do what he wanted to be and do, and he wasn't going to let anyone say otherwise. Out of that often selfish pursuit, he pulled his people, as he liked to call them, right along with him. Then he gave of his time and his money to make sure they stayed there.

Call him a civil rights pioneer, because he was, well before there was a civil rights movement. Call him the world's greatest entertainer; few would argue with that either. He wasn't Frank Sinatra, but only Davis himself cared about that. He was Sammy. And, for everyone else, that was plenty. And, you know what? It still is.

Notes

Research for this book was based on three principal sources: (1) Interviews conducted by the author, principally during the winter and spring of 2002, with the friends, relatives, and professional colleagues of Sammy Davis, Jr., whose names are cited in the acknowledgments. All quotes and information attributed to these individuals in the text were derived from those interviews, unless otherwise indicated. (2) Books and periodicals. Those works referenced in the bibliography are identified below by the author's last name followed by a P for periodical or B for book. Citations involving authors with more than one relevant book or periodical include the date of the work from which the quote or information is derived, as in "MacLaine, 1991/B." Citations drawn from articles or books reprinted in *The Sammy Davis, Jr. Reader* edited by Gerald Early include the name of the author, the title of the book or name of the publication in which the article initially appeared, followed by "/Early/B." Periodicals of only passing interest, such as reviews from Davis' films, television shows, or nightclub appearances, are cited in full below. All unattributed quotes from chapters 1 through 14 are derived from Davis' first autobiography, *Yes I Can,* and all unattributed quotes from chapters 15 through 30 are derived from Davis' second autobiography, *Why Me?* Quotes derived from his book *Hollywood in a Suitcase* are attributed to "Davis/B." Quotes derived from the memoir of his daughter are designated "Davis, T./B." (3) Primary source materials. These include quotes derived from (a) oral histories conducted with Howard W. Koch and Charles Strouse by Ronald L. Davis, part of the Ronald L. Davis Oral History Collection, DeGoyer Library, Southern Methodist University, and on file at the Margaret Herrick Library of the Academy of Motion Picture Arts and Sciences (RLD); (b) Davis' interview with Pete Martin preparatory to Martin's profile of Davis in the *Saturday Evening Post,* which reside in the Hollywood Museum Collection of the Cinema-TV Library of the University of Southern California, designated below as "HMC"; and (c) quotes derived from Davis' interview with Alex Haley preparatory to, and not necessarily included in, Haley's published interview with Davis in *Playboy,* which reside in the Alex Haley Collection of the Schomburg Center, a branch of the New York Public Library, designated below as "AHC." Quotes from the final, published texts of Martin's profile and Haley's interview are attributed to "Martin, P./P" and "Haley/P." Finally, a few quotes are drawn from Davis' appearances on television programs, transcribed by the author. These include an appearance on the *Sally Jessy Raphaël Show,* seen at the Museum of Television and Radio in New York City and designated below as "SJR."

INTRODUCTION

"Penn Station at rush hour" (Cook, 3/12/56/P); "I'm not going to hang on to" (Cabot/P); "Sammy was a man who would" (MacLaine, 1991/B); "I didn't like me" (Bennett/P); "all the floats" (Champlin/P); "is something in my makeup" (Bennett/P); "the greatest entertainer" (King/B).

CHAPTER 1: HARLEM AND THE ROAD

"Many Harlemites lived more" (Jervis/B); "thought of little besides" (ibid.); "steely-eyed" and "lantern jawed" (Hue, October 1957); "the black show producer" (Sampson/B); "He hadn't even seen" (Smith, P./P); "My first birthday" (Davis and Feldman/P);

"From the beginning" (Smith, P./P); "Are you a little kid or a midget?" (Shepard/P); "I didn't spend a lot of time" (Smith, P./P).

CHAPTER 2: THE FORTY-FOUR-YEAR-OLD MIDGET

"I was the most pint-sized" (Davis/B); This time Sam: *Variety*'s report of Sam Davis' arrest in 1931 (*Variety*, May 27, 1931, reprinted March 11, 1959); "To me Robin Hood" (Davis/B); "What Bill Robinson really" (Cook, 3/13/56/P); "the best tap dancer" (Torme/B); "That might sound like" (Haley/P); "wanted to go in the army" (HMC); "There were little kids" (Rader/P).

CHAPTER 3: FORT WARREN

But by the end of 1942 (Lee/B); "I found the Negro soldiers" (letter from the Civilian Aide to the Secretary of War to the Under Secretary of War, 10/23/42, Records of the Office of Secretary of War, Records of the Civilian Aid to the Secretary of War, Modern Military Records, National Archives); He recalled, for example (Martin, P./P); Indeed he told Jim Cook (Cook, 3/14/56/P); His sobs caught the attention (ibid.); "I lost the accent" (ibid.); "Until the Army, nobody" (Haley/P); "horrible and very, very frightening" (Witt/P).

CHAPTER 4: "HUNGRY AND MAD"

"hungry and mad, baby" (Morgan/P); "Frank had no artistic" (Watkins/B); "the most illustrious showplace" (ibid.); "There was no rush" (Fox/B); "It really was kind" (ibid.); Price may have reinforced (Robin Callot, *Capitol Collectors Series: Sammy Davis Jr.*, liner notes for CD, 1990); "crowding the big three" (Paul Grein, "The Birth of a Dream," Capitol Records publicity release, c. 1992); Sammy told Dorothy (Boggle/B).

CHAPTER 5: THE BIG TIME

"I still don't know what" (Mesmer/P); "I know I'm dreadfully ugly" (Oriana Fallaci, *The Egotists*, 1968 [interview dates to 11/64]/Early/B); "It was the start" (Davis/B); "a superlative hoofer" (Herm., *Variety*, August 1, 1951); "a brilliant new act"; "If Sammy isn't the fastest"; "a sure-fire talent" (quotes cited in *Variety* ad, December 26, 1951); "lived up to the extravagant" (*Variety*, February 18, 1952); "You know how most" (Mesmer/P); the Trio's weekly asking price (Smith, B/P); "nice" and "amusing," "no romantic interest" (Kitt, 1978, 1989/B); "The word was quickly" (Cook, 3/11/56/P); "I like him" (ibid.); "The closest I ever came" (Davis, 2/56/P).

CHAPTER 6: A CRUCIAL YEAR

"He wasn't optimistic" (Cook, 3/16/56/P); "We felt they would identify" (ibid.); "That's my *pleasure*, man" (Haley/P); "God, please don't let me" (AHC); "Anything he needs" (*Daily Variety*, May 24, 1989); "I was all mixed up" (Davis and Feldman/P); "I'd reach out for something" (AHC); "When I had the bad" (Christy/P); "I've become fatalistic" (Cabot/P).

CHAPTER 7: THE RETURN

"not to see if I look" (Mosby, 1/11/55/P); "lost none of his zest" (Abel., *Variety*, March 23, 1955); "Sammy Jr. was so great" (Earl Wilson, *New York Post*, March 25, 1955); "crowded room shouting" (Frank Quinn, *New York Mirror*, March 27, 1955); "It was a perfectly innocent thing" (Davis, 2/56/P); "We made sure" (ibid.); Instead, they wound up (Horton Streete, *Confidential*, March 1955/Early/B); "This is a rag" (Gardner/B); "one of the hottest acts" (*Time,* April 18, 1955); "It was Humphrey Bogart" (AHC); "a stamp you've arrived" (Mosby, 11/10/55/P); "It's a fine house" (Morgan/P); "At first, reading" (Davis and Feldman/P); "despised" and "rejected," "equality and human dignity" (Haley/P); "I found something" (Davis and Feldman/P); "I wanted to be a Jew" (ibid.); "the greatest thrill" (ibid.).

CHAPTER 8: *MR. WONDERFUL*

his relationship with Cordie King (Tubbs/P); "I already have a husband" (Cook, 3/15/56/P); "I want her to be happy" (Tubbs/P); "The chunky diamond ring" (Cook, 3/15/56/P); *Confidential* published a story (Matt Williams, *Confidential,* March 1956/Early/B); "Each writer made excuses" (Taylor/B); Will objected to a line of Carter's (ibid.); "We're not trying to prove" (Ross/P); "shoddy and tasteless" (Robert Coleman, *New York Daily Mirror,* March 24, 1956); "For a solid act" (Walter Kerr, *New York Herald Tribune,* March 23, 1956); "it's a pain" (Haley/P); "Ease up on us" (Schaap/P); "The most prejudiced" (Martin, P./P); "I believe" (Osborn, 8/11/62/P); filed suit against Sammy (*Variety,* November 23, 1960); "Oh, I've learned" (Donnelly/P).

CHAPTER 9: KIM, HARRY, AND LORAY

"It wasn't the facilities" (Rose/B); "a tall, slightly menacing" (Torme/B); "a beautifully run room" (Horne and Schickel/B); "the most blatantly run" (Thomson/B); "They both came over" (Kashner/P); "I doubt we exchanged" (Haley/P); "Which top female" (Kashner/P); "the biggest Hollywood scandal" (Brown/B); "Sammy, if Kim Novak ever" (Kashner/P); "Negro press started" (Haley/P); "just how deep" (Kashner/P); "Although everyone involved" (Brown/B); "You better ask Kim" (ibid.); Bacon phoned a friend (Bacon, 7/18/76/P); "I felt like a man being" (Haley/P); Then Harry Cohn (Brown/B; Rose/B; Thomas/B); Mickey Cohen who delivered (Cohen/B); "We can protect you here" (Kashner/P); "a beautiful woman" (ibid.); initially met in 1955 (Mrs. Sammy Davis Jr./P); "she couldn't play it" (Haley/P); "Nor was there any pressure" (Mrs. Sammy Davis Jr./P); Gordon White of *Motion Picture* (White, c. 1960/P); "Sammy and I are still" (Brown/B); She spelled her first name (Crawford/P); The ceremony was conducted (*Los Angeles Mirror,* January 11, 1958; *Los Angeles Times,* January 11, 1958); "singing love songs" (*Los Angeles Mirror,* January 11, 1958); "We were never lovers" (Ebert, 2/17/81/P); "I didn't really have an affair" (Grice/P); "serious love affair" (Brown/B); "having a very deep" (Davis/B); "That's how much things" (Kashner/P).

CHAPTER 10: BIG SCREEN, LITTLE SCREEN

"You know, there were times" (Crawford/P); "I don't know what happened" (Thomas/P, 3/4/59); "There's no divorce" (Wilson, 4/25/58/P); "a new adventure" (Davis/B); "It was doomed" (Haley/P); Loray resented the constraints (Mrs. Sammy Davis Jr./P); "That woman has broke" (Crawford/P); Once, Sammy's limousine (Mort Nathanson, United Artists' press release to promote *Anna Lucasta,* n.d.); "a thoroughly engrossing" (Arthur Knight, *Saturday Review,* January 10, 1959); "If somebody dug down" (Bosley Crowther, *New York Times,* January 15, 1959); "just a shade of" (Mrs. Sammy Davis Jr./P); she would seek a divorce (*New York Herald Tribune,* September 21, 1958); she filed in the Santa Monica Superior Court (*Los Angeles Mirror News,* 2/3/59); she and Sammy had agreed to a settlement (*New York Times,* April 24, 1959); "There's no denying" (Kovner/P); "I don't mind admitting" (Davis/B); "had everything on it" (Zehme/B); "Directors I can fight" (*Variety,* 5/23/00); "When everything settled down" (Davis/B); "Bobby spent an awful" (Quirk and Schoell/B); "the epitome of evil" (Davis/B); "You're going to steal" (ibid.); "Let me tell you" (Morgan/P); "a rich and devoted filming" (Paul V. Beckley, *New York Herald Tribune*, June 25, 1959); "a handsome, intelligent" (Land., *Variety*, July 1, 1959); "a stunning, exciting" (Bosley Crowther, *New York Times*, June 25, 1959); "serpentine, acrobatic" (*Cue*, July 4, 1959); "My finest piece of movie acting" (Davis/B).

CHAPTER 11: LOVERS AND FRIENDS

"the racial barrier" (Tube., *Variety*, November 16, 1959); "I'd like to do three" (George E. Pitts, *Pittsburgh Courier*, October 11, 1958/Early/B); "heftiest palming" (Newt., *Variety*, October 21, 1959); *The Jack Eigen Show* (Quirk and Schoell/B); "Give me the check" (*Chicago Defender*, March 7, 1959); "often made Sammy feel" (Quirk and Schoell/B); "was tired of feeling" (ibid.); an MGM picture called *Never So Few* (Taraborrelli/B); "that Sammy was ready" (Wilson, 3/5/59/P); "kind of hit it off" (AP, *Los Angeles Mirror-News*, November 5, 1959); "went to coffee shops" (ibid.); "When I began to talk to Joan" (*Tan*/P); "When you meet the right" (*New York Daily News*, November 6, 1959); "I'm riding on cloud nine" (ibid.); "Naturally, we don't approve" (AP, *Los Angeles Mirror-News*, November 5, 1959); "bounced boyantly" (Morrison/P); Sammy told Hy Gardner (Gardner/P): "Once again he was" (Morrison/P); "We knew and realized" (Gardner/P); "Our decision makes both" (ibid.).

CHAPTER 12: THE RAT PACK

"We were all terribly young" (Quirk and Schoell/B); "one who does not give" (MacLaine, 1995/B); "The guy's always good" (Quirk and Schoell/B); "The idea is" (ibid.); "a ten-million dollar home movie" (Spada/B); "I saw my movie breakthrough" (Quirk and Schoell/B); "broke their backs" (McKinlay/P); "I've never seen so much" (Radcliffe/P); "It would have taken" (Spada/B); "Ah, that movie!" (Quirk and Schoell/B); "you'd have to look hard" (Tosches/B); "We do it because" (Young/P); "It was always clear" (Sinatra, T./B); "For the times, yeah" (Taraborrelli/B); "an energy there" (MacLaine, 1995/B); "the greatest comedy act" (*Ebony*, August 1960); "Sammy was the one" (Taraborrelli/B).

CHAPTER 13: MAY

"Is Sammy Falling for" (*Chicago Defender*, April 30, 1960); "I love Sammy" (Lane/P); "He was clearly feeling" (Rich., *Variety*, May 25, 1960); "I can't let a lot" (London AP, *New York Post*, June 8, 1960); "It is possible we" (Hy Steirman, *Confidential*, January 1961/Early/B); "to lift her marriage" (Gordon White, *Motion Picture*, September 1960/Early/B); "life has been on" (ibid.); "I'm not trying to prove" (transcript of interview with Mike Wallace which aired on WNTA, Channel 13, in New York, printed in the *New York Post*, January 17, 1961); "Why doesn't he stay" (George E. Pitts, *Pittsburgh Courier*, June 25, 1960/Early/B); "about to become the most" (Gordon White, *Motion Picture*, September 1960/Early/B); May's employer announced (*New York Post*, June 21, 1960; *New York Morning Telegraph*, June 23, 1960); Sir Oswald Mosley (UPI, *Beverly Hills Citizen*, June 8, 1960); "I really expected to" (Thompson, T./P); "We got word" (Osborn, 7/28/62/P); "do no wrong" (Duke, *Variety*, December 21, 1960).

CHAPTER 14: "A ONE-MAN BAND"

"It's a gas" (George E. Pitts, *Pittsburgh Courier*, February 18, 1961/Early/B); "The one time when Davis" (Will Friedwald, liner notes for CD release of *The Wham of Sam*); his passport had expired (*Hollywood Citizen News*, April 21, 1961); "My advice to everybody"

(Levy, 1998/B); May went into labor (Davis, T./B); "He's too nervous to talk" (*New York Post,* July 6, 1961); "a good story" (Davis/B); "principal cast members" (A. H. Weiler, *New York Times,* February 12, 1962); "*Sergeants* wasn't to be taken" (Osborn, 7/7/62/P); "seems to be entering" (Army., *Variety,* November 8, 1961); "more than a mere star" (*New York Amsterdam News,* October 21, 1961); "I didn't know what to say" (Biggs/P); "one of the superior" (Jose., *Variety,* August 15, 1962); "Right now things" (Osborn, 7/28/62/P); "real and terrifying" (Jerry Tallmer, *New York Post,* August 22, 1962); "I want people to stop" (*Variety,* October 24, 1962); he earned $30,000 (George E. Pitts, *New York Courier,* February 2, 1963); Principal photography (*Variety,* November 28, 1962; *Variety,* December 6, 1962); Audiences in a Memphis theater (Howard/P); "greatest triumph of them all" (*New York Post,* April 9, 1963); "one of the most impactful shows" (Otta., *Variety,* May 15, 1963); "well informed and genuinely concerned" (Davis, O. and Dee/B); "Millions of white Americans" (Clayborne/B); "I'll work for the NAACP" (Osborn, 8/4/62/P); "We only need about 25" (Young/P).

CHAPTER 15: PALLIES

"woeful, dreary, stupid" (*Newsweek,* October 14, 1963); Frank's daughter Tina (Sinatra, T./B); "I thought you owned" (Tosches/B); "a sucker trap" (Kelley/B); "Baby, let me say this" (ibid.); "I want to talk about your" (Taraborrelli/B); "If you're the producer" (Lefkowitz/P); "being in a Vegas nightclub" (Quirk and Schoell/B); he had tried to remove Sammy (Heymann, 1998/B); "an artless and obvious" (Bosley Crowther, *New York Times,* August 6, 1964); "a zinging, swinging" (Dorothy Masters, *New York Daily News,* August 6, 1964); "The Clan thing" (Marks/P).

CHAPTER 16: *GOLDEN BOY*

Still, Sammy's participation (Trevor Armbruster, *Saturday Evening Post,* February 13, 1965/Early/B); "In its 24-year" (Robert Alden, *New York Times,* May 9, 1964); "*Mr. Wonderful* was just a series" (*New York Post,* May 17, 1964); "I don't go for the unfairness" (ibid.); "tendency was to make" (RLD); they actually came to blows (Thompson, T./P); "People didn't know what" (RLD); the producer estimated the overage (Nick Lapole, *New York Journal-American,* October 18, 1964); "For the first time in months" (Trevor Armbruster, *Saturday Evening Post,* February 13, 1965/Early/B); "Maybe Frank didn't send" (Thompson, T./P); "serious, expert, affecting" (Walter Kerr, *New York Herald Tribune,* October 21, 1964); "snap, speed and professionalism" (Howard Taubman, *New York Times,* October 21, 1964); "I'm ten feet tall!" (Thompson, T./P).

CHAPTER 17: "ON THE SEVENTH DAY, HE WORKS"

the Davises moved into (*Newsweek,* August 9, 1965); "I love doing *Golden Boy*" (Roy Newquist, *Showcase,* 1966/Early/B); "I never worked so hard" (*Ebony,* April 1966); "a strange and repelling" (*New York Herald Tribune,* November 26, 1965); "Chief Justice [Earl] Warren might fail" (Clayborne/B); "smell of victory" (ibid.); "We were reminded that" (ibid.); King equated the demonstration (ibid.); "Some people think Davis" (Schaap/P); "As a jack of all trades" (Leonard Harris, *New York World-Telegram & Sun,* July 2, 1965); "Sammy's trying to kill" (Schaap/P); "I wanted to prove the world" (Christy/P); he collapsed in his apartment (Wilson, 9/24/65/P); "It was absolutely marvelous" (Stuart W. Little, *New York Herald Tribune,* October 6, 1965); "Sammy Davis, Jr. musical" (Hedda Hopper, *Los Angeles Times,* September 24, 1965); "That's what they say" (Wilson, 9/24/65/P); "I respect my wife" (Roberts/P); "We seldom saw" (Davis, T./B).

Chapter 18: A Book, a Film, and a TV Series

"a gigantic jigsaw puzzle" (*Newsweek*, August 9, 1965); "one of the most candid" (Marice Dolbier, *New York Herald Tribune*, September 29, 1965); "I did not type" (*Newsweek*, August 9, 1965); "We took the camera" (Davis/B); "This is the best part" (Schaap/P); Sammy collapsed (ibid.); "On the movie set, Davis is" (Weintraub/P); "We literally bounced" (press book for *A Man Called Adam*); "a very creative, spontaneous" (ibid.); "savage intensity" (Thompson, H., 8/4/66/P); "was getting something he had" (Adams/P); "I'd have walked over" (Ebert, 7/16/66/P); "Rather than a variety show" (NBC press release for *The Sammy Davis, Jr. Show*, December 3, 1965); "Listen, baby. Few people" (Ebert, 7/9/66/P); a mere $50,000 (NBC press release for *The Sammy Davis, Jr. Show*, n.d.); "The dynamic personality" (Jack Gould, *New York Times*, January 8, 1966); "a shambles" (*Time*, January 14, 1966); "From now on, baby" (Ebert, 7/9/66/P); "light, fast-moving" (Mor., *Variety*, February 9, 1966); Ebert kept telling him, "Great." (Ebert, 7/9/66/P); "Whatever had been seriously" (Les, *Variety*, February 16, 1966); "having trouble getting really" (Ebert, 7/16/66/P); "looked so awful that" (ibid.); "Outside of my wife" (Davis, 7/25/65/P); "I'm going to go back" (Haley/P); "Here's a guy who's won" (Ebert, 7/16/66/P); "They're my people" (Ebert, 7/16/66/P); "The promise to return" (Shayon/P); "I've got no cop-out" (Haley/P).

Chapter 19: That's All!

"arguably the most famous" (Early/B); in excess of $6.5 million (Davis, T./B); "I still remember the first day" (ibid.); "A performer realizes" (Eliot Tigel, original liner notes for *Sammy Davis, Jr.: That's All*, reprinted in the CD liner notes); gave "the audience a show" (Kahn, *Variety*, November 18, 1966); "It's a little romantic" (AHC); "I'm not going down there" (*New York Times*, June 22, 1966); "had lent support" (Johnson/B); While in Atlantic City (Thomas, 8/17/66/P); "a large assemblage of Rothschilds" (*New York Times*, June 3, 1967); "display of dramatic intensity" (Helm., *Daily Variety*, November 22, 1967); the setting had to be re-created (Spada/B); Although there were women (Quirk and Schoell/B); "Sammy and Peter were very undisciplined" (Spada/B); "It cost us fifty thousand dollars" (ibid.); "Both stars should be ashamed" (Archer Winsten, *New York Post*, September 19, 1968); According to Earl Wilson (Earl Wilson, *New York Post*, n.d.); "Sammy's shock wasn't an act" (Guild/P); "MAY TO SAMMY" (*New York Daily News*, November 25, 1967); Granting her petition (AP, *New York Times*, December 20, 1967); "a very, very special lady" (SJR); "I have loved twice" (Pacter/P).

Chapter 20: Sad Times and Swinging Times

Sammy owned more than (Mosher/P); "Soon after that" (MacLaine, 1991/B); "the first such SRO" (*Hollywood Reporter*, June 6, 1968); "But this is providential" (Reuters, *New York Post*, June 6, 1968); "At times like this" (Green/P); "I attended a performance" (Graham, S./P); "I've seen nothing like it" (unidentified columnist, unidentified New York publication, August 10, 1968); "two or three girls with him to bed" (Quirk and Schoell/B); "My first impression" (Patrick William Salvo, interview with Altovise Gore, *Sepia*, September 1978/Early/B); Davis' ability to pack in (Long., *Variety*, November 13, 1968).

Chapter 21: Altovise

"Although there are several flaws" (Bill Ornstein, the *Hollywood Reporter*, March 28, 1969); The idea for the trip (Jones/B; Poitier, 1980/B); "When Altovise Gore stepped out" (Poitier, 1980/B); "a brilliant director" (Davis/B); allowed "Davis to display" (Richard

Cuskelly, *Los Angeles Herald Examiner,* November 6, 1970); Less enthusiastic was Milt Ebbins (Spada/B); "It was a crying shame" (Davis/B); "Let's fervently hope" (Howard Thompson, *New York Times,* June 11, 1970); "My interest in Michael X" (Davis/B); "Even then he looked good" (Rich, *Variety,* September 3, 1969); "I think acting is" (Smith, C./P); Jimmy Bowen, one of Reprise's (Bowen and Jerome/B); "I'm a performer" (Frankel/P); "pull out all the stops" (Torme/B); "This was war" (Davis, T./B); "Only my father would spring" (ibid.); "in what Sammy could do for her" (Quirk and Schoell/B); "That's the reason he married" (Kashner/P); Davis admitted to talk show (SJR).

CHAPTER 22: ENTERING THE SEVENTIES

"Well, he was marvelous" (Harriet Van Horne, *New York Post,* March 14, 1970); "Maybe that was a dream" (*New York Amsterdam News,* February 16, 1974); "I met the whole Cabinet" (Bacon, 10/15/71/P); "I lost a lot of friends" (DeLeon/P); "Anyone who drinks as hard" (*Newsweek,* October 11, 1971); *TV Guide* ranked it thirteenth (*TV Guide,* June 28–July 4, 1997); "wasn't an all-black show" (Davis, 6/72/P); "Timmie Rogers is just funny" (ibid.); "pull my coat to what was" (ibid.); "In all my 45 years" (ibid.); "The most vital one" (Davis/B).

CHAPTER 23: THE CANDY MAN AND THE MAN IN THE WHITE HOUSE

"walking into a whole different planet" (Cornyn/B); he wanted to do an R&B album (Bowen and Jerome/B); "an ill-advised attempt" (Gregg Geller, e-mail to author); "Theatre-in-the-round concerts are" (Clark/P); offered to make Davis a partner (Reuters, *New York Times,* August 30, 1972); "These were clean, neat people" (White/B); "It's a marvelous feeling here" (*New York Post,* August 22, 1972); "Nothing in my life ever hurt" (Bennett/P); "lackey" and an "ass-kisser" (ibid.); "They're really trying to infer" (Gilliam/P); "104% sure" (*Variety,* January 10, 1973); "good pace" (Bok., *Variety,* February 14, 1973); "pleasantly and attractively entertaining" (John J. O'Connor, *New York Times,* September 23, 1973); "It was the greatest thrill" (*Ebony,* May 1973); "My support of the man continues" (*Variety,* July 4, 1973); "Nothing's being done" (DeLeon/P); "Nixon is not to be explained" (*New York Amsterdam News,* February 16, 1974); "My egomania told me" (Bennet/B).

CHAPTER 24: AN OPEN MARRIAGE

asking price was $4.25 million (*Los Angeles Times,* December 23, 1990); When the work was finished (*Ebony,* June 1981); "Though none of the rooms" (Slansky/P); "There's a lot of memorabilia" (ibid.); "Pop was very hard on Altovise" (Davis, T./B); "Oh yeah, we had a crucial" (Patrick William Salvo, interview with Altovise Gore, *Sepia,* September 1978/Early/B); "I'll never forget that first night" and all other quotes attributed to Kathy McKee (Kathy McKee with Rudy Maxa, *Penthouse,* September 1991/Early/B); "For a time he seemed intrigued" and all other quotes attributed to Linda Lovelace (Linda Lovelace with Mike McGrady, *Ordeal*/Early/B); "Sammy has become Linda's biggest fan" (Bacon, 7/13/73/P); "I was trying to act" (Taraborrelli/B); "I started going to Sammy's" (Luft/B); "When he was working" (ibid.); "This was a hard time" (Taraborrelli/B); "I didn't like what I" (Rothstein/P); "created a lifestyle" (Bruning/P); "My performances were mediocre" (Davis/B); "Well, folks, some nights" (Albin Krebs, *New York Times,* June 1, 1977); "Davis' habit of losing control" (Shie., *Variety,* October 9, 1974); "In previous appearances, Sammy" (Hud., *Variety,* February 18, 1976); "Davis . . . was so loose" (Toy., *Variety,* July 7, 1976); "The gamblers are taking odds" and other quotes attributed to Joyce Haber (Haber/P).

CHAPTER 25: A NEW SHOWROOM, A NEW SHOW, AND AN OLD MUSICAL

"There will be a lot of changes" (DeLeon/P); But, in the end (author interview with John Climaco); "I went through my super black" (unidentified publication, December 12, 1974); "free and easy" (Will., *Variety,* December 4, 1974); "As himself for real" (Har., *Daily Variety,* December 9, 1977); Earnings of the MDA (Levy, 1996/B); "He never said 'no'" (Gerald C. Weinberg, letter to author, June 12, 2002); "In fine voice" (Stan., *Variety,* April 13, 1977); "Look," Sinatra said (Rader/P); "Ok, I was an ass" (Carr/P); sell-outs in some venues (*Los Angeles Times,* May 18, 1978); Dan Sullivan of the *Los Angeles Times* (dated June 5, 1978); "a sort of disaster" (Clive Barnes, *New York Post,* August 4, 1978); "an intolerably cute show (Douglas Watt, *New York Daily News,* August 4, 1978); Brendan Gill disliked it (Brendan Gill, *the New Yorker,* n.d.).

CHAPTER 26: DIFFICULT ADJUSTMENTS

"Davis, 52, still has it" (Bill Kaufman, *Newsday,* May 8, 1979); "Sammy Davis, Jr. at 53" (Will., *Variety,* March 14, 1979); "At one time I used to think" (Carr/P); Davis had earned in excess (Sloane/P); "I love to live a particular life-style" (Robinson/P); Tracey Davis maintained (Davis, T./B); "Sammy and I spend the holidays" (Makel/P); "My relationship with my wife" (Winters/P); "lack of communication between" (Dillon/P); "I once told Alto" (Davis, T./B); "pressures of being with" (ibid.); a bill for $227,483 (AP, *New York Post,* July 19, 1966); These deductions were disallowed (*Variety,* June 9, 1976; *Los Angeles Herald Examiner,* January 9, 1988).

CHAPTER 27: "I'VE NEVER FELT BETTER"

"everyone pretty well lubricated" (Reynolds/B); "Prosaic, superficial" (Jack Slater, *Los Angeles Times,* September 26, 1980); "I've never felt better" (*Los Angeles Herald Examiner,* October 22, 1980); "You're gonna get your money's" (Dago., *Variety,* 12/9/81); "I've seen him 30" (Ruth Robinson, *Hollywood Reporter,* April 21, 1982); "my religious homeland" (*Newsweek,* July 26, 1982); "the greatest experience of my life" (ibid.); "All my life I've been" (*New York Daily News,* November 26, 1982); "the show, upstaging" (Richard Gertner, *Motion Picture Product Digest,* December 15, 1982); "He had been working" (*New York Post,* March 15, 1983); "Atlantic City had a real impact" (Thomson/B); "a pleasant, low-key affair" (Dennis Hunt, *Los Angeles Times,* April 28, 1983); "in top form" (Will, *Variety,* October 5, 1983); "overlong" (Mel Gussow, *New York Times,* November 2, 1983); "And Bill was there for me" (SJR).

CHAPTER 28: TURNING SIXTY

"up to the task" (Will, *Variety,* March 20, 1985); "If you have any Christmas" (Kay Gardella, *New York Daily News,* December 9, 1985); "some fun visualizing" (Quin., *Variety,* June 17, 1986); Not knowing how to start (Davis, T./B);

CHAPTER 29: "THE ALTERNATIVE IS SOMETHING ELSE AGAIN"

"a new and mellower man" (Leonard Feather, *Los Angeles Times,* August 8, 1986); some $12 million (*Daily Variety* ad paid for by the St. Louis Variety Club, May 24, 1989); "Now I *like* me" (Bennett/P); "That person you saw" (Graham, J./P); "Slowly—and somewhat painfully" (*Newsday,* May 17, 1990); "We represent the end" (Leerhsen/P); "The two stylists did" (Zimm., *Variety,* August 8, 1987); "a wry self-parody" (Michael Wilmington, *Los Angeles Times,* September 9, 1988); "It was like someone" (Cynthia Gorney, *Washington Post,* n.d.); "Well, the alternative" (Burden, 10/7/87/P); "Frank designed the tour" (Taraborrelli/B); "I didn't want to do it" (ibid.); "You think he'll last" (ibid.); "detectable loss of vitality" (Dennis McDougal, *Los Angeles Times,* March 15, 1988); "When'd you get so" (Taraborrell/B);"The story making the rounds" (Stephen Williams, *Newsday,* October 5, 1988); "Mort arranged for a private" (MacLaine, 1995/B); "a night of triumph" (Stephen Holden, *New York Times,* April 8, 1988); "So powerful was Davis' performance" (Bob Harrington, *New York Post,* April 7, 1988); "a kind of urban fantasy" (Lawrence Van Gelder, *New York Times,* February 10, 1989); "It's a startling moment" (Frazier Moore, *New York Post,* February 15, 1989); "These were the kinds" (production notes for *Tap*); "I've only done a couple" (Gallo/P); "I really do feel like" (Davis/B); "It was like the most" (*Daily Variety,* May 24, 1989).

CHAPTER 30: "I DON'T THINK THIS IS THE WAY I'M SUPPOSED TO GO OUT"

According to the *Star* (*Star,* March 26, 1991); Tracey wrote in her memoir (Davis, T./B); "very painful. The guy" (Graham, J./P); "SAMMY DAVIS FIGHTS CANCER" (*New York Post,* September 15, 1989); "If it had to happen" (Army Archerd, *Variety,* September 15, 1989); "Everything he ate" (Smith, A./P); "I've never seen a turnout" (*People,* November 27, 1989); "Mention the name Sammy" (Paul Green, *Los Angeles Times,* November 15, 1989); "happiest day of my life" (Aldore Collier, *Jet,* December 4, 1989); "the quintessential performer" (Walker, 5/19/90/P); "They can't keep me away" (Smith, A./P); "I'll be back" (*New York Daily News,* February 14, 1990); *Entertainment Tonight,* for one (*Los Angeles Times,* February 28, 1990); "Those stories are not" (Smith, A./P); "If you take one day" (Davis, T./B); "Poor thing looks just" (*Star,* May 15, 1990); "I was told when I went in" (Walker, 5/19/90/P); "I felt totally helpless" (*Star,* May 15, 1990); "After a little while" (Sinatra, N./B); "Pop, if you want to die" (Davis, T./B).

EPILOGUE

"a durable fixture" (*New York Times,* May 17, 1990); "*the* consummate entertainer" (Jarrett/P); "Although he gained fame" (Shuster/P); "The world has not only lost" (Martinez/P); "He's not the last" (Mydans/P); "It was a moment in my life" (ibid.); "The outpouring of love" (*New York Post,* May 19, 1990); "While his last role was" (Irv Letofsky, *Los Angeles Times,* December 14, 1990); approximately $4 million (Schermerhorn and Kranes/P); She was also the beneficiary (Tayman and Bacon/P); Sammy's indebtedness exceeded (ibid.; Pristin/P); The first to go (Pristin/P); "I wouldn't feel right" (Martin, H./P); auction of Sammy's paintings (Pristin/P); just over $2.7 million (Curtiss and Lieberman/P); "The debt has cast" (Tayman and Bacon/P); "We were shocked" (Pristin/P); "Some of the questions were" (ibid.); The cache to which (Curtiss and Lieberman/P); "I'm sick of all" (Tayman and Bacon/P); reached a settlement with the IRS (Walter Scott, *Newsday,* January 21, 2001); she told *Variety*'s Army Archerd (Army Archerd, *Variety,* November 25, 1997).

Bibliography

BOOKS

Anderson, Jervis. *This Was Harlem: A Cultural Portrait, 1900–1950*. New York: Farrar, Straus and Giroux, 1982.

Batterberry, Michael, and Ariane Batterberry. *On the Town in New York: From 1776 to the Present*. New York: Scribner, 1973.

Bennett, Tony, with Will Friedwald. *The Good Life*. New York: Pocket Books, 1998.

Berg, A. Scott. *Goldwyn: A Biography*. New York: Knopf, 1989.

Blumenthal, Ralph. *Stork Club: America's Most Famous Nightspot and the Lost World of Café Society*. Boston: Little, Brown, 2000.

Boggle, Donald. *Dorothy Dandridge: A Biography*. New York: Amistad, 1997.

Bowen, Jimmy, and Jim Jerome. *Rough Mix: An Unapologetic Look at the Music Business and How It Got That Way—A Lifetime in the World of Rock, Pop, and Country as Told by One of the Industry's Most Powerful Players*. New York: Simon and Schuster, 1997.

Brown, Peter Harry. *Kim Novak: Reluctant Goddess*. New York: St. Martin's Press, 1986.

Carroll, Diahann, with Russ Firestone. *Diahann!* Boston: Little, Brown, 1986.

Carson, Clayborne, editor. *The Autobiography of Martin Luther King, Jr*. New York: Warner Books, 1998.

Cohen, Michael Mickey, as told to John Peer Nugent. *Mickey Cohen: In My Own Words*. Englewood Cliffs, NJ: Prentice-Hall, 1975.

Cohen-Stratyner, Barbara Naomi. *Biographical Dictionary of Dance*. New York: Schirmer Books, 1982.

Condon, Jack, and David Hofstede. *Charlie's Angels Casebook*. Beverly Hills: Pomegranite Press, 2000.

Cornyn, Stan, with Paul Scanlon. *Exploding: The Highs, Hits, Hype, Heroes, and Hustlers of the Warner Music Group*. New York: HarperCollins, 2002.

Davis, Ossie, and Ruby Dee. *With Ossie & Ruby: In This Life Together*. New York: William Morrow, 1998.

Davis, Sammy, Jr. *Hollwood in a Suitcase*. New York: William Morrow, 1980.

Davis, Sammy, Jr., Jane Boyar, and Burt Boyar. *Why Me? The Sammy Davis Jr. Story*. New York: Farrar, Straus and Giroux, 1989.

———. *Yes I Can: The Story of Sammy Davis Jr*. New York: Farrar, Straus and Giroux, 1965.

Davis, Tracey, with Dolores A. Barclay. *Sammy Davis Jr., My Father*. Los Angeles: General Publishing Group, 1996.

Douglas, Mike, with Thomas Kelly and Michael Heaton. *I'll Be Right Back: Memories of TV's Greatest Talk Show*. New York: Simon and Schuster, 2000.

Earley, Pete. *Super Casino: Inside the "New" Las Vegas*. New York: Bantam Books, 2000.

Early, Gerald, editor. *The Sammy Davis Jr. Reader*. New York: Farrar, Straus and Giroux, 2001.

Eisner, Joel. *The Official Batman Batbook*. Chicago: Contemporary Books, 1986.

Erenberg, Lewis A. *Steppin' Out: New York Nightlife and the Transformation of American Culture, 1890–1930*. Westport, CT: Greenwood Press, 1981.

Epstein, Daniel Mark. *Nat King Cole*. New York: Farrar, Straus and Giroux, 1999.

Fisher, Eddie, with David Fisher. *Been There, Done That*. New York: St. Martin's Press, 1999.

Fleischer, Richard. *Just Tell Me When to Cry: A Memoir*. New York: Carroll & Graf, 1993.

Fox, Ted. *Showtime at the Apollo*. New York: Holt, Rinehart and Winston, 1983.

Furia, Philip. *Ira Gershwin: The Art of the Lyricist*. New York: Oxford University Press, 1996.

Gardner, Ava. *Ava: My Story*. New York: Bantam Books, 1990.

Gavin, James. *Intimate Nights: The Golden Age of New York Cabaret*. New York: Grove Weidenfeld, 1991.

George-Graves, Nadine. *The Royalty of Negro Vaudeville: The Whitman Sisters and the Negotiation of Race, Gender and Class in African-American Theater, 1900–1940*. New York: St. Martin's Press, 2000.

Giordano, Gus, editor. *Anthology of American Jazz Dance*. Evanston, IL: Orion Publishing House, 1975.

Gordy, Berry. *To Be Loved: The Music, the Magic, the Memories of Motown. An Autobiography*. New York: Warner Books, 1994.

Gottfried, Martin. *All His Jazz: The Life and Death of Bob Fosse*. New York: Bantam Books, 1990.

Gray, Barry. *My Night People*. New York: Simon and Schuster, 1975.

Guralnick, Peter. *Careless Love: The Unmaking of Elvis Presley*. Boston: Little, Brown, 1999.

Heymann, C. David. *Liz: An Intimate Biography of Elizabeth Taylor*. New York: Birch Lane Press, 1995.

———. *RFK: A Candid Biography of Robert F. Kennedy*. New York: Dutton, 1998.

Horne, Lena, and Richard Schickel. *Lena*. Garden City, NY: Doubleday, 1965.

Hughes, Langston, and Milton Melter. *Black Magic: A Pictorial History of the African-American in the Performing Arts*. Englewood Cliffs, NJ: Prentice-Hall, 1967.

Johnson, Rafer, with Philip Goldberg. *The Best That I Can Be: An Autobiography*. New York: Doubleday, 1998.

Jones, Quincy. *Q: The Autobiography of Quincy Jones*. New York: Doubleday, 2001.

Kelley, Kitty. *His Way: The Unauthorized Biography of Frank Sinatra*. New York: Bantam, 1986.

Kessler, Susan E. *The Wild Wild West: The Series*. Downey, CA: Arnett Press, 1988.

King, Alan, with Chris Chase. *Name-Dropping: The Life and Lies of Alan King*. New York: Scribner, 1996.

Kisseloff, Jeff. *You Must Remember This: An Oral History of Manhattan from the 1890s to World War II*. San Diego: Harcourt Brace Jovanovich, 1989.

Kitt, Eartha. *Alone with Me: A New Autobiography by Eartha Kitt*. Chicago: Henry Regnery, 1978.

———. *I'm Still Here*. London: Sidgwick & Jackson, 1989.

Lawford, Patricia Seaton, with Ted Schwarz. *The Peter Lawford Story: Life with the Kennedys, Monroe and the Rat Pack*. New York: Carroll & Graf, 1988.

Lee, Ulysses. *United States Army in World War II: The Employment of Negro Troops*. Washington, DC: Office of the Chief of Military History, United States Army, 1966.

Levy, Shawn. *King of Comedy: The Life and Art of Jerry Lewis*. New York: St. Martin's Press, 1996.

———. *Rat Pack Confidential: Frank, Dean, Sammy, Peter, Joey & the Last Great Showbiz Party*. New York: Doubleday, 1998.

Lewis, Jerry, with Herb Gluck. *Jerry Lewis: In Person*. New York: Atheneum, 1982.

Lhamon, W. T., Jr. *Raising Cain: Blackface Performance from Jim Crow to Hip Hop*. Cambridge, MA: Harvard University Press, 1998.

Lovelace, Linda, with Mike McGrady. *Out of Bondage*. Secaucus, NJ: Lyle Stuart, 1986.

Luft, Lorna. *Me and My Shadows: A Family Memoir*. New York: Pocket Books, 1998.

MacLaine, Shirley. *Dance While You Can*. New York: Bantam, 1991.

———. *My Lucky Stars: A Hollywood Memoir*. New York: Bantam, 1995.

Mahar, William J. *Behind the Burnt Cork Mask: Early Blackface Minstrelsy and Antebellum American Popular Culture*. Urbana: University of Illinois Press, 1999.

Manso, Peter. *Brando: The Biography*. New York: Hyperion, 1994.

McCrohan, Donna. *Archie & Edith, Mike & Gloria: The Tumultuous History of All in the Family*. New York: Workman, 1987.

McWhorter, Diane. *Carry Me Home: Birmingham, Alabama. The Climactic Battle of the Civil Rights Revolution*. New York: Simon and Schuster, 2001.

Poitier, Sidney. *The Measure of a Man: A Spiritual Autobiography*. San Francisco: HarperSanFrancisco, 2000.

———. *This Life*. New York: Knopf, 1980.

Preminger, Otto. *Preminger: An Autobiography*. Garden City, NY: Doubleday, 1977.

Pryor, Richard, with Todd Gold. *Pryor Convictions and Other Life Sentences*. New York: Pantheon Books, 1995.

Quirk, Lawrence J., and William Schoell. *The Rat Pack: The Hey-Hey Days of Frank and the Boys*. Dallas: Taylor Publishing, 1998.

Reynolds, Burt. *My Life*. New York: Hyperion, 1994.

Riis, Thomas L. *Just before Jazz: Black Musical Theater in New York, 1890 to 1915*. Washington, DC: Smithsonian Institution Press, 1989.

Rose, Frank. *The Agency: William Morris and the Hidden History of Show Business*. New York: HarperBusiness, 1995.

Sampson, Henry T. *Blacks in Blackface: A Source Book on Early Black Musical Shows*. Metuchen, NJ: Scarecrow Press, 1980.

Sanders, Coyne Steven, and Tom Gilbert. *Desilu: The Story of Lucille Ball and Desi Arnaz*. New York: William Morrow, 1993.

Shaw, Arnold. *Black Popular Music in America: From the Spirtuals, Minstrels, and Ragtime to Soul, Disco, and Hip-Hop*. New York: Schirmer Books, 1986.

Shipman, David. *Judy Garland: The Secret Life of an American Legend*. New York: Hyperion, 1993.

Sinatra, Nancy. *Frank Sinatra: An American Legend*. Santa Monica, CA: General Publishing Group, 1995, 1998.

Sinatra, Tina, with Jeff Caplon. *My Father's Daughter: A Memoir*. New York: Simon and Schuster, 2000.

Southern, Eileen. *Biographical Dictionary of Afro-American and African Musicans*. Westport, CT: Greenwood Press, 1982.

Spada, James. *Peter Lawford: The Man Who Kept the Secrets*. New York: Bantam Books, 1991.

Spelling, Aaron, with Jefferson Graham. *Aaron Spelling: A Prime-Time Life*. New York: St. Martin's Press, 1996.

Stearns, Marshall, and Jean Stearns. *Jazz Dance: The Story of American Vernacular Dance*. New York: Macmillan, 1968.

Stein, Charles W., editor. *American Vaudeville as Seen by Its Contemporaries*. New York: Knopf, 1984.

Taraborrelli, J. Randy. *Sinatra: A Complete Life*. New York: Birch Lane Press, 1997.

Taylor, Theodore. *Jule: The Story of Composer Jule Styne*. New York: Random House, 1979.

Thomas, Bob. *King Cohn*. New York: G. P. Putnam's Sons, 1967.

Thomson, David. *In Nevada: The Land, the People, God, and Chance*. New York: Knopf, 1999.

Thorpe, Edward. *Black Dance*. Woodstock, NY: Overlook Press, 1990.

Torme, Mel. *It Wasn't All Velvet: An Autobiography*. New York: Viking, 1988.

Tosches, Nick. *Dino: Living High in the Dirty Business of Dreams*. New York: Doubleday, 1992.

Watkins, Mel. *On the Real Side: Laughing, Lying, and Signifying—The Underground Tradition of African-American Humor That Transformed American Culture, from Slavery to Richard Pryor*. New York: Simon and Schuster, 1994.

White, Theodore H. *The Making of the President 1972*. New York: Atheneum, 1973.

Woll, Allen. *Black Musical Theatre: From Coontown to Dreamgirls*. Baton Rouge: Louisiana State University Press, 1989.

Zehme, Bill. *Frank Sinatra and the Lost Art of Livin'*. New York: HarperCollins, 1997.

PERIODICALS

Adams, Val. *New York Times*, October 18, 1965.

Bacon, James. *Los Angeles Herald Examiner*, October 15, 1971.

———. *Los Angeles Herald Examiner*, July 13, 1973.

———. *Chicago Sun-Times*, July 18, 1976 (excerpt from his book, *Hollywood Is a Four Letter Town*).

Bennett, Lerone, Jr. *Ebony*, March 1980.

Biggs, Clark. *Variety*, November 15, 1961.

Boxoffice, May 1981.

Bruning, Fred. *Newsday*, May 17, 1990.

Burden, Martin. *New York Post*, January 5, 1984.

———. *New York Post*, October 7, 1987.

Cabot, Tracy. *National Enquirer*, January 20, 1976.

Carr, Jay. *New York Times*, July 30, 1978.

Champlin, Charles. *Los Angeles Times*, May 17, 1990.

Christy, Marian. *Los Angeles Daily News*, May 18, 1990.

Churm, Steven R., and Jocelyn Stewart. *Los Angeles Times*, May 19, 1990.

Clark, Paul Sargent. *Hollywood Reporter*, February 18, 1972.

Collier, Aldore. *Esquire*, February 1990.

Cook, Jim. *New York Post*, March 11–16, 1956.

Crawford, Marc. *Tan*, August 1959.

Curtiss, Aaron, and Paul Lieberman. *Los Angeles Times*, December 4, 1991.

Davis, Mrs. Sammy, Jr. *Ebony*, June 1959.

Davis, Sammy, Jr. *Ebony*, February 1956.

———. *Los Angeles Times Calendar*, July 25, 1965.

———. *Ebony*, June 1972.

Davis, Sammy, Jr., as told to Trude B. Feldman. *Ebony*, February 1960.

DeLeon, Robert A. *Jet*, November 22, 1973.

Dillon, Barry. *National Enquirer*, June 14, 1977.

Donnelly, Tom. *New York World Telegram*, December 24, 1956.

Dowling, Kevin. *National Enquirer*, August 11, 1974.

Ebert, Alan. *TV Guide*, July 9, 1966.

———. *TV Guide*, July 16, 1966.

———. *US*, February 17, 1981.

Frankel, Haskel. *National Observer,* October 4, 1965.

Gallo, Hank. *New York Daily News,* January 5, 1989.

Gardner, Hy. *Beverly Hills Citizen,* April 11, 1960.

Gilliam, Dorothy. *New York Post,* June 9, 1973.

Graham, Jefferson. *USA Weekend Magazine,* March 19, 1989.

Graham, Sheila. *Newark Evening News,* September 1, 1968.

Green, James. *Evening News* (London), June 6, 1968.

Grice, Elizabeth. *Daily Telegraph,* April 14, 1997.

Guild, Leo. *National Enquirer,* January 7, 1968.

Haber, Joyce. *Los Angeles Times Calendar,* July 29, 1973.

Haley, Alex. *Playboy.* December 1966.

Harford, Margaret. *Los Angeles Times–Washington Post* Service, March 10, 1968.

Howard, Edwin. *Hollywood Reporter,* November 2, 1964.

Humphrey, Hal. *Los Angeles Times,* January 5, 1965.

Jarrett, Vernon. *Chicago Sun-Times,* May 20, 1990.

Kashner, Sam. *Vanity Fair,* April 1999.

Kovner, Lee. *Hollywood Reporter,* n.d.

Lane, Bill. *Chicago Defender,* June 18, 1960.

Leerhsen, Charles. *Newsweek,* April 13, 1987.

Lefkowitz, Bernard. *New York Post,* October 18, 1963.

Makel, Chris. *Black Stars,* October 21, 1980.

Marks, Sally. *Los Angeles Times Calendar,* September 3, 1967.

Martin, Hugo. *Los Angeles Times,* September 23, 1991.

Martin, Pete. *Saturday Evening Post,* May 21, 1960.

Martinez, Michael. *Hollywood Reporter,* May 17, 1990.

McKinlay, Colin. *Los Angeles Mirror,* April 8, 1961.

Mesmer, Marie. *Los Angeles Daily News,* October 15, 1952.

Morgan, Thomas B. *Esquire,* October 1960.

Morrison, Allan. *Jet,* January 28, 1960.

Mosby, Aline. *New York Morning Telegraph,* January 11, 1955.

———. *New York Morning Telegraph,* November 10, 1955.

Mosher, Jo. *California Living* magazine, *Los Angeles Herald Examiner,* August 18, 1968.

Mydans, Seth. *New York Times,* May 19, 1990.

Osborn, Tek. *New York Courier,* July 7, 1962.

———. *New York Courier,* July 28, 1962.

———. *New York Courier,* August 4, 1962.

———. *New York Courier,* August 11, 1962.

Pacter, Trudi. *Daily Mail* (London), June 1, 1968.

Pristin, Terry. *Los Angeles Times,* September 10, 1991.

Pryor, Thomas M. *New York Times,* June 8, 1958.

Radcliffe, E. B. *Cincinnati Enquirer,* July 7, 1960.

Rader, Dotson. *Parade Magazine,* September 24, 1989.

Roberts, Stanley. *New York Journal-American,* July 9, 1965.

Robinson, Louie. *Ebony,* February 1976.

Rothstein, Mervyn. *New York Times,* May 30, 1989.

Ross, Don. *New York Herald Tribune,* March 18, 1956.

Salmaggi, Robert. *New York Herald Tribune,* October 18, 1964.

Sanz, Cynthia, and Doris Bacon. *People,* January 29, 1990.

Schaap, Dick. *New York Herald Tribune,* February 6, 1966.

Schermerhorn, Terry, and Marsha Kranes. *New York Post,* September 19, 1991.

Shayon, Robert Lewis. *Saturday Review,* May 21, 1966.

Shepard, T. Brooks. *American Visions,* August 2000.

Shuster, Fred. *Los Angeles Daily News,* May 17, 1990.

Slansky, Paul. *Sunday News* (New York), November 15, 1981.

Sloane, Leonard. *New York Times,* November 25, 1973.

Smith, Alan Braham. *National Enquirer,* December 5, 1989.

Smith, Bill. *Billboard,* July 11, 1953.

Smith, Cecil. *Los Angeles Times,* November 4, 1969.

Smith, Patricia. *Chicago Sun-Times,* October 4, 1990.

Tan, April 1960.

Tayman, John, and Doris Bacon. *People,* October 7, 1991.

Thomas, Bob. *New York Post,* March 4, 1959.

———. *New York Post,* August 17, 1966.

Thompson, Howard. *New York Times,* November 26, 1965.

———. *New York Times,* August 4, 1966.

Thompson, Thomas. *Life,* November 13, 1964.

Tubbs, Vincent. *Jet,* February 9, 1956.

Variety, October 24, 1962.

Walker, Jesse H. *New York Amsterdam News,* December 9, 1989.

———. *New York Amsterdam News,* May 19, 1990.

Warga, Wayne. *Los Angeles Times,* May 28, 1978.

Weintraub, Bernard. *New York Times,* January 2, 1966.

White, Gordon. *Motion Picture,* c. 1960.

Wilson, Earl. *New York Post,* April 25, 1958.

———. *New York Post,* March 5, 1959.

———. *New York Post,* September 24, 1965.

Winters, Jason. *Black Stars,* July 1978.

Witt, Linda. *People,* n.d.

Young, A. S. (Doc). *Negro Digest,* June 1963.

Filmography

Dates of feature films and Broadway shows reflect openings in New York. A * denotes a film's availability on videotape. A + indicates a film's availability on DVD.

FEATURE FILMS

Anna Lucasta (Longridge Enterprises/UA). January 14, 1959. Produced by Sidney Harmon. Directed by Arnold Laven. Written by Philip Yordan, from his play. With Eartha Kitt, Frederick O'Neal, Henry Scott, Rex Ingram, Georgia Burke, James Edwards. 97 minutes. b&w.

Porgy and Bess (Columbia). June 24, 1959. Produced by Samuel Goldwyn. Directed by Otto Preminger. Written by N. Richard Nash, based on the folk opera with music by George Gershwin, libretto by DuBose Hayward, lyrics by Hayward and Ira Gershwin, based on the play *Porgy* by DuBose and Dorothy Hayward. With Sidney Poitier, Dorothy Dandridge, Pearl Bailey, Brock Peters, Leslie Scott, Diahann Carroll. 146 minutes. color.

Ocean's Eleven (Warner Bros.). August 10, 1960. Produced and directed by Lewis Milestone. Written by Harry Brown and Charles Lederer, from a story by George Clayton Johnson and Jack Golden Russell. With Frank Sinatra, Dean Martin, Peter Lawford, Angie Dickinson, Richard Conte, Cesar Romero, Patrice Wymore, Jose Bishop, Akim Tamiroff, Henry Silva, Ilka Chase. 128 minutes. color.* +

Pepe (Columbia). December 21, 1960. Produced and directed by George Sidney. Written by Dorothy Kingsley, from a screen story by Leonard Spigelgass and Sonya Levien and a play by L. Bus-Fekete. With Cantinflas, Dan Dailey, Shirley Jones (Davis has a cameo) 197 minutes. color.*

Sergeants 3 (E-C/United Artists). February 10, 1962. Produced by Frank Sinatra. Executive Producer: Howard W. Koch. Directed by John Sturges. Written by W. R. Burnett. With Sinatra, Dean Martin, Peter Lawford, Joey Bishop, Henry Silver, Ruta Lee, Buddy Lester. 112 minutes. color.

Convicts 4 (Allied Artists). October 3, 1962. Produced by A. Ronald Lubin. Directed by Millard Kaufman. Written by Kaufman, based on *Reprieve*, the autobiography of John Resko. With Ben Gazzara, Stuart Whitman, Ray Walston, Vincent Price, Rod Steiger, Broderick Crawford, Dodie Stevens, Jack Kruschen. 105 minutes. b&w.

Johnny Cool (United Artists). October 2, 1963. Produced and directed by William Asher. Executive producer: Peter Lawford. Written by Joseph Landon. With Henry Silva, Elizabeth Montgomery, Richard Anderson, Jim Backus, Joey Bishop, Brad Dexter, Wanda Hendrix, Hank Henry, Marc Lawrence, John McGiver, Gregory Morton, Mort Sahl, Telly Savalas. 101 minutes. b&w.

Robin and the 7 Hoods (Warner Bros.). August 5, 1964. Directed by Gordon Douglas. Produced by Frank Sinatra. Executive producer: Howard W. Koch. Screenplay and story by David R. Schwartz. Songs by Sammy Cahn and James Van Heusen. Cinematography by William H. Daniels. With Sinatra, Dean Martin, Bing Crosby, Peter Falk, Barbara Rush, Edward G. Robinson, Victor Buono. 123 minutes. color.* +

The Threepenny Opera (Embassy). October 14, 1964 (Detroit). Directed by Wolfgang Staudte. Produced by Kurt Ulrich. Screenplay by Staudte, Gunter Weisenborn, based on *Die Dreigroschenopera* by Kurt Weill and Berthold Brecht and *The Beg-*

gar's Opera by John Gay. With Curt Jurgens, June Ritchie, Hildegard Knef, Marlene Warlich, Lino Ventura, Gert Frobe, Hilde Hildebrandt, Walter Giller. 83 minutes. color.

Nightmare in the Sun (Zodiac/Afilmco). December 1964 (Los Angeles). Produced by Marc Lawrence and John Derek. Directed by Lawrence. Written by Ted Thomas and Fanya Lawrence, from the story by Lawrence and George Fass. With John Derek, Aldo Ray, Arthur O'Connell, Ursula Andress, Allan Joslyn, Keenan Wynn, Chick Chandler, Richard Jaeckel, Robert Duvall. 80 minutes. color.

A Man Called Adam (Embassy Pictures). August 3, 1966. Coproduced by Ike Jones and Jim Waters. Directed by Leo Penn. Written by Les Pine and Tina Rome. With Cicely Tyson, Ossie Davis, Peter Lawford, Frank Sinatra, Jr., Johnny Brown, Louis Armstrong, Mel Torme, Lola Falana, Jeanette Du Bois, George Rhodes. 96 minutes. b&w.*

Salt and Pepper (Chrislaw Trace-Mark/United Artists). September 18, 1968. Produced by Milton Ebbins. Directed by Richard Donner. Written by Michael Pertwee. With Peter Lawford, Michael Bates, Ilona Rodgers, Robertson Hare, William Mervyn. 101 minutes. color.

Sweet Charity (Universal). April 1, 1969. Produced by Robert Arthur. Directed by Bob Fosse. Screenplay by Peter Stone, based on the play by Neil Simon, Cy Coleman, and Dorothy Fields. With Shirley MacLaine, John McMartin, Ricardo Montalban, Chita Rivera, Paula Kelly, Stubby Kaye, Barbara Bouchet. 157 minutes. color.* +

One More Time (Chrislaw Trace-Mark/United Artists). June 10, 1970. Produced by Milton Ebbins. Directed by Jerry Lewis. Screenplay by Michael Pertwee. With Peter Lawford, Percy Herbert, Bill Maynard, Lucille Soong, John Wood, Anthony Nichols, Allan Cuthbertson, Dudley Sutton, Glyn Owen, Sidney Arnold, Maggie Wright. 93 minutes. color.

Save the Children (Paramount). September 19, 1973. Produced by Matt Robinson. Directed by Stan Lathan. Narrative written by Robinson (who also narrates). With Marvin Gaye, the Staple Sisters, the Temptations, the Chi Lites, the Main Ingredient, the O'Jays, Isaac Hayes, Zulema, the Rev. Jesse Jackson, the Cannonball Adderly Quintet, the Push Mass Choir, Albertina Walker, Loretta Oliver, the Rev. James Cleveland, Bill Withers, Curtis Mayfield, Roberta Flack, Quincy Jones, Gladys Knight and the Pips, Jerry Butler, Brenda Lee Eager, the Ramsey Lewis Trio, Nancy Wilson, the Jackson Five, Jackie Vardell, Dick Gregory. 123 minutes. b&w.

Sammy Stops the World (Special Event Entertainment). September 19, 1979 (Atlantic City). Produced by Mark Travis and Del Jack. Executive producers: Saul Barnet, Hillard Elkins. Directed by Mel Shapiro. Book, music, and lyrics by Leslie Bricusse and Anthony Newley. With Dennis Daniels, Donna Lowe, Marian Mercer. 105 minutes. color.

The Cannonball Run (20th Century Fox). June 19, 1981. Produced by Albert S. Ruddy. Directed by Hal Needham. Screenplay by Brock Yates. With Burt Reynolds, Roger Moore, Farrah Fawcett, Dom DeLuise, Dean Martin, Jack Elam, Adrienne Barbeau, Terry Bradshaw. 95 minutes. color. * +

Cannonball Run II (Warner Bros./Golden Harvest). June 29, 1984. Produced by Albert S. Ruddy. Executive producers: Raymond Chow, Andre Morgan. Directed by Hal Needham. Written by Needham, Ruddy, and Harvey Miller, based on characters created by Brock Yates. With Burt Reynolds, Dom DeLuise, Dean Martin, Jamie Farr, Merilu Henner, Telly Savalas, Shirley MacLaine. 108 minutes. color.* +

That's Dancing! (MGM/UA). January 18, 1985. Produced by David Niven, Jr., and Jack

Haley, Jr. Written and directed by Haley. With special appearances by Davis, Mikhail Baryshnikov, Ray Bolger, Gene Kelly, Liza Minelli. 105 minutes. color and b&w.*

Moon over Parador (Universal). September 9, 1988. Produced by Paul Mazursky. Directed by Mazursky. Screenplay by Leon Capetanos and Mazursky, based on a story by Charles G. Booth. With Richard Dreyfuss, Raul Julia, Sonia Braga, Jonathan Winters, Fernando Ray, Michael Greene, Polly Holiday, Charo, Marianne Sagebrecht, Carlotta Gerson (Mazursky), Lorin Dreyfuss. 105 minutes. color.*

Tap (Tri-Star). February 10, 1989. Produced by Gary Adelson and Richard Vane. Directed by Nick Castle. Screenplay by Castle. With Gregory Hines, Suzzanne Douglas, Savion Glover, Joe Morton, Dick Anthony Williams, Sandman Sims, Bunny Briggs, Steve Condos, Jimmy Slyde, Pat Rico, Arthur Duncan, Harold Nicholas. 110 minutes. color.*

TELEVISION FILMS

The Pigeon (Thomas/Spelling Production/ABC). November 4, 1969. Produced by Alex Gottlieb. Executive producers: Aaron Spelling, Danny Thomas. Directed by Earl Bellamy. Teleplay by Edward Lasko, from the story by Stanley Roberts. With Dorothy Malone, Victoria Vetri, Ricardo Montalban, Pat Boone, Roy Glenn Sr., Patsy Kelly. 90 minutes. color.

The Trackers (Aaron Spelling Productions/ABC). December 14, 1971. Produced by Aaron Spelling and Davis. Directed by Earl Bellamy. Written by Gerald Gaiser, from a story by Spelling and Davis. Photography by Tim Southcott. With Ernest Borgnine, Julie Adams, Connie Kreski, Jim Davis, Arthur Hunnicut, Caleb Brooks, Norman Alden, Leo V. Gordon, Ross Elliot, Dave Reynard. 90 minutes. color.*

Poor Devil (NBC). February 14, 1973. Produced by Robert Stambler. Executive producers: Earl Barrett, Arne Sultan. Directed by Robert Scheerer. Written by Barrett, Sultan, and Richard Baer. With Christopher Lee, Gino Conforti, Jack Klugman, Adam West, Madlyn Rhue, Emily Yancy. 120 minutes. color.

Alice in Wonderland (Irwin Allen Prods./P&G Prods./Columbia/CBS). December 9–10, 1985. Produced by Irwin Allen. Directed by Harry Harris. Teleplay by Paul Zindel, based on Lewis Carroll's *Alice in Wonderland* and *Through the Looking Glass*. Songs by Steve Allen. With Natalie Gregory, Sheila Allean, Scott Baio, Red Buttons, Sid Caesar, Imogene Coca, Sherman Hemsley, Arte Johnson, Roddy McDowall, Jayne Meadows, Robert Morely, Anthony Newley, Donald O'Connor, Martha Raye, Telly Savalas, Ringo Starr, Shelley Winters, Steve Allen, Ernest Borgnine, Beau Bridges, Lloyd Bridges, Carol Channing, Patrick Duffy, George Gobel, Eydie Gormet, Merv Griffin, Ann Jillian, Harvey Korman, Steve Lawrence, Karl Malden, Donna Mills, Pat Morita, Louis Nye, John Stamos, Sally Struthers, Jack Warden, Jonathan Winters. 240 minutes. color.*

The Kid Who Loved Christmas (Eddie Murphy Television Enterprises). December 14, 1990. Directed by Arthur Allan Seidelman. Produced by Mark McClafferty. Teleplay by Sam Egan. Story by McClafferty, Clint Smith, Mark E. Corry, and Lynn Marlin. With Cicely Tyson, Michael Warren, Trent Cameron, Gilbert Lewis, Charles Q. Murphy, Ken Paige, Ray Parker, Jr., Della Reese, Esther Rolle, Ben Vereen, Vanessa L. Williams. 120 minutes. color.*

THEATER

Mr. Wonderful (Broadway Theatre, New York). March 22, 1956. Produced by Jule Styne and George Gilbert. Book by Joseph Stein and Will Glickman. Music and lyrics by

Jerry Bock, Larry Holofecner, and George Weiss. Directed by Jack Donohue. With Kay Medford, Chita Rivera, Jack Carter, Pat Marshall, Will Mastin, Sam Davis, Sr. 388 performances.

The Desperate Hours (Hollywood Center Theatre, Los Angeles). November 8, 1958. Produced by Tim Baar. Directed by Michael Ferrall. Written by Joseph Hayes. With Buddy Bregman, James Waters, Morry Erby, John Dennis, Roy Glenn, Anne Barton, Olive Sturgess. 24 performances (approximately).

The Desperate Hours (Mineola Playhouse, Mineola, Long Island, NY/Westport Country Playhouse, Westport, CT) August 1962. Produced by Henry T. Weinstein and Laurence Feldman, in association with Will Mastin. Directed by Lloyd Richards. Written by Joseph Hayes. With Kathleen Maguire, James Waters, Remo Pisani, Roy E. Glenn, Moris Erby, Judith Robinson, Val Avery. 24 performances (approximately).

Golden Boy (Majestic Theatre, New York). October 20, 1964. Produced by Hillard Elkins. Directed by Arthur Penn. Book by Clifford Odets and William Gibson, based on the play by Odets. Music by Charles Strouse. Lyrics by Lee Adams. With Billy Daniels, Kenneth Tobey, Paula Wayne, Roy Glenn, Johnny Brown. 569 performances.

Golden Boy (The Palladium, London). June 5, 1968. Produced by Hillard Elkins. Directed by Michael Thoma. Book by Clifford Odets and William Gibson, based on the play by Odets. Music by Charles Strouse. Lyrics by Lee Adams. With Gloria De Haven, Mark Dawson, John Bassette, Al Kirk, Hilda Haynes. 116 performances (approximately).

Stop the World—I Want to Get Off (New York State Theatre, New York). August 3, 1978. Produced by James and Joseph Nederlander, in association with the City Center of Music and Drama, Inc./Hillard Elkins. Directed by Mel Shapiro. Book, music, and lyrics by Leslie Bricusse and Anthony Newley. With Marian Mercer, Donna Lowe, Debora Masterson, Joyce Nolen, Wendy Edmead, Shelly Burch, Charles Willis, Jr., Dennis Daniels, Patrick Kinser-Lau, Edwetta Little. 29 performances.

Discography

The following are the principal long-playing albums released during the artist's lifetime. A + indicates current availability on CD.

Starring Sammy Davis, Jr. Decca (8118). April 18, 1955.
Sammy Davis, Jr. Sings Just for Lovers. Decca (8170). August 15, 1955.
Mr. Wonderful (Original Broadway Cast Recording). Decca (9032). May 6, 1956.
Here's Looking at You. Decca. (8351). August 13, 1956.
Sammy Swings. Decca (8486). May 27, 1957.+*
Boy Meets Girl (with Carmen McRae). Decca (8490). August 12, 1957.
It's All Over but the Swingin'. Decca (8641). November 25, 1957.
Mood to Be Wooed (with Mundell Lowe). Decca (8676). February 17, 1958.
All the Way . . . and Then Some! Decca (8779). August 11, 1958.
Sammy Davis Jr. at Town Hall. Decca (78841). January 11, 1959.
Porgy and Bess (with Carmen McRae). Decca (78854). March 23, 1959.
Sammy Awards. Decca (78921). January 6, 1960.
I've Gotta Right to Swing! Decca (78981). July 1, 1960.
The Wham of Sam. Reprise (2003). March 1961.+
Mr. Entertainment. Decca (74153). August 7, 1961.
Sammy Davis, Jr. Belts the Best of Broadway. Reprise (2010). February 1962.
The Sammy Davis, Jr. All-Star Spectacular. Reprise (6033). July 1962.
What Kind of Fool Am I—and Other Show Stoppers. Reprise (6051). August 1962.
Sammy Davis Jr. at the Cocoanut Grove. Reprise (6063). January 1963.+
As Long As She Needs Me. Reprise (6082). March 1963.
Sammy Davis Jr. Sings Forget-Me-Nots for First Nighters. Decca (74381). April 13, 1963.
A Treasury of Golden Hits. Reprise (6096). September 1963.
Finian's Rainbow: Reprise Musical Repertory Theatre (with various artists). Reprise (2015). November 1963.+**
Guys and Dolls: Reprise Musical Repertory Theatre (with various artists). Reprise (2016). November 1963.+**
Kiss Me Kate: Reprise Musical Repertory Theatre (with various artists). Reprise (2017). November 1963.+**
South Pacific: Reprise Musical Repertory Theatre (with various artists). Reprise (2018). November 1963.+**
Johnny Cool (Motion Picture Soundtrack). United Artists (5111). January 1964.
Sammy Salutes the Stars of the London Palladium. Reprise (6095). 1964.
The Shelter of Your Arms. Reprise (6114). February 12, 1964.
Robin and the 7 Hoods (Original Motion Picture Soundtrack). Reprise (2021). May 1964.+
Sammy Davis Jr. Sings Mel Torme's California Suite. Reprise (6126). August 1964.
Sammy Davis Jr. Sings the Big Ones for Young Lovers. Reprise (6131). October 1964.
Golden Boy (Original Broadway Cast Recording). Capitol (2124). November 1964.+

* *Sammy Swings* and *I Gotta Be Me* are on the same CD, part of MCA's Twofer series.
** These four albums have been released as a CD box set under the title *Reprise Musical Repertory Theatre.*

When the Feeling Hits You: Sammy Davis Jr. Meets Sam Butera & the Witnesses. Reprise
(6144). January 1965.

Our Shining Hour (with Count Basie). Verve (8605). March 1965.+

If I Ruled the World. Reprise (6159). March 1965.

The Nat King Cole Song Book. Reprise (6164). May 1965.

Sammy's Back on Broadway. Reprise (6169). August 1965.

The Sammy Davis Jr. Show. Reprise (6188). February 1966.

A Man Called Adam (Motion Picture Soundtrack). Reprise (R6180). 1966.

The Sounds of '66 (with Buddy Rich). Reprise (6214). September 1966.

Sammy Davis Jr. Sings, Laurindo Almeida Plays (with Laurindo Almeida). Reprise
(6236). November 1966.

That's All! Reprise (6237). January 1967.+

Sammy Davis Jr. Sings the Complete Doctor Doolittle. Reprise (6264). October 1967.

Lonely Is the Name. Reprise (6308). August 1968.

Salt and Pepper (Motion Picture Soundtrack). United Artists (5187). September 1968.

I've Gotta Be Me. Reprise (RS6324). November 1968.+*

Sweet Charity (Motion Picture Soundtrack). Decca (71502). February 1969.+

The Goin's Great. Reprise (6339). August 1969.

Something for Everyone. Motown (710). May 1970.

Sammy Steps Out. Reprise (6410). August 1970.

Sammy Davis Jr. Now. MGM (4832). April 1972.

Portrait of Sammy Davis Jr. MGM (4852). September 1972.

Sammy (Original Television Soundtrack). MGM (4914). September 1973.

That's Entertainment. MGM (4965). August 1974.

The Song and Dance Man. 20th Century. 1977.

Stop the World—I Want to Get Off (Original Broadway Cast). Warner Bros. (3214). July
7, 1978.

Sammy Davis Jr. in Person 1977. RCA. 1983.

Closest of Friends. Applause (1016). 1984.

Index